My Roosevelt Years

MY
ROOSEVELT
YEARS

Norman M. Littell

Edited by Jonathan Dembo

UNIVERSITY OF WASHINGTON PRESS

Seattle and London

Library of Congress Cataloging-in-Publication Data

O Littell, Norman M. (Norman Mather), 1899–
  My Roosevelt years.

  Includes index.
    1. United States—History—1933–1945. 2. World War,
  1939–1945—United States.   3. Littell, Norman M.
  (Norman Mather), 1899–   .   4. Lawyers—United States—
  Biography.   5. United States. Dept. of Justice—
  Officials and employees—Biography.   I. Dembo, Jonathan,
  1948–   .   II. Title.
√ E806.L59   1987   973.917   87-10523
  ISBN 0-295-96525-8

Contents

Illustrations

Introduction

While most American historians of the 1941–45 period understandably direct their attention to world affairs and military compaigns, events of unprecedented significance also took place in domestic affairs. Vast transformations, far surpassing the much better known reforms of the New Deal period, affected American society while its men were away at war. Unemployment declined sharply, the Depression ended, for the first time large numbers of women and minorities entered the industrial work force, and the economy boomed as never before in American history. Meanwhile, dramatic population shifts occurred as millions migrated from the South and Midwest to the coastal areas to work in the war industries that sprang up there. The federal government grew enormously in size and in its effect on the everyday lives of the people. It enforced rationing, allocated scarce resources, directed production, controlled most wages, prices, and rents, strictly limited the ability of workers to change jobs, and censored the news. Its power for good or ill grew pervasive. During the war, the government evacuated 110,000 Japanese Americans, suspected of being disloyal, and confined them to concentration camps.

Despite the recent publication of a number of useful works on American politics and society during the war, however, the home front remains a neglected field of research.[1] Much less is known about wartime politics than about politics in the 1920s or 1930s. Yet politics did not adjourn during the war. Congressmen and senators continued to pass laws, to represent their constituents, to campaign for reelection, and to investigate other branches of government. Bureaucrats continued to maneuver, to make alliances, to seek advantages for their agencies. Private interests continued to seek profits, favorable laws, and administrative decision. Newspapermen continued to hunt for stories, to expose wrongdoing, and to promote ideologies and favored personalities. Partisanship, personal rivalry, ambition, jealousy, and political intolerance did not cease merely because the nation was at war. Indeed, the war may well have intensified the passions of politics.

---

1. Richard Polenberg, *War and Society: The United States, 1941–1945* (Philadelphia: J. P. Lippincott Company, 1972); John Morton Blum, *V Was for Victory: Politics and American Culture During World War II* (New York: Harcourt Brace Jovanovich, 1976); Richard R. Lingeman, *Don't You Know There's a War On: The American Home Front, 1941–1945;* (New York: G. P. Putnam's Sons, 1970).

No better window on the wartime political life of the nation's capitol exists than the Justice Department. Its role, in keeping track of aliens and foreign agents, in investigating violations of federal criminal laws, in enforcing or not enforcing the antitrust laws and in breaking up cartels and monopolies, in defending the federal government against suits against it, and in acquiring millions of acres of land and other property needed by the federal government for the war effort, made it a central focus for domestic politics. In the Justice Department, few men were better situated to observe and record events than Norman Mather Littell, who served as assistant attorney general in charge of the Lands Division from March 1939 to November 1944. During this period, Littell dictated a diary in which he recorded his daily contacts, his conversations with friends and enemies, his perceptions of the great and the small, and their comments and intrigues against one another. He tells of the dinner parties, court cases, and the political and social conflicts of the day, as well as his own official responsibilities. In the process, he sheds much new light on domestic politics and society during the war years.

Norman Mather Littell was born 8 September 1899 in Indianapolis, Indiana, the son of Dr. Joseph Littell, a Presbyterian minister, and Clara Safford (Munger) Littell, the daughter of an Ohio county judge. After graduating from the Indianapolis public schools, Littell entered Wabash College in Crawfordsville, Indiana, in 1917. While in college, he was a reporter for the school newspaper and competed for the college as a debater. In 1920, his oration, "The Path to Peace," won first prize in an interstate regional contest held in Michigan. He graduated in June 1921, with an A.B. degree.[2]

In his senior year, Littell was awarded a Rhodes Scholarship, the first ever given to an Indianian. Following graduation, he attended Christ Church College at Oxford University from 1921 to 1924. He received a B.A. in modern history from Oxford in 1924. In the summer of 1923, he also served as a correspondent for the *Philadelphia Public Ledger* Foreign News Service covering the League of Nations at Geneva.

Upon his return from Europe, Littell determined to improve his financial prospects. To this end, he abandoned his intention to become a foreign correspondent and decided to become a lawyer. Despite insufficient funds, he enrolled at Harvard Law School in the autumn of 1925. At first it appeared to be the right decision, but the experience soon soured. Littell described what happened in a letter to me (8 June 1985):

---

2. "Norman Littell Goes to Holland Michigan," clipping, n.p., n.d.; "Degrees Granted at Wabash Exercises," *Indianapolis News*, 21 June 1921, in Littell scrapbook. Additional biographical information: *Marquis' Who's Who in America*, vol. 43 (Chicago, 1984–85), p. 1997.

Roscoe Pound, dean of the law school, told me that I was eligible for the Richard W. Hale Scholarship, established by the senior member of a leading law firm in Boston. He also told me, with what seemed to me a feeling of disappointment, that the cases of two or three students who had received the scholarship had not worked out well in the law school. In giving the scholarship to me, it seemed to me that he, perhaps, thought he was now going to have satisfactory results since he was dealing with an ex-Rhodes Scholar.

One of the alleged advantages of the so-called scholarship was supposed to be personal contacts with an outstanding member of the Boston bar, meeting his wife, visiting at his home for a night or weekend, and consulting on law problems from the classroom. However pleasant these so-called advantages seemed to be, in a month or two, the truth finally dawned on me. I was a plaything for this leading legal light. He did not seek to help me with a legal question but enjoyed confusing a new, young mind in the law.

Actually, there was a good deal of the old, widely known, social snobbery in the donor's attitude. The constant flow of young, "self-made" men, especially from the Middle-West, was an irritant. He could vent his spleen in his professional field, in which he was an expert, by confusing a selected student.

If this sounds like a fairy tale, it was not. When I reported it to Dean Pound, as I could then give him examples of cultivated confusion on a legal issue (none of which examples I can recall now) the scholarship was abolished by the dean. But, in the meantime, I was demoralized as well as exhausted by intensive work.

Emotionally disturbed by the collapse of his law school career and badly in need of rehabilitation, Littell went to New York where he found a job as an "ordinary seaman" on an American freighter bound for the Far East and around the world.[3] Returning to Harvard Law School when the cruise was over, he finished "first year law," but remained troubled. Seeking renewal, he went to the Far West, where he worked as a timber faller in the Douglas fir country for the Long Bell Lumber Company. It was during this time that he developed the pugnacious attitude of life that was to characterize most of his personal and political contacts. As he later put it: "I long ago learned by experience at sea and in a logging camp that there is no way to deal with a human rat except to stamp on him. A man of such despicable character that he will drop a monkey wrench on your head 'by accident' cannot be dealt with politely. He must be invited out on deck or made to feel that at any moment you will take him on deck."[4]

---

3. Norman Mather Littell, *Trails of the Sea* (New York: Vantage, 1983).
4. See diary entry for 7 April 1943.

(He was able to do so if necessary, for he had won the light heavyweight boxing championship at Oxford.)

His health and stability finally restored, and with no desire to return to the East, Littell enrolled in 1927 at the University of Washington Law School, where he became a classmate and friend of future congressman and senator Warren G. "Maggie" Magnuson, and was introduced to Democratic Party politics. Graduating in 1929, Littell was admitted to the Washington bar and became an associate in the Seattle admiralty law firm of Bogle, Bogle and Gates, where he remained from 1929 to 1934.

Soon after joining the firm, Littell married Katherine Franch Maher LeBlanc, a brilliant classics student whom he had met and fallen in love with at Oxford. Upon return to her home in New Orleans, she had extended and enlarged their comradeship by studying law at the Tulane University Law School.[5] As soon as Littell's income could support a family, she joined him in Seattle, where they were married 14 June 1930. Although she never practiced law actively, she served as Littell's closest legal and political adviser. The Littells became only the second couple in history to be admitted to the bar of the U.S. Supreme Court.[6] Establishing their home in Seattle, they became active in both social and political arenas. Avid outdoorsmen, they enjoyed an active life of hiking, camping, sailing, hunting, and fishing. On one camping trip, Littell rescued two bear cubs whose mother had been killed by hunters, and gave them to the Seattle zoo.[7]

In Littell's first case after graduating from the University of Washington Law School, Bogle, Bogle and Gates assigned him to the case of Alaska Steamship Company against the United States for the cost of transporting a shipwrecked crew from one of its own vessels from the coast of Alaska back to Seattle. Littell argued the case before the U.S. District Court, which decided it for the government. On appeal, the U.S. Court of Appeals for the Ninth Circuit affirmed the District Court decision. Littell was always grateful to the officers of the Alaska Steamship Company because they did not ask the law firm to have one of the older men in the firm, experienced in operating on the high legal level of the U.S. Supreme Court, take over the case, but stood by Littell's appealing and arguing the case in the Supreme Court. There he won a unanimous judgment reversing the two lower courts in an opinion by Chief Justice Stone (*Alaska Steamship Company v. U.S.*, 290 U.S. 16 [1934]). This was

---

5. "Leading Ladies of Seattle," clipping, 24 October 1937, in Littell scrapbook.
6. "Littell Nomination; Assistant U.S. Attorney General," *Seattle Post-Intelligencer*, 17 March 1939, in Littell scrapbooks.
7. "Loaded for Bear," photo clipping, n.p., n.d., in Littell scrapbook.

the first of eleven cases he would argue before the Supreme Court, winning ten with one divided court in the eleventh case.

As a rising Democratic attorney and a supporter of the New Deal, Littell's public career also progressed rapidly. In 1934 he was appointed as special assistant to the U.S. attorney general, assistant solicitor to the secretary of the interior, and Pacific Northwest regional director of the National Petroleum Administration. As regional director, he was responsible for assuring compliance with the price codes in the petroleum industry established under the National Recovery Administration (NRA).[8]

In 1935, after the Supreme Court ruled the NRA unconstitutional, Littell returned to private life as a partner in the Seattle law firm of Robert H. Evans, W. G. McLaren and Littell.[9]

The next year, however, he was appointed part-time special assistant to the U.S. attorney general to argue the government's case in *United States v. Northern Pacific Railway Company*, 311 U.S. 317 (1940). The government had charged the railroad with having overreached its 2.9 million-acre land grant and argued that the railroad should be forced to divest itself of these lands. Again, after a four-year battle, the U.S. Supreme Court upheld Littell's arguments.

On 16 March 1939, after Attorney General Frank Murphy and Presidential Assistant Benjamin V. Cohen jointly implored Littell to accept the position of assistant attorney general to help break up what they thought was improper control over federal land litigation and land acquisition policies, he relented and accepted President Roosevelt's renewed offer. He was sworn in 21 April 1939.[10]

The Lands Division of the Justice Department, with over five hundred attorneys and numerous other personnel in Washington, D.C., and operations scattered over every state and territory, was the largest and, in some ways, the most important division in the Justice Department.[11] Littell's diary details how, as head of this division during World War II, Littell supervised the acquisition, through condemnation or purchase, of more than twenty million acres of land from private owners. No hint of corruption attached to his administration of the division. He successfully argued some of the most important of the department's cases before the Supreme Court. Even his greatest enemies acknowledged that he had turned a moribund division of the department into a model of efficiency and effectiveness.

---

8. "Littell Named Aide to Murphy," *New York Times*, 17 March 1939.
9. "Rights of Way Deemed Coming; New Attorney Aide Tells Bonneville Plans," n.p., n.d., in Littell scrapbook.
10. Ibid.
11. See diary entry for 8 September 1941, note 6.

Littell's diary also reveals a constant battle within the administration and with Congress to attain the original goals of the New Deal in good government and to prevent inroads by private interests into the policy-making process. Through his daily entries, one may glimpse the constantly shifting tide of the intra-administration battle for position and bureaucratic control of policy, for publicity and for the ear of the President.

As a high official of the administration, Littell also performed political functions. He was called upon to explain and defend government land acquisition and other policies to the public and to Congress. He was both a Democratic Party partisan and a member of a faction within the administration. He was a vigorous opponent of big business domination of the war effort, opposing monopolies and special favors for the powerful. A strong internationalist, he was an advocate of military preparedness in the months preceding Pearl Harbor and, as chairman of the Foreign Investment Committee of the International Bar Association, favored postwar aid to the Allies. He took a leading part in the struggle against fascist and nazi penetration of American business. Toward the end of the war, he argued forcefully for reconversion policies that would favor small businessmen, farmers, and demobilized servicemen rather than powerful, established interests. He was a leading proponent of civil rights and a co-founder of the National Committee Against Persecution of the Jews, which struggled against anti-Semitism.

Littell was close, both personally and politically, to the wing of the Roosevelt administration led by Vice President Henry A. Wallace. Throughout the war years, he was one of Wallace's strongest advocates in the administration and played an important role at the 1944 Democratic convention as a Wallace organizer among western state delegations. Littell also admired Supreme Court Justices Robert H. Jackson and Frank Murphy, both former attorneys general under whom he had served. He and Katherine were also close to the Roosevelt family. They had developed a warm friendship with Roosevelt's daughter, Anna, whom they had met during their Seattle days. Anna's husband, John Boettiger, publisher of the *Seattle Post-Intelligencer* since 1935, was also a friend and political ally, at least until the election of 1940. In addition, the Littells had many of the same convictions and humanitarian interests as Eleanor Roosevelt and were occasional guests at White House social gatherings, although they were not personal friends.

At first, Littell's relations with his colleagues in the administration were amicable, but his convictions, uncompromising honesty, and unwillingness to avoid a good fight made him many enemies. He soon came into conflict with Thomas G. "Tommy the Cork" Corcoran, who had been a behind-the-scenes political "fixer" in the administration since early New

Deal days.[12] After leaving the administration in 1940, Corcoran became a political lobbyist using his ties with members of the administration to promote the interests of his clients. Corcoran was allied with the increasingly conservative Supreme Court Justice Felix Frankfurter, his former professor at Harvard Law School, and Frankfurter's allies in the administration, including Secretary of the Interior Harold L. Ickes, the Texas businessman and Reconstruction Finance Corporation chairman Jesse H. Jones, and their respective supporters. Time after time, on a variety of issues, these groups clashed.

After Solicitor General Francis B. Biddle's appointment as attorney general, Corcoran gained increased influence in the Justice Department in promoting the interests of his clients, for Biddle was another of Frankfurter's many protégés scattered throughout the administration. Littell felt that Biddle, whose interest in the administration of the Justice Department seemed to be restricted to civil liberties, failed to "take charge" of the department. Biddle's failure to attend to personnel and administrative matters, his inexperience, his apparent ignorance of the law, and his ineptitude in dealing with the U.S. attorneys, the press, and the public soon aroused Littell's contempt. On the other hand, Littell's frequent statements to the press and to Congress, which undermined Biddle's efforts to harmonize relations with other departments of government, contributed to Biddle's loss of confidence in Littell. A palpable atmosphere of distrust soon poisoned their relations. The Biddle-Littell relationship, which forms the centerpiece of this diary, was thus punctuated by a number of increasingly spectacular clashes which culminated in Biddle's dismissal of Littell in November 1944. The Sterling Products, Savannah Shipyards, Elk Hills, Breakers Hotel, and Surplus Properties cases are little remembered today, but in their time they were significant political milestones in domestic politics. After his retirement from government, Biddle omitted all references to Littell from his several works on his experiences as attorney general.[13]

During the war, the faction in the administration to which Littell belonged—the Wallace wing—increasingly found themselves outnumbered and outmaneuvered by the men President Roosevelt brought into the government after 1940 to help in the war effort. Backed by a strong coalition of Southern Democrats and Republicans in Congress, the new men in the administration moved behind the scenes to promote business interests, to maintain racial segregation, to restrict labor unions, and to

12. William E. Leuchtenburg, *Franklin D. Roosevelt and the New Deal, 1932–1940* (New York: Harper and Row, 1963), pp. 148–49, 327; Booth Mooney, *The Lyndon Johnson Story* (New York: Avon Books, 1964), pp. 46–47.
13. See, for example, Francis Biddle, *The Fear of Freedom* (Garden City, N.Y.: Doubleday, 1951)

end many of the social reforms of the 1930s. Increasingly preoccupied with foreign and military affairs, and in poor health, Roosevelt paid less and less attention to domestic affairs. Without his continuing protection, the Wallaceites fared badly. In 1943, when bickering between the Reconstruction Finance Corporation and the Board of Economic Warfare over the conduct of foreign economic policy exploded in public, Roosevelt abolished the BEW and transferred its functions, together with some of the RFC's to an entirely new agency. The chief victim of the affair was Vice President Henry Wallace, who had been chairman of the BEW. The hopes of his followers were finally shattered at the 1944 Democratic convention, so poignantly described by Littell. Heeding the advice of advisers, who argued that Wallace would be a liability on the ticket, Roosevelt agreed to have Wallace replaced as his running mate with Senator Harry S. Truman. With their leader eliminated from the top of the ticket, many of the lower-ranking Wallaceites, like Littell, found their positions untenable and were forced out of the government. Wallace became secretary of commerce in the new administration, but it was an office shorn of many of its former powers. Truman's elevation to the presidency, following Roosevelt's death in April 1945, hastened the trend.

Following his dismissal as assistant attorney general (30 November 1944), Littell established a Washington, D.C., law firm, but he did not lose all interest in politics. In 1946 he joined with Ickes in successfully opposing the nomination of Edwin W. Pauley, a California oilman and Democratic Party fund-raiser who had worked to defeat Wallace at the 1944 Democratic convention, to be undersecretary of the Navy. Ickes, who had resigned from the administration in protest of the nomination, and Littell charged in congressional testimony that Pauley had offered to raise large amounts of money for the Democrats in 1944 if the Interior Department showed greater sympathy for the oil industry. They also alleged that Pauley had played an important role in stopping a government suit to obtain title to important offshore oil reserves.[14]

Littell's law practice, which he maintained until his retirement in 1982, was wide ranging and lucrative. He also helped organize and served as the first president of the American Youth Hostels in the late 1940s and early 1950s.[15] As chairman of the Committee for Development of Foreign Investment Laws of the International Bar Association, 1949–54 (and later as chairman of similar committees of the American Bar Association and the Inter-American Bar Association), he testified before Congress to protect American investment abroad and wrote the sections of the

---

14. Alonzo L. Hamby, *The Imperial Years: The United States Since 1939* (New York: Weybright and Talley, 1976), pp. 145–46; Thomas J. Hamilton, "Pauley Requested Favor on Oil Lands, Says Ickes," *New York Times*, 2 February 1946.

15. *New York Times*, 6 January 1953, p. 20.

Marshall Plan of 1948 and the Economic Cooperation Act of 1951 that accomplished that end. This led to one of the most important developments in his career. Chiang Kai-shek learned of his testimony and invited him to become a consultant to write Taiwan's (Republic of China's) Foreign Investment Encouragement Law, which proved very important in Taiwan's subsequent economic rise. He also served as a legal consultant to the State Department on foreign trade and to the governments of Taiwan in 1960 and Turkey in 1961.

Perhaps Littell's most important client, however, was the Navajo Tribe, the largest tribe of Indians occupying the largest Indian reservation in the United States. As general counsel, Littell represented the tribe in its dealings with Congress and the Interior Department from 1947 to 1967. In addition to drafting a new tribal constitution, he reformed the tribe's method of leasing its mineral resources. Before that the Interior Department had "negotiated" such leases "with favored developers," much to the benefit of the latter. Littell advised the tribe to open the leases to competitive bidding. The tribe followed his advice and thereby increased the tribal treasury from $200,000 to over $100,000,000, converting the Navajos from among the poorest to richest tribe in the nation. Littell also successfully defended the Navajos in the U.S. Supreme Court.[16] In the case of *Warren Trading Post v. Arizona Tax Commission* Littell defeated the efforts of the state to tax Navajo reservation trading posts, and in the case of *Littell v. Nakai* he defended the Tribal Council against the newly elected tribal chairman who sought to annul the Council's prohibition against the use of peyote, and won.[17] His activities angered many state officials and businessmen and led to a third series of court cases, between 1964 and 1966, when Secretary of Interior Stuart Udall attempted to force his dismissal as general counsel for the tribe. Littell won a permanent injunction against Udall, which the Supreme Court upheld.[18]

Finally, Littell is notable for being the only person ever to win a libel action against syndicated columnist Drew Pearson.[19] Littell and Pearson had once been on good terms, politically and personally. Pearson had praised Littell in his column for his actions against Tommy Corcoran, and Littell had been a frequent visitor at Pearson's farm in Maryland. In April

---

16. Letter from Norman M. Littell to the editor, 9 January 1985 (in the editor's possession).

17. *Warren Trading Post v. Arizona Tax Commission*, 85 S. Ct. 1242; 380 U.S. 85; 14 L.Ed. 2nd 165 (1965). *Littell v. Nakai*, 34 LW 3074 (1966).

18. *New York Times*, 1 December 1963, p. 83. *Udall v. Littell*, 385 U.S. 1007 (1966).

19. Douglas A. Anderson, A *"Washington Merry-Go-Round" of Libel Actions* (Chicago: Nelson-Hall, 1980), pp. 143–48; Oliver Pilat, *Drew Pearson: An Unauthorized Biography* (New York: Harper's Magazine Press, 1973), pp. 251–53; Tyler Abell, ed., *Drew Pearson: Diaries, 1949–1959* (New York: Holt, Rinehart and Winston), 1974, pp. 160, 267–68, 270, 272.

1949, however, without confirming his information with Littell, Pearson published the following report: "The Justice Department is casting a quizzical eye on ex-Assistant Attorney General Norman Littell. They have reports that Littell is acting as a propagandist for the Dutch government although he failed to register as a foreign agent." Because this was a crime punishable by a $5,000 fine or ten years' imprisonment, or both, Littell sued Pearson and the Bell Syndicate, Inc. for $300,000 in damages.[20]

Instead of apologizing to Littell, Pearson compounded his error by repeating and expanding on his charges in a radio broadcast, 21 May 1950, in which he was commenting on Senator Joseph R. McCarthy's claims that there were communists in the State Department:

> I would like to urge a full investigation of all subversives, all attorneys for Communists and of our national security, perhaps by a committee of prominent citizens. As a sample I suggest that such a committee look into the attorney for a Communist embassy and ascertain how, after Gerhart Eisler [whom Pearson identified as an undercover agent of the Comintern, a Communist Party organization] was spirited out of New York on the Polish steamer *Batory*, this attorney arranged for Polish Communists to board the returning steamship and interview the crew ahead of the U.S. officials who wanted to find out how Eisler escaped. This attorney was a former high official of the Justice Department and because, unlike McCarthy, I believe in naming names without Congressional immunity, [I reveal] that gentleman is Norman Littell.
>
> His activities and that of others could be a start in ascertaining what lawyers, lobbyists, Congressmen, ex-members of the Truman Committee, or sons-in-law, or anyone else, are working for the Communists or the Fascists, for Poles, or Peron, or Franco, or for any government which does not believe in letting Democracy live.[21]

Littell, who had quite openly worked for the Polish Embassy in 1949 and 1950, argued that any American lawyer was entitled to advise a foreign government without being accused of being subversive, and he sued Pearson for an additional $300,000.

The trial of the consolidated cases, which ended 15 May 1953, lasted six weeks. The jury was unable to agree on the Polish charges but granted Littell $50,000 damages on the Dutch charges. The judge reduced the award to $40,000. For a while, Pearson seemed prepared to appeal, but he decided not to on the advice of his tax accountant and the knowledge that eleven of the twelve jurors had wanted to award Littell $100,000 in the Polish case and the lone holdout was the son of one of Pearson's old friends.[22]

---

20. Anderson, p. 143.
21. Pilat, pp. 252–53.
22. *New York Times*, 16 May 1953, p. 9.

Since the death of his wife Katherine in 1980, Norman Littell continues to live at his home in Deale, Maryland, on the shores of Chesapeake Bay. Although in poor health, he remains alert and corresponds with old friends and business acquaintances. He hopes that this memoir of life in wartime Washington will contribute to a growing understanding of that era in our nation's history.

The manuscript of *My Roosevelt Years* is based on a series of "diary" entries which Littell recorded by dictaphone and had transcribed by a number of secretaries from 1938 to 1955. In fact, however, the entries took a variety of forms. Most were in straightforward log book format which record the daily occurrences of the wartime Justice Department. Another large percentage consists of notes Littell took at Justice Department staff meetings and record the day-to-day decision-making process of the attorney general and his aides. In addition, Littell filed a number of memoranda in these notebooks. These contain a blow-by-blow account of his major battles within the administration. Last, but by no means least, Littell periodically used the format of a father's letter to his daughter, Katherine Mather Littell. He began these letters while recuperating in the Pacific Northwest from the heart attack he suffered in August 1941. The lengthy period of separation and enforced idleness provided a perfect opportunity for extended letter writing. Furthermore, as Littell put it to me in a letter: "She was a child of unusual intelligence who in my eyes would grow into maturity of great grasp and understanding. My urge to write found an outlet in this personality of the future who would eventually appreciate my accounts of many events in the years she had passed through without knowing of them." The letters are, in many ways, the most interesting and illuminating of the entries. They tend to be more analytical and to encompass a greater period of time and a greater variety of subjects than the other entries.

Littell filed each entry in chronological order in a series of looseleaf notebooks.

Notebook		Pages
No. 1	21 July 1941–30 April 1942	1–134
No. 2	6 May 1942–11 July 1942	135–262
No. 3	15 September 1942–26 July 1943	1–204
No. 4	17 October 1943–17 July 1944	205–366
No. 5	23 July 1944–24 September 1944	367–445
No. 6	10 October 1944–15 August 1945	446–592

Littell and Samuel R. Blate, of Gaithersburg, Maryland, who performed the initial editing work, trimmed the manuscript, eliminating the earliest entries, from 1939 to mid-1941, and the latter entries, after

January 1945. According to Blate, they also made the following changes to the original text: (1) Portions of the diary that relate either to family affairs or social occasions of no historical import were deleted. (2) A few words whose meaning would require footnotes in the 1980s were changed to contemporary terms where the meaning of the text would not be altered. (3) In several instances, observations concerning some people were made which might be considered libelous in a published document. Such passages were revised slightly to bring the memoir out from under the shadow of possible legal action. Littell and Blate state that, apart from these changes, the manuscript "is a candid verbatim account of Mr. Littell's experiences as Assistant Attorney General of the United States. The typescript of the edited original manuscript has been verified against the original."

In my editing of the manuscript, I have made additional changes based on both the edited version and the original notebooks. I have reduced the length of the manuscript significantly, chiefly by eliminating repetitious and less important material. I have indicated all such cuts with ellipses. I have also attempted to regularize spelling, capitalization, punctuation, and format to maintain consistency throughout the document, since each of the secretaries who transcribed the original dictation followed her own rules. In cases where I have corrected the manuscript, or supplied new or missing material, I have indicated as much by enclosing the new or altered material in brackets, to distinguish them from parenthetical passages in the original text, which are set apart by parentheses. In every instance I have attempted to remain faithful to the manuscript as I received it. In certain cases, I have corrected obvious historical errors, such as inconsistencies in dates from one page in the manuscript to another. It has also been my policy to supply, wherever possible, the full names of persons at their first mention in the text. I have indicated this by enclosing the supplied material in brackets. In cases where some doubt may exist, I have supplied footnotes. In a few cases, where the transcription was obviously garbled, I have reworded the text in the interests of understanding. Again, I have enclosed these passages in brackets.

Since the manuscript was not originally intended for publication, and was intended rather as a means by which a busy government official might keep track of his own far-flung affairs, it contains many arcane references to legal terms, legislation, publications, historical events, and circumstances that would be mysterious to the average reader. In such cases, I have provided footnotes wherever possible. For reasons of space, however, I have not cited every such reference, but only enough to confirm statements in the text. Generally, I have cited only published material, but in a few cases I have cited Littell's scrapbooks and notebooks. These are currently in my possession, but Mr. Littell has willed them to the

University of Washington Library along with the rest of his papers and records.

At the end of the text, I have appended a Biographical Notes section. Here I have supplied thumbnail biographical sketches of prominent persons mentioned in the text. For reasons of space, I have eliminated from the section all world leaders, whose biographies are very well known or easily available elsewhere. The biographies emphasize the New Deal and World War II period, and provide other information only as needed to amplify the text. I have not attempted to include persons who played minor roles in the text. Persons not cited in the Biographical Notes section, however, are cited in the index.

I would like to thank Robert E. Burke and Frank Freidel of the University of Washington for their advice and assistance in the editing of *My Roosevelt Years*. Without their support, its publication would not have been possible. I would also like to thank Julidta Tarver of the University of Washington Press, who had charge of the publication and who provided key support to the project. At every stage in the editing process, Norman Littell provided welcome assistance and support. It goes without saying that I take full responsibility for any errors which may have crept into the manuscript since I received it from Mr. Littell.

JONATHAN DEMBO
Seattle, Washington

My Roosevelt Years

1941

. . . I missed the swearing in of Bob Jackson in a ceremony at the White House—as he was elevated from the attorney general's office to the Supreme Court—a real disappointment. He is one of the great Americans, and as a great lawyer is potentially a great judge, although he has not been a good administrator, as he himself has admitted. There is much which ought to be done to the Department of Justice, which has not been done, to put it on a more businesslike basis and deliver its full power.

I called on [Mr. Justice] Frank Murphy at the Supreme Court as a result of persistent rumors that he is to resign and become the attorney general. I learned from a frank talk:

1. That the rumors are false. He has been offered the post for the last six weeks by the President, but believes it improper to leave the Court, before which the attorney general practices, and take the post. He wishes to remain and master the present job.

2. The President will not appoint [Solicitor General Francis B.] Biddle—reasons not defined.[1]

3. Paul McNutt is said to be making a strong drive for the post due to his sacrifice of the vice presidency at the Chicago convention when Vice President [Henry A.] Wallace was nominated.

Murphy was greatly interested in my statement that Biddle had said my name had been mentioned on several occasions, stating that the President had run out of his old-line leaders due to the appointments to the Supreme Court, and other factors.

I have had an exchange of correspondence with Vice President Wallace to whom I sent copies of my speeches, "The German Invasion of American Business" and "American Business and the New Order."[1] . . . Thurman

---

1. Since Jackson's nomination to the Supreme Court, Biddle had served as acting attorney general.

---

1. Norman M. Littell, "The German Invasion of American Business," *Mid-Winter Banquet of the Indiana State Bar Association, Riley Room, Claypool Hotel, Indianapolis, Indiana* (25 January 1941); "American Business and the New Order," *Graduating Banquet*

Arnold, assistant attorney general in charge of Anti-trust,[2] has an article
in the current *Reader's Digest* [3] dictated largely out of the former address
and, curiously enough, even the testimony of Assistant Attorney General
Frank Shea, in charge of the Claims Division,[4] quoted in Arnold's article,
was obviously taken verbatim from one of the addresses. Wallace was very
much interested.

I had some concern over Murphy's advice yesterday. He suggested a talk
with Wallace, [so] I met with him today . . . [I] also [spoke with him] on
the subject of economic warfare. . . . Wallace must be the key figure by
reason of being next in command under the President and above the
cabinet members. Therefore, [he is] above the jurisdictional jealousies and
tugs of war which, even in these tragic times, must prevail in government.
He gave me an executive order for suggestions and criticisms and asked
that I telephone him that night. He wondered about Justice participation,
fearing the assignment of Frank Shea to an advisory board on economic
defense, proposed in the order, of which Wallace would be chairman.[5]

Regarding the attorney general's post, a certain measure of eligibility
attache[s], should I say, to my geography. I am now the highest-ranking
man from the West in the government and the only one from the Pacific
Coast. There has long been a hue and cry for more recognition for that
area which led the progressive fight for the President. [I] was discussed—
so far as I'm concerned—only because Biddle and Murphy seem to be
out. A stranger to the department would be a poor appointment now. It
is really an unenviable post, for no man could go through the next few
years without being cut down mercilessly in the end. He will have to take
a firm stand against communists and firmer even against the more
formidable representatives of Nazi Germany, and it would be difficult to
emerge without a "Palmer" of "Red Raid" reputation.[6]

I talked with Secretary [Harold L.] Ickes immediately afterwards

---

of the University of Chicago School of Business Administration, 1941, in Littell scrapbook.

2. During the early 1940s, the Anti-trust Division of the Justice Department enforced
the anti-trust laws and handled legal proceedings arising from thirty other major laws
involving business regulation. It also conducted investigations and criminal prosecutions, or
suits in equity, to break up monopolies, restraints of trade, cartels, agreements with foreign
corporations, and restrictive patent arrangements.

3. Thurman W. Arnold, "How Monopolies Hobble Defense," *Reader's Digest,* July
1941, pp. 51–55.

4. The Claims Division of the Justice Department was in charge of all civil suits and claims
against the federal government that had not been specifically assigned to other divisions. It
was also responsible for all shipping and admiralty matters, war contracts, and contractors.

5. The Economic Defense Board (EDB) was established by Executive Order No. 8839,
30 July 1941, to advise the President on economic defense measures and to prepare for
postwar economic reconstruction. By Executive Order No. 8982, 17 December 1941,
President Roosevelt renamed the EDB the Board of Economic Warfare (BEW).

6. The "red raids" occurred during the anticommunist hysteria, 1919–20, and were an

regarding Puerto Rico—the housing problem in particular—and unsatisfactory relations as outlined to me by [Luis] Munoz-Marin, . . . the most
powerful figure in Puerto Rico. . . .

Ickes also advised me that within the next week he was making Rexford
Tugwell governor of Puerto Rico and bringing Mr. [John J.] Dempsey[7]
back to the Bureau of Insular Affairs[8]—a fortunate change. Mrs. Dempsey
is miserably unhappy there. . . . She is reported to be actually afraid of
living in Puerto Rico, which feeling communicates itself to proud
residents. I have understood also that she occasionally falls asleep when
the ladies of Puerto Rico call on her. . . .

Tuesday, 29 July 1941

In a conference with Mr. Biddle, I explained our problems in Hawaii
regarding condemnation cases, and he read the proposed letter to
Secretary [Frank] Knox explaining that we could not be put in a position
of defending a $481,000 deposit in court as insisted upon by the Navy,
when the Navy produced no witnesses and we could find none who would
testify to less than $925,000 as the value of the 1,000-acre site in the next
Mokapu land case. Mr. Biddle wholly agreed with my solution in sending
a [government] appraiser on the [Boeing] clipper ship today, in advance
of my own investigation there the ensuing week.

Wednesday, 30 July 1941

I conferred again with Mr. Biddle, presenting him with a memorandum
showing the serious situation which confronts us in the handling of
condemnation cases for lack of judges in various points in the country. . . .
I urged Mr. Biddle to take up these appointments with the President in
case any of them were ready for action, and he indicated that he might do
this tomorrow. . . .

---

outgrowth of the wartime fear of German subversion, labor turmoil, and antiwar activism.
They were led by U.S. Attorney General A. Mitchell Palmer, who alleged that a communist
plot existed to overthrow the government. During a series of midnight raids under Palmer,
the Justice Department arrested 6,000 citizens, without warrants or trials, and deported 556
radical aliens, but failed to uncover any grand plot.

7. Littell is probably referring to Mr. and Mrs. Guy J. Swope. Rexford G. Tugwell
replaced Swope as governor of the Territory of Puerto Rico. John J. Dempsey was an
Interior Department official but was not stationed in Puerto Rico.

8. The Bureau of Insular Affairs (or Division of Territories) was the Interior Department
agency responsible for civil government in such island territories of the United States as
Puerto Rico, the Virgin Islands, Hawaii, and the Philippines. Guy J. Swope served as
director, 1941–43.

We also gossiped a few moments about the current article by Thurman Arnold in the latest [Reader's] Digest, entitled "How Monopolies Hobble Defense," . . . Mr. Biddle was very much interested in the fact that both Arnold and . . . Shea had used portions [of my address to the Indiana Bar Association]. . . .

---

8 September 1941
Hunts Point, Bellevue, Washington

The gap between this and the last entry in July covers a great many events and considerable mileage, but most significant of all is the mileage covered in regaining my own equilibrium of outlook with which to face the ironies of those events and circumstances which confront me on my forty-second birthday—lying on my back for the fourth week, the first two having been spent in a hospital. . . .

That last week in July, upon which I dictated such sketchy, hasty notes, was an intense and exhausting one, the strain of which was greatly aggravated by the continuance of Washington heat in which I had never learned the technique of living. Behind it lay many months of continuous tension—in fact, two and one-half years of hard driving in Washington, D.C., broken up only by field trips and two periods of two weeks vacation each, the latter being spent, unfortunately, in other intense activities which precluded the type of rest and exercise which alone can break up tension and strain. There is no Puget Sound around Washington, D.C. . . .

Most trails of thought led back to the office, but I spent a lot of time on extra-curricular as well as curricular activities. In the last two and one-half years, I have argued in the Supreme Court four great cases: the Hetch-Hetchy case,[1] which is the great public power case from San Francisco; the Alabama tax case;[2] the Dam Five case;[3] and the Northern Pacific

---

1. In United States v. City and County of San Francisco, 310 U.S. 16–32 (1940) Justice Black overruled the decision of the 9th U.S. Circuit Court of Appeals, and upheld the District Court of Northern California, which had ruled in favor of the United States, in seeking to prevent the city of San Francisco from selling power from the Hetch-Hetchy Dam to private companies.

2. In United States v. State of Alabama, 313 U.S. 274–83 (1941)—the Alabama Tax Case—Chief Justice Hughes dismissed the efforts of the United States to prevent the state of Alabama from taxing lands the United States had acquired, because of preexisting liens on the property.

3. In United States v. Chicago, Milwaukee & St. Paul Railway Company, 312 U.S. 592–99 (1941)—the Dam Five Case—Justice Roberts reversed the lower courts and held that the United States did not have to pay compensation to the railroad when the government raised the water level of a river to improve navigation even though it damaged railroad-owned structures. The decision confirmed the supremacy of federal jurisdiction over navigable streams up to the line of mean high water.

case.[4] On the latter case, I argued one issue only; namely, the "agricultural point," which I tried in the District Court[5] and lost, but which I won in the Supreme Court. These were all invaluable experiences, for there is no pleasure to the lawyer like arguing a case in the Supreme Court—at least not to this lawyer. This is one of the invaluable prerogatives of the office of assistant attorney general, and I could not bear to neglect it in spite of the pressure of administrative duties. . . .

However, on the Dam Five case, I was compelled to leave the office for a week, taking briefs and books to Warm Springs, Virginia, to master that argument. . . . [I arrived] there on a Saturday in the first week of March, 1941. . . . It was not until after midnight on a Sunday night [a week later] that the pattern of the argument for the Dam Five case cleared in my mind, a stage which should be reached at least a week or ten days before the argument. It was a painful and disturbing experience to operate that close to the deadline, and I almost called a member of the Appellate Section who had written the brief for him to take over the argument.

The final draft of my argument (the second, only) came out of the typewriter as I picked up my hat and left for the courtroom, and I reviewed the argument once in the Department of Justice car while being driven to the Supreme Court.

Nevertheless, the oral argument of that case was one of the most satisfactory I have delivered. . . . [It] laid down clearly the unequivocal rights of the federal government in the exercise of a servitude over navigable waters below the high water. I argued up to the hilt the doctrine that the railroad company built at its peril below the high water on the Mississippi, risking any future changes in the plan of rendering the river more navigable (i.e. any future exercise of the federal government servitude). We won the case and resolved a confusion of conflict of authority, but I was pretty well burned out.

The Alabama tax case was also an expensive one in terms of day and night work, and I lost it, not anticipating that Justice [Charles Evans] Hughes would, with great pleasure, favor tax relief to the local, state, or municipal governments, and that the part of the New Deal part of the Court would, with pleasure, offset the charges made against the Court of supporting increased central power in the federal government, by leaning, in this case, toward relief of the state government. There being no other Supreme

---

4. In *United States v. Northern Pacific Railway Company*, 311 U.S. 317–76 (1940) the federal government had sued the railroad for preempting lands illegally under the terms of its 1864 land grant, and Littell had won the case in the District Court of Eastern Washington. Justice Roberts dismissed the company's appeal and returned the case to the District Court. Ultimately, on 29 August 1941, the company agreed to a settlement and returned approximately 363,000 acres of its original 2,900,000 acre land grant to the government and paid $300,000 in cash.

5. United States District Court for Eastern Washington.

Court decision on the subject, the Court could do as it pleased. Perhaps this is a defensive explanation, but I think there is much merit in it. . . .

In addition to the trip-hammer duties of the Lands Division[6] and its fast-moving problems, I endeavored to write, at night and on weekends, an article on the technical subject of land acquisitions in the attorney general's office, which would be sufficiently interesting to be readable and would tell to the public the story which we really have to tell there. The article is in the hands of an agent now. These extra-curricular activities consumed all extra hours at home and during weekends. . . .

The virtual trial of my close associate, Ewing Wright, during the last week before I left Washington on August 1, was the torpedo which sank the much-battered ship. Without recounting that incident now, the . . . facts seemed to indicate that he had utilized the position as my general assistant to have a higher valuation recognized on lands which he owned in a condemnation case. It was the first incident of that sort I have ever encountered and was as close to me as it could possibly arise; it made me sick all over. I virtually tried him, having in mind that my own reputation, the reputation of the Department of Justice, and the reputations of those involved and their families were at stake. . . . We found him technically not guilty, but it would not be a happy situation to have him remain in Washington, so he was permitted to return to Indiana to his old job upon renouncing any advantages [in] the transaction. In other words, he stuck to the lowest appraisal figure in order to clear the record of any possible implication.

Somehow I got through with the remainder of that week, until the evening of August 1, when I caught a plane for Los Angeles. . . . I was ill on the plane that night to the extent of having acute pains in high altitude. At Los Angeles, I dropped into a bed at the Biltmore immediately. . . . In the late afternoon, I called the house doctor, . . . He . . . said there was unquestioned indication of a heart attack . . . requiring immediate rest and escape from the tension under which I had been operating. It was a warning only, he said, and at my age a fortunate one—it would teach me to slow up a bit.

. . . I decided to skip Los Angeles engagements and knock off for the weekend, and since I had to go to San Diego anyway, I flew down the next morning and went out to La Jolla to the Casa de Manana . . .

I did not, however, get the old familiar lift out of exercise, the longest

---

6. The Lands Division of the Justice Department, of which Littell was the head, handled all legal matters—except criminal cases—pertaining to the public domain, land condemnations, titles, forest reserves, reclamation and irrigation projects, conservation of natural resources, and Indian lands and property; it also controlled similar work in the insular and territorial possessions of the United States, its federal reservations, and on public works; and it handled boundary disputes.

walk being . . . about three miles up the shore and back during which time I had to sit down a couple of times. "Exercise," the doctor had said in answer to my inquiry, "but not too intensely, and get plenty of rest just now. You will be all right in a little while."—It was bum advice and, as subsequent events proved, might have been fatal.

. . . The [5th, 6th, and part of the 7th of August] were spent in business in the Los Angeles office. . . . I postponed land acquisition matters in our other office there until returning from Honolulu, but lined up a number of apprentice attorneys suggested by deans of California law schools, all for interviewing upon my return. . . .

I cannot begin to cover those eight days in Honolulu with any adequacy, even the business of the occasion, which was to attempt to understand the almost incomprehensible differences between valuations on lands there and the perpetual struggle which we have had to prevent the exaction of exorbitant profiteering prices for land taken by us for the United States government. . . .

. . . We then went . . . down the entire coast over some of the most lovely scenery I have seen any place in the world to Makapu Point, where the big problem which primarily brought me to Honolulu was centered: A deposit of $481,000 in court, which we are instructed by the Navy to defend, whereas we could not find a witness on the island who would testify to a value of less than $925,000—and the defendants were claiming $1,300,000!

I had advised Secretary Knox of the Navy Department that we could not, in effect, make bricks without straw, and we had continued the trial of the case until I could investigate the whole matter. It all boiled down to a perfectly stupid and incredible mistake of the admiral in command in reaching a valuation of $481,000 based upon "assessed valuations," an utterly incompetent method of determining the market value. We reviewed every site on the island where land acquisitions were involved, and the entire problem cleared up immensely and quickly in my mind as wheelbarrow loads of correspondence could not have cleared it. A virtual state of land monopoly by a few large owners results in inordinate demands for land and very grudging sales—even to the government for the purposes of national defense. . . .

In flying away from that exquisite island, I could not be too happy about what I had seen there, not only on my own business of land acquisitions where we confront the tightest little monopoly and the most consistently resistant and selfish attitude on land acquisition of any place under the American flag, but also as to national defense itself and the general firm-ness of grasp of the federal government in this remote island of the Pacific.

On the latter point, our U.S. personnel are not strong, with occasional exceptions such as Judge [Ingram M.] Stainback, who is a stalwart, forth-right and courageous soul, if not brilliant. I met all the principal members

of the judiciary at a cocktail party given for me at the colonel's [Col. Elmer
E. Kirkpatrick, Jr.] house and, with a few exceptions, I was not impressed.
A requirement of three years' residence in Honolulu before appointment
to the judiciary weakens our power to put strong men in. The governor
[Joseph B. Poindexter] was away, but I gathered from calling on the acting
governor the general impression that he is an old man, not too well, and
that the administration is weak all the way down the line. . . .

A long conference with General [Walter C.] Short at Fort Shafter
showed me a fine old gentleman who certainly must be past sixty, not too
keen, whose moderation in attacking power I quickly suspected. [I] confirmed my opinion in the district attorney's office by examining a letter of
General Short's sent to Secretary of War [Henry L.] Stimson and, in turn,
sent by Secretary Stimson to the attorney general, asking that we not
prosecute Japanese consular representatives who had failed to register
under the Alien Registration Act,[7] or under the act requiring the registration of foreign agents, because he was working out a propaganda program of good feeling and cordial relations between the Americans and
Japanese in Hawaii. Without vast experience with orientals, I know that
was wrong. Only force is recognized, and the small minority of law-
breaking Japanese present there should be indicted vigorously. Old men
are essentially appeasers, and I could not understand a man of Short's
character being in charge of this vital defense post.[8]

Similarly in the Navy, Admiral [Claude C.] Bloch was a fine old three-
star admiral who had taken a demotion rather than be retired. I had lunch
with him in regard to land acquisition problems, at which time his responsibility for the Mokapu fiasco was practically admitted. He wanted the
land in order to exclude all foreign elements, including a few Japanese
fishermen, and obviously strove to make a low deposit and a low appraisal
to convince the Navy it could be had for that amount, taking the assessed
valuation rather than an appraisal of market value; all of which I think is
fairly typical of his ability. He has a lovely berth, in a fine spot in the naval
program, where authority is everything and critics not too numerous under

---

7. The Alien Registration Act of 1940 (Public Law 670), approved 28 June 1940,
empowered the attorney general to register and fingerprint all aliens within the United
States and its territories. The Foreign Agents Registration Act of 1938 (Public Law 583),
approved 8 June 1938, had previously required nondiplomatic representatives of foreign
governments to register with the attorney general.

8. Mr. Littell appended the following comment to this diary entry. "History has since
recorded the correctness of these observations in the bombing of Honolulu by the Japanese
on December 7, 1941. General Short was removed and is under investigation by a
committee appointed by the President (and headed by Supreme Court Justice Owen
Roberts) at the moment of writing this footnote (Jan. 1, 1942) and Admiral Block at Pearl
Harbor is involved in the same investigation. . . . " For the text of General Short's letter,
see Code Radiogram, General Short to War Department, 22 July 1941, Log Book Entry,
Littell Log Book No. 8, p. 20.

naval regulations. His most telling admission to me was that he had difficulties staying awake after 9:00 at night and frequently went to bed early—another grand old man, rising by seniority, occupying one of the most vital posts in the defense program. I really can't understand it in the face of the lessons which the Nazis have taught us.

The return trip was without event, save for a conversation with an American businessman just closed out of his embroidery manufacturing business at Swatow and a representative of the Chase National [Bank] returning from Hong Kong. With both of them I tested out my judgment on the question of policy as to indicting Japanese, due to their long experience in the Far East. Both concurred 100 per cent. I should add, however, that the Japanese problem in Hawaii is greatly magnified on the continent. The head of the FBI,[9] military authorities, lawyers, judges and others confirmed that the great mass of the Japanese would not go back to Japan if they could; are fearful of possible Japanese intervention; and that only a small minority of them, who are being watched and are allegedly detectable, would be Japanese fifth columnists or representatives. Vigorous indictment against these would, it seems to me, insure the loyalty of the majority who see action being taken.

I arrived at San Francisco on the 18th at 11:15 and spent a very busy day with Special Assistant M. Mitchell Bourquin, . . . The appointment of an attorney general had still not been made, and I found my name being bandied about quite a bit, Paul Mallon having said unequivocally in his column that Biddle would not be appointed but that a memorandum on the President's desk gave the name of the most probable successor to Bob Jackson, a young assistant attorney general from Seattle.[10] Then also, Hugh Fraser, . . . to whom I had given a very hasty and somewhat impatient ten-minute interview in Washington, . . . came out with a column, with nice ironies involved in his description of what was needed for the attorney general's post.[11] I refer particularly to the equation he lays down requiring "a tireless, vigorous, almost driving personality" and describing me as "a man of dynamic energy"—language with grim irony in it considering my present predicament.

I told my friends in San Francisco, including Governor [Culbert L.] Olson, . . . that Biddle, as solicitor general, was the man at this time, that

9. The Federal Bureau of Investigation was a bureau of the Justice Department. Under its director, J. Edgar Hoover, the FBI was responsible for all investigations into violations of federal laws, except for matters that were specifically assigned elsewhere, such as counterfeiting, postal violations, customs violations, etc. Robert Shivers was head of the FBI in Honolulu in August 1941.

10. Paul Mallon, "Hitler's Mounting Losses," Seattle Post-Intelligencer, 9 August 1941; "Norman Littel" [sic], Minneapolis Star, n.d., in Littell scrapbook.

11. Hugh R. Fraser, "Inside Washington," n.p., 30 August 1941, in Littell Log Book No. 1, after p. 19.

the President could not pass him over in my opinion. . . . It is a matter of constant disappointment and frustration to the westerners that we have no man in the cabinet, and they see no excuse for it now that some of them think roughly as outlined in the column of Fraser's that the West has no man who should be recognized, except me. . . .

I wound up a number of personnel problems, which are always the most exacting, leaving the interviewing of new applicants to [Robert E.] Mulroney the next day, and I flew to San Francisco on the 21st, where I spent another day, concluding with calls on the available judges in the federal building in the late afternoon, finally interviewing a half a dozen applicants and visiting Dudley Field Malone, who is on my roll assisting Mr. Bourquin there. There is a tragic story which I have not time to tell— one of the greatest lawyers in American life during the period of the Wilson administration, destroyed by drink and now seeking a footing in practice again, apparently in full control of himself and reaching out to do good work. I was impressed by his fine quality of mind, understanding and real modesty and appreciation of the very humble role we have given him, instead of demanding, through his intimate friendship with the President, bigger and better things.

I had dinner at Judge [William] Healy's, of the Circuit Court, at night, with Superior Court Judge [Edward P.] Murphy and Supreme Court Judge Parker and Bourquin and their respective wives. It was a stimulating and interesting occasion, but I was troubled throughout with the now familiar ache in my chest, and resolved that would have to skip Portland and make directly for Seattle and for Dr. [Nils A.] Johannson's office to see what in the devil was wrong with me before I could fly to Spokane the following week on the 28th to conclude the Northern Pacific case in the District Court there. . . .

Fortunately, Katherine met me at Seattle, . . . and we went immediately to Dr. Johannson's office, where I was ordered to bed until a cardiograph could be taken the next morning, and Dr. [Eric M.] Chew, a heart specialist, brought in. The verdict came quickly and was more of a shock to Katherine than to me because I had somehow, in those final days between Los Angeles and Seattle, felt that a complete reorientation was going to be dictated. There had been a definite occlusion during the last week of July—Dr. Chew named the date from the cardiograph. Both he and Johannson damned the advice I had received in Los Angeles, saying that while the injury was extremely slight and that I would completely recover from it and need never have another one, still the only treatment, particularly in the ensuing ten days, is complete and immediate rest.[12] . . .

It is one hell of an assignment considering the irons I had in the fire which are now getting cold, . . .

---

12. "Norman Littell in Hospital for Rest," *Seattle Times*, 25 August 1941; "Norman Littell in Swedish Hospital," *Seattle Post-Intelligencer*, 26 August 1941.

The world goes on so quickly and easily without any of us. Friends are the chief consolation . . . John and Anna Boettiger have been in to see us twice at the hospital and their expected call this weekend was cut off by the death of Grandmother [Sara Delano] Roosevelt at Hyde Park yesterday. John and Anna were on the water in their power cruiser taking Secretary Ickes and his wife [Jane] to Port Angeles and then returned to hear the news. Note Mrs. Roosevelt's comment in "My Day" in my scrap book.[13] There are volumes behind certain lines in that statement. . . .

---

11 September 1941
Hunts Point, Bellevue, Washington

I broke training and listened to the President's speech—electrifying in its cold statement of facts and conclusions. It is spraying the world, today, on broadcasts of many languages, with the incisiveness of machine gun bullets, evoking similar reactions in South America.

Almost the only noise which consistently interrupts the peace and quiet of this little cove on Lake Washington is the clank of steel on steel at the Washington Shipyards at Kirkland, when the heavy blow of a drop-forge, hammering out some angle-iron for steel rib, echoes down the shore. . . . There is a twenty-four hour shift at the shipyard for, no matter at what hour I have awakened, I have, from time to time, heard that echo. Far from being a disturbing sound, it is, in fact, a reassuring one—as stern and metallic as the President's speech today: Full of decision, strength, and persistent cooperation. Hitler already has under his domination, in Europe, shipbuilding capacity approximately four times the production capacity of this country, in terms of ships—although many may not be operating either willingly or effectively under his control—whereas here, in as remote a point as Lake Washington, a small shipyard is doing its utmost all of the time.

---

15 September 1941
Bellevue, Washington

After one or two unsuccessful tries, I caught up with the new attorney general, Francis Biddle, at Santa Monica, California, this morning.[1] After expressing concern over my situation, about which he had learned appar-

---

13. Eleanor Roosevelt, "My Day," *Washington Times-Herald*, 7 September 1941.

---

1. "Biddle Is Named Head of Justice Department," *Washington Evening Star*, 25 August 1941; "Biddle Takes Oath of Office," *Washington Times-Herald*, 6 September 1941, in Littell scrapbook.

ently through Melvyn and Helen Douglas and Mr. [Rensen DuB.] Bird,
. . . I told him that the doctor had prescribed at least six weeks of vacation
and that I had a great deal of unused, accumulated leave which I felt
inclined to draw upon if this met with his approval. He was, of course, most
cordial and urged that I take all the leave I had coming or any amount that
I thought proper and, when I stated that the Lands Division was in good
shape and in good hands under the direction of J. Edward Williams, chief
of the Condemnations Section, he assured me that he was entirely satisfied
with that, having had two or three contacts with Williams in my absence,
which he said were entirely satisfactory. . . .

I said that I particularly wanted to advise him of the administration's
loss of face with our forthright liberal friends in the West, particularly in
California, in view of the widely current rumor that Ed [Edwin W.]
Pauley of the [Pauley] Petrol Corporation had apparently been able to
stop the filing of a suit by the federal government to test the federal
government's interests in oil deposits in the tidelands along the coast of
California.[2] Francis Biddle and I knew the inside story better than anyone
else. I had introduced Ed Pauley to Mr. Biddle as a representative of the
owners interested in the wells located in the tidelands. As an old-line
Democrat, who had helped in the campaign, he had, through Ed Flynn,
secured an appointment or two with the President, unbeknownst to me or
to Francis Biddle, who was handling the tidelands case after the matter
had been thoroughly briefed in the Lands Division, pursuant to an order
of the President that we study the problem. Pauley had come back from
his appointment with the President to my office in great satisfaction at
having won the chief over to the injustice and futility of attempting to file
suit in California. Apparently, the President had said that his chief
interest was in the Gulf tidelands off of Texas and Louisiana where, in
certain locations many miles to sea, there were still only a few fathoms of
water and dome structures which indicated substantial oil possibilities
which ought to be protected if the interests were properly in the United
States government. No doubt this leaked out in oil circles for it was
widely rumored that the case had been blocked by Ed Pauley.

Francis said that he had picked that up already in California and intended to see the President about it when he got back to Washington to
determine what could be done. We all know that the case is an extremely
difficult one, except as to our rights in the marginal sea beyond the
three-mile limit, but it strikes me now as a case which, in spite of all legal
doubts, should be disposed of conclusively in court, whether we take a

---

2. The issue had arisen several years previously. While cruising in the shallow waters of
the Gulf of Mexico, President Roosevelt had become interested in who had title to the oil
tidelands. He had endorsed both a congressional joint resolution and a suit claiming federal
title to all oil lands lying beyond the three-mile territorial limit.

licking or not, in order to remove the cloud on title and definitively settle the matter. Now, above all else, we should remove the impression that special interests have reached through to our basic policies to prevent the litigation. . . .

After concluding the conversation, I must say that I had a feeling of some satisfaction at having dealt with Biddle's appointment as attorney general in a forthright manner as it should have been dealt with. There were so many *prima donnas*, particularly Thurman Arnold, who were in search of this appointment and used every device, including the use of well-tamed columnists, to get it. There is a practice in Washington much like the medieval practice of using falcons which were carried on the wrist and then released at the appropriate time to pounce upon the prey. . . . Similarly, there are trained newspaper writers who, in exchange for news . . . champion the cause of one person or another and pounce upon his enemies at will. So [Frank C.] Waldrop, a friend and booster of Thurman Arnold's, pounced upon Biddle the very moment that Bob Jackson went up to the Supreme Court, describing Biddle as an "aristocrat of Philadelphia who had broken out with a rash of liberalism," and damning him throughout, concluding the article with a strong plea for the appointment of Thurman Arnold.[3] This was repeated later as the delay in Biddle's appointment dragged out.

I wrote promptly to the President, advocating the Biddle appointment, and only became interested in the equation which made my appointment a possibility when every indication was that Biddle would not be appointed and I was definitely advised to this effect. . . . The President could not pass over the solicitor general[4] without deeply hurting him and, while he is not starting off with a show of popularity and has what we must describe as a "poor press," he will make a good attorney general as his mind works with quick flashes and he gets things done. The above discussion about the oil controversy[5] . . . [is a case] in point.

---

17 September 1941
Hunts Point, Bellevue, Washington

John and Anna Roosevelt Boettiger . . . were out to dinner last night. . . . I must say they have been cheery, faithful friends, in spite of any mis-

---

3. Frank C. Waldrop, no title, *Washington Times-Herald*, 9 August 1941, in Littell scrapbook.
4. The solicitor general is the second ranking officer of the Justice Department. His main function is to represent the Justice Department before the Supreme Court and other federal courts and to serve as acting attorney general in the absence or incapacity of the attorney general.
5. During the war, the oil tidelands issue was not resolved. In January 1942, Biddle

understandings or differences of opinion which I have had with John—particularly the one last fateful event in which I found myself squarely in between him and the President just before the election. I differed flatly with John as how the [Stephen F.] Chadwick–[Monrad C.] Wallgren campaign for the Senate should be handled.

However, bit by bit, we have patched up any differences that seemed to hang over from the last exciting year; and as far as the priceless Anna is concerned, it is a homecoming. She again told me during a long visit at the hospital that she had never been devoted to any woman as she is to Katherine, my wife. . . .

John's and Anna's visits, singly or together, bring in the eddys and currents of Washington's life at this remote distance from the capitol. Secretary Ickes and Jane, his young wife, have been vacationing in a rain-bound cabin at Lake Crescent after spending some gloomy days with John and Anna. [The] secretary [is] depressed over his loss of power and exclusion from the national defense picture.[1]

He is described in this week's *Time*[2] as "nobody's sweetheart" and, indeed, he is such a professional oppositionist and inveterate fighter or slugger, and such a feudist by preference, that he is preferred only by his own following of satellites. Now, when cooperation and personnel organization are needed, he is not wanted. They left with imperfect rest, Jane having wished to leave before their time was up because of the gloomy, incessant rain. . . .

John brought a handful of files last night—the Paul Appleby–Claude Wickard clash in the Department of Agriculture—to discuss Wickard's nomination of Appleby for a post on the [Federal] Reserve Board. Both the secretary and his undersecretary, Appleby, deny any conflict which they say is created by newspapers (particularly the *Merry-Go-Round*) but knowing both men well, I can imagine there is a basic incompatibility there—temperamentally and intellectually.

The question of the division of the Ninth Circuit into two circuit courts

<hr>

announced that the government's proposed suit was "Dead." Later, in August 1946, President Truman vetoed a bill to give the states jurisdiction over the tidelands on the grounds that the matter was before the Supreme Court. Eventually, on 16 May 1949, the Supreme Court ruled the federal government could file suit against the states to settle the question. See Thomas J. Hamilton, "Pauley Requested Favor on Oil Lands, Says Ickes," New York Times, 2 February 1946.

1. This is a reference to the growing importance of Jesse H. Jones in financing the national defense program and to Ickes's relative decline. Jones had negotiated a contract with the Aluminum Company of America, by which the Reconstruction Finance Corporation (RFC) financed construction of several plants at concessionary terms, and had signed it without Ickes's consent. See Drew Pearson and Robert S. Allen, "Washington Merry-Go-Round: Jesse Jones Power Next to Roosevelt," *Seattle Post-Intelligencer*, 27 October 1941.

2. "Nobody's Sweetheart," *Time*, 15 September 1941, pp. 14–16.

of appeals is a raging controversy of the moment on which John has sided
vigorously in editorials . . . with the one advocate of the division, Judge
Healy. Judge [William] Denman argued the matter with me extensively
in San Francisco, . . . attacking Judge Healy most mercilessly. Senator
[Homer T.] Bone and Congressman [Warren G.] Magnuson have introduced bills to divide the circuit.[3] I have taken no position and will take none
until I have examined the statements of both Judge Healy and Judge
Denman and considered the matter fully. John has grown somewhat in
stature and astonished me with a modesty on this issue, wholly unexpectedly; he usually makes up his mind and takes the bit in his teeth.

"I am going to be guided by what you conclude in this matter,
Norman," he said. "If you think this bill should not be supported and the
circuits should not be divided, after you have had time to study the
matter, then I will not support it any further."

I told him I would reach my best judgment whenever time permitted
because I anticipated that the attorney general would wish to know my
opinion in the matter if I got back in time.[4] . . .

Of course, the further incident of a visit by George A. Henrye and Bill
Durkee . . . contributed somewhat. . . . Durkee and Henrye confirmed
overwhelmingly that Ed Pauley was dominated by the Signal Oil
Company. Durkee spoke of Ed's suddenly blossoming into prosperity in
1938, with new trucks and an outlet for his Santa Clara crude which had
always been denied him . . . —a *rapprochement* for Signal Oil, subsidiary
of the Standard Oil Company of New Jersey. Hence, Ralph Davies,
deputy administrator for the oil industry now under Ickes[5] and former
director of the Standard Oil Company of New Jersey, gets on splendidly
with Ed Pauley whom he used to damn as the crookedest man in the
business, largely because he was a struggling independent. Wheels
within wheels! I have so advised Mr. Biddle by memorandum. . . . and
the problem is his. I am not the attorney general, and perhaps one
difference between Biddle and me is that, . . . I would file the case to test
ownership of the tidelands and tell the President about it later. So many

3. The Magnuson (H.R. 5489) and Bone (S. 1793) bills to divide the 9th U.S. Circuit and
to create an eleventh circuit were introduced in Congress. *Congressional Record*, vol. 87
(28 July, 4 August 1941), pp. 6330, 6734.

4. Both bills to split the 9th Circuit were referred to the judiciary committees of the
respective houses but went no further.

5. Ralph K. Davies was deputy petroleum coordinator of the Office of Petroleum
Coordinator for National Defense, 1941–46. Harold Ickes was coordinator. Originally
established in May 1941 as an advisory office in the Interior Department, it was transformed
by President Roosevelt into a powerful central control over petroleum by Executive Order
No. 9276, 2 December 1942. It was intended to "coordinate and centralize the war policies
and actions of the government relating to petroleum with a view toward providing adequate
supplies of petroleum."

explanations could be offered afterwards, and there is nothing like a *fait accompli* to stand on its own feet.

Anna recounted many fascinating incidents in the life of her family, and particularly her father—how the President flew to the convention in 1932 to make his acceptance speech and how, while Anna was waiting with others in the airport control station, the plane was frequently lost overhead in the stormy weather which prevailed, . . . and how her father on the plane re-wrote his acceptance speech three times.

In the 1936 acceptance speech, while [John Nance] Garner was beginning to mumble his speech through the microphone and the wind was blowing his script away, the President had almost fallen face forward due to one of the iron braces on his left leg having slipped. The President was holding onto his son Jimmie's arm and Jimmie's other hand held the President's manuscript, which he had to drop with the pages scattering all over the platform behind the President, while he supported the President in an inconspicuous manner so that no one in the audience knew what had happened. His bodyguard behind saw immediately what had happened and bent quickly and snapped the brace back into position so that the President could steady himself with Jimmie's aid and the fall was avoided. It was a real job getting the manuscript back into place, however, before it was time to speak, and beads of perspiration were standing out on the President's brow.

There are many other things in the life of that fascinating family which I cannot recount; I only hope I will not forget them—a priceless incident being Franklin's search for his missing pants on the night of the first inauguration, going up and down the hall on the second floor of the White House in full dress, lacking only the said pants, looking for sympathy and the pants also. . . .

---

2 October 1941
Spencers' House, West Vancouver, B.C.

[Dear Katherine Mather,]

The magic carpet upon which I seem to have made a series of fateful moves of late—as a submissive and somewhat awed passenger—lands again in a new and unexpected spot at Pansie[1] and David Spencers'[2] house in Vancouver. What I expected to be a hasty visit and a week's

---

1. Catherine Grace "Pansie" Spencer was the widow of Thomas A. Spencer (1874–1937), formerly director of the David Spencer (Department) Stores, Ltd. of Vancouver, B.C., 1920–37. Littell served, without pay, as the executor of her husband's estate.
2. The son of Catherine and Thomas Spencer.

leave seems to be a sentence of at least six weeks of convalescence. . . .

. . . It was almost a necessary escape because people and events had been rapidly closing in on me . . . after a general discovery of where my place of hibernation was. . . . So we drove away after reviewing the state of the universe with John and Anna, where I could not resist a very gentle "I told you so" about Tommy Corcoran upon whom I had futilely put my mark on previous occasions in discussions with John and Anna, only to encounter some slight resistance. The conclusion to be drawn from the whole Tommy Corcoran incident is one which I drew long ago in my observations as to Tommy himself, and I stated it simply to John and Anna: "No quality is so essential in government as simple integrity and forthrightness. Ability and brilliance of mind are not enough."

I recall the case of Alex Cravens, one of Tommy's good friends, whom I had known at Oxford as one of the most brilliant of the Rhodes Scholars then in attendance, although almost removed from our common walk of life by frequent visits to Buckingham Palace, where he played tennis with the Prince of Wales, now the Duke of Windsor. We always felt that, like some of the American girls who had been kissed by that same worthy representative of English nobility (and these were legion) Alex Cravens was never the same thereafter. Employed by the RFC[3] during the NRA period,[4] Alex Cravens left the administration under embarrassing circumstances. It seems that he had accepted a fee of one thousand dollars or so for assistance in getting an RFC loan while an attorney on the staff of that agency. . . .

Tommy Corcoran was of the same pattern, and he once defended Alex Cravens to me, giving some explanation of his conduct as elaborate as the current explanations of Tommy's influence on the Department of Justice in behalf of the Sterling Products Corporation which was indicted under

3. The Reconstruction Finance Corporation (RFC) was a federal agency established by Congress (Public Law 2), 22 January 1932. Congress empowered it to lend money to banks, agricultural credit associations, and other corporations in an effort to end the Depression. Under the New Deal the RFC received greatly enlarged financial resources and was empowered to lend money directly to individuals. Under Jesse Jones, the RFC became both the nation's largest bank and its largest investor. It bought stock in banks, thereby adding to their capital. It also expanded to include a large number of subsidiaries, including the federal mortgage agencies, the Commodity Credit Corporation, the Electric Home and Farm Authority, and the Export-Import Bank. During World War II, it was heavily involved in financing the war effort.

4. June 1933–May 1935. The National Recovery Administration (NRA) was a federal agency authorized by the National Industrial Recovery Act (Public Law 67) approved 16 June 1933. The basic principal of the NRA was self-help. It established a framework by which industry, labor, and government could cooperate to reduce cutthroat competition and stabilize wages, prices, and employment. In May 1935 the Supreme Court ruled the NRA unconstitutional in the "Sick Chicken" case, *Schechter Poultry Corp., et al. v. United States*, 295 U.S. 553, on the grounds that Congress had delegated too much power to the President.

the anti-trust laws for its affiliations with the *I.G. Farbenindustrie* of Germany.[5] Even John and Anna had to agree that the situation was scandalous, very hard on the administration, and that it left both Thurman Arnold and . . . Francis Biddle, in an extremely awkward position. . . .

Affectionately,
Your Father

---

6 December 1941
Boettigers' House, Mercer Island, Washington

[Dear Katherine Mather,]

The long interlude at Vancouver, B.C., staying with your Aunt Pansie, has come to an end. Mother and I have been away from you . . . [for] four months—our longest absence from you and Norman, Jr., and we shall find you quite changed when we return.

The period of convalescence at your Aunt Pansie Spencer's house has been remarkable in many respects, aside from the fact that it is the longest period of sheer idleness and reflection I have ever known in my life, but most particularly for the discovery of a diet through a doctor in Vancouver, which must be listed as one of the principal events in my life, for we fully expect to put the household on this diet on our return even though our hearty Norman, Jr. does not seem to require such refinements. . . .

You will find that your own life develops in stages. We have reached a new stage [in] our relationships with John and Anna. We are divorced from, or have outgrown, some of the feverish differences of opinion which antedated the election. John has grown in stature with the success of the *Post-Intelligencer* of which he and Anna are the publishers. While John worked on his new boathouse, your mother and I went for a walk and a ride with Anna. I think we have always been something of an outlet— either or both of us—for Anna, and the observations of her recent visits to Washington, D.C., and Hyde Park poured out unrestrainedly. There had been only one hurried day in Washington with brief visits with the President and Mrs. Roosevelt, John having lunch with Mr. [William S.]

---

5. The Justice Department subpoenaed the books of Sterling Products, Incorporated, on 9 April 1941, along with the records of its subsidiaries and those of several other major drug and chemical firms, to ascertain whether they were controlled by German firms. On 26 September, Sterling and its subsidiaries signed a consent decree to avoid a trial. Sterling paid a fine and agreed to have no further contact with the German firm I. G. Farbenindustrie. See Joseph C. Goulden, *The Superlawyers* (New York: Dell, 1973), pp. 163–64; *Congressional Record*, vol. 91 (22 January 1945), pp. A295–A297.

Knudsen and the President as a rather self-conscious invader of what was intended as a *tête-à-tête* between the President and Mr. Knudsen. . . .

Anna and John were invited by the President to go with him to the Eustises[1] in New York. Anna knew at once that their function, literally translated, was to chaperone the President in seeing Princess Martha of Norway, a Swedish princess whose name is pronounced "Merta." Her husband [Crown Prince Olav] is abroad in London attached to King Haakon's [King Haakon VII of Norway] staff, namely his father's staff in exile in London. Princess Martha seems to be a sore spot in the family as far as Mrs. Roosevelt is concerned, although there is no conceivable impropriety in the relationship between the President and Princess Martha; there is only that keen enjoyment and relaxation in her company which men from time to time find in women whose particular mentality or charm appeals to them.

"He is entitled to any relaxation he can find," I said, "and most particularly of that bantering relaxing type which a charming woman alone can supply." We parked the car looking out over Lake Washington down by the Boys' School on Mercer Island.

"Of course he is," Anna said, "and I wish I could get mother to see it that way. The truth is that mother after all these years is deeply in love with him and feels the situation keenly. As a matter of fact, Princess Martha is neither a brilliant intellect nor a great beauty. She is simply a highly cultivated, charming woman who listens to the President and keenly enjoys his conversations. She is the kind of woman, and the proper kind, with whom he can unbend and relax completely, and he needs that kind of relaxation."

Anna spoke of the awful ordeal through which her mother had recently been during the long illness and final death of Hall, the brother to whom she was most devoted, and who in turn would see and recognize no one but Mrs. Roosevelt during his last illness. The public little knows of the violent tragedy of that prolonged death—how Mrs. Roosevelt slept for days in her clothes, coming home from the hospital only to take a shower and go about her duties, but for the most part remaining at the hospital and at the bedside where the agonized, tortured suffering of her brother kept her constantly on the rack; violent hemorrhages exploding involuntarily from the sick man actually splattered the walls of the hospital room with blood. It was vain for nurses to reassure Mrs. Roosevelt that Hall was unconscious and did not suffer during these frightful attacks, and she herself suffered attacks of illness and nausea almost daily from what she went through.

---

1. William C. and Edith M. Eustis were neighbors and old family friends of the Roosevelts.

As an example of the difficult relations, hopes, satisfactions and disappointment, which the sensitive Mrs. Roosevelt has enjoyed and suffered all of her life with the President, is the incident regarding Hall's funeral. The day before the funeral, the President was most thoughtful and gentle and said that he was going to set aside all appointments and go with her to the funeral. It was, however, a passing moment of thoughtfulness, and he quite forgot all about it the next day and instead invited Princess Martha to Hyde Park for the weekend with John and Anna. It was an unintentionally brutal blow at Mrs. Roosevelt's most tender spots, for it hit both the soreness of her loss of her brother, from which she was recovering weakly, after his tortuous death, and her companionship with the President. What desolation of heart must have been hers at the funeral—alone.

At Hyde Park, the President said he wanted to have dinner in his new cottage, recently completed as his own private retreat, and instructed Anna and Princess Martha that he wanted them only to get the dinner. Anna had it arranged as much as possible in advance knowing full well that neither she nor Princess Martha would be able to spend much time in the kitchen, at least after cocktail hour was reached, and sure enough the President called to them from the living room to come out of the kitchen and have cocktails. They did the usual old-fashioneds. Harry Hopkins and John Boettiger were the only other men present.

It was one of those completely off-the-record periods of hearty relaxation, with stories and wisecracks both good and bad, laughter and sheer fun. Harry Hopkins, who looked terribly ill, with pouch, sagging skin over a sallow face, drank his liquor nevertheless and was as gay as the rest—living up to the hilt. I notice that he is back in the hospital for treatment again in the last few days. It is difficult to see how he can last long, and this, too, is a tragedy as he is the most companionable of the men around the President. Even in my obscure little post, I know what that means to have a man close to you who is utterly and completely loyal and faithful. . . .

Missy Le Hand, the President's secretary, for example, has gone completely to pieces and has been in a sanatorium, although she is now at Warm Springs. She was in the Doctor's Hospital at Washington when Anna was there, and Anna called upon her, finding her mind reduced to that of a small child. She, too, has taken a beating in recent years, and relied too much upon sleeping tablets to quiet the high strung, nervous temperament. The climax came when she fell on her face one night at a dinner at the White House and was carried away, a casualty of battle which closes another chapter of companionship which likewise has its history in the personal life of the President and Mrs. Roosevelt.

As Anna very wisely said, it is fine to have a woman of Princess Martha's good breeding and background because she brings associates not from the secretarial level. There are always associates who are hangers-on. Indeed the intrigue of the White House has been due somewhat to that very factor for two camps existed there. How well I know that Missy Le Hand represented one of them and that the Tommy Corcoran school worked through Missy Le Hand and did everything they could to court the influence of Mrs. Roosevelt. Whatever be the differences of opinion which may arise from time to time between the President and Mrs. Roosevelt, there is never a need for the violent conflict of cliques which has existed in the Missy Le Hand days.

Even Harry Hopkins fell victim to those cliques. Having been first taken up by Mrs. Roosevelt because of his social service experience and background—and introduced through this channel to the President—he attained to such position . . . that he was considered the likely candidate for the President in 1940. . . . In 1939 Hopkins himself frankly admitted to Anna, in a conversation, that he was the most likely candidate for the presidency in 1940. Health and other factors disposed of that ambition but, in the meantime, he passed completely into the President's camp and into the anti-Eleanor group.

It would be wrong to leave an inference that the great community of public interest between Mrs. Roosevelt and the President do not bind them together. He would not for one moment consider parting with her. This issue arose once before in their lifetime, and he made it very clear that he would make no change and wanted her by him.

---

7 December 1941
[Continuation of letter to Katherine Mather]

This includes one of the most eventful days in the history of your country. John and Anna have gone to the office of the *Post-Intelligencer* to select articles and pictures for the morning paper, for war between Japan and the United States became an accomplished fact with bombing of Honolulu today. We had been out on a long walk—Anna, your mother, "Sistie," "Buzzie,"[1] and I—while John was working on his boathouse with one of the Secret Service men[2] who constantly watches the place. When we got back we were advised that the incredible attack [was] apparently staged by the military powers in Japan without knowledge of the civil government, for fifty planes flew in from an airplane carrier lying at sea and

---

1. Eleanor "Sistie" Dall and Curtis "Buzzie" Dall were Anna Boettiger's children by her first husband, Curtis Dall.

2. The Secret Service is the division of the Treasury Department charged with protecting the President, the Vice President, and their families. It is also responsible for enforcing the laws against counterfeiting of currency, the forgery of securities, and other laws enforced by the Treasury Department.

bombed both Honolulu and Pearl Harbor, setting fire to and ultimately sinking the battleship *Oklahoma* and damaging the new battleship *West Virginia*, which as Buzzie advises with great precision, had six sixteen-inch guns.

One bomb struck a barracks at Hickam Field killing 350 enlisted men, all of which indicated that the military forces of Hawaii were certainly not ready, although apparently pursuit planes did get into the air and engage the invaders.

In writing recently to Marvin H. McIntyre . . . in regard to the successor for Governor Poindexter, I pointed out the inadequacy of government personnel in the Islands during these days of tension, showing that Poindexter, himself, was old and enfeebled by recent illness, and was incapable of the executive attentions necessary for the chief of government to serve this principal base of supplies should hostilities break out in the Far East. . . . I went on to point out that Admiral Bloch, in charge of naval operations there, was also past sixty; and in one of the most exciting posts under the American flag, he found it impossible to stay awake after 9:30 P.M. as he advised me at luncheon one day. He was apparently still asleep when the Japs came in with no listening posts functioning and no observers out.

General Short, who was in command at Hickam Field, was another nice old gentleman of wide experience, past sixty in years. . . .

Mrs. Roosevelt telephoned from the White House shortly after we returned from our walk at about 11:30 A.M., explaining that a transport had been sunk and adding that the attack had occurred while the Japanese ambassador[3] was negotiating in Washington for an agreement between the United States and Japan. Typical Nazi tactics.

Of the rumble of guns off the coast of Hawaii, indicating a naval engagement, no concrete information has been made available, but the rumble of guns here is indeed audible. In a single day, the nation has been united. Even the most recalcitrant isolationists,[4] like [Burton K.] Wheeler and Governor [Alfred M.] Landon of Kansas, are driven into camp with declarations of national unity and determination under this attack.

"I am glad it came this way, since it had to come," Katherine said. . . .

"It's that old Roosevelt luck," I said to Anna, somewhat grimly over the application of it to these tragic circumstances. "His enemies are com-

---

3. The Japanese ambassador to the United States at the time of Pearl Harbor was Kichisaburo Nomura.

4. Isolationists were persons and groups who favored U.S. neutrality in world affairs and who opposed U.S. participation in international agencies that might commit the U.S. to foreign military action without congressional approval. They opposed FDR's policy of preparedness for war and of aid to the Western Allies. Many isolationists supported the aims of the German, Italian, Japanese, and, prior to June 1941, the Soviet regimes.

pletely routed, and all of his policy of preparedness and firmness in the Far East is vindicated."

I was a little astonished at Mrs. Roosevelt's suggesting somewhat anxiously that perhaps the children ought to come to Washington to stay in the White House, fearing the possibility of bombing Sand Point [Naval Air Station] and the Boeing Airplane factory. The possibilities were rushed upon us by the daring nature of the Japanese attack which had sunk a transport 1,300 miles from San Francisco. A solution applicable to the Boettiger children would scarcely be applicable to all the other children in danger, but the mind of the grandmother had obviously not thought this matter out. She simply telephoned Anna involuntarily and in an obvious state of nervous anxiety. . . .

We hung over the radio all evening listening to pros and cons and speculations as to whether we would have the use of Vladivostock as an airplane base or not. We had heard just before leaving Vancouver, from the sister of Mrs. Glassford,[5] that her husband had been put in command of the allied fleet in the Pacific, a startling bit of news with implications which came to challenge our credulity. John Boettiger could not believe it, and we had sent a telegram of congratulations to Mrs. Glassford in Los Angeles also asking for a letter advising of the scope of Admiral Glassford's command. I hope we shall hear, but events may have overtaken her before she will reply. Such younger men should be in command all the way down the line, replacing an old fellow like Admiral Bloch who has no real ability anyway, as operations at Pearl Harbor seem clearly to indicate. Such great executive capacity is demanded in a place like that. A man either has it or hasn't it, and he might be a good navigator or naval strategist without being able to run a big show like that going on at Pearl Harbor. We do not know Glassford except through his wife, and vital discussions with her indicate a hard driving, able, fearless man. I hope he is in command from all I know of him. . . .

All my love to you my darling daughter.

Affectionately,
Daddy [signed]

---

8 December 1941
[P.S.]

As we sat at breakfast this morning, we heard over the radio the meeting of both houses of Congress to hear the President's message, asking for a

---

5. Eleanor Phelps "Doddie" Glassford was the wife of Admiral William A. Glassford, Jr. She was originally from Vancouver Island.

declaration of war on Japan. As the President spoke, Johnnie Boettiger, aged 2 years and 6 months, toddled into the dining room with a pingpong ball in one hand and a paddle in the other. I had been playing with him, teaching him how to hit the ball the preceding evening. He looked up for a playmate but his mother said, "Sh. . . . ! Grandpa is speaking. Listen to Grandpa's voice!"

Johnnie listened while his grandfather's resonant voice and cutting words came over the radio into the breakfast room at Seattle:

> It will be recorded that the distance of Hawaii from Japan makes it obvious that the attack was deliberately planned many days or even weeks ago. During the intervening time the Japanese government has deliberately sought to deceive the United States by false statements and expressions of hope for continued peace. . . .

Little Johnnie looked up as if he had had enough of that serious and incomprehensible subject and said, "May I play now?" looking at this mother.

His mother nodded and gave him an encouraging pat in the direction of the dining room door where he vanished for pursuits more to his interests.

---

30 December 1941

At the attorney general's staff meeting, this morning the following principal matters were discussed:

Alien Property: The question as to whether or not there should be an executive director or a board provided for in the proposed executive order of the President was apparently the issue delaying finality or organization.[1]

War Labor Policy Board: A very real question of policy was presented as to whether or not the Department of Justice ought to be represented on this board in view of the fact that the Department of Justice will inevitably be involved in the enforcement of whatever law may be passed restricting strife and regulating labor during wartime.[2] Mr. Arnold thought

---

1. President Roosevelt signed Executive Order No. 9095 establishing the Office of Alien Property Custodian on 11 March 1942. The Alien Property Custodian was ordered to seize the assets of enemy nationals in the United States and to use these to the fullest extent in the war effort. In April 1942 the President directed the Alien Property Custodian to seize enemy-controlled patents and make them available to American companies."

2. President Roosevelt established the National War Labor Board by Executive Order No. 9017, 12 January 1942, to replace the National Defense Mediation Board. Its function was to settle labor disputes and regulate wages so as to maintain war production. Its membership consisted of four representatives each from industry, labor, and government. William H. Davis was chairman.

the Department should not be on the board in view of the fact . . . that continual demand for snap judgments and legal options . . . are presented to the representative of the Department on such boards, frequently on matters . . . which ought to be given thought and consideration in the Department. [Charles] Fahy pointed out that it would only be a board advisory to the President, and it seems that Jerry Reilly, general counsel for the Department of Labor, is preparing the executive order. The consensus of opinion was definitely opposed to membership on the board in view of the Department's respective functions in prosecuting cases.

Executive Orders and Emergency Legislation: The cumbersome character of the old method of proposed executive orders and legislation through the Bureau of the Budget[3] to this and other departments was discussed, and the attorney general pointed out the existence of the new committee consisting of Judge [Newman A.] Townsend of this Department, Ed Kemp of the Bureau of the Budget, and Oscar Cox of the Office of Emergency Management,[4] authorized to hear and clear promptly all emergency legislation and executive orders for immediate reference to Congress. I mentioned two bills now ready for referring to this committee, a Bill for the Ready Acquisition of Personal and Real Property,[5] (Pub. 164 of October 16, 1940, being by no means adequate) and a bill, which we call our "Dive Bomber Bill,"[6] to avoid delays to title work on the seizure of real estate by simply serving notice on occupants, posting notice on the land and publishing notice—converting condemnation to a strict *in rem* proceeding.[7] The latter bill, I explained, was to meet the increasing pressure for payment of compensation to dispossessed property owners throughout the country where the resources for preparing title evidence are either exhausted or so strained that conventional title evidence cannot be prepared without great delay, and consequent postponement of payments to owners.

---

3. The Bureau of the Budget was brought into the Executive Office of the President by Executive Order No. 8248, 8 September 1939. Its function was to assist the President in preparing the annual federal budget and fiscal program, to supervise the administration of the budget, and to try to improve the administration of the executive branch of the government.

4. President Roosevelt established the Office for Emergency Management (OEM) by Administrative Order on 25 May 1940, in the Executive Office of the President, to coordinate and direct all emergency agencies during the war.

5. Attorney General Biddle sent Littell's draft "Bill to Expedite Payment for Land Acquired During the War Period" to Congress 21 May 1942. It was referred to the House Judiciary Committee, which took no action on it.

6. Attorney General Biddle sent Littell's draft "Dive Bomber Bill," or a "Bill to Provide Speedy and Summary Notice in Proceedings to Condemn Land for War Purposes, . . . " to Congress 16 June 1942. It was referred to the House Judiciary Committee, which took no action on it.

7. An *in rem* proceeding is a legal proceeding "against a thing" rather than "against a person."

The Settlement of United States v. [Arthur V.] Brown, Indianapolis, Indiana:[8] This famous case has at last been *nolle prossed*[9] by the Criminal Division[10] after extended consideration and considerable embarrassment because a former assistant attorney general, [James O'Brien] Brien McMahon, was counsel for Brown. The overwrought and over-conscientious United States attorney,[11] Howard Caughran, opposed settlement to the point of insubordination, reading in court a statement that he personally did not agree with the dismissal of the case and was strongly opposed to it, although his responsibility had been lifted from him by sending a special representative from this Department (our former Mr. [Oscar A.] Provost of the Lands Division). The whole incident was so violently insubordinate that he was roundly denounced, especially in view of the fact that his statement had been given to the press. It was agreed that he ought to be dismissed. It was a sad case to me in which the voltage of that particular case was too great for the transmission line and it burst asunder Caughran's judgment, I am afraid, to his ultimate discredit.

The attorney general closed the meeting with a very interesting letter from a female applicant for a position in the FBI who described herself as a specialist in "marriage hygiene," endocrine glands, vitamins and hoped she could be of service to the government.

---

30 December 1941

Had luncheon with the attorney general after staff meeting today. Aside from health and diet and personal matters, which constituted our first visit since my return to Washington, we covered other matters rather candidly. He asked my opinions of how the Department was going, or whether I had been long enough back to get the feel of it. The question

---

8. *United States v. Brown, Indianapolis, Indiana.* Arthur V. Brown, the president of the Union Trust Company in Indianapolis, was charged with conspiracy to use Works Projects Administration funds, or influencing others to use the funds, to build a road past property in which he had an interest. Biddle settled the case out of court, 23 December 1941. "Biddle Wants Ouster of U.S. Prosecutor in WPA Conspiracy," *Washington Post,* 17 Jan. 1942, in Littell scrapbook.

9. That is, the case was dismissed.

10. The Criminal Division of the Justice Department handled all matters involving criminal practice and procedure, including questions related to indictments, grand juries, search warrants, passports, and extradition. It also handled crimes on the high seas, cases under the federal banking, immigration, kidnapping, and racketeering laws, and had overall jurisdiction of the U.S. attorneys in criminal cases.

11. A U.S. attorney (or district attorney) is assigned to each federal district court. They are responsible for prosecuting violations of federal law. They operate under the supervision of the administration assistant to the attorney general.

was a little awkward because I frankly hadn't got the feel of it, although I could say it was "clicking." The outbreak of war is sufficient to guarantee that everybody has his shoulder to the wheel, but there are, as a matter of fact, many tensions within the Department and many weak spots.

The attorney general mentioned that he had favored Tommy Corcoran for solicitor general and had so advised the President but the President had said that this was out of the question. Francis also stated that the President had promised Tommy the solicitor general's position "a long time back." I thought myself that it must have been a very long time back, and I observed that I had not thought Tommy's appointment possible for precisely the reasons that it proved to be impossible, although they [i.e. the reasons] were greatly accentuated by the exposure of his lobbying activities while the vacancy existed. I favored the faithful old public servant Charles Fahy, as Francis Biddle well knew. I must say he stuck to Tommy through thick and thin, if it is a virtue in public office to stick through thick and thin to a man who ought not to be stuck to in the public interest.

"Do you know that Murphy was actually offered the attorney general's position?" Francis asked, in a somewhat incredulous tone of voice as if this could not really be.

Of course, I did know all about it from Murphy himself, but listened while he continued.

"I think it would have been perfectly awful, don't you?" he asked. "Murphy was a very poor attorney general from the point of view of administration in the Department, according to what [Ugo] Carusi and the boys all tell me around here."

There are many answers to this statement, first and foremost of which is the fact that those who thus spoke of Murphy hated him as the "pious" successor of [Homer S.] Cummings. Carusi had been removed by Murphy from his position as close assistant to the attorney general. I was tempted to remind Francis that some of the men he quoted would say the same thing of him after he left. . . . I hesitated to say so on the general practice and theory of "The king is dead, long live the king," which prevails in petty offices and large offices as well.

Undoubtedly, there were failures in Murphy's administrations, as there would be in any, but once having been loyal to a man I cannot bring myself to strike him down, even though my mind operates critically and even relentlessly on every servant in high public office and refuses to be blinded by personal loyalties or affections. A sound and gentle rule to follow is to state the affirmative of the case.

"There is this to be said about Murphy," I said. "No man in this administration, other than the President, has such a genius for political insight. He has a celtic quality of imagination and shrewd discernment into public forces which control the flow of events in the destiny of the country, a quality which has been greatly needed in the turbulent days of violent domestic conflict, now temporarily resolved by a unity of purpose on the elemental front of national defense."

Francis agreed, but said that Murphy was really not qualified to be a judge on the Supreme Court; that he didn't wish to be there; that he didn't know he was to be nominated; and that the President just sent his name up.

There were errors in these statements. I know of the actual conversation between the President and Murphy in which the President pointing one thumb over his shoulder toward the Supreme Court, when the vacancy occurred after the death of Justice [Pierce] Butler, said something to the effect: "Frank, you know what this means for you, don't you?"

He was consulted all right. I might have added that Francis' intimate friend, Tommy Corcoran, was once highly enthusiastic about Frank Murphy and only abandoned him when Frank refused to do what Tommy wished done.

"Frank Murphy is certainly more of a man of action," I said, "and I have no doubt was happier on the battle line of political life than in Court."

"He really wanted to be secretary of War, you know," Francis added.

"He would make a good one, too," I said.

Murphy has really outstanding capacity for leadership, subject to two or three reservations as to integration of his outlook which have always bothered me. How rapidly things dim!

We were interrupted by a message from Mr. Justice [James F.] Byrnes, who is serving on one of the committees appointed by the President with Biddle. . . . [He] advised that he wished to postpone the appointment with Biddle to hear Churchill over the radio making his address to Ottawa. We adjourned to Biddle's office, which had the radio in it, and heard this masterful address with his classic, down-to-earth, vitalized, American touches, such as the German boast to the French government that within six weeks they would handle England like wringing the neck off a chicken. "Some chicken! Some neck!"

We spoke of the President, and Biddle said the President "had really been very nice to him—had called him over for consultation on a number of things."

After the long wait before Biddle's appointment, I felt just a wee bit sorry for him on this statement. I think perhaps he feels pretty much buffeted about in the terrific currents of the time—and how could it be otherwise, particularly after the basic insecurity which must have been created by the long delay in his appointment.[1] He has a brilliant mind

1. Attorney General Robert H. Jackson was nominated to the Supreme Court 11 June

and could acquit himself rather admirably on the bench. But a lone picture of Justice [Felix] Frankfurter on his wall, coupled with his vigorous defense of Tommy Corcoran, confirms him as part of a passing trio.

1942

6 January 1942

I attended the attorney general's press conference at 11:00 today. It is better than all of the official releases of the Department, which take so much time to read, for getting perspective on the matters of major importance in the Department. I was particularly interested to see how the attorney general would handle the [Harry] Bridges case.[1]

I was sorry for him as the questions flew. Judge [Charles B.] Sears, a retired circuit court judge, had filed a report to the Immigration Board recommending Bridges' deportation [because of his communist affiliations]—at long last after a second protracted trial[2]—[but] Dean [James M.] Landis, of the Harvard Law School, reached a contrary conclusion on the first trial, after which re-enforcing statutes had been passed which

---

1941 and was confirmed 7 July 1941. Biddle was not nominated to replace him until 24 August 1941. The Senate confirmed his appointment 5 September 1941.

---

1. Secretary of Labor Frances Perkins had originally ordered Bridges arrested 2 March 1938, because he was an alien who was a member of the Communist Party. She appointed James M. Landis, the dean of Harvard Law School, to be the trial examiner. Bridges's first trial lasted from 10 July to 14 September 1939. On 28 December 1939, Landis ruled that the evidence did not show that Bridges was a communist when he arrived in the United States. Perkins upheld the decision and dismissed the proceedings 8 January 1940. The Immigration and Nationalization Service was transferred to the Justice Department 14 June 1940. The INS administered the immigration laws, investigated alleged violations, and recommended prosecution where necessary. It also supervised the naturalization procedures.

2. After the transfer of the INS from the Labor to the Justice Department, Attorney General Jackson directed the FBI to make a new investigation of Harry Bridges. As a result, Bridges was rearrested 14 February 1941. Jackson appointed Judge Charles B. Sears, of the New York State Court of Appeals, as an INS inspector to preside over the hearings, which lasted from 31 March to 12 June 1941. He delivered his report 26 September, concluding that Bridges was indeed a member of the Communist Party and should be deported. Bridges appealed and, 24 November 1941, received a hearing before the Board of Immigration Appeals, which on 3 January 1942 ruled that the record did not show that Bridges was a communist. See also the entry for 3 June 1942, note 2.

supplied Judge Sears with a different approach.[3] However, the Immigration Board unanimously recommended against deportation, finding "no evidence" in the records of his having been a communist. And, from them, the matter goes to the attorney general, who is the final authority to pass on the matter.

What a spot! Indeed, poor Biddle seems to be the ill-starred, ill-fated man in these successive misfortunes. . . .

"I am reviewing the records," answered the attorney general. "It is a long record and will take me some time, with my other duties, to get through it. However, I have done a great deal of judicial work and I am accustomed to examining records. I shall take it in my stride when and as I can."

So the issue was postponed in a pleasant, off-hand, way which belies the silent conflict of forces which are presented in the Bridges case. The griddle was just lighted, and the press could wait patiently while the unfortunate recipient of the primary responsibility in the Bridges case could, and would be, slowly roasted. . . .

. . . As to alien enemies apprehended by the Department, the attorney general stated there were four thousand in the clean-up since the Pearl Harbor attack on December 7th, and there was a general scurrying about of the representatives of the Department press room to correct the figures to a little over three thousand.

The *New York Times* representative, Mr. [Edwin L.] James, came back to the Bridges case: "Doesn't the trial examiner who hears a case know the evidence better than anyone else, being in a position to appraise the witnesses because he actually hears them?"

"That is generally true," Biddle replied. Someone raised the point that that's what Madame [Frances] Perkins, secretary of labor, said at the time of the Landis decision after he had heard the evidence and acquitted Bridges.

"Yes," said James, "but the statement was then made in support of Landis' decision acquitting Bridges." There was a subtle question pregnant in his statement. Was the rule also good as to Sears' judgment when Sears had decided exactly to the contrary under the newly presented evidence?

The press conference broke up, and we went into staff meeting which was gathering as the press men left the room at 11:30 A.M. No matters of great importance arose during the staff meeting. It developed that the executive order on alien property custody was still debated. The question was whether a board or a single man director should be the form of

---

3. Following Bridges's first trial, Congress passed the Nationality Act of 1940, approved 28 June 1940, which provided for the deportation of aliens who became communists after they entered the United States. See also 10 March 1942, note 3.

organization, other departments contending for the board form. Leo Crowley was not present at the meeting.

Judge Townsend reported that the Second Emergency War Powers Act[4] now was being completed.

A provision for the taking of realty and the personalty located thereon, drafted by our Division, was embraced, which we discussed for a moment.

The attorney general asked me to send him a memorandum as to eliminating the legal branches of the Army and Navy[5] in land acquisition work, although I had explained on more than one occasion that we were now functioning most effectively with the Army, following the blowing up of the old real estate section under Colonel Valliant following the Indiana scandal from last January.[6]

It was Carusi who intervened to say that, "The Army work is all straightened. It is only the judge advocate general of the Navy[7] which intervenes between Justice and the land acquiring work of the Navy."

And so I have commenced the drafting of a memorandum with data being gathered in the Condemnation Section, showing not only that the judge advocate general of the Navy is a fifth wheel in land acquiring operations (How, for example, can he say whether adjustments should be made when he has no contact with the witnesses, no knowledge of the property, except what we tell him, and no experience in court?) and that a great preponderance of the work is incompetently done. We should operate directly by supplying them with complete legal services from the field to the seat of government.

---

13 January 1942

There was no staff meeting today, but the attorney general sent for me at noon, possibly on his own initiative or possibly because I had applied for

---

4. The Second Emergency War Powers Act (Public Law 507), approved 28 March 1942.

5. Each of the two armed services had an Office of the Judge Advocate General. The JAG of the Navy had responsibility for all legal matters concerning the Navy Department. He administered justice in the naval service and was responsible for boards of promotion, retirement, and examination of candidates for appointment to the naval service. He drafted proposed legislation and reviewed cases affecting international law and admiralty law. He advised and reviewed all Navy contracts concerning public buildings, lands sales, purchases, and condemnations. The JAG of the Army had similar responsibilities. He was the official legal adviser of the secretary of war on matters concerning military administration and justice, and the financial, contractual, and other business affairs of the War Department and the Army.

6. The Indiana scandal arose in January 1941, following an exposé of seemingly fraudulent commission agents' fees and charges for title evidence in Army land acquisition cases. The case led to a complete reorganization of the Army's Real Estate Section and the appointment, 6 February 1941, of Littell's general assistant, John J. O'Brien, as head of the Real Estate Section. See Drew Pearson and Robert S. Allen, "The Washington Merry-Go-Round: Army Acquisition of Land Attacked," *Seattle Post-Intelligencer*, 28 January 1941.

7. Walter B. Woodson was judge advocate general of the Navy, 1938–43.

an appointment two or three days before. . . . [I wanted] to explain the confidential character of the rather critical memorandum supplied to him in regard to the Judge Advocate General's Office of the Navy which, if released in the wrong quarters, would have a most devastating effect upon our cooperation with the judge advocate general. . . .

"How should the reorganization to eliminate the judge advocate general from your condemnation work be effected, in your opinion?" the attorney general asked, as I sat down by his desk. His secretary [was] still in the room [and] apparently in the course of taking dictation. That, itself, was a damper on anything I might say—one instinctively draws in in the presence of a third party.

"I believe you yourself discussed it with Secretary Knox about a year ago in connection with Terminal Island and submerged oil land problems, and you probably can appraise better than I can how far you would get with the secretary," I replied. "I think the only remedy is by executive order under Public Law No. 703 (the Overton Act, I think) giving power to the President to reorganize these agencies for the sake of efficiency."[1]

We discussed the matter further for a moment or two, and the attorney general agreed that that was probably the only approach. He agreed to take it up with Judge Byrnes and a third member of the committee appointed by the President to handle various emergency matters of this sort including legislation.

I explained that for every fault set forth in the memorandum which could be explained away by the Judge Advocate General's Office . . . by digging back into the files we could substitute a dozen more pieces of evidence of inefficiency, delay or sheer incompetence. We were too busy in the Condemnation Section to draft a memorandum with the care of an indictment and merely gave a handful of examples to show the general character of our problem in dealing with the judge advocate general of the Navy.

The personal equation, incidentally, always intrudes into one's mind. Judge Advocate General [Walter B.] Woodson is a nice old man. In the extraordinary policy of the Navy of having its men serve in many capacities, he has been rotated from actual command at sea into this post. He is supposed to have had two years of law training at some time or another, and with that experience behind him he is legal counsel to the

---

1. Littell is probably referring to the Government Reorganization Act of 1939 (Public Law 19) approved 3 April 1939, which allowed the President to reorganize the Executive Branch of the government by executive order, with certain limitations, and allowed him to appoint up to six administrative assistants without senate confirmation.

Navy in spending millions and millions of dollars! There is no real grasp by the judge advocate general or any of his regular staff whom I have ever met.

"We are buying Bennett Field from the City of New York," he explained to me over the telephone today, "and Mayor [Fiorello H.] La Guardia is coming in here tomorrow to close the deal. We are paying a few million dollars for it, but we wish to hold out enough money to pay for private interests within the Field which we may have to condemn. Your Department of Justice rules for direct purchase require full consideration to be recited in the deed, but we can't tell what the full consideration will be until the condemnation cases subduing the private interests are concluded. How can I get around that rule?"

It was a pathetic question which a scared bureaucrat like Buettner, who handles land acquisitions for the Navy, had been too timorous to ask me himself, and had had the judge advocate general himself call me.

"Forget it," I said. "Put in any consideration you wish. Whatever the sum is that you are going to pay him in cash on the initial installment is good enough for us. The rule is to protect the government in getting enough revenue stamps on deeds, but in a purchase from the City, there are no revenue stamps so it really doesn't matter. . . ."

I mentioned the memorandum sent to him on the appointment of a district attorney in Hawaii—another weak spot which ought to be strengthened immediately. I also mentioned feeling deeply conscious as I do of the importance of those two strategic posts in these strenuous times in both territories, that there was another such vacancy now in Puerto Rico due to A. Cecil Snyder having been confirmed for the Supreme Court of Puerto Rico.

"[Lewis] Lebaron seems to be the man, doesn't he?" the attorney general said.

"Lebaron is in Hawaii, not in Puerto Rico," I said, "and Lebaron is a candidate for the Supreme Court, not for the United States attorney post."

Well, I cannot blame a harassed man for lack of grasp of these details, but where they are not grasped, the matters ought to be delegated to someone else. As it is, I have the impression that these far-flung appointments knock around among Carusi and [A. Devitt "Gus"] Vanech and Linton Collins until one of them decides the matter on the basis of the written evidence or pull. No doubt they decide the issue very conscientiously and carefully, but that makes good the charge in the territories that no one of importance takes keen interest or shows sympathetic understanding of their problems.

The impression is unavoidable that the attorney general is hurried, harried, and is ridden by his job rather than being firmly in the saddle riding his job. There is an absence of a firm grasp. He said again in the discussion of the first problem as to the legal work of the Navy, "Well, I suppose if we prepared a memorandum for submission, it would simply be sent to Judge Advocate General of the Army [Emory S.] Adams for his consideration."[2]

"No, Mr. Attorney General," I said. "It would not go to the Judge Advocate General Adams because he is . . . [adjutant] general of the Army, and our relations with the Army are entirely satisfactory.[3] We operate directly with the Real Estate Section of which my old general assistant, Mr. [John J.] O'Brien, is in command. We are talking about the judge advocate general of the Navy."

I am frankly not sure whether he realized until that moment that there were two judge advocate generals, one for the Army and one for the Navy; or, perhaps, his mind had slipped again, as it had in staff meeting, and he thought we were working on our problem of doing legal business with the Army.

These fundamental distinctions ought now to be clear, but his background is in the solicitor general's office and, perhaps, he was not close enough there to government operations to feel intimately at home with the organizational set-up.

I went away feeling very discouraged in spite of the undoubted sincerity with which he urged me to make recommendations on appointments at any time. I could visualize them landing on Carusi's desk. With his quiet vanity, he loves to feel that he is running the Department, to a certain extent anyway, through the filter of his particular allotment of personal prejudices. What I brought to him was not too much detail for wartime; it was vital matter lying at the very heart of government in the now highly important, far-flung territories of Puerto Rico and Hawaii. I felt, instinctively, that Biddle was reaching out to lean on the nearest reed. And as I passed Carusi, in the cathedral-like antechamber of the attorney general's office, sitting behind his enormous glass-top desk, I felt myself in the presence of one of the reeds most conveniently at hand.

It is clear that mere intellect is not sufficient in government. There must be capacity for power. The transmission line must be equal to the load. A ten-volt line cannot carry a two hundred and ten voltage. There is no disloyalty here. I shall continue to support Francis Biddle right up to the hilt every conceivable way, but I cannot help being honest with myself. . . . I shall be interested to see how . . . he can deal

2. Emory S. Adams was the adjutant general of the Army, 1938–41.
3. Major General Myron C. Cramer (1881–1966) was judge advocate general of the Army, 1 December 1941–45.

with the current issues—other than civil liberties, of which he is a great champion.

Sunday, 17 January 1942
4101 Lorcom Lane, Arlington, Virginia

Dearest Katherine Mather:

One month and ten days have elapsed since your mother and I got on board the train in Seattle on December 8 to come back, and during every one of those days since then history has rushed past as precipitantly as the mountain streams we left behind in the West. . . .

. . . One thing was sure: The country had been united in twenty-four hours by the attack on Pearl Harbor. The butcher, the baker, and the candlestick maker all thought the same on this issue, summed up in time by the shocked and perfectly typical exclamation of ordinary citizens: "Why, the little yellow bastards!" There was just one verdict—a unanimous one—to go and clean up on them!

At a blow, the isolationists had been routed, and even those who had called Roosevelt a "warmonger" now saw an international pattern too big for their previous horizon. On Thursday, the 11th, Hitler declared war on the United States under the obligations of their pact with Japan, gloating over the triumph of the Japs in that first treacherous attack and openly boasting of it in the German press, thus completely letting the cat out of the bag to the American public that this was a general Axis plan all along. The President, and our school of thought, generally, rose in stature. . . .

Those of us who felt that we had carried the responsibility of the affirmitive side in the great public debate could relax and enjoy what we saw about us, no matter how grim the implications of the event were. It would be interesting to know how many of our 130,000,000 people in the country scrambled for atlases to see just where Manila, Batavia, Singapore, Thailand, Burma, and Borneo were, as the lightning drama of the Pacific unfolded. We had heard about tin and rubber from some of those places, but no American could conceive of his automobile without tires. Somehow, the unlimited optimism and self-confidence of people who have never had to do without things which the rest of us hold most dear had caused us calmly to assume that we would be able to continue to get these things, no matter what happened. Only during the last week has the full realization been brought home to Mr. Average American that he may have to do without his dearest possession—his automobile—for the private purchase of tires has been completely forbidden by our erstwhile New Deal friend, Leon Henderson, who has now risen to be the

Czar of the price world.[1] Well, at any rate, the horizon of Mr. Average American, even in the valleys of the Middlewest, has been so suddenly expanded that it must make his head swim.

The complacent sentiment, which held us—as it did the English in the pre-Dunkirk days before that awful debacle of the evacuation from Dunkirk stripped England of her military supplies and left her absolutely helpless—had been shattered. Had Hitler followed through to an attack on the Island at that time, we would have gone to England's aid. Japan ended our complacency. *Pearl Harbor was our Dunkirk.*

There still remained another kind of complacency, however—a complacent confidence that we could "mop up" on these little yellow men. Many of us on the Pacific Coast had realized that the Japanese had been greatly underestimated, . . . as to intelligence, endurance, determination, toughness, and the grim inspiration of necessity in population's pressure and economic need. It will be a long war and a tough one. They have millions of men to spare; life is cheap and its sacrifice has a religious sanction behind it which makes suicide squads quite ordinary in the Japanese military forces. We are now in the parade days of war, full of gusto and determination, but the thin dribble of wounded men and the reports of the dead are only beginning to filter through. The ultimate probable fact that millions of men can only be stopped by millions of men has not really dawned upon us with all of its horrible implications. . . .

---

27 January 1942
Attorney General Staff Meeting

The attorney general has been at home ill for the last week, so there was no staff meeting until today. . . .

The attorney general was greatly concerned about columnist [John P.] O'Donnell's attack on the FBI responsibility for successful fifth column operations in Honolulu as shown in Mr. Justice [Owen J.] Roberts' report on the bombing of Pearl Harbor.[1] [Before] Mr. [J. Edgar] Hoover entered

---

1. Leon Henderson became director (i.e., "Czar") of the Office of Price Administration and Civilian Supply, within the Office for Emergency Management (OEM), when it was established by Executive Order No. 8734, 11 April 1941. The OPA and CS assumed the duties and the staff of the adviser on price stabilization of the National Defense Advisory Commission. On 28 August 1941, responsibilities for civilian supply were transferred to the Office of Production Management (OPM) by Executive Order No. 8875. Under provisions of the Emergency Price Control Act of 1942 (56 Stat. 26) approved 30 January 1942, the OPA was transformed into an independent agency, primarily concerned with price and rent control, and rationing.

---

1. The Roberts Report was the result of an inquiry ordered by President Roosevelt, 18

the meeting, . . , Mr. [Edward A.] Tamm explained that under the President's directive, the Navy was to have primary control of the Japanese population. The Roberts report, as O'Donnell said, "puts the finger directly on the FBI," but Tamm explained that in the division of responsibility between the Army, Navy and FBI intelligence services, the primary responsibility for covering the population of Hawaii *other than Japanese* was on the FBI.

When Hoover came in, later, having appeared for two hours in executive session of the Appropriations Committee, he described Justice Roberts' report as to the intelligence services as "ambiguous" and "unfortunately worded," and stated that it did not follow the testimony given at Hawaii and is "not a correct finding of fact," and that this was most unfortunate to the intelligence services.

The question was whether the Department should make a release on the subject, and the attorney general, while not wishing to take issue with a columnist of limited circulation, who was previously far from sympathetic for the democratic cause, wondered whether or not the matter should be made clear to the public.

I, frankly could not help recalling quite clearly, in the face of Hoover's very indignant denial of responsibility for the Japanese in Hawaii, the fact that Bob Shivers, the FBI agent in charge in Honolulu, took a most reassuring view in talking with me at Colonel Kirkpatrick's house just before I left Honolulu in August.

"You people on the continent take this Japanese problem too seriously here," he said. "The situation is absolutely under control. The most of the Japanese population are entirely loyal American citizens and, only a very small number (I believe he said less than 1%) are disloyal, and those are under strict observation."

He continued in almost these precise words, because they impressed me so vividly. "You can scratch it off! Just forget the problem." . . .

The attorney general called attention to the *Washington Star* editorial attacking the Congress for refusing to pass a wire-tapping bill[2] when the attorney general and the President had recommended it last summer, with the result that the Japanese telegrams and telephone messages

---

December 1941, into the Pearl Harbor disaster. Supreme Court Justice Owen Roberts, who headed the probe, delivered his report 24 January 1942. The report did not establish clear-cut blame, but did accuse Rear Admiral Husband E. Kimmel (1882–1968) and Lt. General Walter C. Short of "dereliction of duty." Rear Admiral Claude C. Bloch, who had advised against installing baffles to protect against aerial torpedoes at Pearl Harbor, received a copy of the report, was reassigned, and retired later in 1942. In 1946, a congressional inquiry cleared Kimmel of the dereliction of duty charges. See *Washington Post*, 25 Jan. 1942, p. 1.

2. The wire-tapping bill of 1941 (H.R. 4228) would have allowed wiretaps in four categories of cases: espionage, sabotage, kidnapping, and extortion. The House defeated it by a vote of 147 to 154 on 30 June 1941.

involving their proposed attack passed unchallenged, and suggested that
we might get that bill by now. However, Hoover replied, rather bitterly
I thought, in answer to the attorney general's inquiry, that, "The
wire-tapping bill would not pass now either—the CIO[3] would oppose it!"
I disagree. I think it would pass like a shot now. . . .

He discussed also the great problem of taking into protective custody
American citizens of Japanese descent and the problems of passing
appropriate legislation authorizing the seizure of these people. . . .

Thursday, 29 January 1942
Washington, D.C.

A letter came to the attorney general and thence to the Lands Division
from Secretary Ickes today, quoting an Associated Press clipping in the
California papers in regard to the proposed suit to test the government's
interest, if any, in the tideland oil deposit.[1] The issue has long been a
subject of bitter controversy and one over which we have spent over a year
of intensive research at great expense to explore the government's position
pursuant to specific instructions from the President to the attorney general
in July 1940. The press reported how Congressman [Álbert E.] Carter had
interrogated me so exhaustively before the Appropriations Committee a
year ago, over the useless expenditure of funds to pursue a sterile, legal
theory, trying to make out a federal interest in these tidelands. I dodged
and evaded in such a noncommittal manner that the chairman of the
Committee[2] congratulated me later on telling Carter "absolutely nothing."

Carter had asked the attorney general at the opening Appropriations
Committee hearing this year whether further funds were to be expended
for this purpose or if the tideland matter was "dormant."

"It is worse than that," the attorney general is reported to have said. "It
is dead."

If this is true, it is a sad comment on the effect of Ed Pauley. . . I was
somewhat aghast upon returning to Washington . . . to find that Ed Pauley
had become secretary of the party in place of Chip Robert. This, I am
afraid, may be a case of "out of the frying pan into the fire." Ed Pauley's
Petrol Corporation is unquestionably dominated by Signal Oil & Gas, a

---

3. The Congress of Industrial Organizations (CIO) was a national labor federation of
industrial unions, which had been expelled from the American Federation of Labor (AFL)
in 1936. It generally supported liberal economic and political causes.

1. See Log Book entry for 15 September 1941, note 5.
2. Congressman Clarence Cannon of Missouri was chairman of the House Appropriations Committee, 1941–46.

subsidiary of Standard Oil of California, according to reliable information passed on to me. There was one occasion when Ed would have gone to the wall had not the Signal Oil & Gas Company bailed him out, actually issuing pay to Ed's employees with Signal Oil & Gas Company checks. This is so well known in the oil world that it is liable to break at any time. . . .

Saturday, 31 January 1942
Washington, D.C.

Yesterday, Brad Schofield, director of Immigration in this Department, came to lunch for a long-deferred visit and, in honor of the occasion, I lit the fire in the fireplace in my office and pulled up two big leather chairs.

A Philadelphian, brought down by Attorney General Biddle, and a successful practicing lawyer there, Brad is from a far distant end of the world in tradition and background from my own, but we have often stood on the same ground in staff meetings. I have sometimes questioned his executive capacity from what I have seen of his organization inherited from the Department of Labor, but I have never questioned his forthrightness and fearlessness.

"One thing I have always noticed about you," Brad said frankly, "is that you take the Department point of view in staff meetings, rather than merely a Division point of view—you look at things from the vantage point of what is needed by the whole Department."

We both agreed that Leo Crowley was wholly right in the last staff meeting when he stated that the struggle between military, naval and FBI intelligence services to settle the responsibility for Pearl Harbor attack on December 7th was wrong from the point of view of the private citizen, and that whether the Roberts report definitively and accurately settled the responsibility or not (Hoover charged that it certainly did not) was wholly immaterial as far as the average citizen was concerned. He only knows that the fifth column worked, and we should let it go at that and not try to show that the FBI, at least, did not fail.

We discussed the Bridges case, which is directly . . . in Brad's province, portions of which he personally tried as counsel for the government. Recognizing the delicacy of the situation, in view of our present fighting alliance with Russia, and the potential embarrassment from deporting someone on the charge of being a "communist," Brad feels strongly that the Sears report—that Bridges is a communist and should be deported to Australia—is wholly correct, based upon: (1) The . . . testimony given by [Harry Lundeberg], the . . . head of the Sailors Union of the Pacific, which has fought communism in the ranks of the maritime workers on the Pacific Coast: and (2) the testimony of one witness who was personally present . . . when Bridges acknowledged his membership in the Communist Party. At the trial, Bridges denied this testimony but did not call as witnesses any of the other people present even though members of his own family were available as witnesses.

It cannot be merely the enthusiasm of a prosecutor who has worked on a case, or the point of view of a conservative Philadelphian which reaches such a conclusion; it is rather the logic of the lawyer's mind confronting the affirmative testimony plus the heavy weight of Bridges' failure to call these witnesses.

"How does the Board of Appeal get around that, in reversing Judge Sears and holding that Bridges is not a communist in their opinion?" I asked. "Is there a lawyer on the Board?"

Brad said there were five members of the Board and lawyers aplenty, but there had been strong feeling in certain quarters that Judge Landis, who had heard the first Bridges case and recommended against deportation, was not only right, but that putting Bridges to a second trial was unfair and un-American. Brad thought that the matter should have been concluded, without more ado, after the Landis decision was handed down. In reviewing the Landis decision, much emphasis had been given to the fact that the trial examiner is in the best position to know what the truth is, and he heard the witnesses and took the testimony, but there now is a great deal of wiggling to get away from that principle of law so long established in judicial proceedings, to explain away the idea that Sears misjudged the evidence.

We agreed, however, as to the tough spot upon which the recommendation of the Board to overthrow Sears' decision convicting Bridges leaves the attorney general. It is an advisory opinion to the attorney general. He must decide.

Furthermore, the martyrdom of Bridges is doubly assured by conduct of the FBI subsequent to his actual trial for, to my astonishment, I learned that wire-tapping of Bridges' telephone line had been continuously practiced since the trial. Bridges had not only found out but had a very good time of it, sending the FBI on all sorts of wild goose chases by receiving and placing telephone calls of a wholly fictitious character for the express purpose of playing ducks and drakes with the FBI. Not only had Bridges' men watched the FBI agents by means of spy glasses through the windows of a hotel room in which the agents were situated, watching them pick up the telephone receiver as soon as Bridges made a call and proceed to take transcription notes all the time he was talking, but they had also caught the FBI red-handed by closing in on the room. Having demanded that the hotel admit Bridges' men to the locked hotel room where the FBI agent was taking the transcription, they stood by outside the room laying siege to the man within it. News reporters and photographers were there, too. Finally, when a waiter, undoubtedly an

FBI agent, himself, brought food to the man in the room, the latter hustled out with a coat drawn up around him and his equipment tucked under his coat and ran down the steps so that the only photograph secured was of his back with his coat collar pulled up!

However, the agent had very stupidly left in the room not only odd pieces of wire for making the necessary connection, but carbon copies of some of the transcribed reports of Bridges' conversation—fatal and conclusive evidence of wire-tapping. A petition was promptly made before Judge Sears (who had the case pending at that time) based upon this evidence and requesting that the proceedings be re-opened to make the government show what portion of the testimony introduced before Judge Sears had been based upon wire-tapping, which is, of course, illegal. In the Roberts report, the non-use of wiretaps was cited as one of the basic reasons for the surprise attack on Pearl Harbor, since the intelligence services could not tap the telephone or telegraph lines of the Japanese in Honolulu. It was a tough spot for the government, as Brad frankly stated. A demurrer[1] was filed, and the matter was argued before Judge Sears; he denied the petition, but it was a close point and one which, if Bridges had prevailed in the petition, would have given him a field day with government witnesses such as J. Edgar Hoover. . . .

In conferring with J. Edgar Hoover, during the period when the petition was being resisted for reopening the Bridges case to prove wire-tapping subsequent to the closing of the case, Hoover stated quite frankly that, if he were put on the stand as a result of the reopening of the case, he would frankly state that he was authorized to tap the wires by the President, himself. "I'd cut my tongue out before I would do that," Brad added, "but that's Hoover for you," meaning that Hoover knows no loyalty to the commander-in-chief. He would just let the chief take the rap for authorizing an illegal act done in defense of the nation in advance of the time when congressional insight reached a stage sufficiently abreast of the times to authorize wire-tapping.

We have reached that stage now. Repentant congressmen, facing elections in this year 1942, faced the record of their votes on several cumulative items, such as the Wire-Tapping Bill which, if it had passed, could have prevented Pearl Harbor; and the fortification of the Island of Guam,[2] the

---

1. A demurrer is a legal pleading which argues that even if the facts are as alleged by the other party, they are not sufficient to sustain the argument built on them.

2. Littell is probably referring to an item in the Naval Authorization Bill of 1939, which would have provided funds to dredge the harbor and construct aviation facilities at Guam. The House defeated it by a large majority, 23 February 1939.

defense of which, in an unfortified condition, is now one of the great epochs of American military history, transcending the Alamo in Texas. . . .

10 February 1942

Miscellaneous matters were discussed at our staff meeting such as the necessity of locking doors or keeping passes to the Department strictly under control, proposed United States attorneys' regional conferences, and the danger of obstructing national defense with anti-trust suits, which Thurman Arnold disposed of by saying that whenever Undersecretary of War [Robert P.] Patterson says an anti-trust suit is hurting the war it will be dropped. . . .

In discussion of the Wire-Tapping Bill, Hoover pointed out that we were the only restricted ones in wire-tapping and that the British and Free French[1] intelligence services, which are enormous in this country, make free use of wire-tapping. The Free French had even suppressed a telegram to the secretary of War, advising of the seizing of St. Pierre and Miquelon islands off the coast of Canada,[2] and the astonishing statement was made that the British had attempted to get Undersecretary of War Burle[3] discharged from the State Department, for reasons which were not stated.

The revised Wire-Tapping Bill[4] authorizes wire-tapping by the attorney general for all the services, as I understand the matter. Anything the Department of Justice thinks proper. There is no question that the War and Navy Departments would go pretty far in the matter if a free hand were given.

Sunday, 15 February 1942
Washington, D.C.

Congress has come in for a great deal of general criticism throughout the country for its bickering, long-drawn fight with the Office of Civilian

1. Free France was the British-supported resistance movement organized by General Charles De Gaulle in London in 1940.
2. St. Pierre and Miquelon islands, off the coast of Newfoundland, were seized by Free French naval forces from the Vichy governor, 24 December 1941, even though De Gaulle had agreed not to do so and the United Sates preferred that the islands be taken by Canadian forces.
3. Littell is probably referring to Assistant Secretary of State Adolph A. Berle, Jr.
4. The wire-tapping bill of 1942 (H.R. 6919) and three House joint resolutions (Nos. 273, 304, and 311), which authorized wire-tapping by the attorney general and the intelligence services, were introduced in Congress but not passed.

Defense,[1] which has really been an attack upon Mrs. Roosevelt and, through her, an attack on the President. Poor Mrs. Roosevelt went in when the enterprise was floundering under the directorship of Mayor La Guardia of New York, who has since before the election of last November, demonstrated such amazing lack of executive capacity in this office that he has frequently been referred to as "The Little Flower that at last faded." Mrs. Roosevelt went in to the OCD to stiffen up the organization and provide some inspirational leadership but, last week, upon the retirement of La Guardia and the appointment of Dean Landis of the Harvard Law School to take over, the long pent-up spleen found its victims.

A Miss [Mayris] Chaney, a dancer who invented the "Eleanor Glide," had been appointed at a $4,600 salary to head up a Children's Division— what to do with children in time of war, etc., etc.! Also, Melvyn Douglas had been appointed to head the Arts Division to muster the talent of the country which has had no channel through which to express itself in moving pictures, dramatic performances, over the radio, and otherwise, to clarify the national opinion now greatly confused, in spite of Pearl Harbor, especially in the Middle West. It was found that Douglas had been put in what is called a P-8 classification, for which the rating is $8,000, although he was to serve without compensation. The press fell upon these two appointments like a pack of hungry wolves on spring lambs, and the savage debauchery which followed in the press and in Congress was a disgraceful spectacle.

Poor Douglas does not have an aptitude for public repartee and, by the time he got around to making a gentlemanly statement, he had waited two or three days too long and the press would not give him the recognition to his denial as far as compensation was concerned and the odious comparison of his "$8,000 salary" with that of General [Douglas] MacArthur fighting in the Philippines was not successfully erased.

A perfect instance and example of what can get by Congress was the Guayule Rubber Bill,[2] which passed the Senate some days ago, which provides for the purchase of the Inter-Continental Rubber Company's patents and processes and bulk supply of guayule seed, the only supply in the country, at two million dollars. In the House, the word "condemna-

---

1. President Roosevelt established the Office of Civilian Defense (OCD) by Executive Order No. 8757, 20 May 1941 "to provide for necessary cooperation with state and local governments in respect of measure for adequate protection of the civilian population in emergency periods." Fiorello La Guardia, the mayor of New York City, was named director and Eleanor Roosevelt was named assistant director. Shortly after Pearl Harbor, both La Guardia and Roosevelt resigned. James M. Landis replaced La Guardia. President Truman terminated it by Executive Order No. 9562, 4 June 1945.
2. The Guayule Rubber Bill of 1942 (S. 2152) provided for the planting of 45,000 acres of guayule plants in order to produce rubber domestically. It passed the Senate 15 January 1942. The House also passed it, 5 February 1942, but President Roosevelt vetoed the bill 17 February 1942 (S. Doc. 182).

tion" was stricken out of the Bill so that seventy-five thousand acres of land necessary for the development of the seed to meet in part the rubber shortage of the present crisis was stricken out. Neither the land nor patented processes nor the property of the company could be condemned. It could only be purchased. And lands for the development could only be leased for not to exceed ten years, with the perfectly obvious result that, after the government had spent several million dollars developing these lands, the landowners would have the entire benefit. Provision for leases for acquisition of land in the "Western Hemisphere" was also stricken out, although it was shown on the floor of the house that profitable operations could not be had in the company's experience in New Mexico or Arizona, but only on the Mexican side of the border, where guayule grows cheaply, and the harvesting and manufacturing are possible on a profitable basis.

Feeling that Vice President Wallace, with the fast flow of bills before him, may not have caught the significant changes, I telephoned to him and, in his absence, dictated a memorandum to his secretary, showing these consequences of the Bill and the fact that the government was wholly at the company's mercy now, when the right of condemnation was stricken from the Bill. If it wished to lease or license the processes, then the government would develop the guayule manufacturer's supply of rubber on terms and conditions dictated by the company. It was what can be accurately described as a steal, faithfully encased in much unctuous debate and dissertation on the need for rubber and the necessity of planting the guayule seed by April 1st.

I thought the matter could be stopped in the Senate if the Vice President would tip off some senator to be on his guard but, to my surprise, having failed to call the Vice President for two days due to the pressure of work in my office, I had a call back from him Thursday morning saying that the Bill had already passed upon the assurance given to the Senate by Senator [Sheridan] Downey of California that Breckinridge Long of the State Department had approved the Bill. Wallace said he had sent a copy of my memorandum immediately to Sumner Welles and another to [Earl N.] Bressman, of the War Production Board,[3] working on the rubber supply problem, and he suggested that I call Welles to see what attitude the Department had taken.

This, too, I did not get around to doing until Saturday morning, feeling a trifle embarrassed that my informal memorandum had gone so far so fast, written as it was in rather candid language which I could use with the Vice President, with edges which might have been trimmed off had I anticipated the course it was to travel. In the meantime, I confess that I sent

<hr>

3. The War Production Board (WPB) was established in the OEM by Executive Order No. 9024, 16 January 1942, to replace the SPAB and the OPM. Its function was to coordinate the production and distribution of raw materials and manufactured goods for the war effort.

the *Congressional Record* and the Bill, as amended, to Drew Pearson, of Pearson and Allen, one of the watch-dogs of Democracy, ever vigilant to an abuse of responsibility in public. Saturday morning, I called Undersecretary of State Welles, saying I was a little embarrassed to find that I had intruded on his province somewhat in a personal memorandum, which I had sent to the Vice President, but he interrupted very promptly. "I am mighty glad you did, and I was grateful for your memorandum. I took the matter up in cabinet meeting yesterday morning and it was very quickly decided that the President would veto this Bill." I was immensely relieved that I had not again stepped on the toes of the State Department, as I did in writing a letter regarding the Mexican embassy to F.D.R., Jr., after the visit there in December 1940. I felt bold enough to ask a question. "Then Breckinridge Long did not have the authority of the State Department in approving that Bill as was stated on the floor of the Senate?"

"No, he certainly did not. I can only say that I wish he had consulted others here." Welles spoke with obvious irritation in his voice and, I suspect, that there has been a bit of a blow-up over this incident, which could rebound to the very great embarrassment of the State Department, particularly in view of the striking out of the clause authorizing development of guayule in the "Western Hemisphere." . . .

Last night, Undersecretary of War [Robert P.] Patterson and Mrs. Patterson came to dinner, a private affair with no other guests, for the purpose of discussing a situation at the Boeing Plant in Seattle and an extraordinary development in Army personnel in Seattle. John Boettiger had telephoned me, on February 9th, the confidential information that General Marsh, of the Interceptor Command in Seattle, and Colonel Griffin, in command of the Army Air Corps' inspection service at the Boeing Plant, were both under investigation by reason of disloyal and viciously anti-Roosevelt remarks made at the home of LeRoy Backus, a Seattle businessman who lives at the Highlands. The matter had been reported by others present at the dinner with the result that General [George C.] Marshall of the United States Army had caused an immediate investigation to be made by the Inspector General's Office by a Colonel [David S.] McLean. . . .

It was decided that court martial proceedings should not be had, but that the men should simply be removed from command and placed elsewhere. John had felt compelled to advise the inspector general's representative of the confidential information I had given him about Colonel Griffin, which I discovered during a short visit in the home of P. G. and Mrs. Johnson,[4] the president of the Boeing Company, when we were in Seattle on the weekend of November 6th. . . . We arrived there on Sunday afternoon with

---

4. Philip G. and Katherine F. Johnson.

Mrs. Spencer, from Vancouver, B.C., also with us, and, a half-hour later, Phil came in swaying drunk, having just returned from a duck club with Colonel Griffin as his only attendant. He was absolutely "blotto" although he did recognize us both.

It was a shocking disappointment to see him in this condition, so reminiscent of earlier days in Seattle, when Phil had, as president of the Boeing Company and United Air Lines, gone the downhill road up until the cancellation of the air mail contracts by the federal government on charges of conspiracy to monopolize and divide the air mail business of the country, in which Phil Johnson was involved. He was one of the many executives thrown out of the company upon the insistance of the government, and he went to Canada as the vice president of the Trans-Canada Airways, where he did an excellent job—after sobering up quite abruptly. He established airports across Canada.

. . . Kate Johnson, whom we had always regarded so highly for her patient treatment of Phil and her general character, was bitterly anti-English, and we suddenly awoke to the fact that she was, when scratched, fundamentally an Irish Catholic and an embittered follower of Bishop [Gerald] Shaughnessy, one of the rabid anti-English Catholics and a man of great influence in Seattle, unfortunately.

"We're not going to fight this war to help England, I'll tell you that!" Kate told Katherine, "and you can ask any of the Army officers about it— ask Colonel Griffin."

Colonel Griffin did not need to be asked. He made his attitude very clear. . . . Griffin frankly stated to me in the study, while demonstrating his two-fisted capacity for drinking another man's liquor, that he supposed he would have to restrain his expression of personal opinions somewhat being in the services, but he made himself quite clear on the subject of Roosevelt and revealed a thoroughly nazified mind. In other words, he would be in favor of putting all the Jews in one place to live—he didn't say where, or how it could be arranged.

"I suppose," I said, "you have an equally simple solution for the Negro problem in this country?"

"They ought to be sent back to Africa—that is, most of them," he said, or words approximately to this effect. He seemed to realize he was heading into deep water and equivocated somewhat.

In the study, playing bridge later with Pansie and Katherine, he made himself much more clear on his anti-British attitude, saying definitely that he was not going to fight this war for England, to which Kate Johnson added, "You see, Katherine, how the Army officers feel."

This conversation, by the way, took place on the second evening, for he was again a guest at dinner the next evening, and on that evening I was the New Deal victim of a united onslaught in the library from four out of five men—Phil Johnson, Colonel Griffin, their attorney Ed Allen, Arthur

Krauss, and another chap, who did not share their views on the anti-English view. Phil Johnson had denounced, in chorus with the others, an executive order of the President requiring equality in the employment of men in national defense industries—no color line and no discrimination on racial grounds.[5] . . .

I was so thoroughly disgusted with the atmosphere which one sensed as well as discerned in many remarks which were made, and with the beating that I took on the executive order in the study with the men after dinner, and on other New Deal policies that I was expected to be the master of on all fronts, that I left the room in disgust. I was particularly disgusted with the Army officer sent out to the Boeing plant to watch this very man whose hospitality he constantly enjoyed and whose good Scotch whiskey traveled up and down alternate lifts on its way to the Colonel's mouth, for his left hand was as dexterous as his right hand in hoisting that tingling glass. He was the inspector for the Army to see that the industry was living up to its contracts, but all he had was a soft berth at the end of a government paycheck, where he lived an easy life (by his own admission, going to the office at ten or later, just as he felt like it) being royally entertained in a state of constant seduction. . . .

Of course, we wouldn't let a destroyer go to sea under the command of men like Johnson, just on the grounds of too much drinking, but he is in command of the most important plant of the country at the moment because the flying fortress is the biggest and best long-range bomber under construction, particularly since they have turned out the new model B-17-E, with a turret at the rear, the lack of which made the ship vulnerable. . . .

I pointed out the complete lack of ideological leadership which resulted at the Boeing plant from the state of opinion at the top and would have been more gravely felt except for the fact communist influences were now wholly behind the war because of Stalin's position, and that communist influences were strong in Seattle and represented at Boeing.

"But they made their quota in January and then some!" said Patterson. "They turned out 84 flying fortresses." That was considerably more than the quota which he mentioned but which I cannot remember. "That is because the boys were mad after Pearl Harbor," he added. "It just shows what can be done when the wheels to produce are there." We agreed that leadership was not particularly important right now, but it might be any time. In this respect, [William S.] Knudsen, [who] recently retired as the

---

5. Executive Order No. 8802, signed by President Roosevelt, 25 June 1941, ordered government agencies, job training programs, and manufacturers accepting defense contracts to end racial discrimination in hiring. It also created the Fair Employment Practices Committee in OEM to investigate complaints of violations.

head of O.P.M.[6] and was made a general in charge of surveying production efforts for the Army, . . . will be very useful to Patterson.

"He works for me now, you know," Patterson said, "and he is a crackerjack on getting production problems ironed out."

"You ought to use him as a talent scout," I said. "You will need to know who the best trained executives are with the right ideas."

We also discussed pretty thoroughly the situation at Pearl Harbor, and I gave my impression of General Short and Admiral Bloch. From that, we went on to the Japanese problem, where Patterson strongly recommended that martial law be declared on the Pacific Coast states in order to reach the problem of controlling the Japanese citizens which under the Constitution we find difficulty in reaching now, although it is impossible, as Pearl Harbor demonstrated, to tell who is a loyal Japanese-American and who is a spy. I concurred and, as a Pacific Coast resident, I dread some terrible acts of sabotage which will bring the failure to handle the Japanese situation down on to the attorney general in an avalanche of public condemnation. Even as to enemy aliens (those who are not yet citizens) Francis Biddle has given them until February 24th to remove from the Coast areas over three hundred miles inland. Anything could happen before that and the responsibility for it is focussed on him. . . .

I am afraid that a single act of sabotage will release the vengeance of the vigilantes and there will be killings aplenty. There have already been several.

---

25 February 1942

At the attorney general's staff meeting today, the attorney general advised of his conference with the Judiciary Committee of the House in respect to the "Official Secrets Bill"[1] which he had proposed to Congress after the publication of several confidential matters which were not specifically mentioned. There had been some very hostile [comment by

---

6. The Office of Production Management (OPM) was established by Executive Order No. 8629, 7 January 1941, within the OEM. Its function was to coordinate national defense purchases, small business activities, research and statistics, and advisers on industrial materials and production. It was given broad powers over the supply of national defense materials. William S. Knudsen was the director general and Sidney Hillman was the associate director general. The OPM's powers were transferred to the WPB by Executive Order No. 9024, 16 January 1942.

---

1. The "official secrets bill" of 1942 (H.R. 7151), which Biddle proposed to Congress, would have amended the First War Powers Act of 1941 (Public Law 354) approved 18 December 1941, to include communications from the United States to any U.S. territories or possessions and between any such territories and possessions. The Senate passed it, but later requested it back from the House and took no further action.

columnists], but also some favorable editorial comment. As the attorney general pointed out, this was no doubt due to the factor that the columnists have their stock in trade in leaks from inside sources, whereas the regular press gets its news in the standardized manner.

The alien property situation was again discussed, because an executive act had been signed,[2] and Leo Crowley has not yet been appointed alien property custodian, which had been anticipated for two or three months. The attorney general advised that the Treasury Department is now exercising the duties and responsibilities provided by law, and that the President had indicated at press conferences that these powers were now reposed in the Treasury Department. As we all know, a tug of war had been going on around the government as to whether these powers would be centered in a custodian, in a board, or in one department.

Arnold expressed the private opinion that it would be a good thing to have full powers reposed in the Treasury Department as it would give too great a burden to the Department of Justice if these responsibilities were placed here and would add too great an investigational burden to the FBI. He stated that he would be glad to have available the investigational facilities of the Treasury Department for investigating the foreign cartel in any anti-trust work. Mr. Biddle said he had always told the President that we did not seek this work, that Justice had lots of work to do, and went on to say that we had trebled in size—that, perhaps, the Department had grown too fast.

Mr. Hoover made it clear that he had no fear of the investigational burden which would be imposed upon the FBI, and Mr. Biddle added that the Treasury investigations in the line of duty on the alien property front would quickly run into subversive activities, resulting in a division of this work between the Treasury and the FBI. Hoover pointed out that divided responsibility along this line in the last war had produced very bad results, and that the responsibility ought to be centered in one place. . . .

Sam Smith, from the Special Defense Unit,[3] brought attention to the new line of isolationist political attack—criticism of the President for sending supplies to other countries, for sending the fleet away from their own shores where it is scattered in isolated operations, and the distribution of "scurrilous sheets" which had become rather numerous. The attorney general said that he was still firmly of the opinion that it was

2. President Roosevelt established the Office of Alien Property Custodian in the OEM by Executive Order No. 9095, 11 March 1942. He appointed as alien property custodian (APC) Leo T. Crowley, who served 1942–44.

3. The Special War Policies (Defense) Unit of the Justice Department, was an intradepartmental committee, established 19 May 1942 as part of the War Division of the Justice Department. It was under the directorship of the solicitor general, who designated Lawrence M. C. "Sam" Smith as chief. Its purpose was to coordinate policy relating to neutrality, foreign enlistments, sedition, espionage, sabotage, and so forth.

unwise to prosecute for this kind of talk, particularly because the country was not divided in this war as it was in the last and was pretty firmly unified since the outbreak of war.

Mr. Hoover pointed out that on the Pacific Coast and in the Middle West areas, it is not understood why this sort of propaganda attack against the government is permitted to go on. Mr. [Max E.] Gilfond expressed the view that the people generally approved the Noble decision,[4] but that they are getting tougher in their attitude all the time. (This was a case of a man in California who said that the President ought to be impeached; Biddle ruled against indicting him for seditious statements, a consistent position for one who has always championed freedom of speech, but a decision much criticized on the West Coast, where the sense of war danger puts people very much on edge.)

Wendell Berge recounted the incident of Mrs. [Evalyn Walsh] McLean (of Hope Diamond fame) and her demand that the Department bring criminal charges against the author of the story in *New Masses*, which was published last week, saying that she was the center of the Cliveden Set in Washington, D.C., which, as in the case of Lady [Nancy] Astor's Cliveden Set[5] in England, was the center of the isolationist talk, and which the President recently denounced in a press conference. He referred to the rumor factory here in Washington. Wendell frankly stated that a case for criminal prosecution could be made, but so also could many cases be made against various columnists or writers from time to time. We would be greatly burdened with such prosecutions, and the decision not to prosecute for criminal libel in such cases was made in the case of Senator [Millard E.] Tydings, when Robert Jackson was attorney general, Jackson having refused to bring criminal libel proceedings against columnists alleged to have libeled Senator Tydings, on the grounds that civil remedies were available to the senator.

The question of policy was again presented by Mrs. McLean's case, Mrs. McLean having just publicly denounced the refusal of the Department to prosecute and having written a letter to the foreman of the grand jury in Washington, D.C., who naturally presented the matter to the United States attorney, asking what, if anything, ought to be done in such a case. It was suggested that a copy of Mr. Jackson's opinion or excerpts from it might be sent to the United States attorney.

---

4. Robert C. Noble was a former old-age pension leader and the head of Friends of Progress, a California isolationist organization that blamed the United States for the war and criticized President Roosevelt. Despite much prodding, Biddle refused to prosecute him. On 31 March 1942, Governor Earl Warren of California had him arrested for libeling General Douglas MacArthur.

5. The Cliveden Set was an anti-Soviet, proappeasement group in England, associated both socially and politically with Nancy Astor, whose country house was at Cliveden in Buckinghamshire.

The Japanese problem[6] on the Pacific Coast was briefly discussed when I asked the attorney general whether properties of those being evacuated inland were to be taken charge of as alien property, to which he replied in the affirmative as to the enemy aliens. "It shows the need for appointing an alien enemy property custodian," he added, and I concurred. I called attention particularly to the fact that these people were compelled to walk away from their properties in the Pacific Coast without provision therefor, and that a greater problem perhaps arose in respect to the property of Japanese American-born citizens, who would be evacuated from some areas by the Army.

In regard to the problem of handling the citizens of Japanese descent, I asked whether consideration had been given to the point that for a generation a greater proportion of Japanese entries into the United States were generally accepted to have been illegal. In fact, both Japanese and Chinese were smuggled in in great numbers on the Pacific Coast, and I well recall the wreck of a Chinese smuggling ship in Puget Sound where we used to land on yachting trips. Would it be possible to contend that, the entry of the parents being fraudulent, birth of children could not give them the constitutional right of citizenship?

The attorney general made short work of the question and said that, of course, they would be entitled to citizenship and that there was nothing in the point.

I recognized the extremely tenuous character of the contention, which the government would have to make but, having explored many tenuous contentions to a successful conclusion . . . it seems to me very much worth exploring, although I must say I never heard of a legal contention based upon fraud benefiting human intercourse. Maybe it could.

The attorney general's abrupt method of disposing of the point was, I must say, opposed to open discussion of doubtful questions. In going around the staff from right to left, most of the men present had nothing to present to staff meeting, which is usually the case. There is not exactly an opportunity of frank and open discussion which, in my opinion, ought

6. After the outbreak of the war, the entire Japanese population in the West Coast states was forcibly evacuated from the coastal areas and resettled in concentration camps for the duration of the war. Lt. General John L. DeWitt, the commanding general of the Western Defense Command, carried out the operation under authority granted to him by President Roosevelt by Executive Order No. 9066, 19 February 1942, which designated the western half of the states of Washington, Oregon, and California, and the southern half of Arizona, as military areas from which persons of Japanese descent would be prohibited. Beginning 22 March 1942, the Army began evacuating the Japanese to camps administered by the War Relocation Authority (WRA). The WRA, established by Executive Order No. 9102, 18 March 1942, eventually had jurisdiction over 110,000 men, women, and children. Nine of the WRA's ten camps housed loyal Americans; the tenth center (Tule Lake, California) housed evacuees who said they were loyal to Japan.

to pervade these meetings to get the best exchange of views on fundamental questions of policy.

Tuesday, 10 March 1942

The staff meeting today was quiet and unresponsive. No comments were made by any man called upon by the attorney general down to Jim [James Van B.] Bennett—at which point we got into a discussion of the Japanese problem which has largely been taken over by the United States Army conducting wholesale evacuations from the Pacific Coast. It was mentioned that the Gallup Poll showed 39 per cent of the voters favored FBI control of the Japanese problem and 31 per cent in favor of the Army, by way of discussion.

Sam Smith of the Special Defense Unit advised that the committee appointed by former Attorney General Jackson (appointed about November 1st) to study the various subversive organizations alleged to be operating in the United States would have a report completed this week which would then go to Mr. [Edward J.] Ennis of the Alien Registration Unit.[1] The report will show whether the Department can move against members of the Bund merely upon the broad general ground that they are members of the Bund.[2] The difficult legal problem confronted is whether the Department could proceed against members solely on the grounds of membership—whether the organization is so conclusively established as to be subversive as an agent of Nazi Germany as to make membership itself sufficient to justify indictment. It seems fairly clear, but there are other organizations too; the principal question is one of good faith and whether the organization is attached by allegiance to another country rather than to the United States. Smith has a bill drafted called the "Nationality Act of 1942"[3] to provide "for the expatriation of dual citizens for conduct establishing allegiance to the foreign country claiming them." The rough draft, subsequently handed to me by Smith on request, provides that any person who shall "engage in a course of conduct which establishes that his true political allegiance is to a foreign state or sov-

1. The Alien Registration (Enemy Control) Unit of the Justice Department was a special intradepartmental committee under the supervision of the War Division. It was established to enforce the Alien Registration Act of 1938 and had charge of the supervision and control of alien enemies in the United States.

2. The German-American Bund was the chief pro-Nazi organization in the United States after 1936. At its peak, in 1939, this quasi-military organization had about 8,300 members.

3. The Nationality Act of 1940 (Public Law 853), approved 3 June 1940, revised and codified the nationality laws into a comprehensive code. A bill to amend the act (H.R. 7746) to deport aliens to countries allied with the United States was introduced in the House in 1942 but was not adopted.

ereignty, such course of action shall be considered *prima facie* evidence that such persons did not, in taking the oath of renunciation and allegiance to the United States, absolutely and entirely renounce and abjure all allegiance and fidelity to any foreign prince, potentate, state or sovereignty," and, "in the absence of countervailing evidence," this would be enough to authorize revocation of citizenship.

The Bill provides that the United States district attorneys should proceed against such persons in the district court. The wife and minor children should be excepted. . . .

11:30 A.M., 24 March 1942
Attorney General Staff Meeting

The attorney general spoke of the increasing problem of seamen's desertions from English, Greek, Norwegian and other ships because of the torpedoing of ships along the Coast. He also stated that the discipline in the merchant marine was terribly demoralized, that some of the ships were scarcely fit to live on, particularly the Greek ships where the quarters were almost unfit to live in and the ships were filthy with garbage and slops on deck. Another factor rendering it difficult to get seamen to return to their trade was the fact that high wages were paid on shore. A committee consisting of Chairman [Emory S.] Land of the Maritime Commission[1] and others were considering the pooling of shipping resources for the allied nations and also the problem of getting seamen to return to their ships. . . .

The conditions at Ellis Island were also discussed upon inquiry from the attorney general to Schofield, and the complaint of certain Japanese now at Hot Springs that the Geneva Convention as to the care of interned citizens of other countries were being violated.[2] Schofield explained that for 10 days there was such a congestion of Japanese that undoubtedly conditions were difficult but that this was being remedied and that he would make a personal inspection soon, which the attorney general encouraged. . . .

The attorney general asked Jim Bennett as to what was being done about

---

1. The U.S. Maritime Commission was established by the Merchant Marine Act of 1936 (49 Stat. 1985), approved 29 June 1936. The Commission was an independent executive agency which administered government subsidies to the U.S. merchant marine to construct and operate merchant ships. It also regulated common carriers. Rear Admiral Emory S. Land was chairman, 1938–46.

2. Ambassador Nomura had been interned along with other enemy diplomats at Hot Springs, Virginia. He alleged that he and other Japanese nationals there had been overcrowded and mistreated. In April the diplomats were shifted to more comfortable quarters at White Sulphur Springs, West Virginia, and, in June, they and 1,095 other Japanese nationals were exchanged for Americans held in Japan. See *New York Times*, 15 September 1942, p. 2, and 9 June 1942, p. 5.

alien enemy criminals being released from state and federal penitentiaries, pointing out the danger of their being logical saboteurs. Jim pointed out that these cases were all reported to him and to the Immigration Service for such action as was deemed appropriate, and the Immigration Service referred them, like other alien enemy cases, to enemy alien hearing boards around the country.

Most members present at the staff meeting made no comment when called upon by the attorney general.

The attorney general, in conclusion, raised the question as to advisability of having any member of the Department appearing before a congressional committee first consult with the attorney general as to the position to be taken. All this was apropos of Thurman Arnold's outburst against labor at the end of last week, and his now famous statement before a congressional committee that labor was ruining small business and throttling production, thereby vastly aggravating the battle going on to repeal protective labor legislation for the duration of the war.[3] It was unanimously agreed, that on questions of policy, the attorney general should be consulted before offering testimony, and I said that the question resolved itself into one as to "how many attorney generals there could be at one time."

---

26 March 1942

I had a long talk with Charles Fahy, solicitor general, in his office this afternoon, in regard to the affairs of the Department about which both of us expressed very considerable concern. While one owes unflinching loyalty to one's chief, as far as the outside world is concerned, within the Department frank discussion of those devoted to the welfare of the Department is a healthy thing, and we both "let our hair down." I stated quite frankly that I felt that the attorney general was "on the run" and had not steadied down to the frightening responsibilities of a wartime attorney general. Instead of reaching out for men in the Department, who could help him on the policy front with a real insight and capacity therefor, he rested on the men nearest to him, who usually happened to be Carusi.

Charlie expressed regret on the same count, giving as an illustration the Alien Enemy Committee[1] to advise the attorney general which had func-

---

3. "Unions Abuse Their Power Thurman Arnold Declares; Biddle's Assistant Tells a House Group They Prevent Efficient Use of Labor and Machines and Hamper the Independents," *New York Times*, 22 March 1942.

---

1. The Special War Policies (Defense) Unit of the Justice Department, headed by Lawrence M. C. "Sam" Smith.

tioned well and laid the foundations for the action which had immediately
followed Pearl Harbor. Charlie, himself, was called on the telephone on
Sunday, December 7th, by the President, in the absence of Attorney
General Biddle, to discuss the apprehension of enemy aliens who had been
investigated by the FBI. Plans were ready, proclamations were ready, and
the FBI was ready. Charlie took the proclamation and the necessary orders
to the White House. (In his article in "Colliers" in March 1942, the
attorney general says he took them to the White House.)

After the appointment of Ennis, as head of the Alien Enemy Section of
the Department,[2] the committee more or less ceased to function, and the
attorney general went off on his own tangent with Jim Rowe, sending Jim
to the Pacific Coast in regard to the Japanese problem. From the point of
view of the Department, the problem was not handled well at all, but
rather it was surrendered, *in toto*, to the War Department, now
conducting a mass evacuation from the Pacific Coast. I reminded Charlie
that I had pressed the attorney general rather strongly in staff meetings
on the Japanese problem, but had not only had my humble thoughts
brushed aside, even though I came from a section of the country deeply
concerned and where some consciousness of the Japanese problems
might be expected. There is no sectional representation without power of
position. One only fans the air and hopes for attention.

Administratively, the Department is at loose ends. The attorney general
does not come to grips with it and does not have the reins of government
firmly in hand. Everyone runs his own show and, we agreed, that staff
meetings had become insignificant. Why, for example, discuss basic policy
in the presence of Tom Quinn, who has no particular capacity for understanding the underlying currents of thought and struggles which are the
essence of government—or before Jim Bennett, director of the Prisons
Bureau?[3]

Charlie agreed that the attorney general was, perhaps, intending to
follow a pattern, visualizing himself as the successor to his early
progenitor . . . and trying to stand firm for his liberal friends, who do not
see that liberalism must give ground in the interest of preserving
liberalism in the world struggle. Thus, Biddle, having sounded off in
regard to freedom of speech and civil liberties at a time when those must
be somewhat curtailed in the interest of united public opinion, is now
compelled to retreat. Even the President has asked him to take action
against seditious statements such as those of Silver Shirt [William D.]

---

2. The Alien (Registration) Enemy Control Unit of the Justice Department, headed by
Edward J. Ennis.

3. The Prison Bureau of the Justice Department was responsible for administering the
federal prison system, except military prisons.

Pelley.[4] Characteristic of his judgment is the fact that he wanted to appoint Maurice Ernst,[5] somewhat of a self-exploiter and attorney for the Civil Liberties Union,[6] to head the Sedition Department in Justice. Both Fahy and Jim Rowe knocked that out, and the idea was abandoned. It was as improper as his desire to have the President appoint Tommy Corcoran as solicitor general.

A man of high purpose, fine instincts and real legal ability, still the attorney general was acting too impulsively, Charles thought, somewhat because of lack of experience under fire—a lack of seasoning. . . . [His] too frequent assertion of civil liberties [was] described editorially as "Biddling" . . . by Walter Winchell on the air. Biddle finds himself in an exposed and unprotected situation.

We also discussed Thurman Arnold who, a few days ago before a congressional committee, made a sensational attack on labor for throttling the small businessman and holding up national defense. I agreed with a great deal that Thurman Arnold said but, as Charlie quietly put the matter, Thurman assigned to the entire labor movement the very worst features which arise in spots throughout the country. That Thurman has an inclination of mind along the fascist pattern I have little doubt, and his quest for publicity is almost abnormal in its apparent hunger. As [Brian] Bell, . . . [head] of the Associated Press here and his wife, frankly and jokingly recognized, the fellow seeks every opportunity to call a press conference or contact a press man privately, with Mrs. [Frances L.] Arnold aiding and abetting even at social gatherings with the wives of the press men. I recall a conversation with Crowthers, a politically minded Unitarian minister in Los Angeles, who came up to me after the address at Town Hall to say that Thurman Arnold had offered him a position as public relations counsel for Thurman Arnold in Washington and that he, himself, thought Thurman should be a candidate for President in 1944, and that "what this country needed was more Thurman Arnolds." I really believe the fellow has the presidential bug—Thurman, I mean. He so clearly falls in the category of those people who are in search of personal power rather than public service.

Today, again, Arnold sounded off against the Standard Oil Company of New Jersey,[7] a favorite and enjoyable target, for its contractual relations

4. The Silver Legion of America was a pro-Nazi organization, founded by William D. Pelley in 1933 and known as the Silver Shirts because of their uniforms. The organization collapsed in 1942, when Pelley was arrested.

5. Littell is probably referring to Morris L. Ernst.

6. The American Civil Liberties Union (ACLU) is a privately funded civic organization established in 1920 to preserve the Bill of Rights.

7. Arnold told the Truman Committee of the Senate that Standard had tried to do business in occupied France, in 1941, and to establish business connections in Japan, in 1939, anticipating the eventual breakdown of U.S.-Japanese relations. See "All Patents

with *I.G. Farbenindustrie*, a story which he had declined to make public pending the settlement of the indictment against the Company, which [was] *nolle prossed* yesterday, Standard having paid its fine. Thurman charges that Standard gave Germany processes for synthetic rubber which were not released to the American manufacturers for use in this country, even though *I.G. Farbenindustrie* was refusing to give Standard other formulas and data.

Sunday, 6 April 1942
4101 Lorcom Lane

I have fallen far behind in this log, or rather, events have gone by with the rapidity and staccato racket of machine gun bullets—with me on the sidelines still convalescing.

Last night Mr. and Mrs. A. J. T. Taylor and Kathleen, a daughter, and a young lady, by the name of Miss Poate, from the English Embassy, and three soldiers from Ft. Dix, sent out from the Recreation Centers, dined with us. I did not welcome the occasion, but it was Kathleen's one night in Washington and Katherine took on the extras at the same time. I sat in the big chair and listened. The high point was Vincente Villamin's arrival. . . . [He] came after dinner. The three likeable American boys . . . listened goggle-eyed to Villamin's story of arbitrating a mutiny on the *Nuccoa* last week in Philadelphia; and the counter-espionage work among the Filipinos on the Pacific Coast; and [his] description of the situation on Bataan Peninsula where his brother-in-law, Lieutenant General Lim, is in command of the Philippine troops. . . .

The last two days have been given up continuously to drafting instructions under the Second War Powers Act, Title II [of] which we wrote in the Lands Division[1]—a strenuous and exacting job, which I could not seem to get anyone else to do adequately. I am paying the price today and staying in bed all day.

So go the important trivia of my own affairs! The press has roared and raged about greater events on the foreign and domestic fronts. At home and in our own backyard, the Thurman Arnold incident has been the most widely debated . . . President [William S.] Farish of the Standard Oil

---

Freed in Rubber Making by Anti-Trust Suit; Standard Group in Consent Decree, Gives Up Data for Synthetic Products; Complaint Charges World-Wide Monopoly with German Dye Firm to Curb Trade," *New York Times*, 26 March 1942; Frank L. Kluckhohn, "Arnold Says Standard Oil Gave Nazis Rubber Process," *New York Times*, 27 March 1942. See also Note 2, 6 April 1942.

1. Title II of the Second War Powers Act of 1942, approved 28 March 1942, amended the Act of 2 July 1917 (40 Stat. 241) governing federal acquisition of property during wartime.

Company of New Jersey [has alleged that] a consent decree has been entered solely upon Thurman Arnold's promise to delete from the consent decree and from the case charges of suppression of vital information and refusal to give the information to the American military authorities while it was being released to *I.G. Farbenindustrie* of Germany under the cartel agreement. Thurman technically complied but, two days later, he made a sensational appearance before the Truman Committee[2] after the consent decree had been entered and the fine paid and repeated the charges in a far more resounding way than would ever have been possible in the lawsuit.

Having attacked labor last week and slugged at big business this week, he hit a nice dramatic balance of attack, well-timed and well-staged according to the popular opinion of newsmen who know him. Following the incident, which of course put the attorney general very much on the spot as to his labor policy, Frank Waldrop, long the columnist champion of Thurman Arnold, makes a vicious attack upon the attorney general, charging him with having left town to avoid the spot upon which Thurman Arnold placed him. Since Waldrop has long been the intimate of Arnold and has done this sort of thing before, particularly during the period before Biddle's appointment when Waldrop was trying to force Arnold on the President as attorney general, everyone knows where the information comes from.

Away, behind the lines, Thurman Arnold's jealousy of Leon Henderson, the price administrator, and his rising power, influence and recognition by this administration, is one of the mainsprings of Thurman's activities. One must have insight and watch closely his great egotism and extraordinarily unsocial relationships with his fellow men—he is with us but not of us. Such a force is a great and impelling one. All of us who know him know that he should no more be attorney general than Eddie Cantor. Both are effective in their respective lines, and Thurman adds a brilliant and stimulating intellect, but he is a bum administrator, unstable and self-exploiting whenever the opportunities are present, and he can't take a place on a team.

With the growing frustration of having reached the top in the administration, and clear realization with Biddle's appointment as attorney general, that he, Thurman Arnold, would not be appointed attorney general (Or does he have hopes that he can force the President's hand with these antics? It would be almost stupid to think so.) he has reached the place where he will advance his personal fame no matter at what price to the administration. His attack on labor is typically all-out

2. Senator Harry S. Truman of Missouri was chairman of the Special Committee to Investigate the National-Defense Program, 1941–44.

Thurman Arnold tactics, at a time when the administration was trying to salvage what gains could be preserved during wartime against the attack of labor-baiters and vigilantes who have rallied full force to this opportunity. That much must be done to straighten out disorder and clean up vices in the labor movement, I have no shadow of a doubt, but even the National Association of Manufacturers,[3] the business executive polls in *Fortune*,[4] and such men as Bernard Baruch have indicated clearly that conservative, level-headed judgment believes in preserving the forty-hour week and the main gains of organized labor. . . .

Tuesday, 7 April 1942

At the outset of this meeting, the attorney general brought up the matter of Negro employees and the current protest of Negro organizations and leaders at the small part Negroes were being given in the war effort. The staff was urged to select and employ a number of Negro lawyers in spite of the difficulties of fitting them into an organization where White stenographers have consistently complained—particularly the Southerners—about having to take dictation from them.

The possible suspension of the anti-trust laws during the war effort was discussed in reference to a memorandum of the President on this subject which was not read or outlined. It was reported that both the House and the Senate were strong for a bill suspending the Statute of Limitations and the anti-trust laws but, of course, that would seem to be utterly futile from the point of view of industry. It cannot be supposed that industry would operate under suspended anti-trust laws, knowing that the axe would fall after the war . . .

The principal subject of discussion was "what had been done about examining into the Dies[1] charges that employees of the government belonged to some 35 subversive organizations," a matter on which the attorney general had asked Jim Rowe to form an interdepartmental committee to weigh the charges and recommend some follow-up action, if any of them were sustained. . . . Jim reported that members of the various departments were "too intelligent" to serve on the committee, and he had

---

3. The National Association of Manufacturers (NAM) was an organization which represented the political interests of major American industrial companies. It lobbied congressmen and senators, published favorable articles, and provided campaign funds to probusiness candidates.
4. For example, "Fortune Management Survey," *Fortune* 25 (March 1942): 10.

1. Martin Dies, Jr., was chairman of the House Special Committee to Investigate Un-American Activities, 1938–45.

been unable to get anything but refusals—and he couldn't blame them much. . . .

. . . In the meantime, pending a decision as to what organizations are deemed subversive, Hoover has thousands of cases being held up, . . . awaiting advice as to what agencies should be the subject of full investigation. . . .

Wednesday, 8 April 1942
4101 Lorcom Lane

This was a tough day. There were conferences with section chiefs this morning regarding the approaching conference of the United States attorneys from the southern and eastern states, and we noted the problems of each area: personnel, procedural and substantive. . . . Shall I give a lawyer from the West, without influence and terrified by the blank wall of unemployment staring him in the face, a job at twenty-six hundred dollars as a title attorney, or live with a haunting fear that less worthy men will prevail; a grave injustice could be done, and a desperate man could possibly commit suicide—a very real possibility in this case? The answer is "yes," and I wish that justice could be so easily bought.

I had a conference with the assistant solicitor general, [Oscar S.] Cox, regarding my revolutionary "Dive Bombing Title Bill." The Bill would blast the preparation of title evidence out of the way so that we could pay dispossessed property owners throughout the country who, by the thousands, are being removed from their properties and being compelled to await payment for lack of title evidence. We would serve those in possession with notice, post notice on each property and publish notice in the papers, concluding all claims against those who did not appear to defend their interests in thirty days. Cox suggests a reserve fund of one per cent of land acquisition funds as an insurance against those unjustly deprived of compensation by reason of the brevity of these notices—a very good idea.

He also suggests partial distribution to those owners we are sure of even before the thirty days run out—an excellent suggestion which completes the Bill. There was something missing in it until that suggestion was made. It fits into place like the missing part of a jig-saw puzzle. . . .

I went with Katherine to a cocktail party at Ed Kemp's, an attorney for the Bureau of the Budget and an inseparable companion of Justice Murphy's. It was in Justice Murphy's apartment at the New Washington Hotel. . . .

I had quite a talk with Mr. Justice Murphy who, I must say, seems genuinely fond of Katherine and myself, expressing the greatest regret at not having seen more of us and a determination to get together very soon.

There is a fine seam of pure quality in the man's makeup, and rare insight. The conversation fell by force of gravity into a discussion of the Department and he expressed regret over the state of things into which Biddle had reduced it, for it is now a matter of common knowledge that the affairs of the Department under Biddle are at a very low ebb.

"Thurman Arnold is the only one down there who has captured the imagination of the entire country," Murphy said, referring to Thurman Arnold's two recent public utterances, now famous. . . .

Murphy asked me about one or two other assistant attorney generals and, in the candor which I have always practiced with him, admitted lack of force and attacking power for present-day needs. "I am compelled to admit," I said, "however much I disagree with Thurman's self-exploiting tactics and absence of loyalty to any living man except Thurman, that he and I are the only two men of the assistants with any real umph, or attacking power, over and above mere legal ability."

Murphy nodded. "Hoover tells me you have developed an able organization," he said, "and I know that anyway."

"I am not running for President and Thurman Arnold definitely is, in my opinion," I said.

Murphy looked surprised and asked, "Is that so?" He agreed every move was calculated to advance the interests of Thurman Arnold. "He completely runs around them down there," he said, referring to Congress, "visiting congressmen and senators and building up his own support in the Hill by patronage and every other method."

I thought of my own conscientious efforts to route all patronage matters through Jim Rowe's office and play ball according to Hoyle—but what is the use when there is no control at the top of the Department?

"He is unscrupulously devoted to the advancement of his own interests," I said.

"Ruthlessly, I would say, instead of unscrupulously," Murphy said. "He has attacked Biddle ruthlessly."

. . . We both agreed that the downfall of Biddle stemmed from the Biddle-Frankfurter-Corcoran clique. "The object was to keep control of Immigration," Justice Murphy said, "and also the Department of Justice—that was Frankfurter's aim in pressing hard for Biddle, although I must say he resisted Tommy Corcoran as solicitor general. He was wise enough for that." . . .

Thursday, 9 April 1942
4101 Lorcom Lane

[I] attended the Conference of United States Attorneys, Southern and Eastern Divisions—about 18 states—meeting here to discuss problems of law enforcement in wartime, mostly alien enemy problems, violations of the Selective Service Law,[1] criminal enforcement problems, and land acquisitions for national defense. Many of them have criticized the Department very bluntly and there is unquestionably a feeling of resentment at some of the attorney general's policies, his failure to silence many of the avowed enemies of the United States, who take advantage of freedom of speech to spread propaganda undermining public confidence. Not until last week was Pelley, the head of the Silver Shirts organization and one of the most out-and-out-pro-Nazi sympathizers in this country, arrested in Indianapolis on orders of the attorney general. I was reliably informed that the President, himself, told the attorney general to tighten up. The district attorneys relfected the hot feelings of their local communities. . . .

Another sore point was the number of alien enemy hearing boards' decisions which had been reversed. The feeling of these men on the boards, for the most part composed of prominent lawyers and citizens, that the department has inadequate bases upon which [to judge] whether a man should be incarcerated for the duration of the war or not, is very well taken, judging from the few files I have seen. Some of my lawyers use spare time to work for the Enemy Alien Unit, . . . reviewing files from the hearing boards. . . . The fact that inexperienced lawyers, here, . . . should even consider reversing on so scanty a record as is available here . . . seems very risky. . . .

I rode over to the luncheon at the Mayflower Hotel, given by the attorney general and the United States Attorney, [Edward M.] Curran, of the District of Columbia, in the attorney general's car.

We walked through the hotel together, and the attorney general asked if I had attended Ed Flynn's affair the preceding day. . . . The attorney general said he kidded Flynn as to when he was going to be indicted for the flagstone fraud of which he is charged in New York—having flagstones laid free of charge by the city in his own garden—a current scandal with a very real stench to it. It savors, as do Ed Flynn's appearances, of the old ward-heeling politician.

"The luncheon was for big-shots," I said, "and the cocktail party in the afternoon was for the little-shots, but I had another engagement and, besides, the notice was altogether too short. The invitation came in the morning."

The attorney general said that he had had no difficulty with Flynn. If Flynn's recommendations on judgeships were no good, Biddle simply

---

1. The Selective Service and Training Act of 1940 (Burke-Wadsworth Act), approved 16 September 1940, required registration for the draft of all men twenty-one to thirty-six, but limited military service to one year. The next year, Congress passed the Service Extension Act of 1941 (55 Stat. 626), approved 18 August 1941, which extended the period of service to eighteen months. The Act passed by a one-vote majority in the House (203 to 202).

turned them down and told Ed he would have to get some better ones, and everything was lovely.

"Have you gotten acquainted with Ed Pauley, the secretary?" I asked, "and do you know whether the current rumor is true that the party was completely broke, and Ed Pauley raised a lot of money?"

He did not know exactly, although he knew the party was two or three hundred thousand dollars short. "It's oil money, you know," I said, "and that worries me a little right in the heart of the party organization," knowing exactly where the money would come from—Signal Oil & Gas, Standard, and other big oil men on the Coast.

"It always has to come from someplace, you know," Biddle replied, laughing it off. "That's one reason I prefer the luncheons because the source is widely scattered."

I never could quite understand the man. He is so casual about things which seem to me fundamental. Of course, one cannot take on all the challenging issues which are presented, but this one is so fundamental.

"He handled the tideland oil situation very skillfully with the President," Biddle said, referring to Pauley having dissuaded the President from going ahead with the suit to determine the ownership of oil in the submerged lands. "I think the President was quite right in not wishing to stir up a fight with the state at this time, and I did not press the matter with him."

We came to the cloakroom by this time, and the crowd of those attending the luncheon, and the conversation broke up. . . .

The awful, sickening story of the day is the fall of our Bataan garrison, commanded by General [Jonathan M.] Wainwright, under the impacts of attacks from 200,000 Japanese. Some 37,000 men, including civilians, capitulated. Even though this has been inevitable for a long time, the shadow of the headlines fell like a gray pall over the evening. . . .

It was a gray day, a very gray day. I might add, with a considerable irony, that, perhaps, the only light of the day was the faint glow—intermittent—of a small red light[2]. . . .

Thursday, 16 April 1942
4101 Lorcom Lane

I asked for an appointment with the attorney general this afternoon. It happened to be one of those quiet days in his office; I got the appointment quickly and went up at 3:00.

"How do you like our cracking down on *Social Justice*?"[1] he asked, before

---

2.   A reference to the continuing effects of Littell's heart attack.

1.   *Social Justice* was a magazine founded and published by Father Coughlin in Royal

I could get started on my business, referring to Father [Charles E.] Coughlin's paper, which has been the subject of hot controversy, particularly in the newspaper, *P.M.*,[2] which has circulated petitions to sign and send to the attorney general on the subversive statements of the Coughlin paper.

I had read that it had been stopped in the mails by the Post Office Department, but the Department of Justice had not filed an indictment or instituted proceedings before a grand jury. [I] assumed that I must be a little bit vague in my information and not up to date. "It is time," I said, "and I am glad the whole matter is under way. The people are of one mind about it."

"I wanted to go slowly on this sedition work," the attorney general went on, "and let the sentiment of the country build up." There has been criticism from all over the country directed at the attorney general for letting "the free speakers" damn or confuse the war effort, while our boys are battling with the soldiers of propagandist countries, and dying. *P.M.* finally took the matter up as a national issue. . . .

"The President gave me a rough time about it in the cabinet meeting last week," the attorney general said, with great candor, "but I felt I ought to wait until sentiment had crystalized in the country."

"Of course, it did crystalize," I replied, "and, perhaps, it was good to have it build up that way. The trouble was that it broke against you. You were the fall-guy." The attorney general nodded assent.

A telephone conversation interrupted, [from] Frank Shea, assistant attorney general [in the] Claims Division, about the Department bill to take patents controlled by foreigners during wartime,[3] a measure slowly drafted . . . last year. [This bill was] finally submitted to Congress. It was a mild measure making it possible to take in used patents during wartime for a "reasonable royalty," but the whole present system to be reinstated after the war.

I had had a visit with Senator Bone, chairman of the Senate Patents Committee, three days before, when I dropped in on him in the office building of the Senate, and was invited to stay to lunch, where we talked

Oak, Michigan. With a circulation of 200,000, it echoed his increasingly fascist policies. Following Pearl Harbor, Coughlin charged in *Social Justice* that Jews and Communists had tricked America into the war. On 14 April 1942, citing the Espionage Act of 1917, Biddle asked the postmaster general to suspend the second-class mailing privileges of the magazine (because it undermined troop morale), which he did on 4 May 1942.

2. *P.M.* was a liberal New York evening newspaper published by Marshall Field and edited by Ralph McA. Ingersoll, 1939–45. For *P.M.*'s campaign against Coughlin, see "P.M. Proves Coughlin Dangerous," *P.M.*, 31 March 1942, pp. 2–10.

3. Congress never acted on the foreign patent seizure bill of 1942. Instead, in April 1942, President Roosevelt ordered the alien property custodian to seize all enemy-controlled patents and make them available to American companies.

until after 3:00. Bone had recognized what I labeled as the supreme opportunity in the history of the patent law. The recent revelations before the Truman Committee of the cartels and German controls in this country by means of patents [were still fresh in the public consciousness.] . . .

I had recommended that Bone get the best informed man that he could find in the Department of Justice to conduct those hearings and guide them, instead of the well trained and likable lawyer from Texas who is doing the work for the Committee, but who is utterly unacquainted with the complex background of the subject matter. Bone had said that it was Department of Justice evidence, and he was going to depend upon the attorney general, and he asked me to tell the attorney general that. So I did, recommending the assignment of Joe Bourkin. . . . He is the head of the Patent Section in the Anti-trust Division and the source of Thurman Arnold's knowledge.

"I would call Senator Bone and, perhaps, [Joseph] O'Mahoney and [Robert M.] La Follette, too, regarding the organization of that committee proceeding," I said to the attorney general. "This is the supreme opportunity in the entire history of patent law in this country to go to the bottom of the whole matter. The present system stands squarely in the path of human progress in suppressing scientific inventions, such as the tubeless radio and innumerable other inventions, which ought to be at the service of mankind, but which are suppressed for purely competitive reasons or because an existing industry is based on the old system of building radio tubes." . . .

"It is a great opportunity," the attorney general agreed. "Perhaps, we should have a conference with those three senators who I think are running the show, with you and Frank Shea and Thurman Arnold and get matters lined up."

"Why not do it yourself?" I asked. "Leave Thurman and Frank and me out of it, and just call those senators for a conference, first satisfying yourself that you have the best informed man in the Department to lift out of the Anti-trust Division and place in charge of the investigation, if the senators will let you do it. To hell with Thurman, anyway! He has been going around you. Why not take ahold of this issue and handle it yourself, lifting whatever man you need out of the Anti-trust Division to guide the proceedings?"

"It's a good idea," Biddle said, "and I will see what I can do about it."

We turned to the subject of the Judge Advocate General's Office of the Navy, on which [James V.] Forrestal, undersecretary of the Navy, had been working supposedly for two or three months. I told Biddle that matters had reached a crucial point with the passage of the Second War Powers Act on March 28th, expediting the taking of real and personal property and the immediate possession of both on filing a petition in condemnation, without depositing any money in court.

"The blundering, inefficient processes of the JAG's office in dealing with settlements, in handling appraisals, and in the whole, entire business of acquisitions, will wreck us," I said. Forrestal has had lawyers studying the problem of eliminating the JAG from land acquisition entirely, since January, but nothing has yet resulted although I drafted an executive order to remove the functions of the JAG in connection with acquisitions. . . . [I further] suggested the establishment of a real estate section in the Navy Department, as an adjunct to the Bureau of Yards and Docks, which does 98 per cent of their land acquisition work, [and] shifting the young officers of the JAG assigned to the field to the public works officers to work on the preliminary steps of developing projects for acquisition, as well as upon settlement under the direction and supervision of Department of Justice attorneys." It is all so clear and so simple, and the struggle to achieve such simple objectives is so complex.

The AG called Forrestal, then and there, after getting clearly in mind what the suggestions were, but Forrestal was out for the moment. The acquisition of the area adjacent to Hunters Point in San Francisco, this very day, is in point. Having thrown out over 50 people, mostly shipyards workers, adjacent to the Navy's drydock, the JAG was leisurely preparing a "declaration of taking," advising us that it would take two or three weeks. In the meantime, no property owners had their money because no money was deposited in court to distribute, and the popular hue and cry was that "even the Japs got better treatment when they were evacuated. The government at least gave them a place to live." It's a sore point in San Francisco. . . .

As I got up to leave, I asked the attorney general how he was "standing the racket" and there is no doubt that this is one of the most merciless positions in the government, a regular man killer. The occupant is damned if he does and damned if he doesn't.

He replied that he had his ups and downs—that last week was a pretty bad week when the President had "been pretty rough" with him "in cabinet meeting" over the sedition problem, but that this week he was feeling fine.

I left after the most complete and satisfactory conference I had ever held with the attorney general. His mind works in quick flashes; it is not a deliberative, reflective mind, and it is difficult to exchange ideas in a thorough way and get satisfaction. Today, however, we concluded every item of business on pretty thorough, solid grounds of discussion. Perhaps he is a fine man, but he is so lacking in insight into the feelings of the people and sympathies of the time, that he cannot act at the right moment. Lack of insight in public life is a fatal defect as far as effectiveness and winning public esteem is concerned.

The great master of it all is the President, from whom, extraordinary to note, at a time when he is running the war effort of the biggest country in the world—I had a personal note today. Not long ago, I was so greatly impressed with *Lanterns on the Levee*,[4] by William Alexander Percy, and its revealing statement of the Negro problem as it appears to the Southerner, that I spontaneously sent the book to the President with the following note:

> I am yielding to an impulse to send to you the accompanying book, *Lanterns on the Levee* by William Alexander Percy, representing reflections of a planter's son in the Delta country.
> This book seems to me excellent reading of an extra-curricular type such as everyone needs occasionally these days. It is also a most illuminating statement of the Southerner's point of view regarding the Negro. No book I have read casts so much light onto the deep, dark Delta country, even though the story runs out in the end like sands in the hourglass of the generation from which it proceeds.

Today, . . . the President took time to write the following personal note:

> Dear Norman:
>
> Ever so many thanks for your nice note and the copy of *Lanterns on the Levee* by William Alexander Percy. I shall have great pleasure in reading it, especially as it relates to a subject about which I know very little. You were more than kind to think of me.
> With every best wish,
>
> Very sincerely yours,
> Franklin D. Roosevelt [signed]

I am struck with his frank statement that he knows very little about the subject. That was the way I felt, and *Lanterns on the Levee* gave me my first glimpse of real understanding. Horizons fell back. Erroneous conclusions dissolved. I hope some day to know how the President reacted to the book.

Sunday, 19 April 1942
4101 Lorcom Lane

. . . At dinner on Friday night, we had Mr. and Mrs. Harold Smith (Budget director);[1] Lt. Col. [Jack W.] Heard (G-2 on the General Staff in

---

4. William Alexander Percy, *Lanterns on the Levee: Recollections of a Planter's Son* (New York: Knopf, 1941).

---

1. Harold D. and Lillian Smith.

charge of Latin American Division); Mr. and Mrs. Oscar Cox (assistant solicitor general, Department of Justice, recently appointed);[2] Mrs. Gifford Pinchot,[3] wife of the former governor of Pennsylvania; and Mr. and Mrs. Van Wyck Mason, a major in the U.S. Army, Public Relations Section.[4] . . .

I found Mrs. Pinchot, who naturally sat at my right, completely absorbing. She is a clear-headed, incisive thinker, and a fearless speaker. I confess she quite took my breath away when she came in. Why must these able, assertive women lean toward the conspicuous? Her hair is dyed red and she wore a bright red jacket, or waist, with beautifully embroidered green dress and very fancy slippers, together with a lot of large beads looking a bit too bulbous and plentiful for me. However, her charm of personality immediately asserts itself and I found her to have an engaging mind, somewhat to the neglect of Mrs. Smith, who sat on my left.

As an old friend of the President's, Mrs. Pinchot felt that she could speak frankly about "Franklin and Eleanor," both of whom she knows intimately. I hesitated at her frank statement that "Franklin is a bad administrator," not because I hesitated on the grounds of loyalty but solely on the grounds of honest doubt. . . .

My every contact with the President showed a remarkable grasp of detail. Furthermore, I know from my own little sphere that once one has launched a policy and delegated its administration, it is impossible to follow it consistently to conclusion. You can only check up now and then, or when someone forces a checkup on you by calling attention to the way matters have worked out. I would like to discuss that point further with Mrs. Pinchot. We were cut off there.

Against Mason's attack on Mrs. Perkins, secretary of labor, couched in polite language of an inquiry as to "why she was maintained as secretary of labor against the unanimous adverse sentiment of the entire country?" I replied that one of the main difficulties on that score was that this period in labor history had proved to be an extremely revolutionary one. "If you have ever seen a rodeo and a breaking of wild horses, you know what I mean when I say that anyone would be shocked to see a woman attempt to break one of those wild horses. There are some jobs in life that women simply are not fitted to do. The physical shock of rough and tumble of it all is just too tough, and it shocks one's sensibilities to see the attempt. Riding the labor issues during this administration was such a job and Secretary Perkins has been thrown a good many times," I said.

"I don't agree," said Mrs. Pinchot. "There is no job a woman cannot do who is really qualified for the post."

2. Oscar and Louise Bryson Black Cox.
3. Cornelia B. (Leila) Pinchot.
4. F. Van Wyck and Dorothy L. M. Mason.

There spoke a clear mind, which had worked out definite conclusions on many subjects, and quite clearly on the subject of women, although, like many an ardent woman leader, she may lean over backwards in her insistence on equality of the sexes. We will have to explore that a little further, too.

There were other vital subjects, but the most significant of all was the conversation between Katherine and Harold Smith, which constitutes an illuminating page of personal history on the most crucial issue of current politics and economics—the prevention of inflation, which has absorbed the public attention with increasing insistence in recent weeks, reaching a climax during the last week, with the appointment of a board[5] by the President to consider what should be done: Harold Smith, Budget director; Henry Morgenthau, secretary of the Treasury; Leon Henderson, price administrator; and Henry A. Wallace, Vice President. Harold Smith had come into the dinner, late, from a meeting of this board. In fact, the Vice President announced that he was adjourning the meeting so that Harold Smith could keep a dinner engagement, knowing, I gathered, where Smith was going.

The conversation is so conclusive, as to the position of the controversial Henry Morgenthau in the current picture of the day, that I have asked Katherine to dictate it for the sake of accuracy:

> Before Harold Smith's arrival, Mrs. Pinchot and I had been talking about Felix Frankfurter as to whether he was a sincere liberal or not. Neither of us thought that he was. Mrs. Pinchot asked if we had read a recent article, which was to have been in the *Yale Law Review*, but which Felix had had suppressed. We both agreed that suppression of any kind was not the earmarks of a liberal.
>
> I turned to Harold Smith, by way of including him in the conversation. I told him we had been discussing Felix and, apropos of his suppression of that article was his attempt last year to have [Arthur H.] Sulzberger of the *New York Times* suppress an article written by Arthur Krock, which criticized Felix severely. He was not successful in the suppression of these articles but, again, I observed to Smith that working by way of suppression was very questionable tactics in a liberal.
>
> Moreover, I said, I very much resented Felix Frankfurter's show-off tactics on the bench of the Supreme Court, in baiting inexperienced or nervous lawyers by raising complicated points of procedure. I said it was a disappointment to me because I had always admired him, during the 1920's, when he led the fight for Sacco and Vanzetti,[6] when we were in college.

---

5. President Roosevelt appointed this ad hoc board 10 April 1942, to draft an anti-inflation program. It resulted in Roosevelt's message to Congress of 27 April 1942, outlining a seven-point Economic Stabilization Program.

6. Nicola Sacco and Bartolomeo Vanzetti were two immigrant anarchist activists who were

He quite agreed with me and said he not only agreed with that but had found Frankfurter meddling in many affairs that were none of his concern. Even [in] his—Smith's—own division, way down among the lesser frys, so to speak, he often found the hand of Frankfurter installing people here and there. "Such meddling," he said, "might be understood, if they were lawyers. Even so, it would be questionable in a Supreme Court Justice. But in many cases the people were not lawyers. He seems to enjoy meddling and having a hand in whatever was going on, which other officers in the government resented and found highly distasteful. Moreover," he said, "in view of his race and religion and the peculiar spot that they are on now, you would think he would not attempt to incur any further resentment or even risk public resentment in having a Supreme Court Justice step out of his reserved official duties. The American public still likes to think of its Supreme Court Justices as quite apart from any devious political meddling."

I quite agreed with him. I said that, while the American people highly approved the President's calling in a Supreme Court Justice for advice and consultation, or even to do a particular job, such as [Owen J.] Roberts' mission to Hawaii, that that was quite a different thing from any backstairs meddling which [Frankfurter] delighted to indulge in. We both agreed that it was only a matter of time until the criticisms would be much more outspoken and his effectiveness, such as it is, [would become] grossly impaired.

At that time, dinner was announced, and we went in. [Smith] sat next to me at dinner, and I asked about the duties of the director of the Budget, in contra-distinction from those of the secretary of the Treasury. I admitted being very vague as to what his duties were, although I realized that they must be very important ones. He said that all legislation, no matter of what type, had first to pass through [his agency's] hands for consideration, and went on into the functions of the director of the Budget. Recently, he said, he had been called upon to help the President in writing letters to [Philip] Murray and [William] Green and other labor leaders, I suppose by way of pointing out the dangers of our inflationary trend.

I then remarked that his position, now, must be a very difficult one in that he had no charter path on which to go as the lawyer has, or the man in other specialized professional fields. "The economist, today," I said, "in addition to his knowledge of past fiscal ideals and policy, must depend a great deal on common sense plus imagination. He cannot rely on the past. The gold standard has gone and, with it, a great many old standbys of world economic policy." A man too closely allied, or devoted to, the old shibboleths would be a distinct detriment now, I thought, and I asked him, in view of that, how Henry Morgenthau was working out on his committee.

He seemed very much interested in that question, and gave me a forthright answer. He said that, of course we were speaking confidentially

---

convicted of murdering two shoe company employees during a robbery in 1920. Despite their pleas of innocence and the lack of conclusive evidence against them, they were executed in 1927. Their defense, conducted by Felix Frankfurter, became a liberal cause célèbre.

and that frankly, Morgenthau was not working out at all. I told him that I was not surprised because, even as a member of the old school of fiscal policy, he never seemed to be a number-one man to me.

Mr. Smith quite agreed with me and said that, only two or three days before, he had done something which not only showed his limitations in his office, but something much worse. The President has recently appointed this committee to study control of inflation. He said all the other members of the committee were in absolute accord. He said we have all the answers. It is merely a matter of working out the method. Even as to method we are in accord. Morgenthau, alone, objected. After one meeting, they found that he not only was not in accord, but had gone behind their backs to congressional tax committees, right from the meeting, giving them his side and giving them an entirely erroneous impression of the side of the rest of the committee, a highly improper and unethical thing to do. Someone interrupted at this point to say that made him a "son-of-a-bitch" altogether.

Henry, it seems, had gone to the President, complained bitterly about Harold Smith's "interference and intrusions into his job" and resented the work of the committee on controlling inflation and went off in a huff to his Hyde Park estate. The President summoned Harold Smith and asked him if he would do him a favor. "Yes, Mr. President," he answered, "of course: anything within reason," and laughed. "Then," said the President, "please go kiss Henry on both cheeks, will you?"

Then I said to Harold Smith, "He evidently uses the same tactics as his wife, Elinor Morgenthau." He seemed extremely interested in that remark and asked me to elaborate. I then told him that, when Anna and John Boettiger visited here two Christmases ago (the Christmas of 1939), Anna told me that Elinor Morgenthau was in a huff because Anna elected to dine with us, instead of with the Morgenthaus, and she said, "Whenever you come here it is always the Littells. When you have so little time, I don't see why you couldn't give us an evening for dinner." Anna said that that annoyed her, but she was used to Elinor's pulling things like that. She said that when Sistie was christened, and she had only a little family christening, she never dreamed of inviting Elinor Morgenthau. Not only was it only a family affair but, because of the religious question, she did not think Elinor would be interested. Elinor went into a pout and wept on Mrs. Roosevelt's shoulder, complained of Anna's hurting her feelings and ignoring her. She was not only invited to the christening, but Mrs. Roosevelt asked Anna to be especially nice to Elinor because her feelings had been hurt.

I observed to Harold Smith that that incident interested me from two angles: It showed she could be extremely "sensitive," where it helped her purposes in getting her own way, but extremely insensitive where it came to the feelings of others. Not to be hurt, she would attempt to force Anna to spend an evening doing what Anna didn't wish to do; when, as a matter of fact, she might have suggested the dinners merge and see if the Littells and the Boettigers would all dine with the Morgenthaus. That would be the logical outcome for a lady with the right instincts.

Harold Smith was extremely interested in that because, he said, that is exactly the tactics that Henry takes. It must be a family method of achieving their end. I observed that it might well be because Anna had often observed to me that one of her father's most outstanding characteristics was his objection to a row. He would do anything to avoid a scene. [He would] put up with scheming secretaries, stand anything rather than face a squabble. Mr. Smith's face brightened at that and, he said, "That is exactly right and I have only found it out recently. She is quite right, he cannot stand a scene and it is one of his most dominant traits. Morgenthau knows that and trades on it by putting on these sulks and not wanting to play anymore when his feelings are so terribly wounded."

Apropos of that trait of the President, I was forced to recall, in my own mind, Anna's statement to me of her father's attitude toward his mother's baitings of [Eleanor,] through the years. Because of his dislike of any kind of a row or scene, [he] permitted it. Many times, Anna said, when they were little, Mrs. Roosevelt left the dinner table in tears because Granny had observed that Franklin could have married so many pretty girls. She never could understand why he picked one as homely as Eleanor.

Her mother endured it patiently, through the years, and Anna said Eleanor, "did not even have support from us kids because we, naturally, looked up to Granny and thought she was right. When we grew old enough to realize the truth and to see how far Granny's malice went and how patient mother had been, we all realized that Granny was just 'an old bitch.'" Through it all, she felt that her father had failed in that he should long ago have risen to her mother's defense. Here is a glaring example of how far the President will go to avoid a row.

Thursday, 21 April 1942
Attorney General Staff Meeting

The [George S.] Viereck trials[1] having been successfully concluded with the able prosecutions, [by] the Criminal Division under Special Assistant [William P.] Maloney, and the *P.M.* attack having resulted in thousands of petitions being sent to the attorney general to proceed against Father Coughlin's paper, *Social Justice*, the grand jury is now about to proceed with further investigations and subpoenas are being issued. The attorney general started the meeting by asking what those subpoenas contained, for it seems that one witness, by the name of Ward, fell dead upon the service of a subpoena. He had been a former lobbyist agent for Coughlin, here in Washington, and a man of obvious pro-Nazi inclinations. . . .

Sam Smith reported that three papers were under examination, and the question was presented as to whether to shut them up or just control

---

1. George S. Viereck, a pro-Nazi German-born poet and editor, was convicted of violating the Alien Registration Act of 1938. The Supreme Court overturned his conviction 12 June 1943.

them through the Treasury Department control of enemy alien property. The opinion was expressed that the government should explore the program of putting in an APC representative to keep the papers alive and control their policy, thereby reaching the foreign element ordinarily treated to subversive statements in that press.

When Gilfond raised the question as to how much publicity should be given to treatments of enemy aliens, I reported the rather bitter observation of alien enemy hearing boards in Florida to the effect that more publicity was given to the indictment of an American boy who had failed to register for the draft than was given to an enemy alien who was interned for the duration of the war, as the attorney general's policy had been not to publicize such matters.

It developed that a committee composed of Gilfond, Jim Rowe, and one other, had been appointed to consider publicity for any enemy alien cases. They had decided against publicity whether the enemy alien was released, paroled, or incarcerated for the duration, after the boards had reported their recommendations to the attorney general and the attorney general had decided.

I also mentioned the bitterness at the number of reversals of enemy alien board decisions and the feeling that these men in the local communities had the enemy aliens before them and could . . . appraise their character better than young attorneys of the Department of Justice reading a paper record. I wholly concurred, I am afraid and feel somewhat embarrassed at the way a board of young lawyers, under Ennis, are reversing these mature, careful, and conscientious citizens throughout the country, who sit on the enemy alien boards and hear the cases first-hand. I made the point [concerning aliens who were released, as differentiated from] those who were paroled, it would be unjust to label all of them with the enemy alien stamp and place them under suspicion in their communities; [and] that as to those who were actually incarcerated, the public should know about it rather than merely have them disappear from their communities without a word of explanation.

Hoover concurred vigorously on these cases, and the pros-and-cons were discussed. Gilfond stated that he had vigorously supported the policy of publicity on those cases which were incarcerated, but Jim Rowe had been against it. How often one runs into the inadequacy of mind for dealing with vital questions of policy! This I label as another clear-cut fumble, just as Jim fumbled his Japanese situation. . . .

The inevitable backwash of the Japanese evacuation problem is here in the form of citizens' groups pressing for the exception of Japanese who are "loyal and perhaps special interests who need labor also." In any event, there is a great division as to the policy of wholesale evacuation, as might have been anticipated. A move was afoot, from some quarters, to classify aliens into grades of loyalty—a most ridiculous and impossible solution—

although strongly advocated by strong immigration associations. As Hoover said, "confusion worse confounded" would result. . . .

After the staff meeting, I waited to see the attorney general for a few moments. He took me into his office and, without waiting for the matter on my mind, asked me what I thought of the staff meeting. I said, very frankly, that I thought they were unresponsive and astonishingly flat, considering that we were in a sense his cabinet on questions of wartime policy in the Department of Justice. He rather agreed and asked me what to do about it. I merely replied that I had staff meetings in the Lands Division which were of very great value, which seemed to interest him a great deal, and he asked further about them.

"Twice a week," I said, "the heads of the six sections of the Lands Division meet in my office to discuss policies of the Division, and those discussion are extremely vital, lasting over two hours, although at times there is little business to transact and we may get through in about 45 minutes."

The attorney general was greatly interested and remarked, "I think I will talk to the staff about these meetings." I almost said, "It is entirely up to you Mr. Attorney General. Staff meetings succeed or fail according to leadership in them and whether you invite and want advice from your staff. Personally, I think it is as valuable to kick these ideas around among us as it is at any board of directors meetings of a private company—and, perhaps, somewhat more so."

"I quite agree," the attorney general [added]. "A very good thing, indeed." He was writing an autograph on a photograph of himself, which I had requested for my rogues' gallery of distinguished citizens, particularly of the four attorney generals under whom I had served. . . .

---

23 April 1942
4101 Lorcom Lane

. . . The event of the day was a knock-down, drag-out battle with Jim Rowe, the assistant to the attorney general.[1] I was tired anyway when I received the royal summons to his office at just before 6:00 P.M. I had called his assistant, Mr. Vanech, in regard to several pending P.R.'s [personnel reports] . . . which had not been signed . . . thus delaying and embarrassing my very rapidly flowing work. This was the echo and I knew it, so I went up.

---

1. The assistant to the attorney general (i.e., deputy attorney general) handled presidential appointments and legislation in which the Justice Department was interested; he served as liaison with Congress and other departments and agencies; he supervised the U.S. attorneys, U.S. marshals, and the major divisions of the Department. He was also responsible for departmental appointments, salaries, and promotions.

One [P.R.]—Sutton. at Amarillo, Texas—[had been] arranged by [Clyde O. Eastus] the U.S. attorney from Ft. Worth, when he was here at the U.S. attorneys' conference, the week previous. I had discussed him with Senator [Thomas T. "Tom"] Connally of Texas, who was the only one around here who knew the man and knew the qualifications which I needed. [Senator Connally] called me last Sunday at home, from Ft. Worth, with Sutton sitting in his office ready to go to work. The project at Amarillo, the Pan-Tex Ordnance, was greatly in need of attention, and property owners needed the service of legal counsel not from a distance of 300 miles at Ft. Worth, but close at hand. So I told both Eastus and Sutton to make their plans to enter on duty the following day—Monday— so they could immediately go to work. I would get the matter approved retroactively, by the Department of Justice, even though his application was being mailed that day and the appointment could not be made until it was received.

Rowe blew up. "What do you think I am, a rubber stamp?" he asked and, to my inquiry as to what he was talking about, he explained the Sutton situation [in] which I left him no alternative but to sign the P.R., without any review of the subject and without any contact on his part with Senator Connally.

I recited the circumstances of the appointment and said that I was entirely justified under the emergent situation which confronted me in making that decision and in expecting that the Department would back me up in it. If he wished to call it a rubber stamp activity, it was up to him. As far as I was concerned, the matter was properly handled.

We went on to one or two other appointments, of which he had the most superficial grasp—the situation in Kansas, for example, in which a national committeeman, [Lynn R.] Broderick, had come in to see me about releasing our chief attorney, whom he wished to make postmaster out there—the eternal problems of change in personnel in the field. I had gone on to discuss the firing of two other men, both of whom had been recommended by the National Committee and both of whom had been complete failures. One of them had written impudent, insolent letters to the attorney general, to which I was about to reply, with his discharge from the service. The matter was a perfect example of the patronage gone rampant, without proper review or control by the assistant attorney general, who must command the field organization.

Here, too, I had apparently had no business in discussing the matter with Broderick, and Jim felt that I was invading his province in sending Mr. Williams down to discuss it with Linton Collins, one of his assistants, whom he explained had nothing to do with such appointments.

"As far as I am concerned, he had plenty to do with it," I said. "Gus Vanech was out of town, and our business doesn't stop. I dealt with the only man in your office having authority, not being able to reach you. As far as I am concerned, that [is] the proper organizational principle to pursue. If you didn't have your men instructed rightly, that's your fault."

"Well, you can always get to me. All you have to do is to telephone me."

"That is not true," I replied. "You have unanswered telephone calls here to this day, calls which I have placed which you never answered." While we were talking, someone called on the phone, who Jim apparently did not consider of importance, and I heard him instruct the girl to "tell him to call some other time—no, it's up to him to get me when he can. I can't be bothered."

"You have brushed me off just as cavalierly as you brushed off that fellow, whoever he was," I said, "in spite of the big volume of business which I am heading for this Department."

"All you have to do is holler 'war' if I am bottle-necking your business," Jim replied.

"I won't do it," I said, "I am through hollering. If you can't attend to your business efficiently, I'm not going to holler at you about it. That's your affair. Furthermore, you do not understand the situation in the field. I've got to talk to the senator, if he is an able man, or the men who know where the projects are and what the character of the work is, and what the personnel existing in the field are. You can't possibly know that and neither can Gus Vanech, and I refuse to try to relay on to you these complicated statements of fact, which require first-hand dealings with somebody that knows the personnel, in this case, Senator Connally and, in the Kansas case, Mr. Broderick.

I paused, then said, "I was entitled to presume that the Department would back me up in making that decision in respect to Mr. Sutton. If you care to consider it as presumptuous, . . ."

"I do consider it as presumption," he said.

There was more to the conversation, but that's enough. That's the gist of it, except that he observed that a week was not too long to wait for an appointment—a week, when I am asking my men to file cases and secure immediate possession of immense areas in a matter of hours, and have to have immediate assistance in the field. I pointed this out rather strongly.

He also said he had had some little trouble with Thurman Arnold, to which I replied that he had had a great deal more trouble with Thurman Arnold and had failed to take him into camp. I suggested that he take him into camp fully, if he was going to make the rule around the Department about the handling of patronage matters and direct contacts with the senators.

As a matter of fact, it's another case of lack of executive capacity, pure and simple. It is a matter of great disappointment that he cannot even see the elemental difficulties confronting him. He has one competent assistant in Linton Collins, whom he told me was working entirely on judgeships and U.S. district attorney appointments (a matter of interest to me as I was the one who suggested that division of work to Jim shortly after he came into the Department) and one exceedingly unstable, shell shocked war veteran with a suspicious, easily shifting mind—Vanech. Jim does not even see that he has the biggest problem in the appointment of personnel in the history of the Department and has not even thought to expand the staff in his own office. That, alone, would account for many of the difficulties. His is a quest for personal authority rather than for efficiency.

Monday, 27 April 1942
4101 Lorcom Lane

Following the Lands Division staff meeting, I conferred with Special Assistant [Joseph E.] McPherson in regard to the Savannah Shipyards condemnation case, in which the Empire Ordnance Company . . . entered into a contract, on December 3d, with the Maritime Commission for the building of 112,000 tons of shipping—10 ships—on 3 ways . . . to be constructed in Savannah. This was one of several subsidiaries of the Empire Ordnance Company. Others . . . are doing work for the British . . . and the United States Army, contracted before Pearl Harbor.

McPherson's preliminary investigation, after which he had the trial continued, revealed faulty construction so shocking that it either amounts to sabotage or a deliberate effort to mulct the government by building such an inferior structure that the Maritime Commission would be compelled to take it over—at a profit to the instigators. Piling was driven in soft mud with no lateral support. . . . The way was so defectively constructed that it could not sustain . . . the weight of a ship. . . .

The Maritime Commission exercised a paragraph in the contract permitting it to call on the company to demonstrate a $750,000 line of credit or have the contract terminated and, as this was quite impossible, the [Commission] took possession at the end of the 30-day period [during] which such provision was to be satisfied, namely on January 2d, and, on the 3d, asked us to file condemnation proceedings, which has been done. . . . The company has dropped its sights [from $2,187,000] to $1,500,000 and, now, since we have wrung an audit out of them which shows construction cost at $1,219,000, they will undoubtedly drop their sights further. The accounts are padded and spread around through various items, we suspect, submerging attorney fees and other costs. It stinks!

There will be no settlement until I have gone into the matter exhaustively and the facts are before a court.

I had an appointment with the attorney general, at 3:00 P.M., to discuss my row with Jim Rowe and the difficulties of getting personnel appointed for rapidly flowing Lands Division work. He was busy, brittle, and not too comprehending as to my problem.

"The trouble is that he is too swamped with other work to give much attention to personnel, and we have been unable to get money to relieve him," he stated.

"He can at least answer the telephone," I said. "I have at least three calls pending up there which were never returned. We cannot do business that way in the Department."

"I know that," the attorney general replied. "Several people have complained about that telephone business, and I am going to have a talk with Jim about it." . . .

Tuesday, 28 April 1942

Further exploration into the Savannah Shipyard matter: No experienced personnel were employed, . . . except one man. . . . Frank Cohen was in the books for $40,000 a year and Charlie West, a lobbyist from Ohio, was in for $7,500 a year. Tommy Corcoran's fee does not directly appear, but was undoubtedly derived through [the company's law firm] here in Washington, D.C. His wife, the famous "Peggy Dowd," . . . has a brother who is an officer of the Empire Ordnance Company. . . .

Wednesday, 29 April 1942
4101 Lorcom Lane

[I found a] sharp memorandum from Jim Rowe . . . on my desk as I came in this morning, dated yesterday, protesting my conferring with the attorney general without him present, in regard to the matter of our dispute, saying that he was under the impression that he had absolute control of personnel matters, and that apparently I did not agree. It is the height of inexperience to expose one's egotism in written form. It is bad enough to let it creep out, anyway, as we all must to some extent. The rule of business, in these times of strain, should be the calm rule of golf—"Keep your eye on the ball." The ball is the public interest. The question is how to advance it. Personal prerogatives be damned.

Thursday, 30 April 1942
4101 Lorcom Lane

[I] spent the entire morning before the Senate Appropriations Committee, where Senator [Patrick A.] McCarran of Nevada presides, and Senator [Kenneth D.] McKellar of Tennessee waves the flag and denounces travel expenses, which he is particularly examining in . . . all departments at this time. McKellar, as an inveterate enemy of the administration, represents the most difficult type of mentality which democracy has to absorb. . . .

Had the session become an ugly one as far as Lands Division travel expense was concerned, which some of the hearings definitely have been for other departments, with McKellar ranting and raging about Department representatives traveling about the country, I would have blasted him to bits. Not long ago, McKellar came down to the Department and spent two hours with Mr. Williams and Mr. [Ralph J.] Luttrell, general assistant and chief of the Condemnation Section, respectively, endeavoring to persuade them to settle a case with a property owner in Tennessee on a tract of land for which the owner was claiming $80,000. Court commissioners had awarded $70,000, another illustration of how convenient it is to have local court commissioners appointed by the court. The Senator had described the birds, the bees, and the wild life, and the fauna in this extension of the Great Smoky Mountains National Park: The irreplaceable loss to the property owners, etc. Mr. Williams felt like weeping on the senator's shoulder.

My men held their position firmly—and that's hard to do against the mighty weight of a U.S. senator—in fact, two senators, for the junior senator, Tom Stewart, also accompanied McKellar, although [he] left, we suspect, in embarrassment before the session was over. We did not settle and, when I was consulted over long-distance telephone about the incident, I said "by no means" will the case be settled. "Try it."

So, when the trial date rolled around, I sent John Courtney out there to try the case and a Tennessee jury brought in a verdict of $36,000. That was a net saving of $44,000 over what the senator wished us to pay to the property owner, and it was still a generous price. We thereby saved the government almost half of our entire travel expenses for a year. [The] travel expenses of John Courtney to Tennessee and back was $153!

I have a precisely similar situation in respect to Senator Tydings of Maryland, another arch foe and thoroughly unscrupulous barroom fighter in the political arena. He had endeavored to persuade an Army negotiator to settle with [a] property owner for $125,000. [He] had the Army negotiator and property owner meet at his, Senator Tydings', own house, thus throwing the full weight of his senatorial prestige and position behind the property owner. The case was put into condemnation and the ball passed to us for handling. We refused settlement at anything like that figure and, even after a partial commitment to the property owner at $85,000, we concluded the case for $82,500.

Such is life in the tide-rip of politics.

In the afternoon, a joint session was arranged between the attorney general, Jim Rowe, and me, and we had a full, free, and frank discussion of the personnel problems, which have distressed the relationships between Rowe and me in recent days. The net result equalled an admission that Rowe was insufficiently staffed, to which I replied that the work should not suffer thereby, and that . . . he should allow us to handle more of his work until he got a greater staff, . . . He will assign Lands Division appointments to Ed Hickey, a third man in his office, hereafter, and, perhaps, we can get the flow going more comfortably. . . .

Monday, 11 May 1942
4101 Lorcom Lane

Two very compact weekends [are] behind me. During the week of April 30th, our condemnation case against Savannah Shipyards, Inc., . . . became headline news requiring my full attention.[1] The company was one of seventeen subsidiaries under Frank Cohen, promoter and organizer of the now-infamous Empire Ordnance Company, brought to the front of public interest by the Truman Committee's investigation and exposure of the operations and manipulations of Frank Cohen. Tommy Corcoran was revealed to have represented the Empire Ordnance Company and helped to secure the contract for the Savannah Shipyards, Inc. So [revealed], also, was Charles West, former undersecretary of the Interior from Ohio, who subsequently sued Frank Cohen for 1 per cent interest on contracts with the British Supply Commission,[2] which were alleged to have been procured with his assistance.[3]

Apparently, the influence of Tommy Corcoran had, at last, reached into a case involving the Lands Division, and I took hold of the matter to see that whatever influence might exist was headed off immediately. A preliminary audit of the books of Savannah Shipyards, Inc., permitted in the hope of effecting a settlement, as to the value of property taken, revealed a more or less fly-by-night operation, and invited search for the real books other than those quite obviously made up especially for our examination. The court refused to give us ample time to prepare and was hurrying the case to trial, undoubtedly under local pressures of those who needed the money which would be forthcoming from the judgment in the condemnation proceeding.

The defendants claimed $2,187,000. The investigations revealed shock-

---

1. See *Congressional Record*, vol. 91 (22 January 1945), pp. 424–26.

2. The British Purchasing (Supply) Commission consisted of Morris Wilson, chairman; A. J. T. Taylor, assistant chairman; and E. S. Herbert, the director-general of Postal Telegraph censorship. They arrived in the United States several days after the passage of the Neutrality Act of 1939, to expedite the purchase of war material for Great Britain. They also helped promote American defense by advancing capital for plant construction and equipment.

3. Thomas L. Stokes, "Tommy Linked to West as Ship Firm Lobbyist," *Washington Daily News*, 26 November 1941.

ingly faulty construction before the Maritime Commission was compelled to take over the entire operation on January 3rd, cancelling a contract with Frank Cohen and associates, after only 30 days in full force and effect.

. . . My oral argument before the court in Savannah, on Monday, May 5th, after two days of hasty review of the voluminous facts and figures involved, . . . exploded in the press around Savannah and brought down a house of cards, accomplishing my main objective of committing us, irretrievably and beyond any conceivable influence which could be brought to bear, to a hard-fought lawsuit. The judge granted our request for added time and gave us until July 6th. . . .

Two days at home—Thursday and Friday—with a great deal of rest to subdue the red light, which glowed rather vigorously after the Savannah fracas, left me feeling very well and ready for the United States attorneys' conference in New York. I went up on Friday afternoon and spoke Saturday morning, just before the attorney general came in. It was a successful meeting, but I learned with interest how seriously Jim Rowe had been attacked by the United States attorneys—for the same thing on which I had gone to the mat with him. They could not reach him on the phone and they could not see him when they were in Washington. He was a "nice fellow" and all that, but at least they could always reach and talk with his predecessor, Matt McGuire. Poor old Jim has to learn that you cannot be a big man by signing releases and sending them to the field.

Attorney General Biddle, in his speech on Saturday morning, took quite a little time to say what a fine fellow Jim Rowe was, how he had been sworn in the day after Pearl Harbor (he did not mention that Jim had been taking three weeks vacation which, of course, he needed, but it was a vacation at a most crucial time) and how he labored under great difficulties without an appropriation. I got the same impression that I had in the last conference with Biddle and Jim Rowe—that Jim lacked executive ability, tact, and understanding for his present office, and that he was helping to drag the attorney general down. He is one of the attorney general's very own selections and, therefore, the attorney general stands by him and wastes a lot of his time and energy trying to make him stand up. . . .

Wednesday, 13 May 1942
4101 Lorcom Lane

. . . The Savannah Shipyards, Inc., case and plot is beginning to unravel thickly. The SEC [Securities and Exchange Commission],[1] which first

1. The Securities and Exchange Commission (SEC) was established by the Securities Exchange Act of 1934 (Public Law 291) approved 6 June 1934, primarily to administer the

offered to open up its available information, seems reticent. Why? What influences have been set to work there? A conference was held with the special counsel of the Maritime Commission, in respect to using the powers of the Commission under the Second War Powers Act of March 28, 1942, to effect a complete investigation. They promised complete support—to the hilt. If we can get those powers and have myself and three counsel, whom I have assigned to the case, appointed as special attorneys, without compensation, in the Maritime Commission, we can conduct the investigation ourselves.

That my fears of special influences are wholly justified is shown by Jim Rowe's telephone call, this evening, asking if there is any reason why the case cannot be settled if the defendants will accept the government's figures. "Why?" I asked, "And who wants to know?"

"Dempsey and Koplovitz[2] have called the attorney general and he asked me to inquire," Jim replied. That is the firm which paid Tommy Corcoran a fee for serving the Savannah Shipyards, Inc., according to [William J.] Dempsey's statement to me, although according to Cohen's testimony before the Truman Committee, Tommy was directly retained by Cohen.

"We can't settle that case as a matter of principle," I said. "Besides, there are no government figures now. We are re-examining the whole matter, including the effect upon the appraisal of grossly defective construction work, and collateral accounting matters which reach into the subsidiary company."

"I wish you would call the attorney general," Jim said, "and tell him so. I don't want to have anything to do with the case."

"I think that is wise, Jim," I said, "and I cannot let the attorney general have anything to do with it either, for his own sake. I shall so advise him."

Aside from the run-of-the-mill work, which is always running and always milling, I went to lunch with Justice Murphy at the Mayflower Hotel. We have always been very frank with each other. . . . [He] is rather difficult to talk with, although excellent to listen to. He discussed the Department quite frankly, and so did I. He mentioned Biddle's extraordinary incapacity for the responsibility he is carrying, and told me quite frankly that the President was most conscious of it.

In reviewing the potentialities of the Department, he pointed out Thurman's recent successes, but also [mentioned] his definitely fascist inclinations of mind and the fact that he would be a dangerous man as attorney general: . . . [He] could not be and would not be attorney

---

Securities Act of 1933. Its function was later expanded to enforce the Public Utility Holding Company Act of 1935 and several other measures. The SEC supervised the registration of securities issues, suppressed fraudulent practices in the sale of securities, and supervised and regulated the practices of stock exchanges and public utility companies.

2. The New York law firm of William J. Dempsey and William C. Koplovitz.

general in this administration. "You could have been put over," he said, in the most candid recognition of such a possibility which he has ever made, although it seemed to me that it is never quite possible for a senior to fully recognize a junior as entirely worthy of the great position which the senior once occupied. He frankly indicated that there were no other possibilities in the Department other than myself, and in the event of a successor to Biddle, an outsider should not be appointed with so short a term left in the administration, . . .

He spoke again of the Tommy Corcoran-Biddle-Frankfurter group how they had endeavored to get him after he refused, point blank, to take orders from Tommy, after he was made attorney general—and, later, how Frankfurter had told columnists of Murphy's ineptitude for work on the bench. . . . [and] tried to undermine him in every way, hoping that he would resign. That was a self-evident fact.

He spoke of Frankfurter's constant meddling in the government, endeavoring to control appointments to such positions as the Federal Communications Commission and others, of his dilettante, nimble intellectualism on the bench, which he said he thought "discerning people now realized," with which I wholly concurred. Discerning people do realize it.

He spoke of Frankfurter frequently pointing out a young man or a couple in the Supreme Court saying, "Aren't those fine faces?" And they were always Jewish faces. "He would never say that of you and Mrs. Littell, although both of you have fine faces quite worthy of notice."

Thursday, 14 May 1942
4101 Lorcom Lane

The call, which I had left for the attorney general yesterday evening, . . . finally came through at 5:00 this evening. The . . . conversation . . . nearly [produced] a *contretemps* between the attorney general and myself. . . . He is obviously conscious of the unique procedure involved in which he candidly admits that Dempsey and Koplovitz (Tommy Corcoran's firm) called him in regard to settlement and not me. I ventured to state that this was most unusual: That suggestions for settlement proceeded from the bottom up . . . and not from the . . . [top] down. This is for the obvious reason that the attorney general never knows the detailed facts. The usual course is to deflect any inquiry . . . to the assistant attorney general in charge.

The matter was left with instructions to me to report back to him when the appraisals were completed. In the meantime, I sent McPherson to Philadelphia for a meeting with the Securities and Exchange Commission, at 2:30 P.M. today, to secure their approval of giving all available information in that investigation to us in the Department of Justice. I noticed a slight cooling off in the SEC attitude the preceding day, allegedly on the grounds that Section XIII of the Second War Powers Act, under which the SEC, by order of the President, obtained access to the books and records of the Empire Ordnance Company, provides that this information shall be confidential and provides a criminal offense for violating the confidence, unless it is in the public interest to reveal the information. . . .

Perfecting another line of attack, in case the SEC fails us, I am arranging with the Maritime Commission to appoint myself, Mr. McPherson, Mr. [James G.] Ewell, and Mr. [S. King] Funkhouser—the three attorneys working on this case—as special attorneys under the general counsel of the Maritime Commission, and I sent the chairman [Rear Admiral Emory S. Land] a letter, over the signature of the attorney general (which Biddle may or may not have actually seen, since Carusi handled the matter last night and sometimes affixes the signature of the attorney general) asking the Maritime Commission to invoke the discovery powers of the Second War Powers Act, giving access to books and records of companies having national defense contracts, and asking the Commission to find that this is a national defense contract (i.e. between the Maritime Commission and the Savannah Shipyards, Inc.) on which to predicate a full investigation. Then, the four of us will conduct the investigation for the Maritime Commission so that no punches can be pulled.

In the meantime, Funkhouser is in Savannah developing the appraisal date and has already asked whether, in view of [the] low value of certain buildings because of defective construction, he can make further deductions for the repairs. . . . I have instructed him to take any conservative position inasmuch as some of the buildings may well be worth nothing but junk value, and the government might have proceeded more rapidly on virgin soil. It would be quite impossible for the defendant to accept the figures which we will propose as the true value.

There has already been an attempt to head off one or another lines of attack and certain parties have conferred with Harry Hopkins to try to put the quietus on the SEC investigation. Each of the subsidiary companies of the Empire Ordnance Company has advised the SEC, officially, that the information it is securing is "confidential" in order to suggest the possibility of a criminal action against members of the SEC disclosing it. Thus, I thought it advisable to head off these lines of counter-attack at the White House, and I called Wayne Coy, secretary to the President,[1] tonight.

He was deeply interested in the whole situation, said it stank to high

---

1. Wayne Coy was one of six administrative assistants (i.e., secretaries) to President Roosevelt, an office he established by Executive Order No. 8248, 8 September 1939, under powers granted him by the Government Reorganization Act of 1939. See William E. Leuchtenburg, *Franklin D. Roosevelt and the New Deal, 1932–1940* (New York: Harper and Row, 1963), pp. 327–28.

heaven, and remarked that, if I would send him a copy of my statement before the Court in Savannah, summarizing the situation, he would speak to the President tomorrow morning at 10:00 and endeavor to secure wide instructions to the SEC to give me all available information. I hope I have beat the enemy to the draw there.

And so it is that I find myself between the old guard and the new guard, between the Tommy Corcoran school and the present adviser to the President. This week's *Time* (May 18th)[2] happens to have a comment on these two schools, all very flattering to the new school of advisers under Harold Smith, the able and forthright director of the Budget, and Wayne Coy. The tag end of the old school is in the Department of Justice and Biddle, faithful to the last, ventures to take up at the behest of Tommy Corcoran's firm the settlement of this controversial case.

[Later today, I had a conversation with Justice Murphy at lunch at the Mayflower Hotel.] I expressed the opinion that Frankfurter's meddling had done the Jewish cause irreparable harm in this country, saying that Hitler had, at least, made a martyr of the Jews, but that there was not compensating feature in what Frankfurter did.

"The three constant and enduring liberals on the Court," Murphy said, "are [William O.] Douglas, [Hugo L.] Black, and myself. Some day, when you go back to your country, or the district, or on the circuit court, as I hope you will, and you look back on these days and the period which will follow, you will find these three standing out on the Court."

The old feud with former Attorney General Jackson still apparently continues, for he expressed the opinion that any number of law school professors could have been found who would have as much ability as Jackson.

In regard to Frankfurter, he said distinctly that Frankfurter wasn't for me. "Perhaps," I said, "because Frankfurter realizes, as Tommy Corcoran learned, that I would not take orders." If I were ever the attorney general, which is extremely unlikely, I would tell him where to head-in, damn quickly, and, no doubt, he instinctively knows that.

"Tommy attacked you violently," Murphy said, "and told me to ask Ben Cohen if I didn't believe he was right. I did ask Ben Cohen, but Ben never sustained him on it. You had some falling out with Tommy at an early date, I believe."

"It was on the Western States Conference,[3] in particular, and on failing

2. "The Administration: Smith & Coy," *Time*, 18 May 1942, pp. 12–13.

3. A conference of political progressives from the Western states in February 1940 organized by Norman Littell and Norman E. Dimock, the second assistant secretary of labor, to promote FDR's reelection. John L. Lewis attacked it as a violation of the Hatch Act, but Attorney General Murphy held it legal and FDR denied knowledge of it. See *Washington Post*, 31 October 1939; *Washington Daily News*, 31 October 1939; *Washington Times-Herald*, 1 November 1939, in Littell scrapbooks.

to take orders from Tommy Corcoran, in general. I was one of the first to label him 'slippery,' and, in those days, when Tommy was in the ascendancy, I was very unpopular for labeling him that way. I principally meant that he lacked the moral quality or integrity which is such an essential ingredient for those in power in the government," [I replied].

"You may claim a priority there, but only a priority. There are plenty who regard Tommy in the same way," [Murphy declared]. . . .

As we walked back to his hotel, I asked if he had seen much of the President and he said, "Yes, frequently—more than anyone thought." [We were then] interrupted by the incredible Mrs. Chip Robert,[4] in a pair of riding breeches, getting into a jeep, after first asking Murphy to go horseback riding with her, as he explained, for the twentieth time in the last three years.

"The Willys[5] people gave it to me," she said, when Murphy asked how she got hold of an Army jeep, and dashed off with the wave of her hand.

"Sheer exhibitionism," Murphy said. Not long ago, she rode an elephant in a parade in the streets of Washington. She is one of the most cold-blooded, calculating, studied, exhibitionists on the Washington scene.

We returned to the subject of the President. "How is he standing it? Is there any weakening of grasp?" I asked.

"He has excellent grasp," Murphy replied, "and there is nothing to any gossip to the effect that he is aging. The trouble is with the crew he is surrounded with—advisers like Frankfurter and Hopkins. The President used to make a fight over men, but the war absorbs him completely now and, in not making a fight, others get their way."

Murphy is very vehement, even stopping on the street in the middle of the sidewalk to face me to drive home a point, making us both very conspicuous to any passersby. He has a little of the air of one who has retired, taking greatness with him and draining a generation. The natural ego in us all inclines us to think that, when we have passed by, lesser beings only must take hold. "Our generation of liberals is done for," Murphy said. "We are through. In another two years, there won't be any of us left." He seems to look down from the vantage point of safe security on the bench with a vital and dynamic career behind him as a completed and accomplished fact. He is working hard and has not the slightest intention of resigning from the Court for more active work. He has real elements of greatness, most conspicuous of which is his insight, slightly clouded now by the fact that he is looking back and is surveying the scene

---

4. Evelyn Robert was the wife of Lawrence W. "Chip" Robert (1889–1976), secretary and treasurer of the Democratic National Committee, 1936–41.

5. The Willys-Overland Company produced the famous general-purpose army vehicle, the "jeep," during World War II.

from a super-critical viewpoint rather than that of a participant guiding
the flow of policy.

Monday, 18 May 1942
4101 Lorcom Lane

. . . I spent the morning, from 10:00 until noon, with Admiral Ben
Moreell, chief of the Bureau of Yards and Docks,[1] in regard to the
long-deferred proposal to eliminate the Office of the Judge Advocate
General from legal work in land acquisition. He stated, quite frankly,
that, when Undersecretary of the Navy Forrestal asked his view, he had
said (quite unexpectedly to me) that he, Moreell, was opposed to sending
any of the functions of the Navy Department to other departments in time
of war. As a matter of principle, he thought that the Navy should
discharge all of its own business if it could. He said that he had come as
a mediator to see if he could smooth the thing out.

"You mean you have come in search of a negotiated peace!" I asked.

It was a great shock to me to rediscover in such an able man that the
Navy lacks vitality with which to slough off its incompetent personnel and
make basic reforms of procedure. The incompetence of the Judge
Advocate General's Office is one of the glaring deficiencies in the military
branches of the government. Everybody knows it. Every able officer in
the Navy knows it. . . .

I so stated to Admiral Moreell.

"In your construction work, wherever I have gone in the field, I have
met men of great ability representing your office. When you find an
incompetent man, the one who can't do the job, you get rid of him, don't
you?"

Moreell assented.

"And yet you wish me to put up with, and carry on with, great
incompetence, which you yourself would not tolerate in your organization
for one moment."

"I am afraid there is something in that," he said, "and I am frank to admit
that I am somewhat selfish about it. We get the land and my construction
work goes forward and that's what I am basically interested in."

"The trouble is that I have spoiled you. We have taken up the mistakes
of the Judge Advocate General's Office, cured them, corrected them,
toiled and sweated with them—all unnecessarily—so that there could be

---

1. The Navy Department's Bureau of Yards and Docks was the Navy's "Public Works
Agency." It was responsible for the design, construction, maintenance, and inspection of all
Navy and Marine Corps public works and public utilities. It also had custody of all Navy real
estate which was not in active use.

no delay in your construction projects in order to help you fight the war. But, one of these days, I am not going to do that. I am going to send the proposed land acquisitions back for correction. And I will send them back so many times that the judge advocate general will learn to do things correctly," I said.

Moreell's proposal, in substance, was that I supply a top-ranking man to work in the Judge Advocate General's Office and take complete charge of land acquisition work. I told him the story of the Army reorganization in February of 1941, and of how I had laid down the condition that the man supplied must have complete authority to hire and fire, pick his own personnel, determine policies of administration, and have backing for these conditions all the way through to the Secretary of War's Office. Moreell agreed that similar conditions could be had and that I would be justified in demanding them; and, in the end, after more thorough discussion than indicated here, he went back to make that proposition to Woodson. He telephoned me in the afternoon to say that Woodson seemed most amenable to [the] suggestion and was going to come and see me immediately.

So the grief comes home to me after all. The Navy lacks sufficient virility to clean its own house, and they are sending the poor old dodo over to me in hopes that I will stand him on his feet with able assistants. I will be damned if I will do so. . . .

Tuesday, 19 May 1942
4101 Lorcom Lane

. . . [Paul] Page, of the Maritime Commission, notified McPherson that the Commission had passed two resolutions: one holding the contracts with the Savannah Shipyards to be defense contracts . . . and the second one appointing myself, McPherson, Ewell, and Funkhouser as employees of the Commission, without compensation, so that we could conduct the investigation in the name of the Maritime Commission in gathering evidence. . . .

However, this evening, at 6:00, McPherson phoned to say that [Joseph R.] Greenwood, of the SEC, had called him and stated that they were to give us no further information by direct orders from the White House. That phrase "the White House" covers a very broad territory, and I find that the order has come from Harry Hopkins. McPherson had learned, in interrogating SEC representatives in New York, that Harry Hopkins had given a conference on or about May 8th (four days after the statement I made in open court at Savannah on May 4th) to Frank Cohen. Mr. [Frank M.] McHale (former campaign manager of Paul McNutt, and big shot

politician and sky-high investor from Indiana) and probably Patrick
(attorney from Indiana) and, possibly, Orgel from Cleveland [also at-
tended]. The sum and substance of that conference was to get Hopkins to
put the quietus on the SEC investigation. However, the quietus was put
upon our investigation for, today, by order of Hopkins, Greenwood of the
SEC was ordered to give us no further information.

I have been unable to reach Wayne Coy at the White House to determine the result of his conference with the President on the same subject.
In any event, we have the powers of the Maritime Commission, which can
now be pulled out of the hip pocket and used. McPherson could not refrain
from telling Greenwood that he didn't give a damn about the withdrawal
of SEC because we had the powers of the Maritime Commission for
investigation. That was a tactical mistake because Greenwood may spill the
beans and try to get the quietus put on that, also. However, I can't blame
him much. We all shoot from the hip on occasions.

The reason assigned by Hopkins was "international complications" were
involved. That is sheer nonsense. Even if it did take bribery for Cohen to
get a contract from the British Purchasing Commission, when he started
the Empire Ordnance Company and secured a twenty million dollar
contract, that need not be brought into our case. I can eliminate the alleged
"international complications" and save the face of the British Purchasing
Commission and still not have all the other information discovered by the
SEC withheld from us. The real object was not to let us get hold of the
information in the hands of the SEC. Cohen and his crowd are busy pulling
every string they can pull. It is a very nice game of chess.

I had a long, painful, interview with the judge advocate general of the
Navy, this afternoon. He proposed that I lend him a man, to help him put
the land acquisition business in order, under command of a captain
whom, he assured me, was a very able man. I said, right off, that I would
not, under any circumstances, furnish a man to him for that purpose, and
that the only circumstances under which I would recommend that a man
join his staff were that he be given complete authority to handle the land
acquisition work, including the power to remove any of the persons now
working on land acquisition, and the power to form a completely new
staff. . . . "He wouldn't mind serving under me, would he?" he asked.
"Under a rear admiral?"

Now what can one answer to a question like that? Could I tell him that
no self-respecting lawyer of ability would belong to his staff if he could
possibly avoid it? Could I tell him that of all legal staffs [in] Washington,
his stank to high heaven?

"I have lost a lot of sleep over this thing," he said. "I have just been
advised, today, that I am to be appointed for another four years, and I
want to start with a clean slate on the problem."

Another four years! Is it possible that, with all we know about the judge advocate general—all that Secretary Knox knows about him and Undersecretary Forrestal (because I have discussed it with Forrestal and I know how Forrestal feels)—is it possible, under all these circumstances that this old dodo will be appointed for four years more to head one of the biggest businesses in the United States Navy, giving legal advice in the multiple business and maritime adventures in the time of war? Sometimes democracy is feeble indeed.

I bowed him out as pleasantly as I could. He is one of those old fools who thinks that difficulties can be overcome by pleasant words and resolving to be nice to each other, while we groan under the burden of his incompetence. I am going to tell Moreell, frankly, that I resent having the burden placed upon me. The Navy should be able to wash its own dirty linen. . . .

Thursday, 21 May 1942
4101 Lorcom Lane

Two very hectic days lie behind me, like a great heap of mixed-up construction materials which have not yet taken form. [It was a] tug of war between personalities in the Navy Department and myself over reorganization of the [Navy] Lands Division.

Admiral Moreell telephoned in the morning to say that he had a long talk with Admiral Woodson, . . . and that he was sure "something could be worked out."

I gave it to him very straight, indeed, over the apparent incapacity of the Navy Department to see the problems and attack them, vigorously, by eliminating *in toto* the incompetence of the Judge Advocate General's Office in handling land acquisitions. . . .

These were the same conditions which were accepted by Undersecretary of War Patterson and General [Brehon B.] Somervell, formerly in charge of the Construction Division[1] and, now, in command of the reorganized Supply Division[2] of the Army, on February 7, 1941, after I

---

1. The Construction Division of the Army was a division of the Office of Quartermaster General of the Army. It was responsible for construction and maintenance of all Army buildings, structures, and utilities, other than permanent fortifications. In 1941, the War Department was reorganized and the Construction Division was renamed the Services of Supply Division.

2. The Army's Supply Division (Services of Supply) was a division of the new General Staff of the Army. The Services of Supply supplied arms and services to the armed forces. It established policies, negotiated contracts, provided transport and traffic control. It was

had laid down the conditions the preceding noon. . . . The Army did its job in 24 hours. The Navy has studied the situation since December 1941, when I returned from the West and precipitated the matter.

Today, a memorandum from Attorney General Biddle said that he had been in touch with Forrestal and that Forrestal "was willing to do whatever I wanted." Biddle enclosed a chit, written by Ben Moreell to Forrestal, saying that negotiations were in progress; Woodson was going to see Littell; and the matter could be worked out. . . .

When Admiral Woodson came, at 3:00—the girls saw him wandering in the hall, looking at pictures, waiting for the exact hour, . . . I sent them down to tell him to come in—I was ready. He laid before me a memorandum, from himself to Forrestal, with a place for Forrestal's approval on the back page, over which, to my astonishment, appeared Forrestal's signature. This memorandum purported to confirm conditions of reorganization of the land acquisition section in the Judge Advocate General's Office, the gist of it being that Assistant Attorney General Littell would propose three names of men in the Lands Division of Justice and the Navy Department would select one of them to head the land acquisition section. That man, "under the direction and supervision" of the judge advocate general, would be the chief of the real estate section and, with the supervision of the judge advocate general, and his necessary concurrence, would recommend the removal of existing personnel and the addition of other personnel, as well as the transfer of persons already drawn in to the business by way of reserve commissions. With the concurrence of the undersecretary of the Navy, the judge advocate general would have the power to change arrangements at any time and issue specific instructions and regulations. My plan was there all right, completely submerged in the vanity and authority of the judge advocate general.

Again, I declined to take vigorous issue and, in answer to his question as to what I thought of it "in principle." I merely said that the memorandum raised serious doubts as to whether the authority to propose a chief of the real estate section[3] was sufficient to accomplish the intended purpose, that I would discuss the matter with the attorney general and advise him later.

"Your objection, then, is to me?" the old boy stated bluntly.

"It's not exactly a matter of personal equation, Admiral," I said. "It's a matter of having sufficient authority to do the job and, no man whom I would recommend to you, would accept such a post unless he had

responsible for Army construction; it secured funds from Congress; and it administered all Army-wide functions pertaining to personnel, both military and civilian.

3. The Land Acquisition Section was more commonly known as the Real Estate Section.

sufficient authority. It's a hot spot. It's a dirty job. He cannot afford to have essential policies vitiated by anyone, and he should have complete line of authority from the undersecretary of the Navy."

"We don't work that way in the Navy," replied the "JAG." "The line of authority comes down to me in command." . . .

The afternoon papers announced the judge advocate general's reappointment for an additional four years. Good God! He is a likable, cooperative, old codger and, perhaps, those qualities fool those people who are responsible. Then, also, Ed Toland, attorney for the Naval Affairs Committee, whispered to me over the telephone, today, that Woodson had been in command of the *Houston*, when the President cruised on it, and that there was a personal friendship there. I did not tell Ed what Secretary Ickes told me in a conversation a few weeks ago—that Woodson used to play poker at the White House until he won too consistently and too amazingly!

So ends a long trail, for the moment, at a dead end.

Lauchlin Currie, secretary to the President, called in regard to the use of SEC information in the Savannah Shipyards case. [Our attorneys'] access to information . . . had been cut off—supposedly by orders from the White House. . . . So clearly did this seem to emanate from the conference with Harry Hopkins, that (as Currie talked to me) I was little surprised at the duplication of effort over there, and rather assumed that Currie could not have known that steps had already been taken to stop [the] SEC from giving us vital information on the Savannah Shipyards discovered in the course of its investigation. I, therefore, gave it to him fairly straight, pointing out that "international complications" might be only a smoke screen for shielding the Frank Cohen crowd and indicating how easily the international situation could be left out, by our merely dropping the issue as to the British Purchasing Commission, and [by] confining ourselves to the financial ramifications affecting the Savannah Shipyards and the valuation of its real and personal properties.

When he pointed out that Harry Hopkins might not have time to take the matter up again, I replied that he had had plenty of time to take it up with our enemies and that he should find time to take it up with friends to get the matter straight, with which Currie agreed, because the position was unanswerable.

Currie called back, later in the day, to say that the whole matter had, apparently, been a misunderstanding from instructions which he, himself, had given to the SEC lest something get out which would be used widely by Nazi propagandists against the British, and that Harry Hopkins had had nothing whatever to do with the matter and had issued no instructions. I was immediately relieved. [Ganson] Purcell, chairman of the SEC, also called to advise of the revised instructions from Currie to the effect that we should have everything discovered affecting the Savannah Shipyards,

Inc., except the information regarding the British Purchasing Commission. That's all we want, and I am sending the attorneys back to New York to resume operations there, examining the SEC data. . . .

Sunday, 24 May 1942
4101 Lorcom Lane

The attorney general's party "to meet Jim Rowe" was held at his home, Friday, May 22. It reached far and wide into official Washington throughout the three branches of the government. . . .

It was quite a gathering. A chart of the tensions and conflicts in that group, during the business part of the day, would have presented a confused and tangled chart, but now they were at peace, under the influence of whiskeys and sodas, and mint juleps, efficiently distributed by colored waiters.

As I came into the room, about 7:00, one of the last to arrive, having left the Department late, a long, lanky figure pulled itself out of the crowd and walked over to the door in one of those impulsive personal reactions which is almost a reflex of the mind. It was Charles Marsh, with whom I had spent two hours with the Vice President many weeks ago. . . .

The rapid flash of his extraordinary mind, commenting on the procession that passed us by in the adjoining hall and the main drawing room, was completely absorbing. I captured a mint julep, on the fly, to fit in with the spirit of the occasion. This serious, rare mind of Marsh's is the source of advice for many diverse minds in Washington, throwing its influence, persistently and cynically, in support of forthright justice and truth. He operates a chain of newspapers, especially, I believe, in Texas. I shall long remember his intimate memorandum on Jesse Jones, of which he gave me a copy when I was talking with him and the Vice President. He has known the Roosevelts, intimately, and was, at one time, called in by the President's mother to handle a delicate situation with Elliott [Roosevelt], who seemed to be wandering from the home hearth, at the time of his first marriage.

After the last national election, as Marsh himself put it, "I have given my attention to the insurance policy," meaning Henry A. Wallace, the next in command.

We made a date for breakfast, at his apartment the next morning, and I drifted back into the big room to do my duty and visit around. The guest of honor, Jim Rowe, to enhance whose popularity the party was given, button-holed me very quickly, much to my astonishment. "I want to get a couple of minutes with you, Norman," he said.

"Any time, any place, Jim," I replied. "Do you mean now?"

"Yes," he said, and pulled me aside into the room which I had so recently left with Marsh. "What are we going to do about the Savannah Shipyards case?" he asked. "The attorney general has instructed me to handle it and I've got to do something about it."

"You had better lay off of it," I said. "It is a hot potato and a good thing for you to let alone—dangerous for you to touch."

"I know it is," he replied, "but I've got to do something. Those fellows are our friends—Dempsey and Koplovitz." (They were well known as the front law firm for Tommy Corcoran.)

"The more reason to let it alone," I said, amazed at his naivete and extraordinary obviousness. "Just tell them I'm handling the case and refer them to me," I said.

"But I can't. The attorney general has told me to handle the matter and look into the settlement. I've got to do something."

"Then you have a short answer for them," I said. "Just tell them the properties are being appraised and there is nothing to confer about. That is the truth. I would not meet with them for that very reason. There is no occasion for a conference of any kind at this stage of the proceedings."

"Will you tell them that if I let them come to a conference in my office?"

I insisted that Jim tell them, himself, but, upon his repeated request that I tell them, I could do no less than agree to do so, although I was astonished at the weakness of the man in wishing me to take him off the spot with the attorney general and with "his friends," Dempsey and Koplovitz, by having me personally tell them that there was no occasion for a conference. We set the time at 3:00, Monday. It was altogether an almost incredible incident. . . .

[Marsh and I] sat together and the entire evening was enlivened by his veteran newsman's analysis of individuals. He was the only one present who was not an official in the United States government.

"The two pure, virginal, men in that crowd before us," he said, "are Vice President Wallace . . . and Ben Cohen."

Later, in making further comments on Ben, he said, "Ben is the female virgin—actually a virgin, you know! Tommy, the Irish boy, was the big strong male who came along and took possession of him." That was in answer to my inquiry as to how he thought the curious combination of Tommy Corcoran and Ben Cohen had ever been made, with such fine moral perception on one side and such total lack of it on the other.

I rode home with Harold Smith and Wayne Coy, director of the Budget and secretary to the President, together with Oscar Cox, assistant solicitor of the Justice Department. They dropped me at home about 10:30 P.M.

Biddle had sat down by us, earlier in the evening, when we were each eating a buffet dinner off of plates held in our laps. He had discussed politics in the state of Georgia, about which he consulted with Marsh with some considerable deference. He moved away as abruptly as he had come, breaking off the conversation in the middle of an incompleted observation from Marsh. . . .

The next morning, at Marsh's for breakfast, was a rare intellectual bath. Marsh's sister-in-law-secretary, Mary Louise [Glass], was also present, taking an occasional telegram or a note as Marsh worked through various subjects with me.

"One of the most stimulating minds I have met in years," I said to her as Marsh was at the telephone.

"As one of our Latin American friends told me the other day," she replied, " 'He is like a great, flopping albatross hovering in the sky and, suddenly, plunging down to take a fish, now and then, and, every once in a while, he drops something as he floats around.' "

I see exactly what Vice President Wallace gets from him.

11:30 A.M., Tuesday, 26 May 1942
Attorney General's Staff Meeting

Thurman Arnold mentioned that the War Production Board had a series of scandals brewing, which could break out at any time [because] small businesses [have been] deprived of necessary materials or, as I understand the matter, adversely affected by arrangements which would normally violate the anti-trust laws. A pending bill was discussed, which provides the WPB will certify, "with the consultation of the attorney general," that the arrangements were not prejudiced by the anti-trust laws, or that the anti-trust laws should be suspended. (I have not read the bill.)[1]

Thurman pointed out that small plants were closing, such as a . . . plant at Pueblo, and Lew Evans plant at Cleveland, which were literally freezing up for lack of equipment. There were other instances at Louisville, St. Louis, and elsewhere. Thurman said that it was unimportant what language was used, just as long as he had a chance to comment on the proposed order before it went into effect, and he gave the example of an order pertaining to sulphuric acid in which he had called to the attention of Robert Patterson, the undersecretary of War, the consequences of the proposed order. Patterson, he said, had written a "nasty letter," withdrawing his previous letter, but the net result was that no order was issued.

The pendency of other legislation was discussed by Oscar Cox, the

---

1. The bill to exempt from the antitrust laws those firms complying with the directions of the WPB was received by the House and referred to the Judiciary Committee, but was not acted upon.

Prize Bill,[2] Patents,[3] and the Lands Division "Dive Bombing" Bill being particularly mentioned. [The] latter bill was not brought up until I reminded the attorney general of the imperative need for this measure, throughout the country, where resources for the preparation of title evidence are at many places exhausted, with the result that we cannot get money to the property owners. This, I said, resulted in great hardship to property owners who were deprived of their property and were paid nothing for it, [until long, long after the property was taken, or not at all!] The gravity of the situation, I observed, would not be apparent to anyone not close to the land acquisition picture, but that actually we were on the verge of a new era in the increasing use of the Second War Powers Act, approved March 28, 1942. Pursuant to that Act, properties were being seized everywhere, without ample preparation of the preliminary steps, most important of which is the preparation of title evidence. Oscar Cox said he had been "dive bombing" the Budget to get that bill out and over to Congress, and the attorney general urged that the matter be pressed because of the hardships and bad feelings created throughout the country.

Mr. Quinn pointed out that the Appropriation Bill[4] had been approved in the Senate and gone to a conference committee, with a cut of ten per cent in travel expenses and twenty per cent in printing funds, together with a limitation that no one could be appointed in the Anti-trust Division over $5,000 without approval of the Senate. It was hoped that this provision could be eliminated. It is clearly wrong in principle. Anyway, the President would not send names over under those conditions because he believes it to be an invasion of the prerogatives of the Executive, in which respect he is 100 per cent right. I mentioned the Lands Division could not stand a ten per cent cut in the allocation of its travel funds and, furthermore, [that it] should be more, not less. Our condition [is] an emergent one as the men have to travel to and from these projects and over them. [The] increase in our travel expense was in direct ratio to the increase in our work and, therefore, perfectly in order. I said I thought it ought to be handled separately, as are the FBI travel accounts.

I said, also, that the present arrangements, whereby members of the

2. The Prize Bill of 1942 (H.R. 7211) to facilitate disposition of prizes captured during the war, passed the House 1 July 1942 and the Senate 10 August 1942. President Roosevelt approved it (Public Law 704) 18 August 1942.

3. The Patents Bill of 1942 (S. 2794) provided for the adjustment of royalties for the use of inventions required for the war effort. The Senate passed the bill 15 October 1942; the House agreed to it 22 October 1942; and President Roosevelt approved it (Public Law 768) 31 October 1942.

4. The Justice Department Appropriations Bill (H.R. 6599) was passed by the House 18 February 1942; the Senate agreed to it 21 May 1942; later a conference committee settled differences between the two versions of the bill and President Roosevelt approved it (Public Law 644) 2 July 1942.

staff, in order to save rubber, are ordered to combine arrangements for traveling to the office and having nobody riding to work in an empty car, but stopping along the street to pick up passengers, are to be followed. However, particularly as to executives, hours are irregular, and it is impossible to make a neighborhood arrangement, or with other members of the staff. This matter is being studied by Palmer, and a report will be forthcoming, . . .

The attorney general confirmed his informal observation, when I was at his house for dinner for Jim Rowe [on] Friday, May 22, in regard to Lands Division reorganization [of the land acquisition] section of the Navy Department, suggesting that I prepare an executive order, with the memorandum attached, and he would take it up with Forrestal, directly, and then send it to the White House. . . .

Tuesday, 26 May 1942
4101 Lorcom Lane

The Savannah Shipyards case is indeed getting sizzling hot. Yesterday, Paul Page, attorney for the Maritime Commission, advised that some of the Savannah Shipyards people—namely Griffiths, the attorney from New York; and [Wilbur M.] Wilson, a former Shipping Board[1] employee during the last war, employed as an executive by the Savannah company—had called upon Mr. Wade, of the Maritime Commission, obviously to feel out the attitude of the Maritime Commission on settlement of this case. They indicated that settlement negotiations were going on with the Department of Justice, directly through the attorney general and the solicitor general, although in mentioning the latter, they undoubtedly meant James Rowe, the assistant to the attorney general, and that settlement was being considered at $1,300,000.

I stated, flatly, that no settlement negotiations were being considered and, certainly, no figure was being considered, since our appraisal work was not even completed, but [I] admitted that proposed negotiations had been opened directly through the attorney general's office and James Rowe. (There may have been figures mentioned to the attorney general, because $1,300,000 is just above the amount of our preliminary audit, after discounting certain factors, but I took it upon myself to negate the assertion, flatly, because I know that no definite figure is under consideration—it could not be without my knowledge.)

1. The U.S. Shipping Board was a five-member board created by the U.S. Shipping Act of 1916, approved 7 September 1916. Its purpose was to promote the development of a naval reserve and a merchant marine by providing subsidies.

James Rowe called, in respect to the proposed appointment in the afternoon at 3:00 at which I had agreed to tell Dempsey and Koplovitz, for him, that no settlement negotiations could be had and that the properties were under appraisal at the present time.

The matter had, apparently, grown more sizzling hot for Jim, too, because he suggested deferring the conference, stating that he felt it necessary "for the attorney general to be present if such a conference was held." I readily assented, reiterating what I had previously said; that there was no need for a conference; and protesting again as to bothering the attorney general, himself, about such matters with a wartime pressure of work upon the Department.

"It's a damn shame," I said, "when all that is needed is a telephone conversation to tell those fellows that there is nothing to discuss at this time." . . .

I confess the day was a depressing one. Even at home, I cannot get away from the oppressive feeling which results from insecurity on so fundamental a matter of principle within the Department. It makes me ill for the Department. The Lands Division has been as clean as a hound's tooth, although we have handled millions and millions of dollars. I intend that it shall remain so, and will take vigorous issue on this case, if I have to do so. . . .

Wednesday, 3 June 1942
4101 Lorcom Lane

There is a change of mental scenery, but no real rest, in a trip out of town on business. As Mrs. Pinchot said, the main idea is to "change your walls," but I think you have to add recreation while you are doing it.

I went up to New York last Thursday morning with Special Assistant McPherson and had a fairly warm session with representatives of the SEC, in regard to supplying us with information on the Savannah Shipyards. There was a very real reluctance to do so and, where the cold breath comes from which chilled their cooperation with us, I don't know. In any event, after a very candid exchange of views, in which I repeated the arrangements made "through the White House" and the orders which I knew they had received from Purcell, chairman of the SEC, the atmosphere cleared. It was agreed that, on Sunday, we would see all of the raw material collected by their investigators of the Empire Ordnance—all pertaining to the Savannah Shipyards, other than information implicating the British Purchasing Commission, which I had agreed with Lauchlin Currie, secretary to the President, should be omitted from our case for fear of international complications. . . .

Tuesday, the griddle seemed to be hot again. A notice waited me, to be with the attorney general at his office tomorrow at 3:00, with Jim Rowe and [William J.] Dempsey and [William C.] Koplovitz, regarding the Savannah Shipyards settlement. It is an extraordinary summons, considering that I have not been asked to confer with the attorney general, alone, to tell him what I know of this case.

Gilfond, public relations representative of the attorney general, called me and was greatly concerned about it, advising me, simply, to "be sure and hold my own."

I thought I had better talk things over with the Vice President and, upon ringing up for an appointment, secured one this afternoon at 3:15. . . .

"My friend Marsh told me he had had a visit with you and that they were trying to put the heat on you in regard to the Savannah Shipyards case," the Vice President said.

I expressed my appreciation of that, and my gratitude for the discovery of Marsh, who I said possessed one of the most incisive, critical minds I had encountered in a long time.

"His mind works in quick, penetrating flashes," I said, "and in spite of his cynicism and disillusioned newspaperman attitude, he had the solid basis of forthrightness, liberalism, integrity, and seeming faith in mankind. I imagine his conclusions are about 85 per cent correct, are they not?"

"I would say about 75 per cent," the Vice President replied, "but perhaps 85 per cent is justified. But in any event, he's right a surprising number of times. He formerly regarded Tommy Corcoran quite highly," he added.

"There's a miss—one shot in the 15 per cent!" I replied.

"A clear miss," the Vice President said. "It was one of those places where we disagreed, but he is coming around to my way of thinking now. I believe he understands my viewpoint now."

"I do not see how anybody could miss that one," I said, "because there is such a great lack of basic integrity of character. There is brilliant ability. I have always credited Tommy with doing magnificent work in the early fighting days of the New Deal in getting through the Holding Company Act[1] and a few other necessary reforms, but his recent lobbying days demonstrate exactly what I have always contended: That there is a lack of moral perception in him which is absolutely fundamental to proper government."

"Tell me about the Savannah Shipyards case," the Vice President said,

---

1. The Wheeler-Rayburn Public Utility Holding Company Act of 1935 (Public Law 333), approved 26 August 1935, required the dissolution of all utility holding companies more than twice removed from operating companies and empowered the SEC to supervise and to eliminate all utility holding companies not in the public interest.

and I told him as quickly as possible, ending with the proposed appointment of tomorrow afternoon in the attorney general's office, with counsel for the defendants, and taking in some of the territory in regard to Frank Cohen's Empire Ordnance. The Vice President said the attorney general "hasn't been seasoned enough to handle a situation like that." He pondered the question as to what I should do and what, if anything, he could do.

"There isn't much I can do in view of my past relations with Tommy Corcoran but, if you need collateral pressure on the attorney general to see the light in this situation, I would call on Leo Crowley, who has a very wise head for politics."

"I don't want you to do anything," I replied. "I just wanted to talk it over with you and get your slant. I also wanted to apprise you of the situation, which is liable to break into a major scandal of the present war effort."

The Vice President said that he was very glad to know about the situation, that he had recently urged the President to solve the ever-present Tommy Corcoran problem by sending him out of the country on some kind of a job for the government, where he could be useful and could do no harm, but that this situation changed the picture. If Tommy's influence on the Maritime Commission to get the Savannah Shipyards contract should be revealed—if the supposed influence was proved—it would be quite impossible to give him any kind of a government post, even to get him out of the way.

The conversation drifted to the Bridges decision, which the attorney general had handed down during the weekend. Bridges was found to have been a communist, most of the evidence having been described as inconclusive until the decision teetered on the testimony of two witnesses, the principal one of whom was a sailor—Lundeberg—whose testimony Judge Sears had described as "hard-bitten" and convincing. Lundeberg had been present with members of Bridges' family and Bridges had told Lundeberg he was a communist; and Bridges had failed to call members of his family to testify in refutation of his conversation. The Communist Party was found to have been organized in the United States in 1919, and to have been in favor of the overthrow of the government of the United States by force and violence. Hence, the attorney general found that Bridges should be deported to Australia.[2]

---

2. On 28 May 1942, Attorney General Biddle reversed the decision of the Board of Immigration Appeals and ordered Bridges deported. Bridges, however, appealed the decision and, because the Justice Department did not press the case, remained in the United States. On 18 June 1945 the Supreme Court ruled that the deportation order had been illegal. See Lewis Wood, "High Court Blocks Bridges Expulsion; in 5-to-3 Ruling, Douglas Says Hearing on Communist Membership Was Unfair," *New York Times*, 19 June 1945.

A terrific hue and cry went up in many labor ranks, although a sigh of relief was also breathed in the conservative elements of society, but of course the complicating factor is that Russia is our ally. The deportation order came down almost simultaneously with the President's commuting of Earl Browder's sentence to prison, for entry of the United States under a forged passport, Earl Browder being the secretary of the American Communist Party.[3]

Even some of the arch-conservatives protested the decision. The columnist, [Westbrook] Pegler, says the language goes far enough to justify the deportation of Mrs. Roosevelt.[4] [Ralph McA.] Ingersoll, editor of P.M., attacked the decision with all his might, and privately expressed grave concern over the effects of the decision on the ranks of labor.

"It's a lawyer-like decision." I said, in the sense of the pure judicial work behind Biddle's reasoning. "But it is unrealistic in view of the present situation." My own formula for the case was to recognize Bridges' present strong support of the United States government, the unity of purpose for the time being with Russia, defeating the Axis, and suspend deportation proceedings, indefinitely, with a warning that resumption of any activities hostile to the United States government at any time in the future would immediately result in deportation. With this Sword of Damocles over him, the country would have been reassured and disunity in the ranks of labor would have been avoided, which has been so carefully and effectively secured in the war effort. No embarrassment would have resulted in relations with our present ally—Russia.

We concluded after a half an hour's visit. I neglected to say [that], in respect to the Savannah Shipyards case, the Vice President's principal advice was as follows: "When you go into your conference tomorrow, keep sweet about the matter and, through the whole case, don't get under tension. I don't know anything else for you to do, Norman, but hold your ground as you are holding it."

There was an interesting comment on temperament in that remark—not only on mine—for the advice was very good and showed some insight, but it also reflected what the Vice President had learned from many battles in the past and it seemed to explain his quiet, imperturbable, long-wearing disposition. It seemed so much better than a statement I had made [to the effect] that I had no real concern about my own welfare, but [that] I could take care of myself in a barroom brawl, if that is what we had to have.

---

3. President Roosevelt commuted Earl Browder's sentence 16 May 1942. He had been sentenced to four years in prison for fraudulent use of his passport, 25 March 1941.

4. Pegler cited Biddle's report, and noted that the American Youth Congress, which Eleanor Roosevelt had supported, had been "identified" as a "front" or affiliate of the Communist Party. See Westbrook Pegler, "Biddle's Definition of Communist Aims," Seattle Post-Intelligencer, 4 June 1942.

Brawls are bad and quite wearing. They could probably be avoided in almost all instances by following the Vice President's advice.

Thursday, 4 June 1942
4101 Lorcom Lane

A message from the attorney general's office called off the meeting at 3:00, with Dempsey and Koplovitz and Jim Rowe, saying the meeting was postponed and that I would be notified.

Judge Stainback arrived from Honolulu today. The attorney general had finally cabled for him. Two conversations with Secretary Ickes, within the last two months have, I think, dissolved some of the latter's objections to Stainback as governor, and the secretary is forced to the conclusion which I drew a long time ago—that Stainback is the only strong man of our liberal faith in the Hawaiian Islands. Poindexter is sinking in health and, according to Stainback, had signed a proclamation which was a virtual abdication of all civil power to the military authorities.[1] The Army rules there, and Poindexter even has Army colonels trying police court cases.

General [Delos C.] Emmons is under the domination of Walter Dillingham, one of the big contractors there, an expert entertainer of public officials, and a skillful manipulator of their organizations, whether in Washington, D.C., or in Honolulu. He maintains a representative in Washington and has been highly successful in blocking the taking of his own warehouse facilities, until I saw the game and undid his carefully laid plans by pulling a few strings. He had the government all set up (when General Short was in command in Hawaii) to leave his warehouse alone on the waterfront, take the next adjacent piece and leave a third adjacent piece, thereby preserving for himself the most valuable industrial front, securing severance damages which the taking of the second piece would have assured, and all the while the government was doing hundreds of thousands of dollars worth of dredging in front of his own warehouse to serve the new property! It was a chess game with an old master playing against boy scouts.

"Dillingham and Emmons are exceedingly close," Stainback said. "Dillingham is the only man who walks into Emmons office without any announcement whatever. Even aides do not do that."

"There is virtually no civil government in Hawaii."

I explained that I thought the seeds which had been planted aided by

---

1. For details of Poindexter's proclamation, see "Tokyo Bombers Strike Hard at Our Main Bases on Oahu," *New York Times*, 8 December 1941.

the current of reason, would now produce results, and it seemed quite likely to me that he would be made governor if he managed to hit it off all right with Secretary Ickes.

Friday, 5 June 1942
4101 Lorcom Lane

The [postponed] meeting between Dempsey and Koplovitz, attorneys in Washington for the Savannah Shipyards, Inc., the attorney general, Jim Rowe, and myself was called for 11:00, and we met in the attorney general's office, without a preliminary conference.

"What's this conference about?" the attorney general asked Jim, passing the ball to the right to where Jim sat in the big leather chair.

"I guess Norman here had better explain it," Jim said, turning to me, passing the ball to his right.

"I don't know, Mr. Attorney General," I said. "There is really no occasion for a conference. There is nothing to discuss at this time."

And so the ball was passed to the right, where Dempsey and Koplovitz sat facing the attorney general. The attorney general looked at the two young attorneys and asked what the object of the conference was.

"It is in the nature of an appeal from Mr. Littell's attitude," Dempsey said. "We feel that he has no intention of settling the case and that he has made unreasonable and arbitrary statements of our position after a conference was held with him to discuss the settlement."

I cannot recall the exact words, but the complaint was that I had misrepresented the position which they took at the conference prior to my going to Savannah on May 4th; the usual sort of statements from attorneys in trouble! They had the shipyards appraised, and the only question was what was the fair market value. Their appraiser was an eminent man and very reasonable, and then Dempsey rather naively expressed the confident hope that the government would accept his figures—about $1,980,000, if I remember correctly.

I hastened to put the attorney general right as to their representation at the conference in regard to executive salaries, legal fees, and other expenses incident to the promotion of the enterprise being charged as part of reproduction costs. I said that for Dempsey to expect us for one moment to accept the opinion of his appraisers was presumptuous in the extreme. The government would prepare its own appraisal evidence in its own manner as it saw fit.

"As a matter of fact," I said, "these men are not even counsel of record in the case. They are here to negotiate about a settlement, but they are not even of record."

"What do you mean?" asked the attorney general. "These men are counsel for the company. It is certainly quite customary for counsel for the company to negotiate."

Jim chimed in to say that I had met with them with the president of the company. He apparently knew about that meeting. Surely that was enough identification.

"Do you want a letter from the president saying that they are authorized to negotiate?" asked the attorney general. "It's most unusual, and I am sure I do not understand what you mean."

"I mean, simply, that counsel of record for the company are negotiating with Mr. McPherson about various matters in Savannah at this time, and these gentlemen are negotiating with us, here, although they are not of record," I replied. "I have presumed that they are authorized to negotiate from the fact that they met with the representatives of the company and if that is satisfactory to the attorney general, it is certainly satisfactory to me."

"You are in favor of settlement if a figure can be agreed upon, are you not?" asked the attorney general of me. "I understand that you settle most of your cases in condemnation."

"Yes, we do, Mr. Attorney General," I said, "over 90 per cent of the tracts are settled without contest, but this case is subject to peculiar factors rendering the appraisal most difficult." . . .

"I suppose it will take you about 30 days to complete the appraisal work before we know what figure the government would be willing to accept, is that not so?" he asked of me.

"I am sure we can complete the work in 30 days," I replied, "and the appraisal figures will be submitted to you at that time."

"But that leaves no time for negotiating a settlement," Dempsey broke in, and Koplovitz agreed. "I do not think we can negotiate before the trial set on July 6th."

"There is nothing we can do about that," the attorney general said, "except to join with you in a request for postponing the trial of the case until the fall, which we shall be very happy to do if there is not enough time to negotiate after the appraisal evidence is completed."

"But I do not think we can persuade our client to continue the case— we have waited so long to have it tried. The government has delayed the matter repeatedly."

I wanted to tell him that if such an occasion arose, we would assist him in endeavoring to "persuade his client," but the attorney general carried the ball and made his point. He stated that that was the concern of the defendants and not the government's; that my estimate of 30 days was entirely reasonable; that if that did not suit the convenience of the defendants, then they could ask for a continuance or postponement of the trial; and that as far as he was concerned, that concluded the matter.

That was the gist of the conversation, except that after Dempsey and Koplovitz went out, I explained for a moment the complications in respect to the personal property which we were having difficulty in tracing, commenting also upon the naivete of the two boys who had just left. "They are babes in the woods, in this matter," I said.

Both the attorney general and Jim agreed to this, saying that the two attorneys had bad clients but were a couple of inexperienced, but very decent boys. "[Theirs is] a most naive suggestion that we should accept their appraisal, in view of the facts of this whole case of which they must be well aware by this time," I said.

"The Frank Cohen outfit is a bad bunch, apparently," Jim replied.

The attorney general observed that he would like to settle this case in view of his past relationship with this firm. I felt that implicit in this statement was a reference to Tommy Corcoran. The wish was predicated on a condition that the case could be properly settled. I agreed that any case should be settled if it can be properly settled, but I had distinct mental reservations that probably this one could not, unless the defendants were willing to take a considerable sacrifice below their present figures. . . .

Tuesday, 9 June 1942
4101 Lorcom Lane

I neglected to say last week that Secretary Ickes put the question to Stainback: Would he consider being governor of the Territory of Hawaii?

Since then, the logic of things has asserted itself step-by-step, as I hoped it would as far back as last November, when I wrote to the President suggesting Stainback's availability as the strongest man the federal government has in Hawaii. When Ickes called me to remind me that I was to send him the FBI report on Stainback, I replied that there was none, only a large file with a lot of letters of recommendation, but I wrote him a summary memorandum. [Ickes'] only observation [was] that he had an impression of Stainback in the University of Chicago Law School which reflected on Stainback's ability. I cleared that up over the weekend—another case of dual or mistaken identity. Stainback graduated *cum laude* with Jerome Frank, now on the Circuit Court of the Second Circuit, and Miss [Burnita S.] Matthews on another circuit bench. They were the three lights of the graduating law school class. (It all goes to show how invaluable a good record is, and how irreparably damaging a bad one is—such as mine at Harvard Law School—causes be damned!)

"Good," said Ickes, when I told him this about Stainback graduating *cum laude*. "So did I."

I also cleared up the dates. Ickes had graduated in 1907, and Stainback in 1912, having entered the law school in 1909, after graduating from Princeton in 1907; so they could not have met each other. The record was straight. . . .

As John Courtney said, when I told him of the possibilities, now imminent, of appointing Stainback as governor: "What a great thing it would be to have a fearless and forthright man in the saddle in Hawaii!"

Regarding the long delayed reorganization of the judge advocate general's office of the Navy, Ed Toland, attorney for the Naval Affairs Committee, called me last week to ask that I defer the submission of an executive order to the President, transferring the legal functions from the "JAG's" office to the Department of Justice (which the attorney general and I had finally agreed upon was our only recourse) until he had talked with Undersecretary of the Navy Forrestal and brought us both together at lunch to discuss the matter.

That has been the trouble for six months. Undersecretary Forrestal has operated from the mountain top, contacting this Department through three special assistants to the undersecretary, who have investigated land acquisitions (and have done a very good job, and turned in reports precisely coincident with my recommendations). Forrestal has conducted negotiations with me through two admirals—Ben Moreell and Judge Advocate General Woodson—with occasional side flashes on the subject to the attorney general. I told Ed Toland that this was one difficulty and it was no wonder that Forrestal still did not understand the problem. He agreed, but added: "Forrestal is killing himself over there. It is just a matter of what he can attend to as you would readily appreciate if you understood the overwhelming odds against him. He is absolutely tops and has done a magnificent job, but he is killing himself."

Fate passed judgment the succeeding day. Ed Toland, and not Forrestal, dropped dead from heart failure.

Another close one was Brian Bell, head of the Associated Press, who died yesterday from heart failure. In both cases, I mean "coronary thrombosis." The beginnings of Washington heat begin to reap its toll, an added drain which some cannot stand in view of the enormous burden of work and intensity of operations here.

I felt depressed over Ed Toland's death and did not touch the issue of the judge advocate general's work until today, when I called Forrestal to tell him what Toland had told me the day before he died, and asked if he wanted to hold the lunch anyway. Something about the incident hit him just right because the chips began to fly. . . . He said he would call me back. He did call me back and asked me to see [H. Struve] Hensel, his special assistant, right away.

I asked, bluntly, whether that was not starting over where we were about five months ago, when I had first seen Hensel, but this time he said Hensel and I could write the formula, and then we would meet and he would approve it. When Hensel came, I found that Forrestal had called in Moreell and Hensel and had also telephoned Bob Patterson, undersecretary of war, from the same conference, learning first-hand what we had done for the War Department in arranging for my general assistant to become head of the land acquisition work for the War Department.

The matter was settled, and Hensel came with no strings on him. We wrote the formula in a memorandum, then and there in my office, for the establishment:

1. of a Real Estate Section in the Bureau of Yards and Docks under Admiral Moreell;

2. the transfer of all functions done by the judge advocate general to the Bureau of Yards and Docks;

3. the rendering of all legal service of advice by the Department of Justice (all the preparatory or preliminary work would be done by the Bureau of Yards and Docks Real Estate Section);

4. the appointment of a chief for the Real Estate Section (I suggested no use of my name, but Hensel insisted upon my approval) who would have the approval of the assistant attorney general in charge of the Lands Division, but who would be acceptable to the chief of the Bureau of Yards and Docks; and

5. the chief of the Real Estate Section, with the approval of the head of the Bureau of Yards and Docks, would have complete control of personnel, the absorption or rejection of existing personnel in the Judge Advocate General's office, and the direction of an organization of their work and their assignment to duty, including the assignment of commissioned officers now in the field, or at the seat of government.

This seems to be a week in which ripe fruit falls from the trees of patience and long-suffering work and planning: I refer to Stainback's appointment (if it is consummated) and to the reorganization of the JAG's office. . . .

Sunday, 28 June 1942
4101 Lorcom Lane

. . . A buffet supper in Fairfax County at the Douglas Hatch's ended a rich day with Katherine Mather and Norman, Jr. In the tire and gasoline shortage, we called Dr. Hu Shih, the Chinese ambassador (for whom the party was given), and he stopped by for us, giving us an occasion for a delightful visit which we had long wished for. The Barnett Novers were with him—a columnist and associate editor of the *Washington Post*. . . .

What makes the intimate, personal, common bond, which one feels with the higher type of Chinese? We agreed that the community of interest between China and the United States was based to a large extent upon what I called "the absence of stuffed-shirtism which perpetually clutters up the Anglo-American relations." As Dr. Hu Shih said, when he and I were discussing this point with Senator McCarran of Nevada as we stood around in the Hatches' yard with the crowd milling around, there is a common freedom from the examples of formalism which monarchy sets in England and an acceptance of the rise of an ordinary man.

"Chiang Kai-shek is the son of a housemaid," Hu Shih said, "but no one thinks anything about that."

"How about the coolie?" Senator McCarran asked. "What is the coolie class?"

Hu Shih endeavored to explain, but I could see that the Western American mind did not grasp it. What Occidental can without seeing the Far East? One's imagination has nothing upon which to rest a conclusion. "Is he a mucker?" asked Senator McCarran, seizing upon the example of the lowest workman in a western mine.

"Much lower than that," I said. "We have nothing like the coolie in American life—there simply is no comparison that you could make."

Even limited visual glimpses of the Chinese quarters at Singapore and visits to other Far Eastern ports like Saigon is sufficient to bring home that truth.

"And yet the son of a coolie can rise, just as the lowest man in the United States can, if he has the ability and the opportunity," said Hu Shih. And he pointed out a former ambassador to Russia, who had served China with distinction—the son of a coolie, recognized and given opportunity by American missionaries.

"I do not know your junior senator from Nevada," Hu Shih said, referring to Senator [Berkeley L.] Bunker, "but I did know Senator [Key] Pittman and heard him deliver an address before a society of international lawyers shortly before his death, defending the Neutrality Act[1] and the policy of isolation. Tears actually came to his eyes as he

---

1. The Neutrality Act was, in fact, a series of several measures enacted during the 1930s to keep the United States out of foreign wars. The Neutrality Act of 1935 (Public Res. 67) banned trade with belligerents for one year. The Neutrality Act of 1936 (49 Stat. 1152) extended the 1935 Act for another year and banned loans to belligerents. The Neutrality Act of 1937 (Public Res. 27), the "Cash and Carry Act," extended the 1936 Act indefinitely and required all sales to belligerents to be on a strict cash and carry basis. The Neutrality Act of 1939 (Public Res. 54) incorporated the previous Neutrality Acts and prohibited American ships from entering war zones.

The Neutrality Act of 1941 (55 Stat. 764), approved 17 November 1941, amended the Neutrality Acts to allow arming of U.S. merchant ships and to permit their entry into the war zones. It essentially repealed the limitations established by the earlier acts.

argued that a measure of sacrifice or our American rights to freedom of the seas was justified if it would save, as he believed it would, the lives of our men on the battlefield."

Hu Shih explained the deep impressions which this incident made as to sincerity of the chief proponent of the isolationist viewpoint in the United States, a champion of ignorance in a world of enlightenment, but a sincere champion; and Hu Shih's understanding was great enough to grasp the real sincerity of the man. It is doubtful whether there is any representative of another country in the United States who has the understanding and knowledge of the states which Hu Shih has acquired. He had been in every state—many of them many times—and, as a man of great stature and humanity, has grown with his experience.

As the guest of honor, Hu Shih was passed around from hand to hand, but drifted back—as did Katherine after a brief sojourn with Thurman Arnold from which she could not escape. The incredible Thurman explained to Katherine that the cartel did not, after all, eliminate the small business. [The] small business could get the license to manufacture if it wanted to—all except the chisel outfit!

"Do you mean to tell me that the American Beryllium Company could have gotten a license for the manufacture of beryllium?" asked Katherine.

But to the specific questions in cross-examination, Thurman is not adapted. He is so used to loose-sprawling generalities, and just plain loud-mouth talking, that he simply does not bother with the specific.

"Would you change the anti-trust laws—the Clayton Act[2] and the Sherman Act[3]—to meet the needs of postwar adjustment?" Katherine asked.

"Certainly not," replied Thurman. "Just go right on enforcing them. They are absolutely all right the way they are. What we need is free competition and no regulation of prices." (I still think the egoist is still shooting at his old enemy, Leon Henderson, head of the Price Administration, but recently fallen low due to his refusal to appoint Democrats in his rapidly expanding organization throughout the country, which is dominated by an overwhelming majority of Republicans.)

"Then how about Argentine and American beef, for example?" Katherine asked.

---

2. The Clayton Anti-trust Act of 1914 supplemented the Sherman Anti-trust Act and attempted to ban price discrimination, corporate holding companies, and interlocking corporate directorates when employed to restrict competition. It also exempted labor unions when engaged in peaceful activities and limited the use of injunctions or restraining orders against strikes.

3. The Sherman Anti-trust Act of 1890 outlawed contracts, combinations, or trusts, in restraint of trade or commerce. The vagueness of the act, however, allowed monopolies to continue virtually unchecked.

"That's just the trouble right now," Thurman replied. "A beefsteak costs you $2.50—all this price regulation is unnecessary."

Katherine tugged at my arm—she was barely within reach—to get me to pull her away from this "hopeless" conversation. The famous Mrs. Arnold was very much in evidence, too, flitting about being the life of the party.

We sat down with Hu Shih at a table in the yard. Chinese General [Shih-ming] Chu, the military attache at the Chinese embassy, had remarked to Katherine that Ernest Lindley's article in the *Ladies Home Journal*,[4] to be presently followed by a book, *How War Came*,[5] pictures the President as playing with his stamp collection album when the news about Pearl Harbor reached him, and Secretary Knox of the Navy Department dressed and about to leave for a weekend in the country— everyone is painted in an off-guard attitude.

How misleading sheer facts can be! Hu Shih proceeded to give a detailed account of his visit to the President as the last visitor to talk with the President before the news of Pearl Harbor came. His interview with the President began at 12:30 on December 7th, and he left the President's office precisely at 1:40 P.M. He had summoned him to see the dispatch which he had already sent to Japanese Emperor Hirohito, having been unable to reach Hu Shih who was out of the city the preceding day.

"It is the last chance, I am afraid," the President had said—or words to this effect. "The Emperor could use his prerogatives. Otherwise, there will be ugly developments—something nasty, in the next forty-eight hours, and a Japanese attack on the Philippines, Thailand, French Indo-China, or the Dutch East Indies."

The President had had no reply from Emperor Hirohito, although this was still a possibility. He also discussed the negotiations of [Saburo] Kurusu and [Kichisaburo] Nomura and the fact that they were seeking an appointment with [Secretary of State Cordell] Hull.

Barnett Nover had said that the principal officials of the State Department were on duty in the State Department that morning, and that he, himself, had seen Secretary Stimson coming out of the State Department with bundles of maps under his arm. He claims to have said to Mr. [Eugene] Meyer, the owner of the *Washington Post*, who dropped into his office, that "things looked very bad—it looks like war."

I can't quite believe it, but that's what Nover claims. He has become quite an armchair admiral, and the temptation is strong.

---

4. Ernest K. Lindley and Forrest Davis, "How War Came," *Ladies Home Journal*, July 1942, pp. 16–17; August 1942, p. 31.
5. Ernest K. Lindley and Forrest Davis, *How War Came, An American White Paper: From the Fall of France to Pearl Harbor* (New York: Simon and Schuster, 1942).

Hu Shih said that the President called him directly at the embassy within the next hour, exclaiming, "Hu Shih, the Japs have treacherously attacked us at Pearl Harbor, and while those Japanese fellows (Kurusu and Nomura) were seeking an appointment with Hull." . . .

As Lindley said, the President may very well have been relaxing his mind by looking at his stamp album—he must resort to some technique of that sort, since he cannot go out and walk around the block, play a game of golf, or do anything else except resort to the playground of the mind. But the conversation with Hu Shih proves conclusively how wholly conscious he was of the impending forty-eight hours.

Arthur Krock, of the *New York Times*, had, as usual, attacked the President in an article, saying that when the President was informed of the attack on Pearl Harbor, he had exclaimed, "No!"[6]

Against the testimony of Hu Shih that the President expected an attack on the Philippines, Thailand, French Indo-china, or the Dutch East Indies, the exclamation "No!" is perfectly clear. He was astonished, not by the attack, but by the attack on Pearl Harbor. So was the rest of the world—even the Nazis, who disapproved of it violently, but had to conceal their feelings.

We were called to get our buffet suppers, and the ambassador was lost to the incredible Mrs. Emil Hurja [Gudrun A. Hurja] and her pro-Finnish husband, who was once supposed to be the great political statistician of the 1936 campaign. As Barnett Nover had said, "Hurja spent an hour explaining to me that President Roosevelt had not been elected at all in 1936." Hurja was slipping over to the Garner bandwagon in 1940 and, among others, took Lew Schwellenbach from my own state with him—a major political misjudgment by Lew proving his devotion to liberalism was purely calculating as long as the President's popularity was supposed to last. . . .

---

30 June 1942
Washington, D.C.

MEMORANDUM
Re: United States v. Savannah Shipyards, Inc.

I requested a conference with Attorney General Biddle and met with him at 4:15, together with Jim Rowe, and made the following proposal:

I said that the appraisal work was nearing completion—in fact, that I expected to have the final figures in hand today or tomorrow, and that I

---

6. Arthur Krock, "Six Months After Pearl Harbor," *New York Times*, 7 June 1942.

would be in a position to discuss possible settlement of the case. I suggested all negotiations be left entirely to me and that the attorney general and Jim Rowe have nothing to do with settlement and that I would take the matter up and handle it as I would any other case but that the effectiveness of my position would be completely spoiled if it were felt, as had already been indicated by Dempsey and Koplovitz, that the matter could be appealed to the attorney general. I stated that I would prefer to hand the case over to Jim Rowe or somebody else and have nothing further to do with it unless I had complete jurisdiction.

The attorney general said that the matter always had been in my hands, that there had been no intention of removing it, but that he had found it better to confer with opposing counsel on many of these cases, and that was why he held the previous conference. . . .

I added that I thought the case ought to be settled if it could be settled at the government figures, as we had nothing to gain from trying the case.

Jim inquired whether I had seen the Securities and Exchange Commission audit, indicating that he had understood from Dempsey and Koplovitz that I had. He turned to the attorney general and said that he understood from Purcell of SEC that the investigation showed a very "smelly" situation in the Empire Ordnance setup.

I said that the final report on the Savannah Shipyards was coming in tomorrow from Savannah from the SEC investigator and I understood that it contained a lot of "smelly" information, but I had not seen it.

The meeting broke up with a definite understanding that I would have complete charge of the settlement and negotiations as stated above.

NML

Sunday, 5 July 1942
Washington, D.C.

MEMORANDUM FOR FILE
Re: Savannah Shipyards, Inc.

I called Mr. [William] Stanley yesterday (Saturday) afternoon to see if he had been able to contact his client pursuant to my notice that the offer of settlement would be revoked at 3:00 P.M., Saturday, unless accepted. . . .

Mr. McPherson phoned me this afternoon from Savannah to say that he had discussed the proposal with Mr. Griffiths, in the morning, who had contacted Mr. Cohen, and that Griffiths had just advised McPherson of rejection of our offer. Both Mr. Griffiths and Mr. Abrams seemed greatly irritated at Mr. Stanley's intervention in the case, saying that he had only represented Mr. Cohen in certain matters with the War Department.

In the course of the discussion, Mr. McPherson read my telegram sent last night confirming my oral instructions to him that no other concessions would be considered and that the offer stood at $1,000,000 plus interest at 6 per cent from the date of taking. . . .

He had told Griffiths to confer with Cohen before submitting an offer to me, but Cohen had rejected his counter-offer.

"It is just as well," I said, "because I would not have accepted the proposal. This case must be tried unless they accept my offer of $1,000,000 plus interest without further concession."

NML

12:30 P.M., Thursday, 9 July 1942

The realities of the struggle over the Savannah Shipyards case are best reflected in the series of conversations upon which, in this case, I kept memoranda. The tension over settlement reached its peak last weekend and collapsed on Sunday, July 5th, when I refused to consider any settlement for more than $1,000,000 plus interest from the date of taking of the property. . . .

The case went to trial in Savannah on Monday morning, and it is a ouija board proposition as to whether we gain or lose by refusing to settle at a higher figure, but the net gain is in the realm of principle—an imponderable which cannot be evaluated in terms of dollars.[1] Subtle values of immeasurable weight in the operations of government were involved in the integrity of the Department of Justice and its reputation with the general public. These are preserved and even with the jury returning a verdict greater than my figure, the cost is cheap. The effect of the Sterling Products (Allied Chemical Company) settlement last fall will last indefinitely in the eyes of the public. I have at least saved the Deaprtment from such a blow, and have done it without offending the attorney general, even as I insulated him and the Department from the influence of Tommy Corcoran.

The long deferred reorganization of the Navy Department land acquisition section was precipitated by the signing of the executive order on the 7th.[2] The matter hung suspended until the attorney general could

1. In the Savannah Shipyards trial, which began 6 July 1942, the jury awarded the company $1,285,000. This was about $200,000 more than the company had been prepared to accept before the trial. See *Congressional Record*, vol. 91 (22 January 1945), pp. 424–426.

2. President Roosevelt's executive order (No. 9194) of 7 July 1942 transferred all naval real estate work from the Office of the Judge Advocate General to the Bureau of Yards and Docks.

personally see the President, and this would be an indefinite delay in view of his complete absorption in the trial of eight German saboteurs who landed from submarines.[3] Upon learning this, I phoned the attorney general, asked that he send the executive order anyway, and to my relief, Miss [Grace G.] Tully phoned back from the President's office advising that it had been immediately signed. I shall send over to Admiral Moreell, John J. Courtney, special assistant to the attorney general and chief of the Field Service Section to do for the Navy land acquisition work what John J. O'Brien did for the Army in February 1941. It is an immense relief to escape from the judge advocate general of the Navy. No amount of work is so hard as carrying the complete confusion of his office on our shoulders.

The Department of Justice is an armed camp these days with FBI agents at every door and special guards examining passes while the eight saboteurs are tried in a secret proceeding upstairs. . . . It seems just a little empty since the evidence is so clear and since it is obvious what is to be done with these men.

The situation has been succinctly stated in this phrase: "Give them a fair trial and then shoot them."[4] . . .

Saturday, 11 July 1942
4101 Lorcom Lane

It is really absurd how much time and trouble is being taken over the eight saboteurs being tried in the Department of Justice. Nine generals and the attorney general of the United States, with the judge advocate general of the Army [Major General Myron C. Cramer], with assistants, are giving their full and undivided attention to this matter. Jim Rowe is assisting the attorney general and simply can't be reached for fundamental matters of business within the Department; [Ebert K.] Burlew of Interior telephoned that he had been waiting for over two weeks for a conference with Assistant Secretary of War [John J.] McCloy and a representative of the Department of Justice to try to work out a division of authority between the civil and military government of

---

3. On 27 June 1942, J. Edgar Hoover announced that the FBI had captured eight Nazi saboteurs, who had landed on the Long Island and Florida coasts. On 2 July 1942 President Roosevelt established a military commission to try them (Proclamation No. 2561). The commission consisted of seven generals and the prosecution was conducted by Attorney General Biddle and Judge Advocate General Cramer. Two colonels conducted the defense. The trials began 8 July.

4. All eight defendants were convicted. Six were executed 8 August 1942. President Roosevelt commuted the sentences of the other two to long prison terms because they helped apprehend and convict the others.

Hawaii; the appointment of Judge Stainback had been delayed while Burlew was waiting for assurances from Justice that Stainback's one-time employment by Japanese in Honolulu, as a matter of legal business, was in no way indicative of pro-Japanese feelings—"a trivial matter which I am almost ashamed to mention," Burlew said, "but the Secretary and I both felt that it should be cleared out of the way for the sake of the record." . . .

I suggested in sympathy with Burlew's impatience over the unjustified delay of Justice in meeting the issue that he call Assistant Secretary McCloy and make an immediate appointment, simply notifying the Department of Justice that a representative should be sent. . . .

Then, suddenly, at 6:00 P.M., on Thursday evening, Carusi asked that I attend a conference at 10:00 the next morning because "Jim will be unable to go." . . . I [was] tempted to decline the assignment but, instead, took home all the information I could assemble from Interior—the opinions of the solicitor, memoranda, and a copy of the M-Day Plan, adopted by the Hawaiian Legislature in October 1941,[1] together with the proclamation of the governor and orders of the commanding general. . . .

An extraordinary incident in American history is revealed in the Hawaiian incident when Governor Poindexter (whose age and inadequacy of grasp I have commented upon in November) had been persuaded under considerable compulsion by General Short on December 7th to sign a proclamation constituting a complete abdication of the civil authorities. Poindexter (who has just arrived in town) has explained to Burlew that he had refused two or three times to sign the proclamation of December 7th, but that Short insisted upon it, even threatening at last that he would hold Governor Poindexter responsible for the slaughter which might at any time take place in the Hawaiian Islands upon the successful invasion thereof by the Japanese unless Poindexter signed the proclamation—and so he did. There were also assurances from General Short that the matter only involved a few weeks when the civil authority would be returned.

The M-Day Plan adopted by the Hawaiian legislature at the instance of the Army was a carefully thought out, meticulously written scheme for mustering the civil authorities under the civil governor in a full streamlined support of the military in the event of invasion—an entirely adequate scheme of things, but having been brushed aside

---

1. The M-Day Plan, approved by the Hawaiian Territorial Senate, 23 September 1941, gave the governor broad powers over the civilian population in case of an emergency in the Pacific. It allowed him to establish civil-military control over traffic and roads and to issue food ration regulations. See "Hawaii's Senate Votes M-Day Bill," *New York Times,* 24 September 1941.

in the holocaust of December 7th, in favor of military government. . . .

A provost court handles all cases up to five thousand dollars fine,
without appeal, and a military tribunal sits on all else, for which there
is no appeal. . . . The extraordinary fact is that no one here, not even
in the Judge Advocate General's Office, knows precisely what is
happening in the administration of justice in Hawaii. Judge Stainback
could only recount to the attorney general what he had read in the
papers and had heard, indirectly, and the Army had had no report on the
matter.

The interview . . . took place in McCloy's office on Friday morning . . .
We were all shocked at the superficiality of McCloy. I finally asked if he
had ever read a brief on the subject of the Army's position in setting up
for the first time in American history, "a military governor" in territory
other than conquered territories, and McCloy replied that he made it a
practice "never to read briefs." He also stated that the Constitution was
in complete confusion as to military authority.

I replied that there were times in life when we all "had to read briefs"
and that I thought this was one of those times. I added, "I was under the
impression that you were a lawyer."

He replied that he was, and at the end of the interview, added a
concession which had apparently been stirred up in his mind by this
almost sharp interchange: That he would read our briefs on this matter if
we would send one over.

We parted in all friendliness after a hasty discussion about the proposed
appointment of a new governor, Burlew wishing to ascertain McCloy's
attitude toward Stainback.

"Do you know Henderson?" he asked.

We both laughed at seeing our suppositions work out so precisely.
Henderson is the son of a former senator of New Mexico and is now
working with the RFC (Reconstruction Finance Corporation) under Jesse
Jones.[2] He married the niece of Walter Dillingham, the biggest government contractor in Hawaii, and the unofficial governor in that his
influence over Emmons is pre-eminent. He is the only man who can walk
in and out of General Emmons' office without an appointment.

I had mentioned to McCloy the influence of special interests in Hawaii
on the military governorship, unacquainted as the military men were
with the intricate background of Hawaii and dominant economic forces
of the place. "Dillingham complained to me about a number of things
that Emmons was doing," McCloy had said, thus assuring us of a real

---

2. This is probably a reference to Charles B. Henderson, who was both Democratic
senator from Nevada, 1918–21, and chairman of the RFC, 1941–47.

conflict and the fact that Emmons was not following Dillingham completely.

"This, by the way, was one of the things Dillingham complained about," McCloy said. "He complained that Emmons paid too much attention to what Stainback said."

Now there was a perfect circle! The influence of Dillingham on Emmons in regard to Stainback had been perfectly apparent to Stainback whose relations with Emmons were at first solid and friendly, but were subjected to a gradual decline. He knew the reason. The reason was Dillingham, who was threatened with court proceedings by the United States government when Stainback was United States attorney, capitulated to the demand, but he also insisted on Stainback giving the names of his employees who had informed Stainback. Stainback had refused, quite naturally. This conflict of wills and morality had remained in the relationships between the two men.

"That is precisely what I would have expected Dillingham to say." I replied to McCloy. "There is a story behind each of these situations which one not at all familiar with Hawaii cannot possibly penetrate." His mind ran to conclusions in the Hawaiian situation like a pinball in a pinball game, bobbing by haphazard chance from one fact to another until it finally lit someplace—not in the objective hole of the truth, but in most instances as a wasted shot. . . .

McCloy was moving off toward the secretary's office, where a conference had been called. "There is a story behind all of these circumstances, I find," he said, as if a little tired of cynical discountings of personalities.

"That is why we come back to Stainback," I replied persistently, "because he is a disinterested man and the strongest representative which the federal government has in Hawaii."

We went out of the conference and stood on the curb waiting for a car after leaving our identification badges at the War Department desk, all of us wondering how in the hell a man like McCloy got into an important post like that with so little grasp of the basic concepts of government, and so dangerously free from a sense of legal restraint. I had said very aptly at one phase of the repartee in the discussion that we must certainly consider the basic legal situation if we are to have a government of law and not men. I was shooting at a man exactly of McCloy's description, and how fascism gets hold and keeps hold seemed very clear to me as I talked with that fellow.

Having surrendered power to arbitrary military rule in Hawaii in all phases of life which most fundamentally affect the lives of the citizens, the problem was to get it back, and one can't just take it away. The McCloys in the picture simply saw no reason to disturb the existing arrangement of authority. No basic principles were issued to them. The officers were just men and meant well—as we all knew. Why shouldn't they carry on? It was in the interest of safety and there was a perpetual danger of invasion of Hawaii. "Not," I said, "since Coral Sea and Midway Island—the Japs came close then."[3] . . .

---

15 October 1942
4101 Lorcom Lane

Dear Katherine Mather:

A rather extraordinary thirty days lies behind, covering approximately 10,000 miles of travel since I flew out of Seattle on a soupy, foggy morning on September 15 aboard a Navy transport bound for Alaska. . . .

Land acquisition in Alaska had long been a mess, and I seized the opportunity of free transportation, sitting on the mail bags and express in Army transports, made available through orders of Admiral [Charles S.] Freeman, to clear up the mystery of Alaska in respect to our work—and at the request of the attorney general to look over also the United States attorneys' offices while I was there. . . .

. . . I got out of Anchorage on an Army transport bound for Kodiak at 9:30 A.M. on Thursday, September 24, having . . . returned from Matanuska Colony[1] . . . during the afternoon.

That was a grand sight to see. A rich valley, settled by two hundred pioneers, it has long been the subject of controversy, but in spite of ups and downs, 50 per cent of them had survived, considering the poor choice of settlement material. The matter should have been in the hands of the Farm Security Administration[2] in the Department of Agriculture instead of in the hands of the Interior Department, which tried to settle mechanics and all manner of tradespeople who had little or no background in agriculture as a way of living—some of them as unadjusted to what they found as the original settlers of Jamestown who suffered and failed and even died as a result.

We visited three beautiful farms. The productive capacity there is

---

3. The Battle of the Coral Sea (7–8 May 1942) and the Battle of Midway (3–6 June 1942) proved to be the turning point in the war against Japan. After the Coral Sea the Japanese advance halted, and after Midway the American offensive began.

1. The Matanuska Colony in Alaska was established by the Federal Emergency Relief Administration's (FERA) Rural Rehabilitation (RR) in the Matanuska Valley. Its purpose was to resettle urban-industrial workers on farms. After much expense and criticism, it succeeded in developing a permanent agricultural settlement.

2. The Farm Security Administration (FSA) was established under the Farm Tenancy Act of 1937 (Bankhead-Jones Act) to replace the Resettlement Administration (RA) and to provide long-term loans to tenant farmers to enable them to buy land. It also aided migrant farm workers.

amazing, but of course until the present emergency, the outlet was limited, particularly when the city available for market was so uneducated in the use of vegetables. Alaska is just about one generation behind the ABC's of vitamin needs. . . .

---

15 October 1942 (continued)
[Notes from] Adak, 1 October 1942

Up at 6:30 in the "guest tent" where I spent the night in a very fancy silk-lined eiderdown which I really hated to use. In fact, I wanted to sleep in the same tent with the squadron leader, Jim Russell, but there was not a single vacancy. Private Reeves, from San Antonio, was lighting a fire in the guest tent.

"That's Maury Maverick's town," I said, after asking him where he had come from.

"Yeah, that's why I'm here," he replied.

"What do you mean?" I asked.

"I was a reporter on the *San Antonio Express* and the *Express* opposed his election.[1] All five of us reporters were drafted by the local board which was controlled by Maury Maverick." Of course, the fact that every other man of the same age was drafted too did not change the conclusion, so strong are political prejudices. . . .

Affectionately,
Daddy [signed]

---

16 October 1942

Having arrived from Chicago day before yesterday, I saw Bob Patterson, undersecretary of War, at lunch today to pass on immediately my account of the conditions I had found at Fairbanks in which both fighter and bomber planes, bound for Russia via Nome and the Siberian air bases, were bogged down in red tape at both Edmonton and Fairbanks. "Judge Patterson," as he is known around the government, is a forthright, fearless, and honest soul. As a staunch Republican [his] unmitigated admiration for the Russians in the Battle of Stalingrad certainly proves his fearlessness. . . .

I recounted to him, after explaining carefully that the commanding officer and the intelligence officer at Fairbanks at Ladd Field should in no

---

1. Maverick was running for mayor of San Antonio.

way be held accountable for this information, that Russian pilots were waiting to take the planes to Nome and the Siberian air fields and thence to the Stalingrad front, but that under instructions of the Signal Corps of the United States Army, no communications could pass by radio between Siberia and Alaska except bare weather reports unaccompanied by operating information or instructions. . . .

All information aside from bare weather reports had to be communicated to the Signal Corps in Washington, D.C., thence to the State Department, from the State Department to the Russian embassy, from the Russian embassy to Moscow, and from Moscow back to the Siberian airports. In the meantime, Alaska weather, which changes every five minutes, liquidated into worthlessness whatever the reports might be. While planes intended for Russia piled up at Fairbanks and Edmonton, one of the most crucial battles in the world's history raged at Stalingrad with air superiority completely on the side of the Germans.

I said, "In my absence, I understand there has been something of a scandal as to the failure to deliver aid to the Russians." Bob said, "And this incident has all the earmarks of deliberate delay somewhere along the line, unless it is crass stupidity." . . .

Patterson was deeply interested and is going to shake the matter down immediately to see what the explanation is, and can be done about it.

"It may be the Russian regulations, themselves." he said. "They are very strict about communicating anything to us, and I don't blame them. Look at the *Chicago Tribune* incident in which so much valuable information was published that the Japs immediately changed their code, knowing, by the public information, that we had intercepted their communications.[1] We Americans like to talk too much and put everything in print, and the Russians know that. I really can't blame them for not wishing to tell us a thing—I quite understand it."

He went on at length to say that "there was extreme doubt as to the advisability of a second front to help the Russians, notwithstanding all current pressure to the contrary, but that they deserve every single thing we can send them and, as Stalin has pointed out, if it were sent as agreed

---

1. This probably refers to a series of articles by Stanley Johnston on the battles of the Coral Sea and Midway, which appeared in the antiadministration *Chicago Tribune*, *New York Daily News*, and the *Washington Times-Herald*. On 7 August, Attorney General Biddle alleged that the articles contained confidential information concerning U.S. ship movements during the Battle of Midway and asked a federal grand jury to look into the matter. The grand jury, however, found no evidence of a crime. See Stanley Johnston, "Witness of Coral Sea Battle Gives Picture from Carrier (USS Lexington)," *New York Times*, 13 June 1942, 15 June 1942, 16 June 1942, 17 June 1942 and 18 June 1942. See also "Midway Dispatch Is Under Inquiry; Biddle Asks a Grand Jury at Chicago to Weigh Story Used by Tribune There," *New York Times*, 8 August 1942; and "Grand Jury Declines to Indict Publishers of Midway Dispatch," *New York Times*, 20 August 1942.

and on time, it would do the job. I am giving them everything we can—they deserve it. They are doing the only great job of stopping the Germans." . . .

<hr />

27 October 1942

<hr />

The attorney general finally got around to calling me ten days after I had returned from Alaska, and I went to lunch with him last Friday, the 23rd. (A terrible lunch, served in his office! I don't know why his health stands up as well as it does—he was home for three days last week "with a cold.")

Far from being critical of my absence, as Jim Rowe had implied to Ed Williams in my absence, he was keenly interested in everything I had to say, particularly about Alaska, and expressed the opinion that the assistant attorney generals should get out into the field oftener, saying that he was very glad, indeed, I had gone.

I told him of the depressing state in which I found the institution of United States commissioners, the judges of all offenses up to felonies, one of whom had operated a house of prostitution at Dutch Harbor as his principal source of income until the Navy had closed it down. Another at Kodiak was a "squaw man" who is drunk almost all of the time. His unmarried daughter served as his secretary, although about eight months pregnant, allegedly by an Indian. That was Justice in Kodiak!

I invited the attorney general's attack on the whole commissioner system in which he had already expressed an interest at the judicial conference, and suggested above all that their appointments be made subject to the attorney general's approval. . . .

[Biddle] is simply rattled and has no firm grasp of the Department's business. He has taken a terrible beating by the press in my absence, and on the front page of the *Washington Herald*[1] it has been suggested that the only reason for his retention as attorney general, instead of his promotion to the Supreme Court in the position of James Byrnes, who resigned to take chairmanship of the President's stabilization committee,[2] is that Frankfurter wants to keep Biddle here in order to keep control of

<hr />

1. The *Washington Times-Herald* also attacked Biddle for issuing a report 3 September 1942 which dismissed the Dies Committee's charges, of 13 August 1942, that 17,000 federal employees were pro-Nazi sympathizers. Biddle reported that, as a result of an FBI investigation of 2,095 federal employees, only 36 had to be dismissed and 13 disciplined.

2. That is, the Office of Economic Stabilization (OES), which President Roosevelt established within the OEM, by Executive Order No. 9250, 3 October 1942. Its purpose was to establish policies to control wages, prices, profits, and living costs and to minimize labor turnover. Supreme Court Justice James F. Byrnes resigned from the Court to become director. He resigned, in May 1943, to head the Office of War Mobilization (OWM) and was replaced by Frederick M. Vinson.

the Department—a nasty crack and fundamentally false in concept, because Frankfurter is no longer always advising the President with the effectiveness he enjoyed two or three years ago. It was, I am afraid, an anti-Semitic crack of the *Washington Herald*.

By sheer chance of fortune, I had missed talking with the attorney general before the Hawaiian incident finally reached the President's desk. Only the day before we had lunch, he advised me, he and Secretary Ickes had gone to the President. . . . The attorney general was a little indefinite about all of the developments in my absence, but piecing them in with what Ugo Carusi, his executive assistant, told me, they were as follows:

A peaceable agreement was, at last, worked out, since Governor Stainback left San Francisco for Honolulu in August, where I last parted with him, after Secretary Ickes had refused to let the new governor issue a proclamation (which he and I had drafted in San Diego) revoking the proclamation of former Governor Poindexter of December 7th, in the panic of the Pearl Harbor attack, establishing martial law in the regular and proper sense, conveying to the military only those matters of authority which pertained to the public security. Poindexter had abdicated all of his powers and sought to convey them quite illegally to the military commander, then General Short.

Wishing a peaceable solution, as Secretary Ickes had told me over the telephone when I called him from Los Angeles to urge the adoption of the proclamation Stainback and I had drafted, a stipulation had at last been worked out with the War Department as late as September, and it was agreed that the governor would issue a proclamation withdrawing certain matters from military authority. Simultaneously, General Emmons would issue an order giving those powers back to the civil government, so that double "face saving" took place. However, General [Thomas H.] Green, the civil governor under General Emmons, having agreed to these conditions in Washington and having stated that he would work out the details with Stainback without difficulty, drafted an order upon his return to Honolulu which practically undid the agreement, and laying it on Stainback's desk all signed, stating that he was about to issue it.

It was this incident of repudiating the understanding in Washington and defying the orders from Washington which had brought the thing to a real crisis. Stainback and his supporters in Interior had demanded the withdrawal of General Green. Secretary Ickes and the attorney general went to the President and the President agreed that Green should be withdrawn, and that the matter should be settled as agreed between Interior and the War Department. I cannot help but say, "I told you so," under these circumstances, for the time to have settled the difficulty was with the appointment of the new governor who could deftly and easily have issued a proclamation without any need of face-saving and without this long protracted trouble and conflict with great loss of time and resulting hard feelings. The time to remove an appendix is before it bursts. Anyway, Governor Stainback is at last, to all appearances, the governor.

I also checked in with the Vice President by calling him last week to make an appointment to see him. Upon offering to come up there or meet him in my office if he would come to lunch, to my very great pleasure he accepted the invitation and to the astonishment of members of the Lands Division, who were somewhat overwhelmed, the Vice President of the United States came to lunch with me last Saturday at 12:30. We visited until 2:45. The Alaska military situation was of great interest to him, particularly the map which I had brought down from Vancouver showing the world from the North Pole, which throws into dramatic relief the strategic importance of Alaska, the channel of communications via Alaskan and Siberian airports, not only to Russia and for a possible attack on Japan, but for communications to Western Europe, and by sea to Siberian airports during those portions of the year when navigation is feasible. . . .

"It has always been my theory," the Vice President said, "that Alaska was the key to the situation, and I have tried hard to convince some of my military friends to that effect." . . .

"From all I hear," I said, "the War Production Board under Donald Nelson is pretty much of a shambles as far as resisting the high pressure groups like the Aluminum Company of American, the copper boys, and others, are concerned."

"No, not so bad as that," the Vice President said, "but Nelson has not been able to control those groups. He says he will, but he just doesn't do it."

The Vice President was greatly interested in Ralph Lemkin's collection of Nazi decrees, and when I told him about Ralph, said he might be helpful in discussing the postwar situation in a speech which the Vice President was writing for November 8th. In conclusion, he made an appointment for me to bring Lemkin to him at 2:30 the following Monday—yesterday—and I did so.

We read, page by page, his manuscript—a first rough draft of a proposed speech to be given at Madison Square Garden on November 8th in celebration, or in honor of, our Russian ally. He pointed out the striking points of comparison and dissimilarity in Russian and American economics—similarities and dissimilarities (see them in his Madison Square Garden speech)[3]—and spoke with a refreshing and astonishing fearlessness, much as I write into my own dictaphone at midnight. To show the Russian superiority in what he called "genetic democracy" and

3. For a text of Henry Wallace's Madison Square Garden speech see *Congressional Record*, vol. 88 (12 November 1942), pp. A3951–A3952.

freedom from racial prejudice as opposed to our "Anglo-Saxon snobbishness," which he warned against lest it bring us to the low level of the
"Nordic myth" of racial superiority, he quoted a statement in the
Catholic Commonwealth saying that unless Americans were prepared in
their minds to see a colored man elected President of the United States,
they had not risen to the standards of true democracy or escaped from
what Mr. Wallace calls "Anglo-Saxon snobbishness."

"That must come out, Mr. Vice President," I said, impulsively. "Some
day you may have occasion to run for the presidency and that statement,
alone, even though quoted from the *Commonwealth*, would be sufficient
to defeat you."

Also the crack at the English, although well deserved, was not calculated to preserve unity of feeling and action among the Allies. A
statement of [Alexis] De Tocqueville, the French historian, as to the
common destiny of Russia and the United States, although the former
worked through absolutism involving "servitude" and the latter through
an entirely different approach, would also not have pleased our Russian
friends just at this time.[4]

His primary assignment of work was to write a section on the postwar
period in which he outlined certain ideas, but I somewhat gratuitously
said that we would have a go at the whole manuscript if he liked. I have
always felt that his manuscripts lacked order although they are rich in
thought and ideas. And so after an hour and a half, we took the manuscript
with us and went home to go to work.

Ralph Lemkin and I had just completed one intensive job, writing an
answer to the article of Earl Warren, candidate for governor of California,
favoring an extension of martial law on the Pacific Coast. I had been asked
in Los Angeles to do so but had not found time until I could hand the
article to Ralph last week and ask for his candid opinion. It was a dangerous
statement, and so we pitched in and wrote an answer after several intensive
nights of work, sending it to a lawyer in Los Angeles for distribution by
pamphlet and radio before the election on November 3rd. And here we
were with another tough assignment, our first for the Vice President. . . .

---

28 October 1942

A very delicate errand for Anna was to see Bernard Baruch. Anna had
discussed with Katherine and me, at great length, the unhappy situation
in which her mother finds herself in the White House, confronting the

---

4. Wallace quoted De Tocqueville's statement that the United States and Russia each
would "sway the destiny of half the globe."

alienating hostility of Harry Hopkins, the President's close assistant and confidante. It's a curious thing that all thrones should be so surrounded with palace intrigue and a struggle of the palace guard and its various cliques for power. The Tommy Corcoran clique was in for a time, dominating the secretarial world with close connections through Missy Le Hand and others. Tommy even tried to get one of Mrs. Roosevelt's secretaries fired so that he could have a channel of information out of her own affairs—anything to keep the President's family safely insulated from him. Jimmy [Roosevelt] was relentlessly maligned and his position was made untenable as a former secretary to the President, not only by public criticism but by attacks from the palace guard. As Mrs. R. herself once said of Jim Rowe, then secretary to the President—one of the "passion-for-anonymity-boys"—he was put in there "to watch Jimmy for Tommy."

And now it's Harry Hopkins jealously guarding his prerogatives as the great and intimate confidante of the President. Mrs. R.'s unfortunate blunder in assuming the responsibility for the Office of Civilian Defense last year, just when the OCD was about to blow up, giving Mayor La Guardia of New York a perfect opportunity to let the whole show blow up in Mrs. Roosevelt's face instead of his face, gave Harry a fine opportunity to say "there, that's what happens when she is out in front," or words to that effect. I gather from Anna that it was pretty rough stuff and that Mrs. R. was very unhappy about the whole situation, as well she might be, but what could be done about it? Anna thought that some responsible assignment such as a position on a regular schedule of radio programs would restore her sense of usefulness and position. The loyalty and affection of Anna for her mother is deep and staunch and strong.

"Good Lord! Anna," I said in Seattle when she had asked whether or not I might not discuss this matter with Elmer Davis, or some other appropriate person, "that is the most delicate problem in Washington and one which could blow anyone higher than a kite. I hope you appreciate that!"

She did. It was Katherine's suggestion that the matter might be discussed with Bernard Baruch who is a close and loyal friend of Mrs. R.'s, and I agreed to undertake it. Of course, the President's companionship with Princess Martha of Norway is also one of the great sources of unhappiness, although I must say I cannot go along with that feeling. . . .

I wrote a note, and Bernard Baruch's secretary called back, giving me an appointment this morning. He is a grand old man, living in bachelor quarters at the Carlton Hotel—white hair and very grey in his features, but with eyes of piercing blue and full of vitality even as he adjusts an earphone in order to hear better.

"That is an extremely delicate situation," he said, when I explained Anna's concern and the character of my errand. "There is nothing more difficult to deal with than intimate family problems like that—fools walk in where angels fear to tread."

"That is precisely what I told Anna," I replied, "but I have not hesitated to discuss it with you because of your friendship with Mrs. Roosevelt and your long intimate acquaintanceship with the family."

He replied that he was thoroughly familiar with the situation, but that the plain fact was that Harry Hopkins was there. It was an accomplished fact. He was the President's closest confidante. "I, myself, had not seen the President for six months prior to turning in my report in regard to the rubber situation, and all because I said something about the formation of SPAB[1] which the President didn't like." It was something about the SPAB being a compromising or vacillating step—I can't remember the exact words.

"I am very sorry to hear that," I said. "I thought you were very much of a factor there—continuously—and I think the people think so also."

"Oh, I am here all right and have a shadow of influence which is more or less effective from time to time. I did have lunch with the President the other day."

I recalled Bob Patterson's words that if he had the say-so, he would put Berny Baruch in charge of the whole war show and let him run it on three or four hours a day, even though he lacked energy to put in full days of real driving power because he is an old man. I could not agree with that abdication of a generation, but it was a fine comment, nevertheless.

"I have intervened once or twice," Mr. Baruch said, "once to take on myself the responsibility for that South Carolina situation [I assume he referred to a Resettlement Project which had been championed by Mrs. R. and proved utterly impracticable] by saying that 'we must all waste some money on experimentation.' I could say it and it would be accepted, and I did. I also warned her against this OCD enterprise, but she would go into it. The President at last gave his consent to her going to England, she has gone, as she long wanted to do. It made her very happy."[2]

"It would seem to be a fitting occasion for her to go on the radio upon her return," I replied. "She would have much to say."

"She will make a speech when she gets back," he replied. "I know all of the circumstances of her going, but of course I never repeat what either Mrs. Roosevelt or the President tell me." I gathered there was a story behind that situation. . . .

On the main problem, he said that the only solution he could think of

---

1. That is, the Supply Priorities and Allocation Board (SPAB), which President Roosevelt established by Executive Order No. 8875, 29 August 1941. Its purpose was to end bottlenecks and increase war production. Roosevelt named Vice President Wallace as chairman and Donald M. Nelson as executive director. He abolished it by Executive Order No. 9024, 16 January 1942, and replaced it with the War Production Board.

2. Mrs. Roosevelt arrived in England 23 October 1942 and returned to the United States 17 November 1942. She delivered several radio addresses, describing her trip, upon her return. See New York Times, 21 November and 23 November 1942.

was having Anna come and stay at the White House. She could get to the President through the phalanx which guarded him and might really change the situation. "It is always that way—all of us have one man who is a close and intimate confidante, and Harry Hopkins is that man. He has long been sending Harry on all of the principal errands. He sent him to Chicago at the convention in the summer of 1940. He sent him here to me to ask if I would take the chairmanship of the stabilization work[3] and, when I declined, Harry asked me if I thought Jimmy Byrnes would take it. Jimmy Byrnes happened to walk in through that door into this room right then, and so I said, "here he is, you can ask him yourself right now. And he did ask him. But he sent Harry Hopkins on all these important errands."

I asked how able Harry was but did not get a conclusive reply although he indicated that there were many capacities which the President claimed for him. In any event, he was there. Possession was nine points of the law. No one could penetrate that situation, except, possibly, the President's daughter, and he, Baruch, had thought for a long time that Anna was the only one who could change that unpleasant conflict between cliques in the White House—the Mrs. Roosevelt clique against the Harry Hopkins clique.

"The irony of it is that she brought him in to the White House after his wife died, took care of his daughter and has been in every way an aid to establishing the intimate relations which he now enjoys," I said.[4]

Mr. Baruch nodded. When I arose to go he asked what I was going to say to Anna, and I replied that I would simply tell her she should come on down here and have a talk with Mr. Baruch, but that I would go no further into detail in a letter. He agreed with that, and we parted most cordially. He is a great calm man of excellent judgment, a pillar of strength now.

The rest of the day [was spent] working on an impending argument in *United States v. Miller*[5] while Katherine and Ralph Lemkin worked in the appointment room reorganizing the Vice President's manuscript. We

---

3. The Office of Economic Stabilization (OES).

4. When Hopkins's second wife, Barbara, died in 1937, Eleanor invited Harry and his five-year-old daughter, Diana, to spend Christmas Eve in the White House so that they would have company. Later her support helped make Hopkins secretary of commerce. From May 1940, Hopkins lived in the White House for the next three and a half years, but as Hopkins's friendship with the President grew warmer, his relationship with Eleanor deteriorated.

5. The case of *United States v. Victor N. Miller, et al.* 317 U.S. 369-382 (1943) arose when the United States condemned a strip across Miller's land to relocate the Central Pacific Railroad because of flooding caused by the Central Valley Reclamation Project in California. Miller et al. complained that they had not received sufficient compensation in the District Court (1938), but lost. They appealed and the Circuit Court of Appeals reversed the decision. Speaking for the Supreme Court, Justice Roberts reversed the Appeals Court and even required Miller et al. to return portions of the money they had received from the government.

are working every night, having dinner downtown, once with Ralph at Harvey's, once in the cafeteria, and once we brought it down from home in a picnic basket, so much do I miss good home food when we have to stay downtown. . . .

---

29 October 1942

I called the Vice President yesterday to say that I thought we would be ready to give him a draft of his proposed speech as revised today, and we chatted a few minutes about the manuscript. He said that he had changed his ideas and decided to strike out the De Tocqueville quotation as too provocative and reorient it a bit. I told him his brain trust had reached the same conclusion.

He also said that, if it were possible to work it in, he would like to make a statement, subject to the President's approval, that all aid for the next two months would be sent to Russia and China. . . . He said that the President had so indicated. He stated the fact quite bluntly that the English had been "hoarding" equipment. He spoke with considerable feeling, and I wondered as he did so how he could ever make so strong a statement in a public address, cut down into such polite language that there would still be life in it.

"What did you think of [Wendell L.] Willkie's statement?" he asked. Willkie had just made a public statement to the effect that laymen's opinion on military affairs were just as good as the military's and that he was tired of hearing this talk about the superiority of military judgments.

I replied that I was afraid that, as a layman, I would have to agree. I had felt constantly—and particularly in reference to the Alaskan situation, which I had now had a chance to see with my own two eyes—that military judgment was simply good executive ability and common ordinary horse sense, and that there was no mystic quality which training in military strategy could develop to outweigh such judgment. "I feel sure you agree," I added, "because of the opinions you have expressed on the Alaska situation." . . .

[I] think we agreed on Willkie, although the Vice President did not say so openly. He said that [Henry] Luce, the editor of *Life*, [had] recently published the open letter to the English people, which has been a wide open subject of controversy, bluntly advising them that we were not going to fight this war to save the British Empire.[1] We both thought that this was behind the Willkie statement.

---

1. "Life on the Newsfronts of the World: An Open Letter to the People of England," *Life*, 12 October 1942, p. 34.

We labored all of yesterday, last night and today on the manuscript, I at last taking part because it has reached a stage of completed raw material where I could no longer escape giving time to it to cut it down and render it somewhat more incisive, although the resulting document was far more cumbersome than I would ever have used myself as a public speech. Still it had brought order into the Vice President's ideas. . . .

The scene changes so rapidly. At cabinet meeting in the afternoon, members had been instructed by the President that he did not wish any of those who were close to him to discuss the postwar situation at this time. I agree with him. While we cannot give too much thought to this subject, it ought not to be discussed now, when the fate of our efforts [is] really hanging in the balance. We are certainly not winning this war at this moment, even though the British, Australians and Americans have crashed through Rommel's[2] line in Egypt, and newspaper headlines report "holding our own in Guadalcanal in the Solomon Islands."[3] (I can scarcely believe the latter and the news may change any day.)

[Wallace] glanced at the first page of flattering comments on the bravery of the Russians, their great losses and valor, most of which was his own language, and then blue penciled it. "[Joseph F.] Barnes, who accompanied Willkie,[4] tells me that Stalin has said in so many words that he does not like to have them flattered with talk about Russian bravery. They want facts and not words—they want supplies."

He was not at all flattering about our changes in his own manuscript, complaining that there was too much of it—it was too long. He would have to cut it down.

"Of course, Mr. Vice President," I said, "this is still raw material, but we left all the material in knowing that you would wish to strike out chunks of it and that only you could decide that."

He seemed restless and hurried [and], as Ralph subsequently said, was undoutedly disturbed by the President's instructions, which completely upset his plans for the November 8th speech in which he wished to dwell mostly on the postwar situation. "Those ideas are good," he said, after glancing through the section on "The New Democracy and the New Peace." "That was what I wanted, something to ferment in my mind on the postwar situation."

Further on, he said, turning to me, "I don't think a lawyer can do the job of cutting down and putting these ideas in simple words. In public speaking you have to use plain simple words."

---

2. The Allies defeated German Field Marshal Erwin Rommel at the Battle of El Alamein, 23 October–4 November 1942.

3. U.S. forces invaded Guadalcanal 7 August 1942, but did not secure the island until January 1943.

4. Joseph F. Barnes accompanied defeated Republican presidential candidate Wendell Willkie on his trip to the Near East and Russia, August–October 1942.

I could not help feeling somewhat amused at that remark, from one who has no natural aptitude for public speaking and whose only chance of effectiveness is in the ideas which he states. . . .

He thanked us for all the work we had done and said he would take the manuscript matter home and dictate it tonight. He also invited us to ride down with him, which we did, waiting at the curb for Mrs. Wallace [Ilo Browne Wallace] to come by. . . .

Sunday, 1 November 1942

. . . The Vice President sent his speech over to the office about noon. It was sent out to me by Robert [probably Robert Wallace, Henry Wallace's son] with a handwritten note attached, which read:

Dear Norman,

My chief question is on next to the last sentence. Will it offend China?

H. A. Wallace

The sentence referred to read:

Russia and the United States have such a significance that the all important thing is whether or not the points of agreement between these two great peoples are sufficiently fundamental to make possible the construction of an enduring peace, based on the humanitarian ideals which are so dear to the heart of the common man.

Ralph Lemkin came out after lunch. Katherine read the speech aloud to us and we discussed it. I must say, I did not expect to hear from the Vice President again, but he telephoned this morning just when I had made a deal with Katherine Mather to read her only three sections of the funny papers before I went to the office. We had finished "Okey Dokes."

"What did you think of it," Mr. Wallace asked, as I hastily pulled my critical faculties together, also my bathrobe.

"We agreed that you were right about China," I replied, "and were wondering just what you could say in that sentence inserting something about 'with collaboration of China.' "

"Yes, they are concerned about Russia in the Far East," he replied. . . .

I also added as "hardly worth mentioning" the possibility of satirical treatment of one sentence in regard to the "United States being the warp and Russia being the woof." If someone wished to pick it up, Russia could be referred to as the "big, bad woof." (Three little pigs and the big, bad wolf.) He laughed and said that was definitely a possibility, and it might give the boys a chance for a little play. . . .

"Was I too strong in the talk about the British?" the Vice President asked, referring to this line in his speech:

From her (Russia) we can learn much for unquestionably the Anglo-Saxon people have practiced racial snobbishness to a point which has made them exceedingly unpopular in many parts of the world. We have not sunk to the lunatic level of the Nazi myth of racial superiority, but we have sinned enough to cost us already the blood of many thousands of precious lives. Ethnic democracy built from the heart is perhaps the greatest need of the Anglo-Saxon tradition.

. . . The Vice President expressed a little doubt as to whether the President would approve so strong a statement in regard to the English. It would probably raise cain in India, for example. "On the other hand," he said, "it might do some good at this time."

"It might," I said, "particularly with the English credit running out so badly everywhere. . . ."

"You probably noticed that I adopted your phrase 'ethnic democracy' instead of 'genetic democracy,'" the Vice President said, laughing, for we had had a vigorous exchange on this in his office. It was Katherine's point. "Genetic" democracy is undoubtedly wrong, "ethnic" being the proper reference for racial equalities. As Ralph quietly suggested in the Vice President's office, "it has broader implications—even religious concepts are involved." . . .

"I want you all to know how much I appreciate your assistance," the Vice President concluded. "You have been a great help to me."

"I didn't think we had," I replied, "at least not very much."

"On the contrary," he said, "You have been of great help. Please thank Dr. Lemkin for me." . . .

In curious contrast to this discussion of democracy in high places: We had the Archduke Otto and his brother Archduke Karl Ludwig of Austria[1] at dinner last night with Vincente Villamin,[2] the leading Filipino in this country, and his friend St. Clair from Los Angeles (who was offered the position of handling British propaganda in this country during the war and declined it because he felt out of accord with their viewpoint) and Ralph.

---

1. Otto and Karl Ludwig de Bourbon Hapsburg. The archdukes arrived in the United States as refugees after the fall of France. When the United States entered the war, they attempted to form a military unit to aid the Allies from among Austrians living in the United States. Despite some official support, the results were disappointing and few volunteers resulted. The archdukes then joined the American army. See "Austrian Noblemen Join Army," *Washington Evening Star*, 30 December 1942; "Otto May Join But Won't Head Austrian Legion in America," *Washington Evening Star*, 2 January 1943, in Littell scrapbook.

2. Villamin was the brother-in-law of Filipino General Vincente P. Lim. A Filipino refugee, he was engaged in counterespionage and antisabotage activities among Filipinos living in the United States.

It was Halloween night, and a succession of child invaders came by with their "trick or treat" injunction. After passing the necessary candies around, I succeeded in prevailing upon the rest of the invading army to wait until later in the evening.

We awoke in the middle of a discussion of Alaska to see an oriental rug disappearing from the front hall and, upon pursuing it to the front, found all of the porch furniture from the side porch stacked up across the front veranda. We had the pleasure of moving it back and, this time, locked the door, but in the course of these events, I pursued a figure from behind a bush and overtook [it] across the street where, to my surprise, I found [it to be a] . . . girl (and a girl it proved to be) [who] was a guest of the Wankowiczes,[3] our Polish neighbors, and with her was Archduke Felix,[4] who had had dinner with the Wankowiczes. So I brought them all back to the party for some refreshments.

Now never would I have dreamed that this world could have become so topsy-turvy that an Archduke of Austria . . . could have been caught assisting in stealing my furniture as a Halloween prank. . . .

. . . At dinner at Barnett Nover's house . . . [the] most interesting fragment of all was St. Clair's account of his interview with Lord Northcliffe,[5] when the latter was in this country during the last war and St. Clair, in a private interview, asked him "How much does it cost to do the propaganda job of bringing a country into a war these days?"

After labeling the reply "off the record" and stating that he did not wish it ever to be used, at least until after his death, Lord Northcliffe replied as follows:

> For a small country of largely pastoral pursuits—for example, like in the Balkans or Central European countries—$1,000,000. For a big country made up of ignorant people, like the United States, $60,000,000. For all other countries in between, you can estimate it according to the figures I have given you. . . .

---

9 December 1942

Dear Katherine Mather:

I have just returned from spending four days in New York where, I am afraid, my own pursuits were not as reminiscent of Pearl Harbor as the

---

3. Mr. and Mrs. Witold Wankowicz.
4. Felix de Bourbon Hapsburg was a younger brother of Archduke Otto.
5. Alfred Charles William Harmsworth.

newspaper headlines and editorials commemorating the anniversary of Japan's attack there on December 7th last year. New York at night, is, however, a dimmed-out monument to Pearl Harbor, for the glare of Broadway is gone, and street lights, store windows and automobile lights are dimmed to such subdued slits of light that the teeming lights of Times Square move in the mystery and obscurity of a half-lighted ballroom at a masquerade party. One could not recognize the face of an acquaintance even if passing elbow to elbow.

There is an atmosphere of subdued excitement, added glamor and excitement, perhaps due somewhat to the fact that the spirit of vice and indulgence is excitingly near the surface in the street traffic.

I went up on the late train Thursday afternoon and went promptly to bed on arrival, being a bit taut with the strain of work here. The next day was largely spent in Jersey City and Hoboken, reviewing with my special assistant to the attorney general there the problems of land acquisition in that vastly complicated real estate market. [We] have taken vital industrial waterfront properties—particularly the Bayonne Terminal—now expanded into a vast supply base for the Navy and dock sites at the foot of 14th Street, for which the City of New York, under the "Little Flower" La Guardia, is pounding us hard on attenuated theories of valuation. There is a bigger treasury here than in New York; corporation counsel are doing their best to get into us! The Little Flower, himself, manipulated a very expert horse trade for Floyd Bennett Field, wangling $9,000,000 out of the judge advocate general of the Navy some few months ago. We could have beaten him down in a condemnation suit, I believe, because the field had no commercial sales value, but it was policy to settle.

An interview at *Newsweek*[1] took part of the time, as they were writing an article on land acquisitions. . . .

---

30 December 1942

The Vice President made a vital statement at the commemoration of President Woodrow Wilson's birthday over a national radio hook-up on the 29th.[1] I read the statement in the paper *en route* to New York on that day. He flayed his critics considerably on the postwar world. Oscar Cox, assistant solicitor general, mentioned to me in passing, "Did you see the

---

1. See "Uncle Sam, Landowner," *Newsweek*, 21 December 1942, pp. 29–30.

1. For a text of Wallace's nationwide radio broadcast on the eighty-sixth anniversary of Woodrow Wilson's birth, 29 December 1942, see *Congressional Record*, vol. 89 (7 January 1943), pp. A26–A28.

reproduction of our discussion at your house in the Vice President's address?" That vital evening's discussion certainly survived in the address. The footprints were unmistakable. I remembered distinctly observing that the soldiers would not forget upon their return that the country had been able to spend millions to send them to war. They would not be able to see why a country as rich as all that could not spend something to create jobs. That is a deadly issue which we should all grasp. The communists will grasp it very quickly if we don't.

There was also a survival of Ralph Lemkin's ideas in the address in November in regard to postwar education, but I give more credit to our dissective discussion on the evening at our house. . . .

1943

4 January 1943

The Supreme Court handed down its decision in *United States v. Miller*, which I argued in November—a sweeping victory for the government with excellent language on all points, particularly on that most important point as to whether or not the government pays enhanced value of realty following from the announcement of a project up to the date when the government actually takes the land. The answer was "No" as to all lands which were "probably" contemplated when the project was authorized by the government. *Erie v. Tompkins*[1] was also driven back into its cage as far as condemnation law is concerned; Federal law controls and not the state law as to substantive matters, and determining just compensation is a substantive matter.

This is the most important condemnation decision in many years and most gratifying to me. . . . I never suffered quite so much in the preparation of an argument. [Owing] to the insufficiency of our brief written in the Appellate Section, . . . a very fundamental stage of the argument was overlooked and had to be presented in oral argument. Oral

---

1. *Erie Railroad Company v. Harry J. Tompkins* (304 U.S. 64–92 (1937) was the case of a man who had been injured while walking alongside the Erie Railroad's right of way. Justice Brandeis delivered the opinion of the Court, reversing the lower courts, which had ruled in favor of Tompkins, and holding that Tompkins had no right to compensation because he had been trespassing.

argument survived in the all important phrase as to lands which were "probably" contemplated or "likely" to have been included. The government pays the original price and not the enhanced price at the date of the taking for such lands. . . .

Tuesday, 16 February 1943

Dearest Katherine Mather,

I have just returned from a somewhat breath-taking but thoroughly soul-restoring trip into the West. From Warm Springs, Virginia, to Olympic Hot Springs in the Olympic National Forest in Washington, there are no mineral springs so thoroughly restorative to me as a sojourn in the West, that everlasting reservoir of American integrity and inexhaustible source of energy and good will.

I left on several major errands, . . . caught the Santa Fe Chief, a model for all trains, the next day at noon for Chicago, and for three days in the privacy of a roomette, slept, read and worked on an impending argument in the Circuit Court of Appeals in San Francisco, . . .

The faithful and beloved Virgil Jorgenson met me at the station at San Francisco, and I stopped at my San Francisco office only long enough to get two brief cases full of books and then proceeded to Laurel Brook Farm near Sonoma in the valley made famous by Jack London's book, *The Valley of the Moon*.[1] . . . Virgil abandoned his study to me, and I hammered away on preparing an argument as to the value of a power site taken above [Grand] Coulee Dam in Washington, in *United States v. Washington Water Power Company*.[2] . . .

On Monday, I went back to the battle line of ordinary existence and to my case in the Circuit Court of Appeals, arguing before Judges [William] Denman, [Clifton] Matthews and [Bert E.] Haney. Having an assistant attorney general was too much for the egocentric exhibitionist and frustrated power-seeker, Judge Denman. He lit into me very soon, advising most unexpectedly that "if I would listen I would get to know what that Court thought of the law and might really learn something." I was dwelling on Supreme Court decisions at the moment and the attack was wholly unexpected. One cannot argue a case in an atmosphere of intellectual egotism as great as his. Haney expressed regret later but said the treatment of me was mild compared to [what] he had seen [Denman do to] young lawyers arguing for the first time. [They would] go away

---

1. Jack London, *The Valley of the Moon* (New York: Macmillan, 1913).

2. In *United States v. Washington Water Power Company* (88 L. ed 44) the Supreme Court denied Littell's request for a hearing. 30 U.S. 747–748 (1943).

from the courtroom and break into tears with the battering treatment of the bullying Denman. He has no business on the Court. The Court is utterly demoralized, and all members of it hate him thoroughly. They do not even hold conferences if they can avoid it. It was perfectly evident that we would have to take this case to the Supreme Court, so great was his hostility to the government's viewpoint.

The old egotist was swanking it over the other judges by showing that he had an invitation to sit in the Court of Appeals in the District of Columbia where there is a vacancy, but I blocked that with a letter to Judge Harold Stephens of that Court, explaining what a ruthless, trouble-making intellect he would invite into the peace and quiet of the Court of Appeals, where a publicity-seeking *prima donna* would give him nothing but trouble. . . .

The next errand was the possible settlement of our condemnation case taking Treasure Island[3] in San Francisco Bay as an airport and general personnel base for the Navy. [The] proposal [was] that proper military expansion of Mills Field,[4] with the extension of runways and other construction work for wartime purposes, might supply an adequate airfield for the City of San Francisco to be surrendered to them after the war in consideration for the conveyance free of Treasure Island to the United States government. The City is asking over $8,000,000 for it so the deal would be a good one even though we do not concede that value. I revived the proposition, which had fallen apart in the push and pull of various factions and differences of viewpoint, and the engineers for both the City and the [Navy] under Admiral [John W.] Greenslade, of the Eleventh Naval District, went to work to put the pieces together. . . . I left to investigate the highly controversial Indian case of *United States v. Courtemanche*,[5] at Palm Springs, on which I had taken such a severe beating in the press at the hands of Judge [Benjamin] Harrison, although I had known nothing whatever of the case, it being one of over 8,000 under my jurisdiction.[6] . . .

---

3. Treasure Island is a small island in San Francisco Bay which the Navy had taken for a naval base. Littell and the Navy were offering to greatly expand and improve Mills Field, a municipal airport south of the city in exchange for permanent title to Treasure Island. After much negotiation, the city eventually agreed to the proposal in April 1944.

4. Now San Francisco International Airport.

5. *United States v. Amelia Courtemanche* was the case of a poor widow who owned an auto court on land leased, illegally, from the Agua Caliente group of Mission Indians near Palm Springs, California. It was one of more than 250 similar cases in the U.S. District Court for Southern California. Littell demanded that she be removed from the land. See "Desert Court Builder Not To Be Penalized," *Riverside Press*, 12 January 1943, in Littell scrapbook.

6. Judge Harrison ruled that Littell had confiscated Mrs. Courtemanche's property illegally and Littell dropped the case against her. See "Judge Blasts U.S. Bureaus in Land Deal," *Los Angeles Daily News*, 18 December 1942; "Judge Says 'No' to Confiscation," *Los Angeles Daily News*, 13 February 1943, in Littell scrapbook.

. . . I found a most extraordinary disorderly state of land tenure on the Indian Reservation at Palm Springs, with predatory lawyers looking forward to additional cases. We successfully completed two test cases now pending, and I wrote a letter to the secretary of the Interior proposing that we sue everybody on the reservation, between five and six hundred leasehold claimants or permittees, and quiet title to the whole thing instead of picking our flyspecks with the point of a pen. . . .

A very intense week in Los Angeles followed, interviewing lawyers of whom I am putting on six more to handle the stupendous land acquisition program in California—over ten per cent of our national business with over 7,000 different properties; meeting with all the judges to consider the problems of handling the consequent volume of legal business; withdrawing an affidavit of prejudice on Judge Harrison upon condition that he grant a new trial in the Courtemanche case and transfer the case to another judge (which I did and which he did); drafting a press release to try to pin his ears down—although the reporters perverted it so that my ears were pinned back instead; and securing a number of names for the attorney general of those who might be candidates for the United States attorney's office. Another major errand was endeavoring to close the acquisition of the Santa Margarita Ranch,[7] the 123,000 acre condemnation case for which we had deposited $4,121,000 with the Flood and Baumgartner people,[8] claiming the proceeds in court. An unvalued clay deposit, for which we refused to pay and with which they refused to part, held up the deal. . . .

This is a hop, skip and a jump account, one of the most important incidences of which was getting home to you and Mother . . .

Affectionately,
[Unsigned]

---

28 February 1943

Two weeks have elapsed since I returned on the 15th from the West, both filled with the tension of an increasing and climactic personal knock-down-drag-out battle for position with Jim Rowe. I never leave town without getting shot at in one way or another by him, and this time with an unforgivable and unforgettable memorandum charging that at a

---

7. The Santa Margarita Ranch near San Diego was a large estate the Marine Corps had taken for use as a training base (Camp Pendleton). The owners were disputing the government's offer of compensation for unexploited mineral resources on the land.

8. The Flood and Baumgartner people were the owners of the Santa Margarita Ranch. Flood owned the southern part and Baumgartner owned the northern part of the ranch.

cocktail party I had told the newspaper correspondent Marquis Childs that the attorney general would "suppress" the Securities and Exchange Commission report on the Empire Ordnance Company . . . when it was received in the Department. . . . The attorney general's memorandum of January 26th, sending Rowe's memorandum to my office, [and] the fact that no presumptions of innocence arose in the attorney general's mind, showed how completely he was under the influence of Jim Rowe.

Indeed, when I called him from Los Angeles to negative most emphatically the scandalous charge, he simply said that no presumptions whatever had arisen in his mind, and he had been waiting to discuss the matter when I arrived. He allowed a week to go by after I reported in on the 15th, I think—deliberately, as a matter of keeping me on the anxious seat. I was not on the anxious seat, and I sent him a sharp memorandum on February 19th, denouncing the memorandum as slanderous and vicious. We conferred immediately thereafter and, like most weak men, [he is] influenced too easily by those around them. My strong attack on the matter brought him to his senses—particularly since Marquis Childs had explained to me over the telephone that Rowe's account of the whole incident was "perfectly cockeyed."

He started the conference by saying that he thought my memorandum a little intemperate, at which I denounced Jim Rowe's memorandum and included somewhat his own in still more intemperate language, explaining that I expected the whole matter to be cleared up. . . . I told the attorney general, quite frankly, that deliberate efforts had been made to alienate him and that these efforts, in my opinion, had completely succeeded, as evidenced by his memorandum of the 26th showing a complete lack of confidence. He half apologized for his memorandum before I left and promised an early conference with Rowe.

Another week went by. I had written a rather devastating answer to Rowe's memorandum but, at the attorney general's request, had not sent it, awaiting a conference. We held a conference a week later, on Friday the 26th. It was a knock-down-drag-out. All of Jim Rowe's pent-up personal spleen came boiling to the surface.

"If you think I'm going to remove that memorandum from the files, you are very much mistaken!" he said angrily, indicating that the attorney general had already talked to him about the unwisdom of putting such matters in memoranda for the files of the Department.

"Very well," I said, "Then here's one for you which will straighten your thinking out in fast time."

I handed him my memoranda of February 20th, mentioning first the reasons why no reasonable person could have said those things with which I had been charged, and secondly pointing out that if he was as jealous about the reputation of the Department as he indicated, this had not been clear when he sought to effect the settlement of the Savannah Shipyards case and, referring to Tommy Corcoran and his crowd, said he had to do something for them because they were "our friends."

When he read that he let out a roar of rage, asking the attorney general if he had read that last paragraph yet. (I had handed one copy to Jim and one copy to the attorney general.) Turning angrily to me, he [asked], "What case are you talking about?"

"The Savannah Shipyards case, of course," I replied.

"I never said any such thing," he denied, hotly.

"You said precisely that, and you said it at the attorney general's house at another cocktail party which he gave for you on May 24th.[1]

"I did not," he denied again.

"Then you were not sober enough to remember it," I replied. "The words made an indelible impression upon me because they were so shocking. Furthermore, I wrote them down afterwards so I know precisely what you said."

That set him back where he belonged. "Just add that memorandum to the other ones," I said, "and I will be entirely content to have the first memorandum in the records of the Department."

I can't remember the exact sequence of the angry conversation which followed. At one place about this time Jim remarked, "I ought to punch you right in the nose," and growing a bit elemental myself, I suggested that he proceed to do so, indicating that he wouldn't last long. Hate and anger and helplessness were all mixed up in his rather pathetic expression.

"I want to know what's going on here," he said—"This looks like an attempt to frame me. I only asked you to confer with those lawyers (Dempsey and Koplovitz, Tommy Corcoran's representatives), that's all."

"And I told you there was nothing to discuss, and to tell them that over the phone."

Jim raged on that they were right all along and that it was only my bull-headedness which insisted on trial of that case—that it ought to have been settled—that my stubbornness in the matter had cost the taxpayers of this country an extra $200,000. (The verdict was $1,285,000, whereas we could have settled it for about $1,100,000.)[2]

"That shows precisely whose side you were on all the time," I said to Rowe, and then turned to the attorney general.

"We brought no pressure on you to settle that case, did we, Norman?" asked the attorney general.

"Not after you knew the facts, Mr. Attorney General," I said. "I have always said, and I say now, that when I presented the facts adequately to you, you made the right decision, but I had an uneasy time up to then."

---

1. In fact the cocktail party for Jim Rowe at the attorney general's residence occurred on May 22; Littell's account of it, however, does appear in his diary entry for 24 May 1942.

2. *Congressional Record*, 91 (22 January 1945), pp. 424–26.

Jim said something about my having charged them both with being under the influence of Tommy Corcoran who "is my friend, although Norman doesn't happen to like him for some reason—and he is your friend, too, I thought," he said, looking at the attorney general.

"No, Jim," the attorney general replied, "Norman merely told us during the conference regarding the Savannah Shipyards case that our relationships with Tommy Corcoran were well known and that if we settled that case it would be another Sterling Products case. . . . He was right about that."

I explained to the attorney general that I had had two telephone conversations with Marquis Childs, both of which I had had my secretary take down, and that in the first one, Childs had called Jim's account "perfectly cockeyed" and in the second had denied any confirmatory statement to Rowe over the telephone to the effect that I had said the indictment would be dropped against Empire Ordnance, or "Suppressed." I said that "while I had no intention of being on the defensive about the matter at all, the attorney general must know that any such statement by any responsible official in the Department of Justice was wholly unreasonable, quite apart from any matter of personal loyalty to the attorney general. The Empire Ordnance case is just too big. It would be like saying the attorney general could suppress Mount Rainier in the state of Washington by throwing his coat over it.

Jim then threw a bombshell into the controversy by saying that he had talked with Purcell of the SEC and that Childs had called on Purcell and had reaffirmed the whole matter, saying that I had done a flip-flop on it, now denying that I had made the statement at [Oscar L.] Chapman's cocktail party on December 18th.

This was, to say the least, confusing and it floored the attorney general as well as me. I said I couldn't believe it, and the attorney general said there was nothing to do but call Childs and Purcell and see what the truth of the matter was. I agreed.

I called Childs right after lunch and, when I explained the new difficulty, he exclaimed, "By God, this is getting ridiculous." He then reaffirmed all of his statements to me and said that there was some animus in the whole matter which he could not put his finger on, with which I strongly concurred. These three conversations are . . . [an] interesting documentation of trivia of consequence, needlessly and wickedly commanding the attention of busy men in time of war. I have covered a lot of ground in my work, through many unhappy, strained and depressed days. It does seem as if Tommy has some friends at the SEC who are bound and determined to lay me low. Jim undoubtedly hoped that he had an issue over which he could get rid of me in the Department of Justice. His consuming hatred, springing largely from jealousy over the popularity which I enjoy with the United States attorneys, supposedly his men, in contrast to their bitter criticism of the conduct of his office, is perfectly transparent.

The solicitor general, Charles Fahy, has paced me through this incident and in his quiet way pronounces that I am "in a very strong position." I hope the incident will somewhat clarify my status with the attorney general and expose his weakness in following a man like Rowe who has done everything he could to insulate the Lands Division, the only conspicuously successful division in the Department, from the favorable consideration of the AG.

---

6 March 1943
4101 Lorcom Lane

Continuing the grand plot, or the tempest in the teapot: I felt that I had to call Marquis Childs to confirm or disaffirm Rowe's statement that Childs had called on Purcell, . . . and reaffirmed everything previously said and that I had done a "flip-flop."

Childs' reply was that "By God, this is getting ridiculous." He continued by saying that there must be "animus" in the situation, with which I fully concurred.

I, therefore, went to see the attorney general on Monday and showed him Childs' statement which my secretary had taken down on the telephone, saying that I fully agreed with Childs that there was "animus" in the situation, and that in my opinion Jim Rowe's statements in our conference demonstrated plenty of "animus." This, I hoped, would dispose of the matter conclusively.

He read the statement without being impressed, apparently, and said that he was going to call in Marquis Childs and Purcell. He pointed out that the conversation with Childs which he held in his hand in transcript form did not deal with my original statement, to which I replied that that was covered in two other conversations with Childs, the transcripts of which I handed him, remarking that they too were too long and I had not bothered him to read them.

He replied that they were pretty long to read, as if irritated with the whole matter. I felt like saying, "You can damn well read them; you raised the issue." But for the time being I held fire.

He again defended Jim Rowe's action in sending him the memorandum and I again stated unequivocally that filling the files of the Department with gossipy memoranda was an immature and unwise thing to do.

"Since Childs and I had the original conversation about which all this mess has been stirred up, it seems to me it would be in order for me to bring Childs in here and you can interrogate us both and satisfy yourself," I said.

"No," he said angrily, "I will bring Childs and Purcell in here and then I will send for you and Jim after I have first talked with Childs and Purcell."

I thereupon walked out.

On Thursday, March 4th, I received notice that the attorney general would meet with Purcell and Childs at 5:00 and would call for me and Rowe shortly thereafter. In the meantime, I had sent Childs a copy of the transcripts of our conversations, which I had had taken down on the theory that if the loose talking was his, I would promptly and effectively pin it down to concrete statements. I went into the conference at about 5:35, and remarked that I presumed that by this time the attorney general was satisfied that I had never made the statements as charged, to the effect that an indictment would be "suppressed" in the Department of Justice if the Empire Ordnance investigation by the SEC was reported to Justice.

The attorney general threw across the desk to me a memorandum of [Sumner] Welles to Purcell of the SEC. At first glance, I noticed that the now famous memorandum charging that Childs had called Welles and reported my conversation with him to the effect that the indictment would be "suppressed" was dated January 23rd, and referred to a conversation with Childs the preceding day. Without reading further, I said: "Why, this is dated January 23rd, reporting a conversation on the preceding day, whereas the conversation between Childs and me was held at Chapman's house on December 18th—almost a month before." Obviously, Childs could not have called Welles immediately, and furthermore, a month's action and reaction in the memory was at work.

Childs repudiated the statement in the last line of the memorandum and referred to his conversation with me, saying that we both agreed that a lot of people would be hurt and get hit and it would be complicated to bring.

"If you were talking about bringing an indictment in the Department of Justice," I said, "I had no such understanding with you. I never discussed the bringing of an indictment. It was never for one moment in my mind," and, turning to the attorney general, I said, "Let me say once more, and I hope for the last time—for the benefit of these two gentlemen, Mr. Purcell and Mr. Childs, who have not heard me before—that I have never for one moment thought, let alone said, that this Department would not seek an indictment in this or any other case. All other factors aside, it would be just as ridiculous as saying that you could suppress Mount Rainier in the State of Washington. You are not big enough to suppress it and no attorney general would be big enough to suppress a case of this sort. It just doesn't make sense that any man with a modicum of judgment would have made such a statement."

I picked up the memoranda again, while the attorney general actually broke a smile at my reference to Mount Rainier. Jim Rowe said nothing. He had obviously been instructed to keep his mouth shut for fear we would get into another cat-and-dog fight.

I neglected to say as to my conference with the attorney general last

Monday that he had asked me not to bring up in the conference with Purcell and Childs the matter of the memorandum I had written to Rowe, charging Rowe with being under the influence of Tommy Corcoran and seeking to do something for his "friends." No doubt this had something to do with his instructions to Rowe to say nothing, for he said not a single word during the whole interview when the five of us were present.

I could not resist, however, from reconstructing the crime exactly as I conceived of it, and I said: "It is quite obvious to me that someone over at the SEC had a bad case of nerves and is chasing shadows. I don't believe Mr. Childs said anything like he is reported to have said in this memorandum, and I do believe that fears and fancies were exaggerated. When we were seeking information from the SEC in regard to the Savannah Shipyards case, before we tried the case on July 6, 1942, I could not get information even though the White House had ordered all information in regard to the Savannah Shipyards case to be given to me. Do you remember that, Mr. Purcell? We had several conversations about it."

"Yes, I remember," Purcell said. "I wasn't going to bring that matter up, but since you mention it, that is the case."

"I not only talked to you but I had to go to New York twice to break open the situation in your office up there and get what information you had about the Savannah Shipyards case, and in one of the last conferences which one of my attorneys—Funkhouser—attended, one of your men said in the conference that the reason we were not getting the information was because men in the SEC were afraid that the information would be given to Tommy Corcoran through the Department of Justice." Purcell nodded his assent. It was a pretty deadly shot at the attorney general, but I couldn't help it. It was true, with one possible reservation: I never could be sure whether it was the influence of Tommy Corcoran in the SEC which prevented us from getting the information, or whether the information was withheld for the reason assigned, that they feared it would reach Tommy Corcoran. I never encountered such a curious and shadowy maze of influence, and it gives me a new concept of the power which that fellow must have had.

"It is that kind of a background which produced this memorandum from Welles to Purcell, in my opinion," I said. "And I think it is just a case of nerves over there in the SEC."

It was perfectly evident that the whole matter was completely washed up after that interview in Biddle's office. I regretted not putting the memorandum of January 23rd from Welles into my pocket as a keepsake until the entire matter was cleared up, but Purcell pocketed it. He also came over and shook hands in a manner which indicated that in his mind I was in the clear, although he refused to so state in the open meeting.

Childs walked out of the anteroom at the same time I did and I asked him to drop in for a minute, which he did. "I warned the attorney general when he came in here," Childs said, "that he must look out for the Tommy Corcoran influence and keep clear, but he only replied that Tommy Corcoran was a loyal friend of his."

It was Childs, I learned yesterday, who had written an article saying that Tommy Corcoran had secured the Savannah Shipyards contract for the Cohen crowd through his influence on the Maritime Commission, so at least he is apparently in the opposition camp as far as the famous Irishman is concerned.

Childs also remarked, as we stood in my office and talked for a few moments, where I found Katherine waiting for me (it being after 6:00 by this time), that Steve Early at the White House had come to hate Jim Rowe, largely because of the Tommy Corcoran influence there, and that they were not on speaking terms when Jim left the White House where he was formerly secretary to the President. (I remember the President's tactful announcement that he didn't need so many assistants. Notwithstanding that, he has just appointed another one today to take Jim Rowe's place.) I have apparently succeeded to Steve Early's position as far as relations with Jim Rowe are concerned because, "he is not speaking." I passed him on the street yesterday and caught only a flash of rather grim hatred. He is fairly well pinned to the wall with that memorandum I sent and naturally is not happy about it.

Yesterday, Friday, March 5th, I applied for an interview with the attorney general and got it as soon as he came back from the Hill at 12:30. "This matter is all washed up, Norman," he said, . . . He said this immediately upon my coming into the office, apparently as if he wished to see me in order to say that.

"No one could reach any other conclusion after listening to that final interview," I said. "I presume you will send through a memorandum saying that in order to clear the record," I added.

"Oh, no," he said rather impatiently. "There have been too many memoranda in this situation now. It has taken too much time."

"I quite agree," I said, "and it all illustrates how wasteful it is to start these things in memoranda form, but it ought to be cleared up since it was so started."

"Jim Rowe remarked after the others went out yesterday that he was satisfied that 'Norman is telling the truth,' and that ought to end it."

A great concession! The great Jim Rowe is conceding at last that I am telling the truth!

"He's tough, you know," the attorney general said, shaking his head, as if in admiration of the great Jim's tough qualities. I felt like laughing in his face. To think how completely fooled that man is as to the character of Jim Rowe. He even gives a virtue to him by reason of his handling this situation with me, which was as badly and ineptly handled as it possibly could have been. I so stated, and the attorney general immediately began to defend Jim Rowe again, pointing out the severity of the memorandum from Welles about "suppressing" the incident of Empire Ordnance.

"Of course, he should have brought it to your attention," I said. "I would too, but orally, as a matter of information to be cleared up, if it could be cleared up, by discussion with your colleagues involved, and not by spreading libelous memoranda around the Department for secretaries and heavens knows who to see."

But it was hopeless. He is a stout and staunch defender of Jim Rowe and he deserves to go down with him if he has no more discernment than that.

"I presume then that Jim will write me a memorandum stating what you have said and clarifying the whole matter, or withdrawing his memorandum," I said.

"I think we have had too many memoranda," the attorney general said, "but you can speak to him about it if you wish, or I will when we are next discussing it." There was some impatience in his attitude as if I were pressing the matter too damned far. That is a natural feeling after it has blown up in his face, I presume, but it is equally natural for me to get the record straight, as I shall surely do before the incident is considered closed. . . .

---

7 April 1943
4101 Lorcom Lane

. . . Jim Rowe's last onslaught having been completely frustrated, his spleen boiled over again when I sent him a sharp memorandum on March 25th, protesting [his] failure to terminate certain of my staff in response to a $250,000 budget cut for the remainder of this year (to July 1, 1943). He sent back a memorandum of March 26th in which all the sheer egotism of a little man stood exposed. I replied at last, when I found the time, on April 3rd, in a memorandum which told him what many people in Washington have long wished to say. . . . I sent a set of the memoranda to the attorney general marked "personal" under a covering memorandum. . . .

It is a shame to take time for such matters, but I long ago learned by experience at sea and in a logging camp that there is no way to deal with a human rat except to stamp on him. A man of such despicable character that he will drop a monkey wrench on your head "by accident" cannot be dealt with politely. He must be invited out on deck or made to feel that at any moment you will take him on deck. Jim Rowe is that kind of character, and I had no alternative but to write my memorandum of April 3rd. Thus far, I can only speculate as to the results because there has been nothing but silence from upstairs, except that today all of my recommendations for terminations and one for a raise came down simultaneously—all granted. The attorney general might for a change have tipped off Rowe for keeping personal issues alive. At least, and at last, I have confirmed in the record the conclusions of the last encounter in which Rowe came off very badly. . . .

A conflict between the Navy Department over a long term contract with Standard Oil Company[1] as to the extraction of oil from Elk Hills,[2] of Teapot Dome fame,[3] and the undersecretary of the interior [Abe Fortas] who protests the proposed contract, was referred by the President to the attorney general to determine which was right, and the attorney general referred it to me.[4] A very hot subject indeed, on which I will get the best technical advice I can get from my attorneys in Los Angeles working on the Kettleman Hills case; an expert employed by them; and [William J.] Kemnitzer, an oil expert employed by BEW, who was a member of Morris L. Cooke's commission which settled the Mexican oil controversy.[5] Kemnitzer is about to leave for Bolivia on an oil mission for BEW, but I will get two or three days of his time to reinforce our advice to the President. I am a little afraid that Admiral [Harry A.] Stuart, in charge of

---

1. The Navy signed the contract with Standard Oil Company of California 18 November 1942. Under the terms of the contract Standard could take a maximum of 27.5 million barrels of oil, worth about $30 million, from the 8,500 acres of the Reserve it leased during the life of the contract. Over the life of the contract, the Navy would receive 64 percent of the oil and Standard would get 36 percent. But during the first five years of the contract, Standard would get all the oil as compensation for its investment in drilling wells and laying pipelines. After the first five years, Standard would only have to pay the Navy from the proceeds of one-third of its 36 percent of the oil. See *New York Times*, 12 June 1943, p. 6, and 14 June 1943, p. 34.

2. The Elk Hills Naval Petroleum Reserve was one of three tracts of government-owned oil-bearing lands set aside by Congress in 1909 as naval petroleum reserves. Naval Petroleum Reserve No. 1 was at Elk Hills, California, No. 2 was at Buena Vista, California, and No. 3 was at Teapot Dome, Wyoming. The oil in them was intended as a sort of insurance policy to provide a supply of oil for the Navy in the event of a future emergency.

3. This is a reference to the Teapot Dome scandal of the 1920s, which arose when President Harding transferred the naval oil reserves from the Navy to the Interior Department. Secretary of Interior Albert Fall then, secretly and without competitive bidding, leased Reserve No. 3 (Teapot Dome) to Harry F. Sinclair's Mammoth Oil Company and Reserve No. 1 (Elk Hills) to Edward F. Doheny's Pan-American Company; and they proceeded to sell the oil to the Continental Trading Company, Ltd. of Canada. In return Sinclair gave Fall some $260,000 in Liberty Bonds and Doheny "lent" Fall $100,000 without interest or security. Both Secretary of Navy Edwin Denby and Fall were forced out of office as a result.

4. President Roosevelt asked the Justice Department to review the contract 26 March 1943.

5. The Mexican oil controversy arose in 1938, when Mexico expropriated almost the entire foreign-owned oil industry, including properties of American oil companies. Cordell Hull and Henry Morgenthau led a concerted attack on the Mexican economy in an effort to force the Mexicans to reverse their decision, but U.S. Ambassador to Mexico Josephus Daniels resisted their efforts and won the support of President Roosevelt. As a result, the conflict was settled amicably by negotiations in 1941.

the petroleum reserves for the Navy, is a naive fellow, far too slow for these fast and sharp-shooting oil men.

Wednesday, 14 April 1943

In reference to the contract between the Standard Oil Company of California and the Navy Department in regard to the alleged "conservation" of oil in Elk Hills Naval Reserve, . . . a study of the legal aspects of this agreement under the law providing for a naval reserve[1] revealed the contract to be, in my opinion, wholly opposed to the public interest. The subtle compulsions which operate in every contract are, in this instance, all in favor of the Standard Oil Company of California, although the contract on its face purports to conserve the oil in the ground.

Upon reaching these conclusions, a delicate problem was presented in that the secretary of the Navy had already signed the agreement on behalf of the United States government, and the signature of the President had also been affixed, in entire good faith and upon recommendations of the Navy person in charge of this reserve, Admiral Stuart, who was one of those who earned [a] reputation for high integrity during the time of the Teapot Dome scandal. As the contract had actually been submitted by the Navy Department to the Appropriations Committee where it is pending before the Naval Subcommittee on a request for an appropriation of approximately $2,000,000 to put the contract into effect and close the purchase of the surface rights of the Standard Oil Company and acquire its equipment, a legal possibility of the agreement going into effect upon action by the committee presented a very real danger. The first condition to putting the contract into effect had already been satisfied, namely, approval by the President on recommendation by the Navy Department. [As] I read the law, there remained only the necessary final commitment of the funds without which, under the language of the act, the contract could not go into effect.

It seemed that we could not risk waiting the additional days necessary to reduce to final form and impregnable clarity the numerous reasons why this contract is opposed to the public interest and, at the same time, I did not wish the matter to become a public football in the legislative branch of the government, where enemies of opposite political faiths could use it

---

1. The Naval Petroleum Reserve Act of 1938 (Public Law 786), approved 30 June 1938, directed the secretary of the Navy to conserve and develop naval petroleum and other fuel reserves. It authorized him to contract with the owners and lessees of land within and adjoining the naval petroleum reserves for that purpose. The 1938 Act also required that all such contracts be approved by the President and reported to Congress. If the secretary of the Navy could not make a satisfactory contract, he could purchase or condemn the lands outright.

if men of ability went behind Admiral Stuart's rather naive defense of the matter.

In the absence of the attorney general, I discussed the matter with Charles Fahy, acting attorney general, who agreed that we were not yet prepared to write memoranda, and that the matter should be handled as delicately as possible by withdrawing, as I suggested, the submission of the contract by the Navy Department to the Appropriations Committee. Someone would have to request that, and do it quickly. I therefore called McIntyre at the White House, who gave me an immediate appointment. [He] quickly perceived the delicacy of the situation, but stated that it was too much responsibility for him to assume. He made an appointment for me with Jim Byrnes, as McIntyre said, "the Assistant President."

I outlined the situation briefly to Mr. Byrnes, with the suggestion that he have Secretary Knox simply withdraw the contract from the Appropriations Committee on the grounds that he may wish to submit additional information later, making no comments on the merits, thereby giving the Department of Justice additional time in which to study the entire matter carefully, while the instrument was withdrawn from the danger of approval by the Appropriations Committee. Whether this is an actual danger or not, I do not know, but it was definitely a legal possibility because the committee was to act on the Navy's request for an appropriation about April 10th, as Admiral Stuart had remarked to me.

I left Mr. Byrnes' office at 12:40, and after a talk with Ben Cohen, returned to my office where a call from Mr. Byrnes' secretary at 1:50 advised that Mr. Byrnes had reached Secretary Knox and that Secretary Knox was immediately withdrawing the contract from the Appropriations Committee.

---

18 April 1943
4101 Lorcom Lane

Dearest Katherine Mather:

This week opened with Thomas Jefferson and closed with Thomas Jefferson and the measles, as far as you were concerned. The monument to that brilliant mind and rare spirit has been in the slow process of construction for the last three years on one side of the Tidal Basin, where you will most surely find it when you grow up, unless Hitler succeeds in bombing Washington and happens to destroy this symbol of our eternal enmity towards tyranny and of our inherent and determined predilection for exploring further the myriad channels of human freedom flowing through the endless domain of "life, liberty, and the pursuit of happiness."

On such occasions as the dedication of the Jefferson Memorial appear the minor compensations to being a little "brass hat" in Washington, because we had excellent seats—five of them. As Ralph Lemkin had not yet seen the President at close range, we gave him two. . . . Several thousand more chairs were spread up the steps of the Memorial to where the towering figure of Jefferson looked down on the whole ceremony.

I stopped to talk with Claude Pepper, senator from Florida, and Edward G. Robinson and Mrs. [Gladys] Robinson, who were with him and Mrs. [Irene] Pepper. Mrs. Pepper congratulated Mr. Robinson on the presentation by the Jews the preceding evening of a profoundly impressive pageant on behalf of the Jews, entitled "We Shall Never Die." Robinson had read a good bit of the script and Paul Muni had read the remaining part in one of the most dramatic scenes of groups symbolizing the dead. He came onto the stage and reported briefly into the microphone their fate in Europe—machine-gunned, packed into freight cars, and shipped like cattle until they died, prepared for a brothel for German soldiers, only to take poison as a last Jewish rite before being removed to barracks. . . .

The President's car arrived behind the speaker's stand covered with Secret Service men and the band played "Hail to the Chief" as he came up the ramp with the inevitable Pa Watson. The crowd cheered. I explained to Norman, Jr., and Sissie[1] that the President stood with a black cape around his shoulders and Mrs. Roosevelt was a few paces away. Ralph's impressions were the best as he had not seen the President before. He spoke later of the rare spiritual quality in the President's fine features, and in those of Mrs. Roosevelt, too.

"How lucky you are in this country to have two people of such unmistakable capacity for spiritual leadership in the nation. How disastrous it would be for the world if you happened to have now a fat-bellied, round-faced man with the concepts of big business."

I had not seen the President, personally, for some time, not since before the outbreak of war. The matters upon which I occasionally saw him before at his motion or mine—usually mine— were rendered trivial by the momentous events following December 7, 1941, and I have not felt at liberty to press in upon his time, although I probably ought to have done so in regard to the Hawaiian situation. He has aged and his face is grayer and more lined. The fine qualities and the power are there, however, with unabated vitality which seems to flow from an inexhaustible source. I agree with what Ralph says about both Mr. and Mrs. Roosevelt, whose faces as he said, "stood out so conspicuously in the entire crowd."

---

1. "Sissie" Haymaker was one of Katherine Mather's playmates.

The ceremonies were of the best for that sort of function. A short prayer; then the President's speech, about fifteen minutes long; another prayer; and the occasion was over. . . . The President's speech, comparing the time confronted by Jefferson and the present battle with tyranny, was vivid and accurate, and concluded effectively with the President touching on eternal enmity to tyranny. . . .

Affectionately,
Father [signed]

---

19 April 1943
4101 Lorcom Lane

This has been a very exciting day in which I have pushed aside a canebrake of detail in order to get into clear, open space for work on the Navy contract with the Standard Oil Company of California for the production of oil in Naval Reserve No. 1 at Elk Hills. I am afraid poor old Admiral Stuart must be very much on the anxious seat. My general assistant, [J. Edward] Williams, reported that Buettner, in the Judge Advocate General's Office in the Navy, . . . telephoned [him] to ask what our position would be on the Elk Hills contract inasmuch as Admiral Stuart had to testify before the Naval Appropriations [Sub]committee this week. That was a "whizzer" because the contract has been withdrawn from the Naval Appropriations Committee for further consideration by the Navy Department at express orders of Secretary Knox.

I telephoned Adlai E. Stevenson, special assistant to the secretary of the Navy, to make sure of the matter, and he confirmed that the contract had been withdrawn, but he stated that the secretary himself would be asked about it when he appeared before the Committee in support of the Navy's request for 1944 appropriations and that he, Stevenson, had prepared a written statement to the effect that the contract had been withdrawn by the Navy Department temporarily; the Department of Justice was giving study to it; and the Navy might wish to re-submit it.

He stated further that Congressman [Harry R.] Sheppard of California, chairman of the committee, was exceedingly curious about the contract. [He] had gone to California and made a partial investigation himself, and would doubtless wish to know all about it. Stevenson would send me the chronological statement of the progress of the contract through the Navy Department, tomorrow, he said, as he had promised over the telephone last week—gratuitously. It was at that time, in my first conversation with him, when he hastened to say that he thought the contract had been signed by the President before it had been signed by Secretary Knox, and that he did not know how such a contract could get through the President's office without being reviewed by the Department of Justice—he thought they "always referred to Justice," etc., etc. How they all run for cover and lay it on the Chief when there is a chance! The clear fact remains that Stevenson's memorandum defending the contract is in the file.

Study of the contract reveals it to be, in my opinion, a shrewd and skillfully drafted instrument, diabolically so. For Standard of California, it is "heads I win and tails you lose." Increased production of about 3,000 barrels per day raising the daily production to 15,000 barrels per day will hasten the decline of the field as far as present wells are concerned, for they are already sixty per cent water, according to production tables I have been examining today. The field is just one jump ahead of the Kern River field, across the valley, which is already 85.8 per cent water during the first six months of 1940 and 86.6 per cent water during the last six months of 1940. Undoubtedly, the water production has greatly increased in 1942 and 1943.

Costs are correspondingly high in the Kern River field until the wells are actually operating at a loss (crude petroleum, reported by United States Tariff Commission, page 66). From twelve to thirteen cents a barrel was lost from 1939 to 1941 in the Kern River field. This field was brought [in] in 1901, and the Elk Hills field was brought in in 1919. Elk Hills is well on the way towards a downward course in increased water production and increased costs, until by the end of the five years of accelerated production under the contract, the existing wells will be has-beens, operating at a loss.

In the meantime, the Navy Department pays all costs of new wells which are the only means of offsetting this steadily increasing exhaustion of existing wells. The contract very carefully arranges that if the Navy is unable to pay the costs from oil produced in Elk Hills Reserve No. 1, it can pay by delivering to Standard Oil from Elk Hills No. 2, or it may pay cash if it so desired.

The most astonishing thing learned today is that notwithstanding the failure of the Appropriations Committee to appropriate the necessary consideration—approximately $2,000,000 to pay Standard for the surface rights and equipment in the field as provided by this contract—the contract has nevertheless been put into effect and actual production is in full force up to the 15,000 barrels per day. Never before have I known any commercial company of any importance to go into a deal without payment of the consideration, particularly where there were so many hazards to the payment as there are in this case. Nothing is more uncertain than the action of Congress in appropriating funds. The precipitate eagerness of the Standard Oil Company of California to get going on this deal is, itself, an exceedingly suspicious fact, although undoubtedly it is all done under the general banner of the war effort and to get into full force and effect this remarkable arrangement for the "conservation" of Elk Hills oil. Examination of the tables of production (California Oil Fields, Summary of Operations, June 1941) shows that the oil in Elk Hills is about two per cent of the daily production in California. It is impossible for this to be indispensable to the war effort since a vastly greater amount of oil is represented by "shut-in" production from other fields. In the interests of Navy conservation, the two per cent, if deemed so essential to the war effort, could easily be secured by opening up the other shut-in fields. . . .

23 April 1943
Attorney General Staff Conference

There were present the attorney general, Ugo Carusi, Jim Rowe, Tom Quinn, a representative of Mr. Hoover, Jim Bennett, M. E. Gilfond, Oscar Cox, Charles Fahy, Sam Clark, [a representative] for Tom Clark, Antitrust [Division], Frank Shea, and Norman M. Littell.

The attorney general precipitated a discussion of the deferment problem, stating that, in his opinion, older men past the draft age, should not be released for commissions as a general policy as they are of more value here. The pros and cons and the difficulties of the Deferment Committee in facing this and other related problems were discussed by Mr. Fahy, chairman of the Deferment Committee.

The matter of commissions seemed to resolve itself into what each assistant attorney general or head of a bureau thought in respect to the individual applying for release from the Department and, in the end, I felt constrained to ask, in view of the attorney general's original statement, what policy he was now settling on.

"That's exactly what we have been discussing for an hour," he replied in a rather snappy manner, as usual. I reminded him of his original statement of policy toward older men, pointing out that we had departed from that considerably in discussion; that one member of the Deferment Committee might favor releasing all men who wished to go, as a matter of his own individual conviction; and other members might not. I personally felt that a man applying for a commission should be permitted to go and that my organization ought, if possible, to absorb his loss rather than frustrate the individual desires for military service. It seemed to shake down to leaving the matter, nevertheless, to the individual judgment of the bureau head.

The attorney general asked Jim Bennett, director of Prisons, how he was getting on with his conscientious objectors, and Jim replied that they were still being subjected to forced feeding by tubes. Curiously enough, a very substantial lot of them, as Jim reported at a previous meeting, are composed of Phi Beta Kappas. Jim also reported that great pressure was being brought to bear against this wasteful and inhuman treatment, and arguments were advanced for more constructive use of this manpower. The attorney general urged Jim to enter into some sort of an agreement with them—what kind of an agreement was not quite clear, but in order to "get rid of the problem," as the attorney general put it. Jim very properly replied that those concerned with the manpower problem felt that they could not send boys to Africa to their death, by drafting them, and leave behind to a comfortable existence these men suffering from conscientious scruples. The conscientious objectors are 12,000 strong and might be much more numerous unless a firm hand is maintained.

Of the 12,000 conscientious objectors in the country, approximately 6,000 are in conscientious objector camps doing special work. These were so classified by the various draft boards. Jim Bennett told me later that [we have] approximately 1,200 in the penitentiaries consisting of about 500 Jehovah's Witnesses who are denied a classification as ministers of the gospel, . . . and some 600 "intellectuals" who have convictions against war, unidentified with religious attitudes. Two of these, . . . are on hunger strikes and have been subjected to forced feedings since February 13, while others go on occasional hunger strikes or fasts, apparently until they get too hungry and then they eat again. These are permitted to operate in this margin of diminishing return, from one side of it to another, without interference.

The most vicious group is that sometimes called "Ishmaelites" or "Moslems" who think they are the lost tribe of Israel. They are Negroes with a conviction that the way to prevent war is to kill people in authority, as Jim says, "like chairmen of draft boards and like me." There are not over 100 of these.

Only those men sentenced for violations of the draft act reach the prisons and Bennett has authority to enter into agreements with them for their release [only] if they will engage in "work of national importance." It was the working out of some such agreement that the attorney general was urging upon Bennett and it appears that these will now be parolled if some such understanding is established. The two serious hunger strikers and many others will agree to go to hospitals as attendants providing a definite agreement is reached "in writing," and the question was whether the prison authorities should be forced into such a stipulation. There is usually no bargaining with prisoners—just simply a parole on terms.

The subject of jurisdiction over crimes committed by soldiers was also discussed, as an officer in Alabama and a private in some other state were held by civil authorities for committing rape. In one New York case, the civil authorities willingly surrendered a soldier similarly charged because his bombing squadron was about to leave for the front and, as the attorney general said, that should be the attitude taken by civil authorities, particularly since the crime is not barred by the statute of limitations, if they wished to bring action after the war. The matter of jurisdiction is finding its way into the courts.

Aside from the above subjects, each member of the staff passed without offering any matter for discussion, including myself.

NML

---

24 May 1943
4101 Lorcom Lane

My Dearest Katherine Mather:

The last few weeks have gone by in a welter of personal and international events, which sometimes seemed all mingled together.

The Tunisian front has collapsed, with mass surrenders of Nazi and Italian soldiers, about 175,000 strong; an impending summer offensive against the Russians is thus far thwarted; and Churchill is here again. . . .

My mind was completely absorbed, and even bled white, by day and night work on the Elk Hills contract between the Navy and the Standard Oil Company of California, a document which unfolds in its subtlety the more one works upon it. . . .

On May 5th, I went to Chicago to meet with the American Institute of Real Estate Appraisers in open discussion of many national appraisal problems on the real estate front.

[I had] a short interview with the Vice President just before I caught the train in the evening. Because I frequently discuss matters of major importance with him—or so they seem in my realm—and had not seen him for some time, I asked for an appointment and quickly got it. He was, however, absorbed in the higher levels of interest in Western Hemisphere affairs. [He had] just returned from a great trip through South America where he was magnificently received with great popular enthusiasm.[1] The papers here carefully played it down, however. Wallace, the visionary, is not to be advanced politically if they can help it. News of this visit appeared on the sixth page in the local papers, although one of the greatest receptions in the history of South America was accorded him.

I told him I was disappointed in his press here and was amazed to have

---

1. Wallace left Washington, D.C. 16 March and returned 26 April 1943. The trip was a great success. Wallace was received with great enthusiasm, especially in Chile, where he addressed large crowds in Spanish.

him reply that he understood the press had been very good in this country. I wonder who his advisers are on that subject. . . .

We had dinner on May 12th for Admiral Bill Glassford and Doddie Glassford. Bill made such a distinguished record at Dakar in Africa in reconciling the English, French and American interests that the State Department is sending him there as American minister to West Africa, and Doddie is in her seventh heaven because there is a prospect of her going, too. . . .

Bill Glassford gave a fascinating account of his months at Dakar, having arrived there about one month after the landing of our troops at Casablanca on November 7th. . . .

Glassford tells how Churchill met Governor Boisson, governor of West Africa, after Churchill had left the north coast of Africa and was stopping en route to England.

"I tried to pay a call on you," said Churchill, referring to the English attack on Dakar (I believe in September 1940) when the English were repulsed and Dakar did not capitulate, "but I did not receive a very hospitable reception."

"You doubted my hospitality, Mr. Prime Minister," replied Boisson, "but I doubted your cordiality."

There was also a most interesting fragment in regard to Churchill's conversation with Roosevelt at Casablanca, when General [Charles] De Gaulle failed to appear on Roosevelt's inviting him to come to the conference in Casablanca.[2] The Free French under De Gaulle felt that we had not given them sufficient recognition. In any event, De Gaulle refused to come. The President turned to Churchill and said, "Whose payroll is he on anyway?"

When Churchill advised the President that De Gaulle was on the English payroll, the President replied: "No come, no pay! How about it?"

Churchill readily assented and De Gaulle was clearly so advised. He came within twenty-four hours. Even on high levels, payrolls do count.

During the dinner, Anna [Boettiger] had to answer the telephone for a call from her mother in New York, and she came back laughing.

"Mother wanted to know if I knew yet when Churchill was going to leave."[3]

2. The Casablanca conference, between President Roosevelt and Prime Minister Churchill and their respective military staffs, was held 14–23 January 1943, in Casablanca, Morocco. Its purpose was to review the war situation and make plans for future operations in all theaters. After the conference, Roosevelt announced the decision to impose "unconditional surrender" on the Axis powers.

3. Churchill was in Washington, D.C. for talks with President Roosevelt to discuss military operations following the capture of North Africa. He arrived in the United States 11 May and departed 26 May 1943. It was his third wartime visit to the United States.

"Could you tell her?" I asked.

"Yes. I told her in two weeks, and she said, 'Oh, God!' "

"Why, is it that bad?" I asked.

"You have no idea how he wrecks the household," Anna replied. "His staying there just disrupts everything." . . .

As a matter of possible assistance to the Jewish refugee problem, Katherine . . . arranged a stag dinner at our house [on the evening of May 21st] so that several Jewish leaders—Ben Cohen, Mr. [Edmund I.] Kaufmann, and a judge from Pennsylvania—could meet Admiral Glassford. Congressman [Louis C.] Rabaut of Michigan and Estes Kefauver and Ralph Lemkin were also there.

In driving out to our house with Admiral Bill Glassford and Congressmen Kefauver and Rabaut, the admiral told a priceless story of his conference with the President scheduled for 12:15 on Wednesday, May 19th. The recently unhorsed politico, Ed Flynn, formerly chairman of the Democratic Party after Jim Farley resigned, had preceded Bill into the President's office and had consumed almost all of Bill's assigned fifteen minutes. The time went by until only five minutes were left with Glassford still waiting, and then Flynn came out and Glassford went in.

Hardly had the President and Glassford commenced talking when at 12:30 a secretary came in, opened a door in the President's desk, produced a radio and turned it on. It was time for Churchill to deliver his now famous address before the House and Senate in a joint meeting.[4]

"If you're not in a hurry, Admiral, perhaps you would like to stay and hear Churchill," the President said.

Of course the admiral was in no such hurry!

And so it came about that . . . Bill Glassford was sitting alone with the President, listening to Churchill in the President's office. His account of the incident was uproarious, although I could see he was holding back some comments as a matter of discretion.

"Great old fellow, Winnie, don't you think?" the President said once or twice after a particularly good passage. And then he would signify disapproval. "He didn't do what I told him to do— I gave him just the material for that point but he didn't use it," the President would exclaim, as he passed one portion or another of the address. And then again, he would say, "There—that's fine! That's just what I told him to say." This lasted a full fifty minutes.

Unfortunately, the mystery will always remain as to just what portions of the address these remarks applied to. . . . Perhaps I can get Bill Glassford in a corner before he leaves for Dakar and pin this information down a little more closely. In any event, it was a highly successful interview—one in

---

4. Churchill addressed the Joint Session of Congress 20 May 1943.

which I know the President was studying his man all the time having never before exchanged words with Glassford. I did learn from Drew Pearson later in the evening that the President himself had seen Glassford's report on West Africa and, largely on the basis of its excellence, considered him appropriate for the position of minister to West Africa—also, of course, on the basis of achievements since December 1941. . . .

Affectionately,
Daddy [signed]

Tuesday, 25 May 1943
Attorney General Staff Meeting

. . . The attorney general said, guiltily, that he thought we should hear from J. Edgar Hoover on the subject of Stalin's dissolution of the Comintern and its probable effect. Hoover replied, succinctly, that his own policy was one of "watchful waiting, with emphasis on the watching." He did observe that the whole incident had exposed the fact that the American party affiliated with the Comintern had been the espionage agent of Soviet Russia in this country.

Someone reported that Dies had said he would dissolve the Dies Committee, but the statement was considered equivocal and we shall have to wait and see. Theoretically, with dissolution of the Comintern he would be out of business. . . .

---

13 June 1943
4101 Lorcom Lane

. . . [I have spent every] possible moment on the elusive Elk Hills contract, between Standard and Navy, subject to several interruptions such as a one-day trip to New York on June 2, in an effort to find additional lawyers for a hot spot in Newark, New Jersey. [My] appointments [there] must dodge the Hague machine[1] in order that millions of dollars worth of condemnation work may be as clean as a hound's tooth. Then there were hearings before the House and Senate Judiciary Committees on my Bill to Expedite Payment to Property Owners; the bill is roughly and thoroughly opposed by the powerful land lobby, headed by the title companies. . . .

---

1. The Hague machine was the Democratic political organization of Frank Hague, the boss of Jersey City, New Jersey.

With my mind bled white again on Elk Hills, I went to Asheville, North Carolina, for the first conference of the United States attorneys on Wednesday evening, June 9th. [I left] behind the first completed draft of the Elk Hills report with the understanding that, after proofreading and correction by two assistants, it would be given to the attorney general. [On] my return . . . I could revise and correct it as much as desired. However, steam was up in Congress on this subject—more so than I thought, although the pot has been boiling vigorously in recent days— and many inquiries from the press have necessarily been turned down because I could make no comment.

Senator [William] Langer attacked the administration, although he had been a good friend—on Friday, June 11th, in the Senate—for the execution of this contract with the Standard Oil Company of California. [He laid] it largely on the Navy, but also to the signing of the President.[2] Katherine telephoned me in Asheville to let me know. Credit was claimed for having stopped the deal in Congress. [I] at once called Mr. Justice Byrnes in the White House from Asheville to suggest the stratagem of having him announce that the contract had been withdrawn at the suggestion of the White House. . . . I expressed my regret at having taken so much time on the agreement—time which I needed for analysis of fuel oil prices and the gathering and assimilation of a lot of data and law. When Mr. Byrnes asked what conclusions I had reached, I told him that in my opinion the contract was illegal and invalid and should be set aside for a number of reasons which would take too long to explain over the telephone. He asked if I could have a copy sent over to him to consider so that he could advise "the Chief" before he left Washington in the near future.

I, thereafter, immediately phoned the Department, but being unable to get hold of the attorney general, who was on the Hill, instructed Williams to send a copy of the report, with the exhibits, to Mr. Byrnes. Not until about 2:00 was I able to reach the attorney general and explain what I had done. I expressed regret at having been unable to reach him. He was obviously a little irritated that I had given a copy of the report to Mr. Byrnes, as I knew he would be.

"It's a little unusual, isn't it, Norman," he said, "to have given the report out before I had a chance to see it?" (I had also had the original sent to him the same morning at 10:00 upon completion of the proofreading, Mr. Williams having signed it for me.)

"Quite, Mr. Attorney General," I replied, "but these were unusual circumstances. Mr. Byrnes asked me for the report and, of course, I could not refuse to send it to him."

Biddle was in the embarrassing position of being really unable to object. How awkward it would be [for him to] say to Mr. Byrnes that he did not wish to have him have a copy of the report—it would be practically impossible.

"I assumed that you would wish to accommodate him," I added.

It was so perfectly evident that he intended to use the Elk Hills situation for his own great advantage, and he promptly proceeded to do so to the best of his ability. He called Mr. Byrnes, after asking me to send Mr. Williams down to discuss the whole situation with him and bring the files to refresh his memory on the origin of the problem. Later in the afternoon, he called me back. He said that he had gone over the matter with Mr. Williams, had read the original memorandum to the President enclosing the memoranda of [Abe] Fortas of the Interior and Stevenson of the Navy Department, and would prepare a statement to the effect that "the Department of Justice" had asked that the contract be withdrawn from the Appropriations Committee so that it could not be approved. It was amusing to read the headlines in the *Times Herald* on Sunday, June 12th. Front page: "Navy drops disputed oil lease deal" and "Attorney General Francis Biddle disclosed yesterday that he had persuaded Secretary of the Navy Frank Knox to withdraw a $1,748,000 appropriation request intended to finance Knox's Naval Oil Reserve contract with the Standard Oil Company of California."

(I pause here in the story of one intrigue to enter this observation: The plain fact is that forces aiming at the defeat of Roosevelt in 1944 are well organized and are utilizing several congressional committees for the achievement of their purposes. Representative Eugene Cox, through his investigation of the FCC[3] is providing the spur for the drive. Cox has stated that he is for Jim Farley for President in 1944. Counsel of the Committee, Eugene L. Garey, of [the] Wall Street firm of Garey, Desvernines—head of the Lawyers Committee of the Liberty League[4]—and Garey, was selected for his position by Mr. Farley, according to Eugene Cox. The new counsel of the Howard Smith Committee,[5] the "blank check investigating committee," having power to investigate anything they wish to, is an associate of Garey's on Wall Street and, according to Mr. Cox, a close friend

3. The Federal Communications Commission (FCC) was established by the Federal Communications Act of 1934, approved 19 June 1934. The FCC regulated interstate and foreign commerce in communications, especially by wire and radio. The FCC also licensed radio stations, assigned frequencies, and regulated their operations. Rep. (Edward) Eugene Cox of Georgia was chairman of the House Select Committee to Investigate the Federal Communications Commission, 1943.

4. The American Liberty League was an organization of disaffected conservative businessmen, from both major parties, established in August 1934 to oppose the New Deal.

5. Congressman Howard W. Smith of Virginia was chairman of the House Select Committee to Investigate Acts of Executive Agencies Beyond the Scope of Their Authority, 1943.

of Garey's. [He] was employed [so] the two of them might then cooperate more readily on all necessary matters.

(The major forces involved in this drive center around Jim Farley and the New York Catholic Democratic politicians who are opposed to President Roosevelt, plus the Southern poll tax axis[6] headed by [Wilbert L.] "Pappy" O'Daniel of Texas, Governor Sam Jones of Louisiana, former Governor Frank Dixon of Alabama, Eugene Cox, "Cotton" Ed Smith, Jack Garner, etc., and a Midwest isolationist group of Democrats, headed by former Secretary of War Harry Woodring, who is also in the soft drink business and a great crony of Jim Farley. He recently toured the Midwest with Farley, lining up state delegates for 1944 and Catholic Democratic wheel-horses [in] a number of Northwestern and Western states, including Mooney of Minnesota, Senator [Guy M.] Gillette, and the friends of the opposition.)

A similar article appeared in the *Washington Post* on the same date, under the heading "Touchy Business—Navy Calls Standard Oil Deal Off." Biddle is again quoted. It was my strategy, suggested to him by Mr. Justice Byrnes, to show that the executive branch of the government moved first; namely, the President. He continued in his release that the contract had been under study and that "a detailed analysis had been completed." It would have been so easy, and so proper, to have recounted something like the truth: That the matter had come over and been referred "to the Lands Division" where an exhaustive study had been made, but that would build up the wrong man, even if I had not been named. Besides, Biddle needs this desperately to reconstruct his feeble position after successive vicious attacks in editorials and articles in the *New Republic*[7] and *The Nation*[8] and in columns for his failure to prosecute Congressman Cox of Georgia. [Cox] accepted $2,500 for securing a radio station license for a client in violation of federal law, and is now personally heading a committee of investigation designed almost wholly to defeat the administration.

Under these conditions, it is increasingly intolerable to friends of the administration that Biddle has failed to act. Naturally, he was looking for some heroic thing to do, and he seized upon the Elk Hills issue as a splendid opportunity to do it. It was to be expected, but I waited for the truth to come out, as a man who puts himself so far out on a limb can

---

6. The "poll tax" was a tax on registered voters, payment of which was required in order to be eligible to vote. Once widespread, it was by the 1930s limited to the states of the old Confederacy. Southern conservatives used the poll tax to limit voting by Blacks and the poor.

7. "Mr. Cox and the F.C.C.," *New Republic*, 3 May 1943, pp. 580–81; "Scandal in the House," *New Republic*, 24 May 1943, p. 700.

8. I. F. Stone, "Mr. Biddle Is Afraid; Cox Case and the F.C.C.," *Nation*, 22 May 1943, pp. 735–36.

usually anticipate that an enemy will happen along right at that time with a saw and go to work on the limb. And so it happened!

In the meantime, Senator Langer had attacked again and has called my office, having heard of my report on the contract.[9] Rather than let anybody else reply to him, I called him from Asheville. He wanted to see me immediately upon my return, and I asked the attorney general during my conversation with him on Saturday morning, when he telephoned me for the second time from Washington, whether I should see him.

"No," he replied. "Do not discuss it with anyone at this time. We will hold a conference on Monday, when you get back, with Stevenson, . . . and Fortas . . . and Stuart, and perhaps I had better give them copies of your report in advance."

That ruling was fair enough as to Langer and of no material importance to me. As to the balance of the suggestion, I objected to Stuart being present at the conference, as he is not a lawyer and, being on the defensive to the point of being offensive, would only be an obstruction in the conference. I objected also to giving him a copy of my report, which I had not personally had time to review, stating that it would be more useful anyway if I explained it to them first and then submitted it later. He agreed, and the conference was set for 2:30, Monday, June 14th.

These innumerable telephone calls, punctuated by two or three from Katherine to keep me apprised of local developments and the increasingly hot press and radio comments, greatly interrupted the delightful visit at Asheville, but I stayed the three days—Thursday, Friday, and Saturday—with the United States attorneys and the conference of judges from the Fourth Circuit, who summoned me to their conference on Friday afternoon, to discuss land acquisition matters. . . .

Sunday's *P.M.* broke the Elk Hills story in all of its glory with a picture of Abe Fortas, myself, and Congressman Sheppard, under the general caption of "Inside Story of Elk Hills Oil Scandal: How New Dealers Exposed Standard Grab."[10] The article spelled out the transaction in great detail, explaining that, during the absence of the attorney general, I was "acting attorney general" (quite erroneously [because] Charlie Fahy, the solicitor general, was then acting attorney general)[11] and, after receiving the contract, had gone within twenty-four hours to Mr. Byrnes to suggest that it be withdrawn from the Naval Appropriations [Sub]committee. That, too, was erroneous and exaggerated, for I worked on it for fourteen days,

9. "Inquiries in View on Elk Hills Deal; Langer Says He Will Ask Senate to Study Navy Contract with Standard Oil; Criticism in House; Justice Agents in a Report to Biddle Attack Set-Up and Urge It Be Voided," *New York Times*, 14 June 1943.

10. Nathan Robertson, "Inside Story of the Elk Hills Oil Scandal: How New Dealers Exposed Standard Grab," *P.M.*, 13 June 1943.

11. In the absence of the attorney general, the solicitor general becomes the "acting attorney general."

and a good many of those were nights, before I was sufficiently sure of my footing that I dared take so extreme an action. We received the President's memorandum on March 27th, and my conference with Justice Byrnes was on April 14th, with a memorandum nowhere near conclusion or in any form that could be reduced to writing. He took my word for it and acted.

The story, as printed, must have been excruciatingly painful to Biddle, who had only the day before stated that he had persuaded Knox, or so left the impression that the papers wrote it up that way, [to withdraw the appropriation]. When it eventually comes out that he wasn't even in town, it will be even more embarrassing. . . .

I talked to Langer, pursuant to my agreement to call him upon my return, and explained that Biddle preferred that I not discuss matters now. I was not at all unhappy about pointing out that *P.M.* article to him and explaining away the statement of Biddle's yesterday in contrast to the *P.M.* article, saying that I had gone to Jimmy Byrnes. I also corrected a statement of his as to the repayment for Navy's oil, for which he was very grateful. I was, therefore, not surprised to learn from the *New York Times* correspondent, who called me later in the day, and from Drew Pearson's broadcast in the evening, that Langer would undoubtedly call for a resolution to investigate the whole matter in the Senate.[12]

A nice touch was a telegram from Josephus Daniels to Drew Pearson, which Drew read over the radio, protesting the matter and reaffirming the necessity of conserving the oil at Elk Hills. I had been reading in the afternoon in *Privileged Characters*,[13] which has a complete summary of the Elk Hills scandal—how Daniels and the assistant secretary of the Navy under him, now the President of the United States, sat up all night one night to watch and see that a bill to transfer the naval petroleum reserves would not be called and passed in Congress.[14] There are always watchdogs. I felt constrained to write Mr. Daniels a letter. . . .

Now I still have the terrific job of mastering a great amount of technical detail before the wolves of [the] opposition and their experts attempt to tear me limb from limb.

---

18 June 1943
4101 Lorcom Lane

Events have moved with the rapidity of an express train since Sunday. The attorney general had declined to let me fly back from the conference

---

12. See *New York Times*, 14 June 1943, p. 34.
13. Morris R. Werner, *Privileged Characters* (New York: Robert M. McBride and Co., 1935). See chapter on Teapot Dome, pp. 27–192.
14. Ibid., p. 49.

at Asheville a week ago [so that I did not miss] my Lands Division conference of Saturday morning, so I flew in [to Washington, D.C.] Saturday night, instead. [I realized] that I needed all available time before the conference on Monday with Interior and Navy. After an intense Sunday and Monday, working on my report on Elk Hills, [I was] reasonably sure that I was not vulnerable as to any language used, [and inserted] qualifying language on the technical section, where I was naturally more susceptible to attack. [We] went into the conference in the attorney general's office at 2:30: Abe Fortas, a little supercilious because he, after all, felt himself to be the daddy of the whole matter; Adlai Stevenson, nervous, apprehensive, and increasingly concerned as I proceeded from point to point; and the attorney general, fidgety and jumpy and anxious to get away for five days at Warm Springs, to which he was going as soon as we adjourned. Another lucky break for me, as he would only have been in the way here. He had obviously read the report and made a number of my points in a loose, general way but, after all, it would take considerable time and attention and close application to really master it in its entirety; it required eight weeks to write.

I had to put Abe Fortas in his place when he commented on the repayment plan for the first five years of oil, which he said could be repaid in oil or in refined petroleum products. He had so stated, as has almost every congressman on the Hill debating the subject, in his memorandum to Secretary Ickes, which precipitated this examination. In fact, he made three points, two of which were dead wrong.

"You are wrong about that, Abe," I said.

"I believe I am," he said apologetically and, turning to Stevenson, said, "I will write you a correcting memorandum on that."

"Don't bother," said Stevenson.

"No, I wouldn't bother, Abe," I added. "That isn't the only mistake you made. The most important thing you said in that memorandum was that this agreement was against the public interest. In that, you were correct."

At another point, when I pointed out the loss of future competitive prices on Bunker C fuel oil for the Navy, on which we had saved over sixteen years about $16,000,000, Abe announced with some astonishment, "I never saw that point," as if this were simply incredible that he could have overlooked it.

"There is quite a lot you did not see," I replied. "We have just got started."

Even Stevenson found indefensible the lack of power to revise the agreement and the respective interests of the parties, fixed at 64 per cent for the Navy and 36 per cent for Standard.

I insisted upon the right, which the attorney general had given me before I left for Asheville, to revise the memorandum before sending it to Fortas and Stevenson. There was some friction over this, but I was adamant and the attorney general had to agree that he had promised me this right. I, therefore, did not give them copies of the memorandum on Monday.

The next day, in my mail—undiscovered in my full mailbox of incoming matters on Monday—was a letter from Congressman [James H.] Peterson, chairman of the Public Lands Committee of the House, requesting me to be present on Thursday, the 17th, and bring all papers and documents respecting Elk Hills Petroleum Reserve and the Navy contract. I witnessed first-hand the power of a congressional investigating committee, for things began to move very rapidly. While the request was very courteous, it raised very delicate questions as to whether or not it could or should be put off. Acting Attorney General Charles Fahy called Mr. Byrnes at the White House as to what should be done about the hearing. In the meantime, I had called [Donald S.] Russell, Mr. Byrnes' assistant, to suggest that, with the matter under such great pressure, I thought it would help him and Mr. Byrnes if Mr. Fahy and I came over and I endeavored to explain the report and the conclusions reached. At that moment, however, he wanted a two-page memorandum—which had been the first request I had received in the morning on coming to the office—summarizing the whole matter. . . .

. . . I worked intensely on the memorandum, getting the principal points down to four pages on the attorney general's stationery, but it was 1:00 by the time we were through. I called Russell again to suggest that Fahy and I could, in fifteen or twenty minutes, explain more than he could get from a memorandum. He replied that Mr. Fahy was coming to a meeting at 2:00, and it would not be necessary to have an advance conference. He should simply bring the memorandum to him.

I noticed a distinct cooling off in Russell's voice from prior conversations. (I shall never forget Leon Henderson's statement that: "In Washington you never know what has happened to you. You only know that someone has cut your throat." And he drew his finger significantly across his throat. "And then after a while everything gets all right again.") I surmised that the Navy boys and possibly effective Standard connections were reaching in to Byrnes or Russell and, possibly Secretary Ickes had gone to work on me personally. [In] fact, it was perfectly evident that every conceivable step would be taken to prevent my going to the congressional hearing. Stevenson had seen enough of the report to be thoroughly embarrassed and exceedingly reluctant to have it exposed before the committee in Congress. I must confess, I felt very badly at not being included in the invitation to the White House, and this meant definitely that some dirty work had been done at the crossroads.

I completed the memorandum, however, leaving off any signature line, thinking that the acting attorney general would wish to add a qualifying paragraph to the effect that the summary was based on my report and that he had personally not had time to verify it. But even this did not do because there were only a few minutes in which to discuss the matter before going to the meeting. I could see clearly that he had no intention of endorsing it.

"The memorandum is enough just the way you have written it," Fahy said, "and I will hand it to Mr. Byrnes just that way." . . .

My concern about the private meeting with Charles Fahy was an entirely erroneous impression, as it turned out. The meeting was of the war cabinet, with Undersecretary of Navy Forrestal there in place of Knox, Secretary Stimson, Byrnes, Judge [Frederick M.] Vinson, the President, Ickes, and Charles Fahy—I believe that was all. They discussed the Elk Hills contract. Forrestal presented it as an effort in entire good faith to meet the conservation problem. However, he said, he understood that the question of its legality had been raised by the Department of Justice and, of course, if it was illegal, then perhaps the matter of terminating it should be taken up with the Standard Oil Company on that ground alone. Charles Fahy said that neither he nor the attorney general had had adequate time to study the matter; but that he had read my report; that I had prepared an exhaustive study of the matter; and that, if he had to decide then, it would be with me that the agreement was a very bad contract and ought to be rescinded.

The President indicated that, from what he had heard (undoubtedly through Byrnes who, I have since learned from Drew Pearson, had read the report and was definitely inclined to concur with it) he questioned whether "enough oil was being conserved." [This], no doubt, had reference to my section showing the necessity of exploring and exploiting the shallow zone almost completely in order to pay the government back for what Standard would owe the government at the end of five years.

Charles Fahy told me this in substance, and in confidence, when he returned from the cabinet meeting. In the meantime, I worked intensely on the report, in which there were some very real revisions.

I neglected to say that Abe Fortas called me on Monday night, after the meeting in the attorney general's office, to ask if he couldn't borrow a copy of the report. [He] had to write another memorandum on this matter and he thought it would be helpful. The sheer, unadulterated nerve of that suggestion, after the superficial job he had done and the supercilious attitude he had at first taken in our conference struck me with consider-able force. Furthermore, he and I had both been summoned to the Lands Committee. He might have the opportunity to be heard first, which he very much wished to be and which would be in accordance with Secretary Ickes' very definite wishes in the matter. He was preparing a memoran-dum for that and for the secretary, without any doubt.

Once in a while, in the course of life, there is a time to be ungenerous. This was one of those times. I was making the revision and could not possibly let him have it out of my office until the revision was complete. I worked that night and two secretaries worked till midnight. . . .

And then I went home to prepare my argument before the Lands Committee the next morning. Suffice to say, that the issue as to what I should say or whether I should say anything at all was a seething hot one the next morning. It was obvious that Ickes was at work trying to keep me off of the stage, and it was considered for a short time the preceding afternoon that Ickes should lead off. It was a great blunder, as I told Charles Fahy, because Ickes had Davies, [deputy-director] of Standard of California, beside him as the oil administrator. . . . Howard Marshall, my old associate of NRA days and a member of Pillsbury, Madison and Sutro, also sat right beside him. A major scandal would almost certainly ensue if Ickes interfered in an endeavor to in any way soften the blows in regard to this contract. This was apparently perceived, for the idea of his appearing was abandoned.

Byrnes did not want . . . it, but in the morning before the hearing at 9:30 it was finally decided that, in view of the fact that I had just submitted my report, . . . and the President . . . had not yet seen [it] . . . the Committee should be requested to continue the matter until the President had had time to consider it and act. Byrnes phoned Speaker of the House [Samuel T.] Rayburn to ask him to have Peterson do this, and I went up on the errand of seeing Peterson before the meeting to effect the same thing.

When Peterson returned from Rayburn's office, he was still bent on opening the hearing, putting the contract in evidence, and making a statement about the continuance of my testimony. There came one of those delicate moments in life upon which so much hangs. Peterson is a good-hearted, forthright fellow who likes to agree with everybody. [A] desk piled high with letters, reports, boxes and whatnot lay between us. He couldn't, he said, disappoint everybody. [The] announcement had gone out; the publicity had been extensive; and he felt that he should open the meeting. He would, or I could, make a statement of my position and ask for a continuance.

When I thought of him making a statement of God knows what import as to the position of the Department of Justice, the dangers of an erroneous statement loomed greater than the dangers of my appearing and making a statement of precisely what the situation was. Most of it has already been stated in the press anyway, picked up from one source or another. Besides, I was thoroughly irritated by the fact that Secretary Ickes called Peterson right while I was there to endeavor to persuade him not to put me on. He also called Congressman [James W.] Robinson, as I learned when I got to the committeeroom, and persuaded Robinson that I should not be put on at all. All of that was due to one of two things:

(1) Desire to soften the blow as the result of influences from his Standard Oil Company friends within the Department of the Interior; or (2) To keep me out of the limelight in a matter which would be of undoubted fame. [He had] endeavored to do [just this] in respect to the Western States Conference so long ago when his conception of his own great leadership among the liberals of the West had to be protected against any rising upstart who might take the play away from him. Here was a real danger [to him]. These were some of the factors in my mind, as well as the abominable treatment I had had at the hands of the attorney general, the lack of recognition and appreciation for work done, and the full knowledge of the fact that I was open to attack from the attorney general and Jim Rowe at any time at all when any reasonable cause could be found.

The dominant fact, however, was that it was our position which was to be stated, and it is a dangerous thing to let any other man ever state one's position on a delicate point. Peterson very much wanted me to appear because he had his stage set and I was the star witness. We went to the committee together, finding a room full of admirals and newspaper reporters when we got there shortly before 10:00. There was much vigorous discussion, particularly by Congressman [James A.] Elliott, to point out that he had nothing to do with the bill pending before the committee to add a belt a mile wide around Elk Hills and terminate the leases therein, so that his constituents would know that he had nothing to do with this in case the Elk Hills matter turned out to be a [new] Teapot Dome scandal in 1943. This laid an exciting foundation for anything which followed.

Robinson moved that I be not called at all, obviously reflecting Ickes' conversation which he had just confessed to. [The] motion at this stage [was] contrary to [a] definite agreement between Robinson, Sheppard and Peterson in the hall [by] which they had all agreed that I make a short statement of my position—all but Robinson. Robinson now tried to head it off entirely.

[Hugh] Peterson from Georgia, however, wanted to know why it should be headed off at all, and [Frank A.] Barrett from Wyoming even wanted a copy of my report brought in before the committee immediately so that they could have the advantages of it if there was an adjourned meeting, before the subject was reopened at the adjourned meeting. In answer to Robinson's motion, Peterson of Georgia stated quite bluntly that I was here and there was no reason whatever why I should not make my own statement.

Therefore, at long last, after Peterson of Florida, the chairman, had made several gracious remarks about me and my ability and the respect which the committee had for me, [he stated] that out of courtesy to the

President who had not had time to read this report and consider it, he was going to suggest that the committee postpone this hearing, but that he would call on me to state the reasons therefor.

I did, in a tense atmosphere. I stated that I had made an exhaustive report, that it had been handed to Mr. Justice Byrnes, but that it had not yet reached the President. [It] represented my own opinion only inasmuch as the attorney general had received the report only a few days ago (June 11th) and that I had reached the conclusion that the contract was illegal and invalid.

Again, the processes of the executive branch of the government could not possibly catch up with the rapidly flowing current of public opinion reflected in this committee. The committee was only interested in days. I had told [James H.] Peterson [privately] that, in my opinion, there was no need to continue it long, because I thought we could reach a conclusion within the Department. [If] the President were advised that the contract was illegal and invalid, he would terminate it forthwith, in my opinion. . . .

The results of those two somewhat redundant words—"illegal and invalid"—were electric. The press picked them up for headlines throughout the country even though it was already known and had even been reported in the press that my report was adverse on the legality of the contract.

I had some anxious moments in a discussion with Charles Fahy in the afternoon as to the propriety of my having stated even as little as I did state, in view of the instantaneous effect of those two words. I personally felt that it was extremely important to give the committee something—that irreducible minimum which I had given them—because the pressure was great and there was no real substantive reason why an effort should be made to divert or suppress the hearing, even for the time being. I think Charles recognized that, although he was deeply concerned that the Department had failed in its mission of having the matter put off entirely. That, I said, was a paper pattern and a theoretical concept. I handled the matter as a trial lawyer handles a trial, making decisions as best I could.

That evening, at about 6:00, Charles called me and I went up to his office. [He] said he had just learned from Mr. Justice Byrnes at the White House that Standard and the Navy were each preparing a release for the press announcing rescission of the contract on the grounds that its legality had been challenged.[1] So ended what was, behind the scenes, like a waterfront brawl—two blows and two men down, and

---

1. C. P. Trussell, "Knox Terminates Elk Hills Oil Deal; Standard Oil Agrees to Drop Contract Declared Invalid by Biddle Assistant," *New York Times*, 18 June 1943; "Navy Oil Deal Dropped," *Facts on File*, vol. 3 (16–22 June 1943), p. 196F.

these two were Standard and Navy. I certainly never anticipated such capitulation.

By Saturday, the 19th, I was so fatigued and so besieged by reporters and harassed by the inter-departmental telephone calls and manipulations that I decided to make a trip to New York to work in, if I could, the selection of men there in New York to assist Special Assistant [Joseph] Kraemer in Newark, and perhaps get Sunday at the Pinchots' estate where Leila has several times invited me to come, at Milford, Pennsylvania. Just before catching the 11:00 train, [Richmond] Keith Kane, special assistant to Secretary Knox, called to ask if he could not give a copy of my report to Standard Oil Company of California; he also requested two additional copies of the report.

. . . [A] half an hour later, when I reached the station and had thought the matter over in transit, I seized a telegraph blank in my chair car and while standing on the platform, wrote a telegram to Kane objecting to Standard having a copy of the report on the ground that it was an intra-departmental communication, not made public, and that this was strictly a naval matter. . . .

Skipping over a meeting with Special Assistant Kraemer from Newark and [Harold] Moscovit . . . in regard to personnel for Newark, I finally escaped in the evening of a sweltering New York day by bus for Milford, Pennsylvania and, after a breakdown up in the hills at Slate Hill, finally got into Milford at dark where the Pinchots' driver picked me up and took me to "Grey Towers." Gifford was in bed—although he hailed me from the upstairs window with his greetings—he lives a very cautious life after a heart attack some time ago. After a late, cold chicken dinner waiting on the table for me, Leila and I went for a walk down through the woods to a magnificent stream flowing three and a half miles through their property, well stocked with trout, surrounded by natural forests, and running over a series of cascades and falls, the like of which I had not seen since I had come from the West. It was all exhilaratingly beautiful in the moonlight, and I almost went for a swim then and there. Leila stopped me on the ground that the slate and rock walls were exceedingly slippery and until I knew the country, it was not safe to go into the pools at night.

What a blessing it was to sleep in one of the tower rooms—for the old stone homestead built by Gifford's father [James W. Pinchot] is like a French chalet with towers at the corners—and to sleep under a blanket, for it was delightfully cool in the evening in spite of the scorching day.

Sunday was one of the most completely satisfying days I have had in four years in the East. I never dreamed of such country here and spent the morning, after walking to the Great Falls with Leila and Gifford, in climbing up to the falls and pools along rock walls, diving in and out of pools with the occasional flash of a retreating trout ahead of me, until I had reached the top of the falls, and then turning back to explore them once again on the downhill trip. . . .

We had lunch—Gifford, Leila, and Gifford's trained nurse, Miss Boyle—in a most extraordinary dining room under a great arbor sitting at the edge of a great pool for all the world resembling a large bathtub about five feet deep, with our plates set on the rock rim of the pool which slanted up like the edges of a bowl, leaving room quite comfortably for the feet beneath. Food floated in the pool in wooden receptacles. . . . It was one of Leila's extraordinary ideas, and a very charming one, for flowers also drifted on the surface of the water and glass balls, such as we pick up on the Pacific Coast after they have drifted over from Japanese fishermen. Peacocks strutted in the yard with their weird cries, characteristic of the lonely, medieval seclusion of the place and its unique charm. A brilliantly colored parrot resides in a tree over the driveway leading up to the front of the house, and one is startled when walking into the grounds to hear a voice from the tree saying "hello." That is Oscar speaking. Next comes the great dane, Nietzsche, an immense dog who comes bounding through the long hall of the manor house with heavy footfalls and powerful eagerness not easy to control. The Pinchots had fled to America after rallying to the cause of Napoleon's Hundred Days preceding his final exile; a bust of Lafayette looks out over the front lawn and down the deep valley which stretches away from the house.

We talked of everything: Elk Hills, diet and personal history of friend, family, and foe. . . .

. . . Just when I was reluctantly bringing the day to a close and throwing things in my suitcase preparatory to catching a bus for New York, the attorney general telephoned from Washington. It was Elk Hills, of course. Adlai Stevenson had called him from the office of Secretary Knox, and requested that we not go into the details in regard to the contract until the Navy had had a chance to study my report. The attorney general thought that entirely reasonable and asked me to take that position before the committee the following day—today. . . .

. . . I assured him that I would do the best I could to keep the discussion on that level, although I had real doubts about the efficacy of doing so in view of the intense public interest in this contract. . . .

The hearing opened again this morning with the full committee present in a crowded committeeroom. I stated that the attorney general's instructions were to ask for a continuance as to the details of the contract until the Navy had a chance to study the matter and even called attention to the fact, when objections were made to a further continuance, that the

Navy was represented by Admiral Stuart, Keith Kane, as well as by many other officers in the room and that Mr. Kane could speak for himself as to the policy of the Navy. Kane did so, explaining that they had only had the report for a short time and wished to make a study of it. . . . The Navy considered it a good contract and definitely in the public interest. It had announced an agreement to rescind the contract only because of the opinion in the Department of Justice as to the invalidity of the deal. In drafting the instrument of rescission they were awaiting only the opinion of the attorney general to confirm the invalidity and illegality of the contract which I had mentioned. That was a new point. When the rescission was announced . . . there was simply a general desire . . . to retreat from the proposition, . . . but now they were growing bolder. They wanted an opinion of the attorney general.

I finally was called on to testify. The committee deferred my testimony as to the practical effects of the contract analyzed and, in deference to my request from the attorney general, heard only a discussion of the reasons why I considered the contract illegal—with much cross-fire and many questions. Congressman [James W.] Mott, [a Republican] from Oregon, who sat on my right, was in the business to defend Standard and the Navy. I analyzed in detail why this contract went further than the contract in the [Albert B.] Fall leases to [Edward L.] Doheny and [Harry F.] Sinclair, primarily because it gave an interest to Standard in the oil content of government land, whereas the Fall leases merely gave oil in exchange for equipment. Also, there is no exchange of "land" in the common law sense; this is rather a merger or partnership. The committee was certainly with me when I quit. . . .

I had applied for an appointment with the attorney general, but did not get to see him until about a quarter of 6:00. He was obviously irritable over the Elk Hills matter having gotten away from him—he had never gotten a chance to write that "blistering memorandum." Furthermore, he was exasperated that I had inherited the honor and glory.

"It was most unfortunate that you testified as to the illegality and invalidity of the contract," he said.

"You mean, it was most unfortunate that the legislative process overtook us before we had completed the normal processes on the executive side of the government," I replied.

"Had I known that this thing was imminent, I would not have gone to Asheville to the United States attorneys conference, but you recall that, when I offered to stay in order to complete this memorandum, you said, 'No,' " . . . [I added].

"It left nothing for Mr. Byrnes to do but to tell them that the contract ought to be terminated," the attorney general replied, irritably.

"Not at all," I replied. "The rescission which followed was a voluntary act of both parties to get off the hot spot which they were on. They used the illegality and invalidity as a way out, in the hope that the investigation would stop right there and not go into the embarrassing terms of this contract. Besides," I said, "there was great pressure in that committee to get the whole report. I had to give them something and I gave them only my personal opinion."

"Well, I doubt whether the contract is illegal," he said. "It might be a bad contract, but I doubt whether it is illegal."

. . . When he asked me what I thought he should now do, I frankly stated that a letter concurring with the conclusion reached [in my memorandum] was all that was necessary, not a formal opinion of the attorney general, in order that the Navy and Standard could draft an instrument rescinding the contract and reciting in it the opinion as to the illegality and invalidity.

At that stage, he called Charlie Fahy to come down because Charlie had participated in the interview in the attorney general's absence, and Charlie made a cool, calm, accurate appraisal of the situation, as usual—so much abler and more worthy of an attorney general than the attorney general's. He explained the meeting of the war cabinet on last Wednesday, the 16th, and how he had advised the cabinet. (The attorney general interjected, "Was the President there?" and that seemed to bother him, too.) . . . [Fahy] was satisfied that the contract was a bad one from the point of view of the government; that he had had insufficient time to study the question of legality; but if he had to make a decision now, he would go along with the opinion of illegality. . . . On that ground, Charlie explained, Standard and the Navy voluntarily rescinded the contract because it was under attack— public attack—and they used the charge of the invalidity and illegality as a basis upon which to terminate the contract.[1] . . .

The attorney general ended by asking Mr. Fahy to write such a letter as he thought ought to be written. "I suppose they're entitled to recite something in their instrument of rescission," the attorney general said. The meeting then broke up, and I walked up the corridor and stopped in at Charlie Fahy's office before going down in the elevator.

"Did Kane ever call you about giving a copy of the report to Standard?" I asked.

"Yes; and I took it up with the attorney general and he said he saw no objections, providing Mr. Byrnes did not object, and I rang Mr. Byrnes who made no objection. He, therefore, had permission last Saturday, the 19th, to give the report to Standard."

"And yet, I was instructed not to give it to the committee and to ask for

---

1. "Elk Hills Oil Field Faces Condemning; Knox in Letter to Senators and House Naval Committees, Insists Issue Be Solved; Backs Standard Project; Contract in Public Interest He Says—House Group Hears Littell on Same Subject," *New York Times*, 23 June 1943.

a deferment of the consideration of the merits of this contract at this morning's hearing. You realize what that means, Charlie. [If] this news gets out that the attorney general has permitted Standard to have it and has refused it to an investigating committee?" . . .

"That's very bad," Charlie observed. "I must advise him immediately."

He telephoned the attorney general then and there and caught him before he left for the evening, pointing out the danger of the situation. The attorney general immediately agreed that the report should be submitted to the committee, but it will be interesting to see what will happen if that committee finds out that Standard has had the report all the time that it was refused to the committee since last Saturday. I would, of course, have warned the attorney general but did not know that permission had been given for Standard to have it until my conversation with Mr. Fahy. . . .

3:25 P.M., Thursday, 24 June 1943

The newspaper *P.M.* was brought to my attention this morning, showing the fact that Standard Oil Company had the report on Elk Hills, and making much of the fact that the report was denied to the Public Lands Committee.[1] Chairman [James H. Peterson] of the committee, after calling me yesterday, had called Mr. Kane of the Navy, and there it was confirmed that the report had gone to Standard on Saturday, the 19th, but after first securing the approval of the attorney general.

Charlie Malcolmson, public relations officer of the Department, called me at 2:30 to say that now that the news was out about my report, it ought to be mimeographed for distribution to the press, tomorrow, because they would want it. I said I was planning on taking enough copies for each member of the committee, if the attorney general approved, since I felt sure that he would under the existing circumstances. Charlie said he would immediately arrange for mimeographing if I would send down the report, and this was done forthwith after minor corrections on the opening statement of facts.

I called the attorney general immediately after Malcolmson telephoned, but my call was not returned until 3:15. The conversation was approximately as follows:

> *Attorney General:* Did you see the statement in the morning paper, and have you any idea how it reached the press?

> *Mr. Littell:* An article was brought to my attention this morning, and all

---

1. Nathan Robertson, "Elk Hills Deal Described as 'Beyond' Teapot Dome; Three Senate Groups Discuss Probes of Navy-Standard Pact," *P.M.*, 23 June 1943.

I know about it is that Congressman Peterson telephoned me yesterday saying that two reporters were interviewing him. He asked that now that the report had been delivered to the Navy, did Standard Oil Company have a copy? I said that Standard did have a copy, but that I had been utterly unaware of it when I testified on Tuesday, the 22nd. I had explained to Mr. Peterson that I only learned that Standard had a copy at about 6:00 on the 22nd when discussing the matter with Mr. Fahy, solicitor general, after leaving your office, at which time Mr. Fahy immediately called you.

Attorney General: It is most unfortunate that you have had to compare this situation with Elk Hills and Teapot Dome. It gives a bad impression, reflecting upon the Navy. No doubt you saw the newspaper accounts of it?

Mr. Littell: Of course I did, but I can't possibly help what newspaper men do with it. It was impossible not to discuss the case of *Pan American Oil Company v. U.S.* (Elk Hills) in 273 U.S.[2] and *Mammoth Oil Company v. U.S.* (Teapot Dome), the latter case in 275 U.S.,[3] because these are the two cases on which we rely. I said, in explaining the legal status of this contract, that it went beyond these cases in [that] the government yielded an actual interest *in the oil content of the Reserve* and not just merely oil produced.

Attorney General: Well, we will not discuss that any further.

Mr. Littell: We can't help it. These are the only two cases to consider. By the way, have you had a chance to read them? (The attorney general did not reply to this last question. I feel perfectly sure that he has not read these cases.)

Attorney General: We will not discuss that any further. . . .

Mr. Littell: After all, Mr. Attorney General, you telephoned me long-distance in Milford on Monday night at 6:00 in order to instruct me to discuss the legal issues in the next morning's hearings before the committee. I did precisely that. It is impossible to discuss the legal issues without discussing the Elk Hills and Teapot Dome decision in the Supreme Court. They are the two cases upon which we rely.

Attorney General: When you go up to the committee in the morning, I see no reason for you to do anything more than submit your report.

Mr. Littell: Charlie Malcolmson phoned and requested that we mimeograph copies of it so the press could have it.

Attorney General: There is no need to do that.

Mr. Littell: Then will you talk to Charlie Malcolmson?

Attorney General: Yes; I will give him his instructions, and when you go

---

2. 273 U.S. 456 (1927).
3. 275 U.S. 13 (1927).

up in the morning, there is no need for you to do anything but submit a copy of your report.

Mr. Littell: But what if the committee demands explanations? I thought that I would make a simplified statement of what the report contains.

Attorney General: Just read from your report.

Mr. Littell: I had expected to simplify it somewhat. Mr. Peterson had just called me when your call came in.

Attorney General: I will talk to Mr. Peterson now.

That was the end of the conversation. . . .

. . . Peterson had made it quite clear that the report must now go in since it was learned that Standard Oil Company already had a copy of the report. The attorney general's conversation, in tone and [content], showed complete exasperation, a desire to hobble my testimony, and a general state of irritation. There was no question as to the pressure he had been under from the Navy Department, and probably from Interior, too.

I called Peterson . . . and he advised that the attorney general had already called him and assured him that two copies of the report would be sent up immediately, one for him and one for Jerry Voorhis, who had demanded a copy that morning . . . I had referred Jerry to the attorney general, saying quite frankly, that I had been in favor of his having it in the first place . . . ; that the matter had been handled by the attorney general as far as giving copies to Standard was concerned; that I had certainly not known about it when I testified on the 22nd; and that the distribution of the report was now entirely up to the attorney general. I told Peterson I would send him the copies promised by the attorney general immediately.

However, no message came from the attorney general's office and, when I finally reached Mr. Carusi on the phone and explained the situation, the attorney general had left for a meeting "on the Hill." Later, Carusi phoned back to say that the attorney general had become his own messenger and had taken two copies of the report with him, one to be delivered to Peterson and one, apparently, to be delivered to Voorhis. By this abject *salaam* and personal call, he was doing his best to wipe out the blunder of having given the report to Standard first.

Mr. Malcolmson then called back and, when I explained that the attorney general did not wish to have the report mimeographed and the copies distributed and had so ordered, he replied that the attorney general must have changed his mind after talking with Peterson because he had . . . instructed him to go ahead.

Such were the hurdles and nimble high jumps and broad jumps and side jumps of a mind in a flutter that afternoon.

I was in such complete confusion as to what my instructions were . . . and particularly conscious of the futility of an instruction requiring me to read from my report—to comply with which I would have had to ignore questions from the committee members—that I called the attorney general in hope of clarifying the matter. My call was not returned by 6:00, [so] . . . I wrote a memorandum to the attorney general stating the issue as far as I was concerned.

By the time it was completed, at about 6:45, he telephoned to me and I explained my position—the impossibility of refusing to answer questions or confining myself to the report. He reiterated objections to my statement that the present arrangement "went beyond the Teapot Dome leases" and I reiterated my statement that I was reading from my report when I made that precise statement, reminding him again that the contract *did* go beyond the Teapot Dome leases, and I was not responsible for what the press did with that phraseology which I had endeavored to confine strictly to its legal implications. I could not get clear what his instructions were, particularly when he ended up with "you will have to use your own discretion, but you know what I want you to do."

Those were his concluding and completely confusing words of instruction, to which I replied: "No, I do not, Mr. Attorney General. I have written a memorandum to you when I thought I was going to be unable to talk to you on the telephone, and I will send that memorandum up to you in the hope of clarifying the situation."

It was apparent to me that the attorney general suffered from a divided state of mind. He was irritated and exasperated that I was testifying at all, with attendant publicity completely out of control. [He] also was under pressure from the Navy to shut me off and moderate my statements, and yet he was confused by the necessities of the committee hearing for going on with the show. [My] memorandum was, therefore, very much needed to clear the air in this whole matter and, in the absence of instructions from him, I will proceed in an unrestricted manner in the morning.

Thursday, 1 July 1943
4101 Lorcom Lane

Yesterday, Wednesday, June 30th, I concluded my testimony on the Elk Hills matter . . . at 1:30, and, upon returning to the Department, received a telephone call from Charlie Fahy, . . . to come up when convenient to confer with him.

. . . [In] the morning, before leaving for the committee hearing, where I succeeded Comptroller General [Lindsay C.] Warren, who strongly and independently had reached the same conclusion [as] I, . . . I had completed a memorandum to Mr. Fahy on the proposed rescission agreement which the Navy had submitted, together with a copy of an operating agreement in the form of a letter to Mr. [Harry D.] Collier of the Standard Oil Company. Both instruments were rather astonishing in view of the comments in my original memorandum, for they ignored the legal questions there pointed out. Waiving the question of policy . . . as to whether Standard should be continued in control of Elk Hills, and confining attention solely to the legal questions, the operating agreement proposed to pay Standard in oil for the wells it had drilled on government lands at the rate of about $35,000 per well, and to continue to pay Standard for operating and development costs out of oil. This is precisely the thing which was fatal to the Pan American Oil Company and the Mammoth Oil Company leases by Secretary Fall, as pointed out in the two Supreme Court decisions, quite aside from the question of fraud. Standard simply cannot be paid for this development work done by mistake under the now to be rescinded contract, without an appropriation from Congress, and I so indicated.

There are clearly only three courses to follow, as I pointed out in my memorandum: (1) An operating agreement, which would obviously be with Standard as the one principally controlling the other private interests in the reserve; (2) Restore a *status quo* to the operations as they were in November, 1942, when the contract went into effect, thereby restoring cancelled leases; and (3) Condemn the properties and operate them for and on behalf of the United States.

My memorandum pointed out the reasons why the first proposed course was illegal, and also mentioned that it raised a principal question of controversy as to policy which Congress would never tolerate. I am on record as favoring the third course as the only practicable one, ending all controversy and bringing the reserves safely within the control of the United States with every barrel of oil—ammunition for war—where it belongs. Obviously, Navy does not favor this course with its great tenderness for Standard.

When I went up to Mr. Fahy's office, he passed another letter across the desk from the Navy Department to the attorney general which, in effect, asked the Department to suggest what form of operating agreement would be legal and asking two specific questions.

"We shouldn't do that for them," I said. "We have told them what the legal objections are and should not approve in advance any certain form—."

At that point, Fahy launched a most unexpected and most violent attack, saying, "That's not your business to say what we should do and not do. Ever since this matter came up, the question is: Who is the attorney general around here, anyway? You are not running this Department. They are entitled to ask these questions and they are entitled to an answer."

That, as nearly as I can remember it, is the gist of the torpedoes which he let loose. While taken completely aback, and suffering from some confusion from this unexpected attack from one whom I had regarded as a friend, no matter how great the differences of opinion might be between us, I nevertheless said:

"You asked my opinion and in the spirit of exchanging ideas before studying the matter, my reply was perfectly justified."

"And my answer to you was perfectly justified, too!" he replied.

The rancor and strong personal feeling in him was perfectly evident, and it slowly began to dawn on me that I had soared too high in this Elk Hills matter. A broadside effort was being made to bring me down to earth. Of course, I was on the earth all the time and I felt like saying, "I quite understand the matter, Charlie, but you know I have no responsibility for the publicity. I can't help that."

He then subsided into a milder discussion of the powers of the Secretary, one of the questions being whether the Navy could enter into a "unit agreement."

"I don't see any authority in this act for a unit agreement," he said, paging through the *U.S. Code.*[1]

"It's there," I replied. "I'll show it to you."

I took the book and looked through the 1938 act, at issue in this entire matter, until I found the proviso specifically mentioning a unit agreement and read it to him. He was clearly not oriented in the whole matter. There was a pause as we thought things over, and I interjected:

"I am puzzled to know what are the grounds of the attack which you made a moment ago. Just what is it about this situation which you specifically criticize in my conduct?"

"This matter should have gone to the President in the regular way."

"But," I said, "we confront a situation, not a theory. The trouble is over here that we sit in our cool offices and do not begin to understand the heat of a public issue on the Hill. Was it my fault that the attorney general elected, at the very crisis of the matter, to go away to Hot Springs for a vacation?"

I ignored the fact, which was undoubtedly burning in Charlie's own mind, that *he* was [then] the acting attorney general. He no more minded the absence of the attorney general than I had and probably was glad of it, but he should have been the one to have gone to the President and saved the day.

"As a matter of fact," I said, "the President came out of this exceedingly well, and it was only because prompt action was taken on the matter, handled while it was hot. Langer's attack on Friday, June 11th, in the Senate specifically attacked and criticized the President. That could have broken into a deluge of criticism all over the country. By prompt action, we headed that off, and only because at every move, I took good care of

---

1. Naval Petroleum Reserve Act of 1938. See 14 April 1943, note 1, for provisions.

the President, explaining first that he had signed it on the representations and responsibility of the Navy, after it came to the White House for only one day, as he does with thousands of other instruments which he has to approve on cabinet recommendation; and, secondly, because at the first question being raised, he referred it promptly to the attorney general for an analysis; and, thirdly, because when we were the least bit suspicious about this contract, we went to Byrnes and had Byrnes ask Knox to withdraw it from the Appropriations Committee. I have emphasized those facts and in the deluge of publicity around the country, criticism has missed the President—which is exactly what I intended and wanted. To guide such matters, they must be taken when they are hot. You cannot put a great public issue on the shelf or in the icebox to wait until the attorney general comes back from a vacation."

The thought which was in his mind, he really could not state; namely, that the immense amount of publicity which I had gotten from all over the country should have been avoided and somebody else should have had it, preferably Charles Fahy. So does a modest, able fellow come out of his shell and admit to ambition, because, of course, he would like sometime to be attorney general, and does not realize that he has really reached his top level now, except for the possibility of a court appointment. He lacks the capacity for leadership, the dynamics necessary to run a big organization, but of course none of us quite adequately recognize our own limitations, I presume.

"And I might add, Charlie," I said, "the attorney general never recognizes a great issue unless it is pointed out to him, either in person or by the press. I dished up the Hawaiian issue to him on a silver platter, shaping it up all of the time while he was engaged in that foolish saboteur trial, which any criminal lawyer in the Division could have handled, and then handed it to him—only to see him muff it for lack of thorough preparation and grasp. I will not do that again. The grossly unfair treatment I have received from him, the utter lack of personal loyalty and justice in his attitude toward me in the issues which have arisen with Jim Rowe, leave my relationship with him on a purely professional and departmental one. I owe him no personal loyalty whatsoever. On the contrary, I am fully entitled to take care of myself in face of the venomous hostility which I have had to encounter upstairs with no defense from the attorney general."

I thought that Charlie subsided somewhat with these remarks, because he is essentially a fair-minded and just man, and a really fine human character to whom I am deeply devoted. . . . The conversation was so long that I had little time left to catch a 4:00 train for Philadelphia to attend the United States attorneys' conference, where I was slated to appear on Lands Division matters on the final day; namely, this morning. . . .

In the few minutes which were left to us, I pointed out that this matter of an operating agreement cannot be divorced from the question of policy:

[Whether] we should go in at all into an operating agreement with the Standard Oil Company of California. The heat came back into his observations and I have since concluded that somebody in the Department of Interior, or possibly the Navy, or possibly both, has worked on him at considerable length in regard to my attitude.

"How about Richfield? Would you be in favor of a Richfield operating agreement?" he asked.

That really let the cat out of the bag because that has been the line of attack which Standard and the Navy have launched against me by reason of my using an exhibit furnished by the Richfield Oil Company of California in my memorandum. . . .

"Of course not," I replied. "There is no solution to this problem consistent with good sound policy except condemning the Standard properties and all other private properties involved. I have so stated before the committee."

"But that is not our problem," he said. "The Navy is entitled to an answer on these questions, and I do not see anything to prevent their having an operating agreement. The secretary of the Navy needs this oil for the war and can go ahead and produce oil under an operating agreement, as I see it."

"I disagree," I replied. "He can conserve oil in the ground—that is the object of the Act of June 30, 1938."

Charlie grew quite indignant at this remark, seized the statute book before him, and read me the language about the power of the secretary to operate the properties, "sell oil," etc.

"That's perfectly ridiculous," he said. "I don't believe there is any court anywhere which would deny under this language the power of the secretary to develop these properties now that we have a war on and need the oil."

"That language is very deceptive," I replied. "It is the same language relied on in the Fall cases of 1922, and again in the Knox contract of 1942. The purpose of that act is conservation in the ground and if the policy is changed, Congress must change it."

With that, I turned and walked out of the room and caught my train for Philadelphia. . . .

Friday night, 2 July 1943
4101 Lorcom Lane

The most disturbing thing about the conversation with Charlie Fahy—the substantive matter which survived over and above personal reactions— was his utter inability to conceive of policy as affecting this whole problem. . . .

To answer the naked legal questions of the Navy and approve some sort of an agreement for operating Elk Hills by the Standard Oil Company of California, which the President would undoubtedly sign, as he will have to do under the act of June 30, 1938, when we approve the contract, would merely place a time bomb underneath the President. This time, full responsibility will be centered directly on him, and unavoidably so. Already this Elk Hills matter is considered ammunition for the Republicans in the 1944 election, but if the President accepts the advice of the Navy as confirmed by his legal advisers, that the Navy has power to enter into an operating agreement with Standard in compliance with the act of June 30, 1938, then there will be a terrific offensive—this time, aimed right at the President.

I am . . . submerged beneath a layer of authority, through which I pierced in this incident only by grace of providence, accidents of the attorney general's absence, and the rapidity of the congressional process. . . . The layer of authority is now carefully reimposed over me and, indeed, battened down with all the thoroughness of a hatch cover prepared for the open sea in rough weather. I can't get out again—a matter of no great importance to me because I've been out—[but] neither the attorney general nor the solicitor general can recapture that lost publicity which they regard with such longing eyes. I've had it. It's mine. Now, my concern is renewed for the President. I took care of him in the first round, but those in charge over me do not clearly grasp the issue. Under undoubted pressure from Secretary Ickes and Secretary Knox, they are going the Navy way. [The] Navy will execute an operating agreement with Standard Oil Company of California—an interim agreement, at first—which will eventually be graduated into a permanent arrangement.[1] The tenacity with which Standard clings to this Elk Hills Reserve is little realized by the public at this moment, but when it is, explosions will begin to go off.

After consulting with the strategy committee—Katherine and Ralph Lemkin—I called Josephus Daniels at Raleigh, North Carolina, the only man in the country whom the President still calls "Chief." Daniels has followed the matter carefully, as one in which he has great personal interest, as well as a definite historic connection. . . . He has written several editorials—the latest one having reached me just before I went to Philadelphia—saying that I should be "knighted" in any other land for service outside the line of duty to my country. Here was the actor on the stage who could go to the President, anytime, and play the essential role of making the President see the policy issues which were outside of my sphere for comment.

---

1. See *New York Times*, 3 July 1943, p. 7.

And so I called Josephus Daniels this morning before going to the office to see if he could come to Washington—thanking him first for his fine editorial.

"I meant every word of it," he replied firmly.

Unfortunately, Mrs. Daniels [Addie] is quite ill, having a little set-back with some heart trouble yesterday so that he could not come to Washington, but he asked for a memorandum first, and expressed the hope that he could come to Washington next week. . . .

Monday night, 26 July 1943
4101 Lorcom Lane

Dearest Katherine Mather:

An extraordinary two weeks lies behind, containing ten of the most delightful days your mother and I have had since we came east over four years ago. . . .

Mrs. Gifford Pinchot invited us to spend a week beginning July 9th with her and the governor at their famous old country place—"Grey Towers"—at Milford, Pennsylvania, . . . but our acceptance depended on the battle of Elk Hills, which was still raging. Congress was, however, about to adjourn, and the Navy Department was asked for a written reply to my report. The reply was filed, suddenly, late in the afternoon of July 7th, the day before Congress was to adjourn, and the committee records were being closed until fall. It was an incredibly naive attempt to make the public believe in the defunct contract. While I did not receive copies of the report until 10:00 the following morning, [I] was invited to make a short reply, if I so desired, before the chairman of the committee, Mr. Peterson of Florida, at noon. There was little time to get at the matter, [but] the soft spots in the report stood out so conspicuously and so vulnerably that your mother and I, with two of my assistants, by dividing up the report, were able to pick out the points of attack very quickly.

As [I] stated to the chairman of the committee and his reporter at noon, I had felt like a Christian in the arena at Rome, waiting for the lions to be loosed to tear me limb from limb, all during the time when the Navy Department and the Standard Oil Company experts had my report and were preparing a reply. But, now that the answer was out and the dreaded hour had arrived, there came charging out of the lions' cages a lot of kittens whose dreadful mewing "filled the public arena."

The Navy report actually endeavored to show that the contract would cost the Standard Oil Company millions of dollars, and that it would have been very "burdensome" to Standard. It also, without mentioning me by name, referred constantly to the criticism of "the assistant attorney general" and even sallied into the realm of facetious personal attack by saying that, in my anxiety to save the Navy from "a shell game," . . . I had "forgotten which shell the pea was under." Then, there was a patent attempt to hide behind the President and say that the contract had been written pursuant to his wishes and suggestions. This [was] in spite of the plain instructions in his letter of March 21st, to the secretary of the Navy, saying to purchase the properties or condemn them. . . . The Navy had [then] written this mongrel contract which was neither fish nor fowl nor good red herring.

My statement, at noon of July 8th, with the press present in the Lands Committee office, particularly Lynn Crost, the intelligent and interested representative of the Associated Press, was therefore a bit vitriolic. I . . . turned the shell game reference back on the Navy and Standard by saying that, while I would not go so far as to call Standard a shell game operator, as the Navy did, at least we were in accord on one thing—it did seem to be a "shell game."

I was, perhaps, a trifle overheated in referring to the attempt to hide behind the President as rising to the proportions of a "major deception," although it actually was just that. The words "grossly misleading" or "patently misleading" would have undoubtedly prevailed, instead, had I had another hour to work over the statement and think the matter out, but the statement was struck off when the iron was hot and, of course, it rang out, as blows do on a real anvil.

The statement was front page [news] in the evening . . . and the morning papers. Lynn Crost's Associated Press story [was] the best, with emphasis on the "mewing kittens" and the attempt to hide behind the President [being] a "major deception." [He] labeled the statement that Standard stood to lose millions on the contract as "extremely naive" [which] burned its way through. The whole statement so seared the hides of my attackers in the Navy Department and Standard that it was, perhaps, more comfortable for me to leave town on the 9th, which I promptly did, as planned, in order to overhaul my office in Newark, New Jersey, which was in bad shape in respect to personnel problems and to proceed from there to the Pinchots'. I left on the 1:00 A.M. train on the 9th, with the kettle boiling violently behind me, and the *Evening Star* coming out with headlines which were, indeed, most unfortunate, but characteristic of heated discussion in the press: "Littell Derides Navy Elk Hills Report."

On the [next] morning of Friday, July 9th, upon landing at Jersey City, the story was in the *New York Herald Tribune* and in the *New York Times*, kittens and all, although reduced and retired in the *New York*

Times to page 13.[1] The *Times* has not taken a vigorous interest in the Elk Hills matter except that it was front page on the day I testified to its illegality.

The morning was spent going over the work of my field office at Newark. [It is a] delicate problem of setting up a field staff immunized from the Hague machine inasmuch as we are taking the great Bayonne Terminal. The case is about to go to trial with Hague's personal attorneys opposing us. . . .

That evening, your mother joined me, and we caught the 7:00 train at Jersey City for . . . the Pinchots' place and the almost medieval chateau of "Grey Towers," looking out over the valley of the Delaware River. . . .

The escape from the tension and the oppressive heat of Washington and New York into that paradise of unexpected wilderness in the heart of the crowded East, was so sudden, and the contrasts were so vivid, that the whole experience was as breathtaking as a plunge into the cold pools. I literally lived in the stream. . . .

The governor is a masterful fisherman, performing feats with a two-and-a-half ounce rod which are incredibly delicate and precise. He also caught trout with which the stream abounds. Imagine having a three-and-a-half mile trout stream in one's own yard, preserved in its original wilderness condition. . . .

. . . The trout which he caught were delicious. We would have starved on those I caught, which were exactly nil. . . .

Most impossible of all to recapture are our many conversations with these two vital, liberal-minded people, Gifford and Leila Pinchot, with Sally[2] on the side taking matters in and participating occasionally. The governor maintained the firm line of puritanism. He will not fish on Sunday, and Leila explained that it was some years before she could prevail upon him to indulge in guests' fishing there on Sunday—a very necessary departure from his standard for those who could only have the weekend at leisure. He cannot stand swearing—of which I was fortunately advised in time. Young Gifford, who came up the following weekend, and who swears like a trooper, . . . walked the chalkline with his father. No risque stories are in order. These, too, have to be saved for better occasions with young Giff and Sally. . . .

Vice President Wallace was dethroned as chairman of the Board of Economic Warfare during this week,[3] with a strong censuring statement

---

1. "Littell Accuses Navy in Elk Hills Deal; Assistant Attorney General Says it Avoided President's Orders," *New York Times*, 9 July 1943.

2. Mrs. Gifford B. Pinchot, Governor Pinchot's daughter-in-law.

3. President Roosevelt abolished the BEW and replaced it with the Office of Economic Warfare (OEW) in the OEM by Executive Order No. 9361, 15 July 1943. The new OEW, under Leo T. Crowley, also gained control of the RFC's various subsidiary corporations,

by the President over the intra-governmental trouble between Wallace and Jesse Jones, whom Wallace had attacked in a twenty-eight page written statement. The President replied, after a vote of the committee of five in his palace guard, apparently consisting of Jimmy Byrnes, Judge Vinson, Harry Hopkins, Harold Smith, . . . and Wayne Coy.[4] The first three voted to transfer jurisdiction of the economic warfare functions, such as there were in RFC, and . . . the BEW, to a new head, Leo Crowley.

The palpable injustice of such an act in not sifting the charges, but simply punishing both men—Jones and Wallace—as if they were of equal guilt, shocked the liberal sentiment throughout the country as nothing which has happened during this administration. Harold Smith fought hard, and so did Wayne Coy, for . . . Wallace and the BEW, but they lost against the conservative Southerners, backed by Harry Hopkins, who has always disliked Wallace. Throughout the country, and at the Pinchots', there were heated discussions among progressives as to the action that Wallace should take. Pinchot drafted a telegram urging a forthright stand against the increasing reaction as personified by such men as Jones.

. . . We were [also] shocked at the unfairness to Milo Perkins, executive director of BEW, who, it was said, would leave or remain according to the wishes of Leo Crowley. The President so stated in a press conference in spite of the years of faithful service of Milo Perkins. This particular issue illustrates so clearly the necessity of knowing all the facts. We did not know, and I did not learn for some time, and then only in strict confidence, that Milo had issued the statement without authority of the Vice President. Wallace did not repudiate it, nor lay the blame on Milo Perkins, but stood squarely behind him and took the whole thing on his own shoulders. [He did] not even [tell] the President that Milo had issued the statement without the Vice President's authority, although of course it had been signed by the Vice President and was ready to issue whenever the President approved it.

This is further evidence of the fact that Milo has grown a trifle hysterical. Who might not, having lost both sons within the last two years,

---

formerly controlled by Jesse Jones. On 25 September 1943, by Executive Order No. 9380, President Roosevelt transferred the OEW's functions, together with those of the Office of Lend-Lease Administration, and the Office of Foreign Relief and Rehabilitation Operations, to the newly established Foreign Economic Administration (FEA) in the OEM.

4. The Wallace-Jones controversy arose from both political and personal differences. It had simmered for two years, with occasional bursts of publicity. Both men, and their subordinates, considered their respective organizations to be the only true defender of the public interest and the other to be wholly in the wrong and controlled by nefarious selfish forces. The crisis arose, 5 June 1943, when Wallace released a thirty-page reply to criticisms of the BEW, by the chairman of the Senate Appropriations Committee, in violation of the President's wishes. On 5 July, Jones issued his own thirty-page reply to Wallace's statement. President Roosevelt issued his executive order ten days later.

given so much and fought for so one of them just recently, in the war? How could such a man, who has much that democracy stands for, tolerate the manipulations of a thoroughly calculating, reactionary, representative of special interests like Jesse Jones? So much of destiny turns upon the fulcrum of one human character at a given moment. The blow was devastating to Wallace, and might mean the loss of the vice presidency in 1944. Some thought it was so designed in order to advance the interests of Byrnes or some other southern conservative Democrat. . . .

Returning to Washington for one day, . . . I learned that the new Elk Hills deal had not yet been submitted by the Navy—this by inquiry of Paul Freund in the solicitor general's office. . . .

Affectionately,
Daddy [signed]

17 October 1943
4101 Lorcom Lane

Dear Katherine Mather:

. . . I was chained here this summer by the Elk Hills controversy. Not until we finally approved a substitute interim operating agreement between Standard and the Navy for a ninety day period (over my protest, but as a matter of expediency) was I free. That occurred on August 18th,[1] and [it was] timely, indeed, because I was scheduled to address the American Bar Association in Chicago on August 24th. There was just time to slip away to New York for an errand there, and particularly to see Frank Walker in regard to an appointment in the organization to take charge of [voter] registration, a principal factor in the oncoming election in view of the tremendous shifts of people to the West Coast war industry [cities], without having changed their registration for voting purposes. . . .

Then, indeed, I was free as I climbed aboard a United Airlines plane at 8:00 that night [August 24th] and relaxed while the country passed beneath me, knowing that I would . . . wake up in a new world. . . . Your mother was already there, as she had left two or three weeks before. . . .

Therefore, no one knew I was coming to Seattle, except Anna

1. The President agreed to the new plan on 8 September 1943. See "President Ends Elk Hills Deal; He Approves Termination of Navy-Standard Oil Agreement in California; 90-Days to Renegotiate; Effort Being Made to Form Permanent Plan for Making Allocations," *New York Times*, 9 September 1943; see also "Roosevelt Ends Oil Deal, Cancelling Company's Rights at Reserve After 90 Day Renegotiation Period," *Facts on File*, vol. 3 (8–13 September 1943), p. 292.

Boettiger, whom I had advised, hoping that I could hide out at her place on the lake. To my great surprise and pleasure, she was at the airport bound for home, having put in an hour or so at the office and picked up some homework. So we sat on the porch overlooking the lake, while Johnny Boettiger played with the Secret Service men who are constantly around the house, and I got up to date on Washington politics—and some, too, from Washington, D.C.

It wasn't known then, but Mrs. Roosevelt would be turning up in Australia or some Eastern point almost any day.[2] Anna knew it but the news wasn't out yet. That, both Anna and I recognized as a great triumph, or perhaps concession, to Mrs. Roosevelt. [She] had struggled somewhat for recognition following the debacle of her heading up [the] OCD. . . .

Well, in any event, the trip to the battlefront of the Far East was undoubtedly a special concession, as was the speech over the radio which Bernard Baruch had advised me Mrs. Roosevelt was at last being permitted to give after her return from England. Having graduated from the ordinary private practices of American life and the attitudes of the average citizen as a lawyer practicing in Seattle, I have come to recognize . . . that there is a stock in trade little dreamed of by the average American citizen and by the overwhelming mass of people. . . . That stock in trade is public recognition or, subjectively, consciousness in the public mind of one's existence on the stage of public affairs. Men barter and sell for it, struggle and scheme for it. As Thurman Arnold put the matter very bluntly one day: "The main thing is to have your name before the public—by any method—whether as the subject of adverse criticism or approval doesn't make a bit of difference! The point is to get the name out before the public constantly." Thurman wasn't even running for office, but I think he did hope to be appointed attorney general at that time. In any event, he knew the value and traded on it commercially through his books and articles.

Men of good will and less calculating intentions are equally insistent on keeping up in this stock in trade. So, Mrs. Roosevelt, who will never run for anything—but like all public figures, needs public recognition as an attribute of personality, as an earned recognition of worth and influence—has struggled against the adverse influence of Harry Hopkins, who could so easily point to OCD and say, in effect: "You see, Chief, what difficulty she got us into." . . .

To resume my story, Anna and I also spent some time reading Hearst editorials, for Anna's position of declining influence in the *Post-Intelligencer*, in which she is still nominally associate editor (after John's

---

2. Mrs. Roosevelt arrived in New Zealand 26 August 1943 and, after traveling to Australia, reached the United States mainland 23 September 1943.

departure for Italy, where he is serving in the AMGOI[3] organization as captain) still permits her to at least protest certain editorials which she considers violently anti-public or anti-administration. I, frankly, had never realized the full force of the Hearst viewpoint, having turned away in disgust from his editorials where I had encountered them, until I sat there with her, reading a whole series of them in galley proof. They were viciously anti-Russian, viciously anti-English, viciously anti-admin-istration, and viciously representative of perverted truth in the form of half-truths, incomplete statements of fact, strained interpretations, bru-talizing, fascist attitudes towards labor. . . .

. . . Dorothy Parker, the famous wit of this generation, summed the matter up when asked to make a comment on San Simeon.[4] The lines are coarse, indeed, but I preserve them in all their realistic comment, for they measure with precision how far from the mark, how very grimly the public has reacted to Hearst's effort to command respect. Here they are:

> I saw a lovely Madonna
> Enshrined in a beautiful niche,
> It was over the door
> Of the room of a whore
> In the home of a son-of-a-bitch.[5]

Anna discussed with me her position at the *Post-Intelligencer,* and heaven knows, she needed a friend of understanding and sound judg-ment, . . . [Charles B.] Lindeman, the editor of the *Post-Intelligencer,* who had been frustrated and disappointed by John's appointment as editor—a wise smooth calculating move by Hearst, [which] had lifted the *Post-Intelligencer* to its hey-day of financial success— . . . and the old crowd, upon John's departure, had closed in upon the management of a successful newspaper. By deliberate conspiracy with reactionary adver-tising firms and business interests around town, . . . Lindeman secured large advertising accounts which had not been available to John Boettiger. This made a fine showing to the Hearst management and erected a barrier against John's return.

Anna fought some grim battles on policy at the outset, and then decided that she had better not wear herself out in futile struggles.

---

3. AMGOI was the acronym for the Allied Military Government of Italy.

4. San Simeon was William Randolph Hearst's palatial but garishly decorated residence south of San Francisco.

5. Dorothy Parker is alleged to have written these lines in the guestbook at San Simeon after seeing a shrine to the Madonna outside the bedroom door of Hearst's mistress, Marion Davies. Parker's biographer believes the poem to be apocryphal, because "she simply was not a person given to making gratuitous insults." See John Keats, *You Might As Well Live: The Life and Times of Dorothy Parker* (New York: Simon and Schuster, 1970), pp. 49–50.

Editorials were still submitted to her, and some of them she blocked successfully, or at least the conservative management deferred to her wishes as a perfunctory matter of courtesy. Personal relations were pleasant, but the paper had become in every respect a "Hearst press," with all of its implications.

Anna could not leave lightly. The salary was important with John drawing a captain's pay in the Army and having bought a home on Lake Washington, so she did the best she could, ran a successful column, and did not beat her fists against the wall. . . .

A legal battle of major proportions awaited me in Seattle over the seizure of a warehouse by the Army at the port of embarkation, through my Condemnation Office, in spite of Judge [John C.] Bowen's refusal to enter an order of immediate possession, claiming that the taking was "arbitrary and capricious" on the part of the secretary of War.[6] It is too long to describe this proceeding, but it involved a great constitutional question as to whether the courts have the power to review the acts of the secretary of War, or the executive, in times of war, and Judge Bowen got completely off the track, as he does at every opportunity. . . . Poor Bowen has a mugwump mind and is about as near incompetent to sit on a federal bench as any man I happen to know on the bench. . . .

. . . And so the matter stands until the case will be argued on full appeal in the circuit court sometime in January or February when I anticipate going back to San Francisco to make that argument unless other matters prevent. . . .

I landed in San Francisco in time for a much needed weekend of rest . . . and I flew on to Los Angeles. . . .

I will not dwell on work in Los Angeles and the review of my offices there, as big as the office of the United States attorney with 18 lawyers and a total staff of over 30. I reorganized [it] somewhat as it had grown a little top-heavy in imitation of our Washington organization, where large numbers make definitive organization necessary. I attended a cocktail party given for me by the new United States attorney, Charles Carr, appointed after a long and heated controversy at the absolute insistence of Helen Gahagan (Mrs. Melvyn Douglas), national committeewoman. Helen was there with her Melvyn, a captain in the Army in the Recreational Division, whatever it is called.

---

6. *Municipal Transfer and Storage Company v. United States* arose in August 1943 when Judge Bowen ruled that the Army had seized illegally the warehouse the company leased from the Skinner and Eddy Corporation. The Army refused to return the property and so the two companies asked Bowen to find the Army and secretary of the Army in contempt of court, which he proceeded to do, 14–23 September 1943. Littell, appearing for the government, thereupon appealed the case to the 9th Circuit of the U.S. Circuit Court of Appeals. See also diary entry for 3 June 1944.

Having become more of a hero than I used to be, because of the Elk Hills battle and that subtle increased stature which goes with sheer publicity, I was more cordially welcomed by many than ever before, but I passed Helen and Melvyn somewhat casually. The fact that I had risen in the estimation of Hollywood stars did not impress me as much as it did them.

I shall never forget Melvyn's cool failure from the standards of down-to-earth Western friendship, when I lay sick in the Biltmore Hotel at the first of August in 1941. I had written for an address of a place to rest up for a little bit. I got it all right—in a note from his secretary, written at the request of Mr. Douglas, unaccompanied by any invitation to spend a night or even have dinner with them, but concluding with the mild hope that they would see me while I was in Los Angeles. I will admit I had been pretty rough with Melvyn in a letter or two from Los Angeles in response to continual requests to do things, unaccompanied by any corresponding or reciprocal services. There is a quarterdeck attitude by those suddenly elevated by chance to the quarterdeck without ever having served in the fo'c'sle, which I find intolerable. Furthermore, I was just not quite big enough for full, all-out parity, though both Helen and Melvyn had at least been unstinting in their praise and expressions of admiration for my viewpoint and character and attitudes.

Helen obviously wished to recapture lost ground, partially out of genuine interest and a reasonable measure of devotion—and partially because I had become a figure which, from her liberal viewpoint and among her friends, it was highly advantageous to have around her.

With many of the small-fry political lights whom Charlie Carr had naturally asked to this gathering—which was essentially one of political friends, fawning somewhat on the Douglasses—I exchanged only a few words. [My conversation] with Helen [was] interrupted by the ex- governor, Culbert Olson, who drew near with obvious intent of getting my support for appointment to the vacancy on the Circuit Court of Appeals for which he is about as well qualified as Judge Bowen is to sit on the District Court in Washington. Then, I drifted on to others in the gathering who are of no particular interest to you. At the end of the party, when Helen and Melvyn were departing, I shook hands cordially—first with Melvyn and then with Helen, at which point she reached out and took the other hand also and said, "You are perfectly grand—you are just swell!" With that, she leaned forward and kissed me—very much, I surmised, to the envy of many stalwarts around the room who watched with interest.

I was utterly and completely indifferent—deliberately so. I felt like saying, "That's quite all right once, but don't ever do it again!" It was such a characteristic gesture of a charming woman who is used to getting her way by charm. . . .

I spent one afternoon with callers, one [of whom was] J. A. Smith, president of the Independent Petroleum Producers and Consumers

Association and his friend, Frank Burke, who owns two radio stations. Smith was the one who published my Elk Hills report and distributed it to every congressman and senator and all the libraries in the country and thousands of other places. I [had] called him in Los Angeles to see what kind of a fellow he was, never having met him before. I [have] since then [been] accused, before the Naval Affairs Committee, of having operated at his behest in the attack on the Elk Hills contract and also being under the influence of the Richfield Oil Company, according to a letter to the attorney general sent to me from Washington. . . .

My leisure time and dictaphone has now run out.

Affectionately,
Daddy [signed]

21 November 1943
4101 Lorcom Lane

Last Monday, the 15th, Congressman [Carl] Vinson, chairman of the Naval Affairs Committee, called me from the Hill to ask if I could testify the following morning at 10:00 in regard to the Elk Hills contract—the new one proposed by the Navy Department.[1] This followed a call earlier in the day from Mr. [Donald C.] Cook, the investigator for the committee and former assistant general counsel of the SEC, borrowed for this purpose, to ask: (1) if I had finished my study of the new contract; (2) if I had any objection to telling him what the results were or showing him the contract; and, (3) if I couldn't show it to him, could I answer certain questions. In view of the supercilious attitude of this young man at the prior hearings, and a somewhat antagonistic attitude which seemed to reflect the attitude of the Naval Affairs Committee in approaching the hearings of the Lands Committee last summer, I did not exactly warm to the subject, but told him that I was prepared to appear before the committee or submit the report to the committee. [I] certainly thought they should have the full benefit of it at the proper time, but that I could tell him nothing at the moment as my report was going to the attorney general.

Being somewhat soft-hearted, I did confirm his somewhat anxious opinion to the effect that a firm commitment on production by, and participation in, Standard, for the first five years, or the first 25,000,000 barrels, prevented the deal from being a unit plan contract.[2] I told him

1. See *New York Times*, 9 December 1943, p. 16.
2. Mr. Littell has appended the following comment to this diary entry: "Simply stated a

that was one of many things which possibly prevented it from being a unit plan contract under the act of 1938, and that we had considered them all.

It was only the next morning that I found out that Mr. Cook himself was to testify, presumably after many months of work on the investigation; that he was somewhat confused and baffled by the contract, as well he might be! It is a confusing deal for anyone to read.

I called Congressman Magnuson, a member of the committee and a classmate of mine in law school, to relate Cook's conversation and expressed some surprise that the committee was proceeding without the Department of Justice—or was it? "Maggie" said definitely not; that he had already spoken to Chairman Vinson about my being called; that the committee intended to call me. This was confirmed by Vinson's call, and I replied very carefully and very properly—balancing on the tightrope as I must in the Department—that I would appreciate his asking the solicitor general, Charles Fahy, or the attorney general in regard to my appearance. I said that I was available at any time and ready to testify when wanted; that I had finished my report and had handed it to the solicitor general who is handling the matter for the attorney general; and that I thought in view of past experience in which the legislative processes had over-taken our executive processes . . . that he, Vinson, ought to first call the attorney general. Vinson agreed, but told me to stand by to appear the next morning.

It was clear that he had promptly called Mr. Fahy, who had in turn consulted the attorney general, who decided—as I anticipated—that the matter should not reach Congress until he and the solicitor general had had a chance to review it. This was so stated in a return telephone call, and I fully agreed that was the orderly process.

I talked with Charles Fahy, relating my conversation with Vinson, which had concluded in a most interesting way. After asking me if I minded telling him, informally, what my opinion was—to which I had again replied that I would appreciate very much his asking that of the attorney general since the Department of Justice had not made up its mind and my opinion was purely my own—Vinson had said:

> "Well, you haven't changed your mind, have you? I mean in respect to condemnation. I am definitely for condemnation of Standard's interest in Elk Hills, although there is a sharp division of opinion in this committee. I read your report carefully and I think you had your feet on the ground all the time, and I hope you haven't changed."

'unit plan' contract arises when two or more competing producers in the same field agree to limit drilling and production to a certain basis, thus preventing excessive drilling and drainage of oil which would normally result if the development were left to unbridled competition."

"That much I can tell you, Mr. Congressman," I said. "I have not changed my opinion one *iota*. Condemnation is the only solution of this problem and I am delighted to find your leadership supports that same conclusion."

I could have cheered to find that Chairman Vinson was on my side, although John J. Courtney, chief of the Real Estate Section of the Navy, had mentioned at a cocktail party the preceding evening, given by Governor and Mrs. Stainback [Ingram M. and Cecile Stainback] before they left for Hawaii, that opinion was divided in the committee but that the majority were in favor of condemnation. That, however, is counting chickens before they are hatched; I believe there is a long, tough fight ahead.

Two or three conferences between Solicitor General Fahy and his assistant, [Paul] Freund, together with my two assistants working on this matter, finally led to a conference in the attorney general's office, from 11:35 A.M. Friday the 19th to 1:00 P.M., between the solicitor general and Mr. Freund, the attorney general and myself. The solicitor general and Mr. Freund outlined what they conceived to be the legal issues, saying that we were all in accord on: (1) That the contract presented obligations for which an appropriation ought to be secured and that the matter ought to be referred to Congress; but that (2) I was of the opinion that the contract was illegal *in toto* as not being a unit plan contract authorized by law. They thought that matter was not "free from doubt" but that it was unnecessary to go into it further because of the first conclusion reached.

We discussed the matter at considerable length and I endeavored to make my position clear to the attorney general, particularly my objections to the division of percentages between the government and Standard as provided in the Engineering Reports upon which the contract was based. I pointed out that my memorandum examined only the legal issue as the Navy had confined us to that sphere, but that I felt very strongly that certain practical aspects of the contract could not be ignored if the public interests were properly served. I spelled that out in terms of the division of percentages which quite clearly start out on the wrong basis inasmuch as an arbitrary line limiting commercial productivity is drawn down the western end of the originally agreed area of commercial productivity, whereas in fact a much greater area of Navy lands to the west should have been included.

The AG wished to know why I thought we could ascertain the interests of the parties for the purposes of condemnation and yet could not do so by this Engineering Report for the purposes of a unit plan contract. I endeavored to explain, largely on the grounds that the Standard Oil Company has the burden of proof in a condemnation case to establish the value of what is taken away from it; an Engineering Report of this character [is] hopelessly inadequate for such a purpose.

"I can't see that," the attorney general said. "It seems to me you are quite inconsistent in saying that we can establish a valuation for the purposes of condemnation, but cannot establish quantities for the purposes of dividing the interests of the parties in this field in this unit plan contract."

I was up against one of those decisions which, devoid of understanding, is nevertheless quite concrete in form and seemingly impervious to attack.

It was further developed that, in view of the shortage of time—for the interim agreement expires December 8th—it could be extended. This is exactly what I told Mr. Fahy would happen if we wrote a short term operating agreement.[3] Nothing would be decided in that time and the agreement would simply be extended so that in effect Standard is continuing to operate the Reserve.

Mr. Freund was requested to draft a letter to the secretary of the Navy expressing the view that the matter would have to be submitted to Congress, the attorney general saying that he preferred to take the matter up with Secretary Knox.

I have seen nothing of the proposed letter nor have I heard in any further respects from the solicitor general or the attorney general since then.

Monday, 22 November 1943

Having heard nothing from the attorney general's office, and being uncertain as to whether Chairman Vinson expected me to come to the committee this morning (I neglected to say in the above entry that the hearing had been adjourned until this morning to give the attorney general and Mr. Fahy a chance to review my memorandum and reach a conclusion) I called Mr. Vinson. He stated that the whole matter had been put off for two weeks at the request of the attorney general to give him time to reach an opinion, at which time Vinson said, "both of you will be heard."

Two weeks from today will bring the matter to December 6th, so apparently the attorney general has already committed himself to Secretary Knox to continue the interim operating agreement. This accomplishes a division of the oil—64 per cent to Navy and 36 per cent to Standard—which is based upon the objectionable division in the Engi-

---

3. For details of this interim operating agreement, see Log Book entry for 1 July 1943.

neering Report. Perhaps it should be 80 or 90 per cent to Navy. Extending the interim agreement is exactly what was anticipated. How easily policy falls into the line of least resistance!

11:00 P.M., Monday, 22 November 1943
4101 Lorcom Lane

A conference was called by the attorney general in his office at 5:00 P.M., regarding Elk Hills. The solicitor general and his assistant, Mr. Freund, and I convened there. The attorney general called attention to a draft of a proposed opinion which was before him on the desk which he had evidently read. [He] asked Mr. Freund at once if he was sure that the secretary of the Navy under the new proposed contract had the absolute power to arbitrate the case if the Engineering Committee of six members—proposed in the contract—did not reach an agreement as to the division of percentages between the government and Standard. There was some speculation on this point. [The] attorney general wondered whether the secretary's power was sufficiently clear to decide the matter after the report of the special petroleum engineer was made, following disagreement in the Engineering Committee, as provided in the contract.

I expressed the opinion that, if the secretary disregarded the report of the petroleum engineer, his decision could be taken into court by Standard on the ground that the secretary had been "arbitrary and capricious" in reaching a decision. [I] believe Mr. Freund and Mr. Fahy agreed that the contract might be somewhat more explicit. After exploring this point somewhat further, the attorney general expressed the opinion that the contract went far toward being fair to the government in a provision which yielded so completely to the decision of the secretary of the Navy.

The attorney general then expressed doubts as to the meaning of the term "cessation of hostilities" which was one of the possible circumstances upon which Standard's right to take 15,000 barrels a day from the field in the primary period was to terminate. It was agreed that this was of somewhat doubtful meaning. [It] might mean after the last belligerent had laid down arms, and I remarked that there [were] one or two decisions on this point from the last war and that the *cessation of hostilities* had not actually occurred in the legal sense for several years after November 11, 1918. It was thought this should be made more definite.

Some place along in the discussion at about this point, when the attorney general was making references to the opinion before him, I said that I had not seen the proposed opinion and therefore knew nothing of the language to which he was referring at one point in the discussion. Mr. Fahy hastened to explain that he had sent it to me. I replied that I had not received it, and the attorney general added: "It has only just now been completed and we are considering it." A copy was handed to me by Mr. Freund, and we all settled down to read it through. I, apparently, was the only one who had not read it, however. . . .

We then proceeded to consider whether the proposed contract was a unit plan contract authorized by the Act of June 30, 1938—which is the meat of the coconut. Freund, at the attorney general's request, outlined the terms of the contract. [He] and Fahy expressed the opinion that: (1) Inasmuch as the contract calls for considerable sums of money to be expended in exploration, development and operation costs to which the government would be ultimately committed (although not immediately so, due to Standard's bearing the costs in the primary period) the contract ought to be referred to Congress for approval and for appropriation authorization, now; and, (2) they believed that the contract was a unit plan contract authorized by the general powers given to the secretary of the Navy by the act, although not falling within the proviso expressly mentioning unit plan contracts. They said there was, however, some doubt about this point.

I explained that that is precisely where we disagreed. [In] my view the contract was not a unit plan contract under the act. [If] it were, it would have to be brought within the proviso specifically mentioning unit plan contracts, but that this was obviously unsatisfactory to the parties because it gave the secretary of the Navy, with the approval of the President, the power to cut down on production in any unit plan contract at any time the secretary saw fit.

"Would you consider it a unit plan contract if it were among private owners?" Mr. Fahy asked.

"It might well be—I think it could be," I said, "but this contract is illegal as being between the United States, direct, and one owner, which is not authorized by the act. Furthermore, it does not comply with the requirements for a unit plan contract in the proviso which was repeatedly enacted by Congress in slightly different forms in various acts, authorizing unit plan contracts."

"I do not understand what you mean," the attorney general said with obvious irritation. "You say it could be considered a unit plan contract [but], if so, why is it not considered so here?"

I cannot recall the precise words of our discussion at this point but, for the moment, we were talking at cross purposes, and I so stated although during the entire incident, I was like one under hostile cross-examination. I pointed out that the last paragraph of the opinion was the one in which our opinions divided sharply. Although we agreed on one point—that the matter should be referred to Congress—I felt that the attorney general should state, unequivocally, that the contract is illegal, instead of merely acknowledging that there was some confusion about the matter, as the memorandum did, . . .

"I do not want to hold this contract illegal and thereby strengthen the hand of Chairman Vinson of the Naval Affairs Committee, who wants to condemn this property, as against Secretary Knox, who does not," said the attorney general.

I felt like saying that it was not the business of the attorney general to take sides in a controversy of this fundamental character, but to render an opinion on the law, letting the chips fall where they may.

The attorney general continued on the subject of condemnation and all the reasons against it: It would take so much money, we have no knowledge of the true value, it was needless to tie up so much money in oil in the ground. They were all the familiar, old-time Standard-Navy arguments. Charlie Fahy chimed in that it would take several years to litigate the case, and we would be bound by whatever verdict a jury brought it. The attorney general added that there was no way of handling the administration of the reserve in the Navy Department.

I replied that the oil was the life blood of the Navy and that we might just as well tie up all the ships of the Navy as soon as there was insufficient oil to operate them, . . . [The interest] of the Standard Oil Company in this reserve in comparison, . . . was trivial indeed and, besides, we were spending millions of dollars currently, . . . Why not take a little of that future expenditure and invest it in an oil reserve in the ground and keep it there, consistent with the Act of June 30, 1938, at least until Congress decided to take the lid off and open up Elk Hills? . . .

I also mentioned that [the] Navy had condemned innumerable other plants, businesses and properties, the cost of which ran into many millions of dollars.

In returning to consideration of the opinion, Freund was asked to draft it up in final form. "Should I send up to Mr. Freund a copy of what I consider to be the proper opinion for the attorney general in this matter?" I asked.

"No. I think that will be unnecessary," the attorney general said. "We will get Mr. Freund's draft and then meet again and consider it."

It flashed across my mind that he did not want any memoranda in the file showing what my opinion was, but apparently the thought bothered him, for he came back to it a moment or two later and remarked that, of course, I could send a memorandum to Mr. Freund, if I so desired, but he thought it was entirely unnecessary. The essential thing for us now was to all four agree on the opinion, and certainly we were in substantial accord in that the matter should be referred to Congress.

I called attention to the consequences of delay, asking if he fully appreciated the fact that the interim operating agreement expired on

December 8th, and that the result of delay would certainly be that it would have to be extended. He replied somewhat impatiently that of course he realized that, but that was inevitable, "wasn't it?"

"Certainly not," I replied. "Congress could act, and my information is that the Naval Affairs Committee is about ready to decide the matter in favor of condemnation."

He indicated utter disagreement with my view; [that] Congress could not possibly act before December 8th; and that he considered the extension of the interim operating agreement inevitable. That is where a decisive opinion of the attorney general on the true state of the law would be most effective. Congress could and would act. He also pointed out that no appraisal was available, and asked what, if anything, had been done on the matter of appraisal work.

I replied that I had heard it rumored that three men had been sent out by Secretary Knox to make a preliminary survey in reference to appraisal conclusions during the summer, but that although we had facilities for making such appraisals, we had not been invited to do so. We had no jurisdiction [in] the case until it was referred to us. I reminded him, too, of one of the last letters to Secretary Knox, in July or August, before the interim operating agreement was approved, suggesting to Secretary Knox that the facilities of this Department were available so that we could well have had the property appraised during the summer and would now know about where we stand. I also stated that a tentative estimate had been competently made at about $50,000,000, but that I did not consider this by any means an adequate basis upon which to predicate a definite opinion as to value.

There was considerable discussion as to whether or not the contract was one for conservation. I expressed a view that it was one for the exploration and development of Elk Hills, but that on the Navy theory of swapping some of its oil for Standard's by letting Standard take all the initial production, it might conceivably be considered conservation. I pointed out that it involved the Navy giving government property to Standard; namely, oil from government land to Standard during the primary period.

The attorney general then tried to explain the arrangement to me but, not knowing too much about it, he did not succeed very well. He concluded that it all boiled down to whether or not this was a contract for conservation and, on that, opinions could differ and this was a question of policy for the Navy. He also wandered off the reservation somewhat by saying that it was now a general problem in which the Army was also involved, and the Department of the Interior had oil lands, itself, which it had never sought to operate. He observed that the whole matter of oil ought to be coordinated now with Secretary Ickes. Didn't I think so?

I remained silent because he was so obviously and so completely on the other side in Ickes' corner. . . . There was nothing to gain by discussion on that general front as the attorney general is utterly uninformed and is clearly trying to play ball with both Secretary Knox and Secretary Ickes. In such an atmosphere, I am obviously a problem child to be spanked whenever he can reach me and whenever he dares.

23 November 1943
4101 Lorcom Lane

I was notified of a meeting in the attorney general's office at 3:30, and met there with Adlai Stevenson, special assistant to the secretary of the Navy; Keith Kane, attorney for the Navy Department; and Admiral [Thomas L.] Gatch, now judge advocate general of the Navy; a lieutenant assisting Kane; and Mr. Fahy and Mr. Freund. I received, just before leaving for the meeting, a copy of a letter to the secretary of the Navy, dated November 23rd, embracing the opinion which Freund had redrafted and which was to be reviewed with representatives of the Navy. . . .

The most curious phase of the discussion was the Navy's naive attitude toward whether an obligation was assumed which would commit Congress to an appropriation, in view of the fact that Standard was to pay all costs during the primary period of the contract which would last for some years, or until 25 million barrels are produced. The fact that, in approving the contract now, an ultimate obligation of the United States government was undoubtedly assumed, if the contract was a valid exercise of power under the act of 1938, did not seem to bother him [Attorney General Biddle], for he said, we may never develop the reserve. There is no commitment to develop the reserve; therefore, there is no commitment to pay any costs on the part of the government. With such unrealistic hocus-pocus reasoning, he got around the fact that an appropriation would be necessary to support the contract—and I will admit that the contract has been most skillfully drafted to avoid reference to Congress on this point.

However, the opinion was on the whole satisfactory except for the conclusions. After reciting all the reasons which would lead to a definite conclusion that the contract would be illegal, the concluding sentence straddled the matter and ran out on the suggestion merely that the contract ought to be referred to Congress. Even the attorney general's mind stopped on that sentence, which Freund frankly admitted was somewhat "elliptical." I ran into the weakness to say that the only conclusion which could follow was that the contract was "illegal." I think the attorney general's professional sense was aroused, for he finally changed the concluding sentence, striking out that portion of it which is enclosed in parentheses:

"In the light of these circumstances, I am compelled to conclude that (while general authority to execute contracts for the protection of the reserve is granted and the proposed contract would have such an object and effect) the contract should not be executed on behalf of the United States without more specific approval by Congress than is found under the present statutes."

I was naturally delighted with the change, and so advised the attorney general. The deleted matter took all the equivocation from the conclusion, and could only have been improved by substituting for it an unqualified and logical conclusion that the contract, as proposed, would be "illegal." . . .

The Navy men seemed to accept the matter in good grace, and even the judge advocate general agreed that it had to be referred to Congress and he so advised the Naval Affairs Committee in an opinion of his own which the attorney general had considered during the discussion. . . .

Sunday night, 28 November 1943
4101 Lorcom Lane

A gathering the night before last at the Gifford Pinchots' presented Orson Welles. . . . Louis Dolivet, secretary of the International Free World Association (who married a Whitney and, therefore, has the wherewithal to back up his convictions) has interested Orson Welles in the Free World Association, whose objectives are not yet clearly defined, but which are—broadly speaking—to back up those objectives which assure a free world after the war. Primarily, such ideas hinge around collective security and the Four Freedoms in the international sphere, where I think the objectives should be confined, although some look longingly toward domestic issues on which the Free World Association would quickly run onto the rocks. . . .

Last night we had dinner for Governor and Mrs. Gruening [Ernest H. and Dorothy Gruening] of Alaska at which the Vice President and Mrs. Wallace were the ranking guests. Helen and Ronnie Graham, who have been with us for a week, were the prime conservatives of the party. Leila Pinchot, Helen Fuller, and Drew Pearson were also there. There was a fairly vigorous discussion of postwar affairs as the men sat at the dining table following the departure of the ladies. Ronnie Graham, who had just finished reading Wallace's *The Common Man*,[1] which he had bought in Vancouver as he was leaving, and which, as he said, changed his ideas

1. Russell Lord, ed., *Henry A. Wallace: The Century of the Common Man, Selected from Recent Public Papers* (New York: Reynal and Hitchcock, 1943).

U.S. Assistant Attorney General Norman M. Littell at his desk at the Justice Department, June 1941

Katherine Maher at Oxford, 1922

Norman Littell and his family in Arlington, Virginia, shortly after his appointment to the Justice Department

President Franklin D. Roosevelt, ca. 1940

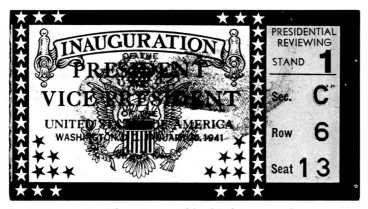

Invitation to President Roosevelt's third inaugural,
January 1941

The President and Mrs. Roosevelt
request the pleasure of the company of
Mr. and Mrs. Littell
at a buffet luncheon at the White House
on Monday, January the twentieth
nineteen hundred and forty-one
immediately after the Inaugural Ceremonies
at the Capitol

Invitation to luncheon at the White House

Mr. and Mrs. Henry Wallace with Mr. and Mrs. Josephus Daniels in Mexico, March 1940

Francis Biddle, Mrs. Claude Pepper, Robert Jackson, and Mrs. Norman Littell, on the occasion of Biddle's nomination as attorney general, February 1941

Former U.S. Ambassador to the Soviet Union
Joseph E. Davies, 1945

U.S. Senator
Joseph C. O'Mahoney
of Wyoming, March 1942

Supreme Court Justice
Robert H. Jackson

Supreme Court Justice
Frank Murphy

U.S. Postmaster General
James A. Farley

Territorial Governor of Alaska
Ernest Gruening, ca. 1940

Former U.S. Attorney General
Homer Cummings, April 1942

*Norman Littell with Territorial Governor of Hawaii
Ingram M. Stainback, ca. 1941*

Autographed Jim Berryman cartoon, Washington Evening Star, *1944*

Norman and Katherine M. Littell, on a cruise ship, ca. 1980

concerning the Vice President because the book was full of such good common sense, [asked] the question, which I had encouraged him to ask: "I cannot understand all this talk about the struggle for raw materials," he said. "Before the war, any country could get raw materials which wanted to pay for them at reasonable cost. Germany was not content with this and wanted to move in and take them without charge."

"That is rather superficial," the Vice President said. "As a matter of fact, neither the United States nor England would purchase Germany's manufactured output, raw materials, or anything else. That is what brought on the war." . . .

"The only possible solution seems to be the enormous expansion of consuming power to absorb more and more of these products, or do you see any other solution?" [I asked.]

The Vice President offered none, except to repeat that we must import goods if other countries are to be able to buy from us, repeating the lesson of the last postwar period in which enormous amounts of capital were loaned abroad while a succession of high tariffs prohibited us from importing foreign goods, thereby cutting off avenues of return for that money.

"The Young Plan[2] certainly added nothing," Ronnie added.

"Only a palliative," the Vice President replied. It was recognized that purely economic factors were not solely responsible for Germany's condition. A substantial share of the responsibility had to be placed upon the warlike instincts of the race, or a substantial portion of it at any rate. . . .

Monday night, 29 November 1943
4101 Lorcom Lane

We convened in the attorney general's office again, at about 4:00, on the subject of Elk Hills, having received by messenger shortly before a proposed statement by the attorney general to the Naval Affairs Committee which he proceeded to review with Mr. Fahy, . . . Mr. Freund, and myself. It was a moderate statement in which he "sought to be fair" as between condemnation and the unit plan contract proposed by Standard and Navy.

---

2. The "Young Plan" was a program developed by an international committee of financial experts, headed by American banker Owen D. Young, to replace the defunct "Dawes Plan" of economic relief for Germany. A fifteen-nation agreement, signed 31 August 1929, it reduced Germany's war reparations to $8 billion to be paid at 5.5 percent interest over 59.5 years. It also reduced Germany's annual payments to $153 million, not coincidentally the amount of the war debts the Allied nations owed to the United States (although it provided for higher payments should German prosperity improve). The Young Plan was expected to be a "final and definitive" solution for Germany's postwar economic woes, but the Great Depression rendered it ineffective.

The fact that I had never seen the draft, as I had never seen his prior legal opinion which went out to the Navy on November 24th, after our conference on November 23rd, was again indicative of the very careful effort to circumvent [me], although of course the circumvention could not go so far as to leave me out entirely in view of my identification with the subject matter. In each and every matter the attorney general would ask Mr. Fahy what he thought, and Mr. Freund what he thought, and, perhaps, he would come around to me to ask me what I thought. My suggestions were largely made in order to avoid being accused later of having remained silent as to any objections which I might have.

For example, in reviewing the differences between this contract and the old contract, of which Freund had listed four, I felt constrained to suggest that there were others which ought to be pointed up. . . .

"What are the things which come to your mind now?" the attorney general asked.

"The attempt to take in the whole reserve of over 43,000 acres is a complete indictment of the contract as a unit plan contract," I said. "It is not simply a unit plan contract, for these are ordinarily confined to the area where there is competing drilling—that is their purpose. There is no competing drilling in the western side of the reserve. The only competing drilling which could possibly be found, or which could arise, is in the eastern, or developed area, now embraced in about 9,000 acres of commercially productive land. [Standard] doesn't even own any property—only two quarter sections of no importance whatever—at the western side of the reserve."

"I think there is something in Norman's point," the attorney general said. "You ought to mention that, Mr. Freund."

"The most conspicuous single piece of unmitigated window-dressing in the whole contract," I continued, "is the provision that Navy may let a contract to any private operator to operate Elk Hills Reserve, or operate the reserve itself but, if Standard should be the contractor operating the field, it must operate at cost. What other operator could ever get the contract if Standard is to operate at cost? It is a meaningless provision. It attempts to get around by words the accusation that Standard is to get the operating control of this field, which was a feature of the last contract."

"You wouldn't take that language out, would you?" the attorney general said. "It still makes possible an alternative contractor—and, after all, Standard is there. It can operate more efficiently than anyone else."

I felt like saying, "So could the private utilities in the power field, which you fought so successfully a few years ago in the TVA battle.[1] They

1. The Tennessee Valley Authority (TVA) was established by the TVA Act of 1933, approved 18 May 1933. The TVA was a multipurpose federal agency, with jurisdiction over

could all operate more efficiently. A question of principle was involved and of basic economic policy—in this case, a question as to whether or not you would increase the already overpowering power of Standard in the West, as a matter of public policy." It was futile to make any comment, however. No one in the room had any concept of the West and of the position which Standard of California has there, except myself. All of them were ignorant of the oil background.

I made one or two more comments as to things which came to my mind, somewhat reluctantly, I confess, because the points can then be played with in a superficial manner without the serious consideration which ought to be given to them.

"That is all I think of at the moment," I concluded, "but I will write a memorandum to Mr. Freund before I leave for New York on Friday."

"It isn't necessary to write a memorandum," the attorney general said. "Just talk the matter over with Mr. Freund."

Again, the same thought as appeared the other day—no memoranda. Someone might discover who was the father of all the critical ideas on the Elk Hills contract if there were too damn many memoranda around the Department. . . .

---

6 December 1943
4101 Lorcom Lane

Dearest Katherine Mather,

. . . This weekend we had a badly needed "change of walls," . . . through the young Gifford Pinchots, who had invited us to New York to see Katherine Cornell. . . .

. . . I finished my [New Jersey condemnation work], ending up with a conference with lawyers in the firm of [Basil] O'Connor and [John C.] Farber, the President's former law firm, where we discussed the rather complex problem of conveying the Hyde Park property to the government as a national monument, and satisfying the President's desire to reserve life estates to himself and Mrs. Roosevelt and the five children in the face of a New York statute limiting life estates to two. John Farber said he had read my brief with very great interest and had a good laugh over the veto measure of Governor Roosevelt vetoing the repeal of the very

---

the multistate Tennessee Valley region. It's main function was to build and operate hydroelectric and flood control dams, but it also built roads and power lines and engaged in social planning. After bitter legal battles, the Supreme Court upheld the constitutionality of the TVA in the cases of *Ashwander v. Tennessee Valley Authority*, 297 U.S. 288 (1936), and *Tennessee Electric Company v. Tennessee Valley Authority*, 306 U.S. 118 (1939).

statutes[1] which now stand in our way. The governor had said that "any intelligent lawyer" can now find a way to accomplish the client's wishes. How ironic!

"Very provocative language!" I said to Farber. "It naturally kept us humping for a while because I hated to give up without finding a solution."

Of course, the solution lay in the creation of trusts on the division of estates, but that is not adapted to this situation in which the estate is not to be divided but is to go to the government, intact, as a national monument. Perhaps, we can accomplish it by retaining a use and occupancy right as an encumbrance to the grant. That is being explored. . . .

Goodnight, my dear,

Affectionately,
[unsigned]

Tuesday, 7 December 1943
4101 Lorcom Lane

The lunch in my office for the Free World Association was the most vital incident of the day. The lunch was for Walter Wanger, the leading producer in Hollywood, head of the Free World Association there. Louis Dolivet, . . . and a number of government officials including Vice President Wallace, Governor Gruening of Alaska, . . . Jim McGranery, the new assistant to the attorney general in Jim Rowe's place—and a blessed relief after Rowe—[attended]. . . .

Wanger . . . is of definitely Republican leanings and had found Willkie quite convincing. As he explained to Dolivet, "He is just as safe on foreign policy but might be better on administration." There will be so many follow that line of reasoning in view of the bad administration in many departments of government during this period—the good administration receiving little attention and appreciation. Many of us have been deeply conscious at this point of the need for sharper executive action in moving incompetent people out of important posts which would have alleviated this situation. It is so clear that no matter how fine a man's viewpoint, if in a responsible position he shows utter lack of executive capacity, he ought to be removed.

Secretary Perkins is a case in point. Elmer Davis, with whom I talked today to invite him to this lunch, is another case in point. OWI [Office of

---

1. Sections 42 and 43 of the New York Real Property Law.

War Information][1] has gotten completely out of his hands. He is a good writer and a good speaker, but in managing that far-flung organization he is a boy scout. His control is so little that the Republicans have captured it completely. As one of the three or four surviving New Dealers in the OWI informed me recently, "We are the very last of the New Dealers. Even the Chief has referred to the OWI in ways which recognize this fact. He said, 'Those fellows over there will not even mention my name, except as Commander-in-Chief.'"

OPA [Office of Price Administration] has similarly gotten into utterly hostile hands as the War Production Board did long, long ago. The camel has come into the Arab's tent and the ejected and dejected Arab cannot get back. This, however, is a digression to another field.

I might add that a staff meeting was held in the attorney general's office this morning at 11:30, there being, as usual, practically no discussion. Almost everyone passed when the attorney general called on them, each saying he had nothing to report. It is for this reason that I have stopped reporting staff meetings. . . .

Sunday, 11 December 1943
Warm Springs Inn, Warm Springs, Virginia

The hearing last Wednesday, the 8th, before the Naval Affairs Committee, in regard to the proposed contract between Standard Oil Company of California and the Navy Department for the development of Elk Hills Naval Petroleum Reserve, was quite a heated affair. Attorney General Biddle and Secretary Knox of the Navy sat beside each other before the committee in the center of the amphitheater, and Mr. Freund, Mr. Fahy and I sat to the left of the attorney general.

The attorney general read his release throughout, embodying his decisions or opinions to the secretary of the Navy. He made a few additional comments in regard to the contract, some of my observations having borne a mild and tasteless fruit. Chairman Vinson, who I learned later is not even a lawyer, pounced upon the principal weakness of his opinion after the reading of it was concluded. . . .

"You really mean that the contract is illegal, don't you?" asked Vinson.

"I prefer to use my own language," the attorney general replied. "I said that the matter was not free from doubt as to whether or not the

---

1. President Roosevelt established the Office of War Information (OWI) by Executive Order No. 9182, 13 June 1942, to direct war propaganda and disseminate official war news both at home and to the troops abroad. The Army News Service, however, soon took over the role of supplying news to U.S. forces abroad. Elmer H. Davis, a popular radio newscaster, was the director of OWI. President Truman abolished OWI 31 August 1945.

contract was authorized by the Act of June 30, 1938," or words to that effect. . . .

I do not think the attorney general could have had much satisfaction from his "play" in the press, which did not leave too clear-cut an impression except that he thought the matter ought to be referred to Congress. Mrs. Pinchot observed to Katherine the next day, after reading the morning paper, "It is quite clear that Norman pushed the attorney general into this position, and that he was reluctant to take a strong position."[1] . . .

I neglected to say that Anna Boettiger arrived in Washington a week ago with the three children. Sistie and Buzzie have been keeping up their school work with Katherine for two hours a day at our house. . . .

Thursday, 23 December 1943
Department of Justice

Among other troublesome matters in recent days has been the problem of settling the disposition of the President's Hyde Park home, which he wished to deed to the government, subject to successive life estates in himself, Mrs. Roosevelt and the five children, respectively. Just prior to the President's departure for Cairo and Teheran,[1] I had advised him in a memorandum and letter, on November 6th, somewhat exhaustively about the obstacles of the New York law which forbade the suspension of the power of alienation for more than two lives in being and restricted successive life estates to two in number.

With all of the complexities presented, the matter could not be concluded before his departure, and we pressed our study somewhat further until I was satisfied that there was no conclusive way around the New York law to accomplish the President's wishes, and that a resolution really ought to be adopted by the New York Legislature, either specifically exempting Hyde Park property from the effect of the law, or a general resolution exempting all real property given to federal, state, or municipal governments because the reason for the rule limiting the power of alienation fails where property is given to the government. . . .

I finally concluded a letter to the President, outlining all possible courses of action in regard to the Hyde Park property, . . . noting on the

---

1. "Navy Defends Deal for Elk Hills Oil; House Group Hears Biddle Ask for More Study by Congress," *New York Times*, 9 December 1943.

1. For the Teheran conference with Churchill and Stalin, the first meeting of the "Big Three," which occurred 28 November–1 December 1943 in the Iranian capital. The leaders established personal ties and reached agreements on the Eastern border of Poland, the future of Iran, and on the support of Tito in Yugoslavia.

envelope: "To the Attention of Miss Grace Tully—Please Forward," believing the President to be in Hyde Park as the papers had announced. Miss Tully called me in the afternoon to say that the President was still there, and to ask me to come to see him at 11:30 today, unofficially, through the East End of the White House, where necessary arrangements were to be made with the Secret Service, as he "wished to settle the Hyde Park matter." . . .

As for the President, when I finally made my way through a labyrinth of Secret Service men and an outpouring of White House employees, who had just come from a short visit with him where he presented them each with a present, I was shown into his office and found the President at his desk in apparently excellent physical condition, in a great good humor and a characteristically jovial mood.

He waved his hand as I closed the door behind me and called, "Hello, Norman." I crossed the room and shook hands with him. "Have you seen Anna yet?" he asked, at once. I explained that, to my regret, I had not, although Katherine had had several visits with her.

He turned at once to my letter, which was before him on the desk, and said he wanted to get the Hyde Park matter cleaned up before January 1, for income tax purposes. "I have read your letter," he said, "and now I have a better plan," he added, laughing and waving his hand in a sweeping gesture as if he were really going to fix things up.

"Splendid, Mr. President," I replied. It flashed through my mind that I was not a damned bit surprised that a better plan should come out of that versatile mind, but I had my doubts, too. We had combed out every possibility so thoroughly. He went on to explain that he thought the thing to do was to sign a straight deed to the Interior Department, reserving life estates in two lives in being, taking the two youngest children, Franklin, Jr. and John. So far, this was right from my letter. Seeing that I had pulled out my notebook and was taking notes, he slowed up so I could cover the instructions in my notes.

"—or grant a life estate to two grandchildren," he said, obviously taking the point from my letter before him in that such a plan would probably give a longer estate in his family. "With the conveyance, write a letter to the secretary of the Interior,"—this was obviously the "better plan" he had thought of—"to the effect that it was clearly the intention of Congress that I and my children should have the privilege of living at Hyde Park, and paying taxes on the property, during the lifetime of my children—however, that legal questions had been raised as to whether the act of Congress was superior to the inheritance laws of the State of New York—."[2] The President interrupted himself at that point to inject,

2. Probably a reference to the Joint Resolution (53 Stat. 1062) approved by Congress 18

"I don't want to go to the Legislature with this." That was to dispose of my first recommended course of action: That a resolution of the New York State Legislature would dispose of the problem. There was a note of impatience in his voice—not with me, but with the Legislature. I could well see that he would not care to inject so delicate a personal matter into the arena of political discussion in a state now dominated by the rising star of Republican [Thomas E.] Dewey. Much could naturally be said by the Republicans about the President erecting his own monument before his death. He resumed outlining a letter to the secretary of the Interior:

"Therefore, I have made this deed, placing in it the names of the two youngest grandchildren, and I desire that my wife and I should live there as long as we wish, and that Mrs. Roosevelt and any of the five children should live there as long as they like after my death—during that time taxes to be paid just as at present. Therefore, I have made this deed to conform with the laws of the state of New York, and even though there is a question as to whether the federal law does not supersede the state law, I am asking the Department of the Interior to accept this deed and to apply it in conformity with the intent of the act, which was definitely that my wife and I live there and that the children, and any of them, should continue to live there at their option."

Then the President explained: "The Department of the Interior could write me a letter that it would be the Department policy to carry out my intention. The present secretary could state that he could not bind future secretaries, but he is sure that the Department would carry out the original policy."

I then pointed out to the President that the only unfortunate feature of this plan was the hazard of having the use by his family concluded by the accidental termination of the second life estate; that the whole scheme was no stronger than the accidents of life and death at that point. That seemed to concern him, and he mentioned that the whole matter might be terminated by a fatal automobile accident. He then proceeded to continue down through my letter to consider other possible courses.

"The leasing proposition is no good," he said. "It would clearly be an attempt to avoid the effect of the New York law." He then reached the proposal that conveyance be made to Mrs. Roosevelt and all the children, thereby creating a joint estate, and the joint tenants could all convey to the United States government, subject to the right of use and occupancy

July 1939, which authorized the Librarian of Congress to accept a tract of sixteen acres donated by the President upon which the Franklin D. Roosevelt Library, Inc. planned to build a library to house the President's papers. The government would maintain the library. The New York State legislature also passed a bill to allow the federal government to acquire and occupy the part of Hyde Park needed for the library. See *New York Times*, 24 May 1939, p. 23, and 20 July 1939, p. 17.

during their lives. That seemed to appeal strongly, but then I pointed out that, if he wished to conclude the matter by January 1st, this course would be impossible because some of the boys were at remote places in the world and could not execute conveyances.

"That leaves open the last possible course—No. 7 in my letter," I said, which contemplates that the President and Mrs. Roosevelt would convey to the government, subject to a life estate in the President, the conveyance to contain a covenant assuring the use and occupancy after the President's death to Mrs. Roosevelt and the five children." The President read it over again.

"That one is all right," he said. "We can do just that, and that is entirely in accordance with the intent of Congress as expressed in the act." I pointed out that Congress had only approved a conveyance subject to "any life estate" of a person or persons "now in being," and that a technical objection could be raised, but that I thought it probably never would be as a practical matter. As a lawyer, however, these objections had to be pointed out. The President thought that the matter could be concluded with the execution of the conveyance such as I had suggested, covered by a letter to the secretary of the Interior, and his reply.

We talked somewhat about the rest of the property, including the personal property, the President observing that he thought it quite unlikely that Mrs. Roosevelt and the children would actually wish to live in Hyde Park—that it was large and expensive to maintain and that, probably, Mrs. Roosevelt would move into her cottage. "There are four or five houses adjacent there, you know," the President said, and I believe he referred to the house of a sister or a half-sister, as well as to Mrs. Roosevelt's cottage.

"This course is really better," the President said. "Mrs. Roosevelt won't want to live there—it is too expensive. The chances are that, when I die, there will be two or three years of straightening out things in general and property matters. If Mrs. Roosevelt had the use during her life, it gives time to adjust matters." The President added:

"There is the personal property, of course. I thought the children perhaps could take ten per cent of it, as each will want certain things, and leave ninety per cent. John and Anna want to leave it all right there."

"That is what ought to be done," I commented. "It is such a struggle to recapture these various things from the family after years have elapsed and you reassemble the home, as at Mount Vernon, Monticello, or at Hermitage."

I was conscious of dealing with items about which there would some day be a great deal of discussion and historical society scrambling, in a perfectly oriented way, with full realization that if the subject became a matter of general discussion at this moment, it would be a heated and bitter discussion, indeed, with roars of indignation that any man should be thinking of preserving his own home as a national monument. As a matter of fact, it is a perfectly cool, un-egotistical, natural thing to do in the light of the bare facts of the President's position in American and world history. It will only take a very few years to surrender him to the textbooks for all time, after which Hyde Park, with its visible evidence of a mind with a thousand facets, will become increasingly significant as a shrine of national historic importance.

"I am leaving this evening for Hyde Park," the President said. Indeed, I suspected that he had remained behind "unofficially" to avoid the official welter of events as Anna had described them to Katherine, as planned by Mrs. Roosevelt. Anna said that, "Every soldier within two or three hundred miles is invited and there will be one event after another." Anna is already being buffeted about in that welter, I am quite sure, while the peace and quiet which reigned around about in the White House must have been a matter of enjoyment to the President. "I expect to be back by next Wednesday (December 29th) but I may be back Sunday as I may have to ask Francis Biddle to prepare the papers for taking over the railroads," he said. "I am going to a conference right now about the impending railroad strike—the men are waiting for me outside." He observed something which, as nearly as I can remember, was that the railroad union men were being pretty tough. "We have offered them twice what we could have settled with them for two months ago—an eight per cent an hour increase and one week's vacation with pay, and they won't take it."[3]

While the nation was reading the headlines, somewhat breathlessly, about the impending railroad strike on the 30th, the President was dealing with the situation in great good health and about as unexcitedly as I deal with a condemnation case in the Lands Division. I suppose it is all a matter of training. One of the first things I learned in the practice of law was that you can handle the big cases with just as little work and strain as you can handle the little cases, and the same goes for public problems, providing you learn the technique—and the President is a past master. God knows how he does it, when the lives and futures of so many millions

3. On 15 December 1943, the five Railroad Brotherhood unions of operating employees had called a strike for 30 December 1943 to press their demands for higher wages. On 21 December, the fifteen nonoperating unions had promised to support them. Between 19 December and 22 December, President Roosevelt attempted to reach an agreement, without success. Therefore, on 23 December, he called on Attorney General Biddle to prepare documents to take over the railroads if the unions did not agree to his arbitration. The crisis eased 24 December, when two of the unions accepted arbitration, but President Roosevelt went ahead and issued Executive Order No. 9412, 27 December 1943. The measure ordered Secretary of War Stimson to seize the railroads. Finally, on 30 December, just hours before the strike was scheduled, the three remaining unions agreed to accept arbitration. Roosevelt completed his awards on 17 January 1944 and, at the same time, returned the railroads to their owners.

of people are really dependent, from time to time, on his mood and determinations of policy.

The President rang the buzzer under his desk and I leaned forward to leave, but asked if he had one more minute about Washington politics and, as Miss Tully came in, he paused in assent to my question. "Particularly because one question you, alone, can answer," I said, "and that is whether you would consent to Anna's running for Congress. I know you have declined to consent to your sons running, but I believe the reasons for that decision are not present in Anna's case, and it would relax a difficult situation in the state."

"To reelect Senator [Homer T.] Bone, if Eric Johnston runs against him, we will have to have a strong team-mate running for governor against [Arthur B.] Langlie. Congressman Magnuson is the only one who can probably be elected governor."

"But," the President broke in, "Senator Bone wants to leave the Senate because of his hip and secure the appointment as United States Circuit Court Judge in the Ninth Circuit—he won't run for the Senate."

"That's news to me, Mr. President," I said, "and bad news, for he is the only one who can be elected."

"I only learned that yesterday," he said, obviously referring to a conference with Postmaster General Frank Walker, the national chairman.

"That would be most unfortunate," I said, "because there is only one man who has a chance of beating Eric Johnston who, after a great deal of fanfare about his becoming Republican candidate for the vice presidency, is generally expected to settle down to running for the Senate in the state of Washington, and he will be a formidable opponent, even for Senator Bone." I was tempted to say that Bone was in as good health as he ever had been, having just come back from [the Mayo Clinic] where he had had a "new hip," as I had been informed by an intimate friend of his, a newspaperman who was in my office, a Mr. Block from the *Washington Daily News*, the *San Francisco Chronicle*, and the *Seattle Star*. I refrained.

"As far as Anna is concerned," I added, "If Magnuson does not run for Congress, but runs for the governorship, he has a reasonable chance of beating Republican Langlie because of his Scandinavian name and background, in view of Langlie's having lost much of that support. If he leaves the congressional race, there will be an awful dogfight for it which will be very hard on the party—unless Anna runs, in which event there will be no dogfight as every one will accept her candidacy."

"I will talk it over with Anna tomorrow at Hyde Park," the President said, without indicating any disapproval of the idea.

As Miss Tully was already waiting and more pressing matters were at hand, I had to stop at that point without making the additional personal comment which I really would like to have left with him that Anna was in a very unhappy situation on the *Post-Intelligencer* which had reverted to form as a Hearst paper, and that a congressional seat would, from all personal points of view, be a highly satisfactory occupation as well as a great gift to the waning forces of liberalism in Congress.

I had observed when I mentioned the proposal that, "Anna has won a great place for herself in her own right in the state of Washington—is greatly beloved by the people there and could, according to general opinion, win."

As I withdrew, saying that I would call Miss Tully when the papers were ready, the President said to confer with the Department of Interior fellows on the matter. As I went out, Mr. Justice Byrnes, director of the Office of War Mobilization,[4] Harry Hopkins, and Judge Vinson, director of the Office of Economic Stabilization, came in and I stopped to shake hands with Harry Hopkins in the anteroom. He looked hale and hearty after his trip to the Near East, in spite of his reputed ill health and the terrific panning he is receiving in the press these days, the latest crack being in the *Washington Merry-Go-Round* yesterday, which observed that one hundred and twenty people had gone with the President to Cairo, but that the seats in the plane for the trip to Teheran were saved for only the important members of the delegation, such as the President, General Marshall, Harry Hopkins, one or two others, and Private [Robert] Hopkins, the son of Harry Hopkins.

Christmas Day 1943
4101 Lorcom Lane

I could not help but speculate as to my own relationship with the President of the United States after finishing my interview with him day before yesterday. However seriously we young men of ambition take ourselves, I am unquestionably only the merest detail in his vast scheme of things, just as able young lawyers in my staff of over four hundred register only in approximate outlines of my mind, conspicuous for ability, for mediocrity, or lack of it—or they do not register at all. I have apparently registered, at least as an able lawyer, for the President once said so at dinner at the White House, apparently under the influence of

4. President Roosevelt created the Office of War Mobilization (OWM) by Executive Order No. 9347, 27 May 1943, at the suggestion of James F. Byrnes, who became director. OWM had wide powers over allocation of civilian labor and resources. It acted primarily, however, as a mediator between the various production agencies. As "Assistant President" Byrnes chaired a White House council consisting of the secretaries of war and navy, and the heads of the WPB, OEC, and the War Food Administration. In 1944, OWM was converted into the Office of War Mobilization and Reconversion by Executive Order No. 9488, 3 October 1944.

conversations with certain Supreme Court justices, who have been good enough to compliment my arguments before the Supreme Court. But that is long ago, and I have sunk into oblivion, without a doubt.

His greeting was cordial enough, as I came into his study—a wave of the hand from behind his desk and "Hello, Norman,"—but [it was] unaccompanied throughout by any personal inquiries or comments, which might, of course, be due entirely to the speed and pressure of his operations for, as stated in the preceding entry, his next appointment was with Mr. Justice Byrnes and Mr. Justice Vinson, who are practically assistant presidents, both taken from the political front for more effective dealings with "The Hill." Hyde Park has plenty of attention, however; it is a subject close to his heart.[1] . . .

Yesterday, I had lunch with Mr. Justice Murphy . . . and I must say the most satisfactory visit we have ever had. He repeatedly expressed his appreciation for the great job of work I had done in the Department—by all odds the best of any job done there among the assistant attorney generals, and spoke with real enjoyment of how, one after another, I had "unhorsed" enemies. (He spoke of the attack on me at the time he wished to appoint me; of Carl McFarland's conversation; of the fact that neither Katherine nor I would wear well; [and] that he, Murphy, would soon tire of us!)

"Why, in the name of Heaven, and what could [McFarland] say about Katherine?" I asked.

"Nothing much," he replied, laughing, "except that [you] told dirty stories; not very serious, but that was the charge."

"He certainly enjoyed the stories on many an evening when we were still friends, long before my appointment came up, such as they were," I said, remembering some of Katherine's specials.

"And the Northern Pacific case," Murphy added. "How they panned you for losing that one phase of the case which you tried out there in Spokane (the agricultural point) and then took it to the Supreme Court and beat John W. Davis on it. One by one, you routed them all—as Ed Kemp and I have frequently observed. You won!"

He went on to say that I should certainly have that circuit court appointment, and the only reason I didn't have it right this minute was that he was not attorney general. He would see the President, if necessary, but he would first talk to Anna. He told me again how the President did not want Biddle as attorney general, and told Murphy so on more than one occasion. [He] had delayed his appointment for six weeks or so; had begged Murphy to come off the Court and take the post again; and Murphy had

1. See "Roosevelts Deed Their Hyde Park Home to Government as National Historic Site," *New York Times*, 4 January 1944.

asked for a week to think it over. [He returned] from Detroit, after a week, with the understanding that he would take the attorney general's post and, late in the fall, would become secretary of War. That was the deal. But when he returned from Detroit, the Frankfurter crowd had done a job on him with the President, who explained that he, on reflection, "couldn't think of pigeon-holing Murphy," as previously suggested.

Murphy was enormously relieved as he did not wish to leave the Court, and was only going to do so because the President requested it. He explained how Tommy Corcoran had tried to "get me"—a story I have heard before; how I would never get any place as long as they could defeat it.

"You are too independent-minded. They left me, too, when I was attorney general, [because] I wouldn't take orders and, after I went to the bench, when Frankfurter found I would not follow him in my opinions, he turned on me there. Biddle, of course, does exactly what Frankfurter wishes, and that's why Biddle is there—to make judicial appointments and other personnel appointments in the Department. Jim Rowe, the first assistant to the attorney general, was constantly in and out of Frankfurter's office, as was [Edward F.] Prichard, 'the big fat boy.' I remember him as the pet of Frankfurter, now some place in Jimmy Byrnes' office. Frankfurter would be glad to see Charlie Fahy . . . as the Catholic on the Court in my place. Frankfurter has run the War Department through the appointment of the major posts there. The President, himself, is too much in the grip of this set of advisers and I told him that, to get back to the confidence of the public, he would have to clean out some of this band who are unpopular from coast to coast, right from the Tommy Corcoran days down to the present time."

"And also take the West into consideration," I added.

"Precisely," he replied. "Those two things must be done, and I have mentioned both to the President on many occasions. The strange part about it is that he always agrees, but nothing has yet been done."

We walked back to the Washington Hotel, discussing everything from Princess Martha to Anna, who remains the idol of his life (of many women, according to popular rumor).

As to Tommy Corcoran, he said: "He is living in a big apartment here and probably making from two to three hundred thousand dollars a year. I think J. Edgar Hoover has plenty on him and some others around here, too."

"Do you know Hoover well?" I asked.

"Yes," he replied.

"A strange fellow, don't you think?" I asked. "But very able and honest."

"Very. He is exceedingly able and has done a magnificent piece of work with the FBI." I interrupted to agree fully and to state that I had always considered his job one of the most efficient in all government service."

"But he is almost pathological," Murphy continued. "He can get something on anybody if he starts investigating him; that is his tendency."

"What is he after?" I asked.

"To become attorney general in the next Republican administration," Murphy replied. "At such a time, he would indict a lot of people around here, perhaps, and certainly Tommy Corcoran. I believe he has the goods on him."

Somehow, the subject of Princess Martha and the President came up, which Murphy labeled as the principal current subject of drawing room or cocktail party gossip. "I hope it's true," he said. "The poor fellow has to have an outlet and means of recreation and relaxation with the terrific load he's carrying, sitting there always, half paralyzed. [And] what if it is true that he is having an affair? History is full of such incidents. Mrs. Roosevelt is a great and good woman, but what a battleaxe to live with." . . .

1944

23 February 1944
4101 Lorcom Lane

It is difficult, indeed, to pack into these few pages the concentrated essence of the last two or three months. Let me dispose, first, of my waning ambition to return to the West by appointment to the Circuit Court of Appeals in San Francisco. My conversation with the President in December, in which he mentioned Senator Bone's interest, is reported in my notes but, thereafter, I was able to confirm definitely that Senator Bone was making a concerted effort, in the ways of politicians—without admitting that he would take the appointment—to secure the nomination.

I, therefore, shifted to his support, particularly in view of his crippled hip, which is giving him constant pain and the need for retirement, and I so advised his mercurial political adviser, Saul Haas, collector of customs at Seattle, when he telephoned recently, ostensibly to chat, but actually to find out what my point of view was. Every cloud has a silver lining, and I take great satisfaction in thinking what a thorn in his side the vitriolic and caustic Senator Bone would be to Judge Denman, the incredible bully in the Ninth Circuit Court.

But this is ahead of my story. First, I finally did see Anna Boettiger after Katherine and I returned from a trip to New York on the weekend of January 15th. She came to lunch at my office, where I lit the fire in the big fireplace on a chilly day and we settled down to lunch.

Anna had seen Mr. Justice Murphy—had been to dinner with him— and he had obviously talked somewhat about me and also the appointment to the Ninth Circuit, which he felt very strongly that I should have.

"You have certainly done a lot of groundwork with Murphy," Anna observed.

Now that was one of those remarks which, like a drop in a test tube, precipitates a vigorous reaction and a permanent change. There was no groundwork and no planning with Murphy. None was needed. Had there been, I would not have had him go to Anna as it was needless for anybody to go, presumably. I did not reply as I was inclined to do, because she was my guest, but the remark simmered for days. . . .

. . . She discussed her talk with the President, while riding around at Hyde Park with him in the car, in regard to the courtship. It was naturally of great interest to know what reaction had been forthcoming.

"I believe the thought is that you are too temperamental for the bench." Now, there were many reasons why I should not go on the bench. The most obvious and the most decent in view of the conspicuously successful job—if I may say so myself—performed here in the last five years, was that I was needed to carry on. Older men could go on the bench and younger men should remain on the firing lines. That was an excellent and adequate reason and a true one; with a dearth of ability in administrative posts in Washington, and the President under constant indictment for bad administration. There were excellent reasons to keep a man who had won recognition in developing the most efficient division in the Department of Justice, tacitly recognized on all sides, . . . in the Department of Justice. Instead, a rather nasty reason had to be assigned which definitely bore the fingerprints of special influence emanating, I think, from I know where.

What interested me most in connection with Anna was that she had quite obviously not gone to bat, but allowed her frail convictions to be borne down by words from the oracle. . . . Two weekends with Harold Ickes would be sufficient, for the increasing viciousness of his attacks upon me, while measuring his fears and the rising importance of my opposition to him in the field of oil . . . would not be wholly transparent to Anna. He told Drew Pearson in a letter, a copy of which I am securing, that he had already saved the day in the Elk Hills controversy and that I had merely "grabbed my fireman's hat" and dashed out yelling "Fire! Fire!" It was all done for self-exploitation, according to Ickes—publicity hunting. . . .

I thought over the conversation for several days and then called Anna at the White House to set the milestone right by the roadside, where no one could mistake it. "I wanted you to know that I consider our conversation extremely unsatisfactory," I told Anna.

"Why? How?" Anna exclaimed in an astonished voice.

And I proceeded to tell her as bluntly as I could that it was utterly immaterial what the President did with the courtship. It was within his province naturally to consider all sorts of possible appointees . . . least of them all I, who certainly had no right to expect such an appointment unless by chance he was considering the abilities and merits of those who had been named as possible appointees. (This was most unlikely as far as the court appointments of Franklin D. Roosevelt are concerned.) I told her that the matter which fundamentally interested me was her own attitude which I thought lacked the elements of loyal friendship and personal interest of the quality which had always marked our relationship. I said that my friendship came very high and could not be had for the asking; that she could no doubt have anything from many in Washington, merely because she was the President's daughter, but that [with me] she stood absolutely on the merits as a human being and nothing would be conceded in the friendship line on any other basis than that.

It was a very frank talk, somewhat deflationary in character. I wonder what the White House operators thought who were listening.

She assured me that she knew all of that and that we must really get together and talk these things out. . . .

And so ends the prospect of returning to the West on the bench.

A feature of this recent period has been the return of Colonel John Leavell, petroleum attache of the State Department in the East (from Afghanistan to Africa) who was sent to Baghdad to explore the Saudi Arabia oil possibilities, ostensibly as part of a commission going from the Department of the Interior and the State Department . . . I had warmly endorsed Leavell to the State Department as an experienced oil man devoted to the public interest. He is a Republican and a former independent oil producer. John's confidential report, which I had read on his return, exposed the fabulous riches of Saudi Arabia in oil; the extent of the Standard Oil of California and Texas Oil Company holdings, by their jointly owned subsidiary called "Cal-Tex Company," and a proposed deal with Secretary of Interior Ickes, whereby the government would loan $125–$150,000,000 to build a pipeline from the Persian Gulf to the Mediterranean and be repaid for it in the transportation of oil through it over a period of twenty-five years. The unrevealed consideration would be the protection which the United States Marines would give to the pipeline as government property; in return for that, we would not only secure desperately needed oil resources for the future of this country, to protect it against becoming a third rate power, but a right to demand 1,000,000,000 barrels of oil at 25 per cent off the Eastern Mediterranean posted price or the Atlantic Seaboard price, whichever is the lesser.

Thus, the greatest oil field in the world would be left the victim of

English and American cartels, in violation of the Atlantic Charter,[1] which assured the distribution of natural resources equitably. Indeed, if the have-not nations do not have access to Saudi Arabian oil, the next world war will be located right there. A vacuum of political weakness invites Russian action anyway. . . .

A team of my Katherine and Mrs. Gifford Pinchot, two of the most effective catalytic agents in Washington, has discussed and advocated for about two months through December and January, the formation of a national group or committee of non-Jewish American citizens to combat the rising tide of anti-semitism in this country and one of the most dangerous and explosive elements in American life. The group would also champion the rescue of those few millions of Jews abroad who are the victims of Hitler's last-ditch campaign of extermination. There is a great void in American life in which there was neither action nor adequate expression of non-Jewish citizens in defense of the American principles of tolerance and religious freedom, or of our historic sense of moral responsibility to aid the victims of massacre.

So desperately was this voice needed in American life that I grew irritable and impatient with Mrs. Pinchot and even Katherine for failure to mature the much discussed plans for a national committee. They delayed for some time asking Chief Justice [Harlan F.] Stone (who had expressed strong sentiment on this subject) to serve as chairman; but when they did see Justice Stone, after deliberating for two weeks, he declined to take the post because of the position he had consistently taken within the Court to keep other justices from meddling in political affairs. His remark on this score was undoubtedly directed at Felix Frankfurter, the stormy petrel of the Supreme Court, whose fine hand reaches into many phases of the executive branch of the government—with power.

In discussing this matter at luncheon with Justice Murphy, he had made clear his own convictions and wondered why those working on the formation of a National Committee Against Persecution of the Jews had not considered the effectiveness of having the ranking Catholic in the country. I could see, instantly that this was correct and that, as the ranking Catholic, Murphy would make a splendid chairman for a national committee, to which the ladies readily assented. . . .

By Thursday night, after using long-distance telephone calls, we had a National Committee organized under the chairmanship of Mr. Justice Murphy consisting of the following:

---

1. The Atlantic Charter was a joint Anglo-American declaration of war aims issued by President Roosevelt and Prime Minister Churchill following their meeting at sea (Placentia Bay, Newfoundland), 14 August 1941.

Frank Murphy, Associate Justice, Supreme Court of the United States, Chairman

Wendell L. Willkie, Vice-Chairman

Norman M. Littell, Assistant United States Attorney General, Secretary

Henry A. Wallace, Vice President of the United States

Gifford Pinchot, Former Governor of Pennsylvania

Leverett Saltonstall, Governor of Massachusetts

Walter S. Goodland, Governor of Wisconsin

Herbert B. Maw, Governor of Utah

Henry St. George Tucker, Presiding Bishop of Protestant Episcopal Church and President of Federal Council of Churches of Christ in America

Bernard J. Sheil, Auxiliary Bishop of Chicago

Henry Sloane Coffin, President of Union Theological Seminary

Eric A. Johnston, President of the United States Chamber of Commerce

Governor [Earl] Warren of California hesitated and did not accept. As Governor Maw said over long distance, "Warren cannot accept. He has a minority problem with the Japanese on which he is taking a position inconsistent with what he would have to take in regard to the Jews. He will not accept." And so it proved to be!

Governor [John] Bricker of Ohio was equally cautious although very cordial over the telephone, giving assurances of his views on this subject. He declined. Bishop [Joseph R.] Hurley of St. Augustine, Florida, also declined with enthusiastic endorsement and offers of help. All others accepted.

Mr. Justice Murphy was able to announce the formation of the Committee on January 30th[2] the [anniversary] of Hitler's rise to power, a day upon which Hitler made another diatribe against the Jews.[3]

The reaction throughout the country was spontaneous and overwhelming, from both Jews and Gentiles, and an avalanche of mail poured in. . . .

I made the principal address at the concluding dinner of the American Jewish Congress in New York, on February 14th, having written most painstakingly among the tensions of official duties and the stress and strain of the office, an address called, finally, "Shadows of the Crooked

2. "New Group Set Up to Protect Jews; Justice Murphy, Willkie and Governors are on Committee to Fight Nazi Persecutors," *New York Times*, 31 January 1944.

3. Hitler became Chancellor of Germany 30 January 1933. On each anniversary of that occasion, he delivered a radio broadcast attacking his enemies and threatening those he hated, particularly the Jews. For a text of his address 30 January 1944, see *New York Times*, 31 January 1944, p. 4.

Cross."[4] Katherine and I worked fairly constantly on it in all spare hours
and some that weren't to spare.

It was a very moving occasion in the Pennsylvania Hotel ballroom. The
emotional content was great, because the address was a milestone of
significance—the statement and assumption of responsibility by non-
Jewish Americans for a minority facing deadly increasing persecution. A
foundation principle of American life was an issue, and the address sought
to place it in its historic perspective. Rabbi Stephen S. Wise, president of
the American Jewish Congress, who has known many Presidents, said it
was the greatest address he had heard since a famous occasion in New
York many years ago. (I lost the reference in the shuffle of conversation.)
He has told many since, that I reminded him of Woodrow Wilson and that
they should keep an eye on me for 1948. I forgive him for the emotional
content of the subject so very vital to him and to his people. . . .

---

4 March 1944
Breakers Hotel (Ream General Army Hospital),
Palm Beach, Florida

[Dear Katherine Mather,]

I seem to find odd places from which to write, and seldom more odd
than this, for I am the only guest at the famous old Breakers Hotel at Palm
Beach, Florida, now serving as a general army hospital and still with
1,038 sick and injured soldiers.

We secured possession of the property in a condemnation proceeding,
December 11, 1942, and it was put in use as a station hospital to service
the far-flung training program of the United States Army Air Forces; but
the departure of those trained men for overseas—for the African and
Italian campaigns and the bombing of Germany—left no need for the
station hospital as such. It was converted to a general hospital on
September 10, 1943, after having had a rather stormy career under
administration of the Air Force, where it had acquired a reputation for
maternity cases more than anything else.

After reorganization under Colonel Charles C. Demmer of the Army
Medical Corps, who took command in September, the hospital has
emerged as a real going concern, but promptly became the object of
heated public controversy on the issue of whether or not it should be
returned to the owners, as other leased properties no longer needed by
the Army are being returned, or whether it should be continued as a

---

4. "U.S. Help Pledged in Combatting Bias; Biddle Aide Declares Federal Prosecutors
'Strike Hard Wherever Facts Justify,'" *New York Times*, 15 February 1944.

general hospital. Powerful and subtly operating influences, stemming chiefly from the Florida East Coast Railway Company, the owner of the Florida East Coast Hotel Corporation, had been brought to bear to secure the return of this priceless old center of social life and gaiety along the Florida coast. A public issue of considerable proportion was raised by several commentators and, more lately, by the newspaper *P.M.*, which charged that wounded veterans were being expelled so that the playboys and the rich could return to their favorite resort at the Breakers.[1]

. . . Finally, two weeks ago, upon the acknowledged failure of the Army to reach an agreement as to compensation, I took complete jurisdiction of the case. The Army had offered as high as $350,000 a year and the owners had come down from about $1,000,000 to as low as $500,000 a year.

If the government had spent about $400,000 for the lease term to June 30, 1944 (now undetermined), and $400,000 in alterations, and [if it costs]—as it admittedly will—over $500,000 to reconvert it to a hotel, plus an undetermined liability for severance damages in the taking of part of the property only, the government would obviously have paid over $1,300,000 for a period of use lasting a year and six months—and a period of effective use of about one year, the first patient having been received here on March 1, 1943. . . .

This graduates the problem from a mere question of how much we pay the owners to a basic issue as to whether or not the property ought to be acquired outright by purchase, or by completing the trial of the condemnation case after amending the petition to take the property in its entirety, rather than for a limited use. I therefore called General B. B. Somervell, chief of the Service and Supply Division, and suggested this latent problem. . . . Somervell recognized the problem; at least, he concurred with my suggestion that I submit a memorandum analyzing the potential liabilities, even though he protested the acquisition of further property. He said the policy was to release surplus property.

I flew down to Miami to look over our office there and went back here by car with my attorney from Jacksonville, Florida, for a meeting with our principal appraiser and to review the unconsidered severance damage problem.

Skipping all these technicalities, opinions could not be completed before Tuesday, the 7th, so we planned to meet the owners of the Breakers at Jacksonville at that time and, in the meantime, I continued on here. Because General Somervell had made a few scornful remarks over the telephone about, "a lot of socialite women at Palm Beach who filed a

---

1. I. F. Stone, "Palm Beach Hotel Men Happy; Wounded Ordered Out; Gen. Somervell Orders Breakers, Now Army Hospital Returned," *P.M.*, 23 January 1944; "Palm Beach Group Backs Army Hospital; Protests Charge Town Wanted Breakers Hotel Returned," *New York Times*, 28 January 1944.

petition for keeping the hospital," and contended they were not really representative—or, at least, he treated their opinions with not only the usual measure of masculine scorn, but with the extra, super-duper measure which goes with high authority in the realm of the military—I thought it advisable to utilize every opportunity to see what local opinion really was. In fact, opportunities were thrust upon me because the community was anxious to redeem itself from a slur by Walter Winchell over the radio to the effect that the rich people down here didn't want the Breakers as a hospital because they did not wish to see injured soldiers hobbling around on crutches, a depressing note in a gay and sunny atmosphere.

I have been lunched and tea-ed and dined in order to be convinced of how this community feels and, I must say, the very rich people whom I have seen and met are as patriotic on this issue and as grateful to these men as I am myself. The mayor, whom I met at lunch and who reflects the more conservative business opinion, would have personally preferred to see the hospital located down the coast at Boca Raton. An inconvenient interruption to the economic life of the community is always more conveniently placed somewhere else. However, he confirmed the sentiment throughout the community that, if the government wishes this hospital for medical and military reasons, the community is delighted to have it here and serve the war purposes and the injured men. That was expressed by innumerable men in uncompromising and obviously sincere terms. . . .

The fact is that I made up my mind very quickly. In endeavoring to get some sun, air and swimming lying on the beach at the Breakers, I found my enjoyment continuously impaired—in fact rendered quite impossible—until I had left no stone unturned in my plans to force the keeping of this hospital for our wounded men. Ambassador Joseph Davies invited me to lunch to discuss the matter and, even though I arrived three-quarters of an hour late, having fallen asleep on the beach at noon, . . . we had a very vital and delightful visit—a visit of discovery which promises enduring friendship, I believe. . . .

I confessed to Davies, at the end of our discussion, the campaign I had laid out to take title to the Breakers, saying that, when an objective was determined, I always felt that a measure of military strategy was advisable. Plan three or four columns. Let them approach and attack the objective at strategic times. No one could tell which column would become fatally or finally engaged, or what combination of columns would take the objective but, if the forces were rightly distributed, the objective would fall.

The first column in the attack on the Breakers is Mrs. Roosevelt. Knowing her humanitarian propensities, [I felt that] she would undoubtedly be in favor of continuing the hospital. However, the direct approach from her to the President as Commander-in-Chief to reverse Somervell and buy the property could not be assured. Many of her objectives failed. The second column would be my own direct approach to Somervell, based upon the economics briefly indicated above—it is simply nonsense to pay $1,300,000 or more for a rental period of one year and then back out. That is too much of a down payment on the purchase of the property. I would hope to convince Somervell that it was to his own interest.

In this latter respect, I was advised over the telephone two days ago by my general assistant, Mr. Williams, that the Truman Committee[2] has just come out with a report severely criticizing the Army and greatly praising the Department of Justice land acquisition programs.[3] In that report, one of the cited failures of the War Department is in not following a consistent policy—it changes its mind too many times. Having taken properties, it would release them again, after the owners had been thrown out. . . .

Somervell was furious and O'Brien (my former general assistant, . . .) was also furious because it attacked his direct purchase program which he had endeavored to conduct to the exclusion of condemnations—for which he was severely criticized by the Truman Committee. My name is undoubtedly mud in the War Department at this moment since they probably attribute some of that report to me. Not so, but I could not honestly dissent from it entirely. . . .

. . . The vacillation continued at the top until finally Somervell himself announced that it would be returned to the owners on January 10, 1944. A later announcement came out on January 15th, having advised that the wounded would be evacuated from here on March 31st, to leave April, May, and June in which to reconvert the property to hotel purposes before the government vacates it on June 30, 1944.

The grim expectation of this evacuation became a reality on February 29th, when Colonel Demmer received a dispatch ordering him to make plans to abandon Ream General Hospital at the Breakers Hotel on March 31st and advising that the Ream General Hospital would be "activated" at Atterbury, Indiana, on that same date. The men here would be scattered to hospitals throughout the country or sent to Camp Atterbury—of all the God-awful places in a mean, small Indiana town of sweltering heat and no available interest or amusement.

I telephoned Somervell the next day and pointed out that there was scarcely any use in my making a special report on the situation to him here when I could not get it in his hands before the 10th or 12th of this month, and by that time if evacuation were going forward, it would be necessary to have trains and convoys practically at the back door of the

---

2. Actually the Senate Special Committee to Investigate the National Defense Program, it was commonly referred to as the Truman Committee for its chairman, Senator Harry S. Truman.

3. The Truman Committee issued its report criticizing the Army's land acquisition program and praising the Justice Department's on 4 March 1944. See *Congressional Record*, vol. 91 (25 January 1945), pp. A295–A297.

hospital ready to go with no time for us to decide on a change of policy if one were to be seriously and sincerely considered. . . .

. . . [He] called back later in the day to say that he had cleared it with the surgeon general and that the evacuation would be put off for a month, giving me time to complete my report and negotiate with the property owners in Jacksonville.[4] Therefore, as the second column is preparing to advance, the enemy had retreated one step already. . . .

The third column is the Truman Committee. It would be only natural for certain citizens here to ask the Truman Committee to take this matter up vigorously and call attention to the fact that Assistant Attorney General Littell had made a special study of the Breakers' problem and that the Truman Committee ought to have the benefit of his report. In view of what they recently said of my work and the standing which I obviously have before that powerful Committee, it would be more than natural to call for my report to Somervell. The report to Somervell, while confidentially on his desk is one thing, but when brought out into public will be a time bomb which will go off with terrific force.

At this stage of the operations, as I told Mr. Davies, the attack should also be covered with a canopy of bombers and fighters as we have well learned from current military history. Certain columnists, such as Drew Pearson, the newspaper P.M., and others, could drop a few bombs around the objective as the operations proceeded.

Davies thought that was splendid and . . . also added a fourth column. He suggested that I see Jimmy Byrnes, . . . just as I did in the Elk Hills case, and point out the political dynamite which is in the return of this hospital to the owners just before the second front really gets under full way, giving him a copy of my memorandum for Somervell based on the merits of the whole matter. I concurred.

After lunch today, Colonel Demmer confirmed that Mrs. Roosevelt (my first column) was arriving on the 4:00 plane; he was meeting her. I wished to dodge the lady, if I could, by reason of various family complications, and made plans to be away when she inspects the hospital tomorrow, Sunday. . . .

Then I came home to dictate on the dictaphone the start of my memorandum to Somervell, but I no sooner got started when I heard from my first column. The colonel called me . . . to say that Mrs. Roosevelt asked me to come out there for a few minutes. . . . I obeyed the royal summons and went forth clad in a Palm Beach suit and wearing a bright red tie. . . .

Mrs. Roosevelt and I retired to a divan at one side to discuss the hospital. There was no reference whatever to the "wife and children,"

4. "Army Reviews Breakers; Reconsiders Decision to Return Palm Beach Hotel to Civilians," New York Times, 15 April 1944; "Army Halts Moving Patients at Palm Beach Pending Inquiry into Abandoning Breakers," New York Times, 19 April 1944.

whom she knew so well, and none whatever by me to Anna or John. We were out for business. She asked if I had reached conclusions as to the hospital. I said I had but could not state the precise figures until I had conferred with the property owners in Jacksonville.

What did I think it best for her to do to help? Should she take it up immediately with the President? I thought not. We should give Somervell a chance to change his mind. I also told her of Davies' suggestion that I see Byrnes, and she thought that was very good. She then concluded that she would write to the President; if I did not get results with Somervell, I could then ask General Watson for an appointment in regard to the matter about which Mrs. Roosevelt had written and see the President myself. In the meantime, I could give a copy of my memorandum to Somervell to Byrnes. I agreed. . . .

Sunday, 5 March 1944

. . . I had quite a different impression of Mrs. Roosevelt than I had ever had before, not having seen her for a considerable time at close range. There seems to me a new sense of what I can only describe as self-importance. Perhaps I should describe it as complacency in power. Possibly no human mind can stand power too long—power and prominence in the public eye. From the obscure, shy, distressed, ugly duckling type of individual described in Mrs. Roosevelt's autobiography,[1] she has perhaps passed through a complete metamorphosis to one who now hungers for activity and prominence in public affairs. In our earlier letter, I mentioned the tensions within the White House over this subject and am constrained now to consider whether or not there might possibly be some merit in the opposition's viewpoint.

Let me also confess, in the interests of honesty and realism, that I sensed in the interview of last evening more definitely and keenly than I ever have before an atmosphere of somewhat oppressive [femininity]—or should I say, more crudely, femalism—in the sense of being repelling to men. There is an atmosphere or climate surrounding certain spinsters whom one meets from time to time which definitely repels the male of the species. It is a slightly stuffy atmosphere like that emanating from a trunk of old lace dresses in a dusty attic when the trunk lid is raised on a hot day. As I felt it, I could more readily understand why Mrs. Roosevelt had surrounded herself with very stuffy ladies such as Betty Lindley to whom she gave a prominent position in the Office of Civilian Defense, when Mrs. Roosevelt tried so disastrously to rescue it from the management of

---

1. Eleanor Roosevelt, *This Is My Story* (New York: Harper and Brothers, 1937).

Mayor La Guardia of New York. Another favorite of hers is at the Democratic National headquarters at $7,000 a year, in an utterly useless capacity; and a prominent hanger-on during the national campaign of 1940 was Mrs. Henry Morgenthau, Jr. [Elinor Morgenthau], who insisted on a big desk and considerable prominence, however futile and ineffectual she proved to be. There are others.

When Mrs. Roosevelt asked me why there had been a change in policy in respect to the Breakers Hotel, and a determination to turn it back, I ventured to confide that I suspected very strongly the influence of the Florida East Coast Railroad and its subsidiary corporation, the Florida East Coast Hotels.

"That is not right," Mrs. Roosevelt had replied in the most serious air. "Special influence should not be brought to bear in such a matter as this." [This was] all said with an air of thinking something new and profound.

There is also a lack of sense of humor, which is almost a fatal defect in any human character. At least it is fatal to insight and is the natural concomitant of a character which takes itself too seriously. I could not help smiling inwardly as I heard her plodding her serious way through her adventures in the Solomons, while I waited for my car and listened as an obedient subject after the business of our conversation was concluded. . . .

Later

. . . Nothing I have said about Mrs. Roosevelt in the full candor of honest recording should detract from what I have said before: That she is one of the great women of history in terms of her power and influence on the generation in which she lives. Certainly, she is possibly the greatest woman in American history, measured in those terms, and her influence would have a high rating among the "do good" people of history. It will take time to appraise the effects of her dealing with the Negro problem into which she moved without the "know how" of those intimately associated with the Negroes—indeed, she has moved in utter disregard of the accumulated human experience of reasonable, intellectual and humane members of our Southern society in the United States. Maybe that was just the thing to do, but maybe it wasn't. We are too close to appraise her methods or the results. . . .

Affectionately
Daddy [signed]

Tuesday, 14 March 1944
4101 Lorcom Lane

I arrived back from Florida on the 4:30 P.M. plane Wednesday, the 8th, after conferences with the president and attorney for the Breakers

Hotel at Jacksonville, Florida, but have been unable to submit my report on the disposition of the Breakers Hotel to General Somervell, until today, although he telephoned about it yesterday. After his secretary had made an appointment with me for 4:30 this afternoon, Somervell called solicitously himself to confirm the appointment and said he would send someone down to the Mall entrance of the Pentagon building to meet me.

He read my report through carefully when I came in, precisely at 4:30. I was offered a cigar out of a new box from Cuba, and the conversation was very lovely and chummy. When he finally got around to the Breakers, he said he had read my memorandum thoroughly and was turning it over to "some of my boys" to go through it carefully and consider the matter, but that the hospital problem revolved around the fact that millions of men have gone overseas leaving hospital facilities empty. He said nothing about expecting those men back on stretchers when the second front got really under way.

"It's like buying your wife a fur coat—or my wife, I should say. If she doesn't need the coat, it doesn't matter how good a bargain it is." That was the straw in the wind indicating his opinion. Obviously, he has already made up his mind and had his back bowed on the thing, and he is trying to break the news gently to me.

He dismissed the Truman Committee report as "pure politics" and said that the secretary of the committee had offered to drop the whole matter if he would pay $250,000 more to the hotel operators in Florida which the Army was accused of having abused and badly mistreated in its negotiations. The report, which came out while I was in Florida, praised my work, mentioning me by name, and the Lands Division, and condemned the War Department in the most castigating statement.

I endeavored to explain to Somervell that his chief of the Real Estate Section, Colonel John J. O'Brien, whom I had recommended to Somervell in February of 1941, had gone adrift on matters of policy.

"You can never tell when you take an able administrator, who is your assistant, out of a subordinate post and put him in one of policy-making decisions," I said. "Until his ability is separated from one's own policy-making capacity, it is impossible to know how able he is in the realm of policy. This is O'Brien's first experience in the sphere of policy, and his experience in court and in condemnation work is wholly inadequate. I expected to continue cooperation with him and supply these deficiencies. He cannot stand on administrative ability alone."

I spelled out the basic errors in policy, primarily in the selection of appraisers consisting of men utterly incompetent to appear in court—of utter disregard for severance damage possibilities, as in the Breakers' case—and other matters reflecting inexperience in actual cases. I blamed it squarely on the colonel's wings which had been put on his shoulders. "As I told Senator [Homer B.] Ferguson on the Truman Committee, when asked what is the matter with O'Brien: "He just flew away from us."

Somervell considered this "one of the best jokes in Washington." . . . [He] had thought his relations with Justice were well established by taking O'Brien; and now he found us in great disagreement. He urged that we get together for lunch and try to straighten it out. . . .

23 March 1944
4101 Lorcom Lane

My appointment with Somervell was put off from yesterday noon—due "to a conference with General Marshall" as Somervell's secretary affirmed—until today at 4:00, and I met with him and Colonel O'Brien in the Pentagon for three and one-half hours—exceedingly wearing hours— because I laid down the rule myself: "Let's pull no punches."

First, as to the Breakers. . . .

The answer to my recommendation that he purchase the Breakers was a polite "No," as I anticipated.[1] He gave me a letter to this effect written, of course, by O'Brien. My figures were disputed. It would cost $250,000 less than I estimated to restore the hotel to as good a condition as it was when the Army took it; however, that still left an investment of $1,600,000 for two years' occupation and only one year's actual use as a hospital, all the rest of the time having been required for conversion and reconversion.

"I have wrestled with this thing and gone over my entire figures on whether we need it or not. I have been on the telephone to London," Somervell said, waving a tabulation which he did not unfold for my examination, "and considered our evacuation needs, but it is just as I mentioned the other day. If you don't need something, it's not a good buy no matter how good a bargain it is. We have enough."

"You mean you have enough hospital beds that you can afford to dispense with these," I asked.

"Yes, I have considered what a fool this would make out of me if, after all, we had to acquire more hospital space after I had let this go, but I have to take that chance," he said. "The gap is too wide between what we have and our expectations."

I did not argue the case at all. His mind was quite clear, and it was perfectly apparent that he had given merely polite consideration to my recommendation. The human factors got no consideration whatsoever— the exodus of 1,038 men to [a] new environment, new doctors. (One soldier told me he had already been to seven hospitals, although I do not think that was quite exceptional.) . . .

1. "Army to Abandon Miami Beach Set-Up; Will Turn Back 139 Hotels There by July 1, Shifting Air Training to Texas," *New York Times*, 21 March 1944.

We passed on to other things—the Hanford Project[2] in Eastern Washington, concerning which I advised that I was making a survey to review the Army's figures. The Army is in the dog house there, having offered people less for their land by far that the crops on the land were worth. This is frequently the case in a good season, but the strain on the credulity of juries is altogether too great and the jury awards have been as high as 200 per cent more than the Army's appraisals of the land.

I cannot review all of that session, which was designed primarily to hear my objections to Army land acquisition policies [and] . . . the man I put there—Colonel John J. O'Brien. I laid it out fairly straight: Failure to consult with the Justice Department on the selection of appraisers so that we had no witnesses in court, or incompetent witnesses; protracted negotiations; inability to approve settlements; failure to satisfy judgments; and bad engineering and descriptions. There is no need to review it all. My work came in for its measure of criticism also. In fact, in one stage of the proceedings, Somervell, to my utter amazement, took out a Bible from the top drawer from his desk and read from it: "Let he who is without fault cast the first stone." To have that hard-boiled go-getter put on that neat little act was really too much for me. [He] had undoubtedly done it before. . . .

Then, I started operations on the Breakers to see if we can undo Somervell's decision. Mrs. [George A.] McKinlock[3] had called and Colonel Demmer, too, the preceding day to say that Mr. and Mrs. Joseph Davies (former Ambassador)[4] had offered their big estate—the former Hutton estate of Mrs. Davies—for use by the hospital as part of its convalescent rehabilitation program.[5] That was undoubtedly a deliberate stroke on Davies' part. He is in entire accord with me, and I sent him—confidentially—a copy of my report to Somervell. I called Mr. [Ernest G.] Howes, at Miami Beach, to urge that that news be released immediately because it had not been announced. A big spread in the press would make it harder to give the Breakers Hotel back. [I.F.] Stone of *P.M.* had been calling me all day from New York. I returned his call and gave him the same information so that he will get a big spread in Sunday's *P.M.* about the estate.[6] At any time, I will go to see Mr. Justice Byrnes, Senator

2. The Hanford Project in eastern Washington was part of the secret Manhattan Project to build an atomic bomb. The E. I. Du Pont de Nemours chemical company, which operated the Hanford Project, was one of three prime contractors on the project and was responsible for producing the uranium explosive for the bomb.
3. Marion Wallace Rappelye McKinlock.
4. Joseph E. and Marjorie Post Hutton Davies.
5. "Veterans to Use Davies' Estate," *New York Times*, 25 March 1944.
6. I. F. Stone, "Davies Gives Estate as GI's Face Ouster; Physicians Also Protest Army Plan to Move Boys from Palm Beach," *P.M.*, 28 March 1944.

[Sinclair] Weeks, and, if necessary, the President, also calling on Senator [Harry S.] Truman. That is enough at the moment.

Tuesday night, 4 April 1944
4101 Lorcom Lane

Last Thursday, March 20, 1944, I suddenly realized that sending my report on the Breakers to the Truman Committee was probably a technical violation of Biddle's pet rule against assistant attorney generals escaping from the Department—a rule against testifying before a committee without advance authority—although strictly speaking the report did not constitute testimony and, furthermore, the Truman Committee had already examined into the Breakers Hotel issue and Truman, himself, had made a personal investigation. However, I went to Acting Attorney General Fahy, as Biddle was in Florida on vacation, and stated the case. It was agreed that I recover the report, immediately, which I did by going to Rudolph Halley. Halley immediately made a formal request to the attorney general, enclosing a personal letter to Fahy saying that the danger of closing the hotel, on April 30th as now ordered, necessitated the request without awaiting the return of the attorney general.

However, Biddle got back, unexpectedly, the next day—Friday—and Fahy turned the matter over to him. I left that afternoon for a weekend with Giff and Sally Pinchot at Frederick, Maryland, where Giff is now stationed on research work for the Navy, leaving the whole matter seething and sizzling in Washington. A parting shot had been sent to General Somervell upon receipt of his letter turning down my recommendation that the Breakers be purchased and pointing out how several hundred thousand dollars of reconversion costs could be saved by acquiring the property outright. [I] failed to see the President, as Mrs. Roosevelt had suggested in Palm Beach, due to the cancellation of the President's appointments on account of the grippe, [so] I called Malvina Thompson, Mrs. Roosevelt's secretary, having noticed in the paper that she and Mrs. Roosevelt had returned from the Caribbean. At her suggestion, I immediately sent my report and the letters exchanged between myself and Somervell over to the White House. Having dispatched the day's routine—including the closing of the Treasure Island–San Francisco Airport deal in San Francisco—I left town. . . .

[On Monday] afternoon, Carusi called from the attorney general's office; stated that he had called on Saturday and found me out; stated that, on the attorney general's instructions, I should take no further action, whatsoever, in the Breakers case [because] the attorney general had taken the matter entirely into his own hands; and stated that I should write no more letters and do nothing about it.

There couldn't have been any cruder or blunter way of telling me to go-to-hell had the attorney general sought one. Whether he seeks to pick off the celebrated case, in time for whatever publicity there is in it, or whether he is up to the old trick of protecting another department, whether right or wrong, as he did the secretary of the Navy in the Elk Hills controversy, remains to be seen; but I surrendered jurisdiction to a brass hat bigger then mine with the comfortable knowledge that I have lighted so damn many fires he cannot possibly put them out or even control them. He can investigate to his heart's content, but he faces two alternatives, neither of them happy ones: He can agree with me and be right, in which case I shall be perfectly happy because I only want to win the objective of keeping the hospital as it would be well worth the price of having him get the credit for it to attain that objective; or, he can dissent from my views, in which case he will throw himself to the wolves.

However, I think others will determine the matter.

This afternoon, Mrs. Roosevelt telephoned me, saying that she had not received my memorandum and was surprised to learn that I had sent it to Miss Thompson on Friday. It developed that it had gone to New York to Mrs. Roosevelt but had missed her there and had just come back in the mail, so Miss Thompson handed it to her. We discussed the matter somewhat on the phone, however, and she asked what Somervell's arguments were. I summarized them briefly. . . .

Miss Thompson rang back to say that Mrs. Roosevelt was now reading the memorandum and would go in to see the President immediately. So this column has come over the horizon and [has] definitely engaged the enemy, in a stronger approach than I had hoped for due to Mrs. Roosevelt's return from the Caribbean. . . .

Tuesday, 11 April 1944
4101 Lorcom Lane

It has not been feasible to keep up with the rapidly moving story of the Breakers. Senator Claude Pepper telephoned to me from Miami Beach Sunday night, regarding his major political campaign weapon, the taking of the Gandy Bridge to make it toll free, between Tampa and St. Petersburg—the longest causeway bridge in the country. The political problem is not for me and the taking raises just another legal question. . . .

The White House had authorized the taking of the bridge, and we have briefed the question for the assistant solicitor general [Hugh B. Cox], who gave the opinion through the attorney general to General [Philip B.] Fleming of the Federal Works Agency,[1] that we could take it under the Second War Powers Act, the Navy having certified that it was needed for the war effort, for the transportation of shipyard and other workers to St. Petersburg. Judge Sam Rosenman, secretary to the President, and long his personal advisor in New York, was handling the matter for the President. He had been over to lunch last Saturday, and we were all in accord but, when the papers came over from Acting Administrator [John W.] Snyder (due to Fleming's absence in South America on the international road problem) it was for an ordinary condemnation and not war purposes. No immediate possession and no title was taken and, of course, no tolls could be cancelled or the bridge made a [toll-free] bridge.

That day, Pepper announced that the bridge would be taken under the War Powers Act and it would be toll free, so the action of the Federal Works leaves him in an embarrassing position, and the enemy is closing in on him for the failure to deliver.

In Eastern Florida, at Palm Beach, he became again very much aware of the Breakers problem. In his conversation with me he had suddenly realized that Ed Ball, one of the owners of the Florida East Coast Railway line, which was trying to get the Breakers back as a hotel, was pouring thousands of dollars into the campaign against him, so he announced the intention of going after him right then and there in a public statement, and in the morning press was his release condemning Ball and those who sought to defeat the maintenance of the Breakers as a hospital for the veterans.[2] Ed Ball in particular! . . .

On Monday, *P.M.* fanned the ever-lively feud between Attorney General Biddle and myself by coming out with a blast against Biddle for refusing to deliver my report on the Breakers Hotel to the Truman Committee.[3] A wealthy manufacturer, E. G. Howes, at Palm Beach, who has led the fight to retain the Breakers, had wired the Truman Committee announcing Biddle's failure to release the report and had wired Biddle asking him why he refused to deliver it. Mr. Howes headed the forces of the rich people who are standing for my position as a matter of principle.

---

1. The Federal Works Agency (FWA) was established by Reorganization Plan I, presented to Congress 25 April 1939. The FWA consolidated four preexisting agencies: the Works Progress Administration (WPA), except for the National Youth Administration (NYA), the Public Works Administration (PWA), the Public Roads Administration, and the Public Buildings Administration. These agencies dealt primarily with public works and administered federal grants or loans to the states and local governments for construction of public works. During the war, FWA was given authority to provide for public works where the war congestion had made local facilities inadequate.

2. "President Asked to Spare Army Hospital and Stop Order to Give Up Palm Beach Hotel," *New York Times*, 8 April 1944.

3. I. F. Stone, "Biddle Bars Report on Retaining Breakers for GIs; Action Asked to Prevent Removal of Wounded from Palm Beach Hotel," *P.M.*, 10 April 1944.

P.M. sounded off in headlines on Biddle's refusal, and today Biddle denied that the Truman Committee had ever demanded it of him.

Now it is simply incredible to me that a man should be so unwise—so damn stupid—as to do that. Ten days ago—a week ago last Friday—Rudolph Halley had written a letter to the attorney general with a covering letter to Fahy, then acting attorney general, saying that the matter was too urgent to await Biddle's return because the men were to be removed from the hospital April 30th. I knew the demand had been sent over by messenger. The truth was ferreted out by I. F. Stone of *P.M.*, who called Halley in New York and learned that Biddle had asked Halley to withdraw the request and this had been done. That will surely come out and, in the face of Biddle's denial that he ever received a demand for the report, will be more damning than if he had frankly admitted a request to have it withdrawn.

He is the most completely inept fellow I know. When Howes' telegram came in yesterday, Carusi . . . again called me and cross-examined me somewhat on why it was that Howes' telegram mentioned Littell's report, in particular, whereas the Senator Pepper telegram of the preceding day, published in *P.M.*,[4] had only said the reports of the Department of Justice. The bristling hostility of the attorney general could be felt behind the questions, but my answers were innocent enough and quite disarming. After all, Mrs. Roosevelt had sent for me down there, and I had discussed the matter with her in a drawing room. There was no question, whatever, but what she had mentioned my view that the hospital should be purchased, outright and, furthermore, Claude Pepper knew it. Everyone down there knew I was making a report for Somervell because it was in the papers. The only thing not generally known was what my conclusion was, and Mrs. Roosevelt very quickly provided that. . . .

He has only started on the Breakers issue and I shall certainly let him fry. . . . Biddle has never yet seen the issues!

When questions are asked and it is discovered that the attorney general took the case away from me ten days ago—the only case he has ever taken away—stopping all processes of appraisal and enjoining any further action on my part, it will be perfectly apparent to everyone that pure unadulterated personal spleen is at the bottom of it.[5] He just took one beating a few weeks ago in refusing to let Mr. [Jonathan W.] Daniels, secretary to

---

4. "Pepper Asks FDR to Act on Breakers; Urges Hotel Be Kept as Hospital for Wounded GIs," *P.M.*, 9 April 1944.

5. For subsequent developments in the Breakers Hotel case, see "Army to Return Breakers Hotel; Decides Finally After Board Calls a Hospital at Palm Beach Unsound Idea," *New York Times*, 28 April 1944; "Army Hotel Deals Face Senate Check," *New York Times*, 7 August 1944; "Ask Why Army Drops Big Hotel as Hospital," *New York Times*, 9 August 1944; "Criticizes Army Breakers Deal; Senate Committee Reports on Taking of the Hotel and Abandoning as Hospital," *New York Times*, 23 August 1944.

the President, testify before a committee—until the President had to overrule him and even [offer] to testify himself. Here is another move designed to conceal vital information from Congress or the Senate. There are plenty of gadflies around to see that he is stung again. My wife is one of them.

Sunday, 3 June 1944
4101 Lorcom Lane

Dearest Katherine Mather:

Your mother and I have just been home for three days from a pilgrimage in the West unique in many respects. . . . [The] last week— before my departure on April 13th for New York—was too hectic to record in detail. Having set all "columns" in motion to take the Breakers, there was little else I could do except prod one or another of them, surreptitiously from the rear. Biddle was in damned hot water. The Truman Committee was mad because he would not give them my report. The Palm Beach colony, in which he had some old connections from Philadelphia, was mad because he responded brusquely to a telephone call and correspondence to the effect that the Breakers issue was none of [their] business. It was a War Department matter. I had made it much too late for the Department of Justice to take that position. Finally, Truman did what Biddle never anticipated. [He] sent a subpoena to the attorney general of the United States to get my report.

To show the extremes to which Biddle will go to save his dignity, he sent the subpoena up to my office with a notation written across the top: "Cancelled." Sensing a fraud, my relentless Katherine took the liberty of calling Senator Truman to find out whether that subpoena had been cancelled and, of course, it had not been. The Senator merely explained that Biddle had called to talk the Senator out of it, saying the report could be secured from General Somervell, to which the Senator had replied, "I only know I want the report. I do not care where it comes from. I want the report right away." Biddle said he didn't have it.

Biddle had then, apparently, arranged with Somervell's office to provide it and, on that slight evasion, said the subpoena was "cancelled."

Promptly, portions of the report were made available and *P.M.* came out with a pretty full account of it and a terrific blast against Somervell and the War Department. Having raised this general hell and shot all my ammunition, I left town.[1]

1. For an account of Littell's report on the Breakers Hotel, see: *P.M.*, 10 April 1944; I. F. Stone, "Biddle Says Stimson Got Breakers Data: Denies Truman Asked for Littell's

I had also suggested the essential strategy to Mr. Truman: Namely, that he call the secretary of War and state that, inasmuch as the Hotel was not to be returned until December, 1944, on the basis of my opinion that the Army was liable for two years' rental, there was no need to vacate the soldiers on April 30th as ordered, but that they should remain until the committee had time to look into the matter. That was done, and the evacuation order was postponed. . . .

These recollections tumbled over each other as [the plane] made a wide sweep over [Seattle], apparently giving right of way to another plane. I even caught a glimpse of our old home on Lake Washington, where dogs and children and even bears had come and gone. I can never measure my debt to the Northwest and its forests, where I found myself after a dissembling experience, by swinging an axe in the woods during one of the hardest and best years I ever had.

There was a warm welcome at the Irving Clarks', across Lake Washington. Young Irving was there, too, for the Circuit Court was sitting in Seattle. [Indeed], that was why I was there: To argue the Seattle Storage and Warehouse case on appeal, on April 19th.[2] Irving is clerk to one of the judges, Judge Healy. . . .

I was desperately tired, and there is nothing one can do about that quickly. Furthermore, I had to pitch in and work day and night preparing an argument which I had never completed in Washington. Although I made many a crack at the administration during the argument of the case in the District Court,[3] while I was there last September, the papers did not even mention my presence there. I could have done something about that but didn't. There were other motives, too. We were nearing election time, and I had frequently been mentioned in various articles as a potential candidate for governor or the senate, and the papers, being Republican, couldn't encourage anybody on our side. . . .

So I argued the case in a practically empty courtroom, and it was a very satisfying argument in which the opposition was completely mopped up, including Judge [James A.] Fee, the District Court judge from Oregon, who sat with [Albert L.] Stephens and Healy because other members of the Circuit Court were too aged or tired to come to the Northwest with Stephens. Fee took the occasion to vent his spleen, long pent up because I had not supported him for the Circuit Court appointment to which

---

Report on Retaining Army Hospital," *P.M.*, 11 April 1944; I. F. Stone, "Secret Probe of Breakers Is Underway; Army Board Reportedly Airing Plan to Abandon Florida Hospital," *P.M.*, 13 April 1944.

2. *Municipal Transfer and Storage Company v. United States* was an appeal from the decision of Judge John C. Bowen in the District Court of Western Washington, 14–23 September 1943, citing the secretary of the Army for contempt. The Court of Appeals upheld the United States and overturned the contempt citation.

3. See diary entry for 17 October 1943, note 6.

Homer Bone had been appointed and because he does not like certain policies we follow in land acquisitions, pursuant to statute. Those antipathies, long pent up, were now freely expressed with the advantage of being on the Circuit Court, quite irrespective of whether they had anything to do with the present case or not, and I answered rather roughly. In fact, both of the [other] judges were somewhat disgusted, and Stephens half apologized to me later for Fee's attitude. I do not care what the Court holds—we won that argument.

To get ahead of my story, the underground rumor from the Circuit Court, which I later received in San Francisco, was that I had, after all, won a unanimous decision due to two factors: [Judge John C.] Bowen's palpable errors and the "excellence" of my own presentation. I am still awaiting the decision, however, and will believe it when I see it.

I could not resist running over to my old favorite stamping grounds at Olympic Hot Springs [in Olympic National Park] for a weekend to recuperate. . . . In forty-eight hours, I slept over twenty-four. . . . I [then took] a quick, hot trip to Yakima, with two of my attorneys. [This] fortunately [justified] the use of an automobile . . . [and] gave me a priceless backtrack through the Snoqualmie Pass, . . . coupled with meetings with the Army at Yakima. The biggest project of the war effort is there—470,000 acres acquired, almost all in fee, although partially in leasehold—for the big Du Pont secret plant. We do not know what is made there, presumably chemicals or secret explosives. The land acquisition program has been abominably handled by the Army and is one of my chief points of struggle with General Somervell and Colonel John J. O'Brien, whom I met in Yakima. But I will not dwell on business. . . .

Here, indeed, begins a rare chapter of my married life, for [after a speaking engagement in Portland, Oregon on behalf of the National Committee Against Persecution of the Jews, May 27th–28th] I left Portland on the 28th and, on arriving the next day in San Francisco was met at the train by Virgil Jorgenson and Katherine, who had arrived two days ahead of me as train reservations dictated. Then began the first complete two weeks' vacation we have had together in five years. . . .

We made camp in an astonishing change of scenery, toward the end of the day. . . . We sat by the campfire until late in the evening. . . . Here at last was one vacation in which Biddle or his ilk did not bother me. I was left strictly alone. Why? Because Biddle had his hands full with his own troubles. It was at this time that the extraordinary incident of Biddle's capture of Montgomery Ward took place. For failure to comply with the War Labor Board order (I will not recount the details) the government had seized the Montgomery Ward plant in Chicago, and the attorney general, himself, had flown to Chicago to order the Army into possession. The stubborn Mr. [Sewell L.] Avery, president of Montgomery Ward, an arch enemy of the administration and a dyed-in-the-wool reactionary of the worst sort, had really scored a tremendous victory and captured the public imagination by sitting calmly at his desk and refusing to go out. Biddle had ordered the soldiers to carry him out and pictures were flashed on the front pages of every paper throughout the land of Avery being carried out by two soldiers. The American people have always been deeply suspicious of a combination of civil and military power, and the attorney general of the United States ordering soldiers to evict the owner was as perfect a symbol of that combination as we have ever had except under martial law. I have learned since that Chatfield Taylor of the Department of Commerce not only did not know of Biddle's coming out, but had not invited him, and was opposed to Army seizure.[4]

Night after night, Fulton Lewis on the radio and other commentators, took my chief to pieces, limb from limb, and the newspapers and magazines dissected those pieces. It was a pathetic case. It was a humiliation such as no man can ever recover from. What little stature he had left was completely destroyed. From a merely ineffectual fellow, he became an object of contempt.

We discussed this and other matters by the campfire, and I could not help but rejoice that Biddle's preoccupation in his own troubles at last prevented him from disturbing a vacation of mine, which was a regular event in the past, particularly when Jim Rowe was there at the Department. In perfect security I smoked a cigar at the campfire and recounted the incident in the Anti-Trust Division Christmas party in which one of the men in a slight state of inebriation had thrown his arm around me and kissed me because of the speech I had made entitled "German Invasion of American Business" in 1941. "You lifted the Anti-Trust Division off the ground with that speech—you started economic warfare for sure," he had said to my amazement.

Just then Biddle came into the room and someone stopped the speaker with a little group around him by saying "Shh-sh. Here comes Biddle," to which my inebriated friend had replied, "Piddle on Biddle!" And then he proceeded to tell me that in an interview with the President two or three weeks before on matters pertaining to cartel penetrations, the attorney

---

4. Throughout 1942–44, Sewell Avery, head of Montgomery Ward, had refused orders from the National War Labor Board (NWLB) to negotiate with its CIO union and terminated their contract with the union. On 12 April 1944, the union struck but the company still refused to negotiate. Finally, 25 April 1944, President Roosevelt ordered the seizure of the company's offices by Executive Order No. 9438. Avery was photographed being carried out of his office by two soldiers. The incident caused much uproar and outrage at the government's seizure of private property. After a National Labor Relations Board (NLRB) election, the government returned the company to its owners 9 May 1944. But the company still refused to negotiate with its union workers and so President Roosevelt seized the entire company by Executive Order No. 9508, 27 December 1944. President Truman returned the company to its owners 25 August 1945.

general's name had come up and he had exclaimed to the President, "Piddle on Biddle!". . . .

The poor devil [Attorney General Biddle] had made matters worse by going into court and making a complete misstatement of the executive power in time of war. A statement such as he made would authorize the President under his "aggregate powers" to seize any business whatsoever in time of war—even a beauty shop or manicure parlor. The statement was too broad, and the next day he had to retract and modify it. . . . He could have saved himself the humiliation. . . . [However], he very carefully let in no competing figure. . . .

. . . We caught the famous Santa Fe Chief at noon [May 30th], and settled down for two and a half days of its comfortable service as we rode across the West. I worked on a brief case full of Elk Hills files, which I had had sent to me upon learning that hearings on a new proposed bill authorizing the development of Elk Hills [were] in full swing. . . .

The hearings had closed when we arrived in Washington on the morning of June 2nd, the Senate Naval Affairs Committee having concluded its work the preceding day and having refused to wait until I could get back to ask the one question they wanted to know from us. The plain fact is that my testifying before either committee was the last thing in the world that was desired by the Navy (which might have been embarrassed by having approved the first, illegal, agreement), by Standard, or by the attorney general. When my general assistant met me at the train in Washington it was to carry oral instructions from the attorney general, through Ugo Carusi: "Tell Norman Littell that he is not to make any statement whatsoever in regard to Elk Hills, and he is not to communicate directly with any congressman or senator." It was quite obvious that I was to be kept in confinement by the attorney general who, incidentally, never asked me what information I might have in regard to Elk Hills. That was quite beside the point. The public interest be damned. The personal equation was the important thing, and Norman Littell was not again to have a chance to go before a committee. Instead, Department of Justice representatives went, pursuant to a summons to me from the Naval Affairs Committee of the Senate, from the chairman[5]—who, when he learned I was out of town, would not continue the hearings one day, until the third. The delegation, handpicked by the attorney general, consisted of Freund, from the solicitor general's office, and [Marvin J.] Sonosky, from my office. . . .

The bill has been reported out of the House Committee favorably and, on the 2nd, the day on which I arrived, had been reported out of the Senate favorably. Passage was a foregone conclusion.[6]

---

5. Senator David I. Walsh of Massachusetts was chairman of the Senate Naval Affairs Committee, 1937–47.

6. See *New York Times*, 3 June 1944, p. 13.

I could have broken through these barriers by various methods, but it wasn't worthwhile. Congress had explored a matter in which they had complete jurisdiction. The bill was not bad and the contract was not bad— it had 90 per cent of the jokers out of it which I had exposed in the contract of November 20, 1942. The Army and Navy needed the oil in the Pacific. Congress was reaching a simple decision that this was the war we had been saving it for. With limitations of production to 65,000 barrels a day for three years and congressional control over any changes, the public interest was reasonably safe, even though there was much to be said which I could have said about the whole transaction.

I shall, however, read the record before the committee with great interest when it comes out.[7] . . .

Affectionately,
Daddy [signed]

Tuesday, 6 June 1944

The invasion news shook the country out of bed this morning even though there were only occasional glimpses through the mists of war of fleet movements, bombardments, landings at undesignated points a few of which since the news broke have been admitted. . . .

. . . I acknowledge . . . a sense of humility that such things are taking place and I am still here shoving papers around over a desk. . . . There is nothing to do but tread our humble paths, however, and I tramped on over to the White House to have lunch with Judge Sam Rosenman, legal adviser to the President on his secretarial staff, and an old and trusted friend, who resigned from the Supreme Court of New York to come to Washington.

Just before leaving for the West, in conversation with the judge—one of several over the condemnation of [the] Gandy Bridge in Claude Pepper's southwestern Florida—I remarked in exasperation that I was tempted to resign and go back to private practice because I was tired of being badgered by brother Biddle. "Don't do it," he replied. "Come and see me when you get back."

This was it. I called and was invited to lunch. We went to the Federal Trade [Commission] executive lunch room. I read the President's prayer

7. For a legislative history of the bill, which authorized joint exploitation of the Elk Hills Naval Petroleum Reserve by the Navy and Standard Oil Company of California, see *New York Times*, 3 June 1944, p. 13; "Senate Passes Bill on Elk Hills Pool; Measure Authorizes New Navy Contract with Standard Oil," *New York Times*, 13 June 1944; "Roosevelt Signs Elk Hills Oil Bill; Approving Increased Output at Navy Request, He Objects to Powers Given to Congress," *New York Times* 18 June 1944.

on the invasion, handed to me by the judge's secretary, as I waited in the executive offices of the White House—a masterfully devout statement and how apt!

"Some wanted the President to make a speech on the invasion," Rosenman said, "but he would not do it. He feels that the honor and glory belong to the boys who are in it. Churchill made a speech in the House of Commons and the King of England will make a speech this afternoon to the troops."

"This is better," I replied, putting the copy in my pocket. "It is really the way we all feel about it down in our hearts. He has the knack of understanding and timeliness."

"There is no one with a nicer sense of the fitness of things and timeliness," Rosenman said.

He explained that the President was hopping mad this morning because a United Press dispatch had gone out saying that the President was unaware of the invasion and, in fact, was asleep during the night, citing the fact that he had made a speech the preceding evening (Monday) on the fall of Rome, which had just taken place, as the retreating Nazis were fleeing into northern Italy. . . .

"The President was fully aware of everything going on," Rosenman said, "and was in constant touch by telephone with the Pentagon Building. This speech on the fall of Rome was a nice bit of psychological warfare. The Germans were caught completely unaware by the invasion, apparently. Steve Early fixed the matter up by contact with the United Press but it did get into some of the papers."

With a quick and precise mind, Rosenman . . . plunged into the subject of Biddle himself. "He is an exceedingly jealous fellow you know," he said. "He made life so miserable for Oscar Cox that he really had to leave the Department. Biddle was jealous of any information that went through Oscar Cox such as executive orders, opinions and so forth. He held the executive order on his desk, which reorganized the Economic Warfare Board [i.e., BEW] in the controversy between Vice President Wallace and Secretary Jones, all day long, until Mr. Justice Byrnes sent a message over to him that the executive order was going to be signed that evening. If Biddle wished to agree with it he had better say so."

He said there were occasions when Biddle would delay matters, just to cross a few "t's" and dot a few "i's"—just to show his authority—so keenly did he resent anyone communicating directly with the White House. I replied that the Gandy Bridge matter was a perfect example. There I had had the entire legal problem briefed and served up the ammunition to the attorney general through the assistant solicitor general, just so we would not get our wires crossed and so no one would get mad. I had explained the matter to Rosenman over the telephone during the heat of battle giving him the low-down on the situation and then telling him to get it officially through Biddle.

"He also resented my appointment as legal adviser to the President and he even went to the President about the title, saying that the attorney general of the United States was the legal officer of the government and there should be no other one. Perhaps, he is right," Rosenman added, "although in New York there is a counsel to the governor provided by statute and it seems to work pretty well."

I agreed. "There is so much day to day stuff flowing along which does not justify reference to the attorney general and, besides, the President ought to have a double-check." . . .

Rosenman asked about our relationships and I explained the high points in [the] deterioration of my relations with the attorney general from the time when he and Jim Rowe endeavored to tell me to settle the Savannah Shipyards case because their great and good friend Tommy Corcoran wanted it done. He was greatly interested in my maneuvering in that story and in my final method of stopping the attorney general in his tracks by telling him that such a settlement, as far as he was concerned and in view of his connection with Tommy Corcoran would simply "be another Sterling Products case." . . . I had won and we tried the case. . . .

Judge Fred Vinson joined us at about this point and we dropped off the personal discussion, which I had not quite completed, in favor of politics. The Texas [Democratic State] Convention displayed a new and somewhat vicious technique in securing the instruction of delegates so that the electoral college could be split in the selection of a President with a group of men with hard and fast instructions not to vote for President Roosevelt for a fourth term. If enough states did that, no matter what happened in the Democratic [National] Convention, the fourth term could be defeated in the electoral college, or possibly the election thrown into the House of Representatives, which could wreck the party system by making the selection of a President, ultimately, dependent solely upon the legislative branch of the government. . . .

. . . Judge Vinson, just back from Kentucky, says there is no question about how the folks will vote down there—all for Roosevelt.

A car was waiting in time to get me over to the budget hearing in the House of [Representatives] for our Lands Division deficiency appropriation.

Wednesday, 28 June 1944
4101 Lorcom Lane

A week ago, today, I left with the other assistant attorney generals and the attorney general for the third United States attorneys' conference, combined with the judicial conference of the Fourth Judicial Circuit at Asheville, North Carolina—the same from which I returned quite suddenly after one day's attendance last year to do battle on the Elk Hills front. There was soon no question about that even having been noted in Asheville, North Carolina; even the U.S. marshal, Charley Price, immediately remarked upon the Elk Hills controversy shortly after I got off the train. . . .

As a further personal slight, emanating beyond doubt from His Nibs, Attorney General Biddle, the Lands Division was not on the program. It had not been at the first and second United States attorneys' conferences, which my general assistant, Mr. Williams, attended for me. . . . It is impossible to say that a division of the Justice Department, which has almost twice as many attorneys as any other division, has, under these circumstances, no place on the program for discussion. Many of the United States attorneys noticed the fact and asked about it and, as usual, there were a large contingent who came up to say that the division doing the finest job in the Department of Justice was the Lands Division. . . .

In the afternoon, I listened to a part of the discussion of the new Criminal Rules of Civil Procedure, in the middle of which the attorney general injected himself into the discussion by moving that a rule, contemplating dismissal of criminal cases in the district courts on motion of "United States attorneys," be changed to make the matter perfectly clear by substituting for the quoted words, "on motion of the attorney general." A storm promptly broke over his head. He stated, in defending his motion, that it was only in accordance with the law: That the attorney general—and only the attorney general—had the authority to dismiss these cases, and that was what was meant by referring to the United States attorneys, who are really only his agents.

Four judges took him on with such vigor as to leave no standing whatever. The statutes, themselves, refer to "the United States attorneys." The courts have the United States attorneys before them and, in liberal translation of the remarks of Judge [Charles C.] Wyche, Judge [Julius W.] Waring, Judge [Joseph C.] Hutcheson, and one of the Circuit Court judges, the courts would be damned if they would permit an attorney to adjourn the discussion in the middle of the court and go out to telephone the attorney general. Furthermore, it was not the law. The attorney general called on one of his own lawyers, [Alexander] Holtzhoff, an authority on the Rules of Civil Procedure, to bear him out as to his statement of the law. As Holtzhoff told me afterward, "I tried, as politely as I could, to tip him off to the fact that he was completely wrong as a matter of law, by saying that the problem was left to the relations between the attorney general and the United States attorneys as a matter of intra-departmental relationships, but he did not see it, and simply went on his own course. He is not a reflective type of mind, you know!" Holtzhoff added moderately.

Tom Clark told me later, by the swimming pool at the Biltmore, that the attorney general had discussed this rule with [him] in frequent conferences in his office and, at no time, had he ever made such a suggestion; that he had thrown in his motion as an impulsive matter, like tossing a handgrenade playfully into a school picnic. It had blown the Department's views completely to pieces as far as that particular rule was concerned, and any change was voted down almost unanimously. The judges voiced the United States attorneys' opinion, who—as Holtzhoff said—"do not really have freedom of speech," inasmuch as they are speaking in the presence of their bosses: The attorney general and the assistant attorney generals above them.

It was a smashing defeat, and a real humiliation to the attorney general of the United States to take such a beating from the judges and the United States attorneys, but it is wholly characteristic of the man, even though somewhat shocking, to find at this late hour in his professional life, he did not know the fundamental matter of law that United States attorneys have the power to dismiss cases. . . .

. . . [After] another game of tennis, I made it back to the train, where Josephus Daniels finally walked down the train to find me, and we sat and talked for over two hours. I was amazed to learn of the battle he had fought in the Wilson administration against the development of Elk Hills and the threat of Secretary of the Interior [Franklin K.] Lane to lease the same petroleum reserve over which we have just had a further extended battle. The new facts, hitherto unpublished, but of which Daniels has testimonial knowledge, were conveyed to him by Secretary of Agriculture [David F.] Houston, who informed Daniels, as secretary of the Navy, that Lane had been offered fifty thousand dollars in cash, and a salary of $100,000 a year as the head of an oil company after he retired from the office of secretary of the Interior. The fact had also been confirmed by [Thomas W.] Gregory, the attorney general, but nobody had the proof of it. Such a fact, however, would naturally account for Lane's persistent efforts to rent the Naval Petroleum Reserve; and, in fact, he did have considerable oil withdrawn from the Reserve, I believe. Daniels went to the President with the information, admitting that it could not be proved, but convinced of the authenticity of it, and of the fact that Lane intended to go right ahead in exercise of his power as secretary of the Interior and sign a lease, after which it would be too late to repudiate the matter. He was going to bull it through, in spite of Daniels' opposition at the cabinet meeting in which he had been strongly supported by Attorney General Gregory.

Lane had said that the lease would be valid and legitimate exercise of his power, and Daniels had consulted with the attorney general, from whom he secured a contrary opinion, and that opinion was expressed in cabinet meeting. This occurred in 1913, I believe. When Daniels went to

Woodrow Wilson with the story of Lane's prospective employment by an oil company, Wilson wrote Lane a letter of definite instructions not to take any action, whatsoever, in respect to the Elk Hills Naval Petroleum Reserve without the approval of the President.

That ended the matter, then, but, of course, all during the war . . . there were determined, consistent, and prolonged efforts to open up the Reserve, just as there has been in this war—and those efforts have now prevailed. Daniels will indicate in his book[1] that parties appealed to him to lease Teapot Dome, on the grounds that the applicant was a Democrat, and then, when the administration changed and the Republicans came in, it would be leased anyway—and, therefore, it might as well be released by Daniels to good, loyal Democrats rather than letting the Republicans get it. He turned down this extraordinary proposition, also, but, subsequently, had a letter from the applicant reminding him of that statement after the fall leases of Teapot Dome and Elk Hills had been made in 1921 to Doheny and Daugherty.

A telegram from Oscar Ewing, assistant to the national secretary of the Democratic Party, requested me to make an address at the "Negro Freedom Rally" in Madison Square Garden on the night of the 26th. . . . Upon returning to the office, I found . . . that it was rather a doubtful assignment. Mrs. Roosevelt had declined to go—was not permitted to go—because such an appearance by her at this time could well be a fatal piece of political dynamite. Her championing of the Negro cause is a major issue in the impending election.

Nevertheless, the meeting was considered an important political one with the Republican convention convening in Chicago. As Jack Ewing said over the telephone, "We have to have someone there." Ickes had declined upon learning that there was no national hook-up on the radio. With a hasty scrambling for materials, I left Washington at 3:00 P.M. on the 26th, and spent the time riding to New York by scribbling notes of an address. It was a radical crowd, I had been informed, and therefore it was a very dangerous front for me, personally.

I arrived about 8:30 P.M., after the speaking had begun, and gazed with some amazement at the throngs of people crowding every seat in all four tiers of that immense amphitheater—three-fourths of them being colored. The house was dark, except for spotlights which were playing on the speakers in the center of the platform, which was located in the middle of the arena. I was taken to a seat beside [Adam Clayton] Powell, the Baptist minister from Harlem, who anyone would mistake for a White man—and a handsome one at that! He is the spellbinder and rabble-

---

1. Josephus Daniels, *The Wilson Era*, 2 vols. (Chapell Hill: University of North Carolina Press, 1944–46).

rouser from Harlem who is now running for Congress—and he will probably be elected.

A succession of labor union Negro leaders spoke in machine-gun bursts of rousing oratory, attacking White supremacy, the Jim Crow tradition, political and economic inequalities, and social discrimination—all while Negro soldiers were fighting at the front. There was terrific applause and shouts during the speaking. There were elements of the old-fashioned Negro revival service, only *en masse*. Over 21,000 people packed the hall.

As I listened, I rapidly reoriented my scribblings which I had made on the train to a line of thought which was the most sobering of the evening. As the administration representative, I certainly could not keep pace, or give this crowd the extremist satisfaction they were there to enjoy.

After eliciting laughter and applause by describing prejudice as, "a state of being down on something you are not up on," and referring to Will Rogers' famous remark when he was referred to as an ignorant "cowboy," to the effect that, "Of course, he was ignorant; we are all ignorant, but on different subjects," I proposed that we adjourn the subject of prejudice for just a moment—in deference to the men dying at the front—in order to explore our liberties at home. After doing so, I said that, "If there was anyone so cynical or so discouraged in outlook as to doubt these values, let him look abroad, where millions of enslaved people looked longingly across the ocean to the United States, to regard American citizenship as the most priceless heritage on earth."

There were cheers and hisses, and one man hollered into the arena, "I don't so regard it—not me!" I was tempted to reply, but why get into a brawl when one was so easily available in the highly excited atmosphere. . . . And then, I explained the rise of Negro employment and the attack on violations of civil liberties in the Department of Justice, giving a few brief figures.

There were more hisses at the conclusion of those figures. Many there were not interested in gains; they were interested in conquests. Many, undoubtedly, had revolution in mind—and the appeal of the Communist [Party] is overwhelmingly clear on this point, because they suggest an orgy of equality—a disorderly, violent, and immediate emancipation from all restraints and restrictions of whatsoever kind or character. . . .

As a matter of interest, and in order to confirm or otherwise dispose of my impressions, I asked a colored man next to me on the speakers' platform, who was a member of the House of Representatives in Pennsylvania, what I had said which elicited hisses.

"You asked them to suspend discussions of race prejudice."

"But only for the moment, just for the moment to consider American citizenship," I replied.

"I understood that perfectly, but it is too fine a point for them. They are not in the mood for that tonight. What you said was perfectly all right, but there are some here would not take it."

The *New York Times* reporter, who said he had "covered" me before, gave a different explanation, when I asked him. . . . "It's a left-wing crowd. There are a lot of communists here. They were bound to hiss you." He showed me a newspaper article in advance notice of this meeting, maintaining that it was organized by communists. . . . [2]

Wednesday night, 5 July 1944
4101 Lorcom Lane

Katherine and I went to dinner with Mr. N. Goldmann. Rabbi Stephen S. Wise had asked him to see us and so had Mrs. Archibald, an unofficial Jewish ambassadress, who has made it her mission in life to examine the attempted Jewish colonies, all of which she says have failed tragically from Brazil to Madagascar—all except Palestine. Goldmann is in charge of refugee work on the part of the American Jewish Congress, and a very vital fellow.

He reported a conversation between [Edward R.] Stettinius, undersecretary of State, and Churchill, in London, . . . in which Churchill said, unequivocally, that Palestine would be created into a national Jewish state after the war. The matter has been soft-pedaled, and a British White Paper[1] limiting immigration to Palestine has been enforced, undoubtedly in deference to the relations with the Arabs, since England has its hands full in the Mediterranean and dares not risk the stirring up of another problem in that area. According to Stettinius, the statement was unequivocal, but Goldmann would like to know also, whether it meant the present territory of Palestine or, after further severance of a portion of its territory, as the Trans-Jordan Territory was removed from the original boundaries of Palestine.[2]

He recounted a priceless incident when he and Rabbi Wise and one or two others called on Secretary Hull in respect to the Saudi Arabia

---

2. "Equality Demanded at Negro Rally Here; Thousands at Garden Session Urge End of Jim Crowism," *New York Times*, 27 June 1944.

1. The British White Paper, 17 May 1939, repudiated the Balfour Declaration of 1917, which promised to allow a Jewish homeland in Palestine. It limited Jewish immigration in Palestine to 75,000 over the next five years and, after 1 March 1944, would permit such immigration only with the approval of the Arabs.
2. On 1 September 1922, the British had divided their League of Nations Mandate lands in the Middle East, which had formerly belonged to the old Ottoman Empire's province of Palestine, into Trans-Jordan, to the East of the Jordan River, and Palestine, to the West of the Jordan River.

pipeline deal. Secretary Hull, in the course of the conversation, remarked that the pipeline was to deliver the oil—that is, [to] terminate—"in the Persian Gulf."

When he was corrected, and his attention was called to the fact that the pipeline was to terminate in the Mediterranean, he said, "That is what I said—the Persian Gulf of the Mediterranean."

It was necessary to get up and go to a map to show him that the Persian Gulf was not the same thing as the Mediterranean, at which point he said, "I must call so-and-so. I have not been in touch with the detail of this matter."

It was an incredible abyss of ignorance as to geography and as to the purpose of the Saudi Arabian pipeline, which was to run from the Persian Gulf, across Saudi Arabia, to the Mediterranean, at about Haifa.

I had the story repeated twice to make sure of it because it was so incredible, and there can be no doubt of the incident having occurred.

Friday, 7 July 1944
4101 Lorcom Lane

One of the most fateful issues behind the scenes of the government at the moment is the disposal of surplus properties. Will Clayton was made administrator of [the] Surplus [War] Properties [Administration][1] and, when I returned from the West, on June 1st, I found that he had appointed an advisory committee. Rather, I found it out some days later. All agencies were represented except the Lands Division, the only disinterested agency which has a view of all operations of all other agencies of government, and a vast amount of accumulated experience in title and appraisal work in acquiring the same properties now to be disposed of. It was preposterous that we had not been invited onto the committee, and I called Clayton, on June 13th, having met him at Mrs. Borden Harriman's [Florence J. Harriman] at dinner.

"It's just plain ignorance on my part, Littell," he said. "I didn't know you had a Lands Division over there. I will take it up with the chairman right away."

"Who is the chairman?" I asked.

---

1. President Roosevelt established the Surplus War Property Administration (SWPA) by Executive Order No. 9425, 19 February 1944. Its purpose was to "expedite the orderly disposition of surplus war property so far as possible under existing law, pending the action of Congress." He placed it under the supervision of the director of OWM. The SWPA consisted of an administrator (William L. Clayton) who was assisted by an advisory board of fourteen members who were drawn from various government agencies having jurisdiction over federal lands.

"Colonel J. J. O'Brien."

"Good Lord!" I exclaimed. "Why, he is a title lawyer of excellent administrative ability who was on my staff here." I explained briefly O'Brien's history, and then stopped. He said he would call me back, or otherwise communicate with me regarding becoming a member of the advisory committee.

It was a great shock to see O'Brien made chairman of such an all-important committee when the properties to be disposed of, and the policies in respect to them, will enormously affect the public welfare, in respect to which O'Brien has no qualities of judgment for the determination of policy. He is simply an administrator.

When the letter came from Clayton, it said that he had discussed the matter with O'Brien and that it "was agreeable" to O'Brien for me to "appoint a representative of the Lands Division." The letter was an extraordinary admission of O'Brien's very definite determination that I was not to be on his committee. And I can well understand it. He would not have a chance in the world of leading that committee under those circumstances, and he knows that I know of his support from the National Association of Real Estate Boards, which has endeavored to run the disposal of this vast aggregation of property for its own profit. They wish it to be handled on a commission-agent basis, and have had a hard drive toward that end from the very start. They endeavored to defend O'Brien after the Truman Committee report; as one of them recently explained to John Courtney in a convention at Newark: "We had to. We set up his organization for him and we had to come to his help."

It was this influence that made O'Brien chairman of the advisory committee. When he discussed disposal problems with Clayton, he laid a plan on Clayton's desk. It was the plan of the National Association of Real Estate Boards and not O'Brien's, because O'Brien is incapable of original thinking along that line. Clayton was so impressed that he wanted to take O'Brien into his office to take charge of it, [but] Somervell refused to release him, after which Colonel [M. J.] O'Byrne, in charge of O'Brien's San Francisco office and a former real estate operator from Columbus, Ohio, was placed in charge at $10,000 a year, with O'Brien as chairman of the advisory committee. . . .

Their influence rides right straight through to the R.F.C. which has now been placed in charge of the disposal of all industrial plants and—crime-of-crimes—even agricultural lands. And so, I wrote to Clayton a fairly sharp letter pointing out that policies had been determined long before the most widely experienced agency in the government had been invited to attend the advisory committee, that I knew O'Brien well and the influence of the National Association of Real Estate Boards, and doubted whether I could be of any material service on the committee. . . .

Fireworks will start fairly soon now because that is virtually a declaration of open war between O'Brien and myself in my laying the cards right on the table in regard to the National Association. . . .

Sunday, 12 July 1944
4101 Lorcom Lane

The long-expected news was announced today by the President: That he would accept the nomination for a fourth term. The announcement was made to a packed press room, obviously with considerable emotion on the President's part. Even he had his "Commander-in-Chief"—the People. If they demanded that he continue, he could no more refuse to do so than the boys in the Armed Services today. It was a classic statement. Critics could hardly get at it, except to complain of his use of the title "Commander-in-Chief."

His statement was unaccompanied by an endorsement of any candidate for Vice President, however, leaving open the greatest quandary in American political life today. Wallace has returned from China[1] and made his speech at Seattle last weekend[2]—not at all a moving address, considering that his political fate hung on it and the whole nation was listening to find a clue as to whether they wanted this man as Vice President or not. The South does not want him. Industrial leaders do [not] want him. Party leaders, although somewhat divided, on the whole do not want him. Only the People want him, as the popular polls clearly show. He runs ahead of all other candidates.

Tommy Corcoran and Joe Kennedy have come back into the battle to try to put over Justice Douglas, and they are working with great effect to defeat Wallace. Other candidates are Justice Byrnes, now assistant president; Senator Alben Barkley ("Bumbling Alben" as he is popularly called as the President's leader of the Senate); Speaker Rayburn of the House; ex-Senator [Sherman] Minton, now on the Circuit Court of Appeals (having been narrowly defeated by failure of the President to step into Indiana in the 1940 elections); and Senator Truman from Missouri. The last two would make excellent vice presidents.

The vice presidency takes on unusual significance in this period because of the President's age and the fear that he might not survive a fourth term. I seriously suspect that the President's recent sickness,

---

1. President Roosevelt sent Vice President Wallace to Russia and China, 20 May–5 July 1944, to make a "first-hand report" of conditions there.

2. "Wallace Calls US to Unity in Pacific with Russia, China; Reporting in Seattle Radio Talk on Trip to China," *New York Times*, 10 July 1944.

which took him on a protracted visit to Bernard Baruch's country estate in South Carolina (where there are not telephones) was a mild heart attack. The long rest period and the restricted hours under which the President is now working indicate that this might have been the case—not just a cold or the usual wear and tear commanding recuperation. The Vice President, whoever he is, is viewed as an insurance policy. It is vitally important to get the right man. . . .

Katherine and I weighed the matter carefully and decided that we ought to do what we could [to help Wallace]. Before calling any friends in the West, I telephoned the Vice President's house through his private number. His secretary summoned him to the phone after inquiring who was calling.

"Welcome home, Mr. Vice President. I hope you're feeling fit after your hard trip."

"Thank you, Norman, I am."

"Before calling friends of mine in the West, I wanted to see what the lay of the land was with you. My understanding is that the President is about to come out with a statement endorsing you."

"Yes. We discussed the matter today," he replied.

His first discussion with the President had been confined, solely, to affairs in the [Far] East—according to the press—and according to my knowledge of Wallace, it would be. His mind would be full of it, irrespective of his personal fortunes in the impending convention.

"The President is going to make a statement endorsing me, but the question is: What kind of a statement [will] it be?"

In view of the fact that the President virtually held the power of life or death over the selection of a Vice President, everything naturally depended upon that statement.

"He said," the Vice President continued, "that he would make a statement, but not one which would produce too strong a reaction."

That could only be interpreted to mean that he would leave the matter somewhat to the convention. The statement would not be a mandate.

"I think a few communications with your friends might help stiffen that statement up," I replied.

"They might," he replied, "if the statements would reach him. I do not believe all the communications are reaching him through the secretaries at the White House. I did not know that the old Tommy Corcoran game of blocking off channels of communication through influence on White House secretaries—who can always decide that a matter is too trivial with which to bother the President under these strenuous circumstances—was still in vogue over there."

The Vice President reiterated that he did not think all the messages were being communicated to the President, although his enemies had had access to the President without great difficulty.

"In that event," I observed, "I know how I can get any messages to him which come from friends of ours in the West, and I will arrange matters so that they do reach him."

I asked the Vice President if he had any other suggestions and he said that he did not; that that would be the most helpful thing which could be done at the immediate time.

It was impossible to reach anybody in the State of Washington because yesterday was election day there, and neither office phones nor home phones seemed to answer, but tonight I talked with Magnuson, who was nominated yesterday to the United States Senate to fill Bone's vacancy. "Maggie" assures me that the Washington delegation was in line for Wallace and that he, himself, had sent a strong telegram to the President. Upon my explaining the situation, he assured me that he would get several more; also, that he would try to arrange for my appointment as an alternate at the convention. Having overlooked the detail of having myself elected a delegate to the convention—which could have been arranged—he thought it was still possible to [find] a vacancy.

I talked to Frank Burke, in Pasadena, owner of two radio stations and one of our liberal Democratic leaders.

"It's too late, I'm afraid," he observed immediately. "The President today has thrown him away."

When I asked what he meant by that, Burke replied that the President had announced his own acceptance of a fourth term nomination, today, without mentioning Wallace, and he was afraid that was equivalent to abandoning him. I assured Mr. Burke that was not the case; that the matter was in balance now with a terrific conflict of forces being brought to bear upon the President in the White House; that his attitude toward Wallace was being determined within the next twenty-four or forty-eight hours; and that it was imperative that the President hear from those who believed in Wallace.

"He is the spark-plug of liberalism in the Party; he is the only assurance of the continuance of the liberal cause in the Democratic Party at this time," Burke replied. "We have had a terrific division here with the delegation evenly split. Half of them, purchased by Standard Oil Company money under the influence of Pauley, are against Wallace; but the other half of us are solidly for him. A group of us are meeting on Friday at the Biltmore to close our ranks and stand pat for Wallace, irrespective of what happens."

"That's too late," I replied. "What is needed is a strong statement from your group to the President right now. Meet tomorrow instead of Friday and send a joint telegram to the President."

"We'll do it," Burke replied. "Wallace's only difficulties are with the official party leaders. There is no difficulty when it comes to common people, as all of the polls show. Our problem is to get him past the party organization to a place where the voters can really vote for him. They will do so."

"That is precisely the point to make to the President in your telegram," I replied. "And send your telegram to the attention of Miss Grace Tully, his private secretary. That will get by any cabal in the White House."

I called the Vice President to report both conversations, saying that I had done nothing in Oregon, as Oregon has been consistently hopeless throughout the whole administration as far as liberals in our ranks are concerned; that, as Vice President, he had stated in his speech from Seattle on returning from China, in referring to [Charles L.] McNary, the ex-senator who died during this last year, that the liberal leadership had been in the Republican Party—first in McNary, who stole the public power issue from under our noses in the Bonneville[3] fight in Oregon, and now in Wayne Morse, who had won the nomination for the Senate against [Rufus C.] Holman. I explained the pro-Wallace reactions in Washington and California.

The Vice President had been sitting in his apartment talking to Sidney Hillman, [the] CIO leader. I got the impression, as I frequently have, that here was an elemental, wholly unsophisticated man who had, by those strange accidents of political life, or by some providential or fateful designs, been thrown into the political picture to become the center of a heated controversy. He is wholly unprepared for the devious type of warfare which is being waged around him, and is almost unaware of it.

"You know that your old friend, Tommy Corcoran, and Joe Kennedy are at work, trying to eliminate you," I said.

"Yes; and I guess they are doing pretty damaging work and making real headway," he replied, apparently without the slightest idea of how to do anything about it.

He was greatly interested in the reaction of Mr. Burke from California, and in the story about his position in the State of Washington, and was relieved when I explained to him that I had had the telegram sent to Miss Grace Tully, because her high professional standards as a secretary would see to it that she faithfully show to the President any communication

---

3. Congress had authorized establishment of the Bonneville Power Administration (BPA) by the BPA Act of 1937 (Public Law 329), approved 20 August 1937, to market the electric power produced by the Bonneville Dam, then being built on the Columbia River. As the Grand Coulee Dam neared completion, liberals campaigned to transform the BPA into a regional reform agency akin to the TVA. President Roosevelt, however, settled the matter by Executive Order No. 8526, 26 August 1940, which placed the power generated by Grand Coulee Dam under BPA jurisdiction, without enlarging its charter.

which she received of that important character, however she might feel personally about the individual issues.

"That will get the communication past any obstacle in the White House," I said.

I agreed to run in and see him in Chicago, and he suggested that I call his secretary to find the name of the hotel, which he had forgotten at the moment. He was very appreciative.

"Is there anything else I can do, Mr. Vice President?"

"You have done more now than I could think to tell you to do," he replied appreciatively. We said good night.

There is a void there—a naive, almost childlike incapacity to cope with the hard fighting forces surrounding him. One has flashes of amazement and anxiety, too, as if a child were walking into a sawmill among a lot of flying buzz-saws. We have weighed carefully that country-boy quality, that ingenuousness, to see whether it is a fatal flaw in a man who might be President of the United States should anything happen to President Roosevelt. Can he be imposed on? Could he be led away and committed on plausible projects? Could he be "taken for a ride?"—in the lingo of the racketeer.

The answer would lie in experience only, as no one could say, in the vast panorama of detail which surrounds a President, but all the brilliance and sophistication of President Roosevelt have not safe-guarded him against incidents of that sort. For example, consider the Elk Hills Naval Petroleum Reserve contract and the Saudi Arabian pipeline deal. He approved both through oil man Ickes. With Wallace, safety would lie in his utter and complete devotion to principle, as distinguished from loyalty to individuals, of which I believe he has very little. He would rigidly apply the test as to whether a project is in the public interest; his penetration is very great there. He is the most selfless man in American politics today. He is not in search of power, except as one must have position to be effective. He does not understand the instrumentalities of power or the machinations which usually surround it in any sphere.

As Charles Marsh said to me quite some time ago, after attending a cocktail party at the attorney general's house: "There are two virginal spirits in this room: Vice President Wallace and Ben Cohen."

I must check in with Marsh and see what the score is according to his brilliant mind. My honest feeling at this moment is that the Vice President has not a chance. Skilled politicians of the first order are against him. Adroit, powerful combinations are driving to defeat him. I do not see how he can possibly make it against such proportions. He has been so completely misjudged and so badly advertised by the conservative class because of his "Milk for the Hot-en-tot" speech and others that people have had it drummed into them that he is really a communist. . . .

Sunday, 16 July 1944
4101 Lorcom Lane

The day before yesterday, I dropped in to see Charles Marsh, the eccentric political savant who lurks behind the scenes in Washington and runs a chain of small newspapers by remote control in the South. He is Wallace's political adviser. He is a rare combination of a thoroughly cynical newspaper man with unfoundering fidelity to liberal causes. I went with his opposite number in the Northwest, Sheldon Sackett—who owns the *Coos Bay Times* and two radio stations—a brilliant young Oregonian of only 41 years, as effervescent as Marsh. . . .

The President has written a letter of endorsement of Wallace saying that, if he were a delegate at the national convention, he would vote for Wallace, and that they had worked well together in these years. The letter is to be released at the convention. Wallace, himself, participated in the drafting of it, and it was signed by the President against overwhelming opposition of the "Palace Guard"—Byrnes, Rosenman, and all, I believe, except possibly Vinson. Even [Robert E.] Hannegan, the party secretary, the new Irishman from St. Louis, had done his best to dissuade the President and, indeed, he has waxed almost loquacious. He boasted at a cocktail party this week in Washington of having had a conference with Wallace in regard to his candidacy and of having told the "plain truth"—in fact, he said: "I told the son-of-a-bitch just where to get off."

In these circumstances, Hannegan could not be trusted with carrying the letter of endorsement to the convention, and has left Washington highly exasperated because last week's letter from the President was given to him, announcing that the President would run for a fourth term. He thought that the Wallace letter of endorsement also should have been given to him.

I read a memorandum covering every state in the union, establishing beyond any doubt that over 50 per cent of the delegates were for Wallace.

It was a comment on the statesmanship of Wallace that he left Marsh with this question when he went to China: "What candidate for Vice President would secure the most votes?"

Shrewd and dissecting research throughout the country by Marsh during Wallace's absence has produced a masterful memorandum of pros and cons. . . .

The news of today is discovering the 28th canon of the Judicial Code of Ethics, which bars judges from participating in political activities— speech-making or activities of any party convention. I talked with [the] assistant editor of *P.M.*, who was carrying the fight against the Tommy Corcoran–Joe Kennedy cabal for the synthetic Westerner, Douglas— *P.M.* having announced that Douglas would actually make the nominating speech for President. If so, this is a shrewd attempt at answering the President's letter endorsing Wallace.

Sunday, 23 July 1944
Chicago Athletic Club, Chicago, Illinois

Dearest Katherine Mather,

While the last few days have burned themselves deeply into American history, they have also burned themselves deeply into my mind, just as they have into the minds of millions of American citizens and men and women throughout the world. Out of a kaleidoscopic shifting of events and violent interplay of forces at the Democratic convention, I must set down for you the principal facts and events in the nomination of a Vice President of the United States which, for the first time in history, was the focal point of public interest and a fulcrum of historic consequences.

I left Washington for Chicago last Monday night, via Detroit, however, to visit my office there. Tuesday morning was adequate for the dispatch of all official business, which I had in Detroit, and I met Justice Murphy at the Book-Cadillac Hotel for lunch, where we primarily discussed affairs of our National Committee Against Persecution of the Jews. I had succeeded in having a talk with both Philip Murray, head of [the] CIO, and [William] Green, head of the A.F. of L., during the intense week which preceded the Democratic convention, and both men agreed to come on the board of directors of the committee together with a representative of each, Mr. [James B.] Carey, secretary of CIO, and Mr. Robert Watt, international representative of A.F. of L. The latter two men would serve on the executive committee also, to which Raymond Gram Swing, the noted radio commentator, has also agreed that his name shall be added. . . .

We covered many subjects, including the national convention and the Tommy Corcoran cabal to put Douglas on the [ticket], which Murphy forecast would be a hopeless flop. He, himself, was nominated by the Michigan delegation as the papers that day announced but, as Murphy said, merely as a favorite-son gesture. He claimed to have advised them over the phone not to propose him. We talked until 4:00 when, through Murphy's arrangements, I went out to the Cadillac plant and did a hasty hour's tour of that plant with Nicholas Druistadt, president of the Cadillac Company. It would probably create a major rumpus if it were known that he was a submarine commander on the German side during the last war, now manufacturing Allison motors for airplanes, tanks, and Cadillac motors for tanks.

It was a really remarkable show, a world-wide phenomenon, at Willow Run, where I was driven by a representative of Mr. [Harry H.] Bennett's office at the Ford plant, after returning to the city. There, a B-24 bomber is turned out every hour and it could be every half hour but the government will not take them that fast. The steady flow of materials through that plant, covering 57 acres, to the end of the assembly line— where converging sections of fully assembled airplanes, complete down to Red Cross boxes, oxygen tanks, earphones and a vast network of wiring, struts, mechanical parts, and four motors, flow into a completed plane— seemed as fluid as water and as complex as the human nervous system. Small wonder that Germany and Japan are reeling under our blows when these giant bombers are delivered off the assembly line, filled with gas, tested right there, and delivered to the Army for immediate transportation to the battle fronts of the world.

But, I must get on with the main story. I arrived in Chicago Wednesday morning and, after settling at the Chicago Athletic Club, which I had chosen for the sake of a swimming pool, proceeded to the Stevens Hotel and into the welter of political forces shaping up to expend themselves during that and the succeeding two days. Having contacted my Washington delegation and found no vacancies for which I could be appointed as an alternate, . . . I nevertheless secured an alternate's badge and book of tickets through my own connections, and also some extra tickets for the delegation, thereby getting access to the floor of the convention.

It is hard to recapture, even at this moment, the intensity of feeling which marked even the opening session of the convention, on Wednesday noon, July 19th. The packed stadium was in great contrast to the Republican convention a month ago, which was dull and listless, perfectly managed, and perfectly vacuous, both in content and in result. Even Herbert Hoover had spoken—the kiss of death to any convention.[1] As one speaker in the Democratic convention said, "The mantle of Herbert Hoover was placed around the shoulders of Thomas Dewey. What was intended as a mantle was in fact a shroud."

Roars of enthusiasm and applause followed the first mention of Franklin D. Roosevelt's name in the welcoming address of Boss Mayor [Edward J.] Kelly of Chicago, one of the great machine bosses of the United States, like [Frank] Hague of New Jersey and [Edward H.] Crump of Tennessee. The fourth member of the Big Four—[Thomas J.] Pendergast of Kansas

---

1. The Republicans held their convention, 26–28 June 1944, in Chicago. They nominated Governor Thomas E. Dewey of New York and Governor John Bricker of Ohio as their presidential and vice presidential candidates.

[City]—is in the penitentiary, put there by Attorney General Murphy.
The nomination of Roosevelt was, of course, a foregone conclusion, fourth
term and all. Nevertheless, there were roars of applause for the standard-
bearer outlasting in duration and in unquestioned enthusiasm anything
which happened at the Republican convention.

Among these kaleidoscopic events was suddenly injected with electric
effect, the news flash announcement by Hannegan that the Japanese
cabinet had fallen.[2] The word was greeted with roars of applause, and no
one could escape the immediate political effect, for the knockout blow was
credited to the standard-bearer—Roosevelt—and rightly so.

With the usual advantages enjoyed by the "party of the poor," . . . we
were welcomed with reasonable weather and not blistering heat such as
that which suffocated the Republicans. Mayor Kelly adroitly aggravated
the situation for them as I learned through Arthur Sullivan, special
assistant to the attorney general, who has my principal trial work here and
who happens to be Kelly's personal attorney. There were occasional
intermittent blasts of cold air shot across the stadium, but otherwise it was
a bake oven. He never misses a trick, particularly a dirty trick, although
I must say no one can fail to enjoy the humor of this particular one.

Even the policemen, who were so helpful and cooperative at the
Democratic convention, were, as Sullivan said, "very much in the way" at
the Republican convention. Little things can make big things so very,
very difficult—and they did. Sullivan swears to me that the heat—which
may have been 100 degrees outside the hall—would rise to 103 and 105
inside.

Weather or no weather, Democratic enthusiasm could not have been
restrained. Mayor Kelly and Senator [Scott W.] Lucas from Illinois were
the principal speakers of the morning. In the night session, after the
chairman, Robert E. Hannegan—the new Irish "Mick" political boss and
secretary of the national party from St. Louis, Missouri—gave an address,
followed by Mrs. Charles W. Tillett [Gladys A. Tillett], chairman of the
Women's Division, who really out-did herself,[3] and vastly out-did Mrs.
Clare Luce at the Republican national convention. However, real competition for Clare Luce was Helen Gahagan (Mrs. Melvyn Douglas)—
running for Congress in Los Angeles—whose natural photogenic qualities
and stage glamor offered the competition for Clare Luce when Helen
spoke the second evening. Mrs. Tillett's speech had a fine take-off on
"Little Red Riding Hood" in which the Republican Party was playing the

2. The Japanese cabinet of Premier Hideki Tojo (1884–1948) resigned 18 July 1944
following the fall of Saipan. On 22 July 1944, Emperor Hirohito replaced them with General
Kuniaki Koiso (1880–1950) and Admiral Mitsumasa Yonai (1880–1948) as premier and
deputy premier.

3. For an account of her speech to the convention, see *New York Times*, 20 July 1944.

wolf, having adopted, as its own, numerous New Deal planks. Mrs. Tillett portrayed them as the New Deal "teeth," with the Republican wolf replying to the Little Red Riding Hood voter who inquired about the size of her teeth—"The better to eat you with, my dear." The keynote address by Governor Robert S. Kerr, in the evening, was really inferior to Mrs. Tillett's in substance. It was full of war and bombast and oratory and wasted too much time—although amusingly, by attacking the Republicans.

These are bare mention of the outward events of the convention. Inwardly, and behind closed doors, it was seething with intrigue. Slowly the competition boiled down to two candidates—Henry A. Wallace and Harry S. Truman, senator from Missouri and chairman of the Committee to Investigate War Expenditures,[4] which he has headed with such marked success. This has been largely due to able investigating counsel, [Hugh A.] Fulton, and to the fact that mistakes in the war effort were so thick that, in the early days of his Committee, they were like ducks flying over in such close formation that one could almost shoot them down with a rifle. The magnificent job done by this Committee made Truman a national figure.

James Byrnes . . . withdrew his candidacy on the first day. He really never had any to withdraw. "Presidentitis" is one of the most powerful diseases to get into the mind of a man. . . . [That] Justice Byrnes, with all of his political acumen, was not immune to "Presidentitis," and, for a man of his intellect and background, this practically proves that no man would be immune to "Presidentitis." . . . [He] ought to know that no period of sojourn in the Supreme Court of the United States could purge his record of the fact that he had not purged his state of the poll tax. Of course, labor was against him for this and other reasons. A letter to Senator [Burnett R.] Maybank, of the South Carolina [delegation] advised him that Byrnes withdrew "in deference to the wishes of the President." Obviously, he was in touch with the President when he made the letter public on the first day of the convention.

The President had been subjected to months of pressure to eliminate Wallace as a man who would lose votes for the party. Wallace had been in China on a mission to Chiang Kai-shek, and those hostile to him, including the entire Palace Guard, from James Byrnes, Sam Rosenman, Gene Casey ("Farmer Casey" from Maryland), Dave Niles, Secretary Ickes, and the political bosses Ed Flynn and Hannegan, had all brought great pressure to bear on the President to drop Wallace as a liability due to his liberalism. Perhaps it is small wonder that the President's endorsement of Wallace was limited to the following inconclusive language:

4. The Senate Special Committee to Investigate the National-Defense Program.

Hyde Park, N.Y.
14 July 1944

My Dear Senator [Samuel D.] Jackson:

In the light of the probability that you will be chosen as permanent chairman of the convention, and because I know that many rumors accompany all conventions, I am wholly willing to give you my own personal thought in regard to the selection of a candidate for Vice President. I do this at this time because I expect to be away from Washington for the next few days.

The easiest way of putting it is this: I have been associated with Henry Wallace during his past four years as Vice President, for eight years earlier while he was secretary of Agriculture, and well before that. I like him and I respect him, and he is my personal friend. For these reasons, I personally would vote for his renomination if I were a delegate to the convention.

At the same time, I do not wish to appear in any way as dictating to the convention. Obviously the convention must do the deciding. And it should—and I am sure it will—give great consideration to the pros and cons of its choice.

Very sincerely yours,
Franklin D. Roosevelt

This was the letter which Charles Marsh, Wallace's Colonel House[5] and intimate political adviser in Washington, had told me of just before I left Washington. In fact, I was reading Marsh's confidential analysis of the political situation throughout the country when a long-distance call came through from Claude Pepper at Chicago, Senator Pepper from Florida being one of the brave and stalwart supporters of Wallace even though hoping that lightning would strike and make him—Pepper—the people's candidate for the vice presidency. I had heard Marsh tell Pepper about this letter, saying it was a strong statement which Wallace himself had drafted and "it came right from his [Wallace's] heart." I had departed at that point feeling that I ought not to be an unwitting eavesdropper when Marsh was compelled to talk in my presence in his drawing room, but I left with the query in my mind as to whether the endorsement came from the President's heart, rather than Wallace's. . . .

Emanating from the Hannegan headquarters, during the first day of the convention, and disseminated by Ed Pauley from Los Angeles, the treasurer of the party, and others supposed to be close to presidential advice,

5. That is, a close personal friend and political adviser. Colonel Edward M. House was among President Wilson's most trusted friends and often served as his unofficial personal emissary.

were rumors of another letter in which the President endorsed Senator Truman and Justice William O. Douglas. Hannegan was supposed to have this letter and the rumors of it were wreaking havoc among confused and bewildered delegates who look up to the Great Gods of Mt. Olympus at the top of the national party organization for light and learning at times like these. Rumors distilled from the Gods were about as strong and effective as machine gun fire in mowing down delegates. We were all angry and ready for blows at such unscrupulous and outrageous conduct which unavoidably implied duplicity on the part of the President. He had already said that, if he were a delegate, he would vote for Wallace. . . .

Any doubts as to the necessity of Wallace being here were resolved by these developments. He arrived from Washington on Wednesday, July 19th, the morning the convention opened. As internecine strife went on within the key delegations of Pennsylvania, New York, Connecticut, California, and many others, all of us Wallace amateurs were working intensely on the floor of the convention or in the corridors, polling delegates from each state, winning converts if possible, trying to consolidate ranks, and attempting to estimate Wallace's support. The "breaks" of that day were that a poll of the Connecticut delegation (only 18 in number, but coming from a significantly located New England state) had divided ten to eight in favor of Wallace, and thereafter had adopted the unit rule so that the whole 18 votes would go to Wallace. That was rather a surprise since former Attorney General Cummings headed the delegation from Connecticut. I had seen him at breakfast in the morning, while I was talking to Mrs. Jeanette Testu, national committeewoman from Washington, who had breakfast with me in the Stevens Hotel. Cummings and his wife had observed that they thought the Connecticut delegation was for Wallace. I considered this surprising in view of Cummings' conservative outlook but, of course, the voters may have determined the matter. His prognostication proved correct.

A poll of the New York delegation in conference that day had indicated that, out of 52 delegates, Wallace would have at least 40 votes, a majority—but the unit rule was not adopted. In the Pennsylvania delegation of 72, Wallace's champion, Senator [Joseph F.] Guffey, also led a majority, and Attorney General Biddle, playing his small part as a delegate from the state, endeavored to sidetrack a motion to support Wallace by moving to table it. This came out in the press and showed quite clearly where Biddle stood, which, of course, I knew, as he was bound to play some sort of a part on Tommy Corcoran's team, even if he was only water boy.

I observed him later walking up and down the floor of the convention. So did Marshall Field, with whom I visited at the Ambassador East, yesterday afternoon (to get a little ahead of my story) for Mr. Field remarked with some evident restraint at his true feeling that he, too, had seen Biddle walking up and down in front of the delegates on the convention floor. "It seemed to me that he simply wished to be seen," Mr. Field observed. He added that actually nobody paid any attention to Biddle. In any event, Biddle's motion was defeated in the delegation, as his motions usually are. . . . Thereafter, Biddle switched his vote to Wallace in the Pennsylvania delegation, although, of course, retaining the primary objective of Tommy Corcoran that William O. Douglas should prove to be a dark horse in the event of a tie vote. Biddle was, unquestionably, ready to shift to the dark horse.

These were rays of light on a very dark day, and we Westerners bestirred ourselves to a gathering of the clan from the eleven Western states. All Western delegates were invited to a "Friends of Wallace" meeting at 10:30 P.M., after the evening session at the convention hall. We met in the afternoon, in the room of Helen Gahagan at the Palmer House, because Helen Gahagan had been asked to chair the meeting. Only a handful of delegates arrived for this meeting on such short notice, but it had been put on the press board and press men and women swarmed around and even into the room. In fact, we were advised that about a hundred were awaiting admission to this meeting which had been somehow reported to them as available to the press as the other conferences had been. We had to turn them away because the meeting, as we advised them, was not to be held until that night—this was merely an organizational step.

I proceeded to Vice President Wallace's headquarters in the Sherman Hotel for two reasons: To see if he would attend the meeting that night—if it were a success; and to see if by any chance he would like to go over to the Athletic Club for a swim. I knew well his propensity for keeping in fine physical trim under all conditions and thought that that might appeal very strongly after the long and strenuous days he had been keeping. I walked through a battery of individuals who in their numerous selves make up the sum total of a whole force for Wallace, but who individually and numerically are difficult for the candidate to deal with. I was admitted immediately to his quarters, however, and took Nels Peterson, a promising young delegate from Oregon, along with me for the lift which it gives to a developing young man to meet the great. Harold Young had us sit down and wait as the Vice President was just taking a bath . . . and would be out in a moment. He came out, finally, and assured us both that, if the meeting were a success, he would be pleased to come over. He declined the swimming invitation, however, but, after sitting for a moment in the big easy chair with the abstract, thoughtful look which sometimes comes over his face, and which is so totally devoid of strain while the simple process of digesting an idea works itself out, he said:

"I really haven't time for a swim, Norman, but I will slip away with you and have dinner." And so he did.

We slipped down the stairway (after I had sent Nels Peterson on the innumerable jobs which had to be done before the evening meeting, which he well appreciated) ducked through the crowd in the lobby, out the side entrance of the hotel and down the street toward Michigan Avenue and the Athletic Club. We came into the dining room, unannounced, and the head waiter found a table for two, where we settled down for one of the most delightful visits I have ever had with the Vice President. It was a moment of relaxation from politics, to which we returned repeatedly. He told me much about his trip to China, the inspection of Russian experimental stations in the field of agriculture, their great progress in developing cotton adapted to the peculiar climatic conditions of the country where there is one hour more of sunlight than is available in our country in the cotton belt, and other natural problems to confront. Experimentation in the breeding of pigs and livestock was also touched upon—how the breed of pigs in Russia were based upon those bought from Yorkshire (I believe) in England, although they had since been crossbred with other stock and improved. He explained that this experimentation work in the field of agriculture was not new in Russia and had been quite well developed even under the Czarist regime.

As to China, his mission had been to see if he could impress upon Chiang Kai-shek the necessity of not getting at odds with Russia. He spoke of Chiang Kai-shek's strongly anti-Russian, anti-communist feeling. . . . Wallace's one concrete achievement while in China, he stated, was getting permission from Chiang Kai-shek to admit American military observers on the front of the Chinese Communist Army. The United States Army has never been able to get such privileges which had been consistently refused.

"I hope you had recognition for that accomplishment," I said.

"Not at all. The Army has never said anything to me about it and I rather suspect that they may even resent the fact that I was able to get it when they were not."

He related an incident, which happened in one of the Chinese provinces in which the party was being carried for about a mile over up-and-down country in sedan chairs, carried by poles extending between the shoulders of two coolies. Wallace had gotten out and offered to take the place of one of the coolies just to see if he could carry the sedan chair on his shoulders carrying some Chinese officials, all of whom had scrambled out of their chairs to walk with him, but had declined to carry the chair.

"I thought it might do some good," he added with a twinkle in his eye.

"Such an incident would go all through China," I added, laughing at the imagined scene of the Vice President of the United States trudging along with a sedan chair on his shoulders carrying some Chinese officials. . . .

"I did do a little digging in the field with the Chinese labor at work there," he said.

"You may have caused a lot of trouble," I said.

"—may have started the Chinese Revolution!" he replied, laughing.

"It seems as if one might be due there. Is it?" I asked.

"It is due," Wallace replied. "There are vast resources for the relief of an immense population but they have suffered from war lords, landlords, and feudal lords." . . .

He spoke also of recent conversations with President Roosevelt. This was *apropos* of a discussion of the existing state of things in the executive branch of the government, which I said was shot through—in fact, riddled through and through—with reactionary forces not interested in the public welfare, but interested only in laying the foundation for profit-making in a big way, with opportunities greater than anything ever known before, eclipsing in potential danger the Harding administration. I gave an example of my present struggle over the disposal of real estate by the Surplus Property Administrator Will Clayton, pointing out how the organization had been dictated by the National Association of Real Estate Boards, right through to RFC, and how the disposal of property on a brokerage basis had been protected in meetings of the advisory committee—also how Clayton had procured the assignment of agricultural lands to RFC for disposal. Administrative methods can never be divorced from policy. Even with the purest-minded businessmen operating on a brokerage basis, interests are set in force which cannot be artificially directed in the proper channels. . . .

"I could tell you that after the election, the President will swing to the left and clear some of those fellows out of Washington," Wallace said.

I recalled that he had told me, earlier, that the President would swing to the left after the primaries were over, and regain a more liberal position, but no such tendencies were evident, and I did not remind him of that conversation. The biggest and most convenient opportunity to swing to the left was in the support of Wallace for the vice presidency.

"This must go no further," Wallace said, "but the President is on to "Jesus" H. Jones, and told me so—also Will Clayton. He said that after the election, he would clean out such fellows as Jones and Clayton and restore full-fledged liberal government."

I wonder! Could it possibly be? Such forces have their roots too deep into the government and such a reformation could only be accomplished by a change of Presidents. . . .

As to the immediate prospects of Wallace's success in the convention, he made this cryptic remark: "I am perfectly happy about the outcome."

"I don't quite understand," I said. "Do you mean that you are now confident of victory, or do you mean that, whichever way it goes, you will be happy about the outcome."

"I mean the latter," he said.

"As a worker in the trenches at this moment, I can't appreciate that," I replied. "I want to win. You will have to spell it out for me a little bit."

"I mean this," he said: "There is only one issue in my nomination and that is the existence of liberal government in the United States. I happen to be the symbol of that issue. I am not wholly convinced that it would be best for us to win now. It might be better to postpone the issue until 1948 or 1952. It is the cause of liberalism which is an issue and not my own fortunes."

He said, in response to my comment that I was out for immediate results and unwilling to take chances on the future if these could be avoided, that he was too. He intended to win if possible. It was obvious, however, that he was quite philosophical about the whole matter and willing to leave things to the determination of destiny.

The waiter brought the check. Wallace pushed two crumpled bills across the table. "Take this as my contribution toward the meal." It was an act of simple and unsophisticated thoughtfulness.

"I am not a rich man, Mr. Vice President," I said, "but under no circumstances could you pay for any part of this meal. I am honored to have you as my guest tonight, and it has been a great pleasure to have this visit with you."

The news had gotten around that he was in the room. In fact, several requests for autographs had been sent over until I put a stop to it by telling the headwaiter that I had undertaken to give Mr. Wallace an uninterrupted quiet hour at the club. The headwaiter said he had already given an order to present no more requests. That had occurred when we sat down, but when we rose to go and walked through the dining room, applause broke out all through the room. It was a singular event considering the conservative character of this club. No doubt, part of the demonstration was in recognition of and in respect for the office of Vice President, but most of it was in recognition, I believe, of the inherent goodness of the man which is widely recognized even by those who are against him.

We walked over to the Sherman House after a brief encounter with a man on the sidewalk who buttonholed Wallace to complain about the tax structure and the renegotiation of contracts. Wallace listened patiently until I rescued him.

"He is partially right," the Vice President said as we walked along. "The tax structure is absolutely wrong. It is calculated to prevent the accumulation of capital so that these small businesses and corporations cannot expand and develop and have needed capital for the postwar period when they will need it."

"I do not think that Henry Morgenthau is a big enough man to see and understand the essential revision of the tax laws," I replied.

Wallace agreed and said that Morgenthau was a good administrator. I observed that he had put over the voluntary sale of bonds when I thought he was certainly licked on his proposed methods.

"I thought so, too," the Vice President said. "He certainly put that over in good shape."

"—Aided by the fact that there is about $5,000,000,000 more in circulation than ever before in the history of the country and marked limitations on places to spend it," I added. "Anyway, his plan worked, and it's better perhaps than compulsory savings."

Jack More, chairman of the Iowa delegation, was waiting on the curb when we arrived at the Sherman House and we all climbed into a taxi for the auditorium. There had been about a thousand Iowa people to take care of, at least three hundred of whom had come all the way from Iowa to be present and give support with the unanimous Iowa delegation, but poor More had only been able to get 219 books, that is, 219 tickets, for each session of the convention. He had had 70 additional single admissions, or 289 for the evening of Wednesday, although he had gone repeatedly to Ed Pauley's office to request more.

What "Babes in the Woods" those people were! Asking Ed Pauley for more seats for the Vice President. "Don't you know he's against you?" I asked. "You'll never get any seats from Ed Pauley. I will help you in the morning through contacts in the national committee."

As we shoved through the crowd with many recognitions, we were aided by the police who recognized Wallace. We walked to a little room underneath the grandstands and I was about to leave, but Wallace beckoned me to come in and sit down. We sat alone for a while, chatting about the individual delegations. After a few minutes, however, I excused myself, saying I had work to do on the Western states meeting of the evening, and I went out on the floor and got to work, checking up on the Washington delegation, the Alaska delegation and the Puerto Rican [delegation; and] also checking with other associates who had worked over their respective delegations for the night meeting.

On the floor of the convention hall, we had all buttonholed the delegates from all Western states—I had been assigned Washington, Alaska and Hawaii and the other states of California, Oregon, Idaho, Montana, Nevada, New Mexico, Utah, and Arizona—and, by special request, Minnesota, had been divided up among other persons. Delegates and alternates both, and the press were to be welcomed. . . .

. . . I waited, with some fear and trepidation, in the Red Lacquer Room of the Palmer House, dubiously counting about 250 chairs, which had been placed in the ballroom. Could we possibly fill them? Could our customers make an impression on that big room? Mrs. Borden Harriman came in with Mrs. Walter Kirk, sister of the ambassador to Italy,[6] and sat in the front row, and, finally, Helen Gahagan and her party came and, little by little, delegates straggled in.

The Wallace support had taken on no great proportions at that moment. Indeed, we were very much in doubt, knowing the machinations of the

6. The U.S. ambassador to Italy from 1944 to 1946 was Alexander C. Kirk.

political managers against him, as to how solid a body of support we could muster even in the West where liberalism is at its best. To our utter amazement, the hall was completely filled shortly after midnight and more chairs had to be brought in [from the stadium], in spite of transportation difficulties . . . and the lateness of the hour after a hard and tiresome day. We agreed that we should start immediately, and Helen Gahagan took the chair, having invited Mrs. Harriman to be a guest speaker, even though she was from New York, and Senator Pepper from Florida, a state which is essentially Western in spirit with a senator of undoubted qualities of greatness. I also had Nels Peterson from the Oregon delegation, an able and intelligent young man, who offers some hope in Oregon, serve as secretary and sit at the head table.

There is no question about it: That was a stirring and significant meeting for Wallace, and it contributed unquestionably toward consolidating Western sentiment. Confusion had been produced among Western delegates by the operations of the high command. Helen Gahagan handled the chairmanship beautifully; Mrs. Harriman made a short, fine talk endorsing Wallace, followed by a stirring comment from Pepper; and the members of each delegation were called upon to give a succession of three- to five-minute talks. (We had, of course, arranged this in advance.)

The symposium of Wallace had great substance to it, and in the middle of it all, Wallace came in to be received with cheers, loud and long. He made a free, natural gem of a talk to the general effect that there was but one issue: The continuation of liberal government in the United States. He personified that issue. He talked about the West, and mentioned our future relations with the Orient and spoke with a direct, translucent simplicity which marked an enormous measure of progress over his original shy, strange, and wholly unsatisfactory delivery. The meeting closed at about 1:15 A.M., with delegates and press, alike, impressed by this profound appreciation which the West has for Wallace. That was the end of the first day.

Sunday, 23 July 1944
Chicago Athletic Club

The Second Day: Thursday, 20 July 1944

Behind the scenes, the struggle over the party platform had been going on steadily. Rabbi Stephen S. Wise stopped me in the lobby of the Stevens Hotel.

"They are refusing to give us a plank on the establishment of an independent state in Palestine," he said, seizing both my hands. "Judge [Joseph M.] Proskauer, through Sam Rosenman at the White House, has influenced the President against such a plan. It will hurt the President. It will lose the President 400,000 or 500,000 votes. The Republicans have a satisfactory plank."

"We must certainly do no less than they did," I replied; and, to Schulman who joined us at that moment as the aide to Wise, I said, "You must make it quite clear that we are legally obligated to such a program as signatories to the Palestine Mandate.[7] Too many people do not know, or only vaguely realize that."

It was quite impossible, however, for anyone to see the members of the Platform Committee during the day as doors were locked. Josephus Daniels was in continuous session. For a man past 80, he possesses extraordinary intellectual vigor, clarity, and real attacking power. In view of my friendship with Daniels, I called upon Wallace at headquarters at the Sherman [House] to see if he did not wish me to explore with Daniels what could be done towards getting the support of the North Carolina delegation. Mr. Wallace was very appreciative and said it was a splendid idea. However, I was unable to reach Mr. Daniels by telephone until I caught him in his room right after lunch, and the first time he could see me was at 9:00 the next morning—Friday—due to the pressure of work on the Platform Committee.

In the meantime, the nomination of President Roosevelt was a foregone conclusion. No struggle revolved around that issue except the minor scrimmage of the protest vote being arranged in support of Senator [Harry F.] Byrd of Virginia. There would possibly be such a vote for Jim Farley, whose waning power and prestige had been exploited through thousands of letters to every description of Democrat throughout the country—in Jim's dying gasp of hope that lightning might yet strike him— and lacking that, strike someone to defeat the fourth term.

The real battle was over the vice presidency. The Hannegan rumors as to a second letter from President Roosevelt, which was supposed to endorse Senator Truman, were ricocheting around the corridors with devastating effect upon the bewildered delegates. Had not the President said, if he were a delegate, he would vote for Wallace? Could Hannegan's statement be true that he had now made another endorsement?

Senator Joe Guffey, a Wallace champion from Pennsylvania, sounded off to denounce Hannegan in no uncertain terms, saying that it was time, as secretary of the party, that Hannegan give at least a portion of his time to delegates other than his personal candidates—Flynn, Kelly and Hague—the big bosses of the convention. It was one of the most

---

7. The Palestine Mandate was the power granted by the League of Nations to Great Britain to administer the former Ottoman Empire's province of Palestine after World War I, pending its ability to become independent. Great Britain surrendered its mandate to the United Nations in 1947.

blistering denunciations ever made of a secretary of the party by an outstanding party leader, but Hannegan had "no comments."

Rumor, rumor, rumor—and still nobody saw the letter. Senator Barkley was angry because he understood that he was not mentioned in the letter, just as Justice Byrnes had been hurt and angry at not having the President's support. He had withdrawn from the race the preceding day "in deference to the President's wishes"—although I have learned since that the quoted statement was something of a face-saving device. The President made no request of him. Byrnes just read the handwriting of failure on the wall, and should have done so months ago.

There were added rumors of direct communication between Hannegan and the President, with alleged instructions to Hannegan "to get Truman nominated," all of which rumors carried the unfortunate implications of duplicity on the President's part and disloyalty to one who had gone through the battle of the administration with him—first, as secretary of Agriculture and, then, as Vice President following the disaffection of Vice President Garner over the third term issue.

I met Pat Jackson, [a] reporter for *P.M.*, in the corridor.

"Of course, there could be no substance to those rumors!" he said. "I have been in almost constant touch in recent days with Anna Boettiger and, occasionally, even with Mrs. Roosevelt at the White House. Anna had all the polls, including the Gallup Poll's latest returns, spread out around her, and she said it is sheer nonsense to assert that Wallace would lose votes in November 1944. The polls were all to the contrary."

In contrast to this bit of testimonial knowledge was the somber realistic approach of Ernest Lindley, a one-time classmate at Oxford, a biographer of the President, and a careful, honest, accurate reporter.

"It's Truman," he said, in answer to my inquiry. "The deal is all set up for Hannegan and Flynn to put Truman over, although a letter to Hannegan from the President says that either Truman or Justice Douglas would be acceptable to the President."

Tommy Corcoran's dark horse, Douglas, had gotten that far!

With the rising confidence given by the preceding evening, and the tabulations of Harold Young and other, more intelligent, supporters of Wallace showing that he would have over 400 delegates on the first vote, . . . Hannegan's alleged manipulations seemed destined to defeat, but it seemed extraordinary that the President did not put an end to them. However, he had said that it would be "a free and open convention." He would not dictate. Rumor thrives where minds are unclear and, as minds were certainly unclear, rumor was riding rampant through the convention, and the President's position was suffering in consequence, not to mention that of Wallace.

I, therefore, telephoned to your mother, having decided on this course in preference to phoning Anna at the White House, because your mother

was in a position to explore the matter so much more thoroughly. I
explained the rumor campaign and said that I thought the President ought
to lay these ghosts by a statement to somebody—perhaps to Senators
Guffey or Claude Pepper. The matter should be clarified.

Your mother confirmed, however, the growing impression that the
President had left Washington for some unknown destination, which had
previously been rumored to be England, or the coast of Normandy (but
which, by evening, when he gave his acceptance address over the radio,
was known to be an air base on the Pacific Coast; namely, San Diego).

"Anna or Mrs. Roosevelt could settle the matter, as they have been
very close to the President in recent days," I said, and related the
conversation with Jackson. Your mother said that she would call Anna and
see if anything could be done about it. I suggested that I would call Anna
if your mother thought it advisable, or Anna or Mrs. Roosevelt could
communicate through some other trusted person.

The program at the convention did not open until 12:30 P.M. that day,
and I was so busy with other Wallace workers that I did not endeavor to
go out. Besides, the heavy engagements were slated for the evening, and
I broke away to go to Mrs. Walter Kirk's for cocktails at 4:45 in a small party
for Mrs. Borden Harriman, and there we listened to Wallace's nominating
speech for Roosevelt over the radio. The speech was electrical in its
courage and dynamic convictions. Here, indeed, was the gauntlet flung
down to the Democratic Party: A clear and unequivocal challenge to
continue liberal government. What Roosevelt would not say he believed
in, Wallace said Roosevelt believed in (just as when Roosevelt, months ago,
hailed the departure of "Dr. New Deal" and welcomed "Dr. Win-the-
War," Wallace had shortly afterwards said, the "New Deal will never
die.").

The entire South was in revolt. The Texas delegation was split between
the anti-Roosevelt Group and the pro-Roosevelt group, the latter having
withdrawn from the Texas convention in protest against the revolt against
Roosevelt, creating a problem over which the credentials committee had
struggled at great length in the convention.[8] The Tennessee delegates, at
first, endorsed Roosevelt for a fourth term and then rescinded the
resolution until they could see the racial plank of the party platform. The
racial issue is one of the most vital of the campaign, fanned to fever-heat
by Mrs. Roosevelt's championship of Negro equality.[9]

8. Roosevelt supporters had bolted the Texas Democratic convention 23 May 1944 to
protest the party's refusal to endorse a fourth term.
9. Mrs. Roosevelt was a liberal on race relations. She opposed discrimination and was
horrified by such incidents as the Detroit race riot in the summer of 1943 which left
twenty-nine blacks dead, but counseled patience and persistence to black leaders. White
Southerners, however, regarded her as a radical in favor of racial equality.

In face of all this—with characteristic political ineptness and utter in-difference to consequences which go hand in hand with extraordinary intellectual and moral courage—Wallace had said: "The poll tax must go." Historically, he is correct. The Supreme Court has recently said so, greatly agitating the fears in the South of the post-Civil War domination by carpetbaggers and Negroes.[10] Everyone knew how Wallace would stand on the poll tax. Why mention it? It was just a red rag before the Southern bulls. . . .

"This is an extraordinary incident in political history," I said to Mrs. Harriman as the speech closed. "In seconding the nomination of Presi-dent Roosevelt, Wallace in this speech is really making his own nominat-ing address. He will stand or fall on that address."

Mrs. Harriman was unstinting in her praise of the Wallace address, although one or two Republican guests, in an exclusive Lake Shore Drive apartment, suffered a state of shock from its liberalism. There is about many Republicans, like Mrs. Walter Kirk, herself, although a professed Democrat, an utter innocence of true issues. They really do not under-stand the conversations going on in the world. Their faces and their minds are blank, or stumped and bewildered over such observations as Wallace made. They simply have no faculties for taking it all into their busy money-making, bridge-playing lives, into which the intrusion of a national convention every four years is sort of a necessary nuisance, tolerated but not wholly comprehended.

I walked around to [the] Ambassador East to a second cocktail party given by Eli Brown, from Louisville, Kentucky, and there joined forces with the *Louisville Courier* crowd: Mrs. [Robert W.] Bingham [Aileen M. Bingham], a principal owner; Mark Ethridge and Mrs. Ethridge [Willie Snow Ethridge], the editor in the absence of Herbert Agar, who is now in London, and the other editors and editorial writers whose names have escaped me at the moment. Here was the royal family of the American liberal press, without prejudice to the newly arrived *Chicago Sun*, founded by Marshall Field, and to the *St. Louis Post-Dispatch*, carrying on the Pulitzer tradition.[11] They were a keen lot. Even the owner, Mrs.

---

10. Probably a reference to the 8-to-1 Supreme Court decision, 3 April 1944, in *Smith v. Allwright*, 321 U.S. 649 (1944). Justice Stanley F. Reed gave the majority opinion overturning a 1923 Texas law which denied blacks the right to vote in Democratic primary elections. See Lewis Wood, "High Court Rules Negroes Can Vote in Texas Primary," *New York Times*, 4 April 1944.

11. The Pulitzer family tradition of liberal, hard-hitting journalism was established by Joseph Pulitzer (1847–1911), the Hungarian-born reporter, editor, and publisher who transformed the *St. Louis Post-Dispatch* and the *New York World* into respected newspa-pers. His sons, Ralph (1879–1939), who was publisher of the *New York World*, 1911–39, and Joseph (1885–1955), who was publisher of the *St. Louis Post-Dispatch*, 1912–55, carried on the tradition.

Bingham, carried on an extended conversation about the disposal of surplus properties, eager for first-hand knowledge of the situation. Mark Ethridge had already dispatched a crack reporter to see me after the convention to get perspectives on this problem.

We were, however, mostly absorbed in the convention and in the discussion of Wallace's speech, which had so clearly laid down the challenge as to whether we were or were not in favor of liberal government in the United States. . . . As we piled into cars and drove out to the convention, after such excellent courses of *hors d'oeuvres* that nobody needed supper—indeed, the *hors d'oeuvres* were for just that purpose as Eli said, because there was no time for dinner—nobody realized what lay ahead of us for the evening. The Wallace speech had touched off deep forces at work in the convention: It had congealed and precipitated them.

The President's acceptance speech boomed over the radio through the stadium with a trifle too much emphasis, I thought, on the fact that he was on duty at an American military base—not politicking at all, but hard at work on his duties as Commander-in-Chief, as it were! Considering his complete absorption in the convention, as we who were officially acquainted with him knew, the military role was a little over-dramatized— but that is all in the great game of politics. It was, however, a fine speech and the crowd roared its applause in enthusiasm such as had never visited the stadium when the Republicans were here, even when a new man and not an old man was nominated.

It was not many minutes after the acceptance speech had concluded, however, that the real pandemonium of the evening broke out, for the mind of the convention proceeded at once to the point at issue: Was it to be Wallace? The fourth term for the President was a foregone conclusion and, therefore, it was disposed of with appropriate applause and enthusiasm as rapidly as possible.

I neglected to say that the first Wallace demonstration occurred when he came into the hall to take his seat as chairman of the Iowa delegation, before the President's acceptance speech, but that was as nothing compared to what occurred after the President's speech. The chant, "We want Wallace! We want Wallace!" broke out all over the hall, on the floor first, and then spread to the galleries. No one had ever seen such a crowd for, apparently, Boss Kelly had permitted seats to be sold on the curb outside of the stadium at $2.00 or $3.00 a head, and the police, by his instructions, had let these pass bearers in without reference to whether they had reservations or not. The aisles were jammed and packed. . . .

I cannot begin to relate how moving this incident was. It was so overwhelmingly clear that Wallace would be nominated. There was nothing synthetic or simulated about his demonstration. It was the real

thing. It was a vote of confidence from the hearts of the people. . . .
None could say that the demonstration was superficial or merely a matter
of combustion in the galleries of the convention; it was combustion
throughout the country supported by fact, for the completed Gallup Poll
had been made public at Princeton, New Jersey, on Wednesday,
showing 65 per cent of the people of the United States were in favor of
Wallace's renomination and, even in the South—a territory where
people were supposed to be hostile to Wallace—support was about 57
per cent.[12]

You can little understand how I felt as an insignificant member of
the crusade of men of good will in the United States: A soldier in the
ranks of those who, like Wallace, believe that the power of government
should be dedicated to the benefit of the common man. As I had stood on
a chair early in the evening in the back of the hall in the space left for
alternates, . . . there was a considerable period when I could not speak,
so overcome was I with emotion at this spectacle and its immense
reassurance of good will and good faith. It was hard to keep the tears
back, and many failed to do so. To see a man so politically inept, without
party machine support, be acclaimed and accepted with such spontaneous and irresistible enthusiasm, was undoubtedly one of the great
events in American political history. Of course, Wallace did have the
support of the Political Action Committee of the CIO,[13] who
undoubtedly had many friends in the galleries, but the party machine
was against him. . . .

It was in vain to try to restore order. It simply could not be done. I
learned later what I could not see from my position, that Senator Pepper
from Florida was on his way to the speakers' platform to move the
nomination of Vice President Wallace by [acclamation], but Hannegan
beat him to the draw and got to the chairman [Senator Samuel D. Jackson
of Indiana] first. He instructed the chairman to adjourn the meeting until
the next day. Through the bedlam and over the partially subdued roar of
the convention, Jackson bellowed through the microphone and loud-
speaker that the meeting was adjourned until the next day. The thump of
the gavel settled it.

On the invitation of the Mark Ethridges, I rode back with them to the
Ambassador East gathering. . . . We were all hoarse with shouting and
tired, too, but not too tired to rejoice over bourbon highballs (the
Kentuckians seldom drink anything else) at the triumph of sheer virtue in

12. "Gallup on Wallace," *P.M.*, 20 July 1944.
13. The CIO established its Political Action Committee (PAC) in 1943 to counter the
rising tide of conservatism in Congress. The PAC was a device to raise campaign funds and
mobilize labor support for the Democratic Party. Sidney Hillman was chairman of the PAC,
1943–46.

Henry A. Wallace over machine politics. I do not drink, except on very special occasions, but this was such an occasion.

I learned that, late that afternoon, Hannegan had taken a terrible beating before the press conference, for they had forced out of him the letter frequently referred to from President Roosevelt which read as follows:

The White House
19 July 1944

Dear Bob:

You have written me about Harry Truman and Bill Douglas. I should, of course, be very glad to run with either of them and believe that either one of them would bring real strength to the ticket.

Always sincerely,
Franklin D. Roosevelt [signed]

The press cross-examined Hannegan over the first line. What had he advised the President? It was on the basis of this advice that the President had replied. [Had] he told him that Wallace had no chance whatever; that he would be a vote loser? Why had he orally mentioned only one name— Truman's—and not revealed that Douglas was also mentioned? How could the letter be reconciled with the President's first letter that he would vote for Wallace if he were a delegate to the convention? . . .

Katherine had not called, when I returned to the Club, regarding Anna. Was there "no comment," or had Anna gone west with the President? No matter! Machine politics and false rumors had all been steam-rollered that night. To all of us, victory was ours without any question.

The Third Day: Friday, 21 July, 1944

I encountered Ernest Lindley again in the Stevens Hotel when I was on the way to Josephus Daniels' room at 9:00 Friday morning. The letter from the President to Bob Hannegan, which had been forced out into public view at 8:00 P.M. the preceding evening, was ricocheting around the press and the convention. While delegates were still confused in trying to interpret the President's first letter, along with his second letter, newspapermen and radio commentators had helped them by tearing the Hannegan machinations to ribbons. The Wallace demonstration the preceding evening had steam-rollered the whole matter and left no doubt about Wallace's nomination, and so I said to Ernie:

"I presume you have changed your views now, Ernie."

In his slow and deliberate way, Lindley replied, "Not at all. The situation is unchanged. Truman will be nominated."

I thought, at first, that this man was exceedingly stubborn and would only have a few short hours to wait until he was deprived of his pride of opinion. But Lindley is always a cautious reporter and so I said:

"You are usually a very careful person and have facts on which to predicate your opinions. Would you mind telling me what they are now?"

"Four men talked to the President on long distance telephone. The gist of the instructions from the President, yesterday afternoon, in that conversation, was that Hannegan should get the lead out of his pants and get that man Truman nominated."

I confess that this was baffling because Lindley is a very truthful fellow.

"You know that beyond all doubt, do you?" I asked.

"Beyond all doubt," he replied. "I know one of the men in on the conversation and I know what was said."

"Do you realize that this is equivalent to charging the President with duplicity?" I asked.

"I do," Ernie replied.

"How do you account for it?" I asked.

"These men have been advising the President for a long time that Wallace would be a liability in the campaign. As Ed Flynn said, 'I am not here to elect two Presidents. I am interested in electing one President. I am a one-man dog.' "

"With the Gallup Poll showing 65 per cent support for Wallace and the demonstration in the convention last night, it is nonsense to say that he would be a vote loser. [There] must be some other reason," I observed. We stood there for a moment, thinking.

"Is the President, by any chance, jealous of Wallace's rising liberal leadership when he himself has been the great liberal President of this generation?" I asked.

Ernie indicated, quite cautiously, that that was clearly a possibility, for Truman, fine man that he is, is of ordinary stature. While very able, he is not one of the great, like Wallace.

I walked on to Daniels' room and sat down with grand old man of North Carolina. "The President should not have written the letter," he said when I referred to it, meaning the second letter mentioning Truman and Douglas.

"How could he do it in the face of the first letter? Has he really advised Hannegan to put Truman in in spite of his first letter saying that would vote for Wallace if he were a delegate?" I asked, knowing that Daniels knew the President, intimately, and his opinion would be a good test of Lindley's.

Perhaps this explanation took the sting out of Lindley's account; for a moment I was convinced that Daniels knew best. He interpreted the second letter merely as a passive statement that either Truman or

Douglas would be acceptable to the President, and he pointed out that the President had been subjected to continuous pressure by Hannegan and Flynn, who had undoubtedly told him repeatedly that they could not put Wallace over. Such an interpretation relieved the President of any implications of duplicity for he would then seem to be justified in indicating second choices. We passed on to the Wallace situation.

I explained that I was there under my own power, but had advised the Vice President that I was coming, as a sort of self-appointed, unofficial ambassador, to determine what, if anything, Mr. Daniels might be able to do when the candidacy of North Carolina's Governor [Joseph M.] Broughton for the vice presidency failed, as it surely would. Could he and would he lead his delegation to the support of Wallace?

Mr. Daniels explained that his position was very delicate; that he had been accused by one paper in North Carolina of not being sincerely for Broughton; and that he would swing the delegation to Wallace. He explained that he was for Broughton, who was splendid vice presidential timber, but that he recognized, as a political fact, that Broughton could not be nominated. He explained, further, that there were conservative members of his delegation, particularly two lawyers, who were strongly opposed to Wallace because of his liberalism. . . . "Lawyers get like that," he said. . . .

"I cannot promise what I can or will do for Mr. Wallace with such a delegation," Mr. Daniels said. "But I am devoted to him." "And," he added with a twinkle in his eye, "I am even more devoted to Mrs. Wallace and would cast a vote for her any time."

He explained that he and Mrs. Daniels and Mr. and Mrs. Wallace had become dear friends in Mexico when the Wallaces were there in December of 1940.

His meaning was perfectly clear, without making a promise which would be in violation of his commitment to the delegation and to Broughton. It seems that Charlie Marsh had had the same thought I had in respect to Daniels for, at that moment, another messenger knocked on the door—one Mitchell from North Carolina—who had come from Marsh to see if he could get the commitment of Josephus Daniels. It was slightly embarrassing, but Daniels, as an old veteran and a dear friend of Wallace, would disregard such incidents. When Mitchell had explained his errand, I told him that we were both there on the same errand and we all three had a laugh about it; although, as I told the Vice President later, it looked for a moment as if messengers from Wallace's headquarters were forming a line outside of the door.

Mitchell asked if Daniels would talk to Wallace—an unfortunate request in view of the delicacy of his relations with the delegation from North Carolina—but Daniels agreed to do so and the conversation took place right then. Daniels explained to Wallace that he had discussed the situation thoroughly with me and had asked me to come and see him after the first ballot and to keep in touch with him. He could clearly have a majority of the 30 delegates from North Carolina and, probably, would not lose more than 6 of the 30. I was appointed messenger between Daniels and Wallace, the matter to be kept very confidential. It sounded very encouraging.

At the end, I said I could now deliver a message for Mr. Wallace: "Tell Josephus Daniels that I love him." I also added that Mr. Wallace had said he considered Mr. Daniels the greatest living liberal of his generation.

Mr. Daniels assured me of his devotion to Wallace and we parted. On the high levels of politics, men do talk in terms of loving each other. . . .

I carried the message back, immediately, to Mr. Wallace at his headquarters, passing through those who waited in the corridor outside and being admitted immediately to the room where Wallace sat in a big easy chair. He drew me down in the chair beside him, taking my hand in both of his and saying:

"You have done a fine job with Mr. Daniels; he has just talked to me on the telephone and told me that he had asked you to keep in touch with him. I understand his situation perfectly. He is for us."

I added what I had learned the preceding evening from Eli Brown, an intimate friend of Senator Barkley, that Barkley would hold out on his own nomination for the vice presidency "until the third ballot," after which he would lead the Kentucky delegation of 24 votes to Wallace. With Georgia's 26 votes, and Florida's 18, probably settling on Wallace under Senator Pepper's leadership, and Barkley adding his 24, and Daniels bringing in a majority of probably 24, which he would undoubtedly lead of the North Carolina delegation, even if the conservative lawyers held out, and with the bloc of New Deal delegates probably going to Wallace, and other isolated gains in the South, Wallace would undoubtedly go over. There would be enough support in the North and West. Spirits were high at headquarters, and confidence was firm. Everyone counted on between 400 and 500 votes on the first ballot; but with split delegations, nobody could be sure.

Hostile papers battled it out in Chicago, giving their confusing impressions to the delegates. The *Chicago Tribune* dared to explain away the preceding evening by the presence of a Wallace "machine" which packed the hall. As a part of that "machine," I had a laugh out of that one. I had battled to get Wallace any tickets at all. As Vice President of the United States, he at least should have had a respectful block of tickets for that convention, but he had 219, plus 70 individual tickets for the first night only, or 289 seats divided between two sessions for the first day. . . .

That was hardly a "packed hall" when each of the bosses—Flynn, Hannegan, Farley, Kelly, Hague—had blocks of tickets running into thousands. Undoubtedly, some of these did reach labor organizations through their organized connections with party officials and among them were unquestionably CIO members—as these would be for Wallace— along with a number of AFL members. The Political Action Committee of the CIO represented solid Wallace support, but these were not on the floor except for isolated members of delegations. They were in the galleries. The Wallace demonstration of the preceding night occurred on the floor as a spontaneous wave, and the enthusiasm spread quickly to the crowds in the galleries.

I had not heard from Katherine, so there would be no word from the White House to anyone that the President had meant what he said in his first letter to Chairman Jackson: "I would personally vote for his [i.e., Wallace's] renomination if I were a delegate to the convention." I will straighten out the mystery about the two letters later.

In addition to the excitement of the preceding evening, the convention was electrified by the news of an attempt on Hitler's life,[14] just as it already had been by the news of the fall of the Japanese cabinet. Today, the papers were full of it—a purge was on. Here was surely the end of Germany. So starkly did the facts stare us in the face as a certainty, it then seemed that political observers soon passed on from the first enthusiasm at the impending fall of the enemy to the political implications of the fact.

If the war was over before November, Roosevelt would not be elected. With his job on the war front completed and the "don't-change-horses-in-the-middle-of-the-stream" argument gone, and the impending peace probably insufficient to continue the argument into a fourth term, a change would be imminent. On the world front, would we repeat the Harding incident?

The afternoon droned on with nominating speeches, all on the same pattern, describing the great virtues of the man that was needed and ending up with the nominee's name. The virtues described were usually about the same, but the name at the end of the speech was different.

Again, the Wallace demonstration broke loose when he was nominated by Judge [Richard F.] Mitchell of Iowa, at 1:37 P.M. and, after many minutes of uncontrolled demonstration, Chairman Jackson persuaded the crowd to come to order so that the work of the day could go forward. The high point was Claude Pepper's seconding address for Wallace—a powerful statement delivered from the floor at the microphone at his delegation—a gem for brevity, clarity, and force.

---

14. The attempt on Hitler's life occurred 20 July 1944 and was made by a group of disaffected German army officers who placed a bomb in his military headquarters. Hitler was bruised and shaken by the explosion but otherwise unhurt. In succeeding days and weeks he reestablished his control.

When Truman's name was first mentioned through the awkwardness of alphabetical arrangement, when one delegation was called upon and passed in order to yield its opportunity for nominating Truman to a Missourian, there was only a mild ripple of applause—surprising indeed—considering the arrangements that were supposed to have been made for Truman. The Truman crowd improved later, when Senator [Joel Bennett] Clark, from Missouri, nominated him. More signs had been purchased, and the Truman crowds were better organized. They put on a very good show, but nothing like the Wallace demonstration.

The favorite sons' nominations droned on. Besides Wallace and Truman, there were Senator Barkley, from Kentucky; Governor Broughton, from North Carolina; Senator Byrd, from Virginia—the "Stop Roosevelt" candidate—Senator Lucas, of Illinois; Justice Murphy, from Michigan; Justice Douglas; Senator O'Mahoney, of Wyoming; Governor [Robert S.] Kerr, from Oklahoma; [Prentice] Cooper; and McNutt from Indiana. What a contrast from 1940 for McNutt, when the whole stadium rocked with his support and only by sheer force of will and McNutt's capitulation to that will, did President Roosevelt rescue the nomination for Wallace. Since then, the President's disposal of Paul McNutt has been one of the most skillful and adroit events in American politics. Roosevelt owed him a position in the cabinet after that magnificent act of self-effacement at the convention of 1940, but he finally got around to making him chairman of the [War] Manpower [Commission][15]—one of the toughest, dirtiest jobs of the war effort, from which no man could survive with popularity. McNutt didn't. The handsome, blonde, man on horseback—the "platinum-haired son-of-a-bitch," as Ickes called him in the midst of the feud—had reached his peak in 1940 and was completely played out at this convention.

About seventeen nominations in all were made and then the balloting slowly proceeded, with resounding cheers every time Wallace got a vote, and cheers for Truman's score. Wallace took 429 1/2 votes and Truman took 319 1/2, the rest being scattered around among the favorite sons. Therein lay the fate of the convention. Where would those votes settle on the second or third ballot? . . .

I passed Farley in the aisles that afternoon. "Hello, Norman," he said, as we shook hands. We had not seen each other for about two years, as nearly as I could remember. He called my name just as he calls thousands of others' names from one end of the country to the other.

---

15. The War Manpower Commission (WMC) was established by President Roosevelt by Executive Order No. 9139, 18 April 1942, to plan and supervise the recruitment, training, and distribution of civilian workers in the face of a growing shortage of labor due to the draft. He appointed Paul V. McNutt as chairman. It was a limited success, owing to its inability to enforce its decisions when opposed by organized labor. In 1945, it was incorporated into the Labor Department.

We passed on, bent upon our opposite ends, but what a contrast! Farley pushed through the throng like a General Grant tank through a cornfield. Just seeing Farley gave me a sense of amateurishness on our side. The Wallace workers were mostly composed of men like myself, working as a matter of principle, but the opposition were professionals, who handled the delegates with the familiar touch of the master. These post-graduates of innumerable conventions—Hannegan, Flynn, Farley, Kelly, and Hague—really controlled the political machinery. It was they who had, daily, weekly, or monthly contacts with the delegations, the National Committeemen and women, the state chairmen. Farley's thousands of letters signed in the famous green ink bore fruit, even though a certain number of them were so gratuitous as to be received with amusement. . . .

The convention droned on into the second ballot. A disturbing incident in the early letters of the alphabet bears mention. "California" had "passed." This big Western block of votes—52 in number—is one of the most significant psychologically in the convention. On the first ballot, it had gone 30 for Wallace and 22 for Truman, representing a split between the liberals and the conservatives. Our meeting of the Western states had consolidated the delegation somewhat, and the preceding evening had given courage, but the work of Pauley and Hannegan could not be ignored and the chairman, Bob Kenny, attorney general of California, had manipulated matters so that California passed, avoiding the psychological effect of admitting again that the 30 Wallace votes held absolutely firm, while other states were to split or cave in under the pounding from the big guns of politics.

The balloting progressed: Again 18 votes from Connecticut for Wallace, 9 from Florida, 26 from Georgia—the most spectacular break in the "solid South"—for, having thrown out the fascist-minded Governor [Eugene] Talmadge, that state had had an impulse of reform, toward liberalism.

Idaho, 5 for Wallace and 5 for Truman; Indiana, 2 for Wallace and 24 for Truman; Kansas, 16 for Wallace; Massachusetts, 11 1/2 for Wallace and 14 1/2 for Truman; Michigan, 35 for Wallace, 2 for Truman, with 2 for Murphy; Minnesota, 24 for Wallace; Mississippi, all 20 for Truman; and Missouri, 32 for Truman. The biggest shift to be announced first on the second ballot was New York, which had been 30 1/2 out of 96 for Wallace on the first ballot, but shifted to 93 for Truman on the second ballot. Farley had won.

The details are tiresome. [It] will suffice to say that, while Guffey held Pennsylvania's 46 out of 72 for Wallace, other states were slipping and the "favorite sons'" shifting vote in the South was moving towards Truman and not towards Wallace.

In the cool light of afterthought, how could it be otherwise? I could see Hannegan at the front edge of the platform motioning excitedly to this delegation and then to that. For all the world, he was like an organ player pulling great stops on a giant organ. First to the left, then to the right and then in the center, as one delegation after another, through its speaker, rose to the microphone standing by the aisle and announced its vote. Hannegan knew what the score would be. It was arranged.

I had climbed back up into the boxes opposite the speakers' platform in the center of the hall to sit with Mrs. Mark Ethridge, while Mark wandered away on the other side of the hall to get the low-down in the press gallery. He had come back once, early in the voting, when my personal hopes were still firm. "It's Truman," he said briefly, "the press boys have the score."

Truman sat with his wife and daughter[16] immediately in front of us in the first tier of boxes next to the floor-level of the hall. They even had to stand boos and hisses in the early stages of the voting when Truman's name came out, but later the votes were like bullets in mowing down the Wallace opposition. Slowly, the tide turned with the unerring instincts of moths flying toward the light. Cameramen gathered in the aisle, immediately in front of Truman's box, and began to flash pictures. There was American life in clear silhouette. It is success that counts.

I had done my best to get Josephus Daniels after the first ballot, but it was quite impossible. Although I drew near to the North Carolina delegation, at the end of the first ballot, he was not there. Doubtless, he was out in conference with other leaders. I waited a long time, but felt exceedingly amateurish. After all, Daniels was an old veteran. He could see what was happening at the convention. Communication between him and Wallace was a trivial matter. It depended on Daniels to make up his mind as to what was politically possible within his own delegation. They stood fast and voted 30 votes for the favorite son, Broughton. Kentucky did likewise—24 votes for Barkley. A shift of those two delegations would have changed the history of the convention. . . .

Why did not Barkley or Daniels perform and make a break in the solid line of the South against Wallace? Here, again, we come to technique. Wallace had said in his speech the day before: "The poll tax must go." Had I seen the speech first, I would have insisted, if I could, upon his striking that expression. (Just as I had struck out of his Madison Square Garden speech, about a year ago, on commemoration of the Soviet Republic, the phrase, "The People's Revolution Marches On.") There was no need for it. Everyone knows how Wallace feels about the poll tax. Everyone knows about how all liberals feel about the poll tax. Daniels himself had put it very neatly: "People might as well stop talking about it—it [has] to go."

However, to the average voter's mind, the conquest of the poll tax was far from complete in the South. To say, there, "The poll tax must go," was

---

16. Elizabeth Wallace (Bess) and Margaret Truman.

like a slap in the face. There is no need to slap faces. Achievements can sometimes be accomplished tactfully. The delegates, and particularly heads of delegations from the South, had to go home from one day in Chicago and live the rest of the 365 days in their hometowns. How could they live there with comfort, having reported their vote for a man who had needlessly slapped them in the face?

Even Daniels and Barkley, whose states had no poll tax, were hesitant to leave the ranks of their Southern brethren. "Why didn't Daniels swing whatever part of his delegation he could?" I asked Harold Young later in the lobby of the hotel."

"He said he couldn't!" Young replied. "Wanted to, but couldn't!"

Slowly, I stopped keeping the score. The man pulling the organ stops on the platform, who had been perspiring furiously, and whom we had given the scare of his life—we amateurs—leaned back to enjoy his handiwork. One by one, the Southern states were coming in for Truman. The tide had turned—turned so convincingly that, finally, a stage was reached where states began to change their votes in order to make the nomination unanimous.

The winning roll call for Truman stood at only 477 1/2 for Truman and 474 for Wallace, with a dozen states passing and yet to be heard from. Then Maine had started the stampede, with its little 10 votes, which had first been split up. It was clear that leaders were simply waiting for a strategic time to pull the props from under the Wallace support and a little block of 10 votes kicked the first prop. . . .

I waited through the welter of voting to the bitter end after Truman had been rescued from his seat by policemen and hustled off to the speakers' platform. Finally, he made an acceptance address, which I waited to hear, to take the measure of the man in such a position. He appreciated the honor; he recognized the responsibility; he would do his best, etc.

He might have been accepting the nomination for presidency of the Kiwanis Club or Chamber of Commerce. It was an unresonant, unmoved voice. It was the voice of a good, plain, solid American citizen. Here, indeed, we had come down from the mountain tops of greatness to the level of the average citizen from a small town in the United States. Was that what the American people wanted? Anyway, it was what they got.

As a headline in the *Chicago Daily News* said: "Men in the Know Helped Put Truman Over"—"Supporters Too Clever for Amateurs Who Aided Wallace." There was the case in a nutshell. As my mind touched bottom in this depression over my country's errors, and I was deluged with thoughts of the grave implications in such a choice should the President die and this man become President of the United States, I struggled vainly for a while to reorient my viewpoint. Then, at last, it came. This man was forthright and fearless, as I knew from his work on the Truman Committee. He was honest. He was far better than the average, run-of-the-mill Vice

President of the United States. The country probably would not be greatly hurt by his nomination. When I thought of what kind of man the bosses could have picked out, I felt relief and reconciliation to the fact.

I got away and caught a bus for town. Force of gravity took me up to Wallace's headquarters in the Shoreham [Hotel]. Passing through a gloomy crowd of about 15 people in the corridor into Wallace's room, [I found him] smiling cheerily and dictating a message for the press:

> I am very happy about it. My own defeat is not a loss to the cause of liberalism—that is obvious in what happened here in the convention.

Then followed a congratulatory message to Truman:

> Congratulations upon your enlarged opportunity to help the President and the people. Both of us will do our maximum for Roosevelt and for what Roosevelt stands.

> Sincerely,
> Henry A. Wallace [signed]

The Vice President laughed up at me as I shook hands with him. Unlike myself, he was not a bit choked up. "It was a fine fight, Norman," he said, "and everything is all right." I remembered our conversation at dinner at the Athletic Club.

"They have defeated a Vice President and elected a President," I said.

Someone read a telegram, from a friend of Wallace's at Chicago University, in which one line emerged: "You are free now." As Burke, from Los Angeles, later said to me, and to the Vice President, "Take no appointments. Remain free. Move about the country and make speeches from time to time so that the people will remember you. That is all you have to do and you will be nominated for President in 1948."

"Order something to eat sent up," Wallace said in answer to his secretary who asked whether he did not want food. "Keep Norman here."

"Scrambled eggs and bacon and some fruit?" asked his secretary.

"That will be fine." Mr. Wallace replied.

"The same," I said.

His secretary started counting heads. "Include three more," Charlie Marsh broke in, motioning to three of his faithful workers who had just come into the room. So supper was ordered for eight and we sat down to it about 10:00. Joe McLeod, city editor of the *Washington Post*, looked very washed up, and I said so in a feeble effort to be funny.

He leaned over to me and confessed that he had cried like a baby—"for the first time in years. I didn't know I could do it."

Wallace was undoubtedly the most cheerful person in the room. Verda Barnes, whom I used to know as an able, vigorous young Democrat from Idaho [and who is] now head of the Women's Division of the CIO, was also very tremulous in her voice. It was a shocking leap from sure success to definite defeat—enough to shake the emotions of strong men—and it did shake them. Quite obviously, many were shaken; all but Wallace. He was the most cheerful of all: Just as sure and firm on his plan of accepting postponement of the issue until 1948 or 1952 as he had been at dinner at the Athletic Club on Wednesday night. "I am entirely happy about the outcome," he had said and I recalled those words clearly. He definitely was happy about the outcome. There was no doubt about it.

I sat at one side of the Vice President at the table set in a bedroom adjacent to the parlor and, at this late date, dictated many days after the convention has concluded (and after my return to Washington, for I did not succeed in completing the dictation in Chicago) I cannot recall all that we talked about. I was too tired and there were many interruptions, such as that of Congressman [Howard J.] McMurray from Wisconsin, who had burst in to shake hands with the Vice President.

"I would fight the same fight again, tomorrow," [McMurray] said cheerily, as they shook hands. "It was a great fight."

That was a brave statement for the defeat of Wallace may well defeat him in Wisconsin.

There were others who filed through, but we had a fairly peaceful dinner, notwithstanding. Shortly afterwards, since there was nothing else to say, I shook hands and said good night.

Well, my dear, that is the end of the story of the convention. I remained in Chicago until the afternoon train, Sunday, attending to some business which I had there and visiting with Sheldon Sackett, editor of the *Coos Bay Times* in Oregon and owner of two radio stations, and also J. Frank Burke, from Pasadena, the two of whom I had brought together and who, as two of similar liberal views, with radio outlets on the Pacific Coast, had much in common. They became fast friends. One common objective came to be to get me back to the Pacific Coast. In a long session with Mr. Burke, he told me he found nobody like your mother and me, that he very much wanted us both back on the Coast and in California, where my type of leadership was needed. There was enough private practice and enough legal fees among my friends to assure a considerably greater income than I was earning here. It was guaranteed. Sheldon Sackett reinforced that statement.

It was tempting, indeed, as I felt at that moment very sick, indeed, of Washington intrigue. My loyalty to the President could scarcely accept the latest decision, although it may have been sound politics—to remain in power at any cost and not invite the attack from the right, which would have accrued had Wallace been nominated, because of his support from CIO, which is openly charged with being "communist-dominated."

I forgot to say that I had seen Sidney Hillman's daughter [Philoine Hillman] while waiting for the Vice President to come out of his room at the hotel, and had innocently cross-examined her as to whether Hillman had ever indicated he would also work for Truman if he were nominated, such an announcement having been immediately made after Truman's nomination. She emphatically denied that there had been the slightest encouragement to Truman. Hillman had stuck by Wallace throughout. Hillman affirmed that when he came out of Wallace's room as one of the succession of visitors who passed through there before dinner.

"We have made history," he said. "We cracked the Pennsylvania delegation, the New York delegation and"—he named several others.

Whatever be the rationalization for the President's action, the record is greatly confused. Anna Boettiger was very much concerned when she talked with your mother. She obviously knew nothing about the [second] Hannegan letter. (Both she and her mother were for Wallace.)

When your mother told her of Hannegan's claiming to have a letter from the President endorsing Truman, Anna said, "Katherine, I know he has been in touch with Father, and he is probably the only one from the convention who has been. As you know, Father is not here; he is on the West Coast. I think it would be a good idea for Claude Pepper to attack him on the floor and make him produce the letter, if he has one. The chances are, though, that he has one."

She evidently was taken by surprise, yet your mother sensed that Anna realized that her father had pulled another "fast" one. The President evidently had taken both Mrs. Roosevelt and Anna for a ride on the Wallace letter—along with many other liberals. . . .

I prophesy that [at the next convention there] will be a vicious battle, for the alliance with Russia will be concluded; that is, the war will be over and the partnership with Russia—which many elements of American society now consider to be strained and in the nature of "walking across the bridge with the devil until you get on the other side"—will no longer have its present strong reasons for existence. The attack will open on Russia. The communists will be out in the open. The "liberals" will be hated by the communists for not going far enough to the left and, at the same time, will be attacked from the right for being communists. That will be the period of greatest challenge to American leadership.

Au revoir, my dear. This is the longest letter I have ever written, to any one at any time, but a crossroad of this character is, perhaps, worthy of a few notes.

Affectionately,
Daddy

Tuesday night, 22 August 1944
4101 Lorcom Lane

Yesterday morning I went to the first meeting of the new advisory committee on the disposal of real estate in the RFC Building. The atmosphere was so tense that it would have vibrated had a door slammed. The general counsel, Bob Hayes, introduced me to the crowd in the room after Colonel O'Brien, chairman and deputy administrator under Clayton, had shaken my hand as warmly as he could.

I could tell from greetings how people felt—most of the feelings were very warm and cordial. I did not speak to Colonel O'Brien, nor he to me. The parting of the ways had arrived. It was inevitable. . . .

The afternoon passed in catching up with a mass of accumulated routine work and drafting a memorandum to Acting Attorney General Fahy [in reply] to his reprimand of Friday the 18th for testifying before the Truman Committee.[1] Another bomb was about to break: The report of that committee on the acquisition of the Breakers Hotel at Palm Beach, Florida. The general counsel called me to ask me to proofread it. I went up in the late afternoon to do so, to Halley's office. It was a blistering report being prepared for publication the next day. Senator Ferguson had insisted on putting in a line about Biddle not cooperating with the committee and the committee's having had to subpoena my report from him. The conclusion reached was that the hotel should be acquired outright: A complete vindication of my report on a much broader basis of evidence because the committee's investigational powers had reached new sources of information.

There were numerous efforts to reach me from Mr. Fahy's office, and rather suspicious inquiries from his secretary as to whether or not I was "on the Hill." I did not bother to answer, although a complete answer was available, in that a representative of the War Department, as well as myself, had been invited to take the committee's report and criticize it.

I found Mr. Fahy in consultation with Assistant Solicitor General [Hugh B.] Cox, trying to reply to a letter of Will Clayton's demanding to know whether my testimony represented the position of the Department or simply my own views as a private citizen, quoting headlines in *P.M.*, and the *Washington Post* with great indignation.[2]

They had obviously been in touch with Biddle in San Francisco by long-distance. I can imagine the blistering comment which passed from the other end, and took a certain amount of pleasure in "reversing the English" on Brother Biddle. He had given me so many uncomfortable times when I had been away from Washington in the West, for one cause or another, and now it was my turn.

---

1. Littell testified before the Truman Committee on the Surplus War Property Bill (S. 2065), 17 August 1944. See *Congressional Record*, vol. 91 (25 January 1945), pp. A295–A297; see also Charles E. Egan, "Proposes Business Aid Surplus Sales; House Tentatively Votes to Have Administrator Name Industry Advisory Committee," *New York Times*, 18 August 1944. For Littell's memo to Fahy, see below, p. 289.

2. Nathan Robertson, "Roosevelt Urged to Fire Clayton as Front Man for Big Business; Patton Calls Him Hostile to Labor, Small Business and Farmers," *P.M.*, 20 August 1944.

He wished to have a line inserted, in the rough draft of the reply to Clayton, that if he had been here in Washington, and had I consulted with him in regard to the facts presented at the hearing, he would have consulted with Clayton, first. Another line would have represented that the views were my "personal views only."

Cox, who has iron in his soul, boldly objected to the last line and struck it out, saying, "I am sure the attorney general will not mind," in a tone which seemed to say, "I do not give a damn whether he does or not—the statement should come out."

I laughed and agreed, saying that I had rather expected a repudiation, but that I, of course, agreed with Mr. Cox in that it was a shame for the Department of Justice to dissociate itself from the testimony of the assistant attorney general in charge of the Lands Division, which was having such wide usefulness and effecting real public service. This was exactly the kind of service the Department of Justice ought to render, and it was a pity to back away from it. The line came out, but the first suggestion stayed in about his preference for consulting with Clayton, first. . . .

The letter which was finally agreed upon by Mr. Fahy and Mr. Cox was altogether acceptable to me, although weak, because it said that the testimony would stand "on its merits," which was just short of saying it represented my personal views.

This morning, Cox telephoned early in the day to say that Fahy had tried to get that line back in the letter again, which is exactly what I would expect of him. Cox had taken it out. . . .

I completed a blistering memorandum to Fahy. The time had arrived to be perfectly clear about my position in the Department. With a swelling tide of approval for my attack on Clayton all around the government, he and the attorney general will have a "hell of a time" expressing their displeasure or disciplining me. There is no doubt whatever that the attorney general thinks this will be the occasion on which to demand my discharge or resignation. If he does, I shall advise him that I consider it in the public interest to remain, albeit for personal reasons I would like very much to go back to the West. . . .

The Breakers report was released to the press today[3]—another bomb for Charlie Fahy—completely vindicating and confirming my previous stand in regard to the acquisition of that hotel. Katherine learned late this evening that Senator Ferguson, in commenting on the Breakers Hotel report on the Senate floor, had blasted Biddle's participation in the entire

3. "Criticizes Army on Breakers Deal; Senate Committee Reports on Taking of the Hotel and Abandoning as Hospital," *New York Times*, 23 August 1944; "Senate Group Assails Army for Breakers Deal," *P.M.*, 23 August 1944.

matter.[4] . . . I can confess to having helped him with that statement at his request—that is, a statement which he intended to reduce to a paragraph for insertion in the Breakers Hotel report, but the general counsel objected to anything more than one line to the effect that Biddle had been subpoenaed. I had no idea that Ferguson was going onto the floor with it, but he did—with a devastating blast which I will read tomorrow in the *Congressional Record*. That also will tone Biddle down quite a little bit, upon his return, and possibly Charlie Fahy, too. I am glad my memorandum reached Fahy before this blast was made on the floor, and before the Breakers report was made public.

Having opened this case, I must win it. At Halley's request, I prepared a list of questions for the examination of Colonel O'Brien, . . . Katherine and I stayed downtown for dinner, kept my secretary, and hammered out those questions which, if asked, will leave him cut to ribbons.

Department of Justice
Washington

Norman M. Littell
Assistant Attorney General

21 August 1944

MEMORANDUM
for Mr. Charles Fahy, Acting Attorney General

I have given considerable thought to your severe reprimand of Friday morning, the 18th, in regard to my testifying before the Truman Committee (Special Committee to Investigate the National Defense Program) on the 17th, concerning the disposal of surplus real property. It seems to me wholly unjustified, and I wish to say why.

The charge that I "deceived" you is unsupportable and most objectionable to me. I had no contact whatsoever with the Truman Committee up to the time when its counsel telephoned and asked me to appear to discuss disposal of surplus as I had done before the Manasco Committee on Public Buildings and Grounds, the record of which has since been well circulated. I advised that the matter must be taken up with you as acting attorney general. Thereafter, a telephone call from you advised that you had approved my appearing before the committee.

While I had shown to you a memorandum regarding the repurchase

---

4. For Senator Ferguson's statement, see *Congressional Record*, vol. 90 (22 August 1944), p. 7185.

rights of prior owners, intended for the Manasco Committee on Expenditures in Executive Departments, which was then considering H.R. 5135, and for delivery to the Senate Military Affairs Committee, then considering S. 2065, it never for one moment occurred to me that you might be confused as to the different functions of these committees and the "Truman Committee." This latter committee is not a legislative committee but an investigational committee. It was reasonable to assume, and I did assume, that you not only understood this but had ascertained from counsel for the committee the subject matter of the inquiry.

You pointed out that this is the "third time" that a similar incident had occurred when the attorney general was out of town: First, in the Elk Hills–Naval Petroleum Reserve matter; second, in the Breakers Hotel case; and now, in the disposal of surplus; that this "didn't just happen;" and that it has now "happened once too often," as far as you are concerned; and that you "didn't care to consider the merits."

I have no regrets and no apologies whatsoever for any of these incidents. The public interest was served in every case. While I regret any personal embarrassment that you may have suffered, as acting attorney general, I see no real grounds for your having suffered any. The results would have been the same whether the attorney general had been in town or not, in my opinion, for you certainly must realize that I would be subject to a subpoena to testify before the committee and would be in contempt should I refuse to answer, regardless of whose instructions I might be following in that refusal. It was very natural that the congressional committees of investigation in the three matters to which you refer should request the presence of one who would have the most testimonial knowledge of the subject matter. Having lived very close to land acquisition work for over five years, for all agencies (with two exceptions) it was quite natural that the Manasco Committee, first, and the Truman Committee, now, should have called me to testify.

The President's letter and order of July 15, 1943, to which you referred in our conversation, to the various agencies of departments of government, in regard to not airing differences of opinion until they had endeavored to reconcile them, expressly excepted furnishing information to congressional committees. The President's instructions could, under no circumstances, apply in the instant case.

In dealing with a man of the high-handed character of Mr. Clayton, in a matter so profoundly affecting the public welfare throughout the United States, I consider it most fortunate that the Truman Committee happened to explore the recent developments in the disposal of surplus property. Mr. Clayton had overruled not only his own advisory committee, but also the secretary of agriculture, who was rudely cut off by Mr. Clayton with the statement that the matter was closed and the lands had been assigned. Quite apart from this, you must surely realize that the congressional committee had the power to investigate these matters at any stage. Except for yourself and the attorney general, the feeling is quite unanimous throughout the government that the inquiry was most timely and fortunate and that the public interests were well served. Both the secretary of Agriculture and the acting secretary of the Interior have called me to extend congratulations and thanks for the public service rendered in laying the facts before the Truman committee.

All of this demonstrates that it is quite impossible to avoid considering the merits.

I am constrained to submit that the objections made in the past in regard to the above three matters have been on a too highly personalized basis. It is quite enough to expend all of one's energies in the public service without being baited and harassed in my own department of government, upon which the handling of each of the above matters has reflected credit.

Norman M. Littell [signed]
Assistant Attorney General

Wednesday night, 30 August 1944
4101 Lorcom Lane

The fast-moving events of these last few concentrated days are very difficult to recapture. Clayton testified a week ago today, opening his case by relying heavily on the letter sent over by messenger from Charles Fahy, acting attorney general, which read as follows:

22 August 1944

Honorable W. L. Clayton
Administrator, Surplus War Property Administration
811 Vermont Avenue
Washington, D.C.

My dear Mr. Clayton:

In the absence of the attorney general, I acknowledge your letter to him dated August 19, 1944, which asks about Assistant Attorney General Littell's testimony before the National Defense Committee of the Senate on August 17, 1944.

As I stated to you on the telephone on August 18th, neither the attorney general nor I reviewed the text or substance of Mr. Littell's testimony prior to his appearance before the Senate Committee, nor have we made an independent study of the problem since he testified. The soundness of Mr. Littell's views, accordingly, is to be judged upon their merits.

Since receiving your letter I have spoken to the attorney general on the telephone and he has authorized me to say that if Mr. Littell had discussed with him the problems involved before testifying, the attorney general would have taken the matter up with you before making any public statement. He also has asked me to say that he appreciates your reference to the spirit of cooperation and harmony that has hitherto existed between this Department and the Surplus War Property Administration and that he hopes that the spirit will continue.

Sincerely yours,
Charles Fahy [signed]
Acting Attorney General

It was fortunate for the positions of Fahy and the attorney general that Hugh Cox prevailed in deleting the line that I had expressed only my "personal views," because the senators tore into Clayton on that point in a relentless manner, as well they might.[1] It was also very easy for me to put two and two together and see that he [i.e. Clayton] had talked with Biddle over the telephone—which he admitted—and deduce that Biddle had assured him that he, Biddle, would advise the committee through Charlie Fahy's letter that my views were only my "personal views" because Clayton tried to make just that impression, irrespective of the language of the letter.

"What do you mean, 'personal views?'" the senators wanted to know. "Mr. Littell is assistant attorney general in charge of the Lands Division, is he not?"

I was not a citizen picked up off the streets to testify. I testified by reason of my peculiar personal knowledge as assistant attorney general.

I will not repeat the cross-examination of Mr. Clayton on this point, which left him, Mr. Fahy and Mr. Biddle hanging on the ropes.

The testimony speaks for itself and is a matter of public record. Clayton made an exceedingly weak defense and again revealed his utter lack of social outlook. He ridiculed my statement that land should sell to the farmers at less than the prevailing market prices.

"How would Mr. Littell determine which, of innumerable applicants, should be sold to, if we were selling at less than the market price?"

It was all so clear, he said, that there was no man wise enough to anticipate the earnings or the productive capacity of any farm land in the future. And yet, under cross-examination by Mr. Rudolph Halley, he had to admit that even on his own plan he might have to make such a determination for, if land worth $150 an acre was to be settled upon by a farmer and his family, how would this be accomplished if a rich

---

1. "Clayton Defends Land Policy," New York Times, 24 August 1944.

man or a large industrialized farmer being determined to get the land, offered Clayton $200 an acre for it? The small man might even have to have a loan, and the veterans also. Would Clayton take the $200 from the man having capital to pay, and let the small farmer or the veteran go?

His answer was a straddle. If the margin was not too great, he would give the doubt to the farmer. But at what point would the margin be too great for Mr. Clayton to stomach as a businessman with a banker's mind and a determination to get everything he could get from the sale as quickly as possible? He would take the cash, of course.

Even as late as this morning's *Washington Post*, this bit of testimony is the subject of a new attack on Clayton. He doesn't even know that the Department of Agriculture has regularly had to anticipate productive capacity of farm lands on a long-term basis and measure value accordingly, rather than determining value on the basis of boom prices of the passing moment. I sent a message to Senator [Homer B.] Ferguson, who was examining on this point, when Clayton testified, to point out as confirmed by one or two of the Department of Agriculture representatives whom I asked, that the Federal Land Bank,[2] on which Mr. Clayton would rely so heavily to distribute these lands, had systematically anticipated earning capacity which Clayton said could not be done, as a basis for determining loan value of farm property. Also private life insurance companies regularly followed the same practice.

Mr. Clayton is just ignorant. Just as he "did not know there was a Lands Division" in the Department of Justice, there is a lot he does not know about government land business. . . .

. . . In arranging for the placing of these lands through private brokers, which was thoroughly and completely exposed, not only by my testimony but by his answers, as was the penetration of the National Association of Real Estate Boards into his whole pattern, he was impaling a stated policy of establishing small-sized family farm units upon a practice inimical to that policy.

As I testified, a broker is interested in commissions: it was only natural for him to be so. But a man interested primarily in commissions is not interested in resettling the small farmer who does not have the cash— who will have to get a loan and a long-term one at that—to get back on the land. He is not necessarily interested in veterans—who will have little money, indeed—and certainly not tenants, with their preferences for resettlement in the same area. This takes out several classes of purchas-

---

2. The Federal Land Banks made long-term mortgage loans to farmers through local and national farm loan associations. Nationwide there were twelve such banks, one for each district of the Farm Credit Administration (FCA) which administered the program.

ers, in which the government is primarily interested. The broker is interested in the man with the cash, and the more cash the better! . . .[3]

His testimony met with fairly devastating criticism in the press. The legend of the big millionaire businessman cotton-broker directing such matters of such profound future significance to the country had been pricked. The general opinion was that Clayton was a "dead duck."

The [ironic] fact, however, is that the next day, after I had testified, the [House] Military Affairs Committee was meeting to consider its Surplus Property Bill.[4] The bill [was] drafted by Clayton and his associates (and, by irony of circumstance, drafted pursuant to the very theories I had outlined in my memorandum to Bernard Baruch; indeed, the footprints of my memorandum are apparent in the reading of the bill) giving highly flexible powers to the administrator. [It] had been adopted by Congress on the 18th, the day after my testimony.[5] The testimony had not had time to percolate and the momentum behind the Clayton Bill carried it right through the House.

I had appeared before an executive session of the House [Military Affairs] Committee, under the chairmanship of [Carter] Manasco, hoping to correct the clauses respecting repurchase rights of former owners and to insert control of supervision of deeds to purchasers by the attorney general, to prevent utter chaos in this end of the business, and I thought I had won. I was well received there in view of my reputation on the Hill as head of the Lands Division. Both suggestions seemed to be adopted when I was there, but the bill emerged without either of them when it went on to the floor of the House. Clayton's power was very great there, or, I should say, that of Jesse Jones standing behind him. They all wanted the favor of the administrator in the disposal of surplus, with piles of surplus in the backyard of each congressman.

It was quite a different story in the Senate. When I went up at noon on the morning of the 18th to the Military Affairs Committee to leave a memorandum in regard to the repurchase rights [to lands] of former owners, which had been so drafted as to paralyze the disposal of surplus, and to submit a clause authorizing the issuance of warranty deeds in order

---

3. For Littell's testimony, see *New York Times*, 18 August 1944, p. 18.

4. The House Surplus War Properties Bill (H.R. 5125) was passed by the House 22 August 1944. It provided a legislative basis for the Surplus War Property Administration and established a three-man Surplus Property Board to formulate disposal policies and exercise overall control of disposal activities. On 28 August the House disagreed to Senate amendments to the bill and appointed a conference committee, which submitted its report (No. 1890) 18 September. On the same day the House agreed to the conference report by a vote of 170 to 19. President Roosevelt approved the measure (Public Law 457) 3 October 1944. In 1946, President Truman replaced the SWPA with the War Assets Corporation.

5. In fact, the House did not approve the bill until 22 August and the Senate did not approve it until 25 August 1944.

to save the government millions of dollars, I was invited to stay, even though I knew Claude Wickard, [the] secretary of Agriculture (who had called me to express his gratitude for the blasting I had given Clayton in defense of the right of the Department of Agriculture to handle the agricultural lands) had been unable to appear before the committee. . . . I intended only to leave the memorandum, but Senator [Warren R.] Austin asked me to remain and appear before the committee, with which two of the others present concurred, and so I did.

It was obvious that I had a very high standing there. The morning *Post* had a full-page column on the front page, "Littell Blasts Clayton," and it went into detail on [what] I had said the previous day about Clayton.

"I almost cut that out to bring it to the committee hearing," Senator [Lister] Hill said, "but I presume others have seen it."

"I am not here to go into that line of testimony," I said to Senator Hill who sat across the table from me, "but to discuss two other matters of vital importance on this bill."

I shied away from opening up on Clayton again, with the echo of the first attack still booming around, and plastered on the front page of the morning paper. He knew how I stood on the Clayton attack and presumed that my action was unpopular in the administration quarters.

I explained fully the confusion of trying to restore, as a matter of absolute legal right, former properties of former owners. The boundary lines have been obliterated by tank maneuvers and artillery practice. It would be particularly difficult in the areas of the original thirteen states which had never been surveyed; natural monuments and old boundary markers would have been destroyed to a very large degree. The matter should be made discretionary with the administrator. Where it was feasible and in the best interests to restore the old lines, he could do so, and where it was not, he would not have to.

Apparently, from the reception which my remarks had, I had completely convinced them. The other section which I had presumed to draft in advance, authorizing the issuance of warranty deeds with the approval of the attorney general, was adopted *in toto*, after very little argument. I was also advised that the section which I had drafted at the invitation of the committee on repurchase rights of former owners had been adopted, but when the bill came out of the committee onto the floor where it now is, this provision was out and the old provision regarding the repurchase rights was in—and in worse condition than before I first saw it.[6] . . .

6. The Senate Surplus War Property Bill (S. 2065) proposed to establish a Surplus War Property Administration to dispose of surplus properties on a more legal basis than Executive Order No. 9425. After several days of debate, on 25 August the Senate indefinitely postponed S. 2065 and adopted the House version of the bill (H.R. 5125), with

The Truman Committee finished the examination of Clayton on Friday, August 25th, and pretty thoroughly deflated him, but he had skirted gingerly around the National Association of Real Estate Boards, which only the examination of Colonel John J. O'Brien could fully expose.[7]

The committee adjourned at 12:30 P.M., Friday, the 25th, and I dashed over to the Department of the Interior for a conference with the mayor of San Francisco,[8] Undersecretary Fortas, then acting secretary, the mayor's associates, and those working on the perennial problem of how to dispose of Hetch-Hetchy power in San Francisco Bay.[9] I neglected to mention several conferences during the last few days up to Friday, August 25th, and the rendering of an opinion by myself [on] the plan proposed by the mayor for distributing 200,000,000 kilowatt hours for the city light, fire department, schools, street railway, etc., by the Pacific Gas and Electric Company, which would keep the balance of 300,000,000 kilowatt hours of annual production from the city's Hetch-Hetchy power plant. [I held that the plan] would violate the Raker Act[10] as much as any of the preceding agreements which the secretary of Interior had disapproved. The matter was crucial because the stay of injunction by the district court against the disposal of power to the [San Francisco] City Gas & Electric Company was to be either raised or continued on Monday the 28th, at which time I had planned to fly out and present the matter in court myself in San Francisco. . . .

It seems it never rains but it pours. Surplus Property Bill, Hetch-Hetchy issue and the Breakers Hotel report were all ricocheting around the Department of Justice, the press, and in interested quarters in Washington, all at the same time. Poor Fahy, as acting attorney general, was on another "hot seat" and Littell was again the cause. However, the reactions to the stand I had taken on the Surplus Property Bill were so favorable that Fahy's attitude necessarily changed. When we finished discussing the Hetch-Hetchy opinion I was about to give to Interior, he brought out

some amendments. A conference committee compromised on a three-man board of co-equal authority with the administrator and the Senate passed the revised measure on 19 September. See *New York Times*, 26 August 1944, p. 9; 16 September 1944, p. 16; 18 September 1944, p. 21; 19 September 1944, p. 17.

7. Nathan Robertson, "Clayton Testimony Verifies Land Disposal Charges; Surplus Property Administrator 'Never Saw' Committee's Report," *P.M.*, 24 August 1944; Nathan Robertson, "Senate Inquiry on Clayton Leaves Many Mysteries; Surplus Property Administrator Admits He Ignored Advisory Group," *P.M.*, 27 August 1944.

8. Angelo J. Rossi was mayor of San Francisco, 1931–44.

9. The city of San Francisco had been selling electric power produced at the Hetch-Hetchy Dam through the Pacific Gas and Electric Company. Secretary of the Interior Ickes asked the attorney general to end this, but after much negotiation, no final decision was taken. An injunction against the city was delayed until March 1945.

10. The Raker Act of 1913 (38 Stat. 242) approved 19 December 1913, required that electricity produced at Hetch-Hetchy Dam not be marketed through a private company.

my memorandum on surplus [property] and asked if I "did not wish to withdraw it." He had never made it a practice to enter into a "war of memoranda" and did not like to start now. Besides, I had misunderstood him. He had not said that I had "deceived" him, as related in my memorandum, but only that I had "fooled" him.

I promptly said I would accept the amendment. It was a distinction without a difference. They meant the same thing to me. I, too, did not believe in a war of memoranda, but had been reduced to it by the low level of the Department of Justice under Biddle, commencing with the incident over the Savannah Shipyards in which I had leveled off the attorney general and Jim Rowe as a matter of protection against Tommy Corcoran. I explained that it had been clear to me that Mr. Fahy had aligned himself with the attorney general in respect to the Elk Hills Petroleum Reserve controversy and the Breakers Hotel issue and now he had done so again regarding surplus property.

He denied this vehemently. He had been in favor of my report on the Elk Hills [case]. I did not remind him of painful incidents when it seemed quite otherwise—when I had been left out of his conferences for a month and a half after my testimony before the committee, and other incidents.

"You were right about the Breakers Hotel," he said. "I agreed with you on that. It is only the procedure for handling these things which I object to. [There] is a way of handling them rightly." . . .

No, I would not withdraw the memorandum. I was sick and tired of being "badgered and harassed" in this Department and, as he had seemingly taken his place with the attorney general on some of these issues, the memorandum would have to stand.

Then, in that event, he would have to reply to it! [he said.]

I have had no reply yet and I think he will find it extremely difficult to reply in an effective way.

The Surplus Property [Bill] hearings closed with the examination of Colonel John J. O'Brien, on Monday, August 28th, in the afternoon, after the committee had heard [Julius A.] Krug, the new acting chairman of the WPB (appointed to succeed [Donald M.] Nelson, who has been sent to China by the President.)[11] There is no time for that issue. I had told Senator [Harley M.] Kilgore and Senator Ferguson—the Republican and Democratic members of the committee who had followed the land issue most closely—that the hearings would have been in vain unless they finished with O'Brien to expose the influence of the National Association of Real Estate Boards. They are two forthright men, and they insisted on additional hearings in order to complete it, although General Counsel

---

11. Donald Nelson traveled to Russia and China, in August 1944, as President Roosevelt's personal representative to Chiang Kai-shek. His mission was to promote better relations between the Nationalist and Communist Chinese forces.

Halley complained that "they were killing" him. Indeed, the committee has never had a more concentrated period, even under Truman's administration, than it has in the last two or three weeks.

O'Brien's examination was pathetic. It was like a boxing match in which you can hear the bones crunch. He tried to lay his advisory committee from the National Association at the door of Undersecretary of War Patterson, but I know Patterson too well to think that [he] would ever have allowed members of the Board to ride right straight through into the realm of policy right into the door of the disposal of surplus with a beautiful provision that land should be disposed of by brokers to be paid at the ordinary accepted rate in the communities where they worked.

Now, I could see why O'Brien had gotten away from our advice on the selection of appraisers. Of his nine regional officers, he had accepted five nominees from the National Association of Real Estate Boards to head those five regions. Four others have been selected on other bases. The story of [Adolphus N.] Lockwood, in charge of the rich industrial area headed up by the office in Brooklyn, was perfectly clear. Yes, he had consulted with them [regarding] exactly the plan submitted to Clayton. He had [consulted] with them frequently. All of his efforts to belittle his acquaintanceship with the various named members of the board were futile. An impression of intimacy was still perfectly clear.

"No," he didn't know "Herb Nelson very well."

"Herb? Herb?" Senator Kilgore had been quick to reply, in one of those subtle moments in the examination of a witness which are so significant and which do not appear clearly in the record. It was apparent that he knew Nelson quite intimately, just by the way he pronounced the name "Herb."

The committee also impeached O'Brien. He had misled them in the Breakers Hotel matter as to whether or not the hotel could be reconverted in four months or two months. When finally asked if he wished to change his testimony of last spring, he said, "Yes."

It was a sickening incident, for I had put him in the War Department. He was my man, crumbling under examination. There could never be a recovery. My major mistake in trying to serve the government lay in pieces before me, and there is nothing more sickening than a crumbled human character. This was the end. I might have anticipated it.

I had had General Somervell over to lunch, within a year after O'Brien's appointment, to explain that I had discovered the man to be unreliable (re: The Ewing Wright incident) and that that fact would come home to roost in the War Department. Here it was now.[12]

---

12. For the testimony of Col. J. J. O'Brien and Col. M. J. O'Byrne, see "Two Top Clayton Aids [sic] Shown Closely Tied to Realty Lobby," P.M., 29 August 1944.

Most of the press ignored the incident as the story had broken with my testimony and that of Clayton's, but *P.M.* castigated O'Brien very thoroughly on the 29th.

In Hetch-Hetchy, the judge granted a six-months' extension on Monday, the 28th, the United States attorney, [Frank J.] Hennessy, having read in court, pursuant to my instructions (he is not very able and I knew of no other way of preventing his getting the matter completely confused) my letter to [him] regarding the conferences in Washington with the mayor.

The Breakers Hotel matter is still unresolved. Today, I talked with Undersecretary of War Patterson and suggested that he come over to lunch, on Friday the 30th, to talk over the whole land acquisition program. There is no reason why the War Department should be sacrificed to a personality like O'Brien. Their relations with the Hill are destroyed. The Senate has no confidence and, if they had, the report now on my desk from the great Hanford Project in the state of Washington, it would blow the lid off the War Department land acquisition program all over again.

In the meantime, the Senate Surplus Property Bill has gone into conference between the House and the Senate, and I must give exclusive time to studying that bill, for I am advised by Senator Hill that I will probably be called, although the conference committees do not usually call witnesses. I still have hopes of getting out the paralyzing clauses on repurchase rights of former owners.

In the meantime, the honorable attorney general of the United States returned from his junket down the West Coast. While I am sure that, on receiving the news that Littell had gotten out of his cage again during his absence, he had high hopes this time of finding a ground for discharging me for raising a rumpus against Clayton, the universal approval of my stand in the press had steam-rollered him.

Furthermore, the vicious attack of Senator Ferguson on the floor of the Senate, expressing regret "that it was necessary for this body to advise the chief legal officer of the government in his duties" had undoubtedly sobered him.[13] I never heard a peep out of him. My proposed letter to the War Department, which had been sent to Charlie Fahy, had been referred to the attorney general and had come back approved from Carusi's office. I have not been sent for. We had an attorney general staff meeting this morning of an unusually vacuous sort. The attorney general told a few funny stories about his trip down the Coast, and Jim McGranery's antics, while Jim in turn told a few funny stories about visiting the Hollywood stars. There was not a serious thought in the whole

13. For Ferguson's attack on Biddle, see *Congressional Record*, vol. 90 (22 August 1944), p. 7266.

matter. Nothing of substance had been brought back—and this in the midst of wartime with all the problems which we confront.

The attorney general, himself, told of Judge [Curtis D.] Wilbur introducing him before the Commonwealth Club of San Francisco as "the greatest attorney in the world." There was a pause and then Wilbur continued—"not of course in intelligence or ability, but in the number of clients." Biddle thought that was great fun, but it was all said with earnest purpose as I well know from the attitude of the bench and bar towards Biddle on the Pacific Coast. With his enormous vanity, it has no effect whatsoever. He was very much amused by the whole incident and by all of his adventures on the Coast.

He called on each member of the staff, as usual, and each reported nothing whatever. Staff meeting was over in a few moments. Everybody has learned that discussion of anything with him in staff meeting is utterly futile. With all that happened to me, how could it possibly be true that I had "nothing to report?" It was the same with everyone. Life is just a gay song to the dilettante Biddle. I left the meeting in disgust. . . .

Sunday night, 17 September 1944
4101 Lorcom Lane

The week has drifted by in a welter of enjoyment of the children at home, of maturing events on the domestic front, and ever-increasing victories abroad until the headlines, today, report our forces within 26 miles of Cologne.

But my front is the domestic front. The Surplus Property Bill has made its way, step by step, through committee until Clayton saw the handwriting on the wall and, yesterday, announced that he would, under no circumstances, serve under a board with a division of authority between the administrator and the board. We have his scalp. By petulant advance resignation, he saved himself the humiliation of not having his name recommended as administrator, and he saved the President the embarrassment of not sending his name over.

Anna came over to lunch on Friday, the 15th: The long-deferred luncheon which I had put off to make sure that my "declaration of independence" over there at the White House was quite clear. The President is in Quebec with Winston Churchill.[1] Anna had explained to Katherine, previously, that, at such a time, she is more free. In fact, she cannot get

1. The second Quebec Conference between President Roosevelt and Prime Minister Churchill, occurred 12–16 September 1944. The two leaders discussed the occupation of Germany, and tentatively approved the Morgenthau Plan of preventing German rearmament.

away from lunch hour at the White House, as a general matter, when the President is there.

The conversation touched on Clayton. "Any reactions over at the White House, pro or con, on Clayton?" I asked, referring to the White House staff.

"I haven't heard any," Anna replied, and that "let the cat out of the bag" if one knows how to interpret. Clearly, the executive staff, from Jimmy Byrnes down, would not discuss the fate of Clayton with Anna Boettiger. There is only one person who would discuss it with Anna, quite naturally and fully, and that is the President. "You see, we did not know what he was doing," Anna carried on. "You knew what was going on, but we did not."

I have noticed a number of times that Anna uses the editorial "we" when she does not wish to refer to the President, directly. The word nevertheless covers joint discussions between them. Coupled with John Boettiger's condescending comments, passed on by Anna over the telephone to Katherine during the midst of the Clayton battle— "Tell Norman he has certainly handled himself well in the Clayton matter"— the straws in the wind as to how the President feels are quite clear.

There was also very frank discussion of Francis Biddle. Anna summed up the state of the weather in the White House on that subject very neatly. "He is a fool," she said. It was quite obvious that understanding of the Biddle problem was universal.

I pointed out Dewey's speech of the 14th, at Sheridan, Wyoming, on the subject of land and the "land grab" of this administration,[2] [and] the fact that a ready reply lay at hand in my files—in fact, on my desk, in rough draft form—but that I could not get through the press room past Biddle. A release, correcting the obvious misstatements of Dewey on the Jackson Hole National Monument[3] and other acquisitions in the West, would be purloined by Biddle—not that I minded, if his statement would be effective, but it would not be! The West despises him. He knows nothing about land. Probably, the press would not take it up. In general, it would be wasted effort.

"Why not give it to some congressman for release on the floor, getting around Biddle in that manner?" Anna asked.

"My dear Anna," I replied, "If you think for one moment that, at this stage, I am going to seek outlets for my opinions in that circuitous route, you have another guess coming. When I make a statement, it will be over

---

2. "Dewey's Talk About Land Brings Reply," *Des Moines Register*, 4 October 1944, in Littell scrapbook.

3. President Roosevelt established the Jackson Hole National Monument 15 March 1943, by Proclamation No. 2578. In 1944 a bill to abolish the monument passed Congress (H.R. 2241), but Roosevelt vetoed it 29 December 1944 and Congress did not try to override him.

my name and with the full impact of such authority as I have accumulated in five years in charge of the Lands Division. It's asking too much of my self-respect for the administration to leave a clinker like Biddle where he is and expect my fire to burn around it. . . . "

"It is perfectly true that I have smashed through resistance [before] . . . and will continue to do so, but in the approaching campaign I [will] be hobbled indeed to pursue that course and [will] have to be given greater freedom, if maximum usefulness [is] to be obtained," I also stated.

Anna saw the point immediately. The smell of battle is in the air and the outcome is by no means certain. The Roosevelts are again campaigning. All support is to be considered.

I explained further that I had very nearly quit on two occasions during the preceding year—to go back to private practice, but had stayed because of the opportunities of public service in such matters as the Clayton battle—because I did not wish to yield the vacancy of this big Division to an appointment nominated by Tommy Corcoran, throwing loyal staff to the wolves, and because I ought to remain there and watch Biddle and Corcoran. Also, I ought to go through the campaign, even though I had said I never would go through another one as assistant attorney general, taking a back seat on radio connections and public meetings before a man like Biddle—of such definitely inferior capacity in every particular, and particularly in respect to public speaking.

Anna said that she could quite understand that viewpoint, but added: "There may be [a] complete shake-up after the election. Really, the whole cabinet ought to tender their resignations if the President is elected again so that there is a chance of making a fresh start. There should be changes and reorganization then."

It was almost an invitation to be patient. Katherine said later that it was, but I doubted it because of the jealous opposition which could be expected from John [Boettiger] at any thought of a cabinet post for myself.

There was a great deal of cross-fire between the three of us [i.e., Anna, Katherine, and me,] and a lot of chitter-chatter which can't be set down here. "What do you think of Truman?" etc. Anna knows and needs no answer: A good, honest, forthright American citizen of sufficient stature. Anna was for Wallace, so she knows what liberals think. . . .

I felt that Anna knows very well she is serving a useful function as any attractive and intelligent daughter might well do with a father pressed with heavy responsibilities.

"It is very difficult, though," Anna said, "as I have no regular position or capacity. Jimmy[4] did when he was here, but was under constant attack for it."

---

4. The President's son, James Roosevelt, was administrative assistant to the President, 1937–38.

I knew that such a position had been contemplated and, in my last conversation with Anna, had understood she was to have such a position, but it had apparently been decided that that would be considered too vulnerable.

"Nepotism, I believe they call it," Anna said, "so I have no regular position and even borrow secretaries from the social secretarial staff, having no regularized function or position."

"And yet, you could handle a big volume of correspondence coming to the President," I said.

"I do," Anna replied, "but I am not part of the staff."

We parted at the car. I must say, both Katherine and I are re-affirmed in our conviction that Anna is a grand personality, even though it is inevitable that her own natural convictions be divided by duties and loyalties to her father.

Yesterday, Congressman Robert Ramspeck came to lunch with me. He is the new chairman of the Speakers' Bureau at the National Democratic Committee and had written to ask what campaigning I could do. We discussed matters for three hours. Dewey had just sounded off at Sheridan, Wyoming, on the administration's "land grab" policies in the West, referring particularly to Jackson Hole National Monument in Wyoming. With the help of one of my staff, I had rough-drafted a proposed reply—disregarding for the moment all reasons why I could not get out in the open to make the reply.

"If I sent this upstairs to Biddle," I said, after reading it aloud to him, while he listened with great interest and expressed keen appreciation, "it would come out over Biddle's name. And what do you suppose that would mean in the West?" I asked.

"Not a thing!" he replied. "I understand that perfectly. As a matter of fact, we have canvassed the cabinet and sub-cabinet very carefully for those who can speak effectively. Biddle is a problem. We do not see where we can use him at all except possibly in one or two spots. As a matter of fact, we find very little speaking material."

"On the cabinet level you find Ickes," I said. "He is the one top-ranking battler—a real campaigner—but he has unfortunately worked out his welcome in the West to a very large extent."

Ramspeck agreed, entirely. "Ickes has the only first-class campaign ability on the cabinet level," he agreed.

It was quite obvious that he included me in what little ability he had found available for, as we explored in detail where I should go in the country, as between the East and the West, and I explained that I thought with Oregon in the balance, and Washington far from clear, I ought to expend my influence there and in California. He agreed, and asked for the schedule of a proposed trip in October from Washington down the Coast to California so that he could schedule speeches from that time in each state. Also, could I stop over in Wyoming and Montana on the way out?

He was also much interested in the reply to Dewey on the subject of lands, where he could readily see that by my being a Westerner and having been in charge of the Lands Division for which I was well-known in the West, I could speak with authority and deliver a real wallop on that vital subject in the West, whereas Dewey appeared as a tenderfoot from the East. If only I could get a clear alley.

"Someone will have to instruct Biddle to that effect," I said. "I will not waste my material on Biddle. I will be glad to give you or any other congressman or senator any information you wish so that you can sound off in the Senate or the House, but I will not dish it up to Biddle."

Ramspeck wholly agreed with that and also thought that would be less effective in the House than having me deliver it with the authority of my position in the Lands Division—although he would be glad to deliver a statement if necessary. . . .

He telephoned to Mr. Justice Byrnes at the White House from my office, while I stepped out, and discussed the matter with Byrnes for over twenty minutes. Byrnes' reply was that he, himself, had examined the Jackson Hole issue in Wyoming and Senator O'Mahoney had assured him that the taking of lands for Jackson Hole might lose the state to the Administration, [but] Byrnes was not at all sure that we were right on that issue. Furthermore, Ickes was the man on the lands and he should make the reply. There was real sense in that, of course, and, as it turned out, Ickes did make a reply which the press apparently did not take up because it had not appeared when I talked with Ramspeck. However, a crack from Ickes about Dewey "beagling for votes in the West" did appear in the Sunday paper, and Drew Pearson, getting his information from Ickes, made an excellent reply on the radio tonight. [He said] that the Jackson Hole National Monument had been urged by both Coolidge and Hoover; that John D. Rockefeller had been urged to buy up lands in that vicinity to give to the government and had done so, but had finally come to Ickes and said that if the government did not do its part, he, Rockefeller, would dispose of those lands. It was then that the President, by executive order, had transferred lands already owned by the government . . . to the National Park Service, thereby withdrawing them from the cattlemen, which is what all the shooting is about. As Drew said, the charge would boomerang on Dewey.

However, the incident was a valuable one, for it leaves unsolved the question of how to dispose of my own influence, such as it is, for the good of the cause.

The conversation with Ramspeck confirmed opinions expressed on all sides about Biddle's uselessness. Why is it that, with casualties abroad and the removal of any officer in leadership who cannot prove his ability to command, we cannot recognize incompetence at home? . . .

Tuesday, 19 September 1944
4101 Lorcom Lane

I talked with J. Frank Burke, in Pasadena, in regard to the political situation in California, over long-distance telephone Sunday night, and he expressed very real doubts. The ranks are divided. The liberals are disgusted and apathetic. The party is in the hands of Ed Pauley, owned body and soul by oil interests in California, whose influence on the chairman of the delegation, Attorney General Bob Kenny, split the California delegation wide open at the national convention. Burke had previously thought that Wallace should not come out before the election to speak in the West, but he reversed himself and urged that he do come.

And so I went to see Mr. Wallace at 11: 00 today.[1] [Paul A.] Porter, the new publicity chairman for the National Democratic Committee, supplanting [Charles] Michelson, was coming in to see Wallace to ask him to go West to California and speak. Ed Pauley had said that it was absolutely necessary.

"There's plenty of irony in that!" I remarked. "Pauley defeats you for the vice presidential nomination, working hand-in-glove with Hannegan, and now he finds he can't get the campaign off the ground in California because the ideas have gone out of it. The liberals are apathetic and won't move and he has to appeal to you."

"The California delegation under Robert Kenny is more responsible for my defeat at the convention than any other," Wallace replied. "They used any kind of tactics."

"Had the delegation not 'passed' on the second ballot, and had thrown its weight of the majority, which was for you, in the Wallace column, it could easily have turned the tide of that second ballot," I replied.

"Bob Kenny did it," Wallace said.

"Speaking quite bluntly, you made a major blunder when you went to the West Coast for those three speeches before the campaign," I said.[2] Wallace looked up in surprise.

"You said you were going to talk with me and you didn't," I continued. "You should have at least talked with someone with some familiarity with

1. For Wallace's account of his talk with Littell, see John M. Blum, ed., *The Price of Vision: The Diary of Henry Wallace, 1942–1946* (Boston: Houghton Mifflin Co., 1973), pp. 380–81.

2. Wallace made three speeches in California—at Los Angeles, San Diego, and San Francisco—in early February 1944.

the West. A man can't go blind-folded into a sawmill with the buzz-saws all going and not get hurt unless he has incredible good fortune. You walked right into the camp of your enemies when you went to California, but had you gone into the camp of your friends and thereby solidified their positions, the story at the convention of the California delegation would have been quite different."

"Harold Young thought Bob Kenny was all right and would go along with us," Wallace replied. "It was just a mistake of judgment."

"He thought—but he had no right to think without getting the best judgment of those who knew. We know Bob Kenny and have known him for years. He is only interested in Bob Kenny. He will play with the extreme left to get votes, but he is always, at heart, on the extreme right and he is taking orders from Ed Pauley and playing with the Pauley crowd right down the road. Harold Young made the same lot of blunders in the Northwest—particularly Seattle. He was sailing blind when he didn't need to."

"You ought to get West for at least one speech," I urged.

"I will have nothing to do with Pauley," Wallace replied. "It all depends on the auspices."

"I quite agree," I replied. "The auspices can be arranged—among your friends."

"As long as Harold Young is my political adviser," Wallace said, "we must agree on it. I suggest that we three sit down together and discuss it at the first of the week."

We made a date for next Tuesday morning, when I would be back from Boston. I neglected to say that, at the outset of the conversation, Wallace reported that Hannegan was accusing Wallace of not cooperating in the campaign, even though Wallace was preparing at this moment a speech for Madison Square Garden next Thursday night in support of Roosevelt.

I left and got back to my office in time for lunch with Raymond Gram Swing, the radio commentator. What a rare, fine spirit and mind he has for equilibrium of judgment, fairness, freedom from personal prejudice, political or otherwise, comprehension, and passionate devotion to the truth. He is without equal on the air. He is the most widely listened-to radio voice in the world. His comments are translated, instantly, into several languages and repeated. Millions throughout the world hear him and, as we talked and got better acquainted, I could understand why.

As he, himself, explained, he lives a celibate life. He has no evening social engagements, whatsoever, but lives entirely to deliver a quality of workmanship and thought in his evening radio comments which have made him famous throughout the world.

He inquired about Dewey's comments on the land situation and listened with an absorbing interest and direct penetrating gaze which bespoke great capacity for absorbtion of information and filtering of viewpoints. . . .

"The outlook on world affairs is very gloomy," he said, when we drifted to that subject. "Dumbarton Oaks[3] is concerned largely with checkmating the power of Russia by England. Plans are being made to check any great power." . . .

I gave an illustration of Phil Johnson, president of Boeing Aircraft Company, who died of a stroke last week, . . . sitting in my office a little over a year ago, saying that our next enemy would be Russia. As soon as we finish off the Germans, we would have to tackle Russia. "Russia, which the greatest military power in history has been unable to defeat; Russia, with her unlimited sources of manpower; with oil many times that which we possess; and with natural resources of every kind at her disposal!" [I said.]

"That sentiment is quite widespread," Swing replied. "Even though we are Russia's natural friends and have been so, historically, for 150 years, irrespective of what government is in power in Russia."

We parted with plans to meet again, in fact, with a sense of lasting understanding and friendship.

Katherine read to me this evening the crowning comment of the day—a gleeful statement in *P.M.*—that the House had passed—179 to 19—the conference [report] on disposal of surplus properties, creating a three-man board and definitely repudiating Clayton.[4] It revealed that last-minute efforts of Bernard Baruch and Jimmy Byrnes at the White House had been made to salvage the Clayton bill and restore the one-man administrator. All had failed. As *P.M.* joyfully observed, Clayton was completely polished off. That is one of the neatest and most complete victories I have ever enjoyed. Nobody has been able to stop that man for four years and he is as dead as a "dodo" around Washington now.

Tuesday night, 26 September 1944
4101 Lorcom Lane

Katherine and I returned this morning from Boston and New York. We spent the weekend with Mr. and Mrs. E. G. Howes, at Cohassett, after clearing up certain appraisal difficulties in my office in Boston. [This followed] a conference with Governor Saltonstall, Friday noon, regarding

---

3. A conference in Washington, D.C., during August and September 1944, at which the United States, the Soviet Union, and Great Britain formalized plans for a postwar United Nations organization.
4. See diary entry for 30 August 1944, note 4.

expanding our National Committee Against Persecution of the Jews, to establish a Boston area group [and] a meeting with the governor's committee of outstanding citizens in the office of the superintendent of schools, to consider the advisability of doing so, [in which] all unanimously concurred.

Saltonstall is a rare revival of a back-bay Boston family into an effective political leader in a community long abandoned to the Irish and others of the common herd. Quiet, composed, without strain, he sat in his desk chair and discussed the anti-semitic problems in Boston. I envied him his composure in a world full of exhaustive excitements. . . .

I visited Democratic Headquarters in New York and am about to do what I said I would never do—go through another campaign as assistant attorney general. I agreed on the western tour and three engagements have already come back in answer to a wire from New York: A speech at Pendleton, [Oregon] on the 17th; Oregon City, on the 18th; and Eugene, on the 19th. [I] am working hastily to conclude a speech for Des Moines, Iowa, on October 3rd, and must then write another for the "Nation's Associates" of liberals from around the country, on October 8th, before starting West that night. . . .

Tuesday, 10 October 1944
Northern Pacific Railway, *en route* Spokane, Washington

Dearest Katherine Mather,

. . . There has been quite a little travel lately. On September 28th, I left for Denver after long hours and late nights preparing an address to deliver at Des Moines on "The Federal Land Bogey," but I took in Denver, too, where we have to appraise approximately four million acres—about the western one-third of Colorado—125 miles west along the southern border and 250 north along the western border, thence east to form a rectangle. The government must pay the Ute Indians for it as a result of wrongful seizures in the past. . . .

Sunday, in Denver, was a real break as our old friends, Sam and Margaret Magoffin, drove me to Estes Park, where they go every Sunday during the shut-down of the tunnel which Sam is drilling through the Rockies—his Big Thompson Tunnel. . . .

I was, in fact, home for only three days, returning on the morning of October 5th, and leaving Washington again on the night of October 7th. I had dreaded those three concentrated days, but Colorado fortified me for them. In the midst of writing a speech for the "Nation's Associates," organized by Freda Kirchwey, publisher of *The Nation*, at the Astor Hotel in New York for the 8th, entitled "Minorities—Keystone of Free Government," I prepared the agenda for the meeting of the board of directors of the National Committee Against Persecution of the Jews to meet on the 6th at my house; prepared the Community Fund War Chest drive in the Department, with a program for a mass meeting of the Department, Saturday morning, the 7th, and another one for the FBI in the armory that afternoon, at 4:00 and dispatched a considerable volume of routine work with the aid of my invaluable general assistant, J. E. Williams.

Just before leaving for Denver, I had gone to see Sam Rosenman at the White House in regard to the greatest current blunder in the government—the announcement of the so-called "Morgenthau Plan"[1] for the treatment of Germany after the war. It was a tough, hard plan against which both Secretary Stimson and Secretary Hull, the two other remaining advisors of the President's advisory committee on the subject, had revolted. It had leaked out to the press—deliberately, no doubt—through hostile forces in the War Department and State Department, possibly even as a deliberate anti-semitic move.

"It was the greatest possible blunder to have Morgenthau have anything to do with it," I told Sam. "Didn't the damned fool know any better than to handle it personally? Can't he see what would happen—what is now happening; that the press is simply setting down his plan as a Jewish desire for revenge, thereby prejudicing one of the gravest problems in the world today—how to treat Germany in order to eliminate generations of training with the single objective of military domination and world conquest?"

"It was probably permitted to leak from within one of the opposing departments for the deliberate purpose of prejudicing the plan," Sam said. "That is the way departments make war on each other around here." He admitted his very grave concern. He had lost sleep over the incident and minced no words about Morgenthau. I surmised that he shared my view that Morgenthau ought to have been kicked out of the cabinet a long time ago; he is a blundering idiot.

"What would you do now?" he asked.

"The President must knock the 'Morgenthau Plan' in the head. It does not matter how he does it; just drop it—smash it—erase it. He can dig up another plan later. Say that the committee is now discharged, having rendered its advice, although having rendered a very great disservice in splitting wide apart over a major issue at the approaching peace confer-

1. The Morgenthau Plan was a Treasury Department proposal for the postwar treatment of Germany, named for Secretary of the Treasury Henry Morgenthau, Jr., and tentatively approved but quickly abandoned by President Roosevelt and Prime Minister Churchill at their meeting in Quebec in September 1944. It proposed to prevent German rearmament and reduce Germany to agricultural and pastoral pursuits by stripping its industrial regions of all heavy industries.

ence. It represented the extremes of divided opinion between a hard peace, a stern peace, and a soft peace."

"I know so little about the merits of that problem," Sam said.

"It doesn't matter," I replied. "Whatever the merits are, the 'Morgenthau Plan' must be discarded—gotten out of the way. The President could do it. He is adroit at moves of this sort, and he will know how to handle it." Because Henry J. Kaiser was waiting in Rosenman's office and we had kept him waiting for fifteen minutes, I departed. I don't know whether that interview had anything to do with the subject or not, but the next day, it was announced at the President's press conference that the "Morgenthau Plan" was dropped. It was too late, however. The horse had been stolen out of the barn. The front page article of *Time* carried a picture of Morgenthau and a somewhat sarcastic account of the "Morgenthau Plan." The rest of the press carried similar articles. He had done a great cause, and his own people, a great harm.

The adjourned portion of [my] conversation [with Rosenman] was resumed on the 7th at 12:00, after finishing the Community War Chest mass meeting. Obviously, the President was gone from the White House—the absence of press men waiting in the executive offices is a sure sign.

I explained that I was going West on business but [would] make campaign speeches down the Coast in my spare time, at the request of the speakers' committee, and I wanted to know if he had any idea of what the President thought should be emphasized in the West. I explained that, as far as I was concerned, I had made the most important speech on Western issues in the lands speech at Des Moines, which answered Dewey's biggest whopper, that the federal government had taken 383,000,000 acres of land. He referred, of course, to the public domain which had always been in the possession of the federal government, as I had explained at Des Moines very effectively and very successfully before the National Association of Tax Assessors. The irony was that, while it was front-page stuff in Des Moines as an "answer to Dewey," . . . it was not front-page stuff, nationally, as it should have been, [because I am only an assistant attorney general]. . . .

I explained that this was my last round-up, that while I had said that I would not campaign again as assistant attorney general, I was doing so because the public interest demanded that I add even my feeble voice for what it was worth. I would definitely leave and return to private practice after the election because I would serve no longer with a plain damn-fool as chief.

"We are all in hopes," Rosenman broke in, "that every member of the cabinet will tender his resignation. In sizing up the situation, however, the only two we were afraid of in following that policy are Biddle and Morgenthau."

"Morgenthau must get out by all means," I said. "He is an old woman at best, but he must not be Treasurer in the postwar period with its multiple financial problems in foreign affairs."

It was perfectly apparent that Rosenman wholly agreed with everything that was said on the score of Morgenthau. As for Biddle, I said that I thought I had absolutely authoritative information that Biddle had written letters to Philadelphia in respect to his returning to private practice after the election—building up his fences a little bit there.

Rosenman said that was excellent news—that he had not heard it—that in fact, they had been concerned about whether Biddle would resign.

"I suppose everyone over here at the White House feels the same way about him, do they not?" I asked.

Rosenman nodded in agreement. "In fact," he said, "I believe Ickes will present his resignation to the President at the next cabinet meeting after the election if the President wins, in the hopes that others will all follow suit."

"It is one of the things I have most to regret out of my period of service here," I said."—the fact that I endorsed Biddle for the position of attorney general after he had served as solicitor general, and wrote a letter to the President to that effect." . . .

Sam took the greatest interest in the fact that I had written to the President—so great that it almost seemed as if he must have been pumped full of rumors to the effect that I had always wanted Biddle's job, but here was conclusive proof to the contrary.

"I feel quite differently now," I explained. "The man is incompetent to the highest degree. I make no bones about saying so and I will not serve under him much longer. I would like to be the attorney general for the sake of putting that Department on its feet. I am already running the biggest Division of it and have reduced it to a streamlined efficiency in the acquisition of land in the war effort, and have won a leadership which is recognized by all United States attorneys (except for a few enemies I have among them because I stepped on their toes) from one side of the country to the other." I related a few examples of the support from that quarter and their recognition of the work of the Lands Division.

"No one will tell anybody at the White House these things," I said, "and I feel quite sure that I have had a job done on me with the President. I used to see quite a little of him, but I have a feeling that Ickes has poured it on, and Ickes is very close to John Boettiger and Tommy Corcoran who. . . . "

"What do you think of him?" Sam asked.

"I think Anna is a very fine person," I replied, "But her judgments are influenced by John, who has no sense at all for public affairs."

"As a one-time reporter for the McCormick press,[2] the *Chicago Tribune*, and a reactionary, he is having a hard time posing as a liberal now, which he tries very hard to do," Sam added.

"That is precisely the case," I said, "but I presume Anna is doing a great job here for her father, as she has real understanding."

"My respect for her has grown immensely since she has been here," Sam said.

"If I am guilty of ambition, so be it," I said, "but I think there is legitimate ambition. A man should wish to reach the fullest capacity of his effectiveness and ability. A simple test which I have devised as to whether a man's ambitions are of this legitimate variety or merely a quest for personal power is this: Will he be just as happy on resuming a private capacity, or will he feel embittered, frustrated and hateful at not getting the position aimed at?

"Applying that test to myself, I shall be perfectly happy to resume private life and see something of my very delightful family. I would know that this is the intent as far as I am concerned and would accept it most happily. However, I would like to do a job on this Department. It is logical. There are thousands of people in the West who think I should. Dewey was right in his attack on the President for not appointing a Westerner to the cabinet in all of this time.[3] The President is absolutely vulnerable there. He has said in the past 'show me a man' and then the West would show him Jefty O'Connor,[4] or someone of that caliber and the President turned away. The reflection on the West is perfectly clear in what the President has done, and the people rightly resent it, as I do. [To] say that one must lop off a whole vast section of the United States as having no man competent for cabinet posts when there are such men as Morgenthau and Biddle and a woman like Mrs. Perkins in the cabinet, is simply grotesque." . . .

The whole Harvard gang down here thinks in terms of each other. Contacts from the West, except for the intimate contact the President had with Senator [William G.] McAdoo, who married Woodrow Wilson's daughter[5] and was considered by the President to be the big man of the West, are simply nil. Of course, the West is to blame in taking things so

---

2. The McCormick press was several newspapers and journals published by conservative Republican-Isolationists: Joseph Medill Patterson (1879–1946), who was editor-publisher of the *New York Daily News*, 1919–46; his sister, Eleanor Medill "Cissy" Patterson (1884–1948), who was publisher of the *Washington Daily News*, 1930–48; and their cousin, Col. Robert Medill McCormick (1880–1955), who was publisher of the *Chicago Tribune*, 1910–55. They were the grandchildren of Joseph Medill (1823–1889), publisher of the *Chicago Tribune*, 1854–99, and a founder of the Republican Party.

3. In fact, George H. Dern, from Utah, served as secretary of war, 1933–37.

4. James F. T. O'Connor.

5. Eleanor Wilson McAdoo.

complacently and so politely. It is so sufficient unto itself and lives in such a happy land that the federal government and the seat of power are far, far away. In contrast to the work of hatchet men like Tommy Corcoran, the West proceeds with polite letters of request and, of course, nobody gives a damn.

"I am glad to have had this talk with you," Rosenman said.

"I don't want you to make any comment or express any opinion in one way or another," I said. "I simply wanted to state my views because I believe in the last year or so I have been completely out of contact with the President, and I believe a job has been done on me by Ickes, who very greatly resented my stand in the Elk Hills matter and does not know that I am aware of his attempts to undermine my testimony; and, possibly, John Boettiger has not been too helpful."

"The President has never shown anything like that in talking to me," Rosenman said in some surprise. In fact, his reaction was quite revealing that I was wrong about the President's attitude. I have no doubt the job was attempted, but, perhaps, it had failed.

We were interrupted once during our conversation by Steve Early, the President's ranking secretary, who came in and dropped a telegram on Rosenman's desk from Negro leaders in Detroit who were putting on a big mass meeting the next day and wanted a telegram from the President endorsing the FEPC [Fair Employment Practices Committee] as a matter of permanent legislation. This hot, controversial measure, which endeavors to secure equality in economic opportunity—compatible with the ability of the Negroes and all other races in the industries of the country— was the subject of bitter attack by the Southerners in Congress. The Republicans shrewdly capitalized on it, having no following in the South anyway, by putting a plank in their platform favoring permanent enactment of FEPC. The Southern Democrats blocked it at the Democratic convention in Chicago. The President was "on the spot," Early said, and he thought he had better telegraph them at once that the President was out of town and could not be reached so quickly.

Rosenman read the telegram carefully. "I think not," he said. "There is no question in my mind how the President would reply to this. He must reply to it in the affirmative. Of course, he is for it—we know that. I think it ought to be put on the ticker to the President (who was undoubtedly up at Hyde Park, although this was not stated) so that he can reply." . . . Steve agreed to send the telegram to the President and went on out.

"That's the way it is around here," Rosenman said. "Somebody has to watch everything. Now Steve Early is a Virginian and his whole point of view is colored by that fact. It would have been a terrible mistake for the President not to have replied to that telegram. It might offend a few Southerners, but the important states are the Eastern industrial states, where the Negro vote is very large. . . .

There was a contrast, however, with the evening before which I present somewhat out of its chronological order. The board [of the National Committee Against Persecution of the Jews] met at my house at 7:00. . . .

Wendell Willkie's secretary had called to say that he was still confined in the hospital and would be unable to come. Little did we realize that death would take this great American a few days later. He had told me over the long distance telephone from New York, about three weeks before, that he would be present at our board meeting as vice chairman of our committee. Governor Maw from Utah was unable to get transportation.

The banter between the CIO representative and the A.F. of L. representative was classic and too long to recount. "You have all the racketeers," Jim Carey [of the CIO] said to Watt [of the A.F. of L.] "and we have all the communists. That is, you have all the racketeers, except those in Eric Johnston's camp," referring to big business. After explaining that the communists would cut his throat, if they had half a chance, and Bob Watt very well knew it, he went on to harpoon Watt, as international representative, for refusing to sit down with representatives of Communist Russia at international conferences. Watt waited patiently and then explained, "I have sat down with them. I do sit down with them, and I will sit down with them, but I will not sit down at conferences to which you refer in which there are to be two representatives of industry, two representatives of labor, and two representatives of the government, only to find opposite me six representatives of the Soviet Government, because the government and labor are all of one point of view. They, therefore, cast six votes to our two on the points of view of labor."

There was an emerging problem of Europe in a nutshell. "But you will have to," Carey replied. "De Gaulle's revived France is certainly going to be similarly set up. The railroads are being nationalized and the mines. It will be a socialistic government and when you sit down to confer with them you would confront the same type of representation."

The discussion launched off into comparative notes on Russia, exchanged between Watt and Eric Johnston, the latter having recently returned from a visit to Josef Stalin. "There are no trade unions there," Watt said, and he and Eric Johnston agreed. There are associations to which the workers belong but they have no bargaining power against the government. . . .

Eric related, confidentially, how Henry Ford had telephoned him before his departure for Russia to ask him to take his particular regards and best wishes to Mr. Stalin, "whom I have always so greatly admired." Eric did so and Stalin was greatly pleased, saying to send his regards and best wishes to Mr. Ford, who he regarded "as the world's greatest industrialist," adding "may God preserve him."

"Did he say 'may God preserve him'?" the Catholic [Justice] Murphy asked, incredulously.

"Just that," Eric replied, and it seems that, when he returned from Russia and gave the message to Mr. Ford in person, the latter was so delighted that he had Eric go into his (Ford's) office and dictate exactly what was said, but later sent the letter back to Johnston to have him place it on his own stationery, quoting Mr. Stalin precisely.

"I saw him last week in Detroit," Eric said, "and I must say he is definitely senile. He is very anti-semitic." We discussed the possibility of getting Edsel Ford on our committee.

I will not endeavor to discuss here the subject of our evening: The rise of anti-semitism throughout the country, partially as a resurgence of Nazi-inspired propaganda, following their thorough work before the war. . . . [This movement was, and is, meant] by Hitler to disrupt order in every free government, partially as a result of encouraged prejudices, witnessing the extermination of Jews abroad, followed by the elemental reaction of the lay mind that "there must be good reason for it"; and, partially, on the merits because the Jew, recently emancipated from the ghetto and political restrictions is, undoubtedly, a shrewder, more astute, and less restrained businessman than the ordinary Anglo-Saxon. I could not admit this, now, as coming from me; it would seem to confess the whole basis for anti-semitism. It does not confess so much. It merely faces the fact realistically. I still maintain that there is no solution except tolerance to any of the racial or religious differences which exist among us. I have stated the matter rather completely in an address for the "Nation's Associates," and I refer anyone to that, if interested. . . .

In Chicago, [on October 8th] I broke a little bomb on the land acquisition front, by depositing $75,000 in court as the estimated value of the Joliet plant for which John W. Galbreath, president of the National Association of Real Estate Boards, has asked the government for $450,000, although he is willing to "commence conversations at $250,000."[6] This is the case I exposed before the Truman Committee in

---

6. Galbreath had purchased a 29.22 acre site near Joliet, Illinois, in June 1943, for $60,000; he had leased it out for one year at $70,000; and wanted the government to pay $450,000 for it. The judge allowed the government to deposit $75,000 in court as full payment for the property. See "Top Realtor Accused of 'Gouging' the Navy," *Washington Daily News*, 10 October 1944 in Littell scrapbooks; "U.S. Accuses Bricker Man of Land Grab; Littell declares the Galbraith [*sic*] Deal Was 'Shocking' Profiteering," *P.M.*, 11 October 1944; "Brickers' Aid [*sic*] Renews Drive on Property Act; Rejoins Jones, Clayton in Attempt to 'Get' Littell," *P.M.*, 21 November 1944.

testimony which blasted Clayton out of office. They have sought a compromise but, by filing a declaration of taking, which vests title in the government, and depositing our estimated $75,000, I have cut off all such discussion. There will be no compromise; we will fight the matter out. I described it as one of the most shocking examples of excessive profit-taking at the expense of the war effort that I had seen in the whole period of the acquisition of property.

Galbreath happens to be the campaign manager for [John W.] Bricker, Dewey's vice presidential running mate. Is this a return to the old Ohio gang of the Harding days?[7] It is a fair question, and I saw to it, after a conversation with Marshall Field, owner and publisher of the *Chicago Sun*, that the point was not overlooked. He sent a special reporter to the press room of the courthouse, where I met the reporters for all of the papers. I am having the entire matter investigated by the FBI, as there may be a conspiracy to defraud the government in the collusive action between Galbreath and the contractor; but, in the meantime, there is no harm in laying this egg while I pass through Chicago.

Having spent the rest of the afternoon and evening in the office of my Special Assistant [Arthur A.] Sullivan, dictating on this dictaphone, I was again glad to climb into this luxurious compartment last night, having secured the same through the special influence of friend Sullivan. And now, having told my story, I must turn to the work of the day: Preparing from a briefcase full of materials, speeches for the impending encounters in Washington, Oregon, and California. Over long distance the director of the Speakers' Bureau said that there was also demand from Salt Lake [City] and [he] hoped I would fly over there to make two addresses, so it will be a strenuous period ahead, of which I shall try to keep you advised because of the momentous importance in American history of this campaign.

The intensity of hatred from the Reich is one of the most frightening things I see on the horizon, and yet I suppose it has always been present in campaigns—certainly in all the campaigns for great presidents, such as Jefferson, Lincoln, Wilson, and Roosevelt; and it is probably to be offset by the enormous reservoir of good will which, fortunately, is to be found in the hearts of the American people.

I do not like a fourth term, but there is no alternative to it. Roosevelt, alone, has the know-how of foreign affairs and even your Uncle George—

---

7. The "Ohio gang" consisted of President Harding's old cronies and poker-playing political friends from his days as an Ohio Republican leader, whom he brought to Washington, D.C., when he became President. Only Harry Daugherty became a member of the cabinet (attorney general), but a number of others received subcabinet and lesser appointments. They were noted for their "courthouse ring" morality.

arch-Republican that he is—recently said so when in Washington. He will vote for Roosevelt. That, perhaps, is the biggest news in this letter.

Affectionately,

Daddy [signed]

Thursday, 19 October 1944
The Gregorian, *en route* San Francisco

In a much needed few hours of respite from my own humble effort in the bitterest campaign in American history, I can bring you up to date on my peregrinations. . . .

After rolling across the country, sleeping, reading, preparing speech material, and gazing out once more at the vast territories of the Northern Pacific land grant which I had helped litigate to conclusion a few years ago, I arrived in Spokane on the evening of October 11th, sans band, sans greeters, and sans hope of any organization with which to do effective work during my week in my own state of Washington.

Ed Connelly, the United States attorney, dropped in on me at the Davenport Hotel, while I was unpacking. There was a Democratic rally at the Masonic Hall. Didn't I even know about it?

"Certainly not, but the National Committee advised Harry Huse, chairman of the State Speakers' Bureau, that I would be here tonight and available thereafter in Washington."

After some discussion, we decided to amble over to the meeting. After all, there is no efficiency among Democrats. We never deserve to win. It is only the people who are for us, in spite of all the blunders. So we went over to the rally—a small group of perhaps 150 people. Congressman Magnuson, candidate for the Senate, was speaking—a loose, not too well organized diatribe against Republicans and in defense of the New Deal.

"The meetings are all running small," Connelly whispered to me as we sat in the balcony and listened. "People are simply not turning out this year in large numbers. The war interests absorb them, I believe."

He introduced me to Joe Drumheller, who is Magnuson's campaign manager. Drumheller knew very well who I was and the greeting was not too cordial. It wasn't until later that I understood why, but I was greatly irritated at the moment. Drumheller has a deal on with Wallgren, [who is] running for the governorship, that if Wallgren wins the governorship and leaves the United States Senate, he will appoint Drumheller in his place. For this consideration, Drumheller is also managing Wallgren's campaign in Eastern Washington.

As a man of considerable national standing and also statewide reputation, it slowly began to dawn on me that I am a vague threat in the State of Washington to the politically ambitious—a definitely uncertain and unknown factor.

Magnuson finally spotted me in the gallery and, at the conclusion of his speech, said that he now had just discovered that I was in the audience and wished to introduce the "brilliant and able assistant attorney general from this state." So I went down stairs and up on to the stage for a moment.

It was not in me to make a speech under all the circumstances but, inasmuch as the Republican candidate for the vice presidency, Bricker, had just left town a day or so before, it was irresistible to remind them of the story of John W. Galbreath to which they listened in very great interest.

The greeting from Vic Meyer, long-time lieutenant governor of the State of Washington and one-time band master at a Seattle night club, was the most cordial of all because, of course, Vic recognizes that I will not run for lieutenant governor.

There was no invitation from Magnuson to join him at the hotel, nor from his campaign manager, Drumheller, so I walked out, after shaking hands with quite a number of people, and returned to the hotel.

The next morning, I saw Dave Cohn, now head of OPA in Spokane, and one of the ablest Democrats in the State of Washington. He was shocked at the reception I had received, . . . at Drumheller's stupidity the preceding evening, and at Magnuson's ineptness. He promptly called Seattle headquarters to protest. A telegram came back immediately inviting me to speak the following Saturday night at Seattle at a mass meeting for Senator Kilgore and at which all local candidates would appear. I accepted.

There was obviously, however, nothing to do in Spokane, although I had made myself available for two days in Eastern Washington. Clearly, the telegram to Harry Huse had been discussed by the master strategists Wallgren and Magnuson. Whereas my help and position in the state was much sought after in 1940 and my open letter to Steve Chadwick, published in the *P.I.*, was the factor which really defeated Chadwick and elected Wallgren—as all of the political critics of competent judgment clearly recognized—my help was not wanted this time. . . . I had acquired too much stature. I was a potential threat, prior to the primaries, when a lot of people were concerned as to whether I would run for the governorship, there having been many suggestions to that effect in the papers, [or] whether I would run for the United States Senate.

I confess to feeling somewhat depressed at finding myself *de trop*, politically, in the State of Washington when there was so much work to be done, [so] I turned my attention to the most pressing land acquisition problem in the country: The immense Hanford Project of the Du Pont Company for the manufacture of something of such great secrecy that nobody yet knows what is going on inside of the project. The area is 470,000 acres, including the protective belt of lease-hold lands. The Army's past practices on appraisal work . . . had borne a vicious crop here. Only 683 options have been taken out of a total of 2,077 tracts. Since I had raised the authorization for settlement of cases in a conference in Yakima, on April 24th, by 20 per cent, we had succeeded in settling 600 more, or thereabouts; had tried 77 cases; and have taken a terrific beating in every one of them, with 771 tracts remaining undisposed of.

Re-examination of the Army's appraisal work, by one of my own staff— a crack government appraiser—disclosed gross errors in the estimates of the Army appraisers. Valuations of grazing lands were based upon estimated grazing capacity instead of sales value. Valuations of houses were estimated upon grossly inaccurate cubic foot capacity of the structures without reference to the true value of the buildings. The owners had been imposed upon. There was nothing for me to do but confess error in court and ask for the continuation of all cases, and I set to work (at 5:00 in the morning of the second day) after several conferences, to draft a statement to the court explaining in advance to Judge [Lewis B.] Schwellenbach what I planned to do.

That statement was unique indeed and, of course, I will be charged by the Army with being purely political about it in order to be popular with the people in Southeastern Washington who were so grossly antagonized by the Army appraisals that the Hanford Project [has become] the liveliest political issue in the state, greatly capitalized upon by the Republicans. My information and my conclusions happened to mature before the election. So much the better, but it was pure accident. Having confessed error and described our services in the trial of cases for our client—the War Department—I announced that a far greater obligation than that to our client bound me upon the discovery of these facts; namely, the obligation of the Constitution of the United States to see that the property owners got just compensation. I would have no more cases tried on the basis of old appraisals.

In conclusion, I warned counsel not to set their sights too high because we would meet them in court if necessary. I also denounced in unequivocal terms a Republican jury before which our last cases had been tried— seven in number—in which ten of the jurors were Republicans and two were Democrats. One of the Republicans had put Dewey-Bricker buttons on every member of the jury except the two Democrats and had offered a button to counsel for the government, taunting him with his refusal to wear it. The verdicts were above the highest value expressed by any appraiser for the owners in three cases and at the highest level in all cases, being 70 per cent above the government appraisals. It was outrageous and I said so. If there is political ammunition in it for our side, so be it.[1]

I left that night on the Northern Pacific for Seattle, wondering just what the political boys would have to say on that side of the mountain.

I was soon informed. No sooner had I settled at the [Washington] Athletic Club than a call from Henneford reached me to explain, with profuse apologies, that the night meeting was overcrowded with speakers and that, when he had presented to the committee the accomplished fact of his invitation to me, they had challenged him to show how it could be done, crowding one more speaker into that crowded program. Magnuson, Wallgren and every congressional candidate wished to speak, including Hugh DeLacey, the Communist nominee for the First Congressional District. I can well imagine his comments upon the suggestion that I was to speak at that rally.

I assured Henneford that I quite understood; that there was nothing worse than a calendar that was too crowded; and that they had plenty on their hands with Senator Kilgore present. So, again, I had nothing to do except my own work.

After conferring with the head of my office in Seattle, I caught the 6:00 train for Vancouver, [British Columbia], to see your Aunt Pansy and Uncle David and look over the affairs of the T. A. Spencer Estate, of which I am a wandering executor. . . . English Bay, stretching away below us, brought back vividly those long afternoons of peace and quiet in which I had convalesced at the Spencer's house in the fall of 1941. . . .

Having checked with Seattle and found that there was still no work for me to do on the political front, I stayed over Monday and Pansy somehow managed to arrange to drive me down Tuesday morning in time to conclude the business in my office, which was light on this trip, before going to Everett to keep a speaking engagement there.

I forgot to mention that, in the sudden concentration of talent in Seattle, with Kilgore and me arriving on the same day, and Senator Truman scheduled to arrive three days later, there was so much major excitement that no speaker was available for a minor engagement at Everett in Snohomish County. . . .

. . . I had called on Kilgore before catching the train for Vancouver and he stepped out of a press conference to talk with me in the bedroom of his suite in the Olympic Hotel. He reported precisely what I had already observed: No organization at all. He had arrived at various places, coming up the coast, without anyone knowing that he was going to be

---

1. "Hanford Area Suits Settled," *Yakima Daily Republic*, 1 November 1944; "Government Settles 58 Land Cases; Agreements Based on Reappraisals of Property at Hanford," *Yakima Morning Herald*, 1 November 1944; "More Hanford Suits End," *Spokane Spokesman-Review*, 1 November 1944, in Littell scrapbook.

there, and had addressed meetings of very small proportions—75 to 125 people.

"The Republicans have all the organization and we have the cause and the candidate, but no organization," he said. "Their machine is clicking as smoothly as anything I have ever seen, from one end of the country to the other, and we have no organization at all." He thrust a telegram into my hand from headquarters at the Biltmore, asking him to stop at Salt Lake [City], but giving no time, giving no suggested meeting places, nor anything definite.

"I am afraid, we are all conducting a lot of one-man campaigns for the re-election of President Roosevelt," I said, and he heartily agreed. He is one of the fine liberal fighters in the United States Senate, but not a well organized man who follows through. He must be pushed back on the track frequently. . . .

So I had told Henneford, over the long distance telephone, when he reached me in Vancouver, that I would fill the engagement at Everett. Eating humble pie is good for all of us and I have eaten so much of it in my life that it really doesn't matter now. I was glad I took the engagement because I shook that crowd of earnest, solid, ordinary citizens from the rural county of Snohomish as they hadn't been shaken up before. I covered three principal points: The Roosevelt preparation for war; . . . the Republican hue and cry about the coddling of labor; . . . and Roosevelt and foreign policy.

Even Clarence Coleman, the state chairman from Everett, who was one of the old guards who must have decided against me upon my coming back into the state, was moved as I have not seen him moved and, as I arose to leave in order to catch the 11:30 train for Portland, he shook my hand with more warmth than he had ever done before, muttering over and over again that it was a fine, very fine, address and he was very grateful, etc., etc. . . .

Oregon was quite different. Here I was not a competitor to anyone. I was a foreigner in the state, as far as political competition was concerned, and a man of national standing. . . . A luncheon had been arranged that noon with a select group of lawyers and a few judges, but the unfortunate timing and general bad management of the speakers' arrangement resulted in my arriving on the same day when Senator Truman, the candidate for vice president, arrived. . . .

In this game, everything goes according to status. Quite aside from local prejudices, Senator Kilgore would have been enough to blanket me out in Seattle, and here, sure enough, the vice presidential candidate did so without any doubt. Even the newspapers follow this classification. . . .

I called on Senator Truman at the Multnomah Hotel, about 11:00 P.M., when I got back from [an] Oregon City meeting on Wednesday the 18th, and was most cordially received. Truman himself [took] me into the back room to extract a bottle of twelve year old scotch from a secret hiding place and had me pour a drink. In spite of better habits, I took it. There was a group of politicos in the room, among them our Senator Mon Wallgren, who got up and came across the room with the greatest gusto and pronounced warmth of greeting.

He is a small, smooth man. I supported him against Chadwick as the lesser of two evils. His record had not been bad, but he is still a small man. I listened patiently while he explained to Senator Truman that he was really going to be elected governor. He was whistling in the dark. I rather regret that I did not tell him so instead of letting Senator Truman be in any respect misled. I should also have told him quite bluntly that he will be elected governor if President Roosevelt carries Washington by 140,000 to 150,000 votes. . . .

I cleaned up work in my office, which is rapidly declining, subject however to the revival of 26,000 acres worth of condemnation cases to be filed on Lake Malheur. That will keep the boys busy for a while longer. . . .

24 October 1944
Later—Palace Hotel, San Francisco, California

. . . Let the record be perfectly clear. My time was available to the party in San Francisco, if they wanted it, but they hadn't wanted it. There were no requests. There was no response from Bill Malone, chairman of the organization in Northern California, so I went off with a clear conscience to the only home on the range I have ever known, for it is a home with these two blessed people, [Floss and Virgil Jorgensen], unique among human beings for their understanding and rich capacity for enjoyment.

A rainy day Saturday and a three hour sleep in the afternoon by myself knocked out the possibility of riding on Saturday, but the sun broke bright and clear on Sunday and we were off to the hills, . . . battling out the election issues as we went, for Virgil is a staunch Republican. PAC (Political Action Committee) and Sidney Hillman constitute one of the principal issues around this section with a deep conviction of their communist domination. I wonder if the word "Republican" was as devastating in its effect when pinned on anyone at the time of the American Revolution as the word "Communist" is today. The foundation for head-on conflict between extreme left and extreme right are surely shaping up even during this truce while the common enemy in the spearhead of Pan-Germanism is defeated. . . .

The next morning, since all good things must come to an end, Floss [and Virgil] Jorgensen drove me into the city, where I still was embroiled in the work of my office there and of Hawaii. . . . [My] representative in

Hawaii was present and John Boyle, chief appraiser, had just returned from there after an inspection of the worst and most difficult condemnation field under the American flag, where we regularly take a beating, in court and out of court. But I will not talk shop. My personal plans had precipitated more firmly in the rides with Virgil and Floss and we had discussed them quite frankly. I would either go up or out after the election. I would no longer remain as assistant attorney general, and I felt curiously happy about whichever way it came out. If the President does not see fit to appoint me to the cabinet, I shall be delighted to return to private practice, although the question as to whether that should be in New York, Seattle, Washington, D.C., or in California—and, if in California, whether in San Francisco or Los Angeles—remains wide open for fate to determine. . . .

. . . The appeal of the West is strong, and there I have Katherine in mind. Floss and Jorgie offer a haven for my family until I get on my feet elsewhere in the transitional state when we will be without income to speak of. It is a very comforting thought; there are loads of fresh vegetables and fruit there, a comfortable little cottage down the road from the ranch house, and [a] new world of fruit and flowers, hills and horses for Katherine, Jr., and Norman, Jr. And, I venture to say, that my abilities are sufficient to permit us to eat after I readjust myself to private practice. And now back to the political battle lines to see what, if anything, there is for me to do in the San Francisco area. I have been met with no brass band, not even telephone calls, so perhaps I shall enjoy three peaceful and quiet days, tending to my knitting in the Lands Division office. Good-bye now.

Affectionately,

Your Father [unsigned]

---

30 October 1944
Union Pacific, *en route* Salt Lake City, Utah

Dearest Katherine Mather:

. . . To resume my story: When I decided that I had better call at Democratic headquarters, knowing the inefficiency of operations these days and thinking it inadvisable to stand upon ceremony and wait for them to call me, it was promptly discovered that nobody knew I was here. "Except Bill Malone," I replied. "The telegram to him was dictated in my presence at the Speakers' Bureau in New York and he knew exactly when I was to be here."

I went to a cocktail party for Congressman [Franck R.] Havenner at the St. Francis Hotel and met many of the leading Democrats. Bill Malone, a bit sheepish about not having recognized my presence and, perhaps, conscious of the fact that he was using all public meetings to give addresses himself, called me to the platform after Havenner had said a word and I spoke for two or three minutes. Others expressed astonishment that I was there and that nobody knew about it, that there were meetings all around the place which I should have addressed during the days when I was there. . . .

With the abject apologies of the publicity director at the San Francisco headquarters of the National Democratic Committee echoing in my ears, . . . for failure to receive me properly and with assurances that I would be most warmly received and would be most helpful in Los Angeles, I flew off the next morning. The situation was precisely the same in Los Angeles. One Mike Fannigan was in charge. Like Bill Malone, he was busy making speeches, himself. These Irish in search of personal power beat anything on earth. The party must get rid of them and get down to the young men of conviction. Politics from now on will be a matter of conviction and not at all of personal manipulations of the old Farley type.

---

5 November 1944
N.Y. Central, *en route* Chicago to New York

I will not bore you with the work done in Los Angeles, consisting largely of reexamining the effect of my reorganizing my office there and placing it in charge of a new head last spring. . . .

Saturday passed with no campaigning engagements and not even a telephone call from the famous Irishman, Mike Fannigan, so that my only engagement in Los Angeles was on Sunday, the 29th, at the program for all candidates on Mr. Burke's radio network lasting one hour and a half. I had been advertised as the principal speaker. Helen Gahagan (Douglas) led off the procession, as usual, using slightly more than her allotment of time. She whispered to me as we sat in a circle of chairs in the studio that she was amazed to see me here; that nobody knew I was coming; that there [would have been] much work to do if my presence had been known. It was the same old story as in San Francisco. The information had been buried.

"Was it because of the stand I had taken for Wallace at the National Convention, helping to lead the California delegation away from its appointed leaders and Chairman Bob Kenny, the attorney general of California?" [I asked.]

Helen had not the slightest doubt that that had much to do with it. "You ought to see what they did to me," she said. "I would like to tell you about it." She had to go to another meeting and we parted there. She has assumed a national importance in this campaign by reason of the National Democratic Committee setting her off against Clare Luce, the vitriolic, indeed, vicious opponent of the President and the administration, [who is] running for reelection as a congresswoman. Helen has shown courage and capacity, but it is difficult to forgive her for not filing in her own district, where she would have had a harder fight, but could have been elected. She filed in a district where there was a very able colored man who could have been elected. If Helen were really sincere on the racial issue, she would have considered that fact. . . .

Burke took me to the train at 5:30 P.M., where I crawled into a roomette for a sound sleep before taking on whatever speaking was scheduled for Utah. . . .

In recounting the events which ensued at Salt Lake City, I must say that nowhere in the United States, within my experience, has the party a more vigorous and healthy status than in Utah. There, it comes more closely to what the party system was intended to be than anywhere in my experience. . . . The basic facts are that a great job is done for the party organization. Arrangements are made far in advance, publicity is given to approaching events and speakers—everything from newspaper and radio announcements to handbills distributed throughout the counties—and the events go off with a reasonable degree of *éclat*. . . .

The governor [Herbert B. Maw] and I had a very satisfactory visit the next morning at the capitol building in which, as an outside ambassador and at the suggestion of one or two of the managers of the campaign, I suggested that he now recognize some of the leaders who [had] opposed him in the primaries in 1940. They were fighting for the united party now.

He agreed. "I routed them," he said. "And when you win a liberal victory there is nothing else to do but go right down the line and throw the old guard out and put your supporters in. I did it."

I knew he had done it because there were too many enemies around the state. I suspected that he lacked any element of tact and even a reasonable capacity for compromise. "Any party always consists of a wide gamut of opinion, from left to right, don't you think?" I asked. "And if the party system is to prevail, we must hold those elements together after the battle for control within the party is over."

"I agree," the governor said, "and I think this would be a good time to recognize some of the men you refer to, who have opposed me, like Cal Rawlings and Joseph Wilson (secretary of the Utah Labor Council) and Frank Marvel (CIO). . . . I think it is time to bring them back into the fold and recognize them," the governor said. . . .

We talked about the National Committee [Against Persecution of the Jews] work and I brought him up to date on the board meeting which he had missed on October the 6th, and then we rode downtown together,

the governor delivering me to the Elks Club, where I was to make an
address at noon. I talked to him on the way down about representation
from the West in the cabinet, explaining to him, frankly, that while I was,
of course, greatly interested, nevertheless, I thought it unlikely that I
would be appointed, but that the principle should be established for
western representation and I thought [that] . . . telegraphing to the
President . . . now, before the election, was a very good idea.

He wholly agreed and went much further, saying that I ought to be the
attorney general and that he would do everything in his power to help. I
explained that that was in the lap of the gods, but that I was quite clear
in my decision either to go up or out. I would not remain much longer—
very definitely not longer under an attorney general whom I considered
one of the weakest and least competent men in the history of the United
States, with which Maw wholly and heartily agreed. . . .

I left Salt Lake at 6:00 P.M. that evening, with a real sense of
achievement. . . . Again, the roomette and a long sleep was welcome, but
not until after I had dropped into the club car and listened to Dewey's
most vitriolic address, in which the whispering campaign against the
President and this administration as communist-inspired, came out with
a whole charge of the Republican candidate. Obviously, the President was
dominated by Hillman and Hillman was dominated by the communists.
The Democratic Party was for sale to the highest bidder. . . . I do not have
the speech before me to bring home some of its passages, but here was
the new and deeper issue on the American front, the ugliest issue of all,
a frank appeal to race prejudice, although our country has been built on
foreign born. . . .

I am afraid, my dear, that there will be no escaping these problems in
your lifetime and, probably not in mine. . . .

Wednesday night, 15 November 1944

Perhaps the best news received since we returned from New York a week
ago, the day after the election, came by the channel of sheer gossip.
"Doddie" Glassford, the wife of Admiral Bill—who last October was sent
to London— . . . had called Katherine several times. Finally, the two
ladies had lunch together and "Doddie" read to Katherine extensive
excerpts from Bill's letters from London. They seemed extraordinarily
indiscreet but extraordinarily illuminating. Bill was on a committee
appointed to set up procedures for the handling of conquered Germany.
Their plan was to be set within the framework of broad instructions from
the State Department to "render Germany impotent."

The "Morgenthau Plan," which has ricocheted around the country in
spite of the President's prompt repudiation of it, and which subsequently

became a major political weapon specifically utilized by candidate Dewey, . . . is now definitely a thing of the past. The details of the plan are immaterial anyway. The heart of the entire matter is, indeed, "to render Germany impotent" if we are faithful to the interests of our children in the next generation and the world in general. What a relief it was to learn that just such instructions had been given!

The Surplus Property battle was resumed immediately upon our return to Washington. The Jesse Jones–Will Clayton–Jimmy Byrnes axis had been busy laying plans while the rest of us were campaigning and, to our utter amazement, it leaked from the White House (deliberately, I think, in order to bring public reaction) that the three-man board was to consist of Clayton's executive assistant, Sam H. Husbands, Colonel Joseph P. Woodlock, and a man named [James C.] Shepherd, the complete Clayton set-up.[1] I took his scalp once in August, and now it seems that he was surviving in alter-ego. As my informant within the National Association of Real Estate Boards advised me, "Jesse Jones has got his hooks into surplus property disposal and he's going to keep them there."

P.M. sounded off with a blast of condemnations, and the liberals went to work, many of them telephoning me. I suggested that they stop firing shot-guns in the air and drill their shots on the target [and agree] upon three men for a panel of 3 to 6 which would meet with the approval of labor, farm interests, and the rest of our heterogeneous gang of liberals struggling for the welfare of the country within the executive branch of the government. They did so. I had to stay on the sidelines because executive decisions were involved and I did not wish to cross swords directly with Jimmy Byrnes. It would have been fatal for the President's first appointment after the election to be of a reactionary character, for the liberals had put him over. Telegrams and letters poured in.

With Russell Smith of the Farmers' Union operating as a central clearing house, it was finally agreed between CIO, AFL and the Farmers that the following three men would be urged:

Cliff Durr (FCC Commissioner) Chairman of the Board
Sumner Pike (SEC Commissioner) Liberal Republican from Maine
[John B.] Jack Hutson (formerly head of the Commodity Credit
    Corporation, Dept. of Agriculture)

These are not wild-eyed liberals, but sound, practical men. I wonder how many—if any—we will net out of this drive.

Drew Pearson, in his column today, pointed out that, due to Jimmy Byrnes opposition, such outstanding New Dealers as myself and two

---

1. I. F. Stone, "Jones–Clayton Appointments Held Up; Protests to White House Keep 'Big Business' Names Off Surplus Property Board," *P.M.*, 15 November 1944.

others had not been named. [2] I called him to tell him he was wrong—that I had refused the job—which he said he knew well but wished to keep the pressure on the President and against Byrnes. He also stated that Senator Barkley advised the President, today, that the appointments submitted by Byrnes probably would not be approved if the President sent them over. The liberals hammered on that point: That the first event after the election should not be a defeat for the President. . . .

Saturday night, 18 November 1944

The attorney general sent for me at 11:30 A.M. this morning. I had a feeling as I walked down the corridor toward his office that this was the "pay-off," and it was.

Ugo Carusi, his administrative assistant, and his two assistants in the big antechamber, motioned me to go right on in. I think they knew it, too. I opened the door and walked into his office without knocking, and as he glanced up from his desk, I sat down in the chair across from him while he put down his pen and leaned back.

The words of this most interesting conversation are given as accurately as I can recall them which, of course, is never precisely correct. They flow too fast. However, the sense of them is exactly correct, and they were as follows:

"Norman, I'm sure you must realize, as I do, that it is time for us to part company. Our relations have been strained for a long time—I am sure you must have felt it as well as I do—is that correct?"

"Entirely correct," I replied.

"I have no confidence in you, personally," he continued. [I tried] as hard as I could to keep perfectly calm in what was obviously to be a complete joinder of issue between us. At long last, I felt my gorge rising. I never knew just what "gorge" was, but I do know what was meant by that phrase, and it has to do with the sharp increase of heart-beats as anger spreads all over the system. Anger and contempt for the man across the desk spread over me. He could have said there were great "personal" differences between us—incompatibility. He did not. He chose to say that he had lost personal confidence in me, using an expression which was slightly of a smear character, with its implications of dishonesty. In the light of the record—his record compared to mine—it was like the use of [Joseph] Goebbels' half-truth or falsehood to create an impression known to be untrue, like "the Poles attacked Germany."

---

2. Drew Pearson, "Washington Merry-Go-Round," *Washington Post*, 16 November 1944, in Littell scrapbook.

I sat there and took it, as he continued.

"You are not loyal to me, and I have known it for a long time. Every member of my staff has told me of your remarks: That I did not dare to ask for your resignation; that I was afraid to ask for your resignation."

"Those are false statements, Mr. Attorney General," I said. While there is no doubt whatever as to the basic fact that no loyalty was lost on him, because it has been forfeited a long time ago by his own conduct, it is quite impossible that every member of his staff should have quoted me. Only with Charlie Fahy, the solicitor general, have I been frank, by way of explaining my resistance. Apparently, Charlie Fahy told "papa." Even so, the statement was hopelessly exaggerated.

"As far back as when Jim Rowe was here—and even Matthew McGuire and now Jim McGranery—it was the same. You just don't fit in here and you are entirely disloyal to me. I ran into your remarks as far away as the Pacific Coast, where you had made remarks to lawyers there which were recounted to me."

I felt like saying that that was "mutual." I had run into his remarks, too. Technically, as a matter of ordinary executive principle, he is quite right. When a subordinate and a superior cannot get on together, there is no alternative but for the former to resign. In fact, I have long thought of doing so. But here, where complete personal loyalty was given to the attorney general as long as he deserved it, and was only forfeited by his conduct in endeavoring to have me settle the Savannah Shipyards case for his bosom friend, Tommy Corcoran; and when and where on every difference between us which has arisen since then, matters of public policy were at issue, in which my position defended the public interest as against his apathetic or supine acquiescence with the opposition, I do not think the general rule holds good.

He said, "You certainly would not wish to remain under such circumstances in view of this relationship between us."

"I might, Mr. Attorney General. I wish to think the matter over."

"It is, of course, reasonable for you to have time to think it over, and I would like to know by Wednesday [November 22nd] as I am leaving town that day and would like to know before I go. I would like to have you leave by January 1st." . . .

"Can you let me know by Wednesday?" the attorney general carried on.

"I cannot say," I replied. "If my mind is made up by Wednesday, I will be very happy to let you know. If it is not made up by Wednesday, I will not let you know. In other words, when I have made up my mind on this matter, I will tell you."

"Do you mean that you might wish to stay on under such circumstances as you and I both recognize in the relationship between us, when I have no personal confidence in you—when I appointed you to this position?"

"You did not appoint me to this position. The President of the United States appointed me to this position."

"But I assigned you, and I am the head of this Department," he replied.

"Let us assume a hypothetical case," I said. "Let us assume that I have no confidence in you. It might be then that I would feel it my duty to continue."

Implicit in that was a lot of unsaid additional thought; namely, the public interest might demand that I stay there to watch an attorney general who, in my opinion, could not be trusted . . . at least as far as my little corner of the big Department was concerned, to prevent him from placing a Tommy Corcoran appointment in my place, where millions and millions of dollars are distributed constantly and where there is plenty of opportunity for bad settlements, as in the Savannah Shipyards case. I might have said I will not throw my fine loyal staff in the Lands Division to the wolves by getting out, but I was resolved to make no commitment in this interview and nothing which he could go away and quote as nasty or insubordinate, so I left my question just as stated.

He snorted rather scornfully at my question as if to say "the insolence of this fellow, thinking for one moment that whether or not he had confidence in the attorney general was of any importance!" But he did not endeavor to explore the point further, and I would have declined to do so.

I neglected to say that, earlier in the conversation, at the time when I was being castigated for my attitude toward the attorney general, as if to offset this and, perhaps, move the way for a more amicable parting, he had said, "I must say in all fairness that I have to commend you for the job you have done in the Lands Division. I really think you have done a most commendable job up there."

I smiled broadly across the desk at him and, in fact, I was smiling during almost all of this interview in a way which must have been a little disconcerting for him, but at this point I smiled very broadly and said "That is very gracious of you, Mr. Attorney General. It is good of you to recognize what everybody around Washington knows about the job in the Lands Division."

"I'm not being sarcastic," he said, a little later in the conversation, returning once more to the job done in the Lands Division. "When I say that you have done a commendable job in the Lands Division I really mean it." I caught a glimpse of the man's enormous conceit in that fragment, for he had expected me to accept his first comment about my commendable job, gratefully, and appreciatively, as a matter of salvaging something nice out of an unpleasant interview. Papa had spanked, but papa had also said a kind word. When I, in effect, laughed at him and said sarcastically, myself, that I was grateful for his appreciating what everybody else knew, he looked a little startled as if he didn't quite get it. And when he came back to the subject later, he did so to explain that he had not been "sarcastic"—he meant it! I had done a "commendable job." He wanted me to appreciate his sincerity.

"I did not for one moment assume that you were being sarcastic, Mr. Attorney General," I said. "It would be strange, indeed, if you did not recognize the job which had been done in the Lands Division."

"I consider that some of the things you have done have been adverse to the public interest," he said.

"Would you be good enough to specify what things I have done which were adverse to the public interest?" I replied.

"No, I will not. I will not go into the particulars. I rest this matter entirely upon the personal relationship between us without getting into specific charges."

"Have you anything to say now?" the attorney general asked.

"Not a thing," I said, smiling at him. "I will think the matter over."

"Can you let me know by Wednesday?" he repeated again. I feel quite sure he and his colleagues, Tommy Corcoran in particular, have pondered over this thing for a long time, and now that they have decided to act— immediately after the election—this thing must be railroaded through as fast as it can. Out by January 1st, with all that it implies: Breaking up one's home, after six years of conspicuous service, [because one is] in the way of a man of piss-ant stature, faithless to the public interest. [His] comments struck me with full force.

"As I said, Mr. Attorney General, I will let you know when I have made up my mind and not before that," and I rose to go, and walked over to the door.

"Just a minute," he called after me. "I am not through. Are you in a hurry?" with that Philadelphia raised-eyebrow inquiring look, as if I had been a little rude.

"Not in the least," I said. "I was through, and I thought you were. I will stay as long as you like." And I walked back to the desk and sat down again across from him.

"Now, I think we ought to part as amicably as possible—" and then he caught himself and said, "Of course, we cannot part as friends, I assume."

"No, I quite agree. We cannot do that, Mr. Attorney General," I said.

"But we can agree to disagree, can we not? You agree with me, don't you, that it would be better all around if we part in—" he was obviously groping for words and I cannot remember just what he did say in the end, but the effect was as if he said, "part in a peaceable manner without stirring up a public ruckus over this incident." "Do you agree with me on this?" he concluded in a most honeyed voice.

"I said I would think the whole matter over, Mr. Attorney General. I have no statement to make now. I do not know what attitude I shall take."

He fumbled with his pencil and sat silent for a moment in the feebleness of a weak man who asks for an easy way out of a tough situation and does not quite know how to deal with a strong man—as indeed he never has.

"Is that all, Mr. Attorney General?" I asked.

He replied in the affirmative and I rose, and, turning my back on his desk, I walked out.

Sunday night, 19 November 1944

These twenty-four hours have been exceedingly thoughtful ones on the part of Katherine and me. . . . I went to see Joseph Davies at the big palatial home where he resides known as "Tregeron" on Macomb Street. I had wanted to see him for a long time, but I particularly wanted his advice on this situation. He was not awake when I arrived and had not been feeling well, his valet said, so I sat and read the *New York Times* insisting that he be not waked up, but I was taken up to his bedroom shortly before 12:00, where his butler was laying the fire in the fireplace. Davies was sitting up in bed with a squirrel-skin cape around him as protection against early-morning chill in the big high-ceilinged bedroom.

"I just can't take it any more, Norman," he said, after greeting me most cordially. "[I] made a speech in New York the other night (the anniversary of the founding of the Soviet Republic). Any added nervous tension starts up my stomach troubles again and I have to take it easy for quite a while to get over it."

I well remembered his story of the trial of the Henry Ford case, in 1926, on which he had wrecked his health.[1] He lived for weeks on bread and milk: As I told him in Florida, the two worst things he could have possibly eaten. Ulcers, of course, resulted during the terrific tension of that case. The case made him a millionaire several times. And then, his first wife—before he went to Russia as ambassador—raised the ante several times. He had been to expensive doctors galore . . . and I could see by the breakfast tray that he was still groping in the dark—that is, the doctors were! The truth was that it didn't work; that, with extraordinary vitality, he still could not get well.

"Of course, I'm an old man, Norman," he said, smiling with a youthfulness of expression and a light in the eyes which belied the fact. "I am 69 years old." . . .

I told him that, when I telephoned to him yesterday, I wanted his advice,

---

1. Joseph E. Davies was counsel for the taxpayers in the Henry Ford stock valuation case, 1924–27.

but in [the] twenty-four intervening hours, I had made up my mind and didn't need it. I also said that I had tried to see him when he came back from Florida, just because I wanted to see him and hoped the desire was mutual—which it seemed to be—except that he had been taken to the hospital with the same old trouble. The second time I wanted to see him, some few weeks ago, was about the matter of returning to private practice—whether in the East or the West—he was out of town. This, the third time, was still a different errand, for I had been fired in the Department of Justice and now had no intention of leaving. [In] fact, [I] had decided to refuse to resign. I said I would still appreciate his suggestions, however.

I wish I had that conversation on a record. It is impossible to summarize it adequately. A lifetime of rich and varied experience was packed into it on the question of how to handle the Biddle controversy. His advice, in effect, was as follows:

There were two courses to follow and the decision was a purely personal one, which I alone could make. I would, of course, in any event reject Biddle's mandate to let him know by Wednesday and get out by January 1st, but Biddle was so anxious for peace, he was quite sure, that I could dictate my own terms, and should do so as far as the time of leaving is concerned, entirely at my own convenience some months from now. Furthermore, Biddle should write me a letter of strong appreciation of my fine work, my integrity and my services to the country in directing the Lands Division during the time of war. Such a letter would be written by way of accepting my resignation. This, No. 1 course, would probably be better from the point of view of my going into practice upon leaving the Department.

The second course was to stay and fight, to refuse to resign . . . (I had already reviewed with him some of the principal instances of my relations with Biddle. . . .)

"This will make a national figure of you without a doubt, if you intend to go into politics or keep on in public life. It will be a good thing to do from your personal point of view but, knowing the Chief (the President) as I do, I do not think you will become attorney general that way. He is not like that. He does not ever want to hurt anybody and he will not remove Biddle on the showing that you could make. He doesn't remove people that way."

"But there is no place to kick him upstairs to," I said. "You know how Biddle is regarded at the White House, I am sure. There might be an ambassadorship, I suppose."

"No, he wouldn't take the ambassadorship," Davies said. "He is aiming directly at the Supreme Court of the United States. Your resistance would, at least, knock him out of the Supreme Court of the United States. I believe he could never be appointed to that position after what you have to say, but I don't think the President would remove him as attorney general."

Davies might be right but, of course, he does not know the whole story within the Department, nor could he evaluate the reaction on the Hill, where there is a great deal of contempt for Biddle. The President will have to work with the Hill from now on. It will be the most important relationship in government from the point of view of establishing the peace. Nevertheless, he is right in his comment on the President's temperament, and he illustrated it by a conflict between a naval intelligence officer and a high Army officer when he was ambassador to Russia. The President sided with the right man, but the right man was subsequently removed by Army processes. Neither of the contestants benefited by the struggle.

I wish I had particularly Davies' full comments on the practice of law and why I should go West without any question whatsoever. "Don't think for a moment of settling in the East," he said. "You couldn't stand it here. The East is decadent. They have no response to moral values. They are like the French—'c'est la vie!'

"In the West, the people respond quickly to a sense of moral values. California, particularly, is the state of opportunity. There is great response there and great opportunity. You can't fail. They can't lick you. You will succeed under any circumstances; it doesn't matter where you go. You will have more business than you can handle and more money that income tax laws will let you keep. How are you fixed, financially?" he paused to interrupt his line of thought.

"Just my salary. That's all," I replied.

"If you need money, let me know. I'll let you have whatever it takes to get you started out there." It was a grand statement for which I felt very grateful. He had already said, in the course of this discussion of my personal position at present, "I like you. I believe in you. I will do anything I can for you."

"Of course," he said, "if you go into a big fight with Biddle, while it will increase your national position, it will not be helpful in respect to big law business of the kind which will really give you income. They will shy away from you as being alienated from the Department of Justice with which they will probably have to do business."

I said that I was afraid that I was already marked as far as big business was concerned, having fought Standard Oil Company on the Elk Hills controversy and the Clayton crowd on Surplus Property. My position was fairly well known. Anyone who was praised by *P.M.* would be a marked man for big business.

"The thing to do is to go out and make your money and then come back into public life," Davies said. And he proceeded to tell how he had done it, himself. When he ran for the Senate in Wisconsin,[2] he had $50,000

---

2. Davies was the unsuccessful Democratic candidate from Wisconsin for the U.S. Senate in 1916.

committed for his campaign, and most of it was cancelled on him by the boys who had the money, because he would not drop Keeney, whom he had employed to head the investigation of the packers. Keeney, himself, had been the subject of a controversy in the Pinchot feud and had been dropped after fighting a winning battle on principle, to which he drew an analogy to my case. Keeney had gone West and had never amounted to a great deal but had been brought back by Davies, who was, along with [Joseph P.] Tumulty, "President Wilson's bright young man."

"They will get you every time unless you are independent," Davies said. "They got me in Wisconsin. I would not withdraw Keeney who did a splendid job on the Packers Association and broke them up, but my financial support was withdrawn in Wisconsin, and I was defeated for the Senate. I had about $30,000 of that money that I had to pay back, anyway, and I set to work to do it. I did it. I worked hard as a lawyer to make money for my family and I did it, and then the Ford suit in 1926 gave me plenty." It was that which had made him a millionaire.

"I wouldn't do it over again any differently," he said. "Of course, now is a bad time for you to make a pile. We can't even keep our fees. I don't want $100,000 fees because I can't keep them. Taxes take it all. You would have a hard time saving up money now, but that situation will change when the tax situation is improved on earned income."

Well, that was the gist of it. His advice on going West was most warming—because that is probably what I wanted to do down in my heart, anyway. We would all be happier there. Katherine Mather said today, as she has frequently said, "I want to go West, Daddy." She is thinking of horses and outdoor things. She loves riding. In fact, we have put her in a children's riding class every Saturday noon, and I rode with her last Saturday, although I despise these Eastern saddles and the awkward position one has to take—so different from the comfortable easy riding position of the Western saddle, with long stirrups and a high pommel.

I could not help but think of the irony of Davies' situation as I went down the big, broad stairway in his palatial home—a sick old man, lying in baronial grandeur. He had made his pile, but had ruined his health. He couldn't escape from the shackles which limited him to the quietest sort of existence, in order to preserve his life. . . .

Tuesday, 21 November 1944

. . . I picked Sam [Rosenman] up at the White House and we drove down to a seafood restaurant. He had discussed the matter with the President this morning as a result of advice over the telephone, Sunday, from Katherine while I was visiting Ambassador Davies, as to the request for my resignation.

"The President was not consulted in advance," Sam said. "he knew nothing about it except that he had received a memorandum from Biddle advising that he had requested your resignation on the grounds of 'personal incompatibility.'"

"If it's a fair question," I said, "did the President react at all to your inquiry?"

"No. He seemed to be very thoughtful about the whole matter. I told him that, as far as 'personal incompatibility' was concerned, that I felt sure it had commenced when you refused to settle a case which Biddle wanted you to settle for Tommy Corcoran, and that your relationship had probably deteriorated as a result of that incident." I was glad he got that point in, and I told him that I was making a memorandum of all such points and I intended to send a copy to the President as I sent it to the attorney general, although with great regret on my part because the President [should] not be burdened with such trivia. And yet, there was no escape from it. He had, by executive order,[1] invited the submission of Department controversies to him before they are aired in public. I would, therefore, comply with the order.

I outlined the general strategy agreed upon, unless Sam advised strongly against it, including the breaking of the information publicly, Biddle's request for my resignation, my refusal to resign, and the writing of letters from Senate committees to the President.

"I suppose I ought to advise you, as counsel for the President, not to cause him this big headache, but I can't do so. I think you may be saving him a bigger headache by exposing this situation now."

"That is exactly my view," I replied. "I think the present situation in the Department of Justice has potentialities of major scandal with a weak and vain man at the head of the Department seemingly completely [under] the influence of Tommy Corcoran."

Sam was especially delighted with my reply to Biddle when he said that surely I would not wish to remain in the Department when he lacked personal confidence in me. . . . That was the strongest remark I had made, as I told Sam, because I did not wish to appear insolent or insubordinate. I would give him the works later, in written form.

"I am afraid I cannot deter you from this course of action," Sam said. "I would do exactly the same thing if I were in your shoes. I do not see how you could do anything else."

He also said that the President was going right ahead with the

---

1. On 21 November 1942, President Roosevelt sent a letter to each federal department and agency, requiring them to submit disagreements to the OWI for clearance. When Jones and Wallace failed to do so and aired their differences publicly, he issued Executive Order No. 9361, 15 July 1943, which abolished the BEW and curbed Jones's powers over the RFC's subsidiary corporations.

Husbands and Shepherd appointments to the Surplus Property Board. There was nothing he could do about it. He had exhausted his efforts to get more liberal appointments. He was up against Jimmy Byrnes and Bernard Baruch. They would have the liquidating bankers' point of view on surplus property, not a long-term social viewpoint directed at employment. That is the battle of the day. It is as simple as that.

I telephoned Harley Kilgore after leaving Sam off at the White House and caught him just as he was leaving for Ferguson's office. He was very much pleased at Sam's reaction, which paralleled his own.

The rest of the day was spent working on the memorandum to Biddle, with a brief interlude for dinner and making a pair of stilts for Norman, Jr. Now the younger members of the family are equipped for any flood and they are the envy of the neighborhood.

It is midnight so I am signing off.

Wednesday night, 22 November 1944

Ugo Carusi told me to come up to the attorney general's office at 3:00. I said there was nothing to discuss, unless he wished to reconsider the request for my resignation as I was reducing my answer to him to writing and it was not completed. The attorney general, himself, rang me upon the inter-communicating system a few minutes later and I said the same thing, whereupon he ordered me to come up.

Not wishing to disobey, I did so. "Your answer is ready, I presume," he said.

"As I told you, Mr. Attorney General, I am reducing it to writing and it is not done. I will hand it to you as soon as I possibly can."

"Well, you know what the answer is. Why can't you state it?"

"Because, as I said, I prefer to give it to you in writing."

"Well, it's dictated, isn't it?"

"Substantially, but not all."

"You can certainly finish in two hours."

"I cannot do so. I would be glad to if I could. It will be done, I think, by Friday, the 24th, but whenever it is done, I will hand it to you."

"It will have to be done in two hours," he immediately said, or words to that same effect. "You realize that you are facing the difference between resignation and being fired."

"No. I did not," I said. "You, yourself, recognized when I was given until today to think over my answer that that ought to be enough time, but possibly it could be extended. It is not enough time in view of my written statement of my case."

"I shall have to proceed to take further steps in the event that your answer is not here in two hours," he said.

"And what might those steps be?" I asked.

"I shall get in touch with the President and get him to dismiss you." At least, he was lawyer enough to recognize that he, himself, did not have that power, as the assistant attorney generals are appointed by the President to serve "at the pleasure of the President."

"You have discussed this with the President?" I asked.

"Yes, several times."

"How recently?"

"Within the last few days."

"And the President approved?" I asked.

"The President does approve."

I felt sure that he was a liar. Sam Rosenman had told me, at lunch the preceding day, that he had talked with the President that morning at his bedside and that the President had indicated he had had no discussions or advance notice from Biddle except a memorandum stating that my resignation had been requested. This is more apt to be true as typical Tommy Corcoran technique. He knows the President is busy, tired, and not too well. Present him with an accomplished fact and get the business out of the way. . . . There must be some very real pressure on Biddle to clean Littell out of there.

"You will have to pursue whatever course you deem proper, Mr. Attorney General," I said. "My statement will not be completed until about Friday but, in any event, you will have it immediately when it is done and not before that. In the meantime, you must take whatever line of action you prefer." And I got up and walked out.

Friday, 24 November 1944

Anna Boettiger called me at home today from the White House in the morning and said she had had a telephone conversation with the President, and would like to talk over the situation with me and with Katherine. Could we come to the White House at 3:00?

Drew Pearson's story of my parting with Biddle was in the morning "Merry-Go-Round."[1] I had not given it to him. He got it from the other side and called here to confirm what had happened. It was a fine boost for my past record. The Associated Press dispatch was also on the front page of the [Washington] Post[2] to the effect that my resignation had been asked

---

1. Drew Pearson, "Washington Merry-Go-Round," Washington Post, 24 November 1944.

2. "'Important Matter of Policy'; Senate Group to Investigate Biddle Move to Oust Littell," Washington Post, 24 November 1944; "Biddle Accused," Facts on File, vol. 4 (22–28 November 1944), p. 377K; "May Investigate Rift on Littell," P.M., 26 November 1944.

but that the Truman Committee was going to investigate the matter, with a statement by Senator Kilgore, one of the members, that they were going to the bottom of the whole matter because they could not have witnesses punished for testifying frankly before them.

We decided, as we drove to the office, that I would go to the White House alone. As Katherine said, "This is no social event. She can't have us in there like a couple of country bumpkins after so long a silence. She did not even return my telephone call after the election—which is not important because calls are lost frequently—but still you should go alone."

I did. I was shown to the Red Room and Anna soon came in. We sat down at opposite ends of the divan, facing each other. I lit a cigar, while she lit up a cigarette.

She had just heard a passing remark of the President on Tuesday evening, speaking to someone else, which indicated that the situation had arisen [on] Tuesday, the 21st, but she had had no chance to talk with the President. She saw the Drew Pearson column in the "Washington Merry-Go-Round" and the *Washington Post* article and telephoned to the President to suggest that, while this was really government business and she would not intrude unless he really wished it, she knew us and would do so if the President wished—talking the whole matter over with us. She then proceeded to tell me her whole position, as she understood it, and that of the President.

"The President told me to tell you that, when he was undersecretary of the Navy under Josephus Daniels, he had resolved that, if ever there was a disagreement on policy with his chief, he would resign before it became a real disagreement. At the slightest shadow of a suggestion of such a disagreement on policy, he would tender his resignation."

"Is that all he said about the matter, Anna?" I asked.

"That was all he said." I invited her to go on with whatever she had to say and I would make my reply after she had finished. So she continued: "You and Katherine told me you had expected to resign and go back to the practice of law," she said. "If only you had tendered your resignation after the election, before Biddle had any chance to do this, it would have been so much better for your personal position, for the children and for everyone. The incident would not have arisen."

I interjected, "That was not exactly a promise I made you, Anna, to retire and go back to private practice. It wasn't a commitment, you know."

I was already shocked at her Roosevelt approach to an easy way out—anything to save trouble and an incident—but I would advise her more fully on that score presently.

"Oh, no, of course not," Anna said, "but I was just thinking how much easier that would have been since you knew about all your disagreements with Biddle. You have told me about them before. It is impossible for you to get on together. This publicity is most unfortunate, and now the Senate Committee is interested in it and Father is in an extremely awkward position. He has to support his cabinet members as long as he is here. He just cannot do anything else but that."

I can't remember all that she said in that opening statement but, when she had finally finished, I said, "Please tell your father, Anna, that I agree with him one hundred per cent about what he said regarding Josephus Daniels and the duty to resign on a disagreement as to policy. If Josephus Daniels were my chief there would be no possible question about it. He is a great man and an intimate friend of mine whom I greatly admire and thoroughly trust. This is not that case."

"Furthermore, please tell the President that I recognize the ordinary rule that every administrator knows: Personal difficulties can rise to the point where personalities must separate, quite irrespective of the merits of any issues between them. Always, in such case, the junior must go. It is the same in a private corporation, or a public corporation: Our organizations are institutionalized and there must be that measure of order. However, this is not that case. I am not to be held accountable, as one who can't get along with his chief, or who has personal difficulties, if all of my difficulties stem from questions of principle which involve the basic integrity of the Department of Justice. Such is the case."

Anna did not seem to be impressed with that. An appeal to high principles seemed almost too inconvenient. They did not solve the problem.

"I suppose your father would be most interested if he had a Daugherty in the Department of Justice as attorney general. He would want to discover that, would he not?" I asked.

That had sufficient shock in it to wake her up. "Of course," she said, as if the significance of the problem hit her with full force, but then she added, "He would have to be pretty bad. You have told me about Tommy Corcoran's influences and things like that—."

"The question would seem to be: Just how bad does he have to be to be bad enough to remove? Is that it, Anna?" (She had known the story of Tommy Corcoran's effect on Biddle trying to settle the Savannah Ship-yards case for two years.)

It was obvious that she didn't think that Biddle was "bad enough" to be bad enough. "He is no good, Anna, and your father ought to perform a housecleaning there. My own personal fortunes are utterly immaterial because I shall go out anyway before long, but the President ought not to tolerate this man any longer."

"I know how Father is," Anna said, "and you do too. He will not make an issue. As long as Biddle is there as a member of the cabinet, he is there and Father will support him."

There is the greatest of all Roosevelt flaws: That fatal weakness for not facing a personal issue. He never faced the issue of the great injustice between his own wife and his own mother, all the years they were living together, and when mother exerted a heartbreaking tyranny over wife. He never faced a personal issue in his cabinet. When, he did, the personal resentment seemed to have accumulated on the wrong side, in favor of Jesse Jones, and he knocked Wallace out of the Economic Warfare Board. Here was another lesser situation in which the liberal was pitted against all of the forces that wanted to get rid of him. What was he going to do with this one?

Anna merely groped for some grand strategy. When I told her the story of how my resignation had been requested and of the later chapter on Wednesday—of how Biddle had threatened to fire me—she was, at last, shocked—or, perhaps, I should say she became acutely conscious of how the situation would look if the President backed up Biddle and fired me, as Biddle obviously [had] requested him to do. . . .

"That was incredibly rotten in handling," Anna said, or words to that effect, which I can't exactly recall. "You should have had all the time you needed in which to make your plans and change."

"Furthermore, Anna, the language used: He did not have 'personal confidence' in me. Do you think I am going to leave the government with the shadow of that cast over my children and my family just because a son-of-a-bitch like Biddle cares to use a slight slur or sneer upon his asking for my resignation?"

"But, somehow, we must get the personal side of this problem solved," Anna carried on. "If we had Biddle eat crow and plenty of it and give you all the time you needed to make your adjustment, could you not, then, resign and solve it that way?"

"I am making a statement of my case in answer to Biddle in a memorandum which I intend to send to the President.[3] It will be done tomorrow morning. I do not think the President should decide anything until he sees that. He is certainly interested in the inside workings of his Department of Justice, I am sure."

"How long is the memorandum?" Anna asked, with the practicability of a tired Washington mind. . . .

"The memorandum will have to be as long as it has to be, Anna," I said. "It will embrace the facts. You can read it, if you like, when it comes over to the President. I am assuming he is interested in the inside operation of his Department of Justice and, while I know the tremendous burden he is carrying of military and diplomatic operations throughout the world, still, he will appreciate, as any executive does, that there are occasionally

---

3. I. F. Stone, "Truman Group Probes Biddle-Littell Dispute; Both Men Asked to Submit Written Reports," *P.M.*, 28 November 1944.

times when a personnel problem must intrude itself onto the higher executive level, even at the cost of a little time. If for no other reason, I am entitled to that much consideration after six years of loyal service. I think you certainly must know that no one has been more steadfastly loyal to your father than I have been."

"But just the same," I said, "a 'job' has been done on me with the President. I have not seen him for two years, due to his illness, and other people have—Ickes, for example."

"I don't think he's ever said a thing," Anna said.

"Why, he's even done a job on you, Anna," I said, laughing.

"He has never said a word to me, although we see a great deal of the Ickeses." That statement was sufficiently revealing in itself. Anna sees a great deal of the Ickeses and we have not seen Anna for quite a long time. Influences do not need to be obvious. They can be quite subtle. Anna seemed so sure that Mr. Ickes had said nothing against me.

"Would it surprise you to know, Anna," I said, "in a conversation with Biddle in regard to Norman Littell, not long ago before the election, Ickes said, 'Why don't you fire the son-of-a-bitch?' and Biddle replied, 'I can't. He's too strong?'" If I had given the complete statement, I would have added, 'too strong at the White House,' but I did not wish to say that to Anna.

Anna seemed shocked at that or, perhaps, she's putting on a little bit of an act. There's no question that she is completely in the other camp. . . . In any event, she was wholly and completely concentrating on getting the problem out of the way for the President, and that's all. She even remarked that there seemed to be a memorandum with "particulars" in it but she hasn't seen it. . . .

. . . She described the President's position very correctly (and to Katherine's very great amusement when I told her, later):

"The President is in a trap in this matter," Anna said.

"He certainly is, Anna," I replied, "and I think you ought to advise him not to get allied with Biddle in this particular battle because Biddle is going to come out very badly. It would only hurt the President to be with him when the shooting starts."

I could see, so clearly, the practical Roosevelt mind trying to squirm out of this situation. If the President supports Biddle and fires me, the rage of the country will be directed at the President as well as at Biddle. If he doesn't support Biddle and fire me, he is, inferentially, leaving me in the office of assistant attorney general to attack Biddle, with notice that I am going to attack and have refused to resign.

Anna came back, again and again, to her feminine day-dreams about solving the personal problems, first. "Wouldn't it be better, Norman," she said, "to get the personal problem out of the way, first, and then, if you want to go ahead and testify before committees and bring pressure to bear to eliminate these other conditions, like Tommy Corcoran's influence and pour it on Biddle, you will be entirely independent and free to do so?" She had said, earlier, that, "perhaps, the committee could be persuaded that this was not the best way to approach the problem," which let the cat out of the bag as to what would happen if I accommodatingly tendered my resignation in order to "solve the personal problem first." The President would then go to work on the Democratic members of those committees, like Senator [James M.] Mead, who wishes to run for governor of New York next year, [who is] chairman of the Mead (Truman) Committee.[4] Wheels within wheels!

It was only a practical problem, not a problem in principle, unaffected by *noblesse oblige* or the slightest measure of personal loyalty or appreciation.

"In any event, Anna, I suggest that your father take no action until he sees the memorandum, a copy of which I will send over as soon as it is completed, probably tomorrow morning."

"I don't think he will do anything now," Anna said, "and Biddle cannot have access to him until Sunday," but she certainly left in the air the indication that the axe might fall after that: At least, that she did not know, specifically, what would develop after that.

Well, so be it. If the President is ever willing to dodge questions of principle, let him dodge as best he can. I can't. Some of us are the complete prisoners of our convictions. If there isn't a desire for integrity in government in high places, such as Biddle's, where do we go from there? Even in the midst of world affairs, there ought to be a flicker of interest long enough to explore the subject. I think there would be, in all fairness, but I believe a job has been done on me so completely that the President has been convinced of allegations which I know nothing about. . . . Whatever happens to me, individually, I will at least have left such a dent in brother Biddle's career that he can never be appointed to the Supreme Court of the United States, and probably cannot even survive as attorney general. I will have done a healthy bit of housecleaning for the President which he does not have the fortitude to do himself. . . .

I left the White House after an hour and ten minutes of discussion with Anna, feeling the last pricks of disillusionment because of her utter barrenness in dealing with questions of principle.

I might add that, perhaps, the whole conversation was best epitomized by Anna's parting remark as we walked down the corridor from an upstairs

---

4. Senator Mead became chairman of the Special Committee to Investigate the National-Defense Program, when Truman resigned from the Senate to seek the vice presidency, 3 August 1944.

drawing room to take the elevator. "It's just unfortunate that the whole situation had to arise—with the publicity and all. I wish it hadn't."

"Anna," I replied, "We cannot wish problems out of the way. There are questions of principle that don't 'wish out' very easily." . . .

I must confess that Katherine had a very good laugh when she heard that expression of Anna's—"the President is in a trap." That is the only way you get Roosevelt's attention. Ordinary loyalty or individual justice are details too trivial for such a busy life. Perhaps it has to be that way. Perhaps those in power get that way—hard and cynical and ungrateful. I don't think it is necessary. Lincoln never got that way and he in many ways faced problems more hardening than the present one because the country was divided. . . .

Linked with my case, right or wrong, is the President's perfectly abominable appointment of Robert A. Hurley, former Democratic governor of Connecticut and, I believe, now national committeeman, and Lt. Colonel Edward H. Heller, of Los Angeles (whose wife[5] succeeds Helen Gahagan, newly elected congresswoman, as national committeewoman) to the Surplus Property Board. All this at a time when he would not be running again and could have made such vital appointments on the merits. It is generally supposed that Senator Gillette, defeated for the Senate, will be the third member. None of them are competent or experienced; all are political appointees charged with the economic destiny of the country in the next few years, to the extent that the surplus property disposal will determine it—to a very large extent.

Wednesday, 6 December 1944

Dearest Katherine Mather,

Inasmuch as I began life in Washington by writing a letter to you, it seems fitting to close this chapter of life with a letter to you. My room is crowded with packing cases full of files and books which accompanied me in the sudden exodus from the Department of Justice. This chapter might be labeled, "Fired by the President," or, if I consider the prevailing thoughts in your mind when I tucked you in bed tonight and the prevailing thoughts in mine as I lie awake in bed, it might be called, "Westward Ho!"

You and I have just one idea in mind as to future plans, and that is to start west as soon as possible. I bought a pair of woolen driving gloves for the long transcontinental trek, and you have been speculating on just what doll and which books you would like best to take in the car.

---

5. Elinor R. Heller.

I will have to refer you to the notes in my "Log" book in regard to the attorney general's request, on Saturday, November 18th; and the developments down to Saturday, the 25th, including the "resign or be fired" order of the attorney general on Wednesday, November 22nd; the breaking of the news in the press, on Thursday, November 23rd; and the conference with Anna Boettiger at the White House, on Friday, November 24th. I left on Saturday night for Cleveland, to keep a speaking engagement made for me by Lecturers, Inc., for the following morning, in the great "temple" of Rabbi [Abba H.] Silver, who has become the most militant zionist in the country and will probably succeed to the leadership of Rabbi Stephen S. Wise of New York. It was my first experience in a synagogue and I followed with interest the Jewish services (in which it seems to be quite a common event to have as principal speaker a lecturer on any subject of current interest—quite contrary to the practices in our Christian churches). . . .

I delivered my Commonwealth Club address, "Nazi Conspiracies in the United States," to an audience of about 1,500 people, and it went well in the perfect acoustic properties of the temple. There was warm appreciation expressed afterward. . . .

Katherine met me at the train in Washington, at the early hour of 8:00, Monday morning. For her to be stirring at that unusually early hour meant something. The principal event was a memorandum, which the President had sent out to me, the preceding day, by messenger. It was a copy of a memorandum, sent to Mr. Biddle, with no covering message of any sort. I had sent Anna a copy of my letter to Mr. Biddle, advising that the Mead Committee was now going into the matter of his request for my resignation. Since the committee had asked the attorney general for a statement of his reasons for requesting my resignation, and had also asked me for a statement of the issues between us, to be delivered to the committee by Tuesday, November 28th, I declined to make my reply to Biddle's request for my resignation on the 22nd, as promised to him, but would defer the matter pending the committee's investigation.[1] Upon receiving the notice from the committee, I had immediately abandoned the preparation of a bill of particulars on the issues between the attorney general and myself, which had absorbed my attention for several days and nights. My immediate task was to convert that draft into a memorandum for the Mead Committee. In sending the letter to Anna, I had merely said, casually, in a transmittal note, in the light of our conversation, "Herewith for your interest a copy of a letter to Mr. Biddle. Kindest regards."

---

1. "Say Littell Balks at Plea to Resign; Some in Congress Defend Aide Biddle Seeks to Oust—Talk of Committee Inquiry," *New York Times*, 25 November 1944; *P.M.*, 28 November 1944.

The President's memorandum was sent even more casually, with no covering letter at all, but, nevertheless, it was sent out to our house by a White House car, the act in itself being a slap at Biddle. The memorandum read as follows:

26 November 1944
MEMORANDUM
for the Attorney General

I am distressed that this matter of Norman Littell seems to have got into an impasse. Many wholly extraneous matters seem to have come into it.

I do not intend to go into them, and I am told that Littell would have been wholly willing to resign if given a little time. Also, I think he is hurt because you said something to him about not having any confidence in his integrity.

Frankly, I think the matter is one of incompatibility between you and him. It would be a pity to have congressional investigations, reports, etc., as this is primarily an executive matter.

I am sure that Norman knows that the head of a department has always been sustained by whoever was President and, if you can make Norman understand that you are doing nothing to hurt his future but that you, as attorney general, have a perfect right to make recommendations in regard to the assistant attorney general under you, he will realize this cannot in common sense be made a *cause célèbre* by any committee in the Congress. As Chief Executive, I have, of course, an absolute right to act as such.

I hope, for Norman's own career and his future, that he will leave your office without any fuss. You can tell him that I would be glad to put him back in some other government work as soon as there is an available opportunity.

I am sending a copy of this to Norman.

FDR

If anything was calculated to reveal how far apart the President and I had become in the last two years, this communication certainly did it. Basically, it was really a reproach to Biddle for getting this situation into an "impasse," warning that the President was "not going into it," and blunt advice that Biddle had handled the matter very badly, as far as I, personally, was concerned, in reflecting on my integrity and not giving me enough time. (Shades of Anna Boettiger!) Still, the memorandum also reflects upon me or, rather, on the President's knowledge of me. It evaluated the whole incident erroneously, by indicating that the President thought I suffered from "hurt feelings." It, again, underestimated me in appealing to self interest of my career, and it reached a contemptible low point, as far as I am concerned, in implying that I sought a "*cause célèbre*" and in saying that he would be glad to put me back "in some other government work as soon as there is an available opportunity."

The President's suggestion was not even specific. With a vacancy on the Circuit Court of Appeals of the District of Columbia and a current conflict going on as to the appointment of members of the Surplus Property Board, for which I am preeminently qualified and for which the President would be most fortunate to secure my services, the President's vague statement was not in the least flattering. It is beside the point that I was interested in neither post. Far more fundamental was my objection to his impression that I could be tempted by any kind of government job if I would leave "without a fuss." All of the Roosevelt indifference to principle and complacency in power was behind that memorandum. He had grown accustomed to moving men around like pawns. The President's power is so tremendous that this, of course, could ordinarily be done.

While I would have accepted neither post referred to above, the fact that neither should be offered seemed to me to indicate the measure of my standing with the President. I recalled what I said to Sam Rosenman and his concurrence:

"A job has been done on me over here," to which Sam had replied, "Yes, and over a period of many months."

It was not a case of little drops of water wearing away stone. Not even the faintest shred of Anna's loyalty remained. What a job!

I had been in constant touch with Governor Ernest Gruening of Alaska—a close and loyal friend and one who despised his senior, Ickes. Ernest had informed me of a conversation—verified through a friend who was present—in which Ickes had said to Biddle, when I was under discussion:

"Why don't you fire the son-of-a-bitch?"

Biddle had replied, "Because he is too strong at the White House."

To which Ickes had replied, "I can fix that."

That had been some time ago. Ickes had undoubtedly set to work in his most skillful manner. . . .

There is no doubt, whatever, of the existence of the Ickes-Corcoran-Biddle axis directed for their joint and respective reasons against Littell. The fingerprints of Ickes' fine hand were all over the case. The President would never have charged that I sought a *"cause célèbre"* unless Ickes' propaganda line had succeeded.

After receiving the memorandum of November 26th from the President, in my absence, Katherine telephoned to Sam Rosenman . . . at the White House and read it to him. She told Sam that, of course, the President was completely wrong if he thought that, for one moment, that I was interested in another job, and would he please tell the President that.

She said, "There isn't a job big enough to bribe him—not even an appointment as ambassador to the Court of St. James! I know Norman well, and he is interested primarily in good government. He thinks there are enough whited sepulchers around here."

She went on to say that we did not wish another job and were going back west, but, for the President's own sake, she hoped that his advisors would inform fully of the danger of his getting into bed with Mr. Biddle on this controversy. The President would suffer a great loss of position and subject himself to the attack which was about to descend upon Mr. Biddle if he took a hand in it. Sam said he wholly agreed with this and would urge the President accordingly.

Katherine drove me from the station out to our house, while I read the President's memorandum she had received the preceding day. She explained to me that, in her opinion, I should not go to the office, nor should my secretaries at the Department of Justice know precisely where I was because there was the danger of Biddle subserviently obeying the President's orders in this memorandum and trying to patch things up with me. This issue was not sharply framed and should be permitted to run its natural course. I wholly agreed.

It so happened that we had a great and good friend who was at the Statler Hotel—E. G. Howes, president of [E. G. Howes] Leather Company in Boston. He had headed the citizens committee at Palm Beach which had fought the battle of the Breakers Hotel. . . . He was a man of great ability and great character (although we differed widely in our economic viewpoint). . . .

E. G. Howes was as staunch a friend as one could have, and he quite agreed with the strategy of [my] not being available. So we moved into his suite at the Statler for daytime operations, and there I composed my reply to the President. I set it forth, here, in full, because it will be of interest in future years. As politely and respectfully as I could, I leveled off the errors in his memorandum and, in that moment of parting, we confronted each other as one citizen to another. Here is my letter:

27 November 1944

Dear Mr. President:

Thank you for sending me a copy of your memorandum of November 26 to the attorney general.

My position in the controversy with attorney general Biddle is so very simple that I join with you heartily in regretting that wholly extraneous matters seem to have come into it.

I concur wholly with the message you sent to me through Anna on the 24th that, as undersecretary of the Navy during the last war, you would have resigned instantly if any difference of opinion in policy had arisen between you and your chief, Josephus Daniels. I also agree that "personal incompatibility" is adequate grounds in itself to require the junior of two officials to resign. These are both elementary rules of administration in private as well as in public organizations, but neither applies in this case.

Unhappily, I do not have as my superior a great public servant like my very dear and deeply respected friend, Josephus Daniels; and there is not involved here mere "personal incompatibility"—unless one is content to describe superficially that personal estrangement which results when the junior will not condone or cooperate with conduct violative of basic principles of integrity and good government. The fact that the attorney general, in asking for my resignation, said that he "lacked personal confidence" in me, is simply an aggravation and not a cause. We are not for one moment dealing with a case of "hurt" feelings. My answer to the attorney general, when he said he was sure I would not wish to remain in view of his lack of confidence, goes to the heart of the matter. I said: "If you assume a hypothetical case in which I do not have confidence in the attorney general, I might well consider it my public duty to remain,"—at least until otherwise removed.

Of course, the Chief Executive has the absolute authority to remove me from office, as the attorney general so forcibly reminded me on Wednesday, November 22, when he said he would have the President "fire" me if I did not resign in two hours. It is equally apparent to me that with the grave and world-wide responsibilities which rest on you as President of the Republic in time of war, you cannot possibly go into the details of the matter to see that individual justice is done, or to see whether or not fundamental principles of good government are really involved, even though in normal times, under ordinary administrative practice, in either private or public organizations, personnel issues do sometimes boil up to a point where for principle's sake they must intrude among major matters and require consideration.

What happens to me as an individual is of no possible consequence, nor have I the slightest interest in "other government work" when there is an "available opportunity." I came to Washington upon persuasion (after first having declined to accept this position) solely to serve you because I believed in you and in what this administration has stood for in the life of the country. In taking my present position, I am serving precisely those same objectives.

It is true that I have hit hard against those things which were wrong, but in each and every instance I was proved right in principle and in results obtained. No one who knows me would think for one moment that I was then or am now in search of a *cause célèbre.*

My motives are very simple. Men are giving their lives to preserve democratic government. Our men are not dying to preserve poor government but preserve good government—faithful to the public interest, conducted for the benefit of all the people. My most humble offering, as one too old to be at the front, is to fight for good government at home in those matters which cross my desk. I would happily risk my life in doing so. Therefore, you can readily see how entirely trivial is the risk of being "fired," when I know that you who have my unswerving devotion would have me follow the same course if in possession of all the facts.

Lest you accept the official statement that my appearances before congressional committees have had nothing to do with the matter, I enclose a copy of a memorandum of August 21, 1944, to Acting Attorney General Fahy, who was then in touch by long distance telephone with the attorney general, the memorandum was written immediately after my testimony before the Mead Committee regarding policies in the disposal of surplus realty. A fundamental issue of government is involved. This is, however, not the only issue with the attorney general.

Naturally, I hope you will not see fit to revoke my appointment pursuant to the attorney general's recommendation, because, as the matter stands, the senators, congressmen, and interested public do not hold you in the slightest degree responsible for whatever Francis Biddle in his widely recognized incompetence has done, and my loyalty to you is such that I hope you will not take sides in the matter to the point where you will share this responsibility.

In deciding the matter, I hope you will consider the fact that I have served under three preceding attorneys general whose confidence and respect I had and still have, that I have worked happily and effectively with my staff in the largest division of the Department of Justice and with my colleagues in the Department, that I have enjoyed the firm confidence of the Bureau of the Budget, of other personnel in land acquisition work throughout the government, and of both houses of Congress, especially the appropriations committees which have consistently expressed appreciation in the efficiency of my work and voted their confidence by approving my annual budgets. Even the present attorney general, in requesting my resignation, said that I had done a most commendable job.

Respectfully,

Norman M. Littell
Assistant Attorney General

I shall never know, I suppose, what the President's reaction to this letter was—although I most certainly would like to, for if he thought at all, it must have effected a complete readjustment in his mind of what he had been taught was true about me. I have no doubt that he read it. As for my own part, I could not help but think, even if facing a losing fight, what a great thing it was to be able to hold to my own convictions and tell one of the most powerful men in the world today exactly what I would do and what I would not do—and get away with it without ending up in a concentration camp.

After it became apparent that Biddle would make no effort to reach me following receipt of the President's memorandum, Katherine and I worked night and day on a memorandum to the Mead Committee, in an atmosphere of increased tension and under continuous inquiry from the press to which neither Biddle nor I replied. I finished my memorandum and sent it to Senator [James M.] Mead, chairman of the War Investigating Committee, on Tuesday, November 28th (it seems to have gotten itself dated November 27th) with copies for Mead, Ferguson, and Kilgore, and the General Counsel [Rudolph Halley].[2]

Your mother and I left the office after a welter of work and sent my two secretaries home after two late and exhausting nights. That night, the news broke of my charges against Biddle being under the influence of Tommy Corcoran and endeavoring to have me settle the Savannah Shipyards case.[3] It broke in the Associated Press. I had said to a messenger taking my confidential report to the Mead Committee: "Don't let it go off in your hands. It's dynamite!"

Well, it went off that night in a preliminary way with a scoop for the Associated Press to the effect that I had charged the attorney general with submitting to undue influence by Tommy Corcoran and that our alleged "personal incompatibility" came from differences of opinion as to basic matters of principle in government. For these reasons I had refused to resign.

It was for all the world like stepping into the ring at the sound of a gong, shaking my opponent up with a left jab, and following through with a right hook that knocked him completely out. However, the right hook did not follow until the next day when, after deliberating much of the day about the problem, the committee finally released my full report to the press. . . .
I hope it will not seem petty to you. Many of the details are, but the case had to be so stated to prove the character of the man. It was not an obvious case like that of Secretary Fall with a "black bag" and $100,000 bribes being handed about. It was a case of the most incompetent man in contemporary public life, with a shifty, evasive, untruthful mind devoid of any real sense of basic principles in good government, viewing the powers of his great office as attributes of personal privilege to be shared with his friends like the other social advantages of knowing a "Biddle from Philadelphia." The case against a dilettante and a fool was in some ways more difficult to prove than Senator [Thomas J.] Walsh's case against Secretary Fall.

While my memorandum does not reflect all of my differences with Biddle, the material ones are there pointing up two main issues:

1. Special influence of Tommy Corcoran in the settlement of cases in the Department of Justice through his great and good friend, Attorney General Biddle; and,

2. Interference by Attorney General Biddle with the free flow of

2. For Littell's memo to the Truman Committee, see "Littell's Story of Attorney General Biddle and Tom Corcoran," *P.M.*, 1 December 1944, pp. 2–3; "Accuses Biddle of Aiding Corcoran; Littell Says Attorney General Acted Contrary to 'Basic Principles of Good Government,'" *New York Times* 29 November 1944.

3. Thomas L. Stokes, "Corcoran's Influence," *Washington Post*, 30 November 1944; Peter Edson, "Biddle's Claim to Fame," *Washington Daily News*, 30 November 1944, in Littell scrapbook; John L. Cutler, "Biddle–Littell Squabble Bounces Back to F.D. as Senators Drop 'Hot Potato,'" *Washington Daily News*, 30 November 1944.

information from the executive and legislative sides of the government in matters which did not involve public security or necessary secrecy.

Unfortunately for Biddle, he was up against someone who knows the subject by chapter and verse, by dates, hours, conversations. Facts are deadly as machine gun bullets. I stated the facts.

It must have been a great shock to the complacent and egotistical Mr. Biddle. I had sent Ed Williams to the attorney general's staff meeting on Tuesday morning, the 28th, and Biddle had asked if I was out of town, to which Ed had replied merely that I had another engagement. Biddle was confident and self-assured. He sailed right up to the brink of destruction with all sails set, confidently walking the poop-deck, the master of all he surveyed, until the bow of the ship splintered in a head-on crash against a reef. Biddle's composure was converted to a state of shock as he floundered in the water trying to save the mere skin of his reputation. Suddenly, a lifetime—his whole position and reputation—was at stake.

Ernest Gruening, who is an old newspaper man, from the *Boston Transcript* days, told me that he had never seen such unanimity of the press. The deluge which broke over Biddle in the ensuing days crowded the war news off to one side of the front pages, and commanded editorial comments which are still ringing around the country.[4] The Associated Press wire photographer came out Wednesday night and succeeded in getting a very attractive picture of the entire family. This also appeared throughout the country.

My picture and Biddle's were also used in juxtaposition, and if I had been an editor, I certainly would have done the same thing. He did not have an exactly reassuring appearance. In contrast to my very ordinary and seemingly honest mug, he really looked quite devious. Looks in this case are not deceiving.

His own statement to the committee was in very simple form: A letter claiming that his request for my resignation was on personal grounds only and not because of any disciplining of me for testifying upon the documentary proof in my memorandum—particularly the memorandum to Charles Fahy attached to my report, written on August 21st, immediately after my testimony in regard to surplus properties, before the Mead Committee—the testimony which unhorsed Clayton. . . . I had been severely castigated by Acting Attorney General Fahy, who stated in perfect proof as to a major cause of my dismissal, that this was "the third time this has happened"—first in the Elk Hills case, next in the Breakers Hotel case, and now in respect to surplus properties. As far as he was concerned, it was "once too often." He "did not care about the merit."

Poor old Charley! The crises did seem to arise with uncanny timing

4. William Moore, "Littell Blows Lid Off Feud with Biddle; Senate Dumps Case in President's Lap," *Washington Times–Herald*, 30 November 1944; Mary Spargo, "White House Action Seen in Biddle, Littell Feud," n.p., 30 November 1944, in Littell scrapbook.

when the attorney general was out of town and Charley, as solicitor general, was "acting attorney general." That fellow Littell always did seem to get out of his cage at the wrong time.

The attorney general also stated that he had requested my resignation on the 18th and had renewed it on the 22nd and that, when I had asked for more time to consider the matter, he had "concurred." This was a lie. He had sent my revocation to the White House on the 22nd after the "resign or be fired" conversation and had thereafter on each day urged the President to take immediate action on my proposed dismissal. We had learned this through White House sources.

In sending the letter to me and inviting my comment, just as the committee sent my report to Mr. Biddle and invited his comment, the committee gave me an opportunity to reply on both points that the attorney general was not telling the truth. . . .

The pressure on the attorney general for a reply to my statement was enormous. Of course, he could not reply to such a breath-taking explosion. He could merely say on Wednesday night that he was in touch with the White House and there would be a statement the next day. There was. The revocation of my appointment as assistant attorney general came over to the department at 11:00 on November 30th.[5]

Of all the communications I have had with the President, this was the briefest and most decapitating. You will find the original in my file, surprisingly enough, on a printed form, leaving only the name of the addressee and the name of the office from which he is removed to be filled in, and the signature line on which was sprawled the President's familiar signature.

The White House
Washington

29 November 1944

Honorable Norman M. Littell
Assistant Attorney General
Washington, D.C.

Sir:

You are hereby removed from the office of assistant attorney general of the United States.

Franklin D. Roosevelt [signed]
Through the Attorney General

---

5. C. P. Trussell, "Roosevelt Ousts Littell in Dispute; 'Insubordination Inexcusable,' Says President—Voorhis Asks House Group Inquiry," *New York Times*, 1 December 1944; "Roosevelt Ousts Littell," *Facts on File*, vol. 4 (29 November–5 December 1944), p. 384 D.

Shortly before this letter was sent to me, I received a telegram from the President, who was at Warm Springs, but the telegram came from the White House, double-starred and somewhat ambiguous in that it only implied removal from office, as follows:

THE WHITE HOUSE   WASHINGTON DC   NOV 29

HON NORMAN M LITTELL
DLR BY BOY DEPARTMENT OF JUSTICE

I REGRET TO HEAR THAT YOU HAVE DECLINED TO RESIGN AS
REQUESTED BY YOUR SUPERIOR OFFICER, THE ATTORNEY
GENERAL. PERSONALLY, I AM SORRY TO HAVE TO DO THIS IN
VIEW OF YOUR LONG SERVICE TO THE GOVERNMENT.

FRANKLIN D. ROOSEVELT

However, the matter was soon subject to correction by a message from the White House which filled out the foregoing telegram as follows:

TELEGRAM

THE WHITE HOUSE
WASHINGTON

30 NOVEMBER 1944

CORRECTION DUPLICATE OF NOV. 29TH.

HON NORMAN M. LITTELL
DEPARTMENT OF JUSTICE
WASHINGTON DC

I REGRET TO HEAR THAT YOU HAVE DECLINED TO RESIGN AS
REQUESTED BY YOUR SUPERIOR OFFICER, THE ATTORNEY
GENERAL OF THE UNITED STATES. UNDER THE CIRCUMSTANCES
I AM COMPELLED TO REMOVE YOU AS ASSISTANT ATTORNEY
GENERAL. PERSONALLY, I AM SORRY TO HAVE TO DO THIS IN
VIEW OF YOUR LONG SERVICE TO THE GOVERNMENT.

FRANKLIN D. ROOSEVELT

Well, that was that! So many members of the press were calling for interviews that I agreed to meet them in my office at 12:00. All of my telephone calls must have been audited by someone in the attorney general's office, for my general assistant promptly received an order to come up to the office of Mr. McGranery. . . . I had also issued orders for a staff meeting of members of the Lands Division staff in the library at 2:00 P.M. to say good-bye to them, and, in the meantime, I was busy packing. Williams returned with instructions from the attorney general, through McGranery, to cancel the press conference at 12:00 and to cancel the staff meeting. Neither was to be held.

I canceled the staff meeting forthwith, lest members of the staff be embarrassed by being accessories to insubordination, but I ordered Williams to return to his office and stay there so that he would have nothing whatever to do with my continuing with the press conference. It was not only too late to call it off, but I would under no circumstances have called it off.

The representatives of the press assembled in my office, and I explained to them that I had been ordered to cancel this press conference but I had declined to do so as it was not convenient for them or convenient for me to meet on the curb outside the Department of Justice, and to please not be surprised if we were ejected bodily from the Department. However, this did not happen.

As far as I was concerned, there was not much to the conference. I merely confirmed the fact that I had been fired by the President, as Biddle had already announced, and, as to future plans, replied that I was going back into private practice, probably on the West Coast in California, but that this was not settled.

As the White House had not released the President's telegram to me, I did not do so either, nor had I released the memorandum to Biddle, or my reply by letter to the President. I handed the press the statement, hastily prepared before they assembled, dated November 30th. . . .

It was just as well that the staff meeting was canceled because I could scarcely have faced them, nor could my associates have met with me under those circumstances. J. E. Williams, who was a great football player and, at one time, before he became a lawyer, a professional baseball player, broke down and cried. Several men, whom I met in the hall did likewise, and many of the girls, too. A meeting of them all would have been too much for all of us. We had operated in the closest teamwork through the war years; had done an immense job in record time; and had raised the prestige of the Lands Division in the Department of Justice to an all-time high in the history of the Department of Justice. All of them knew it, particularly the old-timers who knew that the Lands Division used to be a dumping ground for political appointees whom it was assumed falsely, could examine titles if they could do nothing else.

When I left, we led in everything from overtime hours and War Bond subscriptions to Community Chest donations and blood plasma donations at the Red Cross. We were over twice as big as any division of the

Department of Justice and handled over a third of the mail of the entire Department of Justice, with business in every state and territory and insular possession of the United States—all running smoothly, with very few bad spots. Morale was high and loyalty to the point of mutual affection bound us in an *esprit-de-corps* which old-timers told me had never been [equaled] in the Department of Justice, reaching, as it did, into the remote corners of the land and out into the territories.

Even though J. E. Williams, . . . one of the finest public servants I have known, was immediately made acting assistant attorney general—my man though he was, heart and soul—everyone knew that it could not be the same again and that things would come tumbling down. So I was told. I counteracted this bad thought to the very best of my ability. Indeed, that was the purpose of holding the staff meeting—to tell them that my quarrel was not theirs; that it was their duty to carry on their work and continue to be loyal to the Department of Justice and the attorney general. And I said that in key places, wherever I could.

The next day, I took the precaution of having the head of the file room in the Department come down and observe every file that I packed so that there could be no argument about my removing anything that was not personal, and properly removed as my own, knowing full well that there was no limit to the pettiness with which I would be attacked by the attorney general. For example, that very day, my pay check had been received, along with other checks for distribution on November 30th, but mine was sent back because it included the entire day's pay for November 30th. The entire machinery of the United States Treasury had to be unwound in order to cut my pay back a few hours to 11:00, when the revocation of my appointment was received from the White House.

To give the devil his due, I quote from that portion of the statement of November 30th, which quotes the President's statement, as follows:

The President has today made the following statement:

'When statements made by Norman Littell first appeared in the papers I wrote to him that it was primarily an executive matter; and that I hoped for his own career he would resign. Since then he has volunteered a long statement, thus substantiating what the attorney general had said about his insubordination. This is inexcusable; and under the circumstances my only alternative is to remove him from office, which I have done today.'

Of course, the President had been completely misinformed over long distance telephone at Warm Springs by Francis Biddle. Had I made the report public, it would have been in violation of his executive order of August 1944, forbidding the airing of interdepartment disputes in public, and requiring that they be settled on the executive side first, but this executive order expressly exempted testimony before congressional committees.[6] My report to the Mead Committee was testimony before a congressional committee. Furthermore, I did not make it public. The chairman of the Mead Committee distributed copies to the press on November 29th, a well-known fact when Biddle made [his] statement on November 30th, although he did not inform the President of this fact over the telephone at Warm Springs.

I can justly so state the matter, and two of the senators of the committee promptly made a public statement to the effect that the committee itself had made public the report, but this was after the die was cast and I had been fired. The cause assigned is immaterial. The result had to be the same. The President was grabbing at something which gave him any grounds at all.

Now, since I make it a point to write with all honesty, I may now confess that your mother should have been "fired" if the grounds assigned are also to be attached to the proper party. Unknown to me and, as a hard fighter knowing well the possibility of suppression of a report of this character, it seems as if on the night of the 27th, when we were completing the last run-off of copies in a neighboring office, she may have slipped a copy to a friend in the Associated Press. (There was even brief anxiety about the possibility of liability for libel in the interval of one day before the committee made public the whole of the report which would then be "privileged" if the committee released it.) I cannot blame her. One can little imagine the intensity and perils of a fight like this and your mother was taking no chances. . . .

1945

Sunday, 28 January 1945
4101 Lorcom Lane

It has been quite impossible to keep up with the welter of events since my dismissal by the President on November 30, 1944. The storm of protests, which broke over Biddle's head in the press after my memorandum of November 28th was filed with the Mead Committee, . . . swept him with

---

6. Probably a reference to Executive Order No. 9631, 15 July 1943. See entry for 21 November 1944, note 1.

one rush beyond the possibility of redemption in the public eye. The detailed story of Tommy Corcoran's efforts to settle the Savannah Shipyards case through Biddle ricocheted around Washington and the country until I had 150 editorials on the subject, without mentioning ordinary press accounts.

Governor Gruening of Alaska, one of those rare people who really show up in a crisis, stood by me like the Rock of Gibraltar. As an old newspaperman, he advised me from time to time. Among other things, he had me subscribe to a clipping bureau for editorials, which I did. That skimmed the cream of opinion. The President must have skimmed it too, to his amazement! It was all one way. Gruening said that he had never seen such unanimity, and the curious thing was that the liberal press, ranging from *P.M.*, *The Nation*, and the *New Republic*, were side-by-side *with the conservative press and even with the reactionary press, like the Chicago Tribune.*[1]

It was impossible for the Mead Committee to drop the matter when its Democratic members found that they were in political hot water after my report of November 28th was made public.[2] . . . Even after it was announced that the committee would do nothing further in the matter, the New York press criticized Chairman Mead so strongly for dropping it that he felt compelled, in view of his ambition to be governor of New York after the next election, to write me a further letter and ask if I had any further information for the committee, presumably in reply to Biddle.

I should say, first, that Biddle had taken such a beating from the press that he was finally smoked out of his Olympian silence to make his reply of December 9th, choosing as his forum the Immigration Committee of the Senate, which was largely composed of his friends, but on which Senator Ferguson, . . . who is also a member of the Mead Committee, was a most interested member.[3]

---

1. For press comment on Littell's dismissal, see "Biddle v. Littell," *New Republic*, 4 December 1944, p. 783; I. F. Stone, "Littell versus Biddle," *Nation*, 9 December 1944, pp. 707–8; "Quarrel in Justice," *New Republic*, 11 December 1944, p. 784; "Question of Pull in Washington Raised by Ouster of Biddle Aide," *Newsweek*, 11 December 1944, pp. 37–38; "This Is Inexcusable," *Time*, 11 December 1944, p. 25; See also "An Ouster that Calls for an Inquiry," *St. Louis Post-Dispatch* (n.d.), and "Mortifying News from Washington," *Louisville Courier-Journal*, 30 November 1944, cited in *Congressional Record*, vol. 90 (6 December 1944), pp. A4645, A4767.

2. In fact, the Senate decided to drop the case almost immediately. See Elizabeth Donahue, "Congress Is Dropping Littell-Biddle Issue; Capitol Hill More Intent in Clearing Agenda for Christmas," *P.M.* 11 December 1944; "Sidetrack Dispute of Biddle-Littell; Senate Investigators Decline to Assume Jurisdiction in the Feud—Leave Doors Open," *New York Times*, 30 November 1944. See also diary entry for 6 December 1944, note 3.

3. "Statement of Attorney General to Senate Committee on Immigration, 9 December 1944," *Congressional Record*, vol. 90 (11 December 1944), pp. A4690-A4692; Lansing Warren, "Corcoran 'Pull' Denied by Biddle; Attorney General Tells Senate Hearing Lawyer Is 'Friend' and 'Completely Honest,'" *New York Times*, 10 December 1944; "Biddle Testifies," *Facts on File*, vol. 4 (6–12 December 1944), p. 392 F.

In that fateful statement of Biddle's—wobbly, weak, and incompetent—he laid himself open by stating that Tommy Corcoran only had to
do with three cases: The Savannah Shipyards case, the Sterling Products
case, and the Rockbestos case; and he told the story of Sterling Products—moonlight-and-roses version!

I couldn't let him get away with it. When Senator Mead's letter came,
asking for my further reply, I wrote a reply of January 8th, filed with the
committee on January 9th, carefully documented.[4] It was a tough job—
particularly in view of the fact that the Sterling Products information was
elusive and had to be revised in a detailed and concrete manner—but I
did it. . . .

In any event, Biddle was caught in a fresh blast, although Halley—
counsel for the Truman Committee—showed up in his true colors at last
by announcing, on January 9th, that the report "contained nothing new;"
that the committee had considered the matter before; that there were
other factors involved; and that the committee would probably consider it
"none of its business." [Was he] another Tommy Corcoran stooge and
party to the rigged plan for suppressing this report? The committee had
not even seen the report when he made that statement. He did not
distribute copies to committee members between Tuesday, the 9th, and
the following Friday, although on Tuesday, he rushed one over to Biddle,
who was reported by the press to be at home studying it.

The leak was a very good thing, for it completely disarmed the advance
plan to squelch my further comments and place me in the role of a
disgruntled employee. I could not be crowded back into that role. The
battle royal was on.

The facts stated respecting the settlement of the Sterling Products case
were devastating in their sequence. For the first time, they were out.
Tommy had suppressed investigations of this company before the Truman
Committee, when his good friend General Counsel Fulton was in charge,
and Halley was next in line. He had suppressed it before the Bone
Committee also.[5] Someone had guided the drafting of the report by the
Treasury Department on Sterling Products Company into mild white-
washing terms. He had knocked out the investigation in the Department
of Justice and settled the case. What a fee Tommy must have received for
all these services, and for betraying his country!

---

4. For Littell's memorandum, of 8 January 1945, rebutting Biddle's statements before the
Immigration Committee, see Lawrence Smith, "Mr. Biddle, the Elk Hills Naval Petroleum
Reserve Contract and His Apparent Dereliction of Duty," *Congressional Record*, vol. 91 (22
January 1945), pp. 426–430; (24 January 1945), pp. A268–A270; (25 January 1945), pp.
A295–A297; "Littell Attack Links Biddle and Corcoran," *New York Times*, 10 January 1945;
"Littell-Biddle Fight Still On," *P.M.*, 10 January 1945.

5. Senator Homer T. Bone of Washington was chairman of the Patents Committee,
1939–44.

I managed to get hold of the secret report of the Department of Justice [which had been] prepared, summarizing the 30,000-odd documents in the Sterling Products case—a devastating story regarding Sterling Products; and I also managed to get hold of the Treasury Department's confidential report. The former impales the latter.

One able Republican, Congressman Lawrence Smith of Wisconsin, took up the issue, publicly suggesting the possibility of the impeachment of Biddle. I urged him to get some Democrats with him on an investigation so that the matter would have a non-partisan approach in the interests of good government rather than the interests of party politics. He did, and Jerry Voorhis of California joined in proposing a resolution for investigation.[6] Jerry had proposed one in the last Congress, having made a public statement on the floor of the House immediately after the news of my dismissal by the President, which was one of the finest tributes I have ever had.[7] That resolution died in the Rules Committee in the dying Congress, but he proposed another one in this Congress.

On Monday, January 22nd, I went up with Katherine and our faithful housekeeper Eda [Mrs. Eda Tracey], to Congress to hear Smith's speech and Jerry Voorhis' proposal of a resolution. The speech was largely based upon my report, which he had procured from the Mead Committee (after which I gave him an extra copy for convenience) and he put in the *Congressional Record* the section on the Sterling Products case.[8] John McCormack, Democratic leader, got up and walked out when Smith started to talk. Hardly any Democrats were present. I think they have thrown Biddle to the wolves and will not even try to defend him.

On Wednesday, the 24th, Smith put another section of my report in the *Record* by consent and, on Thursday the 25th and Monday the 29th, the remaining sections were put in; so now it is all a matter of public record and the press can help themselves.[9] Some of them breathe easier because they published the Sterling story on the basis of the first "lead" and were concerned about libel action. (Part of the statement of Congressman Smith in the *Congressional Record* . . . states the sequence of events better than I can do, so here it is quoted below:)

---

6. "Two Bills Demand Inquiry on Biddle; Voorhis and Smith of Wisconsin Press Issue—Charges Made by Littell Are Cited," *New York Times*, 23 January 1945.

7. Congressman Jerry Voorhis introduced a resolution (H. Res. 666) to investigate "all the circumstances" surrounding Littell's dissmissal, but the Judiciary Committee did not act on it. *Congressional Record*, vol. 90 (30 November 1944), p. 8649; Elizabeth Donahue, "Dispute To Be Aired Despite Littell Ouster; Voorhis Describes Biddle Assistant as 'Fearless Public Servant,'" *P.M.*, December 1944.

8. For Congressman Smith's comments on the Sterling Products settlement, see *Congressional Record*, vol. 91 (22 January 1945), pp. 424–26.

9. *Congressional Record*, vol. 91 (24 January 1945), pp. A268–A270; (25 January 1945), pp. A295–97.

BIDDLE, CORCORAN, AND SETTLEMENT OF STERLING CASE

Mr. Smith of Wisconsin. Mr. Speaker, I have today introduced a resolution calling for a full and complete investigation of the conduct of the attorney general of the United States, Francis Biddle, in connection with certain charges made by one Norman M. Littell, formerly assistant attorney general. The resolution also provides for the investigation into the activities of the Department of Justice also as a result of the same charges, and the activities of one Tommy Corcoran.

At this point, Mr. Speaker, I ask consent to have inserted at the conclusion of my remarks the statement of Mr. Littell pertaining to the settlement of the Sterling Products case as contained in the memorandum filed in another body on January 8, 1945.[10]

Without reviewing all [the] complex facts as to the intimate relationship between Sterling Products Company and the German [company], *I.G. Farbenindustrie*, it is sufficient to quote:

> . . . The record is clear that from this point on, in violation of the pledge made by Sterling, that the I.G. Farben companies and Sterling inaugurated a scheme in violation of law to control the international drug market and contrary to law and agreement with our government. This grew to be one of the most powerful international cartels in existence. A reading of the correspondence between the president of the Sterling Co. and the head of the German Bayer Co. bears out this fact. . . . But there was no interruption in the business of these concerns when this war broke out, as the subservient Sterling Products Co. promptly served the Nazi purposes by holding the German market in South America. . . . In the United States, the activities of this group were becoming so involved and the effort to cover up so intent, that fake offices were established in New York and in New Jersey. These secret hideouts were places to which funds could be transferred in an effort to cover up the real intent behind this entire scheme. The time came ultimately when these companies became so bold as to bring pressure to bear upon newspapers who dared to be critical of the German government. . . .

It was in the fall of 1939 that the Anti-trust Division of the Department of Justice started an investigation of these companies, and went on to full development of facts and the filing of a case against Sterling. Then what happened?

> . . . On May 9, 1941, Attorney General Jackson froze the *I.G. Farbenindustrie* funds in the National City Bank of New York and on June 19, 1941, all German assets in this country were tied up by executive order of the President. . . .

10. *Congressional Record*, vol. 91 (22 January 1945), pp. 425–26.

Then the able Robert Jackson, then attorney general, was appointed to the Supreme Court of the United States. Biddle, as solicitor general, became acting attorney general.

> . . . At this time it was well known throughout the Department that Tommy Corcoran was in the case and that he was spending a great deal of time in the office of the attorney general. Mr. Biddle was then only the acting attorney general and was in no position to make an important decision relating to a settlement of the case.

As Congressman Smith pointed out:

> . . . So flagrant were the violations of law by Sterling and its subsidiaries that it was a matter which called for the presentation of facts to a federal grand jury. But what actually happened? On September 4, 1941, Mr. Biddle's appointment as attorney general was confirmed, and, mind you, on the very next day, September 5, the Sterling Products case was settled, and all papers required for a dismissal prepared and ready for execution. Some speed for a law suit. . . .

I was forcefully reminded of what Mr. Justice Frank Murphy of the U.S. Supreme Court had told me at lunch in 1943: That President Roosevelt did not want Biddle as attorney general; had asked Frank Murphy to step down from the Supreme Court and again become attorney general and later be appointed secretary of war. . . .

The crowning fact, not generally known at the time, was that the President offered the vacated post of solicitor general to Tommy Corcoran. A man of Roosevelt's experience should have known, and probably did know, that Tommy would not give up a lucrative position as the leading lobbyist in Washington, with fees running into hundreds of thousands, for a salaried job paying perhaps $25,000 a year. (The President might well have thought that this was a chance for Tommy "to take the job" and escape the public charges as to his lobbying and special influence operations.)

In the meantime, the Wallace-Jones feud struck Washington—the major battle of personalities, as Drew Pearson said tonight, "in the last decade."[11] Congressman Smith moved too slowly and did not take

---

11. This was a continuation of the feud that had caused Roosevelt to oust Wallace as chairman of the BEW in 1943. The liberal Wallace and the conservative Texan Jones disliked one another's politics. Moreover their chief assistants—Milo Perkins and William L. Clayton—also disliked one another and could not work together. After giving the vice presidential nomination to Truman, Roosevelt offered Wallace a cabinet post as consolation. Wallace requested the Commerce Department, which required the removal of Jones as secretary of commerce. Roosevelt complied and requested Jones' resignation 20 January 1945. Jones tendered his resignation but then testified before the Senate Commerce

advantage of the lull in the news during the preceding week. The Wallace-Jones feud broke Monday, the 22nd. For this reason, Smith's rather startling speech in Congress did not get the big play which it otherwise would—but no matter. The facts will stew and boil on Capitol Hill. There is no escaping their [penetrating] effect!

I will not endeavor to set forth the letter from President Roosevelt to Jesse Jones, secretary of commerce and head of RFC, asking for his resignation, because Henry Wallace wanted the place and Henry had served the President well in the last campaign.[12] It was one of the most cynical maneuvers I have ever seen and completely eclipsed what was done at Chicago at the national convention.

All the President had to do was to accept Jones' resignation, which was tendered, and some time later appoint Henry Wallace; but he wrote Jesse Jones a long letter, simply saying that Henry wanted the job and thought he was entitled to it because he had worked so hard for the President's re-election. It threw Jesse to the wolves and Henry, too, for the long pent up forces of conservatism behind Jesse Jones, and of liberalism, behind Henry Wallace, came into open battle in the most violent impact Washington has seen for years.

The first round ended yesterday with the rejection of the Wallace nomination by a vote of 15 to 4 in the Senate Committee,[13] and by approval of the George Bill—proposing to separate the [Reconstruction Finance Corporation] from the Department of Commerce and make it again a separate loan agency—a Bill designed to prevent the possibility of Wallace having direction of these large financial affairs which Jones has dominated for years.[14] The Wallace nomination now goes into its final stages on the floor of the Senate with recommendation of the committee, 15 to 4, that it not be confirmed—a humiliation for Wallace—but he will not withdraw his name. He will possibly be defeated and rejected—a

Committee that Wallace lacked the business acumen to run the Reconstruction Finance Corporation, which was under the jurisdiction of the secretary of commerce. See "Jones Quits; Wallace to Get Commerce Job; Cabinet Member Accedes to Roosevelt's Request," *P.M.*, 22 January 1945.

12. For a text of President Roosevelt's letter to Jesse Jones dismissing him as secretary of commerce, see Edward L. and Frederick H. Schapsmeier, eds., *Prophet in Politics: Henry A. Wallace and the War Years, 1940–1945* (Ames: Iowa State University Press, 1975), p. 118.

13. The vote rejecting Wallace's nomination as secretary of commerce was by the Senate Commerce Committee. For more on Wallace's confirmation fight, see Schapsmeier, *Prophet in Politics*, pp. 121–24; U.S. Senate, 79th Cong., 1st sess., Committee on Commerce, *Hearings on S. 375* (Washington, D.C., 1945), pp. 24–25, 54–56.

14. The George Bill (S. 375), introduced by Senator Walter F. George of Georgia on behalf of a coalition of conservative Southern Democrats and Republicans who hated Wallace, stripped the Department of Commerce of the lending powers that Jones had exercised when he was secretary of commerce.

most unusual event in history because the President is entitled to select
his own cabinet, as a general rule. [15]

The curious and inescapable fact is that Henry Wallace made no
personal friends, even though he was in the Senate for four years,
presiding over it. There is a curious absence of human qualities in the
man—with all of his greatness of mind and vision. I have observed before
an absence of individual loyalties. Perhaps he feels his loyalty is on a
higher plane—to God and history—for the individual equation never
gives him a moment's pause. During all of my crises, I did not have one
call from him, although he was undoubtedly for me through it all. He
never goes to bat for a friend. He did not do so for Paul Appleby, who
served him for years as undersecretary of agriculture, and was a very
intimate friend; nor for Frances "Ma" Perkins.

I have no feeling of personal loyalty whatsoever towards Wallace. He is
the best the liberals have and so they rally around and fight for him,
although it is a scattered, informal engagement and, as usual, without the
impact of a concerted plan.

The best statement on Wallace was made tonight by Drew Pearson on
the radio, who pointed out that, with all Jones' great reputation as a loan
director of RFC, his many millions had not been as great as the many
millions loaned by Henry Wallace, as secretary of Agriculture, for rural
rehabilitation. And, that Jones' recovery on his loans had been about 76
per cent, while Wallace's had been above 80 per cent. (I can't recall the
exact figure.) That somewhat shatters the accepted illusion that Jones is
the better businessman, but the argument comes too late. It should have
been advanced a long time ago in the battle. The tide is running out and
Wallace is being carried away with it—he thinks, undoubtedly, to a
greater destiny, later. I rather doubt it because of his utter lack of
[capacity for] the personal equation which is such a vital factor in political
leadership.

I can add a note here on the Chicago convention which was missing in
my information then. At lunch with Justice Murphy last Tuesday at the
Supreme Court, he told me that when Wallace was sent to China before
the convention, the whole matter was rigged by Hannegan, Flynn . . .
and Frank Walker . . . to oust Wallace. When Wallace came back, the
President asked Wallace not to run—not to be a candidate at the national
convention, but in the course of the discussion the President said that if
he were a delegate at the convention, he would vote for Wallace.
Nevertheless, his information from political sources all over the country
was that it would be to the best interest of the party for Wallace not to

15. Ultimately, on 1 March 1945, Wallace was confirmed as secretary of commerce by a
56 to 32 vote, but only after passage of the George Bill. He served as secretary of commerce
until fired by President Truman in 1947.

run. Wallace declined to drop out and was quick enough to say to the President: "Will you say in a letter to me that you would vote for me if you were a delegate?" to which the President had to reply in the affirmative. He couldn't do anything else. So that was how Wallace got the letter from the President to the effect that the President would vote for Wallace if he, the President, were a delegate at the convention.

Behind the scenes, the President worked with Hannegan, Flynn, and Walker, and was ready to have them settle the shift away from Wallace as a vice presidential candidate, in spite of the evidence that Wallace did have the votes. The liberal flock in the country had shifted to him. . . .

Wednesday, 15 August 1945
4101 Lorcom Lane

Dear Katherine Mather:

You and Norman, Jr., are at this moment safe and sound and undoubtedly asleep in a rustic cabin in the mining town of Jamestown, Colorado, with the faithful Mrs. Tacey. Probably your most serious thoughts today were in regard to your spelling lessons, which Eda faithfully insists upon your pursuing even during holidays, but I venture to say that both of you grasp a little of the significance of the day when the news of Japan's surrender came to Jamestown, for both of you have more than once expressed concern over our soldiers getting killed in the war and have wondered when it would be over. . . .

The sudden passing of Roosevelt at Warm Springs, Georgia, rocked the nation and, indeed, the world, for the San Francisco conference to write a charter of a future world organization was scheduled for the end of that very month—the summation of Roosevelt's efforts and strategy—over which he, himself, was to preside. It is difficult to recapture, now, the sickening anxiety with which we all regarded the shabby leadership he had left in command of various cabinet posts, the greatest danger of all being Stettinius, secretary of state, who was put there because he was acceptable to Secretary Hull, lying on his deathbed but, nevertheless, seeking to control with a dying hand the direction of foreign policy and, because the President was equally willing to have him there, as a man who could not emerge in his own right as a great figure, but who would take orders.

Then, suddenly, Harry S. Truman was President, as overwhelmed with the fact as the country was. Could this plain citizen from a small town [in] Missouri, with no background whatsoever in the intricacies of European diplomacy, possibly succeed to the burden of the Roosevelt mastermind? Truman, himself, in all humility, was overwhelmed with these grave responsibilities.

History has obliterated these anxieties for, while Stettinius could not possibly serve as mediator between the English and the Russians, as Roosevelt had stood between Churchill and Stalin at Yalta, . . . the fundamental achievements of San Francisco were great indeed. . . .

Truman's remote role in Washington was a powerful one for, while President Roosevelt's leadership had been greatly weakened by innumerable tensions between himself and the Senate and the House of Representatives, to which he had grown increasingly indifferent in his later years of power, Truman was one of the fraternity on the Hill. Indeed, he carried it almost too far by dropping into the cloak rooms and visiting with the boys just as he used to in the Senate. He was "Harry" to almost everyone on the Hill and that was a tremendous asset, compensating enormously for any weakness arising from his unfamiliarity with the fifth dimensional qualities of diplomacy.

All these things you can read in the history books. The purpose of my letter is to tell you something of the relatively insignificant incidents in my own affairs. I knew Mr. Truman as a senator. You will find in my accounts of the battle of the Breakers Hotel how strongly he figured in that investigation by the Truman Committee. . . .

Although Mr. Truman had ceased to be chairman of the Truman Committee at the time of the surplus property hearings in August of 1944, when I knocked Will Clayton off of his perch as surplus property administrator, he was nevertheless quite conscious of that public battle as presiding officer of the Senate and Vice President of the United States. He was undoubtedly on my side.

I felt that we saw eye to eye on the Biddle battle and wanted to have a visit with him about that subject so, a few days before I left for Tampa, Florida, on February 18, 1945, on a matter of legal business which had arisen there, I telephoned to Mr. Truman to see if we could meet. He was exceedingly cordial over the telephone; said he was anxious, indeed, to talk with me; but that he was leaving for New York that afternoon, and since I was leaving for Florida in two or three days, as I had mentioned to him, he suggested that I telephone him as soon as I got back from Florida, and so our visit was deferred.

I also wrote to him from Florida and sent him a copy of a news clipping I had cut out, reporting a talk I made to the Board of Directors of the Chamber of Commerce, in which they undoubtedly expected me to do a "Raymond Moley"[1] and lambaste the Democratic administration, but in which I had disappointed them by saying that I regretted very much the

---

1. An original member of FDR's "brain trust," Moley (1880–1975) left the administration in 1933 to become an editorial writer for *Newsweek*. His writings grew increasingly critical of the New Deal.

[implication] of dishonesty which was left by my attack upon Mr. Biddle and that in truth and in fact I had found the great rank and file of government employees to be honestly and faithfully serving the public welfare. . . .

He replied to that letter, . . . I would say, somewhat perfunctorily, on the part of a man with his eye on the presidential nomination in 1948, except for my personal acquaintanceship with him, which places the letter on a higher valuation.

To skip over . . . the events in Florida, I finally got around to telephoning Mr. Truman's office on April 2, 1945, and was immediately given an appointment. He was exceedingly cordial in greeting me. Had I known he was going to be President within two weeks, I would have gone home and written down our conversation, but some of it is indelibly clear in my mind, anyway. It was about as follows:

I said, "From my numerous contacts on the Truman Committee and my knowledge of your forthright attitude and insistence on integrity in the transaction of government business, I have felt sure that we saw eye to eye in the matter of my fight with Attorney General Biddle. As I wrote to you from Florida, I wanted you to know I have not attacked the administration as such. I feel very strongly that when we discover a mess in our own house we ought to clean it up ourselves and not let the opposition come along and do it for us at a later date."

"I quite agree with you, Norman," he interposed, and waited for me to go on.

I continued: "President Roosevelt was too preoccupied with international affairs or, perhaps, indisposed towards a bit of housecleaning, which was very badly needed, so I just took on the job in the Department of Justice myself. It had to be done!"

"You were quite right about it," Mr. Truman said, "and, besides, that fight between you and Biddle was inevitable. It was brewing for a long time."

I cannot remember the precise tenor of his remarks thereafter, except that they were derogatory in regard to Mr. Biddle and wholly cordial towards my attitude and they ended up with this expression which I quote precisely:

"Besides," he concluded, "Biddle is just a pinhead." . . .

I had an appointment to meet Mr. Truman and introduce a friend who was interested in the possible appointment as ambassador to Cuba, on April 14th but, by that time he had been whisked up off my level on to the presidential level and such trivial matters were, naturally, swept aside before the tremendous new responsibilities which confronted him. . . .

I should add, that the night of the President's death, we drove to the White House to leave a note for Anna to express our sympathy and offer our assistance, in any manner which might be useful to her, as the surviving Roosevelts stood on the threshold of a precipitous descent out of the limelight. Poor John and Anna were soon struggling for an apartment in Washington, like ordinary citizens, a fact which columnists announced with some glee. . . .

To resume my own personal story for such interest as it may be to you: Right after my discharge from the department, after being persuaded by Ernest G. Howes, president of the Howes Brothers Leather Company— whom I had grown to know intimately during the battle of the Breakers Hotel as a resident of Palm Beach—to remain and practice in Washington, where my status would be the greatest, I was also retained by the Association of Independent Cigar Manufacturers, of Tampa, Florida, and proceeded to Florida as stated above, in February, taking your mother along. Two weeks of intensive work in Tampa were followed by two weeks in Palm Beach, Florida, where Mr. Howes had a winter home, and we stayed at the Whitehall Hotel, the owners of which promptly became clients of mine in respect to the taking of the Palm Beach Biltmore Hotel, which they also owned, by the Navy Department. . . .

As I told your mother, I suppose I am the only man who ever started a law business by spending a month in Florida at the height of the season, but that is what we did and the two weeks of almost solid play at Palm Beach were two of the most delicious weeks of sheer leisure your mother and I have had since we came to this strenuous city of Washington. . . .

The complete revival in sun and surf at Palm Beach, Florida, was followed on my return to Washington by very intensive work . . . on the filing of cases against OPA, protesting their cigar leaf tobacco regulations and by the continued effort to organize a law office. . . .

Truman made short work of Biddle after the period of mourning for President Roosevelt had elapsed and, to Biddle's utter amazement, he waked up one morning to find that Tom Clark, assistant attorney general in charge of the Criminal Division, was to succeed him. He was about to fire Tom Clark, as he had fired me, and Tom's elevation to the attorney generalship was a devastating blow on top of all he had suffered. I sent Tom a congratulatory telegram, concluding, "You will have to admit that I cleared the deck for you." . . .

With one cabinet member from the State of Washington [Secretary of Labor Lewis B. Schwellenbach]—a small state of less than two million people—no other appointment to the cabinet from that state could be politically considered even had President Truman thought about me for one moment. . . .

And so, I was comfortably and happily left on the side lines, where my income for the first five months was over three times my annual income as assistant attorney general and, even though income taxes make it impossible to keep very much of it, it is a comfortable feeling to have it pass through one's fingers for a change, with more in prospect and the very great pleasure of building a law firm of my own. . . .

These have not been my true reflections on this greatest of days, August 15, 1945, but on the evening of a holiday which President Truman declared yesterday upon the capitulation of the Japanese, I took up my dictaphone by my bed to reflect on this world-shaking event, and instead relapsed into the task of bringing you up to date. . . .

Pandemonium broke loose in Washington. Never have such crowds massed in the streets or pressed against the iron fence of the White House, where President and Mrs. Truman walked down to see them, and the President made a brief statement as to the significance of that day. The fall of tyranny and the victory of democracy. . . . Bitter years lie ahead in your lifetime, in which the "have-nots," dispossessed completely by this war against tyranny, will scheme and conspire and invent until they, too, have secretly acquired the atomic bomb for, what our intelligence has discovered, other intelligences can rediscover, so that the destructive forces of this great power may yet be loosed in your lifetime. Peace can only be maintained, now, at the point of a sword, and peace at the point of a sword, even in the hands of men of good will, who wish justice and human dignity to prevail, may still not be peace in your time.

Affectionately,

Daddy [signed]

Biographical Notes

ADAMS, EMORY S. (1881–). Army officer (major general); adjutant general of the Army, 1938–42.

AGAR, HERBERT S. (1897–1980). Editor of the *Louisville Courier–Journal*, 1940–42; special assistant to the U.S. ambassador to Great Britain and director of the British Division of the Office of War Information, 1943–46.

ALLEN, EDWARD S. (ED) (1885–1976). Seattle lawyer and U.S. member of the International Salmon Fisheries Commission, 1937–51.

ALLEN, ROBERT S. (1900–1981). Newspaper columnist and coauthor of "Washington Merry-Go-Round," 1932–42, with Drew Pearson.

APPLEBY, PAUL H. (1891–1963). Editor and publisher of the *Des Moines Daily Reporter*; executive assistant to the secretary of agriculture, 1933–40; undersecretary of agriculture, 1940–44; assistant director of the Bureau of the Budget, 1944–47.

ARNOLD, THURMAN WESLEY (1891–1969). Special assistant to the U.S. attorney general, 1937–38; Justice Department representative on the Temporary National Economic Committee, 1938–41; assistant U.S. attorney general in charge of the Anti-Trust Division of the Justice Department, 1938–42; associate justice of the U.S. Circuit Court of Appeals for the District of Columbia, 1943–45.

ASTOR, NANCY (LANGHORNE) (1879–1964). American-born viscountess; wife of the publisher of the London *Times*; first woman member of Parliament, 1919–45; advocate of appeasement in the 1930s.

AUSTIN, WARREN R. (1877–1962). Republican U.S. senator from Vermont, 1931–46; U.S. representative to the United Nations, 1946–53.

AVERY, SEWELL L. (1873–1960). President of the Montgomery Ward Company, 1937–51; president and chairman of the U.S. Gypsum Company, 1905–51.

BACKUS, LEROY M. (1879–). President of the Backus Improvement Company, a Seattle insurance and investment firm.

BARKLEY, ALBEN W. (1877–1956). Democratic U.S. senator from Kentucky, 1923–49; majority leader, 1937–49; Vice President, 1949–53.

BARNES, JOSEPH F. (1907–1970). Reporter and foreign editor for the *New York Herald Tribune*, 1935–41, 1944–48; deputy director of the Overseas Branch of the Office of War Information, 1941–44.

371

372   BIOGRAPHICAL NOTES

BARNES, VERDA W. (1907–). Head of the Women's Division of the Congress of
Industrial Organizations, 1944.
BARRETT, FRANK A. (1892–1962). Republican representative from Wyoming,
1943–50; governor, 1951–53; U.S. senator, 1953–59.
BARUCH, BERNARD M. (1870–1965). Wealthy businessman and contributor to
Democratic candidates; chairman of the War Industries Board, 1917–18;
adviser to the War Mobilization Board, 1943–45.
BELL, BRIAN (1890–1942). Reporter and editor; chief of Washington bureau of
Associated Press, 1939–42.
BENNETT, HARRY H. (1893–). Personnel director of Ford Motor Company,
1918–.
BENNETT, JAMES VAN B. (JIM) (1894–1978). Lawyer; director of the U.S.
Bureau of Prisons, 1937–64.
BERGE, WENDELL (1903–1955). Assistant U.S. attorney general in charge of
the Criminal Division of the Justice Department, 1940–43, and of the
Anti-trust Division, 1943–47.
BERLE, ADOLPH A., JR. (1895–1971). Member of FDR's original "brain
trust"; special counsel to the Reconstruction Finance Corporation, 1933–38;
assistant secretary of state, 1938–44; U.S. ambassador to Brazil, 1945–46.
BIDDLE, FRANCIS B. (1886–1968). Former law clerk to Justice Oliver Wendell
Holmes; special assistant U.S. attorney for the Eastern District of Pennsylvania, 1934–35; chairman of the National Labor Relations Board; chief counsel of
the joint committee to investigate the Tennessee Valley Authority, 1938–39;
judge of the U.S. Circuit Court of Appeals, 1939–40; U.S. solicitor general,
1940; U.S. attorney general, 1941–45; judge at the Nuremberg trials, 1945–46.
BINGHAM, AILEEN M. (–1953). Former Mrs. James B. Hilliard and third wife
and widow of Robert W. Bingham (1871–1937), the pro-Roosevelt president-
publisher of the Louisville Courier-Journal and Louisville Times and U.S.
ambassador to Great Britain, 1933–37); she was the leading organizer of the
Bundles for Britain charity.
BIRD, RENSEN DUB. (1888–1971). President of Occidental College, 1921–46,
and of the Association of American Colleges, 1941.
BLACK, HUGO LAF. (1886–1971). Democratic U.S. senator from Alabama,
1933–37; associate justice of the U.S. Supreme Court, 1937–71.
BLOCH, CLAUDE C. (1878–1967). Judge advocate general of the Navy,
1934–38; commander-in-chief of the U.S. fleet, 1938–40; commandant of the
14th Naval District (Hawaii), 1940–42; he helped prepare the coastal defense
plans for the islands; following Pearl Harbor, he was promoted to rear admiral
and retired for physical disability.
BOETTIGER (HALSTEAD), ANNA ROOSEVELT DALL (1905–1975). Franklin
and Eleanor Roosevelt's eldest child and the wife of John Boettiger, the
publisher of the Seattle Post-Intelligencer; after the spring of 1944, she resided
in the White House and became FDR's confidante.
BOETTIGER, JOHN (1900–1950). Reporter for the Chicago Tribune; married
Anna Roosevelt Dall in January 1935; editor and publisher of Hearst's Seattle
Post-Intelligencer, 1936–45; editor-publisher of the Phoenix Arizona Times,
1947–48; lieutenant colonel in the Army, 1943–45.

BONE, HOMER T. (1883–1970). Liberal Democratic U.S. senator from Washington, 1933–44; judge of the U.S. Circuit Court of Appeals, 9th Circuit, 1944–56.

BOURQUIN, M. MITCHELL (1894–1966). Special assistant U.S. attorney, San Francisco, 1940–.

BOWEN, JOHN C. (1888–1978). Collector of internal revenue for Washington State, 1933–34; judge of the U.S. District Court for Western Washington, 1934–78.

BRICKER, JOHN W. (1893–). Conservative Republican governor of Ohio, 1939–45; U.S. senator, 1947–59; unsuccessful Republican vice presidential nominee, 1944.

BRIDGES, HARRY (ALFRED R.) (1900–). Australian-born president of the International Longshoremen's and Warehousemen's Union, 1937–78; vice president of the Congress of Industrial Organizations, 1938–56; until the U.S. entered World War II, there were persistent efforts to deport him on grounds that he was a communist.

BRODERICK, LYNN R. (1892–1958). Democratic national committeeman, 1934–42; internal revenue collector for Kansas, 1940–58.

BROUGHTON, JOSEPH M. (1888–1949). Democratic governor of North Carolina, 1941–45; U.S. senator, 1948–49; unsuccessful favorite son vice presidential candidate at the Democratic convention, 1944.

BROWDER, EARL (RUSSELL) (1891–1973). General secretary of the American Communist Party, 1930–44; expelled for "revisionism," 1946.

BROWN, ARTHUR V. (1863–1949). President of the Indiana National Bank, 1932–42, chairman, 1942–49; president of the Union Trust Company, Indianapolis, 1916–42, chairman, 1942–49.

BROWN, ELI H., III (1906–1974). U.S. attorney for Western Kentucky, 1938–45.

BUNKER, BERKELEY L. (1906–). Democratic U.S. senator from Nevada, 1940–42.

BURKE, J. FRANK. Liberal southern California Democratic Party leader and radio station owner.

BURLEW, EBERT KAISER (E.K.) (1885–1945). Lawyer; administrative assistant to the secretary of the interior, 1923–38; first assistant secretary of the interior, 1938–43.

BUTLER, PIERCE (1886–1939). Conservative railroad attorney; associate justice of the U.S. Supreme Court, 1923–39.

BYRD, HARRY F. (1887–1966). Conservative Democratic governor of Virginia, 1926–30; U.S. senator, 1933–66.

BYRNES, JAMES F. (1879–1972). Democratic congressman from South Carolina, 1911–25; pro-FDR U.S. senator, 1931–41; associate justice of the U.S. Supreme Court, 1941–42; director of the Office of Economic Stabilization, 1942–43; director of the Office of War Mobilization, 1943–45; secretary of state, 1945–47; negotiated the peace treaties with the minor Axis powers.

CAREY, JAMES B. (1912–1973). Founder and president of National Radio and Allied Trades Union, 1933–40; secretary of the Congress of Industrial Organizations, 1938–73; president of the United Electrical, Radio and Machine Workers of America, 1936–41, 1950–65.

CARR, CHARLES H. (1903–1976). U.S. attorney for the Southern District of California, 1943–46.

CARTER, ALBERT E. (1881–1964). Democratic congressman from California, 1925–45.

CARUSI, UGO J. A. (1902–). Private secretary and special assistant to the U.S. attorney general, 1925–30; administrative assistant to the attorney general, 1930–44; commissioner of the Immigration and Naturalization Service, 1944–48.

CASEY, EUGENE B. (FARMER CASEY) (1904–). Maryland businessman and dairy farmer; deputy governor of the Farm Credit Administration, 1940–41; administrative assistant to the President, 1941–45.

CAUGHRAN, B. HOWARD (1890–1973). Assistant U.S. attorney, 1933–40; U.S. attorney for Southern Indiana, 1940–42.

CHADWICK, STEPHEN F. (1894–1975). Seattle lawyer and national commander of the American Legion, 1938–39; a leader in the conservative wing of the Democratic Party; unsuccessful candidate for the Democratic U.S. Senate nomination, 1932; in the 1930s he switched parties and was the unsuccessful Republican senatorial nominee in 1940.

CHANEY, MAYRIS (TINY). Dancer and personal friend of Eleanor Roosevelt's; assistant in the physical-fitness program of the Office of Civilian Defense, 1941–42.

CHAPMAN, OSCAR L. (1896–1978). Assistant secretary of the interior, 1933–46.

CHEW, ERIC M. (1907–1970). Seattle physician and heart specialist, 1940–70.

CHILDS, MARQUIS W. (1903–). Journalist for United Press, 1923, 1925–26, and the St. Louis Post-Dispatch, 1926–44.

CHU, SHI-MING (1902–1965) Chinese Nationalist army officer (lieutenant general) and military attaché of the Nationalist Chinese embassy in Washington, D.C., 1941–45.

CLARK, IRVING M. (1882–1960). Seattle lawyer and conservation leader.

CLARK, IRVING M., JR. (1921–1978). Seattle lawyer and civic activist, 1942–78.

CLARK, JOEL B. (CHAMP) (1890–1954). Son of the former speaker of the House, James B. (Champ) Clark; Democratic U.S. senator from Missouri, 1933–45; associate justice of the U.S. Circuit Court of Appeals for the District of Columbia, 1945–54.

CLARK, TOM C. (1899–1977). Assistant U.S. attorney general for the Anti-trust Division, 1943, and for the Criminal Division of the Justice Department, 1943–45; U.S. attorney general, 1945–49; associate justice of the U.S. Supreme Court, 1949–67.

CLAYTON, WILLIAM L. (WILL) (1880–1966). Texas cotton broker, 1904–40; deputy federal loan administrator and vice president of the Export-Import Bank, 1940–42; assistant secretary of commerce, 1942–44; administrator of the Surplus War Properties Administration, 1944; assistant secretary of state, 1944–45; undersecretary of state for economic affairs, 1945–47.

COFFIN, HENRY SLOAN (1877–1954). President of the Union Theological Seminary, 1926–45.

COHEN, BENJAMIN V. (1894–1959). Lawyer and Zionist activist; counsel for the Public Works Administration, 1933–34, and the National Power Policy Committee of the Interior Department, 1934–41; special assistant to the U.S. attorney general, 1936–38; general counsel of the Office of War Mobilization, 1943–45; played an important role, with Tommy Corcoran, in drafting much of the early New Deal legislation.

COHEN, FRANK (1893–1959). President and chairman of the Empire Ordnance Company, 1940–45, and its subsidiaries, including the Savannah Shipyards Company.

COLLIER, HARRY D. (1876–1959). Director of the Standard Oil Company of California, 1924–56, and president of the company, 1940–45.

COLLINS, LINTON MCG. (1902–1972). First assistant to the assistant U.S. attorney general and special assistant to the U.S. attorney general, 1935–44.

CONNALLY, THOMAS T. (TOM) (1877–1963). Democratic congressman from Texas, 1917–29; U.S. senator, 1929–53.

CONNELLY, EDWARD M. (1892–1947). Spokane lawyer and U.S. attorney for the Eastern District of Washington, 1942–47.

COOK, DONALD C. (1909–1981). Assistant director of the Public Utilities Division of the Securities and Exchange Commission, 1943–45; special assistant to the U.S. attorney general, 1945–49; investigator for the House Naval Affairs Committee, 1943.

COOKE, MORRIS L. (1872–1960). Consulting engineer; administrator of the Rural Electrification Administration, 1935–37; headed a commission to settle the Mexican oil controversy, 1942.

COOPER, PRENTICE (1895–1969). Democratic governor of Tennessee, 1938–46; chairman of the Tennessee delegation to the 1944 Democratic national convention, receiving 29 favorite-son votes for vice presidential nomination on the first and second ballots.

CORCORAN, THOMAS G. (TOMMY) (1900–1981). Protege of Felix Frankfurter and law clerk to Justice Holmes, 1926–27; worked for the Reconstruction Finance Corporation, 1932, 1934–41; special assistant to the U.S. attorney general, 1932–35; played a major role in the drafting and passage of New Deal legislation with Ben Cohen; engaged in corporate law from 1941 until his death.

COUGHLIN, CHARLES E. (1891–1979). Catholic "radio priest" who attracted a large following in the 1930s with his populist, isolationist, antilabor, anticommunist, and anti-Semitic message; his National Union for Social Justice, founded in 1934, promoted these ideas.

COX, (EDWARD) EUGENE (1880–1952). Democratic congressman from Georgia, 1925–52; second ranking Democrat on the Rules Committee.

COX, HUGH B. (1905–1973). Special assistant to the U.S. attorney general, 1935–43; assistant U.S. attorney general, 1943; assistant U.S. solicitor general, 1943–45; general counsel for the Surplus War Property Administration, 1945.

COX, OSCAR S. (1905–1966). Assistant to the general counsel of the U.S. Treasury Department, 1938–41; general counsel of the Lend Lease Administration and of the Office of Emergency Management, 1941–43; assistant U.S. solicitor general, 1942–43; general counsel of the Foreign Economic Administration, 1943–45.

COY, (ALBERT) WAYNE (1903–1957). Indiana journalist, radio and TV executive; assistant administrator of the Federal Security Agency, 1939–42; administrative assistant to the President and White House liaison with the Office of Emergency Management, 1941–43; assistant director of the Bureau of the Budget, 1942–44; chairman of the Federal Communications Commission, 1947–52.

CRAMER, MYRON C. (1881–1966) Army officer (major general); judge advocate general of the Army, 1941–45.

CROWLEY, LEO T. (1890–1972). Wisconsin paper manufacturer; chairman of the Federal Deposit Insurance Corporation, 1934–45; Alien Property Custodian, 1941–43; head of the Office of Economic Warfare, 1943; director of the Foreign Economic Administration, 1943–45.

CRUMP, EDWARD H. (1874–1954). Bookkeeper and businessman; Democratic political boss of Tennessee, 1909–48; mayor of Memphis, 1910–16, 1939–48; Democratic congressman from Tennessee, 1931–35; Democratic national committeeman, 1936–45.

CUMMINGS, HOMER S. (1870–1956). Connecticut Democratic leader, 1900–48; U.S. attorney general, 1933–39.

CURRAN, EDWARD M. (1903–1963). U.S. attorney, Washington D.C., 1940–46.

CURRIE, LAUCHLIN (1902–). Canadian-born economist; administrative assistant to the President, 1939–45; member of the U.S. Economic Mission to China, 1941; deputy administrator of the Foreign Economic Administration, 1943–45.

DANIELS, JONATHAN W. (1902–). Reporter and editor, for the *Raleigh News and Observer* 1933–42, 1944–70; son of Josephus Daniels; administrative assistant to the President, 1943–44; press secretary to the President, 1945.

DANIELS, JOSEPHUS (1862–1948). Editor of the *Raleigh News and Observer*, 1894–48; secretary of the Navy, 1913–21; U.S. ambassador to Mexico, 1933–42.

DAUGHERTY, HARRY M. (1860–1941). Ohio politician and friend of Warren G. Harding; U.S. attorney general, 1921–23; forced to resign in the Teapot Dome scandal, but was acquitted of fraud charges in 1927.

DAVIES, JOSEPH E. (1876–1958). Wealthy Democratic lawyer; counsel for the taxpayers in the Ford stock valuation tax case, 1924–27; U.S. ambassador to the Soviet Union, 1936–38, 1943.

DAVIES, RALPH K. (1897–1971). Vice president of the Standard Oil Company of California, 1935–; deputy administrator of the National Petroleum Administration, 1941–46.

DAVIS, ELMER (HOLMES) (1890–1958). Broadcaster and news analyst for the CBS radio network, 1939–42; director of the Office of War Information, 1942–45.

DAVIS, JOHN W. (1873–1955). Democratic congressman from West Virginia, 1911–13; U.S. solicitor general, 1913–18; U.S. ambassador to Great Britain, 1918–21; unsuccessful Democratic nominee for the presidency, 1924.

DELACY, HUGH (1910–1986). Seattle city councilman, 1937–40; executive officer of the communist-dominated Washington Commonwealth Federation,

1940–42; a machinist at Todd Pacific Shipyard, 1943–44; and Democratic congressman from Washington, 1945–47.

DEMMER, CHARLES C. (1883–). Colonel in the U.S. Army Medical Corps; in charge of Ream General Army Hospital, Palm Beach, Florida, 1943–44.

DEMPSEY, JOHN J. (1879–1958). Democratic congressman from New Mexico, 1935–41; member of the U.S. Maritime Commission, 1941; undersecretary of the interior, 1941–42; governor of New Mexico, 1943–47.

DEMPSEY, WILLIAM J. (1906–). General counsel of the Federal Communications Commission, 1938–40; after 1940, partner in the law firm, Dempsey and Koplovitz.

DENMAN, WILLIAM (1872–1959). Chairman of the U.S. Shipping Board, 1917; judge of the U.S. Circuit Court of Appeals, 9th Circuit, 1935–59.

DEWEY, THOMAS E. (1902–1971). Republican district attorney for New York City, 1937–40; governor of New York, 1943–55; unsuccessful Republican nominee for the presidency, 1944, 1948.

DIES, MARTIN, JR. (1900–1972). Democratic congressman from Texas, 1931–45, 1953–59; chairman of the Special Committee to Investigate Un-American Activities (Dies Committee), 1938–45.

DILLINGHAM, WALTER F. (1875–1963). Honolulu construction company owner and government contractor.

DIXON, FRANK M. (1892–1965). Democratic governor of Alabama, 1939–43.

DOHENY, EDWARD L. (1856–1935). Southern California petroleum producer whose oil leases helped precipitate the Teapot Dome scandal in the 1920s.

DOUGLAS, HELEN GAHAGAN (1900–1980). Mrs. Melvyn Douglas. Actress and liberal Democratic National Committeewoman, 1940–44; Democratic congresswoman from California, 1945–51.

DOUGLAS, MELVYN (1901–). Hollywood actor who served as head of the Arts Division of the Office of Civilian Defense, 1941–42.

DOUGLAS, WILLIAM O. (1898–1980). Professor of law at Columbia and Yale law schools, 1927–36; member of the Securities and Exchange Commission, 1936–39; chairman of the SEC, 1937–39; associate justice of the U.S. Supreme Court, 1939–75, where he was known as a strong advocate of civil liberties; in 1944 conducted an unsuccessful campaign for the Democratic vice presidential nomination.

DOWNEY, SHERIDAN (1884–1961). Democratic U.S. senator from California, 1939–50.

DRUMHELLER, JOSEPH (JOE) (1900–1970). Spokane chemical engineer and Democratic political leader; served as Democratic state senator, 1934–42.

DURR, CLIFFORD J. (CLIFF) (1899–1975) Assistant general counsel for the Reconstruction Finance Corporation, 1933–41; member of the Federal Communications Commission, 1941–48.

EARLY, STEPHEN T. (STEVE) (1889–1951). Journalist with United Press and Associated Press; FDR's advance man during his 1920 vice presidential campaign; assistant secretary to the President 1933–37, secretary to the President, 1937–45; undersecretary of defense, 1949–50.

EASTUS, CLYDE O. (1886–). U.S. attorney for the Northern District of Texas, 1933–53.

ELLIOTT, JAMES A. (1895–1973). Farmer and publisher of the *Tulare Daily News*; Democratic congressman from California, 1937–49.

EMMONS, DELOS C. (1888–1965). Officer in the U.S. Army Air Corps (major general); commander of the Hawaiian Department, 17 December 1941 to 1943, of the Western Theater of Operations, 1943–44, and of the Alaska Department, 1944–46.

ENNIS, EDWARD J. Lawyer in the U.S. solicitor general's office, 1934–41; general counsel for the Immigration and Naturalization Service, 1941–42; director of the Alien Enemy Control Unit in the Justice Department, 1942–45.

ERNST, MORRIS L. (1888–1976). New York labor and civil rights lawyer; member of the State Banking Commission, 1935–45; general counsel of the American Civil Liberties Union, 1929–55.

ETHRIDGE, MARK F. (1896–1981). Newspaper executive; vice president and general manager of the *Louisville Courier-Journal*, 1936–42; publisher, 1942–62; chairman of the Fair Employment Practices Committee, 1941–42.

ETHRIDGE, WILLIE SNOW (1900–). Mrs. Mark F. Ethridge.

EWING, OSCAR R. (JACK) (1889–1980). Special assistant to the U.S. attorney general, 1942; assistant to the secretary of the Democratic National Committee, 1940–42; vice chairman of the DNC, 1942–47; administrator of the Federal Security Agency, 1947–52.

FAHY, CHARLES (1892–1979). First assistant solicitor for the Interior Department, 1933; member of the Petroleum Administrative Board, 1933–34; chairman of the PAB, 1934–35; general counsel to the National Labor Relations Board, 1935–40; U.S. solicitor general, 1941–49.

FALL, ALBERT B. (1861–1944). Republican U.S. senator from New Mexico, 1912–21; secretary of the Navy, 1921–23; his oil leases to Doheny and Sinclair precipitated the Teapot Dome scandal, his resignation, and his conviction for bribery in 1929.

FARBER, JOHN C. (1893–1969). New York lawyer; partner in the law firm of (Franklin D.) Roosevelt, O'Connor and Farber, 1929–33, and of O'Connor and Farber, 1933–69.

FARISH, WILLIAM S. (1881–1942). President of Standard Oil Company of New Jersey, 1937–42.

FARLEY, JAMES A. (1888–1976). Bookkeeper; served concurrently as chairman of the New York State Democratic Committee, chairman of the Democratic National Committee, and U.S. postmaster general, 1932–40; in 1940, he broke with FDR over the third-term issue.

FEE, JAMES A. (1888–1959). Judge of the U.S. District Court for Oregon, 1931–53.

FERGUSON, HOMER B. (1889–). Republican U.S. senator from Michigan, 1943–55.

FIELD, MARSHALL, III (1893–1956). Chicago department store owner and bank director; liberal publisher of both the New York *P.M.*, 1937–, and the Chicago *Sun Times*, 1941–.

FLEMING, PHILIP B. (1887–1955). Engineer and army officer (major general); administrator of the Wage-Hour Division of the Labor Department, 1940–41; administrator of the Federal Works Agency, 1941–49.

FLYNN, EDWARD J. (ED) (1892–1953). Lawyer; chairman of the Bronx, New York Democratic Committee, 1922–, and of the Democratic National Committee, 1940–42; a grand jury acquitted him of using city paving blocks to upgrade his own property, 1941–42, but he remained under a political cloud.

FORD, HENRY (1863–1947). Isolationist, anti-labor, president of the Ford Motor Company, 1903–47.

FORRESTAL, JAMES V. (1892–1949). Investment banker, 1916–40; administrative assistant to the President, 1940; undersecretary of the Navy, 1940–44; secretary of the Navy, 1944–47; first secretary of defense, 1947–49.

FORTAS, ABE (1910–1982). Protege of William O. Douglas at Yale; assistant chief in the legal division of the Agricultural Adjustment Administration, 1933; counsel to the Securities and Exchange Commission, 1934–39, and to the Interior Department, 1939–42; undersecretary of interior, 1942–46; he then returned to private practice; associate justice of the U.S. Supreme Court, 1965–69.

FRANK, JEROME N. (1889–1957). General counsel of the Agricultural Adjustment Administration and of the Federal Surplus Relief Corporation, 1933–35; in 1935 dismissed from the AAA for his radical stand on tenants' rights; in 1937 appointed a member of the Securities and Exchange Commission; judge of the U.S. Circuit Court of Appeals, 2nd Circuit, 1941–57.

FRANKFURTER, FELIX (1882–1965). Assistant U.S. attorney for the Southern District of New York, 1906–10; assistant to the secretary of war, 1911–13; professor of law at Harvard Law School, 1914–39; associate justice of the U.S. Supreme Court, 1939–62, where he was noted for his strong belief in judicial restraint.

FRASER, HUGH R. (1901–). Journalist; author of *Democracy in the Making* (1938) and of a newspaper column entitled "Inside Washington," 1939–45; served on the staff of the U.S. Office of Education, 1940–43.

FREEMAN, CHARLES S. (1878–1969). Naval officer (vice admiral); commandant of the 13th naval district (Seattle), 1942; retired for physical disability.

FREUND, PAUL A. (1908–). One of Frankfurter's proteges; law clerk to Justice Brandeis, 1932–33; counsel in the Treasury Department, 1933; general counsel for the Reconstruction Finance Corporation, November 1933–35; when Stanley Reed became U.S. solicitor general, in 1935, Freund followed him to the Justice Department, where he remained until 1939, at which time he became a law professor at Harvard; assistant U.S. solicitor general, 1942–46.

FULLER, HELEN (1914–1972). Journalist; editor of the *New Republic*, 1941–62; assistant to the administrator of the National Youth Administration, 1939–41.

FULTON, HUGH A. (1908–1962). Special assistant to the U.S. attorney general, 1938–41; chief counsel for the Truman Committee, 1941–44.

GALBREATH, JOHN W. (1897–). Realtor; president of the John W. Galbreath and Co., real estate firm, Columbus, Ohio, 1924, and of the National Association of Real Estate Boards, 1944.

GAREY, EUGENE L. (1891–1953). Partner in the law firm of Garey and Garey, 1925–53, and general counsel for the House Select Committee to Investigate the Federal Communications Commission, 1943–44.

GARNER, JOHN NANCE (1868–1967). Democratic representative from Texas,

1903–33; speaker of the House, 1931–33; Vice President of the United States, 1933–41, until he broke with FDR over the third-term issue.

GATCH, THOMAS L. (1891–1954). Lawyer and naval officer (vice admiral), and judge advocate general of the Navy, 1943–45.

GEORGE, WALTER F. (1878–1957). Conservative Democratic U.S. senator from Georgia, 1922–57.

GILFOND, MAX E. Executive assistant to the U.S. attorney general and director of publicity for the Justice Department, 1940–43.

GILLETTE, GUY M. (1879–1973). An isolationist Democratic representative from Iowa, 1933–36; U.S. senator, 1936–45, 1949–54; chairman of the Surplus Property Board, 1945.

GLASSFORD, ELEANOR PHELPS (DODDIE) Canadian-born wife of Admiral William A. Glassford II.

GLASSFORD, WILLIAM A., II (1886–1958). Naval officer (vice admiral); commanded U.S. naval forces in the Southwest Pacific, 1942; U.S. minister to French West Africa, 1943; deputy commander of U.S. naval forces in Europe, 1944; commander of U.S. naval forces in Germany, 1944–46.

GOLDMANN, NAHUM (1894–). Polish-born publisher of the *Encyclopoedia Judaica*, 1928–34; radical Zionist leader of the World Zionist Congress, 1936–; U.S. representative of the Jewish Agency for Palestine, 1940–46.

GOODLAND, WALTER S. (1862–1947). Republican governor of Wisconsin, 1943–47.

GREEN, THOMAS H. (1889–). Army officer (brigadier general); civil governor of Hawaii under martial law administration after Pearl Harbor, 1941–43; assistant judge advocate general of the Army, 1943–.

GREEN, WILLIAM (1872–1952). President of the American Federation of Labor, 1924–52.

GREENSLADE, JOHN W. (1880–1950). Naval officer (vice admiral) and commandant of the 11th Naval District, San Francisco, 1942–44.

GREGORY, THOMAS W. (1861–1933). U.S. attorney general, 1914–19.

GRUENING, ERNEST H. (1887–1974). Physician and journalist; administrator of the Puerto Rico Reconstruction Administration, 1935–37; governor of Alaska Territory, 1939–53; Democratic U.S. senator from Alaska, 1959–69.

GUFFEY, JOSEPH F. (1870–1959). Public utility company official, 1899–1918; member of the Democratic National Committee, 1920–32; liberal Democratic U.S. senator from Pennsylvania, 1935–47.

HAAS, SAUL (1898–1972). Journalist and broadcasting executive; collector of customs for Seattle, 1933–46.

HAGUE, FRANK (1876–1956). Democratic political boss of New Jersey and mayor of Jersey City, 1917–47; member of the Democratic National Committee, 1922–47.

HALLEY, RUDOLPH (1913–1956). Assistant U.S. attorney for the Southern District of New York, 1937–42; assistant counsel for the U.S. Senate War Investigating Committee (Truman Committee), 1942–44, and its chief counsel, 1944–45.

HANEY, BERT E. (1879–1943). Judge of the U.S. Circuit Court of Appeals, 9th Circuit, 1935–43.

HANNEGAN, ROBERT E. (1903–1949). Democratic political boss of St. Louis,

1933–; chairman of the Democratic National Committee, 1944–49; U.S. postmaster general, 1945–47.

HAPSBURG, OTTO DE BOURBON (1912–1954). Eldest son of Charles IV of Austria and the pretender to the throne of Austria after his father's death in 1922; he was a refugee in the U.S. after the fall of France in 1940 and the president of the U.S.-supported Military Committee for the Liberation of Austria, 1942.

HARMSWORTH, ALFRED CHARLES WILLIAM (1865–1922). Viscount North-cliffe. English journalist, publisher, and politician.

HARRIMAN, FLORENCE J. (1870–1967). Mrs. J. Borden Harriman. U.S. ambassador to Norway, 1937–41; Democratic National Committeewoman from Washington, D.C., 1944.

HARRISON, BENJAMIN (1888–1960). Judge of the U.S. District Court for the Southern District of California, 1940–60.

HAVENNER, FRANCK ROBERTS (1882–1967). Democratic congressman from California, 1937–41, 1945–53; member of the California Railroad Commission, 1941–45.

HEALY, WILLIAM (1881–1962). Judge of the U.S. Circuit Court of Appeals, 9th Circuit, 1937–62.

HEARD, JACK W. (1887–1976). Army officer (major general); intelligence officer (G-2) on the General Staff of the U.S. Army, in charge of Latin American Division, 1942, and on the Manpower Board, 1943–46.

HEARST, WILLIAM R. (1863–1951). Wealthy editor and publisher of a chain of newspapers and magazines.

HELLER, EDWARD H. (1900–1961). San Francisco corporate executive; lieutenant colonel in the U.S. Army Finance Department in Los Angeles, 1943–44; member of the Surplus Property Board, 1944.

HELLER, ELINOR R. (1904–). Mrs. Edward H. Heller. Democratic National Committeewoman from California, 1944–.

HENDERSON, CHARLES B. (1873–1954). Democratic U.S. senator from Nevada, 1918–21; member of the board of the Reconstruction Finance Corporation, 1934–41; chairman of the RFC, 1941–47.

HENDERSON, LEON (1895–). Economist; adviser and director of the Research and Planning Division of the National Recovery Administration, 1934–35; consultant to the U.S. Senate, the Democratic National Campaign Committee, and the Works Progress Administration, 1935–38; executive secretary of the Temporary National Economic Committee, 1938–41; administrator of the Office of Price Administration, 1941–43; director of the Division of Civilian Supply of the War Production Board, 1941–.

HENSEL, H. STRUVE (1901–). Special assistant to undersecretary of the Navy, James V. Forrestal, 1941–45.

HICKEY, EDWARD J. (ED) (1912–). Special attorney in the Lands Division of the Justice Department, 1938–41; special assistant to the U.S. attorney general, 1942–46.

HILL, (JOSEPH) LISTER (1894–). Liberal Democratic congressman from Alabama, 1923–38; U.S. senator, 1939–69.

HILLMAN, SIDNEY (SIMCHA HILLMAN) (1887–1946). Lithuanian-born president of the Amalgamated Clothing Workers Union, 1914–46; pro-FDR chairman of the Congress of Industrial Organization's Political Action Committee, 1943–46; member of the Defense Advisory Committee and director of the Office of Production Management, 1940–42.

HOLMAN, RUFUS C. (1877–1959). Republican U.S. senator from Oregon, 1939–45, until defeated for renomination in 1944.

HOLTZHOFF, ALEXANDER (1886–1969). Special assistant to the U.S. attorney general, 1924–45; executive assistant to the attorney general, 1945; judge of the U.S. District Court for Washington, D.C., 1945–69.

HOOVER, J. EDGAR (1895–1972). Career bureaucrat; special assistant to the U.S. attorney general, 1919–21; assistant director of the Bureau of Investigation of the Justice Department, 1921–24; director of the Federal Bureau of Investigation, 1924–72.

HOPKINS, HARRY (1890–1946). Social worker; directed relief operations in New York State when FDR was governor, 1931–32; administrator of the Federal Emergency Relief Administration, 1933–35; administrator of the Public Works Administration, 1935–38; secretary of commerce, 1938–40; administrator of the Lend-Lease Administration, 1941; administrative assistant to the President, 1941–45; gradually came to be FDR's closest adviser, personal messenger, and confidant—becoming, in everything but title, "assistant president."

HOUSE, EDWARD M. (COL.) (1858–1938). Wealthy Texas railroad developer and adviser, friend, and confidant of President Wilson, often serving as his personal messenger; given honorary title "colonel" by Texas Governor Hogg.

HOUSTON, DAVID F. (1866–1940). Political scientist; chancellor of Washington University, 1908–16; secretary of agriculture, 1913–20; secretary of the treasury, 1920–21.

HOWES, ERNEST G. (E.G.) (1871–1956). Boston manufacturer; president and director of the Howes Leather Company, 1895–1938, and chairman, 1938–56.

HUGHES, CHARLES EVANS (1862–1948). Republican governor of New York, 1907–10; associate justice of the U.S. Supreme Court, 1910–16; unsuccessful Republican presidential nominee, 1916; secretary of state, 1921–23; chief justice of the U.S. Supreme Court, 1930–41.

HULL, CORDELL (1877–1955). Democratic congressman from Tennessee, 1907–21; U.S. senator, 1923–31; secretary of state, 1933–44; in 1944 he won the Nobel peace prize.

HURJA, EMIL E. (1892–1953). Journalist; executive director of the Democratic National Committee, 1932–36; financial analyst for the DNC, 1936–39.

HURLEY, JOSEPH R. (1894–1967). Catholic priest, 1919–67; bishop of St. Augustine, Florida, 1940–49, and archbishop, 1949–67.

HURLEY, ROBERT A. (1895–1968). Civil engineer; Democratic governor of Connecticut, 1941–43; Democratic National Committeeman, 1944–.

HUSBANDS, SAMUEL H. (SAM) (1891–1955). Banker; director of the Reconstruction Finance Corporation, 1939–46; president of the Federal National Mortgage Association, 1938–46.

HU SHIH, DR. (1891–1962). Professor of philosophy and literature; Nationalist Chinese ambassador to the United States, 1938–45.

HUTCHESON, JOSEPH C., JR. (1879–1973). Judge of the U.S. District Court for the Southern District of Texas, 1918–30, and of the U.S. Circuit Court of Appeals, 5th Circuit (Houston), 1931–64.

HUTSON, JOHN B. (JACK) (1890–1964). Department of Agriculture bureaucrat; assistant administrator of the Agricultural Adjustment Administration, 1936–40; director of Agricultural Defense Relations, 1940–41; president of the Commodity Credit Corporation, 1941–44; director of the War Food Administration, May 1943–December 1944; deputy director of the Office of War Mobilization and Reconversion, December 1944–January 1945; and undersecretary of agriculture, 1945–46.

ICKES, HAROLD L. (1874–1952). Lawyer and writer; active in Chicago progressive politics from 1897, serving as chairman of the Cook County Progressive party, 1912–14, and chairman of the Illinois Progressive State Committee, 1914–16; secretary of interior, 1933–46.

INGERSOLL, RALPH MCA. (1900–). Journalist; publisher of *Time*, 1937–39; editor of New York *P.M.*, 1939–45.

JACKSON, ROBERT H. (1892–1954). General counsel for the Bureau of Internal Revenue, 1934–36; assistant U.S. attorney general for the Anti-trust Division, 1936–38; solicitor general of the U.S., 1938–41; associate justice of the U.S. Supreme Court, 1941–54.

JACKSON, SAMUEL D. (1895–1951). Attorney general of Indiana, 1940–41; Democratic U.S. senator from Indiana, January–November 1944; chairman of the 1944 Democratic National Convention; unsuccessful Democratic candidate for governor of Indiana, 1944.

JAMES, EDWIN L. (1890–1951). Journalist; managing editor of the *New York Times*, 1932–51.

JOHNSON, PHILIP G. (1894–1944). Engineer; president of the Boeing Airplane Company, 1926–33, 1939–44.

JOHNSTON, ERIC A. (1895–1963). Spokane retailer; unsuccessful candidate for Republican U.S. Senate nomination, 1940; president of the U.S. Chamber of Commerce, 1942–46, and of the Motion Picture Association of America, 1945–63.

JONES, JESSE H. (1874–1956). Lumber manufacturer and banker; in 1932, became director of the Reconstruction Finance Corporation, serving as chairman of the board, 1932–39; member of the National Emergency Council, 1933–39; chairman of the First and Second Export-Import Banks of Washington, 1936–43; administrator of the Federal Loan Agency, 1939–45; secretary of commerce, 1940–45; member of the Economic Defense Board, 1941–45; member of the War Production Board and the Economic Stabilization Board, 1942–45.

JONES, SAM H. (1897–1978). Democratic governor of Louisiana, 1940–44.

KAISER, HENRY J. (1882–1967). Construction company owner, 1914–, he managed seven West Coast shipyards and many other war-related enterprises, 1941–45.

KANE, (RICHMOND) KEITH (1900–1974). Special assistant to the U.S. attorney general, 1940–42, and to the secretary of the Navy, 1943–45.

KEFAUVER, (CAREY) ESTES (1903–1963). Democratic congressman from Tennessee, 1939–49; U.S. senator, 1949–63.

KELLY, EDWARD J. (1876–1950). Democratic political boss and mayor of Chicago, 1933–47.

KEMNITZER, WILLIAM J. (1898–). Economic geologist and consultant, 1927–; government witness during the naval petroleum reserve litigation, 1936–37;

member of the U.S.-Mexico Oil Commission, 1942, and of the U.S. industrial mission to Brazil, 1942–43; chief fuel specialist for the U.S. Office of Economic Warfare, 1942–45.

KEMP, EDWARD G. (ED) Michigan lawyer; adviser to Frank Murphy, 1933–38; assistant U.S. attorney general, 1939; general counsel for the Bureau of the Budget, 1940–45.

KENNEDY, JOSEPH P. (1888–1969). Wealthy banker, financier, and important financial contributor to the Democratic Party, 1932; chairman of the Securities and Exchange Commission, 1934–35; U.S. ambassador to Great Britain, 1937–40; he resigned in opposition to U.S. aid for the allies; father of President John F. Kennedy.

KENNY, ROBERT W. (BOB) (1901–1976). Judge of the Superior Court of Los Angeles County, 1932–38, 1966–75; Democratic state senator, 1939–42; attorney general of California, 1943–47.

KERR, ROBERT S. (1896–1963). Lawyer and oil well contractor; Democratic National Committeeman from Oklahoma, 1940–48; governor of Oklahoma, 1943–47; U.S. senator from Oklahoma, 1949–63.

KILGORE, HARLEY M. (1893–1956). Democratic U.S. senator from West Virginia, 1941–56.

KIRCHWEY, FREDA (1893–1976). Writer, editor, and publisher for *The Nation*, 1918–55.

KIRK, MRS. WALTER. Sister of Alexander C. Kirk (1886–), the U.S. ambassador to Italy, 1944–46.

KIRKPATRICK, ELMER E., JR. Army officer (captain) in the Quartermaster Corps, stationed at Pearl Harbor, 1941, he was chief of staff, Northwest Service Command, 1944, and established the atomic bomb assembly base in the Marianas Islands, 1945.

KNOX, WILLIAM FRANKLIN (FRANK) (1874–1944). Publisher of the Chicago *Daily News*, 1931–; unsuccessful Republican vice presidential nominee, 1936; secretary of Navy, 1940–44.

KNUDSEN, WILLIAM S. (1879–1948). Danish-born president of General Motors Corporation, 1937–40; director-general of the Office of Production Management, 1941–42; member of the War Production Board, 1942–44; serving as a lieutenant general, 1942–44, he was also director of the Army's Air Technical Service Command, 1944–45.

KOPLOVITZ, WILLIAM C. Lawyer for Frank Cohen in the Savannah Shipyards case with his partner, William J. Dempsey.

KROCK, ARTHUR (1887–1974). Editor and conservative Washington columnist for the *New York Times*, 1927–67.

KRUG, JULIUS A. (1907–1970). Public utilities expert; chief of the Power Branch of the Office of War Utilities, 1943–44; chairman of the Requirements Committee of the War Production Board, 1943–44; acting chairman of the WPB, 1944–45; secretary of interior, 1946–49.

KURUSU, SABURO (1888–1954). Japanese diplomat, considered to be an expert on the U.S., who took part in last-minute peace negotiations, November and December 1941.

LA FOLLETTE, ROBERT M., JR. (1895–1953). Republican U.S. senator from Wisconsin, 1925–47; reelected in 1934 and 1940 as an Independent.

LA GUARDIA, FIORELLO H. (1882–1947). Republican congressman from New York, 1917–19, 1923–33; mayor of New York City, 1934–45; director of the Office of Civilian Defense, 1941–42.

LAND, EMORY S. (1879–1971). Naval officer (rear admiral); chairman of the U.S. Maritime Commission, 1938–41; administrator of the War Shipping Administration, 1942–46.

LANDIS, JAMES M. (1899–1964). Professor at Harvard Law School, 1926–34; chairman of the Federal Trade Commission, 1933–34; member of the Securities and Exchange Commission, 1934–37, and chairman after 1935; dean of Harvard Law School, 1937–47; director of the Office of Civilian Defense, 1942–43; director of American economic operations and minister to the Middle East, 1943–45.

LANDON, ALFRED M. (1887–). Republican governor of Kansas, 1933–37; unsuccessful Republican presidential candidate, 1936.

LANE, FRANKLIN K. (1864–1921). Secretary of the interior, 1913–20.

LANGER, WILLIAM (1886–1959). Republican governor of North Dakota, 1933–34, 1937–39; U.S. senator, 1941–59.

LANGLIE, ARTHUR B. (1900–1966). Republican governor of Washington State, 1941–1945, 1949–57.

LEAVELL, JOHN H. (b.1883). Mining and consulting engineer, 1907–17; independent oil operator and consultant, 1921–43; U.S. attaché at Baghdad, 1943, and Cairo, 1944–45.

LEBARON, LOUIS (1897–). Judge of the U.S. Circuit Court for Hawaii, 1937–42; associate justice of the Supreme Court of Hawaii, 1942–55.

LE HAND, MARGUERITE A. (MISSY) (1898–1944). FDR's stenographer and personal private secretary, 1920–44.

LEMKIN, RAPHAEL (RALPH) (1900–1959). Polish-born lawyer, legal scholar, and refugee from the Nazis, he taught law at the University of Stockholm, 1940–41, and Duke University, 1941–42; chief consultant to the Board of Economic Warfare and the Foreign Economic Administration, 1942–44; adviser on foreign affairs to the War Department, 1944–47; an army prosecutor at the Nuremberg trials, 1945–46.

LEWIS, FULTON, JR. (1903–1966). Radio news commentator with the Mutual Broadcasting System, 1937–66.

LINDEMAN, CHARLES B. (1891–1969). Associate publisher of the *Seattle Post-Intelligencer*, 1930–43, and publisher, 1943–65.

LINDLEY, BETTY GRIMES (1900–1976). Mrs. Ernest K. Lindley. Eleanor Roosevelt's personal friend, radio agent, and chief of staff, 1937–43; member of the Program Planning Committee of the Office of Civilian Defense, 1941–42.

LINDLEY, ERNEST K. (1899–1979). Journalist; chief of *Newsweek*'s Washington Bureau, 1937–61; author of *The Roosevelt Revolution* (New York: Viking, 1933), *Halfway with Roosevelt* (New York: Viking, 1936), and *The New Deal for Youth* (New York: Viking, 1938); he often reflected White House viewpoints.

LITTELL, NORMAN M. (1899–). Seattle lawyer; special assistant regional attorney for the Petroleum Administrative Board, 1934–35; assistant U.S. attorney general for the Lands Division, 1939–44.

LOCKWOOD, ADOLPHUS N. (1888–1968). New Jersey realtor; head of the North Atlantic Region of the Surplus War Properties Administration, 1941–45.

LONG, BRECKINRIDGE (1881–1958). Assistant secretary of state, 1917–20, 1940–44; U.S. ambassador to Italy, 1933–36.

LUCAS, SCOTT W. (1892–1968). Democratic congressman from Illinois, 1935–39; U.S. senator, 1939–51.

LUCE, CLARE BOOTHE (1903–). Mrs. Henry R. Luce. Journalist, playwright, and Republican congresswoman from Connecticut, 1943–47; U.S. ambassador to Italy, 1953–57.

LUCE, HENRY R. (1898–1967). Publisher of *Time, Life,* and *Fortune.*

LUNDEBERG, HARRY (1901–1957). Norwegian-born president of the Sailors Union of the Pacific, 1938–57.

LUTTRELL, RALPH J. Chief of the Lands Condemnations (Acquisitions) Section of the Lands Division of the Justice Department, 1942–62.

MACARTHUR, DOUGLAS (1880–1964). Army officer (general); commander of allied forces in the Philippines and the Southwest Pacific Theater during World War II.

MAGNUSON, WARREN G. (1905–). Democratic congressman from Washington, 1939–44; U.S. senator, 1944–1981.

MALLON, PAUL (RAYMOND) (1901–1950). Journalist; author of syndicated newspaper column, "News Behind the News," 1930–47.

MALONE, DUDLEY FIELD (1882–1950). New York lawyer; collector of the Port of New York, 1913–17.

MANASCO, CARTER (1902–). Democratic congressman from Alabama, 1941–49.

MARSH, CHARLES E. (1887–1964). Editor and publisher of a chain of Texas newspapers, 1916–46.

MARSHALL, GEORGE C. (1880–1959). Army officer (general of the armies); chief of the General Staff, 1939–45; secretary of state, 1947–49; secretary of defense, 1950–51.

MARSHALL, J. HOWARD, II (1902–). Member of the Pillsbury, Madison and Sutro law firm, 1938–; member of the Petroleum Administrative Board and assistant solicitor of the Interior Department, 1933–35; special counsel for Standard Oil Company of California, 1935–37; chief counsel of the Petroleum Administration for War, 1941–45.

MASON, F. VAN WYCK (1901–1978). Author of numerous historical and mystery novels and a major in the Army Public Relations Section during World War II.

MATTHEWS, BURNITA S. (b. 1884). Judge of the U.S. District Court for Washington, D.C., 1949–70.

MATTHEWS, CLIFTON (1880–1962). Judge of the U.S. Circuit Court of Appeals, 9th Circuit, 1934–62.

MAVERICK, (FONTAINE) MAURY (1895–1954). Democratic congressman from Texas, 1935–39; mayor of San Antonio, 1939–41; director and vice chairman of the War Production Board and chairman of the Smaller War Plants Corporation, 1941–46.

MAW, HERBERT B. (1893–). Democratic governor of Utah, 1941–49.

MAYBANK, BURNETT R. (1899–1954). Cotton exporter; Democratic governor of South Carolina, 1939–41; U.S. senator, 1941–54.

MCADOO, ELEANOR WILSON (1890–1967). Daughter of President Wilson, wife of William G. McAdoo.

MCADOO, WILLIAM GIBBS (1863–1941). Secretary of the treasury, 1913–18; director general of the U.S. Railroad Administration, 1917–19; Democratic U.S. senator from California, 1933–38; unsuccessful candidate for the Democratic presidential nomination, 1920, 1924.

MCCARRAN, PATRICK A. (PAT) (1876–1954). Farmer, rancher, and politician; Democratic U.S. senator from Nevada, 1933–54; strong supporter of the silver industry and chairman of the Judiciary Committee.

MCCLOY, JOHN J. (1895–). Special assistant to the secretary of war, 1940–41; assistant secretary of war, 1941–45.

MCCORMACK, JOHN W. (1891–1980). Liberal, pro-New Deal Democratic representative from Massachusetts, 1928–71; majority leader, 1940–47, 1949–53, 1955–61; speaker of the House, 1962–1971.

MCCORMICK, ROBERT R. (1880–1955). Politically powerful, isolationist, conservative Republican publisher of the *Chicago Tribune*.

MCFARLAND, CARL (1904–). Montana rancher; assistant U.S. attorney general, 1937–39; on the federal administrative reform committee, 1939–41.

MCGRANERY, JAMES P. (JIM) (1895–1962). Democratic representative from Pennsylvania, 1937–43; assistant to the U.S. attorney general, 1943–46; judge of the U.S. District Court for the Eastern District of Pennsylvania, 1946–52; U.S. attorney general, 1952–53.

MCGUIRE, MATTHEW F. (1898–). Assistant to the U.S. attorney general, 1940–41; judge of the U.S. District Court for Washington, D.C., 1941–.

MCHALE, FRANK M. (1891–1975). Indiana businessman; member of the Democratic National Committee, 1937–52.

MCINTYRE, MARVIN H. (1878–1943). Public relations assistant to the secretary of the Navy in 1914, he became a friend of Franklin D. Roosevelt; business manager and publicity representative in the 1932 election campaign; assistant secretary to the President, 1933–36; secretary to the President, 1936–45.

MCKELLAR, KENNETH D. (1869–1957). Democratic congressman from Alabama, 1911–17; isolationist U.S. senator, 1917–53; president pro tempore of the Senate, 1945–47, 1949–53.

MCKINLOCK, MARION WALLACE RAPPELYE. Widow of George A. McKinlock (1857–1936).

MCLEAN, DAVID S. (1898–). Army officer (lieutenant colonel) in the Judge Advocate General's Office, 1940–.

MCLEAN, EVALYN W. (1886–1946). Widow of Edward B. McLean (d. 1941), former publisher of the *Washington Post*, and the wife of Robert R. Reynolds, U.S. senator from North Carolina, 1933–45; a celebrated Washington hostess, she was the owner of the Hope Diamond.

MCMAHON, JAMES O'BRIEN (BRIEN) (1903–1952). Assistant U.S. attorney general for the Criminal Division, 1936–44; Democratic U.S. senator from Connecticut, 1945–52.

MCMURRAY, HOWARD J. (1901–1961). Democratic congressman from Wisconsin, 1943–45; unsuccessful candidate for the U.S. Senate, 1944, 1946.

MCNARY, CHARLES L. (1874–1944). Republican U.S. senator from Oregon, 1917–44, and minority leader, 1933–44; unsuccessful Republican vice presidential nominee, 1940.

MCNUTT, PAUL V. (1891–1955). Democratic governor of Indiana, 1933–37; administrator of the Federal Security Agency, 1939–45; chairman of the War Manpower Commission, 1942–45; U.S. high commissioner/ambassador to the Philippines, 1937–39, 1945–46, 1946–47.

MEAD, JAMES M. (1885–1964). Democratic congressman from New York, 1919–38; U.S. senator, 1938–47, where he succeeded Truman as chairman of the Special Committee to Investigate the National-Defense program, 1944; unsuccessful candidate for the Democratic gubernatorial nomination, 1942, and for the governorship in 1944.

MEYER, EUGENE (1875–1959). Member of the Federal Reserve Board, 1930–33; chairman of the Reconstruction Finance Corporation, 1931; editor, publisher, and chairman of the *Washington Post*, 1933–59.

MICHELSON, CHARLES (1869–1947). Editor and writer; director of publicity for the Democratic National Committee, 1929–44.

MINTON, SHERMAN (1890–1965). Democratic U.S. senator from Indiana, 1935–41; administrative assistant to the President, 1941; judge of the U.S. Circuit Court of Appeals, 7th Circuit, 1941–49; associate justice of the U.S. Supreme Court, 1949–56.

MITCHELL, RICHARD F. (1889–1969). Associate justice of the Iowa Supreme Court, 1932–47, and chief justice, 1934–39; pro-Wallace delegate to the 1944 Democratic convention and nominated Wallace for Vice President.

MOREELL, BEN (1892–1978). Civil engineer and naval officer (rear admiral); chief of the Bureau of Yards and Docks of the Navy Department, 1937–46.

MORGENTHAU, ELINOR (1892–1949). Mrs. Henry Morgenthau, Jr.

MORGENTHAU, HENRY, JR. (1891–1967). Publisher of *American Agriculturalist*, 1922–33; FDR's friend and neighbor; chairman of Federal Farm Board, 1933; chairman of the Farm Credit Administration, 1933–34; undersecretary of the Treasury, 1934; secretary of the treasury, 1934–45.

MORSE, WAYNE L. (1900–1974). Member of the National War Labor Board, 1942–44; a Republican (and later an Independent and still later a Democratic) U.S. senator from Oregon, 1945–69.

MOSKOVIT, HAROLD R. (1906–). The Hungarian-born president of the First Voters League of America, 1936–44; state director of the Office of Government Reports, New York, Connecticut, and Rhode Island, 1940–41; assistant to the national director, OGR, 1943–45.

MOTT, JAMES W. (1883–1945). Journalist and lawyer; Republican congressman from Oregon, 1933–45.

MULRONEY, ROBERT E. (b. 1890). Special assistant to the assistant U.S. attorney general for the Lands Division, 1936–39; chief of the Trial Section of the Lands Division, 1939–59.

MUNI, PAUL (MUNI WEISENFREUND) (1895–1967). Austrian-born Hollywood actor.

MUNOZ-MARIN, LUIS (1898–1980). President of the Territory of Puerto Rico's senate, 1941–48; governor of Puerto Rico, 1949–65.

MURPHY, EDWARD P. (1904–1958). Judge of the San Francisco County Superior Court, 1942–45.

MURPHY, FRANK (1890–1949). Democratic mayor of Detroit, 1930–33; governor-general of the Philippines, 1935–36; governor of Michigan, 1937–38; U.S. attorney general, 1939–40; associate justice of the U.S. Supreme Court, where he was a member of the liberal bloc, 1940–49.

MURRAY, PHILIP (1886–1952). Scottish-born vice president of the United Mine Workers of America, 1920–36; in 1936, he became vice chairman of the UMWA's Steel Workers Organizing Committee and, later, president of the United Steel Workers of America; president of the Congress of Industrial Organizations, 1940–52; strong FDR supporter, active in the campaigns of 1936, 1940, and 1944 through the CIO's Political Action Committee.

NELSON, DONALD M. (1888–1959). Realtor; editor of *Realtor's Headlines*, 1942–55; secretary of the American Institute of Real Estate Appraisers, 1932–55; secretary of the National Institute of Real Estate Brokers, 1942–55; executive vice president of the National Association of Real Estate Boards, 1942–55; chairman of the War Production Board, 1942–44.

NELSON, HERBERT U. (HERB) (1886–1956). Executive vice president of the National Association of Real Estate Boards, 1922–55.

NILES, DAVE K. (DAVE) (1892–1952). Administrative assistant to the President for political affairs, 1942–51.

NOMURA, KICHISABURO (1887–1964). Japanese naval officer and naval attaché; foreign minister of Japan, 1939–40; ambassador to the U.S., 1940–41.

NORTHCLIFFE, VISCOUNT. See HARMSWORTH, Alfred Charles William.

NORWAY, CROWN PRINCE OLAV OF (1903–). Son and heir of King Haakon VII; King of Norway, 1957–.

NORWAY, KING HAAKON VII OF (1872–1957). King of Norway, 1905–57; head of the Norwegian government in exile in London, 1940–45.

NORWAY, PRINCESS MARTHA OF (1901–1954). King Haakon VII's daughter-in-law, and wife of Crown Prince Olav.

NOVER, BARNETT (1899–1973). Journalist; columnist, associate editor, and foreign correspondent of the *Washington Post*, 1936–47.

O'BRIEN, JOHN J. (1904–1955). Attorney in the Lands Division of the Justice Department, 1936–39; general assistant to the assistant U.S. attorney general for the Lands Division, 1939–41; head (colonel-brigadier general) of the Real Estate Section of the Army, 1941–45.

O'BYRNE, MICHAEL J. (M. J.) (1878–). Retired army officer (colonel); headed the San Francisco office of the Surplus War Properties Administration, 1944.

O'CONNOR, BASIL (1892–). Partner in the New York law firm of (Franklin D.) Roosevelt, O'Connor and Farber, 1925–33, and, thereafter, with John C. Farber.

O'CONNOR, JAMES F. T. (JEFTY) (1886–1949). Los Angeles lawyer; U.S. comptroller of the currency, 1933–40; judge of the U.S. District Court for the Southern District of California, 1940–49.

O'DANIEL, WILBERT L. (PAPPY) (1890–1969). Democratic governor of Texas, 1939–41; U.S. senator, 1941–49.

O'DONNELL, JOHN P. (1896–1961). Journalist; Washington and war correspondent for the *New York Daily News*, 1933–45.

OLSON, CULBERT L. (1876–1962). Democratic governor of California, 1939–43.

O'MAHONEY, JOSEPH C. (1884–1962). Democratic U.S. senator from Wyoming, 1934–53, 1955–60.

PALMER, A. MITCHELL (1872–1936). Democratic congressman from Pennsylvania, 1909–15; alien property custodian, 1917–19; U.S. attorney general, 1919–21.

PARKER (ROTHSCHILD), DOROTHY (1893–1967). Noted American poetess, wit, and short story writer.

PATTERSON, ROBERT P. (1892–1952). Judge of the U.S. District Court for the Southern District of New York, 1930–39, and of the U.S. Circuit Court of Appeals, 2nd Circuit, 1939–40; undersecretary of war for procurement, 1940–45; secretary of war, 1945–47.

PAULEY, EDWIN W. (ED) (1903–1981). California Democratic Party leader; president of the Pauley Petrol Corporation, 1929–; president of the Independent Petroleum Producers Association, 1934–38; secretary of the Democratic National Committee, 1942–44; treasurer of the DNC, 1944–45.

PEARSON, DREW (1897–1969). Journalist; coauthor of the syndicated daily column, "Washington Merry-Go-Round," in the *Washington Times-Herald*, 1932–42, with Robert S. Allen, which was noted for its political exposés; after 1942, he continued the column on his own in the *Washington Post* until his death.

PEGLER, WESTBROOK J. (1894–1969). Politically conservative syndicated columnist for the *Chicago Daily News*, 1933–44.

PELLEY, WILLIAM D. (1890–1965). Leader of a pro-German, fascist-type organization, the Silver Legion of America, known as the Silver Shirts, 1933–42.

PENDERGAST, THOMAS J. (TOM) (1872–1945). Democratic political boss of Kansas City, Missouri, mid-1920s–1939; jailed for tax evasion, 1939–45.

PEPPER, CLAUDE D. (1900–). Liberal, strongly pro-FDR Democratic U.S. senator from Florida, 1936–51, and congressman, 1963–.

PERCY, WILLIAM ALEXANDER (1885–1942). Lawyer and plantation owner; author of *Lanterns on the Levee* (1941), a work on the "Negro problem" in the South.

PERKINS, FRANCES (1880–1965). Social worker; member of the New York State Industrial Commission, 1918–33; when FDR became governor, in 1929, he made her chairman; secretary of labor, 1933–45; member of the U.S. Civil Service Commission, 1945–57.

PERKINS, MILO R. (1900–1972). Texas manufacturer; president of the Federal Surplus Marketing Administration, 1939–41; executive director of the Board of Economic Warfare, 1941–43.

PETERSON, HUGH (1898–1961). Democratic congressman from Georgia, 1935–47.

PETERSON, JAMES H. (1894–1978). Democratic congressman from Florida, 1933–51; chairman of the Public Lands Committee, 1941–47, 1949–51.

PIKE, SUMNER T. (1891–1976). Corporate official; member of the Securities and Exchange Commission, 1940–46.

PINCHOT, CORNELIA E. BRYCE (LEILA) (1881–1960). Mrs. Gifford Pinchot.

PINCHOT, GIFFORD (1863–1946). Forester, conservationist, teacher and political reformer; professor of forestry at Yale University, 1910–36; director of the U.S. Forest Service, 1898–10; progressive Republican governor of Pennsylvania, 1923–27, 1931–35.

PINCHOT, GIFFORD B. (GIFF) (1915–). Son of Gifford Pinchot.

PINCHOT, JAMES W. (1831–1908). Merchant; father of Gifford Pinchot.

PITTMAN, KEY (1872–1940). Isolationist Democratic U.S. senator from Nevada, 1913–40; chairman of the Foreign Relations Committee and president pro tempore of the Senate, 1933–40.

POINDEXTER, JOSEPH B. (1869–1951). Democratic governor of the Territory of Hawaii, 1934–42.

PORTER, PAUL A. (1904–1975). Reporter and lawyer; Washington correspondent for the CBS radio network, 1937–42; publicity chairman of the Democratic National Committee, 1944; deputy administrator of the Office of Price Administration, 1942–44; chairman of the Federal Communications Commission, 1944–46.

POWELL, ADAM C. (1908–1972). Black civil rights leader and minister of the Abyssinian Baptist Church, in Harlem, New York, 1937–60; Democratic Congressman from New York, 1945–1967, 1968–69.

PRICE, CHARLES R. (CHARLEY). U.S. marshal for the Western District of North Carolina, 1934–44.

PRICHARD, EDWARD F., JR. (b. 1915). Law clerk to Justice Frankfurter, 1939–40; special assistant to U.S. attorney generals Jackson and Biddle, 1940–41; general counsel of the Office of Economic Stabilization, 1942–46.

PROSKAUER, JOSEPH M. (1877–1971). Justice of the New York State Supreme Court, 1923–30; spokesman for the American Jewish Committee, which opposed demands for an immediate establishment of a Jewish State.

PULITZER, JOSEPH (1879–1955). Journalist and publisher of the *St. Louis Post-Dispatch*.

PURCELL, GANSON (1905–1967). Counsel for the Securities and Exchange Commission, 1934–36; chairman of SEC's New York Stock and Trading Division, 1937–41; chairman of SEC, 1942–46.

QUINN, THOMAS D. Administrative assistant to the U.S. attorney general, 1933–43.

RABAUT, LOUIS C. (1886–1961). Democratic congressman from Michigan, 1937–47.

RAMSPECK, ROBERT C. W. (1890–1972). Democratic congressman from Georgia, 1929–45; Democratic whip of the House, 1942–44; chairman of the Speaker's Bureau of the Democratic National Committee, 1944.

RAYBURN, SAMUEL T. (SAM) (1882–1961). Democratic congressman from Texas, 1913–61; Democratic majority leader, 1937–40; speaker of the House, 1940–47, 1949–53, 1955–61, twice as long as any other speaker in history.

REILLY, GERARD D. (JERRY) (1906–). Solicitor of the Labor Department, 1937–41; member of the National Labor Relations Board, 1941–46.

ROBERTS, OWEN J. (1872–1955). Associate justice of the U.S. Supreme Court, 1930–45; initially a conservative, he became a key swing vote in the late 1930s and early 1940s.

ROBINSON, EDWARD G. (1893–1972). Rumanian-born Hollywood actor.

ROBINSON, JAMES W. (1878–1964). Democratic representative from Utah, 1933–47.

ROCKEFELLER, JOHN D[AVISON], JR. (1874–1960). Wealthy oil magnate and philanthropist.

ROGERS, WILL (1879–1935). Oklahoma-born cowboy humorist and political commentator.

ROMMEL, ERWIN (1891–1944). German army officer (field marshal) and commander of German forces in North Africa in World War II, 1941–42.

ROOSEVELT, (ANNA) ELEANOR (1884–1962). Mrs. Franklin Delano Roosevelt. A political figure in her own right, she helped organize women for the Democratic Party in New York in the 1920s and served as finance chairman of the party, 1924–28; as First Lady, she traveled extensively to help promote the New Deal and gather information for the president; she was deeply interested in liberal causes, the interests of minorities, women, children, education, and social reform, especially the National Association for the Advancement of Colored People and racial equality; during World War II, she served as assistant director of the Office of Civilian Defense, 1941–42; she also served as a member of the U.S. delegation to the United Nations and helped write its charter.

ROOSEVELT, ELLIOTT (1910–). Second son of Franklin and Eleanor Roosevelt; advertising executive.

ROOSEVELT, FRANKLIN DELANO (1882–1945). New York lawyer; New York state senator, 1910–13; assistant secretary of the Navy, 1913–21; governor of New York, 1929–33; 32nd President of the U.S., 1933–45.

ROOSEVELT, FRANKLIN DELANO, JR. (1914–). Third son of Franklin and Eleanor Roosevelt; lawyer and businessman; Democratic congressman from New York, 1949–55.

ROOSEVELT, HALL (1890–1941). Eleanor Roosevelt's younger brother.

ROOSEVELT, JAMES (1907–). Eldest son of Franklin and Eleanor Roosevelt; insurance company executive; FDR's unofficial aide in 1933 and administrative assistant to the President, 1937–38; he later became president of an insurance company, a motion picture executive, and a colonel during World War II; unsuccessful candidate for governor of California, in 1950, he served as Democratic congressman from California, 1955–65.

ROOSEVELT, JOHN A. (1916–1981). Youngest son of Franklin and Eleanor Roosevelt; department store executive, investment banker, and contributor to Republican candidates.

ROOSEVELT, SARA DELANO (1854–1941). President Roosevelt's mother.

ROSENMAN, SAMUEL I. (SAM) (1896–1973). New York State Democratic legislator and unofficial counsel to FDR, 1929–32; associate justice of the New York State Supreme Court and adviser-speechwriter to FDR, 1932–43; special counsel to the President, 1943–46.

ROSSI, ANGELO J. (1878–1948). Democratic mayor of San Francisco, 1931–44.

ROWE, JAMES H., JR. (1909–1984). Counsel for the National Emergency Council, 1934; law clerk to Justice Oliver Wendell Holmes, 1934–35; administrative assistant to the President, 1938–41; assistant to the U.S. attorney general (a position now known as deputy U.S. attorney general) in the Justice Department, 1941–43; in 1943, he left to serve in the Navy; technical adviser at the Nuremberg trials, 1945; after 1946, partner in the law firm of Corcoran, Youngman and Rowe.

RUSSELL, DONALD S. (1906–). Assistant to the director (James F. Byrnes) of the Office of Economic Stabilization, 1942–45; assistant to the director (James F. Byrnes) of the Office of War Mobilization, 1943–45.

SACKETT, SHELDON F. (1902–1968). Liberal, pro-Wallace publisher of the *Coos Bay Times* (Oregon), 1930–68; owner of Oregon radio stations KOOS and KVAN, 1937–68.

SALTONSTALL, LEVERETT (1892–1979). Republican governor of Massachusetts, 1939–44; U.S. senator, 1945–67.

SCHOFIELD, LEMUEL B. (BRAD) (1892–1955). Special assistant to the U.S. attorney general and director of the Immigration and Naturalization Service of the Justice Department, 1941–42.

SCHWELLENBACH, LEWIS B. (1892–1948). Democratic U.S. senator from Washington, 1935–40; judge of the U.S. District Court for Eastern Washington, 1940–45; secretary of labor, 1945–48.

SEARS, CHARLES B. (1870–1950). Judge of the New York State Supreme Court, 1917–40; presiding judge of its Appellate Division, 1929–40; associate justice of the Court of Appeals, 1940.

SHAUGHNESSY, GERALD (1887–1950). Catholic bishop of Seattle, 1933–50.

SHEA, FRANCIS M. (FRANK) (1905–). Chief of the Legal Opinion Section of the Agriculture Adjustment Administration, 1933–35; dismissed for his left-wing sympathies; general counsel for the Securities and Exchange Commission, 1935; general counsel for the Puerto Rico Reconstruction Administration in the Interior Department, 1935–36; dean and professor of law at the University of Buffalo, 1936–41; assistant U.S. attorney general, 1939–44; associate prosecuting attorney at the Nuremberg trials, 1945.

SHEIL, BERNARD J. (1886–1969). Catholic priest, 1910–69; auxiliary bishop of Chicago, 1928–69.

SHEPHERD, JAMES C. (1898–1964). Los Angeles attorney; West Coast regional finance director for the Democratic National Committee, 1944; director of the 9th Region of the Office of Civilian Defense, 1942–44.

SHEPPARD, HARRY R. (1885–1969). Labor leader and businessman; Democratic congressman from California, 1937–65.

SHORT, WALTER C. (1880–1949). Army officer (lieutenant general); commanded the Hawaiian Department, February–December 1941; following Pearl Harbor he was charged with "dereliction of duty" by the Roberts report; he then retired and headed the traffic department of Ford Motor Company, until his retirement in 1942.

SILVER, ABBA H. (1893–1963). Rabbi of The Temple in Cleveland, 1917–63; president of the Zionist Organization of America.

SINCLAIR, HARRY F. (1885–1956). President of Sinclair Oil and Refining Company, 1901–56; his oil leases from Albert B. Fall precipitated the Teapot Dome scandals.

SMITH, ELLISON D. (COTTON ED) (1864–1944). Merchant and agricultural businessman; founder of the Southern Cotton Association, 1905; Democratic U.S. senator from South Carolina, 1909–44.

SMITH, HAROLD D. (1898–1947). Engineer and lawyer; budget director of Michigan, 1937–39; director of the Bureau of the Budget, 1939–46.

SMITH, HOWARD W. (1883–1978). Extremely conservative, antilabor lawyer and judge; Democratic congressman from Virginia, 1931–67.

SMITH, LAWRENCE H. (1892–1958). Republican congressman from Wisconsin, 1941–58.

SMITH, LAWRENCE M.C. (SAM) (1902–1975). Chief of the Special War Policies (Defense) Unit and assistant to the U.S. attorney general for the War Division of the Justice Department, 1941–43.

SNYDER, A. CECIL (1907–1959). U.S. attorney for Puerto Rico, 1933–42; associate justice of the Puerto Rico Supreme Court, 1942–53, and chief justice, 1953–59.

SNYDER, JOHN W. (1895–). Banker; U.S. comptroller of the currency, 1931–37; manager of the St. Louis Loan Agency of the Reconstruction Finance Corporation, 1937–43; assistant to the director of the RFC, 1940–44; director of the Office of War Mobilization and Reconversion, 1945–46; secretary of the treasury, 1946–53.

SOMERVELL, BREHON B. (1892–1955). Army officer (general); chief of the Construction Division of the Army in the Office of the Quartermaster General, 1941–42; member of the U.S.-Great Britain Munitions Assignment Board, 1942–45; commander of the Army Service Forces, 1942–45; following his retirement in 1946, he became chairman and president of Koppers Corporation.

STAINBACK, INGRAM M. (1883–1961). U.S. attorney for the Territory of Hawaii, 1934–40; judge of the U.S. District Court for Hawaii, 1940–42; Democratic governor of Hawaii, 1942–51.

STANLEY, WILLIAM (1891–1946). Assistant to the U.S. attorney general, 1933–35; law partner of former U.S. Attorney General Homer S. Cummings, 1939–46.

STEPHENS, ALBERT L., SR. (1874–1965). Judge of the U.S. District Court for Southern California, 1935–37, and of the U.S. Circuit Court of Appeals, 9th Circuit, 1937–65.

STEPHENS, HAROLD M. (1886–1955). Associate justice of the U.S. Circuit Court of Appeals for the District of Columbia, 1935–48, and chief justice, 1948–55.

STETTINIUS, EDWARD R., JR. (1900–1949). Corporate executive and chairman of the board of U.S. Steel Corporation, 1935–39; chairman of the War Resources Board, 1939; member of the National Defense Advisory Committee, 1940; director of priorities of the Office of Production Management, 1941; administrator of Lend-Lease, 1941–42; undersecretary of state, 1943–44; secretary of state, 1944–45.

STEVENSON, ADLAI E. (1900–1965). Special assistant to the secretary of the Navy, 1941–44; Democratic governor of Illinois, 1949–53; U.S. ambassador to the United Nations, 1961–65; unsuccessful Democratic presidential nominee, 1952, 1956.

STEWART, ARTHUR THOMAS (TOM) (1892–1972). Democratic U.S. senator from Tennessee, 1939–49.

STIMSON, HENRY L. (1867–1950). Republican lawyer; secretary of state, 1929–33; secretary of war, 1911–13 and 1940–45.

STONE, HARLAN F. (1872–1946). Dean of Columbia Law School, 1910–23; U.S. attorney general, 1923–25; associate justice of the U.S. Supreme Court, 1925–41; chief justice, 1941–46; member of the Court's liberal bloc.

STONE, ISIDORE F. (I. F.) (1907–). Liberal journalist; associate editor, 1938–40, and Washington correspondent, 1940–46, of *The Nation*, and Washington correspondent for the New York *P.M.* and other papers, 1942–52.

STUART, HARRY A. (b. 1882). Naval officer (rear admiral); director of Navy Department's Office of Petroleum Reserves, 1934–44.

SULZBERGER, ARTHUR H. (1891–1968). Publisher of the *New York Times*, 1935–61; chairman of the board, 1957–68.

SWING, RAYMOND GRAM (1887–1968). Radio commentator for the British Broadcasting Corporation, 1935–45, for the Mutual Broadcasting System, 1936–45, and for the American Broadcasting Company, 1942–48.

SWOPE, GUY J. (1892–1969). Democratic congressman from Pennsylvania, 1937–39; auditor of the Territory of Puerto Rico, 1940–41; governor of Puerto Rico, 1941, resigning to become director of the Division of Territories in the Interior Department, 1941–43.

TALMADGE, EUGENE (1884–1946). Extremely conservative, segregationist lawyer and farmer; Democratic governor of Georgia, 1933–37, 1941–43; governor-elect for the 1947–49 term at the time of his death.

TAMM, EDWARD A. (1906–). Assistant for investigations to the director of the Federal Bureau of Investigation, 1941–45; judge of the U.S. District Court for the District of Columbia, 1945–65.

TAYLOR, (WAYNE) CHATFIELD (1893–1967). Banker; assistant secretary of the treasury, 1936–39; undersecretary of commerce, 1940–45; acting secretary of commerce, 1945; president of the Export-Import Bank, 1945–46.

TESTU, JEANETTE M. (1899–1964). Mrs. Homer J. Testu. Democratic Washington state legislator, 1943, 1949–62; community service director for Seattle in the Office of Price Administration, 1944–48; Democratic National Committeewoman for Washington State, 1944.

THOMPSON, MALVINA C. (1893–1953). Personal secretary to Eleanor Roosevelt, 1928–53.

TILLETT, GLADYS A. Mrs. Charles W. Tillett. Chairman of the Women's Division of the Democratic National Committee and assistant chairman of the Democratic National Convention, 1944.

TOLAND, EDMUND M. (ED) (1898–1942). General counsel for the House Naval Affairs Committee, 1941–42.

TOWNSEND, NEWMAN A. (1883–1951). Special assistant U.S. attorney general and chief consultant to the assistant U.S. solicitor general, 1934–44.

TRUMAN, ELIZABETH WALLACE (BESS) (1885–1982). Mrs. Harry S. Truman.

TRUMAN, HARRY S. (1884–1972). Democratic U.S. senator from Missouri, 1935–45; chairman of the Special Committee to Investigate the National-Defense Program (Truman Committee), 1941–45; Vice President of the United States, January–April 1945; 33rd President of the United States, 1945–53, following FDR's death.

TUCKER, HENRY ST.G. (1874–1959). Protestant Episcopal bishop of Virginia, 1927–40, and presiding bishop, 1938–46; president of the Federal Council of Churches of Christ in America, 1942–44.

TUGWELL, REXFORD GUY (1891–1979). Political scientist, economist, and journalist; one of FDR's original "brain trust"; assistant secretary and undersecretary of agriculture, 1933–36; administrator of the Resettlement Administration, 1936–38; governor of the Territory of Puerto Rico, 1941–46.

TULLY, GRACE G. (1900–). FDR's assistant private secretary, 1928–41; private secretary, 1941–45; after FDR's death, became executive secretary of the Franklin D. Roosevelt Memorial Foundation.

TUMULTY, JOSEPH P. (1879–1954). New Jersey lawyer and Democratic state legislator, he served as private secretary to President Wilson, 1913–21.

TYDINGS, MILLARD E. (1890–1961). Civil engineer and lawyer; Democratic congressman from Maryland, 1923–27; anti-FDR U.S. senator, 1927–51.

VANECH, A. DEVITT (GUS) Administrative assistant to the director of the Bureau of War Risk Litigation, 1938–41; special assistant to the U.S. attorney general, 1941–50.

VIERECK, GEORGE S. (1884–1962). German-born pro-Nazi poet and editor; jailed, in 1942, for violating the Foreign Agents Registration Act of 1938; in 1943 the Supreme Court overturned his conviction.

VINSON, CARL (1884–1981). Democratic representative from Georgia, 1914–65; chairman of the Naval Affairs Committee, 1931–65.

VINSON, FREDERICK M. (FRED) (1891–1953). Democratic representative from Kentucky, 1924–29, 1931–38; associate justice of the U.S. Circuit Court of Appeals for the District of Columbia, 1938–43; resigned to become director of the Office of Economic Stabilization, administrator of the Federal Loan Agency, and director of War Mobilization and Reconversion, 1943–45; secretary of the treasury, 1945–46, chief justice of the U.S. Supreme Court, 1946–53.

VOORHIS, (HORACE) JERRY (1901–). Liberal Democratic congressman from California, 1937–47.

WAINWRIGHT, JONATHAN M. (1883–1953). Army officer (major general); commanded the U.S. Philippine Division, 1940–42; forced to surrender to the Japanese, he was a prisoner of war, 1942–45.

WALDROP, FRANK C. (1905–). Newspaper reporter, writer, columnist, and editor for the *Washington Times-Herald*, 1932–52; friend and booster of Thurman Arnold's.

WALKER, FRANK C. (1896–1959). Treasurer of the Democratic National Committee, 1932–33; chairman of the DNC, 1943–44; U.S. postmaster general, 1940–45.

WALLACE, HENRY A. (1888–1965). Agricultural scientist and reformer; published and edited *Wallace's Farmer and Iowa Homestead*, 1929–33, an agricultural journal; owned a profitable seed hybridization business; originally a progressive Republican, he joined the Democratic party in 1928; from 1933 to 1940, secretary of agriculture; Vice President of the U.S., 1941–45; secretary of commerce, 1945–46; in 1948, the Progressive Party's unsuccessful candidate for president.

WALLACE, ILO BROWNE (1888–1981). Mrs. Henry A. Wallace.

WALLGREN, MONRAD C. (MON) (1891–1961). Liberal Democratic congressman from Washington, 1933–40; U.S. senator, 1940–44; governor of Washington, 1945–49.

WALSH, THOMAS J. (1859–1933). Democratic U.S. senator from Montana, 1913–33; led the Senate investigation into the Teapot Dome scandal, 1923–24.

WANGER, WALTER (1894–1968). Hollywood film producer; president of Walter Wanger Productions, Inc.; president of the Academy of Motion Picture Arts and Sciences, 1939–45.

WARING, JULIUS W. (1880–1968). Judge of the U.S. District Court for the Eastern District of South Carolina, 1942–52.

WARREN, EARL (1891–1974). Attorney general of California, 1939–43; Republican governor of California, 1943–53; chief justice of the U.S. Supreme Court, 1953–69.

WARREN, LINDSAY C. (1889–1976). Democratic congressman from North Carolina, 1925–40; U.S. comptroller general in the General Accounting Office, 1940–54.

WATSON, EDWIN M. (PA) (1883–1945). Army officer (colonel–general); military aide and appointments secretary to the President, 1933–34; assistant secretary, 1934–36; secretary, 1936–45; died aboard ship returning from the Yalta Conference.

WATT, ROBERT J. (1894–1947). Scottish-born secretary-treasurer of the Massachusetts State Federation of Labor, 1929–37; international representative of the American Federation of Labor, 1936–47.

WEEKS, SINCLAIR (1893–1972). Banker; mayor of Newton, Massachusetts, 1930–35; Republican U.S. senator from Massachusetts, January–December 1944; secretary of commerce, 1953–58.

WELLES, ORSON (1915–). Actor, director, and film producer.

WELLES, SUMNER (1892–1961) Career diplomat; specialized in Latin American affairs; assistant secretary of state, 1933–37; undersecretary of state, 1937–43.

WEST, CHARLES F. (1895–1955). Political scientist; Democratic representative from Ohio, 1931–35; following an unsuccessful campaign for the U.S. Senate in 1934, served as special assistant to the governor of the Farm Credit Administration, 1935; undersecretary of the interior, 1935–38; lobbyist whose clients included Savannah Shipyards, Inc., 1940–47.

WHEELER, BURTON K. (1882–1975). Isolationist Democratic U.S. senator from Montana, 1923–47; unsuccessful candidate for Vice President on the La Follette-Wheeler ticket, 1924.

WICKARD, CLAUDE R. (1893–1967). Indiana farmer; undersecretary of agriculture, February–August 1940; secretary of agriculture, 1940–45; administrator of the Rural Electrification Administration, 1945–53.

WILBUR, CURTIS D. (1867–1954). Judge of the U.S. Circuit Court of Appeals, 9th Circuit, 1925–45; senior judge, 1931–45.

WILLIAMS, J. EDWARD (ED) (b. 1902). Attorney in the Lands Division of the Justice Department, 1935–42; general assistant to the assistant U.S. attorney general for the Lands Division, 1942–52.

WILLKIE, WENDELL L. (1892–1944). Anti-New Deal corporate lawyer; president of Commonwealth and Southern Utility Corporation, 1933–40; unsuccessful Republican presidential candidate, 1940; during World War II, supported FDR's foreign policies.

WILSON, WILBUR M. (1881–1958). Civil engineer and professor of engineering at the University of Illinois, 1921–; testing engineer in the Concrete Ship Section of the U.S. Shipping Board, 1918; consultant to the Savannah Shipyards, Inc., in 1942.

WINCHELL, WALTER (1897–1972). Sensation-seeking syndicated newspaper columnist and radio commentator.

WISE, STEPHEN S. (1874–1949). New York City rabbi and president of the American Jewish Congress, 1925–49; president of the Zionist Organization of America, 1918–21, 1936–38; FDR's principal political contact among Jews.

WOODRING, HARRY H. (1890–1967). Kansas banker; assistant secretary of war, 1933–36; secretary of war, 1936–40.

WOODSON, WALTER B. (1881–1948). Naval officer (rear admiral); judge advocate general of the Navy, 1938–43; retired for physical disability.

WRIGHT, EWING E. (1903–1961). Special assistant to the U.S. attorney general, 1935–53; general assistant to the assistant U.S. attorney general for the Lands Division, February–August 1941.

WYCHE, CHARLES C. (1885–1966). Judge of the U.S. District Court for the Western District of South Carolina, 1937–66.

Index

399

C

speech, 271, 273; Southern delegations, 271, 281, 282–83; Tennessee delegation in 271; Texas delegation, split in, 271; Truman supporters in, 280; vice presidential nomination, 276–86 passim; candidates for, 251, 252, 253, 261–62, 269–70, 280; first ballot, 280, 282; second ballot, 281, 282, 283; Henry Wallace's nomination, 279–80, 364–65, supporters of, 251, 252, 253, 263, 267–68, 273, 274, 275, 278, 279; Washington delegation, 253, 254, 258; Western delegations, 263, 267–68
—election of 1944, 308, 321; role of Biddle and Ickes in, 303; in California, 305, 306, 322, 323–25; in Utah, 325; in Washington State, 317–22 passim
Dempsey, John J., 5, 377
Dempsey, Mrs. John J., 5
Dempsey, William J., 84, 101, 377
Dempsey & Koplovitz: and Savannah Shipyards case, 85, 96, 100, 104, 105–7, 114, 141
Denman, William, 17, 137–38, 217, 377
De Tocqueville, Alexis, 126, 130
Dewey, Thomas E.: biog., 377; and John W. Bricker, 316; and election of 1944, 306, 307, 310, 312, 326; and Hyde Park National Monument, 210; statements on Jackson Hole National Monument, 301, 303, 304; and Morgenthau Plan, 326–27; presidential nomination of (1944), 258
Dies, Martin, Jr., 61–62, 159, 377
Dies Committee, 123n
Dillingham, Walter, 104, 118–19, 377
District attorneys. See United States attorneys
District Courts, U.S.: Eastern Washington, xii, 7n, 319, 320, 321; Southern California, 138–39; Western Washington, 237n, 238
Dive Bomber Bill of 1942, 27, 62, 98
Dixon, Frank M., 162, 377
Doheny, Edward L., 173, 246, 377
Dolivet, Louis, 202, 206
Douglas, Helen (Gahagan), 14, 191–92; biog., 377; congressional campaign of 1944, 259, 260, 324, 325, 344; at Democratic convention (1944), 259–60, 263, 267, 268
Douglas, Melvyn, 14, 45, 191–92, 377
Douglas, William O.: biog., 377; Frank Murphy's description of, 87; vice presidential campaign of (1944), 251, 256–57, 262–63, 270, 275, 276, 280
Downey, Sheridan, 46, 377
Druistadt, Nicholas, 257–58
Drumheller, Joseph, 317, 318, 377

Dumbarton Oaks conference, 307
Du Pont, E. I. de Nemours, & Co., 231n, 238. See also Hanford Project
Durkee, Bill, 17
Durr, Clifford J., 327, 377
Dutch Harbor, Alaska: prostitution in, 123

E

Early, Stephen T., 146, 242, 313, 377
Eastern Front: German offensive in, 156
Eastus, Clyde O., 77, 377
Economic Cooperation Act of 1951, xvii
Economic Defense Board (EDB), 4n. See also Board of Economic Warfare, U.S.
Economic Stabilization Program, 71n, 72–75
Edward VII, King of England, 19
E. G. Howes Leather Co., 348, 368. See also Howes, Ernest G.
El Alamein, battle of, 131n
Election of 1916: in Wisconsin, 334–35
Election of 1940, 113
Election of 1944, 301–7 passim, 316; and German propaganda, 316; and Hanford Project cases, 319–20; in Los Angeles, 324; in Oregon, 321–22; in San Francisco, 322, 323–24; in Utah, 325; in Washington State, 312–22 passim; and western public opinion, 312–13, 326. See also Democratic Party; Republican Party
Elk Hills case, xv, 153, 156, 159–70 passim, 173, 175–86 passim, 192, 193–202 passim, 218, 244, 290, 297, 334, 352; and Francis Biddle, 203–5, 233; and Breakers Hotel case, 226; House Naval Affairs Committee hearings, 203–5, 207–8; and Justice-Interior-Navy conferences, 165, 166, 167, 197, 198; and NML, hero status of, 192, reports of, 172, 179, 184–86, 192–93; Navy Dept.–Standard Oil Co. of California contract, 148, 149, 150, withdrawal/rescission of, 153, 170–71, 173–74; Navy-Standard reply to NML's report, 184–86; passage of new bill on, 241n; Public Lands Committee hearings, 185–86; FDR's role in, 255; Senate Naval Affairs Committee hearings, 240; and Teapot Dome scandals, 164, 176, 178, 245–46; settlement of, 188n; War Cabinet meeting on, 167; and Wilson administration, 245–46
—unit operating agreement on, 179–83

I

116–17, 124; Hyde Park National Monument, 209, 210; Jackson Hole National Monument, 304; Matanuska Colony, 120; Middle East oil policy, 219–10; railroad strike threat, 214. *See also* Hyde Park National Monument
International Bar Association: Foreign Investment Committee of, xiv, xvi
International Free World Association, 202, 206–7
Ishmaelites: imprisonment of, 155
Isolationists and Isolationism: described, 24n; and Pearl Harbor attack, 24, 37; policy on, 110–11; press comment on, 52; opposition to FDR, 162; wartime tactics of, 51

J

JAG's Office, U.S. *See under* Navy, U.S. Dept. of
Jackson, Pat, 270, 271
Jackson, Robert H., xiv, 3, 11, 15; biog., 383; and criminal and subversive organizations, 54; and Sterling Products case, 361–62
Jackson, Samuel D.: biog., 383; and Democratic convention (1944), 274, 279–80; and FDR's letter endorsing Wallace, 261, 279
Jackson Hole National Monument, 301, 303, 304, 305
James, Edwin L., 32, 383
Japan: cabinet of, 259, 279; consular officials in Hawaii, 10; Far East attacks feared, 112; and Pearl Harbor, 23–25; relations with U.S., 11; surrender of, 369; U.S. underestimation of, 38
Japanese in U.S.: citizenship of, 53–54; control of, 38–39, 50; evacuation of, 53n, 54, 57, 75–76; Gallup poll on, 54; internees, 55; loyalty of, 50; property of, 53; protective custody of, 40; support for release of, 75–76
Jefferson, Thomas: campaigns of, 316
Jefferson Memorial: dedication ceremonies, 150–52
Jews and Judaism, 309, 315; colonies of, 248; and Democratic convention (1944), 268–69; extermination of, 220; and Felix Frankfurter, 87; holocaust portrayed by, 151; leaders of, 158; refugees, 158; religious services of, 345; and Republican Party, 269. *See also* Great Britain, Palestine mandate of; National Com-

mittee Against Persecution of the Jews; Palestine
Jehovah's Witnesses: imprisonment of, 155. *See also* Conscientious objectors
Johannson, Nils A., 12
Johnson, Catherine F. (Kate), 47–49
Johnson, Philip G.: biog., 383; character of, 47–49; death of, 307; racism and antisemitism of, 49; on U.S.-Soviet relations, 307
Johnston, Eric A.: biog., 383; election of 1944, Washington State, 213; and National Committee Against Persecution of the Jews, 221; trip to Soviet Union, 314–15
Joliet land case, 315–16
Jones, Jesse H., xv, 95, 118; and Francis Biddle, 242; biog., 383; and Board of Economic Warfare, 187, 341; character of, 188; and national defense program finances, 16n; Reconstruction Finance Corporation, 364; FDR's replacement of, 265, 363, 364; and Surplus War Properties case, 294, 327; feud with Henry Wallace, 187, 362, 363, 364
Jones, Sam H., 162, 383
Jorgenson, Floss, 322, 323
Jorgenson, Virgil, 137, 238, 322, 323
Justice Dept., U.S., x, xv; administrative looseness in, 57; Alaska personnel, 123; Alien Registration (Enemy Control) Unit, 54, 57; Appropriations Bill of 1942, 98; Francis Biddle's appointments, 216; Bureau of Prisons, 55, 56, 57, 154–55; Claims Division, 4n, 66–67; and Fr. Coughlin case, 66; Criminal Division, 28n, 74; Martin Dies' charges, 61–62; Deferment Committee, rulings of, 154; Elk Hills case, 170, 194–202 *passim*; Felix Frankfurter's influence, 123–24, 215–16; German saboteurs' trial, 116; Immigration and Naturalization Service, 31–32, 41, 42, 55–56; Japanese evacuation, 57; libel prosecutions, policy on, 52; and Navy Dept., transfer of land acquisition functions to, 109; Negro employees of, 61; patronage, and Pearson-Littell libel case, xviii; Sedition Division, 58, soldiers' crimes, jurisdiction over, 155–56; solicitor generals, functions of, 15n; Special War Policies (Defense) Unit, 51–52, 56, 57; staff meetings of, 26–28, 38–40, 44, 50–57 *passim*, 61–62, 74–76, 97–99, 154–56, 159, 207, 299–300, 352; and Sterling Products Corp. case, 359, 360; and subversive organizations, 54–55; U.S. attorneys, in

O

P

S

Y, Z

ABA-5297